**ELEMENTS OF
PHOTOGRAMMETRY**

(*Courtesy Rapid Color, Inc.*)

McGRAW-HILL
BOOK COMPANY
New York
St. Louis
San Francisco
Düsseldorf
Johannesburg
Kuala Lumpur
London
Mexico
Montreal
New Delhi
Panama
Paris
São Paulo
Singapore
Sydney
Tokyo
Toronto

PAUL R. WOLF, Ph.D.
Professor of Civil and Environmental Engineering
The University of Wisconsin, Madison

Elements of Photogrammetry
(WITH AIR PHOTO INTERPRETATION AND REMOTE SENSING)

This book was set in Times New Roman by Scripta Technica, Inc.
The editors were B. J. Clark and Michael Gardner;
the cover designer was Pedro A. Noa;
the production supervisor was Sam Ratkewitch.
The drawings were done by John Cordes, J & R Technical Services, Inc.

Cover photograph courtesy of Pacific Resources, Inc.

Library of Congress Cataloging in Publication Data

Wolf, Paul R.
    Elements of photogrammetry.

    Includes bibliographies.
    1. Photogrammetry.   2. Aerial photogrammetry.
3. Photographic interpretation.   I. Title.
TR693.W64   526.9′82   73-21856
ISBN 0-07-071337-5

**ELEMENTS OF
PHOTOGRAMMETRY**

90 HDHD 854321

CONTENTS

PREFACE

This book has been prepared primarily for use as a text for an introductory course in photogrammetry at the college level. This includes courses given at universities, junior colleges, colleges of applied arts and technology and military schools. The book should also be a valuable addition to the libraries of practicing photogrammetrists, cartographers, surveyors, engineers, foresters, geologists, geographers, landscape architects, and others who use photographs in their work.

The book provides a modern introduction to the broad and dynamic field of photogrammetry. It includes topics traditionally found in photogrammetry textbooks such as cameras, photographic geometry, stereoscopy, parallax, radial-line triangulation, flight planning, ground control, and stereoscopic plotting instruments. In addition, this book provides introductory coverage on the subjects of orthophotos, terrestrial photos, oblique photos, panoramic photos, photography and photographic processing, photogrammetric optics, control extension by photogrammetric bridging, photographic interpretation, and remote sensing. This broad treatment of the subject is directly in line with photogrammetry curriculum resolutions adopted at a recent conference of the American Society for Engineering Education.

The material in this book has been written using elementary terms as much as possible, and extensive use has been made of illustrations and diagrams. Example problems have frequently been included to clarify computational procedures. In view of the impending adoption of the metric system in the United States, metric equivalents are generally given in parentheses following foot and inch values. In order that the book might be suitable for students of varying levels of mathematical competence, the body of the text has been presented so that knowledge of only elementary algebra, geometry, and trigonometry is necessary. More challenging mathematical developments have been placed in the appendixes, where they are available either for reference or for students having the necessary mathematics background.

Chapters are arranged in an order found most convenient by the author during many years of teaching photogrammetry at the Universities of California and Wisconsin. Early chapters establish fundamental principles, while later chapters discuss the more specialized aspects of photogrammetry with emphasis on practical applications. In general each chapter is arranged so that the more important material is presented first. This makes it convenient to cover only the first parts of certain chapters if course-time limitations will not allow covering the entire book.

A selected list of references is given at the end of each chapter, and from the materials cited, students may expand their knowledge on particular subjects of interest. To conserve space, only a limited number of key references have been given, but many of these also have excellent bibliographies that will lead the student to numerous additional articles. A variety of homework problems are included after each chapter, and a solution manual is available to instructors from the publisher. In addition to providing answers to all numerical problems, this solutions manual contains FORTRAN program listings together with examples of their use in solving several of the more time-consuming computational photogrammetry problems.

Although the author is an engineer, the material is presented here in a general manner so that the book would have appeal not only for engineering photogrammetry courses, but also for nonengineering courses taught in schools of forestry, geography, geology, agriculture, etc. With its coverage of photography, photo processing, cameras, photographic measurements, photographic interpretation, and remote sensing, the book could also serve satisfactorily for courses in interpretative photogrammetry.

While the material has been kept as elementary as possible, the depth of coverage is sufficient to make the book suitable for an advanced course in photogrammetry as well. The coverage of the latter chapters and the appendixes would be particularly useful in an advanced course. Appendix A deals with random errors and least squares adjustment; Appendix B covers the subject of coordinate transformations; and Appendix C gives the development of the collinearity equations. This material forms the basis of modern computational photogrammetry.

The author wishes to express his sincere appreciation to the many individuals who have contributed to this book. Specifically, thanks are due to Professor Arthur J. McNair of Cornell University, whose thorough review of the entire manuscript and numerous suggestions were invaluable; to Professor James P. Scherz of the University of Wisconsin, Madison, who authored Chap. 3 and made numerous other contributions throughout the book; to Mr. L. R. Evans of Alster and Associates, Madison, Wisconsin, Professor Leonard F. Hillis of the University of Wisconsin, Milwaukee, and Professor R. B. Buckner of the Ohio State University, who read and commented on the entire manuscript; to Professor Samuel Sailor of the University of Wyoming and Professor Porter W. McDonnell, Jr., of the Pennsylvania State University (Mont Alto), who reviewed substantial portions of the manuscript; to Professor Ralph W. Kiefer of the University of Wisconsin, Madison, who authored Chap. 19; to Professor Thomas M. Lillesand of the State University of New York, Syracuse, and Dr. Alan R. Stevens of the Tennessee Valley Authority, Chattanooga, Tennessee, who coauthored Chap. 20; to Professor James L. Clapp, Professor Eldon C. Wagner, and Dr. Frank L. Scarpace of the University of Wisconsin, Madison, and Professor David F. Mezera of Texas A and M University, who reviewed portions of the manuscript; to Mr. Victor G. Zsilinszky of the Ontario Department of Lands and Forests, who supplied valuable materials for Chap. 19; to Dr. Donald R. Graff, President of Engineering Computer Services, Hoffman Estates, Illinois, who first instructed the author on the subject of photogrammetry and who also made several valuable suggestions for this book; and to the many graduate and undergraduate students who have made numerous valuable contributions.

The author also wishes to thank the instrument manufacturers, government mapping agencies, and commercial photogrammetric firms who provided many of the illustrations and diagrams used in this book.

And finally, special recognition is due the author's wife, Kaye, and children Paul, Tim, and Jodie, who endured three years of neglect while this book was in preparation.

PAUL R. WOLF

1

INTRODUCTION

1-1 DEFINITION OF PHOTOGRAMMETRY

Photogrammetry may be defined as the art, science, and technology of obtaining reliable information about physical objects and the environment through processes of recording, measuring, and interpreting photographic images and patterns of recorded radiant electromagnetic energy. The definition may be extended to include analysis of radiated acoustical energy patterns and magnetic phenomena. As implied by its name, the science originally consisted of analyzing photographs. Although photogrammetry has recently expanded to include analysis of other records, photographs are still the principal source of information. In this text "photographic" photogrammetry is emphasized, but other sources of information are also discussed.

Included within the definition of photogrammetry are two distinct areas: (1) *metric* photogrammetry, which involves precise measurements and computations to determine sizes and shapes of objects, and (2) *interpretative* photogrammetry, which deals with the recognition and identification of objects. The first area, metric photogrammetry, is applied primarily in the preparation of planimetric and topographic maps from photographs. The photographs are most often *aerial* (taken from an airborne vehicle), but *terrestrial* photos (taken from earth-based cameras) may also be used. Interpretative photogrammetry includes branches of *photographic interpretation* and *remote sensing*. Photographic interpretation involves the systematic study of photographic images for purposes of identifying objects and judging their significance. Remote sensing is a rather new branch of interpretative photogrammetry, which, like photographic interpretation, applies to recognizing and identifying objects without physical contact with them. However, unlike photographic interpretation, which is confined to the analysis of photography, remote sensing uses data gathered from a wide variety of sensing instruments including multispectral cameras, infrared sensors, thermal scanners, and side-looking radar. Remote sensing instruments, which are often carried in vehicles as remote as orbiting satellites, are capable of providing quantitative as well as qualitative information about objects. At the present time, with man's recognition of the importance of preserving his environment and natural resources, photographic interpretation and remote sensing are both being employed extensively as tools in management and planning.

1-2 HISTORY OF PHOTOGRAMMETRY

Developments leading to the present-day science of photogrammetry occurred long before the invention of photography. As early as 350 B.C. Aristotle had referred to the process of projecting images optically. In the early eighteenth century Dr. Brook Taylor published his treatise on linear perspective, and soon thereafter, J. H. Lambert suggested that the principles of perspective could be used in preparing maps.

The actual practice of photogrammetry could not occur, of course, until a practical photographic process was developed. This occurred in 1839, when Louis Daguerre of Paris announced his direct photographic process. In his process the exposure was made on metal plates which had been light-sensitized with a coating of silver iodide. This is essentially the photographic process in use today.

A year after Daguerre's invention, Arago, a geodesist with the French Academy of Science, demonstrated the use of photographs in topographic surveying. The first actual experiments in using photogrammetry for topographic mapping occurred in 1849 under the direction of Colonel Aimé Laussedat of the French Army Corps of Engineers. Among Colonel Laussedat's experiments were the use of kites and balloons for taking aerial photographs. Due to difficulties encountered in obtaining aerial photographs, he curtailed this area of research and concentrated his efforts on mapping with terrestrial photographs. In 1859 Colonel Laussedat presented an accounting of his successes in mapping using photographs. His pioneering work and dedication to this subject earned him the title Father of Photogrammetry.

Topographic mapping using photogrammetry was introduced to North America in 1886 by Captain Deville, the Surveyor General of Canada. He found Laussedat's principles extremely convenient for mapping the rugged mountains of western Canada. The U.S. Coast and Geodetic Survey adopted photogrammetry in 1894 for mapping along the border between Canada and the Alaska Territory.

Meanwhile new developments in instrumentation, including improvements in cameras and films, continued to nurture the growth of photogrammetry. In 1861 a three-color photographic process was developed, and roll film was perfected in 1891. In 1909 Dr. Carl Pulfrich of Germany began to experiment with stereo pairs of photographs. His work formed much of the foundation for the development of many instrumental mapping techniques in use today.

The invention of the airplane by the Wright Brothers in 1902 provided the great impetus for the emergence of modern aerial photogrammetry. Until that time almost all photogrammetric work was, for the lack of a practical means of obtaining aerial photos, limited to terrestrial photography. The airplane was first used in 1913 for obtaining photographs for mapping purposes. Aerial photos were used extensively during World War I, primarily in reconnaissance. In the period between the two World Wars, aerial photogrammetry for topographic mapping progressed to the point of mass production of maps. During this period many private firms and governmental agencies in North America and in Europe became engaged in photogrammetric work.

During World War II photogrammetric techniques were used extensively to meet the great new demand for maps. Air photo interpretation was also employed more widely than ever before in reconnaissance and intelligence. Out of this war-accelerated mapping program came many new developments in instruments and techniques.

Contributions in instrumentation and techniques during the past 25 years have been too numerous to itemize. All the contributions taken collectively, however, have made photogrammetry so accurate, efficient, and advantageous that at the present time, except for mapping small parcels, very little topographic mapping is done by other means. Although topographic mapping constitutes the major use of photogrammetry, it is also being employed in many other fields. Many of these special applications are discussed in Sec. 1-6.

1-3 TYPES OF PHOTOGRAPHS

Two basic classifications of photography used in the science of photogrammetry are *terrestrial* and *aerial.* Terrestrial photographs are taken with ground-based cameras, the position and orientation of which are usually known. A *phototheodolite,* as shown in Fig. 1-1, is a combination camera and theodolite mounted on a tripod. It is used for taking terrestrial photographs. The theodolite facilitates alignment of the camera in a desired or known azimuth. Figure 1-2 shows a terrestrial photograph.

Another type of terrestrial camera is the *ballistic camera,* an example of which is

FIGURE 1-1
Phototheodolite used for taking terrestrial photographs. (*Courtesy Wild Heerbrugg Instruments, Inc.*)

shown in Fig. 1-3. These large cameras are mounted at selected ground stations and are used to obtain photographs of orbiting artificial satellites against a star background. The photographs are analyzed to calculate satellite trajectories, the size, shape and gravity of the earth, and the precise positions of the camera stations. This procedure utilizes precisely known camera constants together with the known positions of the background stars at the instant of exposure. It is currently being used to establish a world wide network of control points and to accurately determine the relative positions of the continents, remote ocean islands, etc.

Aerial photography is commonly classified as either vertical or oblique. *Vertical photos* are taken with the camera axis directed as nearly vertically as possible. If the camera axis were perfectly vertical when an exposure was made, the photo plane would be parallel to the datum plane and the resulting photograph would be termed *truly vertical*. In practice the camera axis is rarely held perfectly vertical due to unavoidable aircraft tilts. When the camera axis is unintentionally tilted slightly from vertical, the resulting photograph is called a *tilted photograph*. These unintentional tilts are usually less than $1°$ and seldom more than $3°$. For many practical applications, tilted photos may be treated as truly verticals without serious consequence. Precise photogrammetric instruments and procedures have been developed that make it possible to account for tilt

FIGURE 1-2
Terrestrial photograph. (*Courtesy Wild Heerbrugg Instruments, Inc.*)

FIGURE 1-3
Wild BC-4 ballistic camera. (*Courtesy Wild Heerbrugg Instruments, Inc.*)

FIGURE 1-4
Aerial camera, model Zeiss RMK 15/23, with electrical controls and aircraft mountings. (*Courtesy Carl Zeiss, Oberkochen*)

with no loss of accuracy. Fig. 1-4 shows an aerial camera with its electrical control mechanism and the mounting framework for placing it in an aircraft. The vertical photograph illustrated in Fig. 1-5 was taken with a camera of the type illustrated in Fig. 1-4 from an altitude of 1,500 feet above the terrain.

Oblique aerial photographs are exposed with the camera axis intentionally tilted away from vertical. A *high oblique* photograph includes the horizon; a *low oblique* does not. Figure 1-6 illustrates the orientation of the camera for vertical, low oblique, and high oblique photography and also shows how a grid of ground lines would appear in each of these types of photographs. Figures 1-7 and 1-8 are examples of low oblique and high oblique photographs respectively.

A rather new classification of photographs called *extraterrestrial* has emerged as a result of space exploration. These are photos taken from high-altitude rockets and spacecraft. Many spectacular extraterrestrial photographs of the moon and near planets have been obtained in recent years. This type of photogrammetry holds great promise for the future. Figure 1-9 is a high oblique extraterrestrial photograph taken over the moon with the earth rising in the background. It was exposed during a recent Apollo mission.

1-4 TAKING VERTICAL AERIAL PHOTOGRAPHS

When an area is covered by vertical aerial photography, the photographs are taken along a series of parallel passes called *flight strips.* As illustrated in Fig. 1-10, the photographs are

FIGURE 1-5
Vertical aerial photograph. (*Courtesy Carl Zeiss, Oberkochen*)

normally exposed in such a way that the area covered by each successive photograph along a flight strip duplicates or overlaps part of the coverage of the previous photo. This lapping along the flight strip is called *end lap*, and the area of coverage common to an adjacent pair of photographs in a flight strip is called the *stereoscopic overlap area*. The pair of photos is called a *stereopair*. For reasons which will be given in subsequent

Camera orientation for various types of aerial photographs

How a grid of section lines appears on various types of photos

FIGURE 1-6
Camera orientation for various types of aerial photographs.

chapters, the amount of end lap is normally between 55 and 65 percent. The position of the camera at any exposure, e.g., positions 1, 2, 3, etc., is called the *exposure station*, and the altitude of the camera is called *flying height*.

Adjacent flight strips are photographed so that there is also a lateral overlapping of strips. This condition, illustrated in Fig. 1-11, is called *side lap*, and it is normally held at approximately 30 percent. The photographs of two or more side lapping strips is referred to as a *block* of photos.

1-5 EXISTING AERIAL PHOTOGRAPHY

Photogrammetrists and photo interpreters can obtain aerial photography in one of two ways: they can purchase photographs from existing coverage or obtain new coverage. It is seldom economical to utilize existing coverage for mapping because it rarely meets the needs of the user. Frequently it may prove suitable for reconnaissance or for photo interpretation purposes. If existing photography is not satisfactory due to age, scale, camera, etc., it will be necessary to obtain new coverage. Of course, before the decision can be made whether to use existing photography or obtain new, it is necessary to ascertain exactly what coverage exists in a particular area.

FIGURE 1-7
Low oblique aerial photograph (note that the horizon does not show). (*Courtesy Wild Heerbrugg Instruments, Inc.*)

Existing aerial photography is available for nearly all of the United States and Canada. Some areas have been covered several times, so that various scales and qualities of photography are available. Most of the existing coverage is single-lens vertical photography taken by or for agencies of the federal government. An index map entitled "Status of Aerial Photography" is available upon request from the U.S. Geological Survey.[1] This

[1] Address requests to Map Information Office, U.S. Department of the Interior, Geological Survey, Washington, D.C. 20242.

FIGURE 1-8
High oblique aerial photograph over Minneapolis (note that the horizon shows).
(*Courtesy Mark Hurd Aerial Surveys, Inc.*)

map shows, by counties, all areas of the United States that have been photographed by various agencies of the federal government. It also shows coverage available from a limited number of state agencies, cities, and commercial firms. The map includes names and addresses of the agencies holding the photography as well as general information regarding photo scales and camera focal lengths. Requests for further information and orders for photos must be sent directly to the appropriate organization. Most state highway departments also have considerable aerial photographic coverage which can normally be obtained by the general public.

FIGURE 1-9
High oblique extraterrestrial photograph of the moon with the earth in the background. (*Courtesy National Space Science Data Center*)

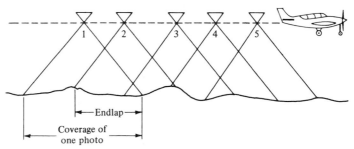

FIGURE 1-10
End lap of photographs in a flight strip.

FIGURE 1-11
Side lap of adjacent flight strips.

1-6 USES OF PHOTOGRAMMETRY

The earliest applications of photogrammetry were in topographic mapping, and today that use is still the most common of photogrammetric applications. At the present time the U.S. Geological Survey, the federal agency charged with mapping the United States, performs nearly 100 percent of its map compilation photogrammetrically. Besides map compilation, much of the needed ground control is extended from sparse networks of control monuments by photogrammetric means. Fieldwork cannot be eliminated entirely because basic control surveying and field checking of photogrammetrically compiled maps is necessary. In addition to topographic mapping, many other special-purpose maps are also prepared photogrammetrically. These maps vary in scale from large to small and are used in planning and designing highways, railroads, bridges, pipelines, aqueducts, transmission lines, hydroelectric dams, flood-control structures, river and harbor improvements, urban renewal projects, etc.

Photogrammetry has become an exceptionally valuable tool in land surveying. To mention just a few uses in this field, aerial photos can be used as rough base maps for relocating existing property boundaries. If the point of beginning or any corners can be located with respect to ground features that can be identified on the photo, the entire parcel can be plotted on the photo from the property description. All corners can then be located on the photo in relation to identifiable ground features which, when located in the field, greatly assist in finding the actual property corners. Aerial photos can also be used in planning ground surveys. Through stereoscopic viewing, the area can be studied in three dimensions. Access routes to remote areas can be identified and surveying lines of least resistance through difficult terrain or forests can be found. The photogrammetrist can prepare a map of an area without actually setting foot on the ground—an advantage which circumvents problems of gaining access to private land for ground surveys.

The field of highway planning and design provides an excellent example of how important photogrammetry has become in engineering. In this field, aerial mosaics are prepared to assist in area and corridor studies and to select the best route; small-scale topographic maps are prepared for use in preliminary planning; large-scale topographic maps are compiled for use in final design; and earthwork cross sections are taken to obtain contract quantities. In some cases the plan portion of the "plan-profile" sheets of highway plans are prepared from aerial photographs. Partial payments and even final pay quantities are often calculated from photogrammetric measurements. The use of photogrammetry in highway engineering has not only reduced costs but has also enabled better overall highway designs to be achieved.

Many areas outside of engineering have also benefited from photogrammetry. Nonengineering applications include the preparation of tax maps, soil maps, forest maps, geologic maps, and maps for city and regional planning and zoning. Aerial photographs are used in the fields of astronomy, architecture, archaeology, geomorphology, oceanography, hydrology and water resources, conservation, ecology, and mineralogy. Stereoscopic photography literally enables the outdoors to be brought into the comfortable confines of the laboratory or office for viewing and study in three dimensions.

Photogrammetry has been used successfully in traffic management and in traffic accident investigations. Its use in the latter area has the advantage that photographs overlook nothing that may be needed later to reconstruct the accident, and it is possible to restore normal traffic flow quickly. Even in the fields of medicine and dentistry, measurements from x-ray and other photographs have been useful in diagnosis and treatment. Of course, one of the oldest and still most important uses of aerial photography is in military intelligence. Space exploration is one of the new and exciting areas where photogrammetry is being utilized.

Photogrammetry has become a powerful research tool because it affords the unique advantage of permitting instantaneous recordings of dynamic occurrences on film. Measurements from photographs of quantities such as beam or pavement deflections under impact loads may easily be obtained photographically where such measurements would otherwise be nearly impossible.

It would be difficult to cover all of the many situations in which photogrammetric principles and methods could or have been used in solving measurement problems. Photogrammetry, although still a relatively new science, has already contributed substantially to engineering and nonengineering fields alike. New applications appear to be bounded only by man's imagination, and the science should continue to grow in the future.

1-7 PROFESSIONAL PHOTOGRAMMETRY ORGANIZATIONS

There are several professional organizations in the United States serving the interests of photogrammetry. Generally these organizations have as their objectives advancement of knowledge in the field, encouragement of communication among photogrammetrists, and upgrading of standards and ethics in the practice of photogrammetry.

The American Society of Photogrammetry (ASP), founded in 1934, is the foremost professional photogrammetric organization in the United States. One of this society's most valuable contributions has been its publication of the "Manual of Photogrammetry," the "Manual of Photographic Interpretation," and the "Manual of Color Aerial Photography." In preparing these volumes, leading photogrammetrists from government agencies as well as private and commercial firms and educational institutions have authored and coauthored chapters in their various special areas of expertise. The American Society of Photogrammetry also publishes *Photogrammetric Engineering*, a monthly journal which brings new developments and applications to the attention of its readers. The society regularly sponsors technical meetings, at various locations throughout the United States, which bring together large numbers of photogrammetrists for the presentation of papers, discussion of new ideas and problems, and firsthand viewing of the latest photogrammetric equipment.

The fields of photogrammetry and surveying are so closely knit that it is difficult to separate them. Both are measurement sciences dealing with the production of maps. The American Congress on Surveying and Mapping (ACSM) although primarily concerned with surveying, is also vitally interested in photogrammetry. Founded in 1941, ACSM is regularly cosponsor with ASP of technical meetings. The quarterly journal of ACSM, *Surveying and Mapping,* frequently carries photogrammetry-related articles.

The Surveying and Mapping Division of the American Society of Civil Engineers (ASCE) is also dedicated to surveying and photogrammetry. Articles on photogrammetry are frequently published in its journal, the *Journal of the Surveying and Mapping Division.*

The Canadian Institute of Surveying (CIS) is the foremost professional organization of Canada concerned with photogrammetry. The CIS regularly sponsors technical meetings, and its journal, *The Canadian Surveyor*, carries photogrammetry articles.

The International Society for Photogrammetry (ISP), founded in 1910, fosters the exchange of ideas and information among photogrammetrists all over the world. ISP sponsors international conferences at four-year intervals. Its official journal is the bimonthly *Photogrammetria.* The International Society contains seven technical commissions, each concerned with a specialized area in photogrammetry. Each commission holds periodic symposiums where photogrammetrists gather to hear presented papers on photogrammetric subjects of international interest. Many foreign countries have professional photogrammetry organizations which are similar to the American Society of Photogrammetry. Together with ASP, these organizations are also members of ISP. They publish journals and offer essentially the same benefits to their memberships as those offered by ASP.

1-8   UNITS OF PHOTOGRAMMETRIC MEASUREMENTS

The solution of photogrammetry problems generally requires some type of length, angle, or area measurement. Length measurements may be in either the English system of inches and feet or the metric system of meters, centimeters, millimeters, and micrometers (microns). Conversion from the English system to the metric system or vice versa is frequently necessary. Photogrammetrists in the United States are rapidly adopting the metric system for linear measure as recommended by the National Academy of Sciences. Textbooks should not lag in this regard, and therefore the metric system is used extensively in this book.

Angle measurements in the United States are usually given in the *sexigesimal* system of degrees, minutes, and seconds. Instruments of European manufacture are very common in photogrammetry, however, and these are graduated in the *grad* angle system. It is often necessary to convert back and forth between these two systems. Electronic computers commonly use radian measure for angles and therefore conversion from degrees or grads to radians and vice versa is also frequently necessary.

The following table of length, angle, and area units should be helpful to the student of photogrammetry:

1) Length equivalents

1 foot = 12 inches
1 yard = 3 feet
1 rod = $16\frac{1}{2}$ feet
1 mile = 5,280 feet
1 millimeter = 1,000 micrometers (microns)
1 centimeter = 10 millimeters
1 meter = 100 centimeters
1 kilometer = 1,000 meters
1 inch = 25.400 millimeters
1 foot = 304.80 millimeters
1 meter = 3.2808 feet
1 meter = 39.370 inches
1 kilometer = 0.62137 miles

2) Angle equivalents

pi (π) = 3.14159265
180 degrees = pi radians
1 circle = 360°
1 circle = 2(pi) radians
1° = 60'

1' = 60"
1 radian = 180°/pi = 57° 17' 44.8"
1 radian = 57.295778°
1 radian = 206,264.8"
1° = 0.01745329 radians
1 circle = 400 grads
1 grad = 100 centigrads
1 grad = 1,000 milligrads
1 grad = 0.9° (exact)
1 grad = 0.01570796 radians
1 centigrad = 0.54'
1 milligrad = 3.24"

3) Area equivalents

1 acre = 43,560 square feet
1 acre = 4,046.9 square meters
640 acres = 1 square mile
247.1 acres = 1 square kilometer

1-9 SIGNIFICANT FIGURES

By definition, measured values have a number of significant figures equal to the number of digits that are *certain*, plus one *estimated* digit. As an example, suppose a distance of 24.37 millimeters is measured with a scale whose smallest graduations are 1/10 millimeters. The first three digits are certain but the fourth (7) is estimated on the scale between the 0.3- and 0.4-millimeter graduations. The value 24.37 therefore contains four significant figures. It is important to record *all* significant figures in measurement. Rounding off or failing to record the last estimated digit is a waste of the extra time spent in obtaining that added accuracy. Conversely, if more than one estimated digit is recorded, an accuracy is implied which in fact does not exist.

Zeros in a recorded value may or may not be significant, depending upon the circumstances. The following rules apply:

1) Zeros to the left of the first nonzero digit serve only to position the decimal point and are not significant.

Examples:

0.003	one significant figure
0.057	two significant figures
0.00281	three significant figures

2) Zeros to the right of nonzero digits and a decimal point are significant.

Examples:

    0.10   two significant figures
    7.50   three significant figures
  483.000   six significant figures

3) Zeros to the right of a nonzero digit but to the left of the decimal point are not significant unless specified by placing a bar over them or by moving the decimal point to the left and expressing the number in powers of ten.

Examples:

$$380 = 3.8 \times 10^2 \qquad \text{two significant figures}$$
$$38\bar{0} = 3.80 \times 10^2 \qquad \text{three significant figures}$$
$$1{,}60\bar{0} = 1.600 \times 10^3 \qquad \text{four significant figures}$$

In computations using measured values, it is important that answers be given to a number of significant figures consistent with the number of significant figures in the data used to compute them. Specifying an answer to less than the proper number of significant figures does not take advantage of the accuracy achieved in measuring the quantities, and giving the answer to more significant figures than are justified implies accuracy that does not exist.

In adding and subtracting, the calculations are carried out without regard to significant figures, but the rightmost significant figure in the final rounded off answer occurs in the rightmost column filled with significant figures.

Examples:

     4.735
     2.05
    24.
    ———
    30.785   answer = 31 (two significant figures governed by 24)

    1,130
   − 83.073
   ————
  1,046.927   answer = 1,050 (three significant figures governed by 1,130)

In multiplication and division, the number of significant figures in answers is equal to the least number of significant figures of any of the data used in the calculation.

Examples:

$$1{,}738 \times 24 = 41{,}712 \qquad \text{answer} = 42{,}000 \text{ (two significant figures governed by 24)}$$

648.1 × 0.0523 = 33.89563   answer = 33.9 (three significant figures governed by 0.0523)

23.985/13 = 1.845   answer = 1.8 (two significant figures governed by 13)

In multiplying or dividing by exact constants, the constants do not govern the number of significant figures in the answer.

Example:

Convert 15.73 feet to inches

Solution:

15.73 × 12 inches/foot = 188.76   answer = 188.8 (four significant figures governed by 15.73, not 12)

In this text the term "nominal" is frequently used to imply nearness to a given value, e.g., a nominal 6-inch focal length camera. "Nominal" in this context may be assumed to imply two additional significant figures (a nominal 6-inch focal length camera lens therefore means a focal length of 6.00 inches).

In intermediate computations it is customary to carry one more than the required number of significant figures and then round the final answer to the correct number of significant figures.

REFERENCES

American Society of Photogrammetry: "Manual of Photogrammetry," 3d ed., George Banta Co., Inc., Menasha, Wis., 1966, chaps. 1, 5, 20, 23, 24, and 25.

Avery, T. E., and D. M. Richter: An Airphoto Index to Physical and Cultural Features in Eastern U.S., *Photogrammetric Engineering*, vol. 31, no. 5, p. 896. 1965.

Brandenberger, A. J.: World-Wide Mapping Survey, *Photogrammetric Engineering*, vol. 36, no. 4, p. 355. 1970.

Eldrige, W. H.: Photogrammetry for Property Surveying, *Surveying and Mapping*, vol. 27, no. 1, p. 63. 1967.

Eliel, L. T.: One Hundred Years of Photogrammetry, *Photogrammetric Engineering*, vol. 25, no. 3, p. 359. 1959.

Kummer, R. H.: A Use for Small Scale Photography in Forest Management, *Photogrammetric Engineering*, vol. 30, no. 5, p. 727. 1964.

Landen, D.: History of Photogrammetry in the United States, *Photogrammetric Engineering*, vol. 18, no. 5, p. 854. 1952.

Parker, L.: Highway Plans from Photogrammetrically Compiled Maps, *A.S.C.E. Journal of the Surveying and Mapping Division*, vol. 90, no. SU1, p. 31. 1964.

Richter, D. M.: An Airphoto Index to Physical and Cultural Features in Western U.S., *Photogrammetric Engineering*, vol. 33, no. 12, p. 1402. 1967.

_____: Urban Photo Index for Eastern U.S., *Photogrammetric Engineering*, vol. 32, no. 1, p. 54. 1971.

Stanton, B. T.: Education in Photogrammetry, *Photogrammetric Engineering*, vol. 32, no. 3, p. 293. 1971.

Stone, K.: World Air Photo Coverage, *Photogrammetric Engineering*, vol. 27, no. 2, p. 214. 1961.

PROBLEMS

1-1 Describe the different classifications of aerial photographs.

1-2 What are extraterrestrial photographs?

1-3 Define the following photogrammetric terms: end lap, side lap, stereopair, exposure station, and flying height.

1-4 What is a ballistic camera and what is it used for?

1-5 Discuss some of the principal uses of aerial photogrammetry.

1-6 Discuss some of the principal uses of terrestrial photogrammetry.

1-7 Describe how you would go about obtaining existing aerial photographic coverage of an area.

1-8 To what extent is photogrammetry being used in highway planning and design in your state?

1-9 Convert the following lengths to inches:
  (*a*) 88.95 millimeters
  (*b*) 152.52 millimeters
  (*c*) 0.68 meters
  (*d*) 23.08 centimeters

1-10 Convert the following lengths to millimeters:
  (*a*) 3.28 inches
  (*b*) 0.74 inches
  (*c*) 1.31 feet

1-11 Make the following length conversions:
  (*a*) Express 44$\overline{0}$ meters in feet
  (*b*) Express 48 miles in kilometers
  (*c*) Express 1,32$\overline{0}$ feet in meters
  (*d*) Express 1 kilometer in rods

1-12 Express the following in degrees, minutes, and seconds:
  (*a*) 48 grads
  (*b*) 172.23 grads
  (*c*) 1.423 radians

1-13 Convert the following to grads, centigrads, and milligrads:
  (*a*) $17° \, 29'$
  (*b*) $85° \, 36' \, 22''$
  (*c*) 0.6172 radians

1-14 Express the following angles in radians:
    (*a*) 282°
    (*b*) 79° 32′ 40″
    (*c*) 303.254 grads

1-15 How many significant figures are there in the following numbers:
23.057; 1,105.062; 0.057; 3,800; 1,62$\overline{0}$; and 417.5?

1-16 Express the following numbers using powers of 10 and retain the indicated number
of significant figures: 8,375.8; 48,30$\overline{0}$; 0.00235; 17.001; and 437,832.

1-17 Express the answers to the following problems to the correct number of significant
figures:
    (*a*) 17.138 + 148.7 + 0.1037 + 4,381
    (*b*) 492.06 − 87.0
    (*c*) 7,948 + 87.34 − 521.075
    (*d*) 88.6 × 380,072
    (*e*) (485)^2
    (*f*) 28.721 ÷ 43.9

OPTICS FOR PHOTOGRAMMETRY

2-1 INTRODUCTION

Practically all photogrammetric instruments depend in some manner upon optical elements for their function. The number and kind of optical elements used varies widely with the type of equipment. Small pocket stereoscopes, for example, use only simple thin lenses; aerial cameras contain highly corrected and expensive compound lenses; and complex stereoscopic plotters often utilize many lenses, mirrors, and prisms.

In analyzing and solving photogrammetric problems, rudimentary line diagrams are often necessary. Their preparation generally requires tracing the paths of light rays through optical elements. These same kinds of diagrams are often used as a basis for deriving fundamental photogrammetric equations. For these reasons a basic knowledge of the behavior of light and of basic geometrical optics is prerequisite to a thorough understanding of the science of photogrammetry.

2-2 REFRACTION OF LIGHT

In geometric optics, light is considered to travel through homogeneous media in straight lines called *light rays*. From any point light source an infinite number of light rays radiate in all directions. The point source is said to be at the center of a *bundle of rays.*

When light rays pass from one homogeneous transparent medium to a second such medium having a different refractive index, the path of the light ray is bent or *refracted* unless it intersects the second medium normal to the interface. If the intersection occurs obliquely, as shown in Fig. 2-1, then the *angle of incidence,* ϕ, is related to the *angle of refraction,* ϕ', by the law of refraction, frequently called *Snell's law.* This law is stated as follows:

$$n \sin \phi = n' \sin \phi' \qquad (2\text{-}1)$$

where n is the refractive index of the first medium and n' is the refractive index of the second medium.

In Fig. 2-1, *IA* is the incident light ray, *AR* is the refracted ray, and *NN'* is the normal to the interface between the two media. The angles ϕ and ϕ' are measured from *NN'* to the incident and refracted rays, respectively. A light ray is refracted such that the incident and refracted rays lie in the same plane. Angle θ is called the *deviation angle* and is given by:

$$\theta = \phi - \phi' \qquad (2\text{-}2)$$

The refractive index for any transparent substance is determined through experimental measurement. Typical values for indexes of refraction of common media are vacuum, 1.000; air, 1.0003; water, 1.33; and glass, 1.5 to 1.7.

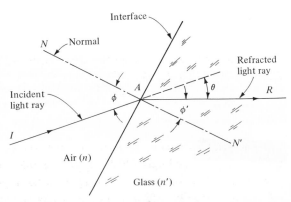

FIGURE 2-1
Refraction of light rays.

If a light ray is directed toward a piece of glass which has perfectly parallel sides, the light ray will emerge from the glass parallel to the direction at which it entered. If the light ray strikes the glass obliquely, it will have been displaced laterally, however, as shown by the distance h in Fig. 2-2. The displaced ray will emerge in the same plane as the incident ray, and the amount of displacement will increase with an increase in the angle of incidence and an increase in the thickness of the glass. The following equation in terms of the thickness t, the refractive indexes n and n', and the angles ϕ and ϕ' may be used to calculate this lateral displacement:

$$h = t \sin \phi \left[1 - \frac{n \cos \phi}{n' \cos \phi'} \right] \qquad (2\text{-}3)$$

EXAMPLE 2-1 Light is directed through air toward a ¼-in.-thick parallel-sided glass plate at a 60° angle of incidence. What will be the lateral displacement of the light ray as it again emerges into air on the other side of the plate? (Assume n of air = 1.000 and n' of crown glass to be 1.520.)
From Eq. (2-1),

$$\sin \phi' = \frac{1.000}{1.520} (0.8660) = 0.5698$$

From trigonometric tables, $\phi' = 34° \ 44'$

From Eq. (2-3),

$$h = 0.25 (0.8660) \left[1 - \frac{1.000 (0.5000)}{1.520 (0.8218)} \right] = 0.13 \text{ in} \qquad ////$$

2-3 REFLECTION OF LIGHT

When a light ray strikes a smooth surface such as highly polished metal, it is reflected so that the *angle of reflection, ϕ''*, is equal to its incidence angle, ϕ, as shown in Fig. 2-3. Both angles lie in a common plane and are measured from NN', the normal to the reflecting surface.

Most surfaces partially refract light rays and partially reflect them, as shown in Fig. 2-3. The greater the angle of incidence, the greater the reflected portion. For a light ray traveling from a medium of higher refractive index to a medium of lower refractive index (e.g., from glass to air), there is a particular angle of incidence where the angle of refraction is exactly 90°. The angle of incidence at which this condition first occurs is called the *critical angle, ϕ_c*. If the refractive indexes of the two media are known, the

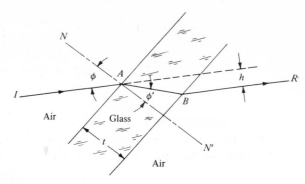

FIGURE 2-2
Refraction through a parallel-sided glass plate.

critical angle can be calculated using the following modification of Snell's law in which the sine of the 90° refraction angle is 1.000:

$$\sin \phi_c = \frac{n'}{n} \qquad (2\text{-}4)$$

In Eq. (2-4), ϕ_c is the critical angle of incidence and n and n' are as previously defined.

EXAMPLE 2-2 Find the critical angle for a light ray traveling from crown glass ($n = 1.520$) to air ($n' = 1.000$).

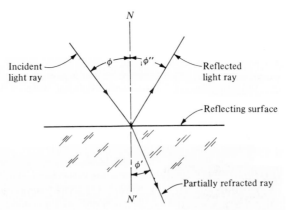

FIGURE 2-3
Reflection of light rays.

By Eq. (2-4),

$$\sin \phi_c = \frac{1.000}{1.520} = 0.6579$$

From trigonometric tables, $\phi_c = 41° \, 08'$ ////

For angles of incidence greater than the critical angle, there will be total reflection and therefore no light loss due to refraction. As will be explained later, this important factor is the underlying basis for the use of prisms in optical systems.

2-4 PLANE MIRRORS

Plane mirrors used for nonscientific purposes generally consist of a plane sheet of glass with a thin reflective coating of silver on the back. The silver coating is usually covered with paint for protection. This type of "back surfaced" mirror is optically undesirable, however, because it reflects rays which interfere with the primary reflected light ray, as shown in Fig. 2-4. These undesirable reflections may be avoided by using *first-surface* mirrors, those which have their silver coating on the front of the glass, as shown in Fig. 2-5. Although mirrors may be made optically acceptable in this manner, they are easily tarnished by fingerprints, smoke, etc., and are not normally used if they can be replaced by prisms.

In certain photogrammetric instruments it is possible to simultaneously view a reflected image and the image of an object which lies behind the reflecting mirror. This

FIGURE 2-4
Back-surfaced mirror.

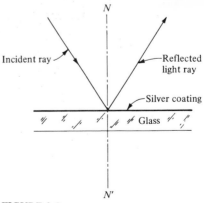

FIGURE 2-5
First-surface mirror.

may be accomplished through the use of *half-silvered* mirrors. These mirrors consist of a piece of glass surfaced with a light coating of silver such that half the intensity of a light ray carrying an image passes through the mirror and half is reflected. In Fig. 2-6, the light ray from A' is reflected by the mirror and the light ray from A passes through the mirror. Thus a half-silvered mirror enables two different objects to be viewed in superposition at the same time. As described in Chap. 9, this is useful for transferring detail from a photo to a map by direct tracing, e.g., tracing planimetric detail on a map at A' from an aerial photo situated at A. This principle is called *camera lucida.*

2-5 PRISMS

For angles of incidence greater than the critical angle, no refraction occurs, but rather every light ray undergoes total reflection. This principle is illustrated with the *right-angle prism* of Fig. 2-7. Light ray IA enters the prism normal to one of the faces, undergoes total reflection at A (ϕ is $45°$, which is greater than ϕ_c), and exits along path AR. An advantage of using prisms rather than first-surface mirrors is that total reflection may be achieved without the use of silver coatings and therefore no surfaces are subject to tarnishing. Consequently prisms are frequently used as reflecting devices in photogrammetric instruments.

Some common types of prisms are illustrated in Fig. 2-8a through d. The *right-angle* type of Fig. 2-8a described above, is the most common prism. Its function is to deflect light rays $90°$. Figure 2-8b illustrates the *porro* prism, a right-angle prism oriented so that reflected light rays are deflected $180°$ from their incident directions. Note that both prisms a and b invert their images. The *dove* prism of Fig. 2-8c rotates the image $180°$ about the longitudinal axis of the prism but does not change the direction of the ray paths. The *pentaprism* of Fig. 2-8d deflects light rays $90°$ regardless of the orientation of the prism. All these prisms are commonly used in photogrammetric instruments to change either the direction of a ray path or the orientation of an image.

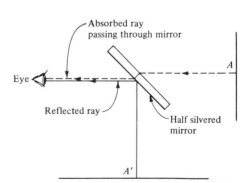

FIGURE 2-6
Use of a half-silvered mirror.

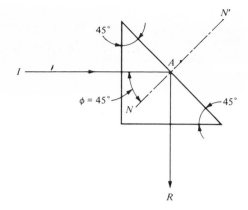

FIGURE 2-7
Total reflection through a right-angle
prism (ϕ greater than ϕ_C).

2-6 SIMPLE THIN LENSES

A simple thin lens consists of a piece of optical glass which has been ground so that it has
either two spherical surfaces or one spherical surface and one flat surface. By definition,
the thickness of a thin lens is considered negligible. Various types of thin lenses are shown

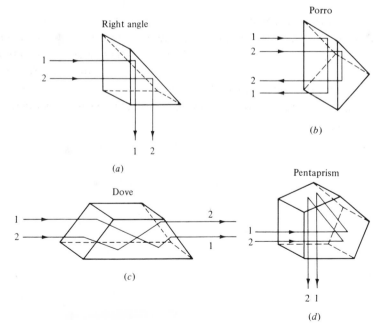

FIGURE 2-8
Common types of prisms.

in Fig. 2-9*a* through *f*. Incident light rays passing through the *converging* lenses *a* through *c* are refracted toward each other according to Snell's law. The *diverging* lenses *d* through *f* refract incident light rays in a diverging manner as illustrated.

The primary function of a lens is to gather light rays from object points and bring them to focus at some distance on the opposite side of the lens. A lens accomplishes this function through the principles of refraction. The simplest and most primitive device which performs the functions of a lens is a tiny pinhole which theoretically allows a single light ray from each object point to pass. The tiny hole of diameter d_1 of the pinhole camera illustrated in Fig. 2-10 produces an inverted image of the object. The image is theoretically in focus regardless of the distance from the pinhole to the camera's image plane. Pinholes allow so little light to pass, however, that they are extremely slow and unsuitable for photogrammetric work. For practical reasons they are replaced by glass lenses.

The advantage of a lens over a pinhole is the increased amount of light that is allowed to pass. A lens gathers an entire *pencil of rays* from each object point instead of only a single ray. When an object is illuminated, each point in the object reflects bundles of light rays in all directions as illustrated in Fig. 2-11. A lens placed in front of the object gathers the pencil of light rays from each point that strikes the lens and brings each pencil to focus at a point in a plane on the other side of the lens called the *image plane*. An

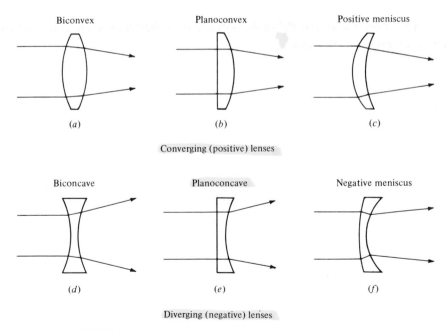

FIGURE 2-9
Various types of thin lenses.

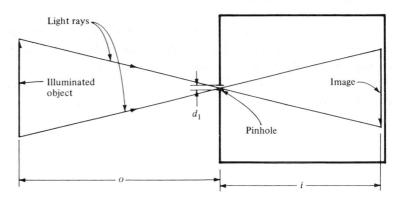

FIGURE 2-10
Pinhole lens of the pinhole camera.

infinite number of image points, focused in the image plane forms the image of the entire object. Note from Fig. 2-11 that the image is inverted by the simple thin lens.

The *optical axis* of a thin lens is defined as the line joining the centers of curvature of the spherical surfaces of the lens. In Fig. 2-12 O_1 and O_2 are the radius points of the two spherical surfaces of the lens, and R_1 and R_2 are the radii of the surfaces. The optical axis is the line O_1O_2. For a lens having one plane surface, the optical axis is defined as the perpendicular to the plane surface passing through the one center of curvature.

Light rays that are parallel to the optical axis as they enter a lens come to focus at f, the *focal point* of the lens. This is illustrated in Fig. 2-12. As a corollary to that description, the focal point of a lens is the point on the optical axis having the property that any light ray passing through it as it enters a lens travels parallel to the optical axis of

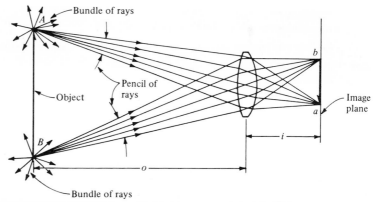

FIGURE 2-11
Pencils of light rays and image formation.

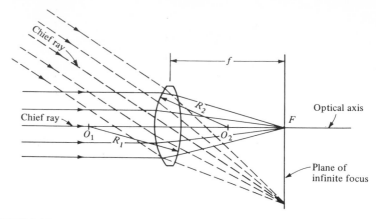

FIGURE 2-12
Optical axis, focal length, and plane of infinite focus of a thin lens.

the lens after being refracted by the lens. Actually any thin lens has two focal points, one on either side of the lens at equal distance from the lens. If light rays parallel to the optical axis were incident to the lens of Fig. 2-12 from the right, they would come to focus at a point on the optical axis a distance f to the left side of the lens.

A plane perpendicular to the optical axis passing through the focal point is called the *plane of infinite focus,* or simply the *focal plane.* Parallel rays entering a converging lens, regardless of the angle they make with the optical axis, are brought to focus in the plane of infinite focus (see dashed rays of Fig. 2-12). The point of focus occurs where the *chief ray* strikes the plane of infinite focus. The chief ray is that light ray passing undeviated in direction through the center of the lens. Note that lateral displacement of the ray due to lens thickness is neglected.

The distance from the plane of infinite focus to the center of a thin lens is f, the *focal length* of the lens. This is illustrated in Fig. 2-12. The focal length is a function of the index of refraction of the glass from which the lens is ground and of the radii of curvature of the spherical surfaces.

2-7 LENS FORMULA

A pencil of incident light rays coming from an object located an infinite distance away from the lens will be parallel, as illustrated in Fig. 2-12, and the image will come to focus in the plane of infinite focus. For objects located some finite distance from the lens, the *image distance* (distance from lens to plane of focus) is greater than the focal length. It is obvious from Fig. 2-13 that the closer the object is to the lens, the farther behind the lens

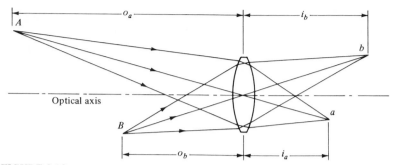

FIGURE 2-13
Image distance increases with decreased object distance.

will be the point of focus. The following equation, called the *lens formula*, expresses the relationship of object distance, o, and image distance, i, to the focal length f of a converging lens:

$$\frac{1}{o} + \frac{1}{i} = \frac{1}{f} \qquad (2\text{-}5)$$

If the focal length of a lens and the distance to an object are known, the resulting distance to the image plane can be calculated using the lens formula.

EXAMPLE 2-3   Find the image distance for an object distance of 50 m and a focal length of 50.0 cm.

By Eq. (2-5),

$$\frac{1}{50} + \frac{1}{i} = \frac{1}{0.50}$$

$$\frac{1}{i} = \frac{1}{0.5} - \frac{1}{50} = \frac{100 - 1}{50} = 1.98$$

$$i = \frac{1}{1.98} = 0.505 \text{ m} = 50.5 \text{ cm} \qquad ////$$

2-8 SCHEIMPFLUG CONDITION

If the image plane is tilted with respect to the object plane when projecting images through a lens, the *Scheimpflug condition* must be adhered to in order to achieve sharp focus of all images. The Scheimpflug condition, as illustrated in Fig. 2-14, states that the image plane, object plane, and lens plane (plane through the optical center of the lens and perpendicular to the optical axis) all must intersect along a common line. (When the

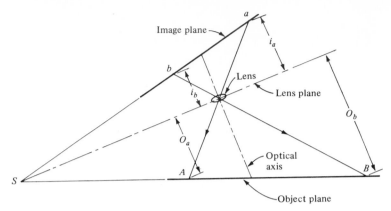

FIGURE 2-14
Geometry of the Scheimpflug condition.

image and object planes are parallel, the lens plane must also be parallel to these planes, in which case the line of intersection of the three planes theoretically occurs at infinity.)

In Fig. 2-14 the image plane is tilted with respect to the object plane and the two planes intersect along line S. Note that, as a result of tilt, object distances of projected images vary depending upon their location in the image plane; e.g., object distance O_b corresponding to image b is greater than O_a corresponding to image a. In order to maintain sharp focus, the lens formula—Eq. (2-5), which relates image distances and object distances for a given lens—must be satisfied for all images. As object distances increase, image distances must be decreased to satisfy the lens formula. This is accomplished by tilting (*canting*) the lens as shown in Fig. 2-14 so that the lens plane passes through S. (Note that image distances and object distances are measured perpendicular to the lens plane.)

Situations in photogrammetry where the Scheimpflug condition must be enforced are in rectification of tilted photographs (see Sec. 13-14) and in orienting oblique photographs in a stereoscopic plotter (see Sec. 16-2). In both of these cases the image plane is tilted with respect to the object plane and object distances are relatively short, so that focus is critical. In exposing oblique aerial photos, it is unnecessary to enforce the Scheimpflug condition because object distances are great with respect to image distances and sharp focus is maintained with image distance set for infinite object distances.

2-9 REAL AND VIRTUAL IMAGES

The image formed by a lens is said to be *real* if it may be made visible by placing a screen in the image plane. Such is the case of the image of Fig 2-11. The converging lenses of Fig. 2-9*a* through *c* all form real images of objects if the objects are located at object

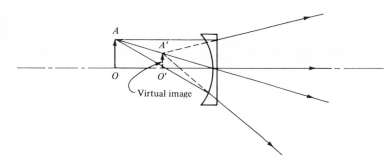

FIGURE 2-15
Virtual image formed by a diverging lens.

distances greater than the focal length of the lens. *Virtual* images are images that cannot be formed on a screen because the rays do not actually come together at a focus point. Instead, the rays must be projected backward to their intersection as indicated by the dashed lines of Figs. 2-15 and 2-16. All diverging lenses form virtual images; so do converging lenses when the object distance is less than the focal length.

In Fig. 2-16 the object distance is less than the focal length of the converging lens. In this case the virtual image is larger than the real image, which illustrates the use of a lens as a magnifying glass. Light rays emanating from A are refracted in a convergent manner by the lens but not enough to enable them to come to focus. To an observer located on the right, light rays appear to emanate from A' and O' instead of O and A. Therefore $O'A'$ is the magnified virtual image of the object OA.

2-10 LATERAL MAGNIFICATION

Lateral magnification of a lens is the ratio of the image size to the object size. For the lens of Fig. 2-11, the lateral magnification is the ratio ab/AB. By comparison of similar triangles, the following magnification equation is obtained:

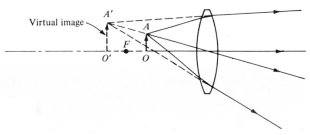

FIGURE 2-16
Virtual image of a converging lens (magnifying glass).

$$M = \frac{i}{o} \qquad (2\text{-}6)$$

Where M is the lateral magnification and o and i are object and image distances, respectively, as previously defined. In Figs. 2-15 and 2-16 lateral magnification is the ratio $A'O'/AO$.

2-11 THICK LENSES

The analysis of thin lens in the previous sections was simplified by assuming that their thicknesses were negligible. With thick lenses this assumption is no longer valid. Thick lenses may consist of a single thick element or a combination of two or more elements which are either cemented together in contact or otherwise rigidly held in place with air spaces between the elements. A thick "combination" lens used in an aerial camera is illustrated in Fig. 2-17. Note that it consists of 12 individual elements.

Two points called *nodal points* must be defined for thick lenses. These points, termed the *incident* nodal point and the *emergent* nodal point, lie on the optical axis. They have the property that any light ray directed toward the incident nodal point passes through the emergent nodal point and emerges on the other side of the lens in a direction parallel to the direction of the original incident ray. In Fig. 2-18, for example, rays AN and $N'a$ are parallel, as are rays BN and $N'b$. Points N and N' are the incident and emergent nodal points, respectively, of the thick lens.

If parallel incident light rays (rays from an object at an infinite distance) pass through a thick lens, they will come to focus at the plane of infinite focus. The focal length of a thick lens is the distance from the emergent nodal point N' to this plane of infinite focus.

2-12 LENS QUALITY

It is impossible for a single lens to produce a perfect image; it will, instead, always be somewhat blurred. These imperfections which degrade the sharpness of the image are termed *aberrations*. Their presence gives rise to the use of combination lenses discussed in the previous section. Through the use of additional lens elements, lens designers are able to correct for aberrations and bring them within tolerable limits.

The primary lens aberrations are (1) spherical aberration, (2) coma, (3) astigmatism and curvature of field, and (4) chromatic aberration. *Spherical aberration,* as illustrated in Fig. 2-19, is the degradation of the axial image. It is caused by faulty grinding of the spherical surfaces of the lens elements and results in rays entering near the outer edge of the lens being brought to focus nearer the lens than the rays which enter near the center

FIGURE 2-17
Cross section of the Super Aviogon lens. (*Courtesy of Wild Heerbrugg Instruments, Inc.*)

of the lens. The image of a point thus formed is a circle called the *circle of confusion*. If spherical aberration exists for a lens, the size of the circle of confusion may be reduced by adjusting the position of the image plane until the smallest possible circle (*circle of least confusion*) is obtained. The image-plane position that produces the circle of least

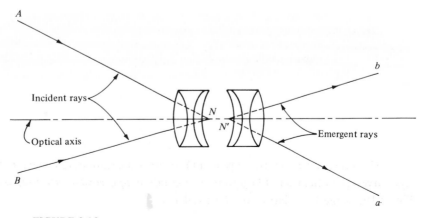

FIGURE 2-18
Nodal points of a thick lens.

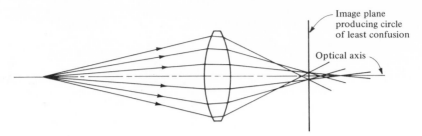

FIGURE 2-19
Spherical aberration.

confusion is illustrated in Fig. 2-19. *Coma* is similar to spherical aberration, except that it applies to the failure of oblique rays, instead of axial rays, to come to focus at a point.

Astigmatism is a condition in which lines in the object that are perpendicular to each other do not come to focus at the same image distance. As shown in Fig. 2-20, rays 1 and 2 from an object line are focused at *a* while rays 3 and 4, which are from a perpendicular line in the object, are focused at *b*. Astigmatism is caused by imperfect grinding of the lens surfaces. Astigmatism is common in the human eye. With an astigmatic lens, images from points of equal object distances will not come to focus in the same image plane. Rather, they will form a curved surface. This condition is called *curvature of field*. Astigmatism and curvature of field can be minimized by using combination lenses composed of converging and diverging elements.

Chromatic aberration is caused by the different refractive characteristics of the various colors which make up white light. As shown in Fig. 2-21, blue light is refracted more than red light, and therefore these two colors fail to come to focus at a common point. The effects of chromatic aberration can also be compensated for through the use of converging and diverging lenses in combination.

The *aberrations* discussed above degrade the quality or sharpness of the image. Lens *distortions* on the other hand, do not degrade image quality but deteriorate the geometric quality (or geometry) of the image. Lens distortions are classified as either *radial* or *tangential*. Radial distortion, as implied by its name, causes imaged points to be distorted

FIGURE 2-20
Astigmatism.

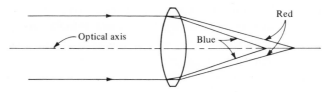

FIGURE 2-21
Chromatic aberration.

along radial lines from the optical axis. It is caused by faulty grinding of the lens elements. Outward radial distortion is considered positive and inward radial distortion is considered negative. Tangential distortion occurs at right angles to radial lines from the optical axis. It is caused by faulty centering of the lens elements of a combination lens. Tangential distortion is generally of much less consequence than radial distortion and can often be disregarded. In Fig. 2-22, instead of the incident light ray being imaged at its correct position a, it is imaged at a'. In Fig. 2-22 the magnitude of radial distortion is Δr (positive in this case because it is outward), and the magnitude of tangential distortion is Δt.

If distortions are present in a camera lens, photogrammetrists will obtain erroneous measurements from the resulting photographs. Distortions present in a lens may be determined by calibration tests, as described in Chap. 4, and corrections can be applied to measurements to eliminate their effect. The correction procedure is described in Chap. 5.

In designing lenses, distortions and aberrations cannot be eliminated completely, but they can be minimized through the use of combination lenses. Often the reduction of one type of distortion or aberration affects another type adversely, and therefore lens design is a science of compromise in attempting to obtain the least possible detrimental

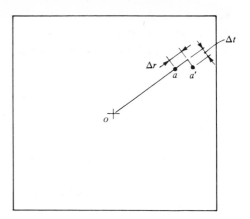

FIGURE 2-22
Radial and tangential lens distortions.

combination of all distortions and aberrations. The quantity of calculations involved in lens design is enormous if the many possible compromises are to be thoroughly investigated. With the advent of electronic computers, lens designers have performed these computations more readily and better and better lenses have resulted. Today distortions of many combination lenses have been reduced to such negligible amounts that they are often referred to as *distortion-free lenses.*

Resolution or *resolving power* of a lens is the ability of the lens to show detail. The measure of lens resolution is the number of *line pairs* (black lines separated by white line spaces of equal thickness) which can be distinguished in the image within a width of 1 millimeter. The method of testing for resolving power is discussed in Chap. 4.

2-13 DEPTH OF FIELD

The *depth of field* of a lens is the range in object distance that can be accommodated by a lens without introducing significant image deterioration. In Fig. 2-23a, light rays from object point B are perfectly focused as a point b in the image plane. Light rays from A and C, on the other hand, are imaged as circles of confusion of diameter x. The larger the circles of confusion become, the more deteriorated is the image. By placing a certain limit on the tolerable diameter of the circle of confusion, depth of field is limited. In Fig. 2-23a, depth of field is limited to the distance AC by the tolerable diameter x of the circle of confusion.

For a given lens, depth of field can be increased by stopping down the aperture of the lens as shown in Fig. 2-23b. This limits the usable area of the lens to the central portion. For aerial photography, depth of field is seldom of consequence because variations in the object distance are generally a very small percentage of the total object distance. For close-range photography, however, depth of field is often extremely critical.

Depth of focus, which is akin to depth of field, is the range in image distances which can be tolerated without introducing significant image deterioration.

REFERENCES

American Society of Photogrammetry: "Manual of Photogrammetry," 3d ed., George Banta Co., Inc., Menasha, Wis., 1966, chap. 3.

Brown, E. B.: "Modern Optics," Reinhold Publishing Corporation, New York, 1965.

Greenleaf, A. R.: "Photographic Optics," The Macmillan Company, New York, 1950.

Habell, K. J., and A. Cox: "Engineering Optics," rev. ed., Sir Isaac Pitman & Sons, Ltd., London, 1953.

Jensen, N.: "Optical and Photographic Reconnaissance Systems," John Wiley & Sons, Inc., New York, 1968.

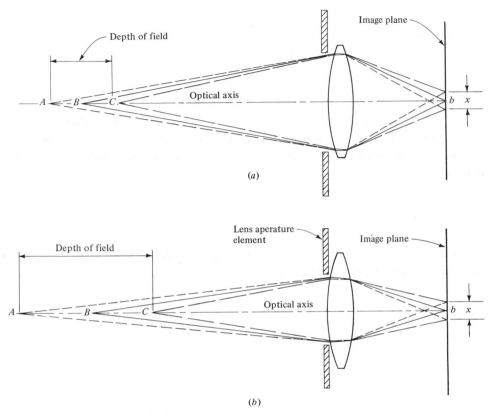

FIGURE 2-23
(*a*) Depth of field of a lens. (*b*) Depth of field increases with decreased lens aperture.

Kissam, P.: "Optical Tooling," McGraw-Hill Book Company, New York, 1962.
Levine, H., and S. Rosin: The Geocon IV Lens, *Photogrammetric Engineering,* vol. 36, no. 4, p. 335, 1970.
Smith, Warren J.: "Modern Optical Engineering," McGraw-Hill Book Company, New York, 1966.
Washer, F. E.: Resolving Power Related to Aberration, *Photogrammetric Engineering,* vol. 32, no. 2, p. 213, 1966.

PROBLEMS

2-1 A ray of light enters glass (index 1.600) from air (index 1.000) at an incident angle of 30°. Find the angles of refraction and of deviation.

2-2 The problem is the same as Prob. 2-1 except that the incident angle is 35° and the index of refraction of the glass is 1.520.

2-3 A light ray emanating from under water (index 1.333) makes an angle of 48° with the normal to the surface. What is the angle that the refracted ray makes with the normal as it emerges into air (index 1.000)?

2-4 A light ray is directed through air (index 1.000) at a 45° angle of incidence toward a parallel-sided glass plate (index 1.520) which is 5 millimeters thick. What will be the lateral displacement of the light ray as it again emerges into air?

2-5 The problem is the same as Prob. 2-4 except that the angle of incidence is 55° and the thickness of the glass plate is 0.30 inches.

2-6 Find the critical angle for a light ray traveling from flint glass (index 1.750) to air (index 1.000).

2-7 Find the critical angle for a light ray traveling from water (index 1.333) to air (index 1.000).

2-8 What is the angle of deviation for a light ray traveling from crown glass (index 1.520) to flint glass (index 1.750) if the angle of incidence is 30°?

2-9 Derive Eq. (2-3) for lateral displacement of a light ray passing through a parallel-sided plate.

2-10 An object located 36 inches in front of a thin lens has its image in focus 12 inches from the lens on the other side. What is the focal length of the lens?

2-11 A thin lens has a focal length of 100 mm. What is the image distance for an object distance of 10 feet?

2-12 An object 10 centimeters high is located 1 foot in front of a lens whose focal length is 3.00 inches. What is the image distance, lateral magnification, and height of the magnified image?

PRINCIPLES OF PHOTOGRAPHY[1]

3-1 INTRODUCTION

Photography, which means "drawing with light," originated long before cameras and light-sensitive photographic films came into use. Ancient Arabs discovered that when inside a dark tent, they could observe inverted images of illuminated outside objects. The images were formed by light rays which passed through tiny holes in the tent. The principle involved was actually that of the pinhole camera of the type shown in Fig. 2-10. In the 1700s French artists used the pinhole principle as an aid in drawing perspective views of illuminated objects. While inside a dark box, they traced the outlines of objects projected onto the wall opposite a pinhole.

In 1839 Louis Daguerre of France developed a photographic film that could capture a permanent record of images which illuminated it. By placing this film inside a dark "pinhole box," a picture could be obtained without the help of an artist. The "pinhole box" used in conjunction with photographic film became known as a *camera*.

[1] By Dr. James P. Scherz, Associate Professor of Civil and Environmental Engineering, University of Wisconsin, Madison, Wis.

3-2 COMPARISON OF PINHOLE AND LENS CAMERAS

Photographic film has improved a great deal through the years, but it still is not sensitive enough to capture an image projected through a pinhole in a short period of time. Therefore it was necessary to increase the size of the opening to allow more light to pass. If the pinhole is enlarged, however, the resulting image is blurred. By replacing the pinhole with a lens it is possible to enlarge the hole and still retain sharp focus.

The geometry of the lens camera of Fig. 3-1 is identical to the geometry of the pinhole camera of Fig. 2-10 if the thickness, t, of the lens is disregarded. Note, however, that the lens opening has been increased from pinhole size d_1 in Fig. 2-10 to diameter d_2 in Fig. 3-1. Instead of object distances and image distances being unrestricted as with the pinhole camera, with the lens camera these distances are governed by the lens formula Eq. (2-5). To satisfy this equation the lens camera must be focused for each different object distance by adjusting the image distance. When object distances approach infinity, as for photographing objects at great distances, the term $1/o$ in Eq. (2-5) approaches zero and image distance i is then equal to f, the focal length of the lens. With aerial photography, object distances are very great with respect to image distance; therefore aerial cameras are manufactured with their focus fixed for infinity. This is accomplished by making the image distance equal to the focal length of the camera lens.

3-3 ILLUMINANCE

Illuminance of any photographic exposure is the brightness or amount of light received per unit area of the image plane surface during exposure. The unit of illuminance is *meter-candles*. One meter-candle is the illuminance produced by a standard candle at a distance of 1 meter.

Illuminance is proportional to the amount of light passing through the lens opening during exposure, and this, of course, is proportional to the area of the opening. Since the area of the lens opening is $\pi d^2/4$, illuminance is proportional to d^2, the square of the diameter of the lens opening.

Image distance is another factor which affects illuminance. As illustrated in Fig. 3-2, radii of areas illuminated by light rays passing through a lens are directly proportional to their image distances. In the figure for example, if i_2 equals $2i_1$, then r_2 equals $2r_1$. The illuminated areas are proportional to the squares of their radii; i.e., $A_1 = \pi r_1^2$ and $A_2 = \pi r_2^2$. Illuminance is inversely proportional to illuminated area, and because of the proportionality of i and r, illuminance is proportional to $1/i^2$. If object distance is infinity so that i equals f, then illuminance is proportional to $1/f^2$. Since illuminance is proportional to both d^2 and $1/f^2$, these two quantities may be combined so that illuminance is proportional to d^2/f^2. The square root of this term is called the

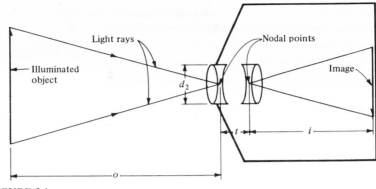

FIGURE 3-1
Geometry of the lens camera.

brightness factor, or

$$\frac{d}{f} = \text{brightness factor} \qquad (3\text{-}1)$$

The inverse of Eq. (3-1) is also an inverse expression of illuminance and is the very common term "f-stop." In equation form, f-stop is:

$$\frac{f}{d} = f\text{-stop} \qquad (3\text{-}2)$$

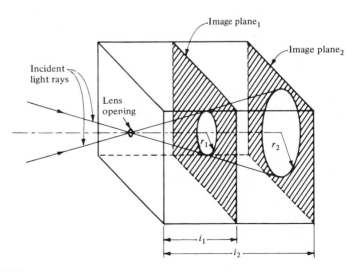

FIGURE 3-2
Illuminance is a function of image distance.

According to Eq. (3-2), *f*-stop is the ratio of focal length to diameter of the lens opening. As the lens opening increases, the *f*-stop number decreases and illuminance increases. Brighter images require less exposure time, i.e., faster shutter speeds. Because of this correlation between *f*-stop and shutter speed, *f*-stop is the term used for expressing *lens speed* or "light gathering" power of a lens. Illuminance produced by a particular lens is correctly expressed by Eq. (3-2), whether the lens has a very small diameter with short focal length or a very large diameter with a long focal length. If *f*-stop is the same for two different lenses, the illuminance of each of their images will be the same.

3-4 RELATIONSHIP OF DIAPHRAGM OPENING AND SHUTTER SPEED

A sunbather gets a suntan or sunburn when exposed to sunshine. The darkness of tan or severity of burn is the product of the sun's illuminance (brightness) and the time of exposure to the sun. *Total exposure* of photographic film likewise is the product of illuminance and time of exposure. Its unit is *meter-candle-seconds*.

In making photographic exposures, the correct amounts of illuminance and time may be correlated using a light meter. Illuminance is regulated by varying *f*-stop settings on the camera, while time of exposure is set by varying shutter speed. Variations in *f*-stop settings are actually variations in the diameter of the *diaphragm*—a circular shield that enlarges or contracts, changing the diameter of the opening of the lens.

With a lens camera, as the diameter of the diaphragm increases, enabling faster exposures, depth of field becomes less and lens distortions become more severe. There are situations when a small diaphragm opening is desirable, and there are times when the reverse is true. In order to photograph a scene with great variations in object distances and yet retain sharp focus of all images, a large depth of field is required. In this case, to maximize depth of field, the picture would be taken at a slow shutter speed and large *f*-stop setting corresponding to a small-diameter lens opening. On the other hand, in photographing rapidly moving objects or in making exposures from a moving vehicle such as an airplane, a fast shutter speed is essential to reduce image motion. In this situation a small *f*-stop setting corresponding to a large-diameter lens opening would be necessary for sufficient exposure.

From the previous discussion it is apparent that there is an important relationship between *f*-stop and shutter speed. If exposure time is cut in half, total exposure is also cut in half. On the other hand, if diaphragm area is doubled, total exposure is also doubled. If shutter time is halved and diaphragm area is doubled, total exposure remains unchanged. This relationship of *f*-stop and shutter speed leads to many interesting problems in determining correct exposures.

EXAMPLE 3-1   Suppose that a photographic film is optimally exposed with an f-stop setting of f-4 and a shutter speed of 1/500 sec. What is the correct f-stop setting if shutter speed is changed to 1/1,000 sec?

SOLUTION   Total exposure is the product of diaphragm area and shutter speed. This product must remain the same for the 1/1,000-sec shutter speed as it was for the 1/500-sec shutter speed, or

$$\text{area}_1 \times \text{time}_1 = \text{area}_2 \times \text{time}_2$$

Rearranging,

$$\text{area}_2 = \text{area}_1 \times \frac{\text{time}_1}{\text{time}_2} \qquad (a)$$

Let d_1 and d_2 be diaphragm diameters for 1/500- and 1/1,000-sec shutter times respectively. Then the respective diaphragm areas are

$$\text{area}_1 = \frac{\pi(d_1)^2}{4} \quad \text{and} \quad \text{area}_2 = \frac{\pi(d_2)^2}{4} \qquad (b)$$

By Eq. (3-2),

$$d_1 = \frac{f}{f\text{-stop}_1} \quad \text{and since } f\text{-stop}_1 = 4, d_1 = \frac{f}{4} \qquad (c)$$

Substituting (b) and (c) into (a),

$$\frac{\pi(d_2)^2}{4} = \frac{\pi(f)^2}{4(4)^2} \times \frac{1/500}{1/1,000}$$

Reducing,

$$\frac{f}{d_2} = \sqrt{\frac{500 \times 16}{1,000}} = 2.8$$

Hence f-2.8 is the required f-stop.   ////

3-5   CHARACTERISTICS OF PHOTOGRAPHIC EMULSIONS

Photographic films consist of two parts: *emulsion* and *backing* or *support.* The emulsion consists of light-sensitive silver halide crystals. These are placed on the backing or support in a thin coat as shown in Fig. 3-3. The support material is usually paper, plastic film, or glass.

Silver halide crystals have the property that when exposed to light the bond between the silver and the halide is weakened. An emulsion that has been exposed to light contains an invisible image of the object called the *latent image.* When the latent image is developed, areas of the emulsion that were exposed to intense light turn to free silver and become black. Areas that received no light become white if the support is white paper.

FIGURE 3-3
Cross section of a photographic film.

Emulsion of
silver halide crystals

Support material

(They become clear if the support is glass or transparent plastic film.) The degree of darkness of developed images is a function of total exposure (product of illuminance and time) which originally sensitized the emulsion to form the latent image. In any photographic exposure there will be variations in illuminance received from different objects in the photographed scene, and therefore between black and white there will exist various tones of gray which result from these variations in illuminance. Actually the crystals turn black, not gray, when exposed to sufficient light. However, if the light received in a particular area is sufficient to sensitize only a portion of the crystals, a gray tone results from a mixture of the resulting black and white. The greater the exposure, the greater the percentage of black in the mixture and hence the darker the shade of gray.

The degree of darkness of a developed film is called its *density*. The greater the density, the darker the film. Density of a film is the measure of the amount of light that can be transmitted through the film; i.e., a black film transmits no light and a clear film transmits almost 100 percent light. Opacity is the reciprocal of transmittance. The unit of density is the common logarithm of opacity. As an example, if 10 percent of the light is transmitted, transmittance is 1/10, opacity is 1/0.10 or 10, and density is the common logarithm of 10 or 1.0. The amount of light incident to a film and the amount transmitted can be measured with an instrument called a *densitometer*.

If exposure is varied for a particular emulsion, corresponding variations in densities will be obtained. A plot of density on the ordinate versus logarithms of exposure on the abscissa for a given emulsion produces a curve called the *characteristic curve* or the *H* and *D curve*. A typical characteristic curve is shown in Fig. 3-4. Characteristic curves for different emulsions vary somewhat, but they all have the same general shape. The lower part of the curve, which is concave upward, is known as the *toe* region. The upper portion, which is concave downward, is the *shoulder* region. A *straight-line* portion occurs between the toe and shoulder regions.

Characteristic curves are useful in describing the characteristics of photographic emulsions. The slope of the straight-line portion of the curve, for example, is a measure of the contrast of the film. The steeper the slope, the greater the *contrast* (change in density) for a given range of exposure. Contrast of a given film is expressed as *gamma,* the tangent of the angle between the straight-line portion of the curve and the abscissa axis, as shown on Fig. 3-4. From Fig. 3-4 it is evident that for an exposure of zero the film has some density. The density of an unexposed emulsion is called *fog*, and on the curve it is the density corresponding to the low portion of the toe region. It is also apparent from Fig. 3-4 that exposure must exceed a certain minimum before density greater than fog

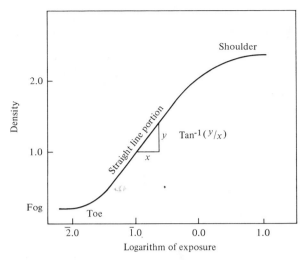

FIGURE 3-4
Typical characteristic curve of a photographic emulsion.

occurs. A properly exposed photograph is one in which the entire range of exposure occurs on the straight-line portion of the curve.

Just as the skin of different people varies in sensitivity to sunlight, so also does the sensitivity of emulsions vary. Light sensitivity of photographic emulsions is a function of the size and number of silver halide crystals or *grains* in the emulsion. When the required amount of light exposes a grain of emulsion, the entire grain becomes exposed regardless of its size. If a certain emulsion is composed of grains half as large as those in another emulsion, it will require approximately twice as many grains to cover the film. This emulsion will also require about twice as much light to properly expose it. Conversely, as grain size increases, the total number of grains in the emulsion decreases and the amount of light required to properly expose it decreases. Film is said to be more sensitive and faster when it requires less light for proper exposure. Faster films can be used advantageously in photographing rapidly moving objects.

As sensitivity and grain size increase, the resulting image becomes coarse and resolution (sharpness or crispness of the picture) is reduced. Film resolution can be tested by photographing a standard test pattern. The pattern consists of groups of *line pairs* (parallel lines of varying thickness separated by spaces equal to the line thickness). The number of lines per millimeter in the smallest line pattern that can clearly be discerned on the developed film is the resolution of the film.

Photographers have developed exposure guides for films of various sensitivities. In the United States the American Standards Association (ASA) system is used. In this system the ASA number assigned to a film is roughly equal to the inverse of shutter speed (in seconds) required for proper exposure in pure sunlight for a lens opening of $f/16$. According to this rule of thumb, if a film is properly exposed in pure sunlight at $f/16$ and 1/200 second, it would be classified ASA 200. This rule of thumb is seldom used today because of the availability of light meters which, given the ASA rating of the film being used, automatically yield proper exposures for particular lighting conditions. In Europe an exposure standard called DIN has been developed. Most light meters today give scales which accommodate both the ASA and DIN systems.

3-6 PROCESSING BLACK-AND-WHITE EMULSION

The five-step darkroom procedure for processing an exposed black-and-white emulsion is as follows:

1) Developing In this first step the exposed emulsion is placed in a chemical solution called *developer*. The action of the developer causes grains of silver halide which were exposed to light to be reduced to free black silver. The free silver produces the blacks and shades of gray of which the image is composed. Developers vary in strength and other characteristics and must therefore be carefully chosen to produce the desired results. Generally the time of immersion of the film in the developer is between 1 and 15 minutes, depending upon the particular film and developer used. The contrast of the final image can be changed somewhat by changing development time and temperature of the developer.

2) Stop Bath When proper darkness and contrast of the image has been attained in the developing stage, it is necessary to stop the developing action. This is done with a stop bath—an *acetic* solution which neutralizes the *basic* developer solution. The emulsion is immersed in the stop bath for just a few seconds.

3) Fixing Not all the silver halide grains are turned to free black silver as a result of developing. Instead, there remain many undeveloped grains which would also turn black upon exposure to light if they were not removed. To prevent further developing which would ruin the image, the undeveloped silver halide grains are dissolved out in the fixing solution. The fixing bath also hardens the emulsion. Normal immersion time in the fixing bath is from 10 to 20 minutes.

4) Washing In this step the emulsion is washed in clear running water to remove any remaining chemicals. If not removed, these chemicals could cause spotting or haziness of the image. Normal washing time is from 20 to 30 minutes. A detergent may be added to decrease washing time, but this is not necessary.

5) Drying In this final step the emulsion is dried to remove the water from the emulsion and backing material. This can be done in a variety of ways, from simply air drying to drying in elaborate heated dryers.

Modern equipment is capable of automatically performing the entire five-step darkroom procedure nonstop. The result obtained from developing black-and-white film is a *negative*. It derives its name from the fact that it is reversed in color and geometry from the original scene which was photographed, i.e., black objects appear white and vice versa, and images are inverted.

A *positive* is obtained from the negative by repeating the photographic process. This reverses color and geometry again, thereby producing an image which is true in tone and geometry. In producing the positive from a negative, printing paper which is covered with a layer of emulsion is exposed by passing light through the negative onto the emulsion. Light is transmitted through the various areas of the negative in proportion to the lightness of the negative; e.g., black areas will not transmit light at all and therefore they will not expose their corresponding areas of the printing paper. As a result of exposure through the negative, a latent image is formed on the printing paper. This latent image is processed using the same five-step darkroom procedure outlined above.

Besides using printing paper, positives may also be prepared on plastic film or glass plates. In photogrammetric terminology, positives prepared on glass plates are called *diapositives*.

3-7   SPECTRAL SENSITIVITY OF EMULSIONS

The sun and various artificial sources such as light bulbs emit a wide range of so-called *electromagnetic energy*. The entire range of this electromagnetic energy is called the *electromagnetic spectrum*. X-rays, visible light rays, and radio waves are some familiar examples of energy variations within the electromagnetic spectrum. Electromagnetic energy travels in regular sinusoidal oscillations called *waves*. Variations in electromagnetic energy are classified according to variations in their wavelengths or frequencies of propagation. The velocity of electromagnetic energy in a vacuum is constant and related to frequency and wavelength through the following expression:

$$c = f\lambda \qquad (3\text{-}3)$$

In Eq. (3-3), c is velocity in a vacuum of electromagnetic energy, f is frequency, and λ is wavelength. Figure 3-5 illustrates the wavelength classification of the electromagnetic spectrum. Visible light (that electromagnetic energy to which our eyes are sensitive) is composed of only a very small portion of the spectrum (see Fig. 3-5). It consists of energy with wavelengths in the range of from about 0.4 to 0.7 micrometers. Energy having wavelengths slightly shorter than 0.4 micrometers is called *ultraviolet,* and energy with wavelengths slightly longer than 0.7 micrometers is called *near-infrared*. Ultraviolet and near-infrared cannot be detected by the human eye.

Within the wavelengths of visible light, the human eye is able to distinguish different colors. The primary colors blue, green, and red are composed of slightly

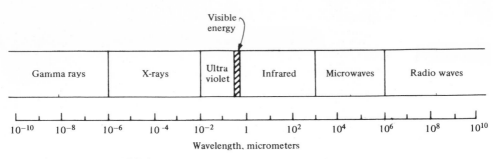

FIGURE 3-5
Classification of the electromagnetic spectrum by wavelength.

different wavelengths; blue being composed of energy having wavelengths of from about 0.4 to 0.5 micrometers, green from 0.5 to 0.6 micrometers, and red from 0.6 to 0.7 micrometers. All other hues are made up of combinations of the primary colors; e.g., yellow is the combination of red and green light. There are multitudes of these combination colors. White light is the combination of all of the visible colors. It can be broken down into its component colors by passing it through a prism, as shown in Fig. 3-6. Color separation occurs because of different refractions that result from energy of different wavelengths.

To the human eye, an object appears a certain color because it reflects energy of the wavelengths producing that color. If an object reflects all the visible energy that strikes it, that object will appear white. On the other hand, if an object absorbs all light and reflects none, that object will appear black in color; and if an object absorbs all green and red energy but reflects blue, that object will appear blue.

Just as the retina of the human eye is sensitive to variations in wavelength, photographic emulsions can also be manufactured with variations in wavelength sensitivity. Black-and-white emulsions composed of untreated silver halides are sensitive only to blue and ultraviolet energy. A red object, for example, will photograph as black on such film. These untreated emulsions are usually used on printing papers for making positives from negatives. When these printing papers are used, red or yellow lights called *safe lights* can be used as a convenience in the darkroom because these colors cannot expose a paper which is sensitive only to blue light.

Black-and-white silver halide emulsions can be treated so that they are sensitive to other wavelengths of the spectrum besides blue. Emulsions sensitive to the blue and green range are called *orthochromatic;* those sensitive to blue, green, and red are called *panchromatic.* Emulsions can also be made to respond to energy in the near-infrared range. These emulsions are called *infrared* or IR. Infrared films make it possible to obtain photographs of energy which is invisible to the human eye. An early application of this type of emulsion was in camouflage detection, where it was found that dead foliation or

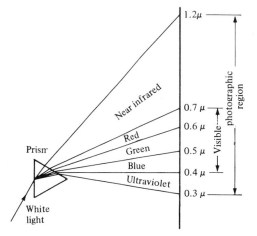

FIGURE 3-6
White light broken into the individual
colors of the visible and near-visible spectrum by means of a prism.

green netting, which had the same green color as live foliation to the human eye, reflected infrared energy differently. This difference could be detected through infrared photography. Infrared film is now widely used for a variety of applications such as early detection of crop diseases, tree species mapping, etc. Figure 3-7 illustrates sensitivity differences of various emulsions.

3-8 FILTERS

The red or yellow safe light described in the previous section usually is simply an ordinary white light covered with a red or yellow filter. If the filter is red, it blocks passage of blue and green wavelengths and allows only red to pass. Filters placed in front of camera lenses also allow only certain wavelengths of energy to pass through the lens and expose the

FIGURE 3-7
Sensitivities of various black-and-white emulsions.

film. The use of filters on cameras can be very advantageous for certain types of photography.

Atmospheric haze is largely caused by the scattering of ultraviolet and short blue wavelengths. Pictures which are clear in spite of atmospheric haze can be taken through haze filters. Haze filters block passage of objectionable scattered short wavelengths (which produce haze) and prevent them from entering the camera and exposing the film. Because of this advantage, haze filters are almost always used on aerial cameras.

Filters for aerial mapping cameras are manufactured from high-quality optical glass. This is the case because light rays which form the image must pass through the filter before entering the camera. In passing through the filter, light rays are subjected to distortions caused by the filter. The camera should therefore be calibrated with the filter locked firmly in place; after calibration, the filter should not be removed, for this would upset the calibration.

3-9 PROCESSING COLOR EMULSIONS

Normal color and *color infrared* emulsions are rather recent advancements which are now finding widespread use in photogrammetry and photo interpretation. Color emulsions consist of three layers of silver halides as shown in Fig. 3-8. The top layer is sensitive to blue light, the second layer is sensitive to green and blue light, and the bottom layer is sensitive to red and blue light. A blue blocking filter is built into the emulsion between the top two layers, thus preventing blue light from exposing the bottom two layers. The result is three layers sensitive to blue, green, and red light respectively from top to bottom. The sensitivity of each layer is indicated in Fig. 3-9.

In making a color exposure, light entering the camera sensitizes the layer or layers of the emulsion which correspond to the color or combination of colors of the original scene. There are a variety of color films available, each requiring a slightly different developing process. The first step of color developing accomplishes essentially the same result as the first step of black-and-white developing. The exposed halides in each layer are turned into black crystals of silver. The remainder of the process depends on whether the film is *color negative* or *color reversal* film. With color negative film, a negative is produced and color prints are made from the negative. Color reversal film produces a true color transparency directly on the film. It is used for making color slides.

In developing color negative film, silver halides in each layer that turned black in the original step are replaced with dyes of the complementary colors of the layer; i.e., the black silver grains of the upper or blue-sensitive layer are replaced with *yellow* dye (yellow is the complementary color of blue and is composed of green and red wavelengths); the black silver crystals in the second or green-sensitive layer are replaced

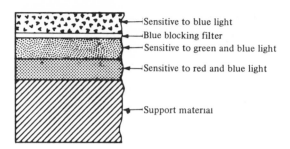

FIGURE 3-8
Cross section of normal color film.

with *magenta* dye (magenta is the complementary color of green and is composed of blue and red wavelengths); and the silver crystals of the third or red-sensitive layer are replaced with *cyan* dye (cyan is the complementary color of red and is composed of blue and green wavelengths).

In producing a color print from the negative, white light (light composed of all wavelengths in the visible range) is directed through the color negative to expose a three-layered color printing emulsion. The color negative acts as a filter, exposing the three layers to the three colors yellow, magenta, and cyan. In developing the exposed print, the complementary colors of yellow, magenta, and cyan (blue, green, and red respectively) are produced. This second color reversal yields the original colors of the photographed scene on the processed print.

With color reversal film, the film is first partially developed to obtain the complementary color layers. The film is then exposed again and the developing process

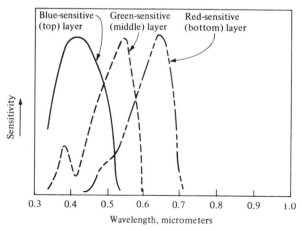

FIGURE 3-9
Color sensitivity of the three layers of normal color film.

repeated to obtain a second color reversal. This is the same process as with color negative film except that both processes are done on the original film. The net result is a color transparency composed of the original colors in the photographed scene.

During World War II there was great interest in increasing the effectiveness of films in the infrared region of the spectrum. This interest led to the development of *color infrared* or *false-color* film. The military called it *camouflage detection* film because it allowed photo interpreters to easily differentiate between camouflage and natural foliage. Like normal color film, color IR film also has three emulsion layers, each sensitive to a different part of the spectrum. Fig. 3-10 illustrates the sensitivity curves for each layer of color IR film. The sensitivity of the top layer peaks both in green and ultraviolet regions. The middle layer has its peak in the red portion of the spectrum, but it too is sensitive to ultraviolet light. The bottom layer has a sensitivity from ultraviolet to infrared. The total sensitivity of the film is from just below the 0.3-micrometer wavelength to above the 0.9-micrometer wavelength. Color IR film is commonly used with a yellow filter, which blocks wavelengths shorter than about 0.5 micrometers. The crosshatched area of Fig. 3-10 illustrates the blocking effect of a yellow filter.

With color IR film and a yellow filter, any object that reflects long-wave red or infrared energy will appear red on the final processed picture. Objects that radiate red will appear green, and objects radiating green will appear blue. It is this mis-representation of color which accounts for the name "false-color." Although color IR film was developed by the military, it has found a multitude of uses in civilian applications.

3-10 PROCESSING BLACK-AND-WHITE AERIAL FILM

Black-and-white aerial film is developed directly on the roll. The simplest and most common method of developing aerial film is the *rewind process*. The equipment for this process, shown in Fig. 3-11, consists of three tanks, one each for developer, stop bath, and fixer. In addition there is a rewind apparatus consisting of two reels mounted on a frame. The apparatus just fits into the tanks. The film is wound onto one of the reels and immersed first into the developer tank. By means of either an electric motor or a hand crank, the film is wound back and forth from one reel to the other during developing. This rewind procedure is repeated for the stop bath and fixer. The film is then washed in clear running water and dried. Aerial film is usually developed in complete darkness because it is sensitive to all wavelengths of visible light.

More elaborate continuous processors are available which automatically develop, wash, and dry rolls of black-and-white film. Equipment is also available for the continuous processing of color aerial films.

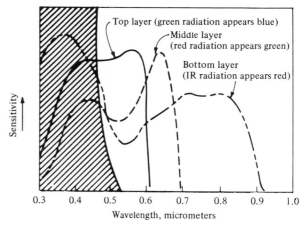

FIGURE 3-10
Sensitivity of color infrared (false-color) film.

3-11 CONTACT PRINTING

Contact printing is the direct process of making a photo positive from a negative. The emulsion side of a negative is placed in direct contact with the unexposed emulsion of a printing paper or glass plate. Together these are placed in a contact printer and exposed,

FIGURE 3-11
Equipment for processing black-and-white aerial film. (*Courtesy Carl Zeiss, Oberkochen*)

FIGURE 3-12
KG-30 single-frame contact printer. (*Courtesy Carl Zeiss, Oberkochen*)

with the emulsion of the printing paper or glass plate facing the light source. Figure 3-12 illustrates a single-frame contact printer. The instrument is equipped with a timing device which automatically makes the exposure for the desired time. Two reel holders on either side of the stage make it possible to handle spools of aerial film easily. The rubber membrane on the cover of the printer is filled with air, so that when the cover is closed and the exposure made, all parts of the paper and negative are pressed firmly together onto the glass stage. Contact printers which are capable of automatically and continuously exposing the aerial negatives of an entire roll of film are also available. In contract printing, the positive that is obtained is the same size as the negative from which it was made.

Uniform lighting throughout the negative during exposure will underexpose the emulsion in more dense areas of the negative and overexpose less dense areas. This can be compensated for in a process called *dodging,* which consists of adjusting the amount of light passing through different parts of the negative so that optimum exposure over the entire print is obtained in spite of density variations. The contact printer of Fig. 3-12 has a bank of lights arranged in a rectangular pattern of rows beneath the exposure stage. Dodging is done manually by turning off lamps in various positions until optimum lighting is achieved.

Log Etronic contact printers are available which automatically perform dodging. With these instruments a spotlight source from a cathode ray tube makes the exposure by scanning systematically back and forth across the negative. A photo tube monitors the light transmitted through the negative and automatically increases or decreases scanning speed to achieve optimum exposure in spite of varying negative density.

3-12   PROJECTION PRINTING

If positives are desired at a scale either enlarged or reduced from original negative size, the projection printing process is used. The geometry of projection printing is illustrated in Fig. 3-13. In this process, the negative is placed in the projector of the printer and illuminated from above. Light rays carry images c and d, for example, from the negative, through the projector lens, and finally to their location C and D on the printing paper, which is situated on the easel plane beneath the projector. The emulsion of the printing paper, having been exposed, is then processed in the manner previously described.

Distances A and B of Fig. 3-13 can be varied so that the positive can be printed at any desired scale, and at the same time the lens formula Eq. (2-5) can be satisfied. The enlargement or reduction ratio from negative to positive size is equal to the ratio B/A.

The easel of a projection printer has many small holes in it which are connected to a vacuum system. When the exposure is made, this vacuum system holds the printing paper flat so that distortions from paper buckling are prevented. The easel and lens of some enlargers are capable of being tilted, which makes it possible to remove the distortions inherent in tilted photographs. A print made with these tilt distortions removed has the same geometry as a vertical photograph and is called a *rectified*

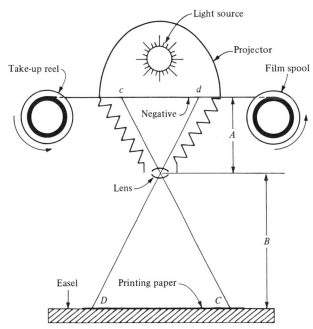

FIGURE 3-13
Geometry of enlargement with a projection printer.

photograph. Rectification is discussed in more detail in Sec. 13-14. A projection printer capable of enlarging and rectifying is shown in Fig. 13-14.

3-13 HALFTONE PROCESS

When ink reproductions are to be made from an original copy which contains varying gray tones, e.g., aerial photos, mosaics, etc., it is necessary to use the *halftone* process. The need for halftone stems from the fact that in reproduction, ink is either printed or it is not printed; there is no "half-ink" process which can produce tones of gray. If ink is printed, the resulting color is black; and if it is not printed, the color is that of the printing paper—usually white.

To get varying tones of gray, halftones are prepared from the original copy using a *screen* in conjunction with a projection printer. The screen is a transparent medium upon which fine black lines have been etched to give a quadrille pattern which, except for the closeness of spacing, would look much like a screen door. The screen is placed on the easel over the emulsion of the halftone film. The screen breaks the light which exposes the film emulsion into small squares, and as a result the image is composed of a mass of small black dots and white spaces. The size of the black dots in any particular area of the halftone depends on the light intensity transmitted through that corresponding part of the negative; i.e., high-intensity light passing through light areas of the negative energizes the emulsion more than low-intensity light and thereby causes larger dots to be formed. In the reproduction process, the dots print ink and the spaces do not. Therefore an area of large dots will reproduce nearly black, while an area of very small dots will appear nearly white.

The dots of halftone copy are generally so small and close together that the human eye is unaware of them and their overall appearance yields smooth and continuous tones of gray. Halftone screens commonly have from about 40 to more than 200 lines per inch. A 100-line screen produces 10,000 small dots per square inch. Coarser screens of about 50 lines per inch are commonly used for rough work such as newspaper pictures, while finer screens such as 100 to 120 are usually used for printing high-quality illustrations, like those in this textbook. Figures 3-11 and 3-12 are but a few of the many examples of the use of halftones in this book. If these figures are examined under magnification, printing dots will actually be seen.

REFERENCES

American Society of Photogrammetry: "Manual of Color Photography," George Banta Co., Inc., Menasha, Wis., 1968.

———: "Manual of Photogrammetry," 3d ed., George Banta Co., Inc., Menasha, Wis., 1966, chap. 6.

Anson, A.: Developments in Aerial Color Photography, *Photogrammetric Engineering,* vol. 34, no. 10, p. 1048, 1968.

Calhoun, J. M. et al.: Physical Properties of Estar Polyester Base Aerial Films for Topographic Mapping, *Photogrammetric Engineering,* vol. 27, no. 3, p. 461, 1961.

Carman, P. D., and H. Brown: Resolution of Four Films in a Survey Camera, *Canadian Surveyor,* vol. 24, no. 5, p. 550, 1970.

Craig, D. R.: Logetronics, *Photogrammetric Engineering,* vol. 21, no. 4, p. 556, 1955.

Eastman Kodak Co.: "Kodak Data for Aerial Photography," Eastman Kodak Co., Rochester, N.Y., 1964.

Harman, W., Jr.: Recent Developments in Aerial Film, *Photogrammetric Engineering,* vol. 27, no. 1, p. 151, 1961.

James, T. H., and G. C. Higgins: *Fundamentals of Photographic Theory,* 2d ed., Morgan and Morgan, Inc., New York, 1960.

Larmore, L.: "Introduction to Photographic Principles," 2d ed., Dover Publications, Inc., New York, 1965.

Mees, C. E. K.: *The Theory of the Photographic Process,* rev. ed., The Macmillan Company, New York, 1954.

Michener, B. C.: Drying of Processed Aerial Films, *Photogrammetric Engineering,* vol. 29, no. 2, p. 321, 1963.

Schallock, G. W.: Metric Tests of Color Photography, *Photogrammetric Engineering,* vol. 34, no. 10, p. 1063, 1968.

Specht, M. R.: IR and Pan Films, *Photogrammetric Engineering,* vol. 36, no. 4, p. 360, 1970.

Sorem, A. L.: Principles of Color Photography, *Photogrammetric Engineering,* vol. 33, no. 9, p. 1008, 1967.

Tarkington, R. G.: Kodak Panchromatic Negative Films for Aerial Photography, *Photogrammetric Engineering,* vol. 25, no. 5, p. 695, 1959.

Tarkington, R. G., and A. L. Sorem: Color and False Color Films for Aerial Photography, *Photogrammetric Engineering,* vol. 29, no. 1, p. 88, 1963.

PROBLEMS

3-1 Discuss the advantages and disadvantages of a pinhole camera.

3-2 A camera has a focal length of 45.00 mm. Its f-stop settings range from $f/3.5$ to $f/22$. What is the maximum diameter of the diaphragm aperature? Minimum diameter?

3-3 An exposure is optimum at a shutter speed of 1/100 second and $f/5.6$. If it is necessary to increase the shutter speed to 1/1,000 second, what should be the corresponding $f/$stop to retain optimum exposure?

3-4 The problem is the same as Prob 3-3 except that it is desired to expose at 1/300 second.

3-5 An exposure is optimum at a shutter speed of 1/200 second at $f/6.3$. In order to increase depth of field, it is necessary to expose at $f/16$. What is the required shutter speed to retain optimum exposure?

3-6 A camera has a focal length of 50.00 mm. What image distance is required for perfect focus if the object distance is 10 feet? 5 feet? 20 feet?

3-7 What is the relationship between film speed and emulsion grain size?

3-8 What is a characteristic or H and D curve?

3-9 What is the relationship between resolution and emulsion grain size?

3-10 Discuss the darkroom procedure for processing black-and-white emulsion.

3-11 Describe the electromagnetic spectrum in terms of the wavelengths of the various types of energy.

3-12 What wavelengths form the primary colors?

3-13 Explain why a "safe light" can be used in a darkroom.

3-14 Explain how a haze filter works and why it is used on aerial cameras.

3-15 On Fig. 3-13 assume that negative distance cd and positive distance CD measure 6.27 and 14.83 inches respectively. What is the enlargement factor for this print?

3-16 On Fig. 3-13, assume that distance A is 153 millimeters and, when the positive is in perfect focus, B is 317 millimeters. What is the focal length of the enlarger lens? What is the enlargement factor for this positive print?

3-17 Describe the halftone process and why it is needed.

3-18 Look at Fig. 3-12 under magnification and determine the number of lines per inch of the halftone screen used.

4
AERIAL CAMERAS

4-1 INTRODUCTION

There are so many important instruments in photogrammetry that it would be difficult to specify the most significant. Surely, however, the camera is one of the most important, since it is used to obtain the photographs upon which photogrammetry depends. In order to understand the science of photogrammetry, especially the geometry of aerial photographs, it is essential to have a basic understanding of the aerial camera and how it operates.

The remarkable success of photogrammetry in recent years is due in large part to the progress that has been made in developing precision cameras. Perhaps the most noteworthy among recent camera developments has been the perfection of lenses of extremely high resolving power and almost negligible distortion. This has greatly increased the accuracy of photogrammetry. There have also been many significant improvements in general camera construction and operation. Because the aerial photographic flight mission is fairly expensive and also since weather and other conditions may prevent aerial photography for long periods of time, it is extremely important that every precaution be taken in the manufacture of aerial cameras to guarantee the quality and reliability of the photography on each mission.

The requirements of aerial mapping cameras are quite different from those of ordinary amateur cameras. The primary requirement of any photogrammetric aerial camera is a lens of high geometric quality. Aerial cameras must be capable of exposing in rapid succession a great number of photographs to exacting specifications. Since they must perform this function while moving in an aircraft at high speed, they must have short cycling times, fast lenses, and efficient shutters. They must be capable of faithful functioning under the most extreme weather conditions and in spite of aircraft vibrations.

Aerial cameras generally use roll film and have magazine capacities of from 200 to 400 feet or more. Cameras have been developed to automatically expose pictures on glass plates, and although this procedure provides highest photogrammetric accuracy, it is not used extensively at this time because it is less convenient and more expensive. The frame or format size of most mapping cameras is 9 inches (23 centimeters) square.

4-2 TYPES OF AERIAL CAMERAS

The four main types of aerial cameras are (1) *single-lens frame* cameras, (2) *multilens frame* cameras, (3) *strip* cameras, and (4) *panoramic* cameras. These are described as follows:

1) Single-lens Frame Cameras These are by far the most common cameras in use today. Single-lens frame cameras are used almost exclusively in obtaining photographs for mapping purposes because they provide the highest geometric picture quality. With a single-lens frame camera the lens is held fixed relative to the focal plane. The film is generally fixed in position during exposure, although it may be advanced slightly during exposure to compensate for image motion. The entire format is exposed simultaneously with a single click of the shutter. In Fig. 1-4 the Zeiss RMK 15/23 aerial mapping camera is shown. Figure 4-1 illustrates the Fairchild KC-6A aerial mapping camera, and Fig. 4-2 shows the Wild RC-10. All three are precision single-lens frame cameras having 9-inch (23-centimeter) square formats and film capacities of approximately 400 feet (120 meters). The KC-6A and the RMK 15/23 both have nominal 6-inch (150 mm) focal length lenses. The RC-10 is capable of accepting lenses of $3\frac{1}{2}$-inch (90 mm), 6-inch (150 mm) or 12-inch (300 mm) focal length.

Single-lens frame cameras are often classified according to their *angular field of view*. Angular field of view, as illustrated in Fig. 4-3, is the angle α subtended at the rear nodal point of the camera lens by the diagonal of the picture format. Classifications according to angular field of view are

(a) Normal angle (up to 75°)
(b) Wide angle (75 to 100°)
(c) Super-wide angle (greater than 100°)

FIGURE 4-1
Fairchild KC-6A aerial mapping camera.
(*Courtesy Fairchild Space and Defense Systems*)

Angular field of view may be calculated as follows (see Fig. 4-3):

$$\alpha = 2 \tan^{-1}\left(\frac{d}{2f}\right) \qquad (4\text{-}1)$$

For a nominal 6-inch (150 mm) focal length camera with a 9-inch (23-centimeter) square format the angular field of view is:

$$\alpha = 2 \tan^{-1}\left(\frac{\sqrt{9^2 + 9^2}}{2(6)}\right) = 93°(\text{wide angle})$$

Single-lens frame cameras are available in a variety of lens *focal lengths,* and the choice will depend on the purpose of the photography. The most common focal

FIGURE 4-2
Wild RC-10 aerial mapping camera. (*Courtesy Wild Heerbrugg, Inc.*)

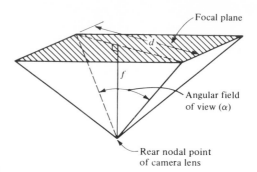

FIGURE 4-3
Angular field view of a camera.

length in use today for mapping photography is 6 inches (150 mm), although $3\frac{1}{2}$-inch (90 mm) and $8\frac{1}{4}$-inch (210 mm) focal lengths are also used. These focal lengths provide the best combination of geometric strength and photo scale for mapping. Longer focal lengths such as 12 inches (300 mm) are used primarily for obtaining photographs for aerial mosaics and for reconnaissance and interpretation purposes. They enable a reasonably large photo scale to be obtained in spite of high flying heights.

From Eq. (4-1), it is seen that for a particular format size, angular field of view increases as focal length decreases. Short focal lengths therefore yield wider ground coverage at a given flying height than longer focal lengths. Short focal length cameras have been in common use in the space program, where the physical dimensions of the camera are somewhat limited by available room in the spacecraft. The Hasselblad camera of Fig. 4-4, for example, has been used extensively for space photography. It uses 70 mm film and can be obtained with focal lengths of 60, 80, or 100 mm. An example of a space photograph taken with a Hasselblad camera was shown in Fig. 1-9.

2) Multilens Frame Cameras   These cameras have the basic characteristics of single-lens frame cameras except that they have two or more lenses and expose two or more pictures simultaneously. In years past, multilens cameras were used to obtain greater width of ground coverage than could be obtained with single-lens frame cameras. The so-called *nine-lens camera* of the National Geodetic Survey, for example, exposed a vertical photo which was surrounded by eight low obliques. Its total angular coverage was 130°. *Trimetrogon* photography was used extensively for small-scale charting from about 1940 to 1960. This photography was obtained with a three-camera system. Two cameras exposed high oblique photos aimed at the flanks while a third camera simultaneously took a vertical photo. The three photos provided horizon-to-horizon ground coverage transverse to the direction of flight.

Multicamera systems such as the one pictured in Fig. 20-6 are becoming increasingly popular. These cameras are used for environmental monitoring,

FIGURE 4-4
Hasselblad MK-70 camera. (*Courtesy Paillard, Inc.*)

mapping of natural and cultural resources, etc. All cameras simultaneously expose the same area, but the different cameras may use different filters or contain films with emulsions that are sensitive to different regions of the electromagnetic energy spectrum. Differences in the resulting photos provide clues that are useful in identifying photographed objects.

Convergent cameras can also be classified as multilens cameras since they simultaneously expose two photographs. These cameras are described in detail in Sec. 4-3.

3) Strip Cameras These cameras expose a continuous photograph of a strip of terrain beneath the path of the aircraft. This is accomplished by passing the film over a narrow slit opening in the focal plane of the camera at a rate just equal to the speed of passage of ground images across the focal plane. Light rays entering the camera lens from a terrain point are therefore focused at a single point on the film during the exposure period. Strip cameras may use a single lens or they may have two lenses—one pointing, say, 20° forward in the direction of flight and the other pointing, say, 20° aft. This arrangement provides stereoscopic coverage. Strip photography is especially useful in route studies for highways, railroads, pipelines, etc.

4) Panoramic Cameras These cameras photograph a strip of terrain from horizon to horizon; the strip being tranverse to the direction of flight. The subject of panoramic photography is discussed in more detail in Secs. 16-12 through 16-17.

4-3 CONVERGENT CAMERAS

A convergent camera, as shown in Fig. 4-5, is actually a special case of two single-lens frame cameras mounted together and operated simultaneously. One camera points forward along the flight line and the other backward. The result is two low oblique photographs taken from the same exposure station. Convergent photography provides a

FIGURE 4-5
Zeiss 2-RMK 21/18 convergent camera.
(*Courtesy Carl Zeiss, Oberkochen*)

high order of photogrammetric accuracy by enabling a large *base-height* ratio to be achieved—a favorable geometric condition for mapping photography which shall be discussed further in subsequent chapters. Convergent photography enables up to 100 percent end lap to be attained; a factor which can reduce the amount of ground control required in mapping projects.

4-4   MAIN PARTS OF FRAME AERIAL CAMERAS

Although all frame aerial cameras are somewhat different in construction, they are enough alike so that a general description can be given which adequately encompasses all of them. The three basic components or assemblies of a frame aerial camera, as shown in the generalized cross section of Fig. 4-6, are (1) the *magazine*, (2) the *camera body,* and (3) the *lens cone assembly.*

4-5   CAMERA MAGAZINE

The camera magazine houses the reels which hold exposed and unexposed film, and it also contains the *film advancing* and *film flattening* mechanisms. Film flattening is very important in aerial cameras, for if the film should be buckled during exposure, image

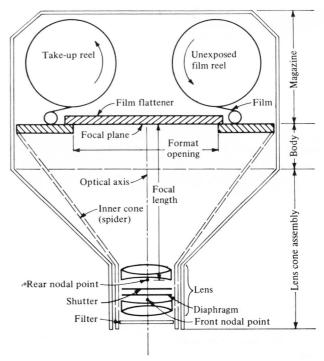

FIGURE 4-6
Generalized cross section of a frame aerial mapping camera.

positions on the resulting photographs would be incorrect. Film flattening may be accomplished in any of the four following ways: (1) by applying tension to the film during exposure; (2) by pressing the film firmly against a flat focal-plane glass which lies in front of the film; (3) by applying air pressure into the air-tight camera cone, thereby forcing the film against a flat plate lying behind the focal plane; or (4) by drawing the film tightly up against a vacuum plate whose surface lies in the focal plane. The vacuum system has proved most satisfactory and is the most widely used method of film flattening in aerial cameras. A focal-plane glass in front of the film is objectionable because image positions are distorted due to refraction of light rays passing through the glass.

4-6 CAMERA BODY

The camera body is a one-piece casting which usually houses the drive mechanism. The drive mechanism provides the force to operate the camera through its cycle, the cycle consisting of (1) advancing the film, (2) flattening the film, (3) cocking the shutter, and

(4) tripping the shutter. Power for the drive mechanism may be supplied by hand, or it may come from an electric motor. The camera body also contains carrying handles and electrical connections.

4-7 LENS CONE ASSEMBLY

The lens cone assembly contains several parts and serves several functions. Contained within the lens cone assembly are the *lens, filter, shutter,* and *diaphragm* (see Fig. 4-6). With most mapping cameras, the lens cone assembly also contains an *inner cone* or *spider.* The spider rigidly supports the lens assembly and focal plane in a fixed relative position. This fixes the so-called elements of *interior orientation* of the camera. These elements are carefully determined through camera calibration (see Sec. 4-13) so that they are available for photogrammetric calculations. The spider is made of metal having a low coefficient of thermal expansion, so that changes in operating temperatures do not upset the calibration. In some aerial cameras which do not have inner cones, the body and outer lens cone act together to hold the lens with respect to the focal plane. The inner cone of an aerial camera is shown in Fig. 4-7.

The *camera lens* is the most important part of an aerial camera. It gathers light rays from the object space and brings them to focus in the focal plane behind the lens. Lenses used in aerial cameras are highly corrected compound lenses consisting of several elements. The lens of Fig. 2-17, for example, is a 90-mm focal length *Super Aviogon* lens used in the Wild RC-9 Super Wide Angle aerial mapping camera.

The *filter* serves three purposes: (1) it reduces the effect of atmospheric haze, (2) it helps provide uniform light distribution over the entire format, and (3) it protects the lens from damage and dust.

The *shutter* and *diaphragm* together regulate the amount of light that is allowed to pass through the lens. The shutter controls the length of time that light is permitted to pass, and the diaphragm controls the size of the opening and hence the size of the bundle of light rays that is allowed to pass through the lens. Shutters are discussed in detail in Sec. 4-9. The diaphragm is located in the air space between the lens elements of an aerial camera. It consists of a series of leaves which can be rotated to vary the size of the diaphragm hole or *aperture*.

The *focal plane* of an aerial camera is the plane in which all incident light rays are brought to focus. In aerial photography object distances are great with respect to image distances. Aerial cameras therefore have their focus fixed for infinite object distances. This is done by setting the focal plane as exactly as possible at a distance equal to the focal length behind the rear nodal point of the camera lens. The focal plane is defined by the upper surface of the focal-plane frame. This is the surface upon which the film emulsion rests when an exposure is made. The focal-plane frame of the lens cone of Fig. 4-7 is clearly visible.

FIGURE 4-7
Inner cone of an aerial camera. (*Courtesy Fairchild Space and Defense Systems*)

4-8 FIDUCIAL MARKS

Camera fiducial marks are usually four in number and they are located either in the middle of the sides of the focal plane opening or in the corners. Side fiducial marks are shown in Fig. 4-7. These marks are exposed onto the negative when the picture is taken. The aerial photographs of Figs. 1-5 and 1-8 have four side fiducial marks; the photos of Fig. 1-7 have four corner fiducial marks. Lines joining opposite fiducial marks should intersect at the *principal point* of the photograph, and every attempt is made in camera manufacture to make this condition exist. The principal point is defined as the point in the focal plane where a line from the rear nodal point of the camera lens and perpendicular to the focal plane intersects the focal plane. As will be demonstrated in subsequent chapters, it is an exceedingly important point in photogrammetric work. Besides locating the principal point, lines joining opposite fiducial marks also provide a rectangular coordinate axis system for measuring image positions on photographs. Some cameras have eight fiducial marks (in the four corners and the four sides)—a favorable condition for analytical photogrammetry.

4-9 SHUTTERS

Because the aircraft carrying a camera moves at a rapid speed, images will move across the focal plane during exposure. If exposure times are long or flying heights low, blurred images may result. It is important, therefore, that the shutter be open for a very short duration when aerial photographs are taken. Short exposure times also reduce the detrimental effects of aircraft vibrations on image quality. The shutter speeds of aerial cameras typically range from about 1/100 to 1/1,000 second. Shutters are designed to operate efficiently so that they open instantaneously, remain open the required time and then instantaneously close, thereby providing uniform light to all parts of the focal plane.

There are a number of different types of camera shutters. Those used in aerial cameras are generally classified as either *between-the-lens* shutters or *focal-plane* shutters. Between-the-lens shutters are most commonly used in mapping cameras. These shutters are placed in the air space between the elements of the camera lens, as illustrated in Fig. 4-6. Common types of between-the-lens shutters are the *leaf* type, *blade* type, and *rotating disk* type. A schematic diagram of the leaf type is shown in Fig. 4-8. It consists usually of five or more leaves mounted on pivots and spaced around the periphery of the diaphragm. When the shutter is tripped, the leaves rotate about their pivots to the open position of Fig. 4-8b, remain open the desired time, and then snap back to the closed position of Fig. 4-8a. Some camera shutters use two sets of leaves, one for opening and the other for closing. This increases shutter efficiency, shutter speed, and shutter life.

The blade-type shutter consists of four blades, two for opening and two for closing. Its operation is similar to that of a guillotine. When the shutter is triggered, the two thin "opening" plates or blades move across the diaphragm to open the shutter. When the desired exposure time has elapsed, two "closing" blades close it.

The rotating disk type of shutter consists of a series of continuously rotating disks. Each disk has a cutaway section, and when these cutaways mesh, the exposure is made. The speed of rotation of the disks can be varied so that the desired exposure times are obtained. This type of shutter is very efficient because no starting or stopping of the parts is required, as with other types.

Focal-plane shutters are so named because they are located in front of the focal plane. The most common type of focal-plane shutter, the *curtain* type, consists of a curtain containing a slit. The curtain width equals the width of the focal plane. When the shutter is tripped, the slit moves across the focal plane. Exposure time is varied by varying

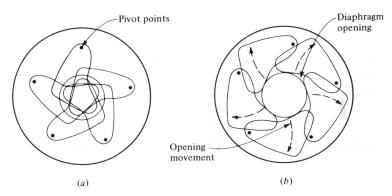

FIGURE 4-8
Schematic diagram of a leaf-type shutter. (a) Shutter closed; (b) shutter open.

either the speed at which the curtain moves or the width of the slit. These shutters expose different areas of the focal plane at slightly different times, and this causes relative image position errors in the resulting pictures. They are therefore not suitable for mapping cameras but are occasionally used in reconnaissance cameras.

Another type of focal-plane shutter is the *louver* shutter. It consists of a number of louvers which are operated simultaneously in a manner similar to the operation of venetian blinds. These shutters are not as efficient as other types, and shadows created by the open louvers cause uneven lighting over the focal plane.

Cameras have been perfected to compensate for image motion which occurs during the time that the shutter is open. *Image motion compensation* (IMC) is usually accomplished by moving the film across the focal plane at a rate just equal to the rate of image movement.

4-10 CAMERA MOUNTS

The camera mount is the device which is used to attach the camera to the aircraft. It has devices which prevent aircraft vibrations from being transmitted to the camera. The mount is also usually designed so that the camera can be rotated in azimuth to correct for *crab*. Crab, as illustrated in Fig. 4-9a, is a deviation in the aircraft's actual travel direction from its direction of heading. It is usually caused by side winds and may be of variable amounts depending on wind velocity and direction. Crab has the undesirable effect of reducing the ground coverage of aerial photos, as shown in Fig. 4-9b. Figure 4-9c shows the ground coverage when the camera has been rotated in the aircraft to make two sides of the format parallel to the actual direction of travel. Aerial cameras are usually equipped with level vials for keeping the camera properly oriented for vertical photos.

4-11 CAMERA CONTROLS

Camera controls are those devices necessary for operating the camera and varying camera settings according to conditions at the time of photography. The *intervalometer* is a device which automatically trips the shutter and actuates the camera cycle at desired times. Older types of intervalometers could be set to automatically make exposures at fixed intervals of time. The time interval could be calculated and depended upon the camera focal length and format size, desired end lap, flying height, and aircraft velocity. The disadvantage of this type of intervalometer is that variations in end lap occur with variations in terrain elevation, flying height, or aircraft velocities.

Newer intervalometers, such as that shown in Fig. 4-10, make exposures at a desired percent end lap in spite of variations in terrain, flying height, and aircraft velocity. This is

FIGURE 4-9
(*a*) Camera exposing aerial photography with crab present. (*b*) Crabbed over-lapping aerial photographs. (*c*) Overlapping aerial photographs with no crab.

done by means of a rotating chain shown in the *viewfinder.* (The viewfinder enables the operator to continually view the terrain beneath the aircraft and to see the ground coverage of each photo.) The chain moves in the viewfinder in the same direction as the passing images. By means of a rheostat, an operator makes the chain move at the same rate as passing images. The desired end lap is set on a dial on the intervalometer, and when the chain has moved the amount which corresponds to the desired end lap, the intervalometer automatically actuates the camera cycle. Of course, an operator can manu-ally actuate the camera cycle at any desired time. The operator can also correct for crab by rotating the viewfinder so that the passing images move parallel to the edges of the picture format. The crab angle is then read from a dial and the camera is given the same amount of rotation.

Another aerial camera control device is the exposure control mechanism. This consists of an exposure meter which measures terrain brightness and correlates it with the optimum combination of diaphragm opening and shutter speed. Exposure control units are available which operate automatically and constantly vary camera settings to provide optimum exposures.

FIGURE 4-10
IRU Intervalometer. (*Courtesy Carl Zeiss, Oberkochen*)

4-12 AUTOMATIC DATA RECORDING

Most modern aerial mapping cameras are equipped with a data recording system which automatically produces pertinent data on the pictures. The usual data consists of date, flying altitude, calibrated focal length of the camera, photo number, job identification, etc. This information is entered on a data block which is exposed onto the film when the photograph is taken. The images of an automatic data recording system are shown along the top border of the aerial photograph in Fig. 1-5. Automatic data recording is a convenience which saves time and prevents mistakes in later use of the photography.

4-13 CAMERA CALIBRATION

After manufacture and prior to use, aerial cameras are carefully calibrated to determine precise values for a number of camera constants. These constants, referred to as the *elements of interior orientation,* are needed so that accurate data can be determined from photographs.

In general, camera calibration methods may be classified into one of three basic categories: (1) *laboratory* methods, (2) *field* methods, and (3) *stellar* methods. Of these, laboratory methods are most frequently utilized. No matter which method is used, however, the approach is basically the same and consists of photographing an array of targets whose relative positions are accurately known. The elements of interior orientation are then determined by making precise measurements of the target images and comparing their actual imaged positions with the positions they should have occupied had the camera produced a perfect perspective view.

Normally in camera calibration at least the following minimum amount of interior orientation information is determined:

1) Equivalent focal length   The focal length which is effective near the center of the camera lens.

2) Calibrated focal length (often called the "camera constant")   The focal length which produces an overall mean distribution of radial lens distortion.

3) Average radial lens distortion   Distortion in image position along radial lines from the principal point.

4) x_o and y_o   Coordinates of the principal point given with respect to the x and y fiducial axes. (Although it is the intent in camera manufacture to place the fiducial marks so that lines drawn between opposite pairs intersect at the principal point, there is nearly always some small deviation from this ideal condition.)

5) Distances between opposite fiducial marks.

6) Angle of intersection of fiducial lines   Should be $90° ± 1'$.

7) Flatness of focal plane   Should not deviate by more than $± 0.0005$ in (0.01 mm) from a plane.

The procedures of determining items 1 through 4 vary somewhat depending upon whether the calibration method is laboratory, field, or stellar. In any case, the mathematics of this phase of camera calibration becomes rather complicated. Items 5 and 6 are obtained from direct precision measurements on an exposed glass plate upon which the fiducial marks are imaged. As discussed in Chap. 5, calibrated x and y fiducial distances are important in correcting photographic measurements for film shrinkage or expansion. Item 7 is measured directly by means of a special gage.

4-14   LABORATORY METHODS OF CAMERA CALIBRATION

The *multicollimator* method and the *goniometer* method are two types of laboratory procedures of camera calibration. The multicollimator method employs a number of collimators mounted in a precisely known angular array. A collimator consists of a lens with a cross mounted in its plane of infinite focus. Therefore light rays carrying the image of the cross are projected through the lens and emerge parallel. If these light rays are directed toward the lens of an aerial camera, the cross will be perfectly imaged on the camera's focal plane because aerial cameras are focused for parallel light rays (those having infinite object distances).

A camera collimator consists of several individual collimators mounted in two perpendicular vertical planes. One plane of collimators is illustrated in Fig. 4-11. The individual collimators are rigidly mounted so that the optical axes of adjacent collimators intersect precisely at known angles such as $θ$ of Fig. 4-11. The camera to be calibrated is placed so its focal plane is perpendicular to the central collimator axis and so that the front nodal point of its lens is at the intersection of all collimator axes. In this orienta-

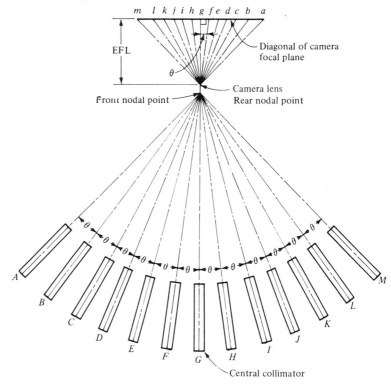

FIGURE 4-11
Bank of thirteen collimators for camera calibration.

tion, image g of the central collimator occurs very near the principal point and intersection of fiducial lines. The camera is further oriented so that when the picture is taken, the collimator crosses will be imaged along the diagonals of the camera format, as shown in Fig. 4-12. Collimator crosses A through M of Fig. 4-11, for example, are imaged at a through m of Fig. 4-12. Crosses from the perpendicular plane of collimators are imaged at n through y of Fig. 4-12.

Distances on the exposed plate between imaged crosses are precisely measured. *Equivalent focal length* (EFL) is that focal length which is effective in the essentially distortion-free central area of the camera lens. In the image plane, this area is considered to be within the circle whose center is at the central collimator image g and whose radius is the mean distance to the four collimator images f, t, h, and s. Equivalent focal length is computed by dividing the average of the four measured distances gf, gh, gs, and gt by the tangent of θ, or

$$\text{EFL} = \frac{gf + gh + gs + gt}{4 \tan \theta} \qquad (4\text{-}2)$$

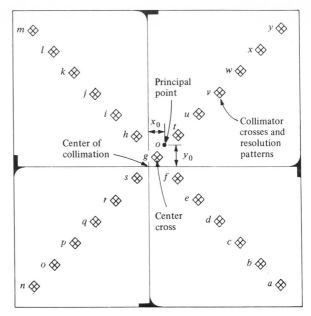

FIGURE 4-12
Images of photographed collimator targets.

Based on EFL, theoretical distances from central collimator image g to all other collimator crosses can be computed. As an example, distances ge, gi, gu, and gr should theoretically be equal to EFL $\times$ tan 2θ. These four distances are measured, and radial-lens distortion at 2θ is obtained by subtracting the *calculated* theoretical distance from the average of the four *measured* distances. Using this approach, radial-lens distortion can be calculated for each increment of θ. A radial distortion curve may be drawn by plotting radial distortion on the ordinate versus radial distance from the central collimator image as the abscissa (see Fig. 4-13). This curve indicates at a glance the nature of the radial distortion of a particular lens, and it also shows maximum positive and maximum negative values. (By definition an outward distortion is positive.)

From the preceeding discussion, it should be apparent that a focal length other than EFL could be used to calculate radial-lens distortion and that a different focal length would produce a different radial-lens distortion curve. *Calibrated focal length* (CFL) of a lens is a focal length which produces some overall mean distribution of radial distortion. It is usually selected so that maximum positive radial distortion is equal to maximum negative radial distortion. Note in Fig. 4-13, for example, that this condition exists. Calibrated focal length is the value used in photogrammetric calculations. Henceforth in this text, the term "focal length," symbolized by f, will be understood to mean calibrated focal length.

FIGURE 4-13
Radial-lens distortion curve for the Zeiss Pleogon aerial camera lens. (*Courtesy Wisconsin Department of Transportation*)

A paradox associated with the multicollimator method of camera calibration is that targets are dense near the center of the format where lens distortion is practically non-existent and sparse in the outer areas of the format where lens distortions are maximum. This problem can be circumvented in either field or stellar calibration.

In addition to determining interior orientation elements, laboratory methods of camera calibration also provide an evaluation of the camera's resolving power. This is done by photographing resolution test patterns using a very-high-resolution emulsion. The test patterns are made up of numerous sets of *line pairs* (parallel black lines of a certain thickness separated by white spaces of the same thickness). The measure of line thickness for each set is its number of lines per millimeter. Line thickness varies, and in a typical test pattern it may range from 10 to 80 lines per millimeter. The test patterns are projected by the collimators simultaneously with the collimator crosses and imaged on the diagonals of the camera format. After the photograph is made, the resulting images are examined under magnification to determine the finest set of parallel lines which can be clearly resolved. The average of the four resolutions at each angular increment from the central collimator is reported in the calibration certificate.

The goniometer laboratory procedure of camera calibration is very similar to the multicollimator method and consists of centering a precise grid plate in the camera focal plane. The grid is illuminated from the rear and projected through the camera lens in the reverse direction. The angles at which the projected grid rays emerge are measured with a goniometer. CFL and radial distortions are then determined by comparing actual measured angles with their theoretically true angles.

4-15 FIELD AND STELLAR METHODS OF CAMERA CALIBRATION

Both the multicollimator and goniometer methods of laboratory camera calibration require expensive and precise special equipment. An advantage of field and stellar methods is that this special equipment is not necessary. Several different field and stellar methods of camera calibration have been developed. Field procedures require that an array of targets be established and that angles subtended by the targets at the camera station be measured using precise surveying techniques. The targets are placed far enough from the camera station so that there is no noticeable image degradation. (Recall that an aerial camera is fixed for infinite focus.)

In the stellar method, a target array consisting of identifiable stars is photographed and the instant of exposure is recorded. Right ascensions and declinations of the stars can be obtained from an ephemeris for the precise instant of exposure so that the angles subtended by the stars at the camera station become known.

In recent years researchers have been investigating "in-flight" camera calibration. Potential advantages of this method are new calibration constants each time the camera is used and the likelihood of greater accuracy due to calibration under actual operating conditions.

REFERENCES

American Society of Photogrammetry: "Manual of Photogrammetry," 3d ed., George Banta Co., Inc., Menasha, Wis., 1966, chap. 4.

Bormann, G. E.: The New Wild RC-10 Film Camera, *Photogrammetric Engineering*, vol. 35, no. 10, p. 1033, 1969.

Carman, P. D.: Camera Calibration Laboratory at N. R. C., *Photogrammetric Engineering*, vol. 35, no. 4, p. 372, 1969.

Hallert, B.: The Method of Least Squares Applied to Multicollimator Camera Calibration, *Photogrammetric Engineering*, vol. 29, no. 5, p. 836, 1963.

Helava, U. V.: New Significance of Errors of Inner Orientation, *Photogrammetric Engineering*, vol. 29, no. 1, p. 126, 1963.

Karren, R. J.: Camera Calibration by the Multicollimator Method, *Photogrammetric Engineering*, vol. 34, no. 7, p. 706, 1968.

Livingston, R. G.: A History of Military Mapping Camera Development, *Photogrammetric Engineering*, vol. 30, no. 1, p. 97, 1964.

McNeil, G. T.: Normal Angle Camera Calibrator, *Photogrammetric Engineering*, vol. 28, no. 4, p. 633, 1962.

Merritt, E. L.: Methods of Field Camera Calibration, *Photogrammetric Engineering*, vol. 18, no. 4, 1952.

Washer, F. E.: The Precise Evaluation of Lens Distortion, *Photogrammetric Engineering*, vol. 29, no. 2, p. 327, 1963.

PROBLEMS

4-1 List the requirements of a precision aerial mapping camera.

4-2 Name and briefly describe the various types of aerial cameras.

4-3 Photography is obtained with a strip camera having a 6-in. focal length from an altitude of 6,000 feet above ground. If the aircraft speed is 150 miles per hour, what must be the rate of passage of the film across the focal plane of the camera (in inches per minute) to prevent image blur?

4-4 An aerial camera makes an exposure at a shutter speed of 1/100 second. If the aircraft speed is 250 miles per hour, how far will the aircraft travel during the exposure?

4-5 An aerial camera having a $3\frac{1}{2}$-inch focal length is carried by an aircraft at 200 miles per hour. If flying height is 3,000 feet above ground and if exposure time is 1/150 second, how far will an image move across the focal plane during the exposure?

4-6 What is the angular field of view of a camera having a 9-inch square format and a $3\frac{1}{2}$-inch focal length? A 12-inch focal length?

4-7 Same as Prob. 4-6 except 70-millimeter square format and 80-mm focal length.

4-8 Name and briefly describe the main parts of a frame aerial camera.

4-9 Discuss briefly the different types of camera shutters.

4-10 What is the function of the camera mount? The intervalometer?

4-11 Why is camera calibration important?

4-12 What are the usual elements of interior orientation that are determined in camera calibration?

4-13 The following table lists the averages of the four measured distances to collimator crosses versus their angular values from the central cross. Calculate the equivalent focal length based on the $7\frac{1}{2}°$ crosses and plot the radial distortion curve based on EFL.

Angle	Average measured distance, mm
$7\frac{1}{2}°$	20.182
$15°$	41.048
$22\frac{1}{2}°$	63.481
$30°$	88.574
$37\frac{1}{2}°$	117.662
$45°$	153.135

4-14 Compute the calibrated focal length for the data of Prob. 4-13. (Make maximum positive radial distortion equal to maximum negative radial distortion.) Plot the radial distortion curve based on CFL. *Hint*: Try CFL = EFL − half of the difference between the absolute values of the maximum negative and maximum positive distortions of Prob. 4-13.

PHOTOGRAPHIC MEASUREMENTS
AND REFINEMENT

5-1 INTRODUCTION

The solution of most photogrammetry problems requires some type of photographic measurement. The measurements may be lengths of lines, angles between points, or positions of points on photos expressed in terms of rectangular coordinates. Rectangular coordinates are the most common type of photographic measurement, and they are used directly in many photogrammetric equations. Photographic measurements may be made directly on negatives or photographic positives printed on paper, film or glass.

In this chapter *monoscopic* measurements are discussed, i.e., measurements made from only one photograph at a time. *Stereoscopic* measurements, on the other hand, require that the observer simultaneously view two different photographs taken of the same area from two different exposure stations. Stereoscopic photo measurements are discussed in Chaps. 8 and 18.

5-2 PHOTOGRAPHIC COORDINATE SYSTEM

For cameras with side fiducial marks, the commonly adopted reference system for photographic coordinates is the rectangular axis system formed by joining opposite fiducial marks with straight lines as shown in Fig. 5-1a. The x axis is usually arbitrarily designated as the fiducial line most nearly parallel with the direction of flight, positive in the direction of flight. The positive y axis is $90°$ counterclockwise from positive x. The origin of the coordinate system is the intersection of fiducial lines. This point is often called the *center of collimation*; for a precise mapping camera, it is very near the principal point.

The position of any image on a photograph, such as a of Fig. 5-1a, is given by its rectangular coordinates x_a and y_a, where x_a is the perpendicular distance from the y axis to a and y_a is the perpendicular distance from the x axis to a. Similarly the photographic position of image point b is given by its rectangular coordinates x_b and y_b.

If the camera is equipped with corner fiducials, as is the case with Wild cameras, the references axis for photocoordinate measurement may be arbitrarily taken as the $x'y'$ system shown in Fig. 5-1b. In this system positive x' is again arbitrarily taken in the direction of flight. The intersection of diagonal lines connecting opposite corner fiducials very nearly defines the principal point. Coordinates measured in the $x'y'$ system are reduced to the conventional xy system with origin at the principal point using the following equations:

$$x_a = x'_a - x_o$$
$$y_a = y'_a - y_o \qquad (5\text{-}1)$$

Where

$$x_o = \frac{x'_B + x'_C}{4}$$

and

$$y_o = \frac{y'_D + y'_C}{4}$$

Recently some cameras have had eight fiducials installed, incorporating both side and corner fiducials. The photographic coordinate system in this case is as defined in Fig. 5-1a. Eight fiducials enable somewhat more accurate corrections to be made for systematic errors in measured image coordinates.

Rectangular coordinates are a very basic and useful type of photographic measurement, for from them distances and angles between points may be calculated using simple analytic geometry. Photographic distance ab of Fig. 5-1a, for example, may be calculated from rectangular coordinates as follows:

$$ab = \sqrt{(x_a - x_b)^2 + (y_a - y_b)^2} \qquad (5\text{-}2)$$

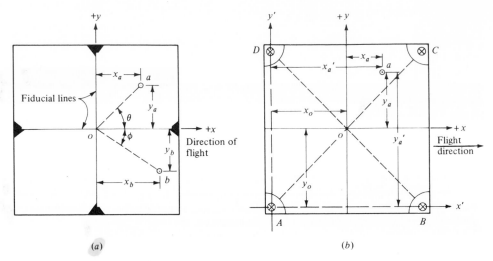

FIGURE 5-1
Photographic coordinate system. (*a*) Side fiducials; (*b*) corner fiducials.

Also, the angles θ and ϕ of Fig. 5-1*a* are readily calculated from the coordinates of *a* and *b* as follows:

$$\theta = \tan^{-1}\left(\frac{y_a}{x_a}\right)$$

$$\phi = \tan^{-1}\left(\frac{y_b}{x_b}\right)$$

(5-3)

Angle *aob* is simply the sum of angles θ and ϕ.

5-3 SIMPLE SCALES FOR PHOTOGRAPHIC MEASUREMENTS

There are a variety of simple scales available for photographic measurements. The particular choice of measuring instrument will depend upon the accuracy required for the photogrammetry problem at hand. If a low order of accuracy is acceptable, an ordinary *engineer's scale* may prove satisfactory. With an engineer's scale, accuracy may usually be increased by using the 50 or 60 scale. Where more accuracy is desired, a device such as the metal *microrule* of Fig. 5-2 or the glass scales of Fig. 5-3 may be used. With any of these scales, measured values may be made more exact by taking the mean of several readings.

The main scale of the microrule is graduated at each inch. It has a movable 1-inch section at the zero end which is graduated each 1/10 inch. A micrometer having 100

FIGURE 5-2
Microrule for photographic measurements. (*Courtesy Theo. Alteneder and Sons*)

divisions is attached to the movable section, and when it is turned through one complete revolution, the 1-inch movable section travels 1/10 inch. Each graduation on the micrometer therefore corresponds to 0.001 inch. Accuracy of measurements with the microrule can be increased by using a magnifying glass. The microrule may be used to lay off distances as well as to measure them.

Glass scales of the type shown in Fig. 5-3 can be obtained in either 6- or 12-inch length with either millimeter graduations (with least graduations of 0.1 millimeter) or inch graduations (with least graduations of 0.005 inch). Readings are taken with the help of magnifying eyepieces which slide along the scale. With a glass scale, photocoordinates may be estimated quite readily to one-tenth of the smallest graduated division. These glass scales cannot be used to lay off distances.

5-4 MEASURING PROCEDURE WITH SIMPLE SCALES

The conventional procedure for measuring photocoordinates when using an engineer's scale, microrule, or glass scale generally consists of first marking the photocoordinate axis system. This may be done by carefully aligning a straight edge across the fiducial

FIGURE 5-3
Glass scales for photographic measurements. (*Courtesy Teledyne-Gurley Co.*)

marks and lightly making a line with a razor blade, pin, or very sharp 4h or 5h pencil. Rectangular coordinates are then obtained by direct measurement of the perpendicular distances from these axes.

If the points whose coordinates are to be measured are sharp, distinct points, they may need no further identification. If not, they may be identified with a small pinprick. This should be carefully done under magnification, however, because systematic error will be introduced into measured photocoordinates if points are erroneously marked.

It is important to affix the proper algebraic sign to measured rectangular coordinates; failure to do so will result in frustrating mistakes in solving photogrammetry problems. Points situated to the right of the y axis have positive x coordinates and points to the left have negative x coordinates. Points above the x axis have positive y coordinates, and those below the x axis have negative y coordinates.

5-5 TRILATERATIVE METHOD OF PHOTOCOORDINATE MEASUREMENT

It is possible to obtain photocoordinates using the simple scales described in Sec. 5-3 but without cutting or scratching fiducial lines. In this procedure, called the *trilaterative method,* distances such as S_a, S_b, S_c, and S_d may be measured from fiducial marks to an image point as illustrated in Fig. 5-4. From photocoordinates of the fiducial marks obtained in camera calibration, coordinates of image points, may be calculated using trigonometry. The procedure is applicable with corner fiducials as well as side fiducials.

EXAMPLE 5-1 Suppose that calibrated coordinates of fiducials A and B of Fig. 5-4a are $x_A = -113.00$ mm; $y_A = 0.00$ mm; $x_B = 0.00$ mm; and $y_B = -113.00$ mm. Calculate x_e and y_e if S_a and S_b are measured as 189.89 mm and 100.47 mm respectively.

SOLUTION By the pythagorean theorem,
$$AB = [(113.00)^2 + (113.00)^2]^{1/2} = 159.81 \text{ mm}$$
From the law of cosines,
$$\cos \theta = \frac{S_a^2 + (AB)^2 - S_b^2}{2(S_a)(AB)}$$
$$\cos \theta = \frac{(189.89)^2 + (159.81)^2 - (100.47)^2}{2(189.89)(159.81)} = 0.848591$$
$$\theta = 31° \ 56' \ 28''$$
Also
$$\delta = \tan^{-1} \left(\frac{113.00}{113.00} \right) = 45° \ 00' \ 00''$$

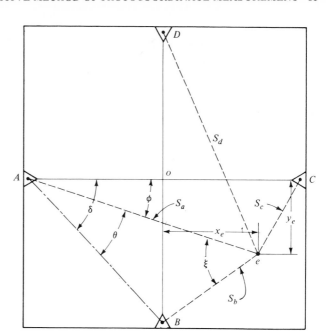

FIGURE 5-4
Trilaterative method of photocoordinate measurement.

Then

$$\phi = \delta - \theta = (45°\ 00'\ 00'') - (31°\ 56'\ 28'') = 13°\ 03'\ 32''$$

$$x_e = S_a(\cos \phi) + x_A = 189.89\,(0.974138) - 113.00 = 71.98 \text{ mm}$$

$$y_e = -S_a(\sin \phi) = 189.89(0.225952) = -42.90 \text{ mm} \qquad ////$$

The trilaterative solution becomes weak as the ξ angle of Fig. 5-4 approaches either 180 or 0°. Strongest solutions are obtained for ξ angles near 90°. Since any two of four possible measured S distances yields a unique solution for the photo coordinates of an image point, the choice should be those two distances yielding an ξ angle nearest 90°. Also, accuracy may be improved by computing photocoordinates in more than one independent solution and then taking the average; e.g., one solution for image coordinates of point e of Fig. 5-4 can be made using S_a and S_b, another can be made using S_a and S_d, etc. A sketch should be used in the calculations to reduce the likelihood of mistakes.

If an electronic computer is available, the trilaterative method can be programmed for solution. As described in a reference cited at the end of this chapter, trilaterative procedures can also be extended to include all measured S distances in a simultaneous least squares solution. Advantages of the trilaterative method over direct measurement from marked fiducial lines are that (1) accuracy is increased, (2) systematic errors of marking fiducial lines are eliminated, and (3) fiducial lines which deface the imagery are not necessary.

5-6 INSTRUMENTS FOR MEASUREMENT OF SHORT DISTANCES

Instruments such as the Zoom Mackroscope shown in Fig. 5-5 make it possible to measure short distances on photographs accurately. This particular instrument has a zoom lens capable of magnifying images from 10 to 30X. A short reticle graduated in units of 0.0001 feet appears superimposed in the field of view. Such instruments are valuable in photo interpretation where short measurements are frequently necessary (e.g., for determining sizes of objects). They are also useful in metric photogrammetry for making corrections for systematic errors that occur in point pricking or in constructing fiducial lines which fail to pass through the fiducial marks.

Faulty fiducial line marking is illustrated in Fig. 5-6. Photocoordinates to point e have been measured from the faulty axis system. The amounts by which the x axis misses the fiducials are measured as y_a and y_c, and the amounts by which the y axis misses its fiducials are measured as x_b and x_d. The measured x and y fiducial distances are x_m and y_m. General expressions for calculating corrected coordinates x'_e and y'_e of point e are as follows:

$$x'_e = x_e + x_d + (x_b - x_d)\left(\frac{y_m/2 - y_e}{y_m}\right) \qquad (5\text{-}4)$$

$$y'_e = y_e + y_a + (y_c - y_a)\left(\frac{x_m/2 + x_e}{x_m}\right) \qquad (5\text{-}5)$$

In Eqs. (5-4) and (5-5), it is necessary to apply correct algebraic signs to y_a, y_c, x_b, and x_d. In the example of Fig. 5-6, these values are all shown positive.

EXAMPLE 5-2 Suppose that in Fig. 5-6 measured photocoordinates x_e and y_e are 38.27 and 49.40 mm respectively. Measured fiducial distances x_m and y_m are 232.68 and 232.43 mm respectively, and $y_a = 0.54$ mm, $x_b = 0.82$ mm, $y_c = 0.69$ mm, and $x_d = 0.48$ mm. What are photocoordinates x'_e and y'_e corrected for the faulty fiducial axis system?

By Eq. (5-4),

$$x'_e = 38.27 + 0.48 + (0.82 - 0.48)\left(\frac{232.43/2 - 49.40}{232.43}\right)$$

$$x'_e = 38.85 \text{ mm}$$

FIGURE 5-5
Zoom Mackroscope for precise measure-
ment of short photo distances. (*Courtesy
Bausch and Lomb*)

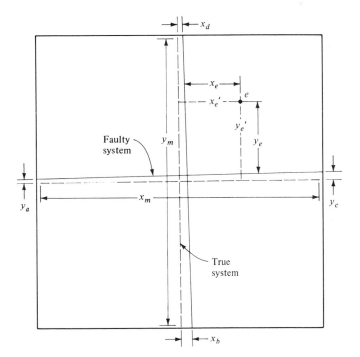

FIGURE 5-6
Systematic error correction for faulty fiducial axis system.

By Eq. (5-5),

$$y'_e = 49.40 + 0.54 + (0.69 - 0.54)\left(\frac{232.68/2 + 38.27}{232.68}\right)$$

$$y'_e = 50.04 \text{ mm} \hspace{5cm} ////$$

5-7 MONOCOMPARATOR MEASUREMENT OF PHOTOCOORDINATES

If the ultimate in photocoordinate measurement accuracy is desired, precise instruments called *comparators* should be used. There are two basic types of comparators, *monocomparators* and *stereocomparators*. Monocomparators, which are discussed in this section, make measurements on one photograph at a time. With stereocomparators, image positions are measured by simultaneously viewing an overlapping stereo pair of photographs. Stereocomparators are described in Chap. 18. Comparators are used primarily to obtain precise photocoordinates necessary for analytical photogrammetry.

A common type of monocomparator is shown in Fig. 5-7. This instrument is classified as a *lead-screw* monocomparator. It is capable of making both angle and coordinate measurements on photos having formats as large as 10 inches square. The film or diapositive to be measured is first mounted on the stage of the comparator. The stage may be rotated about a vertical axis and is equipped with a slow-motion screw for fine settings to the nearest $20''$ of arc. The stage may be moved longitudinally along the x axis of the instrument by means of a lead-screw drive mechanism actuated by the hand wheel on the right side. A similar lead-screw drive and hand wheel on the left side moves the stage transversely along the y axis of the instrument, the y axis being perpendicular to the x axis. The instrument can be obtained with small motors for driving the lead screws. The pitch of the lead screw is 1 millimeter. A micrometer which records the nearest 0.001 turn of the lead screw makes it possible to read X and Y coordinates to the nearest 0.001 millimeter (nearest micrometer). The instrument is equipped with a binocular microscope, having variable magnification of from 10 to 40X, which facilitates setting the reference mark on points at which measurements are to be taken.

There are two basic approaches to measuring photocoordinates with this instrument. In the first of these, the photo is mounted firmly on the stage and the stage is rotated to make the x axis of the photograph parallel with the x axis of the instrument. This is accomplished by trial and error, using the rotary slow-motion screw until the Y coordinates of both side fiducial marks A and C of Fig. 5-8 are equal. Once the stage is set, X and Y readings are taken on the four fiducial marks as well as on all other points whose photographic positions are desired. Owing to setting errors, reading errors, and nonorthogonality of the photo and comparator axes, X readings of fiducials B and D, and Y readings of fiducials A and C of Fig. 5-8 will rarely be equal. Therefore photocoordi-

FIGURE 5-7
Mann type 422-F monocomparator. (*Courtesy David W. Mann Co.*)

nates x_e and y_e of a point e are reduced from the comparator axes to the photographic coordinate axes by subtracting the mean of Y coordinates of fiducials A and C from all Y readings, and by subtracting the mean of X coordinates of fiducials B and D from all X readings, or

$$x_e = X_e - \frac{X_B + X_D}{2}$$
$$y_e = Y_e - \frac{Y_A + Y_C}{2}$$

(5-6)

The second basic method of measurement with a lead-screw type of monocomparator is preferred if an electronic computer is available. In this method no attempt is made to orient the plate so that the Y coordinates of fiducials A and C are equal. Instead, the plate is placed on the stage in the approximate orientation of Fig. 5-8. Then measurements are taken to all fiducials and all image points whose coordinates are desired. The coordinates are later reduced numerically from the comparator measurement axis system XY to the conventional photographic xy axis system of Fig. 5-1. One method of reduction is called *affine coordinate transformation*. The method is discussed in Sec. B-6 of Appendix B and a numerical example is presented.

Another type of monocomparator known as the *multilaterative* comparator is shown in Fig. 5-9. It operates on essentially the same trilaterative principle as that discussed in Sec. 5-5. The measuring apparatus of this comparator consists of a glass scale measuring arm which is precisely graduated at 1 millimeter intervals. This measuring arm is free to rotate about a pivot at its base. The instrument is equipped with a microscopic

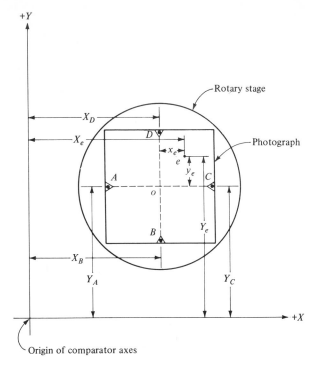

FIGURE 5-8
Measurement of photocoordinates with a monocomparator.

eyepiece having a range of magnification from 10 to 30X. Distances are measured from the pivot point to images whose photocoordinates are desired. Measurements are made by rotating the measuring arm about the pivot and simultaneously moving the eyepiece so that the point to be measured comes within a circular reticle seen through the eyepiece. Rotation of the micrometer drum at the top of the measuring arm causes the glass scale to translate longitudinally, and once the point is within the circular reticle, the drum is rotated until an even millimeter graduation bisects the point. The whole millimeter reading is then made directly from the glass scale and the fractional part is taken from the micrometer drum to the nearest half micrometer.

Figure 5-10 illustrates a generalization of the theoretical basis of the multilaterative comparator. Distances R_1, R_2, R_3, and R_4 are measured from the pivot to point e. In the actual measuring process, the pivot remains fixed in position while the measuring stage to which the photograph is attached is rotated four times, each rotation being approximately 90°. Distances are measured at each of these four positions, and thus the geometric equivalent of Fig. 5-10 is created.

From the measured R distances, the coordinates of the four pivot points, fiducial

Glass scale
measuring arm

Micrometer
drum

Microscopic
eyepiece

Pivot

FIGURE 5-9
Multilaterative comparator. (*Courtesy D.B.A. Systems, Inc.*)

marks, and all image points are computed in the arbitrary XY system shown in Fig. 5-10. The calculations are performed with an electronic computer. After these calculations are made, the coordinates of the fiducial marks are known in both the arbitrary XY comparator system and the calibrated photographic xy system. Using these two sets of coordinates for the fiducial marks, all points may be converted to the fiducial (photographic) coordinate system using a coordinate transformation such as the two-dimensional affine transformation described in section B-6 of Appendix B.

Both types of monocomparators described in this section can be equipped with encoders for direct digital readout of comparator coordinates on punched cards, punched paper tape, or magnetic tape. If a large number of measurements are required, digital equipment can save a great deal of time and eliminate costly mistakes in reading and recording.

5-8   REFINEMENT OF MEASURED IMAGE COORDINATES

Regardless of the instrument used to measure photocoordinates of image points, these coordinates will contain systematic errors from various sources. These systematic errors are:

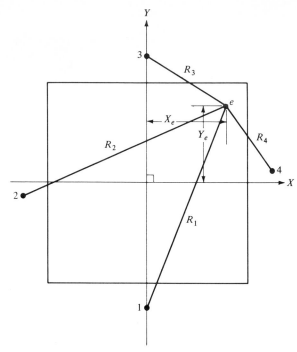

FIGURE 5-10
Generalized geometric equivalent of the multilaterative comparator measurement system.

1) Failure of fiducial axes to intersect at the principal point
2) Shrinkage or expansion of photographic materials
3) Lens distortions
4) Atmospheric refraction distortions
5) Earth curvature distortions

Corrections may be applied to eliminate the effects of these systematic errors. However, all corrections need not be made for all photogrammetric problems; in fact, for crude work they may all be ignored. If, for example, an engineer's scale has been used to make the measurements, uncertainty in the photocoordinates may be so great that the small magnitudes of these systematic errors become insignificant. On the other hand, if precise measurements for an analytical photogrammetry problem have been made with a comparator, all the corrections may be significant. The decision as to which corrections are necessary for a particular photogrammetric problem can be made after considering required accuracy versus magnitude of error caused by neglecting the correction.

5-9   REDUCTION OF COORDINATES TO AN ORIGIN AT THE PRINCIPAL POINT

It has been previously pointed out that the principal point of a photograph does not necessarily occur at the intersection of fiducial lines. The actual coordinates of the principal point with respect to the fiducial axes are x_o and y_o, as shown in Fig. 5-11. These coordinates are obtained through camera calibration.

Photogrammetric equations which utilize photocoordinates are based on projective geometry and assume an origin of photocoordinates at the principal point. Therefore it is theoretically correct to reduce photocoordinates from the measurement or fiducial axis system to the axis system whose origin is at the principal point. These principal point axes are shown on Fig. 5-11 as x' and y'. For any image point a, reduction from fiducial axes to principal point axes is simply

$$x'_a = x_a - x_o$$
$$y'_a = y_a - y_o$$
(5-7)

Manufacturers of precision mapping cameras attempt to mount the fiducial marks and camera lens so that the principal point and intersection of fiducial lines coincide.

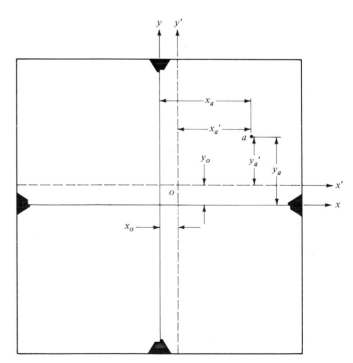

FIGURE 5-11
Reduction of measured photocoordinates to origin at principal point.

Normally they accomplish this to within a few micrometers, and therefore in ordinary photogrammetric work this reduction can usually be ignored.

5-10   SHRINKAGE AND EXPANSION OF PHOTOGRAPHIC FILMS AND PAPERS

In photogrammetric work, true positions of images in the picture are required. Photo-coordinates measured by any of the previously discussed methods will unavoidably contain small errors due to shrinkage or expansion of the photographic materials which support the emulsion of the negative and positive. Photocoordinates must be corrected for these errors before they are used in photogrammetric calculations, otherwise errors from this source will be present in the computed results. The magnitude of error in the computed results will depend upon the severity of the shrinkage or expansion error, which depends upon the type of emulsion support materials used.

Most photographic films manufactured for photogrammetric work have excellent dimensional stability, but some small changes in size do occur during processing and storage. Dimensional change during storage may be held to a minimum by maintaining constant temperature and humidity in the storage room. The actual amount of distortion present in a film is a function of several variables, including the type of film and its thickness. Typical values may vary from almost negligible amounts up to approximately 0.20 percent.

A variety of materials are available upon which positive photographic prints are made. Glass is unsurpassed in dimensional stability; when it is used, shrinkage or expansion may be considered nonexistent. If polyester is used, the same high degree of dimensional stability exists for the positive as for the negative. If the material is paper, however, a much lower degree of dimensional stability exists. For this reason, paper prints are not used for precise photogrammetric work. The amount of paper shrinkage or expansion is a function of temperature, humidity, and paper type and thickness, but to a larger degree it is a function of the method of drying the prints. If a hot-drum dryer is used or if the prints are hung to dry, greater distortions can be expected than if the prints are air-dried lying flat at room temperature. Paper shrinkages or expansions of up to 1 percent are not uncommon, and it is sometimes as large as 2 or 3 percent for single-weight papers which are hung to dry. Distortion in the x direction often is markedly different from distortion in y, and this type of "differential" distortion can lead to serious consequences if neglected.

5-11   SHRINKAGE CORRECTION

The amount of shrinkage or expansion present in a photograph can be determined by comparing measured photographic distances between opposite fiducial marks with their corresponding values determined in camera calibration. Photocoordinates can be corrected if discrepancies exist. If x_m and y_m are measured fiducial distances and x_c and y_c are corresponding calibrated fiducial distances, then the corrected photocoordinates of any point a may be calculated as

$$x_a' = \left(\frac{x_c}{x_m} \right) x_a \qquad (5\text{-}8)$$

$$y_a' = \left(\frac{y_c}{y_m} \right) y_a \qquad (5\text{-}9)$$

In Eqs. (5-8) and (5-9), x_a' and y_a' are corrected photocoordinates and x_a and y_a are measured coordinates. The ratios x_c/x_m and y_c/y_m are simply scale factors in the x and y directions respectively.

EXAMPLE 5-3 For a particular photograph, the measured x and y fiducial distances were 233.85 mm and 233.46 mm respectively. The corresponding x and y calibrated fiducial distances were 232.60 mm and 232.62 mm respectively. Find the corrected values for the measured photocoordinates which are listed in columns (b) and (c) below.

SOLUTION From Eq. (5-8):

$$x' = \frac{232.60}{233.85} (x) = 0.99465(x)$$

From Eq. (5-9):

$$y' = \frac{232.62}{233.46} (y) = 0.99640 (y)$$

Each of the measured values are multiplied by the appropriate constant above and the corrected coordinates are entered in columns (d) and (e) of the table below:

Point no. (a)	Measured coordinates		Corrected coordinates	
	x, mm (b)	y, mm (c)	x', mm (d)	y', mm (e)
1	− 102.57	95.18	− 102.02	94.84
2	− 98.43	− 87.77	− 97.90	− 87.45
3	16.28	− 36.06	16.19	− 35.93
4	65.72	61.84	65.37	61.62
5	104.88	− 73.49	104.32	− 73.23

////

Shrinkage or expansion corrections may also be applied through the x and y scale factors of a two-dimensional affine coordinate transformation. This method is particularly well suited for analytical photogrammetric calculations and requires an electronic computer. The procedure is described in Sec. B-6 of Appendix B, and a numerical example is presented.

5-12 CORRECTION FOR RADIAL-LENS DISTORTION

As described in Chaps. 2 and 4, radial-lens distortion causes imaged positions to be distorted along radial lines from the principal point. If the radial distortion characteristics of the camera lens are known through camera calibration, image positions can be corrected.

Three different methods of correcting for radial distortion are (1) reading required corrections from a radial-lens distortion curve, (2) interpolating corrections from a table, and (3) numerical methods in which the radial-lens distortion curve is approximated by a polynomial. Each of these methods assumes distortions to be symmetric about the principal point. Corrections for radial-lens distortion should theoretically be applied after images have been corrected for shrinkage or expansion.

The following example illustrates the method of reading corrections from a curve:

EXAMPLE 5-4 Suppose that the photocoordinates of Example 5-3 were measured on a photograph taken with the camera whose radial-lens distortion curve is represented in Fig. 4-13. Calculate coordinates of point no. 4 of Example 5-3 after correcting for radial-lens distortion.

SOLUTION (Calculations are based on shrinkage-corrected coordinates.) The radial distance r from the principal point to point no. 4 is

$$r = \sqrt{(65.37)^2 + (61.62)^2} = 89.83 \text{ mm}$$

Entering the abscissa of Fig. 4-13 with an r value of 89.83 mm, moving vertically to intersect the distortion curve, and then moving leftward horizontally to the ordinate scale (see dashed line of Fig. 4-13), radial-lens distortion Δr of $+ 0.004$ mm is read. (Positive values indicate outward distortion.) The corrected radial distance to point no. 4 is obtained by subtracting the positive distortion from the radial distance, or

$$r' = r - \Delta r \qquad (5\text{-}10)$$

For this example, r' is

$$r'_4 = 89.83 - 0.004 = 89.826 \text{ mm}$$

Now the corrected x' and y' coordinates are calculated in proportion to the ratio of r'/r, or

$$x' = \left(\frac{r'}{r}\right) x \qquad (5\text{-}11)$$

$$y' = \left(\frac{r'}{r}\right) y \qquad (5\text{-}12)$$

Applying Eqs. (5-11) and (5-12) to this example,

$$x'_4 = (89.826/89.83)65.37 = 65.367 \text{ or } 65.37 \text{ mm (rounded)}$$
$$y'_4 = (89.826/89.83)61.62 = 61.617 \text{ or } 61.62 \text{ mm (rounded)} \qquad ////$$

Although radial-lens distortion is essentially negligible for the Zeiss Pleogon lens of the above example, it is quite significant for some camera lenses. The Metrogon lens, for example, has radial-lens distortions in excess of ± 0.100 mm. Photogrammetrists should therefore ascertain the magnitude of radial-lens distortion for their camera lenses and make corrections if it introduces an intolerable error in any given problem.

The method of approximating radial-lens distortions with a polynomial is the most complex; however, if an electronic computer is available, it is also most convenient. The polynomial method is especially well suited for analytical photogrammetric calculations. The method consists of approximating the radial-lens distortion curve with a polynomial of the form

$$\Delta r = k_1 r + k_2 r^3 + k_3 r^5 + k_4 r^7 \qquad (5\text{-}13)$$

In Eq. (5-13), Δr is the radial-lens distortion at a radial distance r from the principal point. The k coefficients define the shape of the curve. They are obtained through a least squares curve fitting computation which matches a curve to known radial distortions at varying radial distances as determined through camera calibration. The method of determining the coefficients is demonstrated in an example problem in Sec. A-11 of Appendix A. Once the k's have been determined, radial-lens distortion for any value of r may be readily calculated by back substitution into Eq. (5-13).

The above procedures all assume radial-lens distortions to be symmetric about the principal point. *Asymmetric* lens distortions can also be accounted for. The assumption of symmetry, however, accounts satisfactorily for lens distortions for all but the most precise photogrammetric work. *Tangential* lens distortions are generally very small and are seldom corrected for.

5-13 CORRECTION FOR ATMOSPHERIC REFRACTION

It is well known that density (and hence index of refraction) of the atmosphere decreases with increased altitude. Because of this condition, light rays do not travel in straight lines through the atmosphere but rather are bent according to Snell's law as shown in Fig. 5-12. The incoming light ray from point A of the figure makes an angle α with the vertical. If refraction were ignored, the light ray would appear to be coming from point B rather than from point A. Photogrammetric equations assume that light rays travel straight paths; to compensate for the known refracted paths, corrections are applied to the image coordinates.

In Fig. 5-12, if a straight path had been followed by the light ray from object point A, then its image would have been at a'. The angular distortion due to refraction is θ, and the linear distortion on the photograph is δr. Refraction causes all imaged points to be displaced outward from their correction positions. The magnitude of refraction distortion increases with increasing flying height and also with increasing α angle. Refraction distortion occurs radially from the photographic nadir point (principal point of a vertical photo) and is zero at the nadir point.

From Fig. 5-12 the basic refraction correction equation may be developed as follows:

$$La = \frac{f}{\cos \alpha} \qquad (a)$$

$$\delta r = \frac{La \times \theta}{\cos \alpha} \qquad (b)$$

Where θ is in radians.

Combining Eqs. (a) and (b),

$$\delta r = \frac{f\theta}{\cos^2 \alpha} \qquad (5\text{-}14)$$

FIGURE 5-12
Atmospheric refraction in aerial photography.

Assuming a standard atmosphere, angle θ may be calculated for a particular flight altitude, average ground elevation, and α angle. (Calculations for θ angles are beyond the scope of this text.) To correct a given imaged point for refraction distortion, the α angle is first calculated based on the measured photo coordinates and camera focal length as follows:

$$\alpha = \tan^{-1}\left(\frac{r}{f}\right) \qquad (5\text{-}15)$$

Where

$$r = \sqrt{x^2 + y^2}$$

After calculating θ for a particular flying height, ground elevation, and α angle, Eq. (5-14) is solved to obtain δr. The correction is applied radially from the photographic nadir point (principal point of a vertical photograph), therefore the corrected radial distance r' to the imaged point is obtained by subtracting δr from r. Corrected x' and y' coordinates may then be obtained by using Eqs. (5-11) and (5-12) except that Δr in these equations is replaced by δr.

Figure 5-13 is a nomogram which has been plotted from numerous solutions of the above equations. The nomogram assumes vertical photos, a nominal 6-inch (150-mm) focal length camera, and a standard atmosphere. The nomogram may be used to obtain

FIGURE 5-13
Nomograph for radial distortions due to atmospheric refraction.

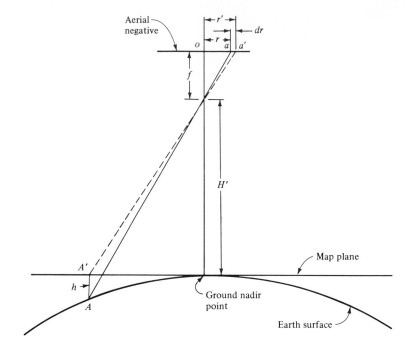

FIGURE 5-14
Distortions in aerial photography due to earth curvature.

refraction distortions for various flying heights and ground elevations above mean sea level (MSL). As an example, if flying height is 10,000 feet above MSL and average ground elevation is 1,500 feet above MSL, refraction distortion is 4 micrometers for an image having a radial distance of 100 millimeters from the principal point. The solution of this example on the nomogram is shown by the dashed line on Fig. 5-13.

5-14 CORRECTION FOR EARTH CURVATURE

If the positions of points in the object space are to be computed in a plane coordinate system, then it may be necessary to account for image distortions caused by curvature of the earth. In Fig. 5-14, A is a ground object point and A' is its position in a map plane which is tangent to the earth at the ground nadir point (point vertically beneath the exposure station). If the map position A' is desired in computation, then it is necessary to use the photo coordinates of the theoretical image position a' instead of the actual image position a. Distance aa' is dr, the distortion for earth curvature. It is radial from the photographic nadir point (principal point of a vertical photo).

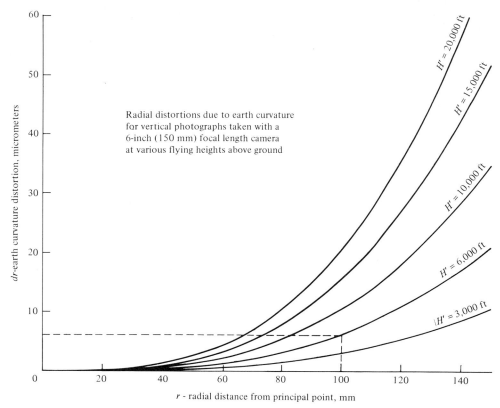

FIGURE 5-15
Nomograph for radial distortions due to earth curvature.

From Fig. 5-14 it is seen that the earth curvature correction must be applied outward. The equation for calculating dr is

$$dr = \frac{H'r^3}{2Rf^2} \qquad (5\text{-}16)$$

In Eq. (5-16), H' is flying height above ground, r is radial distance from principal point to image point, R is the earth's radius, and f is the camera focal length. Corrected radial distance r' to an image point is obtained by adding dr to r. As with radial-lens distortion and refraction distortion, corrected photocoordinates may then be obtained using Eqs. (5-11) and (5-12) except that Δr is replaced by dr.

Earth curvature distortions become more severe as radial distance from the ground nadir point to the object point increases. This distance increases if radial distance r increases, if flying height is increased, or if focal length is decreased. The nomogram of Fig. 5-15 shows radial distortions due to earth curvature for vertical photographs taken with a nominal 6-inch (150-mm) focal length camera for various flying heights above ground. As an example of the use of this nomogram, for a flying height of 6,000 feet above ground, an image of a radial distance of 100 millimeters from the principal point has an earth curvature radial distortion of 6 micrometers. This example is shown dashed on the nomogram.

REFERENCES

American Society of Photogrammetry: "Manual of Photogrammetry," 3d ed., George Banta Co., Inc., Menasha, Wis., 1966, chap. 10.

Bertram, S.: Atmospheric Refraction, *Photogrammetric Engineering,* vol. 32, no. 1, p. 76, 1966.

Brock, R. H.: Methods for Studying Film Deformation, *Photogrammetric Engineering,* vol. 38, no. 4, p. 399, 1966.

Brown, D. C.: Computational Trade-offs in The Design of a Comparator, *Photogrammetric Engineering,* vol. 35, no. 2, p. 185, 1969.

Gugel, R. A.: Comparator Calibration, *Photogrammetric Engineering,* vol. 31, no. 5, p. 853, 1965.

Jaksic, Z.: Deformations of Estar-base Aerial Films, *Photogrammetric Engineering,* vol. 38, no. 3, p. 285, 1972.

Jeyapalan, K.: Calibration of a Comparator, *Photogrammetric Engineering,* vol. 38, no. 5, p. 472, 1972.

Keller, M., and G. C. Tewinkel: "Aerotriangulation: Image Coordinate Refinement," Technical Bulletin no. 25, U.S. Coast and Geodetic Survey, Washington, D.C., 1965.

Kraus, K.: Film Deformation Correction with Least Squares, *Photogrammetric Engineering,* vol. 38, no. 5, p. 487, 1972.

Kreckel, K. H.: Roll Film Mensuration, *Photogrammetric Engineering,* vol. 31, no. 6, p. 1003, 1965.

Lampton, B. F., and M. J. Umbach: Film Distortion Compensation Effectiveness, *Photogrammetric Engineering,* vol. 32, no. 6, p. 1035, 1966.

Schut, G. H.: Photogrammetric Refraction, *Photogrammetric Engineering,* vol. 35, no. 1, p. 79, 1969.

Van Roessel, J.: Estimating Lens Distortion with Orthogonal Polynomials, *Photogrammetric Engineering,* vol. 36, no. 6, p. 584, 1970.

Vlcek, J.: Systematic Errors of Image Coordinates, *Photogrammetric Engineering,* vol. 35, no. 6, p. 585, 1969.

Wolf, P. R.: Trilaterated Photo Coordinates, *Photogrammetric Engineering,* vol. 35, no. 6, p. 543, 1969.

Ziemann, H.: Image Deformation and Methods for Its Correction, *The Canadian Surveyor,* vol. 25, no. 4, p. 367, 1971.

PROBLEMS

5-1 Assume that photocoordinates of points a and b of Fig. 5-1 are x_a = 57.28 milli-meters, y_a = 51.84, x_b = 83.71 millimeters, and y_b = −60.48 millimeters. Calculate the photo distance ab, the radial distances oa and ob, and the angle (less than 180°) aob.

5-2 The problem is the same as Prob. 5-1 except that the photocoordinates are x_a = 2.875 inches, y_a = 2.648 inches, x_b = 3.780 inches, and y_b = −3.008 inches.

5-3 In Fig. 5-4, assume that x_a = −112.70 millimeters, y_a = 0.00 millimeters, x_b = 0.00 millimeters, and y_b = −112.82 millimeters. Calculate x_e and y_e if S_a and S_b are measured as 145.28 and 160.43 millimeters, respectively.

5-4 The problem is the same as Prob. 5-3 except that x_a = −113.000 millimeters, y_a = 0.00 millimeters, x_d = 0.00 millimeters, and y_d = 113.00 millimeters. Also S_a and S_d are measured as 76.460 and 112.485 millimeters, respectively.

5-5 Name and briefly discuss the various systematic errors which may exist in photo-graphic coordinates.

5-6 In Fig. 5-6, assume that a faulty x and y axis system was constructed such that y_1 = −0.24 millimeters, x_2 = 0.08 millimeters, y_3 = 0.04 millimeters, and x_4 = 0.37 millimeters. Calculate the corrected coordinates of a point e whose co-ordinates measured with respect to the faulty axis system were x_e = 84.27 milli-meters and y_e = 49.81 millimeters. Calibrated fiducial distances x_m and y_m are 226.00 millimeters.

5-7 Calculate the acute angle of intersection of fiducial lines for a camera if comparator measurements of the fiducial marks on a flash plate were as follows:

Mark	X, mm	Y, mm
A	− 112.706	0.223
B	− 0.174	− 113.004
C	113.054	− 0.445
D	0.512	112.768

5-8 If the intersection of fiducial lines of the camera of Prob. 5-7 defines the principal point exactly, what are the x and y photocoordinates of the four fiducial marks in the photo system?

5-9 On a paper-print positive, measured distances between x fiducials (A and C) was 226.07 mm and between y fiducials (B and D) was 225.38 mm. These x and y distances determined in camera calibration were 225.89 and 225.93 mm, respec-tively. Calculate shrinkage-corrected coordinates of points 1, 2, and 3 whose co-ordinates were measured on the paper print as follows:

Point	X, mm	Y, mm
1	10.71	− 70.77
2	86.65	95.53
3	− 109.52	− 76.91

5-10 The following $x'y'$ coordinates (see Fig. 5-1b) were measured for a diapositive having corner fiducials. Calculate coordinates of points 1, 2, and 3 in the conventional xy photocoordinate system. Assume the principal point to be at the intersection of lines joining opposite corner fiducials.

Point	x', mm	y', mm
Fiducial A	0.00	0.00
Fiducial B	212.40	0.00
Fiducial C	212.40	212.42
Fiducial D	0.00	212.42
1	38.27	40.23
2	105.41	91.85
3	184.66	201.48

5-11 Calculate shrinkage-corrected coordinates for points 1, 2, and 3 of Prob. 5-10 if the calibrated coordinates of fiducials obtained through camera calibration are as follows:

Fiducial	Calibration x, mm	Calibration y, mm
A	-106.51	-106.52
B	106.51	-106.52
C	106.51	106.52
D	-106.51	106.52

5-12 A diapositive was placed on the stage of a lead-screw monocomparator and oriented so that the y readings of fiducials A and C of Fig. 5-8 were equal. The following measurements were taken:

Point	X, mm	Y, mm
Fiducial A	25.486	135.285
Fiducial B	138.604	22.173
Fiducial C	251.724	135.285
Fiducial D	138.610	248.397
1	203.486	92.073
2	187.228	174.982
3	83.291	64.480

(a) Reduce the photographic coordinates of points 1, 2, and 3 to the fiducial coordinate axes.

(b) If the calibrated coordinates of the principal point of the camera are $x_o = 0.020$ millimeters and $y_o = -0.012$ millimeters, what are the coordinates of points 1, 2, and 3 corrected to the origin at the principal point?

(c) Assume that the calibrated x and y fiducial distances for the camera are 226.005 and 225.996 mm, respectively. Using the method described in Sec. 5-11, apply shrinkage corrections to coordinates of points 1, 2, and 3 that were determined in (b).

(d) Assume that the radial-lens distortion curve of the camera is given in Fig. 4-13. Apply radial-lens distortion corrections to the coordinates of points 1, 2, and 3 that were determined in (c).

5-13 Use the nomograph of Fig. 5-13 to determine photocoordinates corrected for refraction image distortions for the following situations. Interpolate where necessary. Assume a 6-inch focal length camera and vertical photos.

	H above MSL, ft	h above MSL, ft	Photocoordinates	
			x, mm	y, mm
(*a*)	10,000	2,000	− 72.00	46.00
(*b*)	10,000	5,000	60.00	38.00
(*c*)	15,000	3,000	105.50	− 86.25
(*d*)	20,000	4,000	79.10	102.65
(*e*)	30,000	5,000	− 100.75	54.85

5-14 Use the nomograph of Fig. 5-15 to determine photocoordinates corrected for earth curvature image distortions for the following situations. Interpolate where necessary. Assume a 6-inch focal length camera and vertical photos.

	H' above ground, ft	Photocoordinates	
		x, mm	y, mm
(*a*)	5,000	61.27	− 94.81
(*b*)	10,000	85.00	− 38.37
(*c*)	12,000	103.66	70.04
(*d*)	15,000	− 98.90	100.73
(*e*)	20,000	− 32.15	105.21

VERTICAL PHOTOGRAPHS

6-1 GEOMETRY OF VERTICAL PHOTOGRAPHS

Aerial photographs capture on film a complete record of the objects appearing within the area of coverage. As long as the negatives are preserved, that record can be reproduced in the form of photo positives whenever desired. A great deal of information can be determined by means of measurements from photographs; in fact, a complete survey of the area covered can be performed in this manner. Such a survey requires only a knowledge of the camera's calibration data and some limited amount of ground surveying to establish control.

As described in Chap. 1, photographs taken from an aircraft with the optical axis of the camera vertical or as nearly vertical as possible are called *vertical photographs*. If the optical axis is exactly vertical, the resulting photograph is termed *truly vertical.* In this chapter, equations are developed assuming truly vertical photographs. In spite of precautions taken to keep the camera axis vertical, small tilts are invariably present. For photos intended to be vertical tilts are usually less than 1° and rarely exceed 3°. Photographs containing these small unintentional tilts are called *near-vertical* or *tilted photographs,* and for many practical purposes these photos may be analyzed using the "truly vertical" equations of this chapter without serious error.

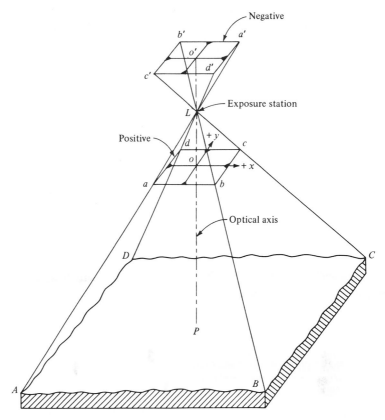

FIGURE 6-1
The geometry of a vertical photograph.

In this chapter, besides assuming truly vertical photographs, other assumptions are that the photocoordinate axis system has its origin at the photographic principal point and that all photocoordinates have been corrected for shrinkage, lens distortion, atmospheric refraction distortion, and earth curvature distortion.

Figure 6-1 illustrates the geometry of a vertical photograph taken from an exposure station L. The *negative,* which is a reversal in both tone and geometry of the object space, is situated a distance equal to the focal length (distance $o'L$ on Fig. 6-1) behind the rear nodal point of the camera lens. The *positive* may be obtained by direct emulsion-to-emulsion "contact printing" with the negative. This process produces a reversal of tone and geometry from the negative and therefore the tone and geometry of the positive are exactly the same as those of the object space. Geometrically the plane of a contact-printed positive is situated a distance equal to the focal length (distance oL on Fig. 6-1) in front of the front nodal point of the camera lens. The reversal in geometry from object space to negative is readily seen on Fig. 6-1 by comparing the positions of object points *A, B, C,* and *D* with their corresponding negative positions a', b', c', and d'. The correspondence of the geometry of the object space and the positive is also readily apparent. The photographic coordinate axes x and y, as described in Chap. 5, are shown on the positive of Fig. 6-1.

6-2 SCALE

"Map scale" is ordinarily interpreted as the ratio of a map distance to the corresponding distance on the ground. In similar manner, the scale of a photograph is the ratio of a distance on the photo to that same distance on the ground. On a map, scale is everywhere uniform because a map is an orthographic projection. An aerial photograph, on the other hand, is a perspective projection and, as will be demonstrated herein, its scale varies with variations in terrain elevation.

Scales may be expressed either as *unit equivalents, dimensionless representative fractions,* or *dimensionless ratios.* If, for example, 1 inch on a map or photo represents 1,000 feet (12,000 inches) on the ground, the scale expressed in the aforementioned three ways is

1) Unit equivalents: 1 in. = 1,000 ft
2) Dimensionless representative fraction: 1/12,000
3) Dimensionless ratio: 1:12,000

It is helpful to remember that a large number in a scale expression denotes a small scale, and vice versa, e.g., 1 in. = 100 ft is a larger scale than 1 in. = 1,000 ft.

6-3 SCALE OF A VERTICAL PHOTOGRAPH OVER FLAT TERRAIN

Figure 6-2 shows the side view of a vertical photograph taken over flat terrain. Since measurements are normally taken from photo positives rather than negatives, the negative has been excluded from this and other figures that follow in this text. The scale of a vertical photograph over flat terrain is simply the ratio of the photo distance ab to the corresponding ground distance AB. That scale may be expressed in terms of camera focal length, f, and flying height above ground, H', by equating the similar triangles Lab and LAB as follows:

$$S = \frac{ab}{AB} = \frac{f}{H'} \qquad (6\text{-}1)$$

From Eq. (6-1) it is seen that the scale of a vertical photo is directly proportional to camera focal length (image distance) and inversely proportional to flying height above ground (object distance).

FIGURE 6-2
Two-dimensional view of a vertical photograph taken over flat terrain.

EXAMPLE 6-1 A vertical aerial photograph is taken over flat terrain with a 6-in. (152.4-mm) focal length camera from an altitude of 6,000 ft above ground. What is the photo scale?

By Eq. (6-1):

$$S = \frac{f}{H'} = \frac{6 \text{ in}}{6,000 \text{ ft}} = \frac{1 \text{ in}}{1,000 \text{ ft}} = 1/12,000 = 1:12,000 \qquad\qquad ////$$

6-4 SCALE OF A VERTICAL PHOTOGRAPH OVER VARIABLE TERRAIN

If the photographed terrain varies in elevation, object distance—or the denominator of Eq. (6-1)—will also be variable and photo scale will likewise vary. Photo scale increases with increasing terrain elevation and decreases with decreasing terrain elevation.

Suppose a vertical aerial photograph is taken over variable terrain from exposure station L of Fig. 6-3. Ground points A and B are imaged on the positive at a and b respectively. Photographic scale at h, the elevation of points A and B, is equal to the ratio of photo distance ab to ground distance AB. By similar triangles Lab and LAB an expression for photo scale S_{AB} is

$$S_{AB} = \frac{ab}{AB} = \frac{La}{LA} \qquad\qquad (a)$$

Also, by similar triangles $LO_A A$ and Loa,

$$\frac{La}{LA} = \frac{f}{H-h} \qquad\qquad (b)$$

Substituting Eq. (b) into Eq. (a),

$$S_{AB} = \frac{ab}{AB} = \frac{f}{H-h} \qquad (c)$$

Considering line AB to be infinitesimal, Eq. (c) reduces to an expression for photo scale at a point. In general, by dropping subscripts, the scale at any point whose elevation above datum is h may be expressed as

$$S = \frac{f}{H-h} \qquad (6\text{-}2)$$

In Eq. (6-2), the denominator $(H-h)$ is object distance. In this equation as in Eq. (6-1), scale of a vertical photograph is seen to be simply the ratio of image distance to object distance. The shorter the object distance (the closer the terrain to the camera), the greater photo scale, and vice versa. For vertical photographs taken over variable terrain, there are an infinite number of different scales. This is one of the principal differences between a photograph and a map.

6-5 AVERAGE PHOTO SCALE

It is often convenient and desirable to use an *average scale* to define the overall mean scale of a vertical photograph taken over variable terrain. Average scale is the scale at the average elevation of the terrain covered by a particular photograph and is expressed as:

$$S_{\text{avg}} = \frac{f}{H - h_{\text{avg}}} \qquad (6\text{-}3)$$

In using an average scale, it must be understood that it is exact only at those points which lie at average elevation, and it is only an approximate scale for all other areas of the photograph.

EXAMPLE 6-2 Suppose that highest terrain, h_1, average terrain, h_{avg}, and lowest terrain, h_2, of Fig. 6-3 are 2,000, 1,500 and 1,000 ft above mean sea level respectively. Calculate maximum scale, minimum scale, and average scale if flying height above mean sea level is 10,000 ft and camera focal length is 6 in. (152.4 mm).

By Eq. (6-2) (maximum scale occurs at maximum elevation),

$$S_{\text{max}} = \frac{f}{H - h_1} = \frac{6 \text{ in}}{(10,000 - 2,000)\,\text{ft}} = \frac{6 \text{ in}}{8,000 \text{ ft}}$$

$$S_{\text{max}} = \frac{1 \text{ in}}{1,333 \text{ ft}} = 1/16,000 = 1:16,000$$

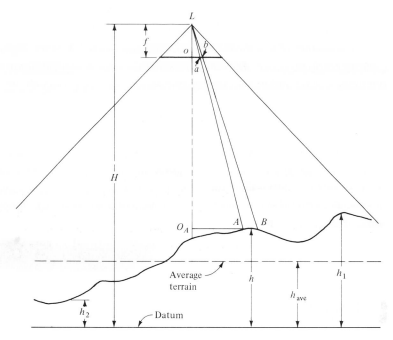

FIGURE 6-3
Scale of a vertical photograph over variable terrain.

(Minimum scale occurs at minimum elevation.)

$$S_{\min} = \frac{f}{H - h_2} = \frac{6 \text{ in}}{(10,000 - 1,000)\text{ft}} = \frac{6 \text{ in}}{9,000 \text{ ft}}$$

$$S_{\min} = \frac{1 \text{ in}}{1,500 \text{ ft}} = 1/18,000 = 1{:}18,000$$

By Eq. (6-3):

$$S_{\text{avg}} = \frac{f}{H - h_{\text{ave}}} = \frac{6 \text{ in}}{(10,000 - 1,500)\text{ft}} = \frac{6 \text{ in}}{8,500 \text{ ft}}$$

$$S_{\text{avg}} = \frac{1 \text{ in}}{1,417 \text{ ft}} = 1/17,000 = 1{:}17,000$$

////

6-6 OTHER METHODS OF DETERMINING SCALE OF VERTICAL PHOTOGRAPHS

In the previous sections, equations have been developed for calculating scale of vertical aerial photographs in terms of camera focal length, flying height, and terrain elevation.

There are, however, other methods of scale determination which do not require knowledge of these values.

A ground distance may be measured in the field between two points whose images appear on the photograph. Having measured the corresponding photo distance, the scale relationship is simply the ratio of the photo distance to the ground distance. The resulting scale applies only at the elevation of the ground line, and if the line is along sloping ground, the resulting scale applies at approximately the average elevation of the two end points of the line.

The scale of a vertical aerial photograph may also be determined if a map covering the same area as the photo is available. In this method it is necessary to measure, on the photograph and on the map, the distances between two well-defined points which can be identified on both photo and map. Photographic scale can then be calculated from the following equation:

$$S = \frac{\text{photo distance}}{\text{map distance}} \times \text{map scale} \qquad (6\text{-}4)$$

EXAMPLE 6-3   On a vertical photograph the length of an airport runway measures 6.30 in. On a map which is plotted to a scale of 1:24,000, the runway scales 4.06 in. What is the scale of the photograph at runway elevation?

From Eq. (6-4):

$$S = \frac{6.30 \text{ in}}{4.06 \text{ in}} \times \frac{1}{24,000} = \frac{1}{15,470} \text{ or } 1 \text{ in} = 1,290 \text{ ft} \qquad ////$$

The scale of a vertical aerial photograph can also be determined without the aid of a measured ground distance or a map if lines whose lengths are known by common knowledge appear on the photo. "Section lines" of a known mile length or a football field or baseball diamond could be measured on the photograph, for example, and photographic scale could be calculated as the ratio of the photo distance to the known ground distance.

EXAMPLE 6-4   What is the scale of a vertical aerial photograph on which a section line measures 5.93 in?

SOLUTION   The length of a section line is assumed to be 5,280 ft. (Actually it can vary considerably from that value.) Photo scale is simply the ratio of the measured photo distance to the ground distance, or

$$S = \frac{5.93 \text{ in}}{5,280 \text{ ft}} = \frac{1 \text{ in}}{890 \text{ ft}} \text{ or } 1:10,700 \qquad ////$$

In each of the methods of scale determination discussed in this section, it must be remembered that the calculated scale is exact only at the elevation of the ground line used to determine that scale.

6-7   GROUND COORDINATES FROM A VERTICAL PHOTOGRAPH

The ground coordinates of points whose images appear in a vertical photograph can be determined with respect to an arbitrary ground coordinate system. The arbitrary X and Y ground axes are in the same vertical planes as the photographic x and y axes respectively, and the origin of the system is at the datum principal point (point in the datum plane vertically beneath the exposure station).

Figure 6-4 shows a vertical photograph taken at a flying height H above datum. Images a and b of the ground points A and B appear on the photograph, and their measured photographic coordinates are x_a, y_a, x_b, and y_b. The arbitrary coordinate axis system is X and Y, and the ground coordinates of points A and B in that system are X_A, Y_A, X_B, and Y_B. From similar triangles $La'o$ and $LA'A_o$, the following equation may be written:

$$\frac{oa'}{A_oA'} = \frac{f}{H - h_A} = \frac{x_a}{X_A}$$

from which we derive

$$X_A = x_a \frac{(H - h_A)}{f} \qquad (6\text{-}5)$$

Also, from similar triangles $La''o$ and $LA''A_o$, we may write

$$\frac{a'a}{A'A} = \frac{f}{H - h_A} = \frac{y_a}{Y_A}$$

from which we derive

$$Y_A = y_a \frac{(H - h_A)}{f} \qquad (6\text{-}6)$$

Similarly, the ground coordinates of point B are

$$X_B = x_b \frac{(H - h_B)}{f} \qquad (6\text{-}7)$$

$$Y_B = y_b \frac{(H - h_B)}{f} \qquad (6\text{-}8)$$

Upon examination of Eqs. (6-5) through (6-8), it is seen that X and Y ground coordinates of any point are obtained by simply multiplying x and y photocoordinates by

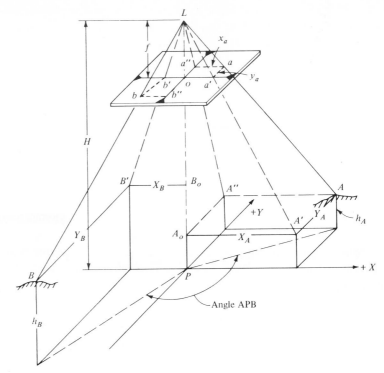

FIGURE 6-4
Ground coordinates from a vertical photograph.

the inverse of photo scale at that point. From the ground coordinates of the two points A and B, the horizontal length of the line AB can be calculated, using the pythagorean theorem, as:

$$AB = \sqrt{(X_B - X_A)^2 + (Y_B - Y_A)^2} \qquad (6\text{-}9)$$

Also, the horizontal angle APB may be calculated as

$$APB = 90° + \tan^{-1}\left(\frac{X_B}{Y_B}\right) + \tan^{-1}\left(\frac{Y_A}{X_A}\right) \qquad (6\text{-}10)$$

In order to solve Eqs. (6-5) through (6-8) it is necessary to know the camera focal length, flying height above datum, elevations of the points above datum, and the photocoordinates of the points. The photocoordinates are readily measured, camera focal length is commonly known, and flying height above datum is calculated by methods described in Sec. 6-9. Elevations of points may be obtained directly by field measurement, or they may be taken from available topographic maps.

EXAMPLE 6-5   A vertical aerial photograph was taken with a 6-in. (152.4-mm) focal length camera from a flying height of 4,530 ft above datum. Images a and b of two ground points A and B appear on the photograph, and their measured photocoordinates (corrected for shrinkage and distortions) are $x_a = -52.35$ mm, $y_a = -48.27$ mm, $x_b = 40.64$ mm, and $y_b = 43.88$ mm. Determine the horizontal length of the line AB if the elevations of points A and B are 670 and 485 ft above datum respectively.

SOLUTION   From Eqs. (6-5) through (6-8).

$$X_A = \frac{-52.35}{152.4}(4{,}530 - 670) = -1{,}326 \text{ ft}$$

$$Y_A = \frac{-48.27}{152.4}(4{,}530 - 670) = -1{,}223 \text{ ft}$$

$$X_B = \frac{40.64}{152.4}(4{,}530 - 485) = 1{,}079 \text{ ft}$$

$$Y_B = \frac{43.88}{152.4}(4{,}530 - 485) = 1{,}165 \text{ ft}$$

From Eq. (6-9),

$$AB = \sqrt{(1{,}079 + 1{,}326)^2 + (1{,}165 + 1{,}223)^2} = \sqrt{(2{,}405)^2 + (2{,}388)^2} = 3{,}389 \text{ ft} \qquad ////$$

Ground coordinates calculated by Eqs. (6-5) through (6-8) are in an arbitrary rectangular coordinate system, as previously described. If arbitrary coordinates are calculated for two or more "control" points (points whose coordinates are also known in an absolute ground coordinate system such as the state plane coordinate system), then the arbitrary coordinates of all other points for that photograph can be transformed into the ground system. The method of transformation is discussed in Sec. B-2 of Appendix B, and an example problem is given. Using Eqs. (6-5) through (6-8), an entire planimetric survey of the area covered by a photograph can be made.

6-8   RELIEF DISPLACEMENT ON A VERTICAL PHOTOGRAPH

Relief displacement is the shift or displacement in the photographic position of an image caused by the relief of the object, i.e., its elevation above or below a selected datum. With respect to a datum, relief displacement is outward for points whose elevations are above datum and inward for points whose elevations are below datum.

The concept of relief displacement is illustrated in Fig. 6-5, which represents a vertical photograph taken from flying height H above datum. Camera focal length is f, and o is the principal point. The image of terrain point A, which has an elevation h_A

FIGURE 6-5
Relief displacement on a vertical photograph.

above datum, is located at a on the photograph. An imaginary point A' is located vertically beneath A in the datum plane and its corresponding imaginary image position is at a'. On the figure, both $A'A$ and PL are vertical lines, and therefore $A'AaLoP$ is a vertical plane. Plane $A'a'LoP$ is also a vertical plane which is coincident with plane $A'AaLoP$. Since these planes intersect the photo plane along lines oa and oa' respectively, line aa' (relief displacement of point A due to its elevation h_A) is radial from the principal point.

An equation for evaluating relief displacement may be obtained by relating similar triangles Lao and LAA_o in Fig. 6-5 as follows:

$$\frac{r}{R} = \frac{f}{H - h_A} \quad \text{rearranging;} \quad r(H - h_A) = fR \qquad (d)$$

Also, from the similar triangles $La'o$ and $LA'P$,

$$\frac{r'}{R} = \frac{f}{H} \quad \text{rearranging;} \quad r'H = fR \qquad (e)$$

Equating expressions (d) and (e):

$$r(H - h_A) = r'H$$

Rearranging the above equation, dropping subscripts, and substituting the symbol d for $(r - r')$, there results

$$d = \frac{rh}{H} \qquad (6\text{-}11)$$

Where h = height above datum of the object point whose image is displaced

$\quad d$ = relief displacement

$\quad r$ = radial distance on the photograph from the principal point to the displaced image (The units of d and r must be the same.)

$\quad H$ = flying height above the datum selected for measurement of h

Equation (6-11) is the basic relief displacement equation. Examination of this equation shows that relief displacement increases with increasing radial distance to the image, and it also increases with increased elevation of the object point above datum. On the other hand, relief displacement decreases with increased flying height above datum. It has also been shown that relief displacement occurs radially from the principal point.

Figure 6-6 is a vertical aerial photograph which vividly illustrates relief displacement. Note in particular the striking effect of relief displacement on the twin chimneys in the upper left of the photo. Notice also that the relief displacement occurs radially from the center of the photograph. This radial pattern is also readily apparent for the relief displacement of all the vertical building corners and for the storage tanks in the lower left of the photo.

Relief displacement often causes straight roads, fence lines, etc., on rolling ground to appear crooked on a vertical photograph. This is especially true when such roads, fences, etc. occur near the edges of the photo. The severity of the crookedness will depend on the severity of the terrain variation. Relief displacement causes some imagery to be obscured from view. Several examples of this are seen in Fig. 6-6; e.g., the railroad tracks in the lower left portion of the photo are obscured by the relief displacement of the large storage tanks.

To calculate vertical heights of objects appearing on aerial photographs, Eq. (6-11) may be rearranged as follows:

know elevation

$$h = \frac{dH}{r} \qquad (6\text{-}12)$$

In order to use Eq. (6-12) for height determination, it is necessary that the images of both the top and bottom of the vertical object be visible on the photograph so that d can be measured. Datum is arbitrarily selected at the base of the vertical object. Equation (6-12) is of particular value to the photo interpreter who is often interested in relative heights of objects rather than absolute elevations.

FIGURE 6-6
Vertical photograph illustrating relief displacements. (*Courtesy Wisconsin Division of Highways*)

EXAMPLE 6-6   The vertical photograph of Fig. 6-6 was taken from an elevation of 1,750 ft above mean sea level. The elevation at the base of the rightmost chimney in the upper left is 850 ft above MSL. The relief displacement d of the chimney was measured as 2.13 in. and the radial distance to the top of the chimney from the photo center was 4.79 in. What is the height of the chimney?

   SOLUTION   Select datum at the base of the chimney. Then flying height above datum is

$$H = 1,750 - 850 = 900 \text{ ft}$$

By Eq. (6-12):

$$h = \frac{2.13(900)}{4.79} = 400 \text{ ft} \qquad ////$$

Equation (6-11) may be used to calculate image displacements with respect to datum, and then corrected datum image positions may be located by laying off image displacements along radial lines toward the principal point as shown in Fig. 6-7. These "datum-corrected" images have true relative planimetric positions, just as they would be on a map plotted at photographic datum scale. Datum scale may be calculated by Eq. (6-1) using H above datum in the denominator. From these datum-corrected image positions, angles, lengths, and areas may be measured just as from a map.

EXAMPLE 6-7   Figure 6-7 represents a vertical photo taken at a flying height of 6,500 ft above datum with a camera having a 6-in. (152.4-mm) focal length. On the photo, points a, b, and c are imaged such that their radial distances from the principal point are 91.42 mm, 83.50 mm, and 70.06 mm respectively. Corresponding ground elevations of points A, B, and C are 835, 600, and 450 ft above MSL respectively. Calculate relief displacements aa', bb', and cc' necessary to locate the datum positions of the imaged points, and calculate datum scale.

SOLUTION   By Eq. (6-11),

$$aa' = \frac{r_a h_A}{H} = \frac{91.42(835)}{6,500} = 11.73 \text{ mm}$$

$$bb' = \frac{r_b h_B}{H} = \frac{83.50(600)}{6,500} = 7.71 \text{ mm}$$

$$cc' = \frac{r_c h_C}{H} = \frac{70.06(450)}{6,500} = 4.85 \text{ mm}$$

By Eq. (6-1),

$$\text{Datum scale} = \frac{f}{H} = \frac{6 \text{ in}}{6,500 \text{ ft}} = \frac{1 \text{ in}}{1,083 \text{ ft}} = 1:13,000 \qquad ////$$

6-9   FLYING HEIGHT OF A VERTICAL PHOTOGRAPH

From previous discussion it is apparent that flying height above datum is an important quantity which is often needed for solving basic photogrammetry equations. For rough computations, flying heights may be taken from altimeter readings. Flying heights may

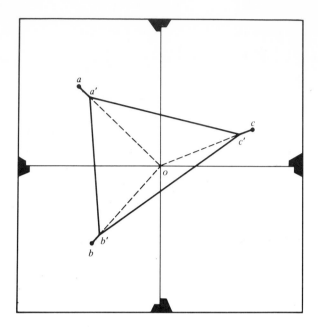

FIGURE 6-7
Relief displacement corrections laid off radially toward the principal point.

also be obtained by using either Eq. (6-1) or (6-2) if a ground line of known length appears on the photograph. This procedure yields exact flying heights for truly vertical photographs if the end points of the ground line lie at equal elevations. In general, the greater the difference in elevation of the end points, the greater the error in computed flying height; therefore the ground line should lie on fairly level terrain. Accurate results can be obtained by this method, however, even though the end points of the ground line are at different elevations, if the images of the end points are approximately equidistant from the principal point of the photograph and on a line through the principal point.

EXAMPLE 6-8   A certain section line lies on fairly level terrain. Find the approximate flying height above the terrain if the camera focal length is $3\frac{1}{2}$ in. (88.9 mm) and the section line scales 3.70 in. on the photograph.

SOLUTION   (Assuming the section line to be 5,280 ft long):
By Eq. (6-1),

$$\frac{3.70 \text{ in}}{5,280 \text{ ft}} = \frac{3\frac{1}{2} \text{ in}}{H'}$$

From which

$$H' = \frac{5,280 \,(3\frac{1}{2})}{3.70} = 5,000 \text{ ft above the terrain}$$

////

approximate

Accurate flying heights can be determined even though the end points of the ground line lie at differing elevations. This procedure requires knowledge of the elevations of the end points of the line as well as the length of the line. Suppose ground line AB has its end points imaged at a and b on a vertical photograph. Length AB of the ground line may be expressed in terms of ground coordinates, by the pythagorean theorem, as follows:

$$(AB)^2 = (X_B - X_A)^2 + (Y_B - Y_A)^2$$

Substituting Eqs. (6-5) through (6-8) into the above equation, there results

$$(AB)^2 = \left[\frac{x_b}{f}(H - h_B) - \frac{x_a}{f}(H - h_A)\right]^2 + \left[\frac{y_b}{f}(H - h_B) - \frac{y_a}{f}(H - h_A)\right]^2 \qquad (6\text{-}13)$$

The only unknown in Eq. (6-13) is flying height, H. When all known values are inserted into the equation, it reduces to the quadratic form of $aH^2 + bH + c = 0$. The direct solution for H in the quadratic is

$$H = \frac{-b \pm \sqrt{b^2 - 4ac}}{2a} \qquad (6\text{-}14)$$

Rather than solving the quadratic equation, a trial-and-error approach is often preferred. In the trial-and-error approach, an initial approximation of H, labeled H_1, is calculated using Eq. (6-2). Then AB in Eq. (6-13), labeled AB_1, is calculated based on the initial H_1. Computed AB_1 is then compared with true AB, and if they do not agree, a revised value of H (labeled H_2) is calculated by the following equation:

$$H_2 = \frac{AB}{AB_1}(H_1 - h_{AB}) + h_{AB} \qquad (6\text{-}15)$$

In Eq. (6-15), h_{AB} is the average elevation of the two end points of the ground line; all other terms are as previously defined. Using the revised value H_2 in Eq. (6-13), a new value AB_2 is calculated which is again compared with the true ground length AB. The process is repeated until satisfactory agreement is obtained between computed and true AB. Usually an agreement within a foot is satisfactory, and if a reasonably good first value of H is used, two iterations are generally sufficient.

EXAMPLE 6-9   A vertical photograph was taken with a camera having a focal length of 5.998 in. (152.3 mm). Ground points A and B have elevations 1,435 and 1,461 ft above sea level respectively, and the horizontal length of the line AB is 1,919 ft. The images of A and B appear at a and b and their measured photocoordinates are $x_a = 0.717$ in, $y_a = -2.414$ in, $x_b = 4.317$ in, and $y_b = -0.835$ in. Calculate the flying height of the photograph above sea level.

SOLUTION

1) Find the photo distance ab:

$$ab = \sqrt{(x_b - x_a)^2 + (y_b - y_a)^2}$$

$$ab = \sqrt{(4.317 - 0.717)^2 + (-0.835 + 2.414)^2} = 3.931 \text{ in}$$

2) Find approximate H_1 by Eq. (6-2):

$$S = \frac{ab}{AB} = \frac{f}{H_1 - h_{AB}}; \frac{3.931 \text{ in}}{1,919 \text{ ft}} = \frac{5.998 \text{ in}}{H_1 - 1,448}$$

$$H_1 = \frac{5.998(1,919)}{3.931} + 1,448 = 4,376 \text{ ft}$$

3) Find AB_1 using Eq. (6-13):

$$(AB_1)^2 = \left[\frac{4.317}{5.998}(4,376 - 1,461) - \frac{0.717}{5.998}(4,376 - 1,435)\right]^2$$

$$+ \left[\frac{-0.835}{5.998}(4,376 - 1,461) - \frac{-2.414}{5.998}(4,376 - 1,435)\right]^2$$

$$(AB_1)^2 = (2,098.0 - 351.6)^2 + (-405.8 + 1,183.7)^2$$

$$AB_1 = 1,912 \text{ ft (The true value of } AB \text{ is 1,919)}$$

4) Using Eq. (6-15), a new approximation of H is calculated:

$$H_2 = \frac{1,919}{1,912}(4,376 - 1,448) + 1,448 = 4,387$$

5) A new value of AB is calculated using H_2:

$$(AB_2)^2 = \left[\frac{4.317}{5.998}(4,387 - 1,461) - \frac{0.717}{5.998}(4,387 - 1,435)\right]^2$$

$$+ \left[\frac{-0.835}{5.998}(4,387 - 1,461) - \frac{-2.414}{5.998}(4,387 - 1,435)\right]^2$$

$$(AB_2)^2 = (2,106.0 - 352.9)^2 + (-407.3 + 1,188.1)^2$$

$$AB_2 = 1919.1 \text{ ft (satisfactory agreement)}$$

Therefore H is 4,387 ft above sea level.

6-10 ERROR EVALUATION

Answers obtained in solving the various equations presented in this chapter will inevitably contain errors. It is important to have an awareness of the presence of these errors and to be able to assess their approximate magnitudes. Errors in computed answers are caused partly by random errors in measured quantities which are used in computation and partly by the failure of certain assumptions to be met. Common sources of errors in calculated values are

1) Errors in photographic measurements, e.g., photocoordinates *how close we measure.*
2) Errors in ground control
3) Shrinkage and expansion of film and paper
4) Lens distortions
5) Tilted photographs where vertical photographs were assumed

Sources 1 and 2 above can be minimized if precise equipment and caution are used in making the measurements. Source 3 can be practically eliminated by making corrections as described in Sec. 5-11. Source 4 is generally comparatively small, but for precise work it can also be eliminated by making corrections as described in Sec. 5-12. Magnitudes of error introduced by source 5 depend upon the severity of tilt. Generally if the photos were intended to be vertical and if paper prints are being used, these errors are compatible with the other four sources. If the photo is severely tilted, or if very high accuracy is desired, the tilted photo equations of Chap. 13 should be used.

A simple and straightforward approach to calculating the combined effect of several random errors in computed answers is to consider separately the effect on the answer of each error source. This approach involves calculating rates of changes with respect to each variable containing error and requires only simple differential calculus. As an example of this approach, assume that a vertical photograph was taken with a camera having a focal length of 6.000 inches. Assume also that a ground distance AB on flat terrain has a length of 5,000 feet and that its corresponding photo distance ab measures 5.00 inches. Flying height above ground may be calculated, using Eq. (6-1), as follows:

$$H' = f\left(\frac{AB}{ab}\right) = 6.000\left(\frac{5000}{5.00}\right) = 6,000 \text{ ft}$$

Now it is required to calculate the expected error dH' caused by errors in measured quantities AB and ab. This is done by taking derivatives with respect to each of these quantities containing error. Suppose that the error dAB in the ground distance is ± 1.0 foot and that the error dab in the measured photo distance is ± 0.01 inch. The error in dH' caused by the error dAB in the ground length can be evaluated by taking the derivative dH'/dAB as:

$$\frac{dH'}{dAB} = \frac{f}{ab}$$

dH' can now be obtained by substituting numerical values into the above differential equation, as follows:

$$dH' = \frac{f}{ab}\ dAB = \left(\frac{6.000}{5.00}\right)(1.0) = \pm\ 1.2\ \text{ft}$$

In similar manner the error dH' caused by error dab is:

$$dH' = \left[\frac{-f(AB)}{(ab)^2}\right](d_{ab}) = \left[\frac{-6.000(5,000)}{(5.00)^2}\right](0.01) = \pm\ 12.0\ \text{ft}$$

In this example the total error in H' due to the combined effects of the two error sources could be as great as 13.2 feet. Total error is not generally the sum of the individual contributing errors, however, because of the compensating nature of random errors. Rather, the total combined effect would be calculated as the square root of the sum of the squares of the individual errors as

$$dH'_{\text{total}} = \sqrt{(1.2)^2 + (12.0)^2} = \pm\ 12.1\ \text{ft}$$

It should be noted that the error in H' caused by the error in the measurement of photo distance ab is the most severe of the two contributing sources. Therefore, to increase the accuracy of the computed value of H', it is necessary to refine the measured photo distance to a more accurate value. Errors in computed answers using any of the equations presented in this chapter can be analyzed in the manner described above, and the method is valid as long as the contributing errors are small.

REFERENCES

American Society of Photogrammetry: "Manual of Photogrammetry," 3d ed., George Banta Co., Inc., Menasha, Wis., 1966, chap 2.

Hallert, B.: "Photogrammetry," McGraw-Hill Book Company, New York, 1960.

Landis, G. H., and H. A. Meyer: The Accuracy of Scale Determinations on Aerial Photographs, *Journal of Forestry*, vol. 52, p. 863, 1954.

PROBLEMS

6-1   The photo distance between two image points a and b on a vertical photograph is 3.68 inches and the corresponding ground distance AB is 5,863 feet. What is photographic scale at the elevation of the ground line?

6-2   The problem is the same as Prob. 6-1 except that photo distance is 52.8 millimeters and ground distance is 3,875 feet.

6-3   On a vertical photograph two section corners appear 3.85 inches apart. What is photographic scale at the elevation of the section line?

6-4 On a vertical photograph a college football field measures 1.08 inch from goal line to goal line (100 yards). What is the scale of the photograph at the elevation of the football field?

6-5 A vertical photograph was taken, with a camera having a 6-inch focal length, from a flying height 8,000 feet above sea level. What is the scale of the photograph at an elevation of 1,250 feet above mean sea level? What is datum scale?

6-6 Aerial photographs are to be taken for highway planning and design. If a 6-inch focal length camera is to be used and if an average scale of 1:3,000 is required, what should be the flying height above average terrain?

6-7 A vertical aerial photograph was taken from a flying height of 12,000 feet above datum with a camera having a focal length of 209.72 mm. Highest, lowest, and average terrain appearing in the photograph is at 6,650, 3,085 and 4,800 feet respectively. Calculate minimum, maximum, and average photographic scale.

6-8 A vertical photograph was taken over the lunar surface from an altitude of 60 miles with a 75-mm focal length camera. What is the actual diameter of a crater whose diameter on the photograph scales 8.27 millimeters?

6-9 Vertical photography for military reconnaissance is required. If the lowest safe flying altitude over enemy defenses is 12,000 ft, what camera focal length is necessary to achieve a photo scale of 1:20,000?

6-10 A distance ab on a vertical photograph is 2.83 inches and corresponding ground distance AB is 4,875 feet. If the camera focal length is 88.75 mm, what is the flying height above the terrain upon which the line AB is located?

6-11 Vertical photography at an average scale of 1:10,000 is to be acquired for the purpose of constructing a mosaic. What is the required flying height above average terrain if the camera focal length is $8\frac{1}{4}$ inches?

6-12 The distance on a map between two road intersections in flat terrain measures 5.03 inches. The distance between the same two points is 3.64 inches on a vertical photograph. If the scale of the map is 1:24,000, what is the scale of the photograph?

6-13 Points A and B are at elevations 1,365 and 1,640 feet above datum, respectively. The photographic coordinates of their images on a vertical photograph are $x_a = 68.27$ millimeters, $y_a = -32.37$ millimeters, $x_b = -87.44$ millimeters, and $y_b = 26.81$ millimeters. What is the horizontal length of the line AB if the photo was taken from 16,000 feet above datum with an $8\frac{1}{4}$-inch focal length camera?

6-14 Images a, b, and c of ground points A, B, and C appear on a vertical photograph taken from a flying height of 7,500 feet above datum. A 6-inch focal length camera was used. Points A, B, and C have elevations of 725, 640, and 1,095 feet above datum respectively. Measured photocoordinates of the images are $x_a = -2.371$ inches, $y_a = 1.864$ inches, $x_b = 2.062$ inches, $y_b = 3.183$ inches, $x_c = 3.704$ inches, and $y_c = -3.138$ inches. Calculate the lengths of the lines AB, BC, and AC and the area within the triangle ABC.

6-15 The image of a point whose elevation is 1,850 feet above datum appears 68.37 millimeters from the principal point of a vertical photograph taken from a flying height of 6,000 feet above datum. What would this distance from the principal point be if the point were at datum?

6-16   The images of the top and bottom of a power pole are 5.083 and 4.961 inches respectively from the principal point of a vertical photograph. What is the height of the pole if flying height above the base of the pole is 3,200 feet?

6-17   An area has an average terrain elevation of 1,000 feet above datum. The highest points in the area are 1,750 feet above datum. If the camera focal plane opening is 9 inches square, what flying height above datum is required to limit relief displacement of 0.25 inches? If the camera focal length is $8\frac{1}{4}$ inches, what is the resulting average scale of the photography?

6-18   The datum scale of a vertical photograph taken from 3,000 feet above datum is 1:6,000. The diameter of a cylindrical oil storage tank measures 4.63 millimeters at the base and 4.78 millimeters at the top. What is the height of the tank if its base lies at 560 feet above datum?

6-19   On a vertical photograph images a and b of the ground points A and B have photographic coordinates $x_a = -12.68$ millimeters, $y_a = 70.24$ millimeters, $x_b = 89.07$ millimeters, and $y_b = -92.41$ millimeters. The horizontal distance between A and B is 3,784 feet and the elevations of A and B are 1,328 and 1,243 feet above datum respectively. Calculate the flying height above datum if the camera had a 6-inch focal length.

6-20   The problem is the same as Prob. 6-19 except that the horizontal distance AB is 5,785 feet and the camera focal length is 88.78 millimeters.

6-21   In Prob. 6-8, assume that the values given for focal length, photo distance, and flying height contain random errors of ± 0.1 millimeters, ± 0.05 millimeters, and ± 0.3 miles, respectively. What is the expected error in the computed diameter of the crater?

6-22   In Prob. 6-10, assume that the values given for focal length, photo distance, and ground length contain random errors of ± 0.005 millimeters, ± 0.01 inch, and ± 1.0 foot respectively. What is the expected error in the computed flying height?

6-23   In Prob. 6-16, assume that the random error in each measured photo distance is ± 0.001 inch and that the error in the flying height is ± 5 feet. What is the expected error in the computed height of the power pole?

STEREOSCOPIC VIEWING

7-1 DEPTH PERCEPTION

In our daily activities we unconsciously measure depth or judge distances to a vast
number of objects about us through our normal process of vision. Methods of judging
depth may be classified as either *stereoscopic* or *monoscopic*. Persons with normal vision
(those capable of viewing with both eyes simultaneously) are said to have *binocular* vision,
and perception of depth through binocular vision is called stereoscopic viewing.
Monocular vision is the term applied to viewing with only one eye, and methods of
judging distances with one eye are termed monoscopic. A person having normal binocular
vision can, of course, view monocularly by covering one eye.

Distances to objects, or depth, can be perceived monoscopically on the basis of (1)
relative sizes of objects, (2) hidden objects, (3) shadows, and (4) differences in focusing
of the eye required for viewing objects at varying distances. Examples of the first two of
these are shown in Fig. 7-1. Depth to the far end of the football field may be perceived,
for example, on the basis of the relative sizes of the goal posts. The goal posts are actually
the same size, of course, but one appears smaller because it is farther away. Also, the
building is quickly judged to be a considerable distance away because it is partially hidden
behind the football stadium.

FIGURE 7-1
Depth perception by relative size and hidden objects.

Monoscopic methods of depth perception enable only rough impressions to be gained of distances to objects. With stereoscopic viewing, on the other hand, a much greater degree of accuracy in depth perception can be attained. Stereoscopic depth perception is of extreme importance in many phases of photogrammetry.

7-2   THE HUMAN EYE

The phenomenon of stereoscopic depth perception can be more clearly understood with the help of a brief description of the anatomy and physiology of the human eye. The human eye functions in much the same manner as a camera. As shown in Fig. 7-2, the eye is essentially a spherical organ having a circular opening called the *pupil*. The pupil is protected by a transparent coating called the *cornea*. Incident light rays pass through the cornea and enter the eye through the pupil and strike the *lens*, which is directly behind the pupil. The cornea and lens refract the light rays according to Snell's law.

The lens of the eye is biconvex in shape and is composed of a refractive transparent medium. It is suspended by many muscles which enable the lens to be moved so that the *optical axis* of the eye can be aimed directly at an object to be viewed. As with a camera, the eye must satisfy the lens formula, Eq. (2-5), for each different object distance. The eye's image distance is constant, however; therefore, in order to satisfy the lens formula for varying object distances, the focal length of the lens changes. When a distant object is viewed, the lens muscles relax, causing the spherical surfaces of the lens to become flatter. This increases the focal length to satisfy the lens formula and

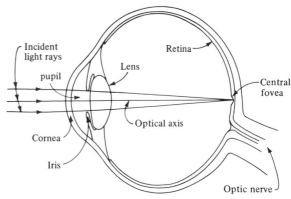

FIGURE 7-2
Cross section of the human eye.

accommodate the long object distance. When close objects are viewed, a reverse procedure occurs. The eye's ability to focus for varying object distances is called *accommodation.*

As with a camera, the eye also has a diaphragm. It is called the *iris.* The iris (colored part of the eye) automatically contracts or expands to regulate the amount of light entering the eye. When the eye is subjected to intense light, the iris contracts, reducing the pupil aperature. When the intensity of the light lessens, the iris dilates to admit more light.

The cornea partially refracts incident light rays before they encounter the lens. The lens refracts them further and brings them to focus on the *retina,* thereby forming an image of the viewed object. The retina is composed of very delicate tissue. The most important region of the retina is the *central fovea,* a small pit near the intersection of the optical axis with the retina. The central fovea is the area of sharpest vision. The retina performs a function similar to that performed by the emulsion of photographic film. When it is stimulated by light, the sense of vision, which is transmitted to the brain via the *optic nerve,* is caused.

7-3   STEREOSCOPIC DEPTH PERCEPTION

With binocular vision, when the eyes are focused on a certain point, the optical axes of the two eyes converge on that point intersecting at an angle called the *parallactic angle.* The nearer the object, the greater the parallactic angle and vice versa. In Fig. 7-3, the optical axes of the two eyes L and R are separated by a distance b_e, called the *eye base.* When the eyes are focused on point A, the optical axes converge, forming parallactic angle ϕ_a. Similarly, when sighting object point B, the optical axes converge forming

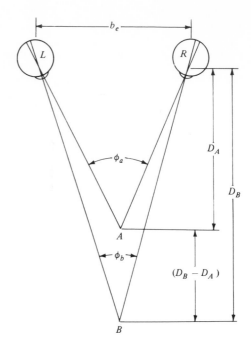

FIGURE 7-3
Stereoscopic depth perception as a function of parallactic angle.

parallactic angle ϕ_b. The brain automatically and unconsciously associates distances D_A and D_B with corresponding parallactic angles ϕ_a and ϕ_b. The depth between objects A and B is $D_B - D_A$ and is perceived as the difference in these two parallactic angles.

The shortest distance of clear stereoscopic depth perception for the average adult is about 10 inches. Objects can be focused at distances as short as 6 inches, but such close viewing causes excessive eyestrain. The eye base of the average adult is between 63 and 69 millimeters or approximately 2.6 inches. The maximum parallactic angle formed by the eyes, assuming 10 inches as the minimum focusing distance, is therefore approximately

$$\phi = 2 \tan^{-1} \left(\frac{1.3}{10} \right) = 15°$$

The maximum distance at which distinct stereoscopic depth perception is possible is not well defined, although for the average adult it is approximately 2,000 feet. Beyond that distance parallactic angles are extremely small and changes in parallactic angle necessary for depth perception cannot be discerned.

7-4 VIEWING PHOTOGRAPHS STEREOSCOPICALLY

Suppose that while gazing at object A of Fig. 7-4, a transparent medium containing image marks a_1 and a_2 is placed in front of the eyes as shown. Assume further that the image marks are identical in shape to the object A, and that they are placed on the optical axes

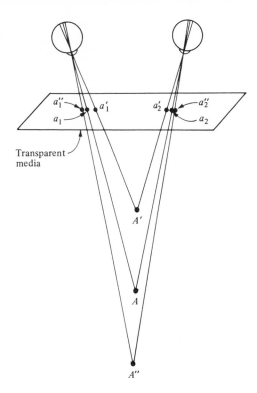

FIGURE 7-4
The apparent depth to the object, A, can
be changed by changing the spacing of
the images.

so that the eyes are unable to detect whether they are viewing the object or the two
marks. Object A could therefore be removed without any noticeable change in the
image that is received in the retinas of the eyes. As shown in Fig. 7-4, if the image
marks are moved closer together to, say, a'_1 and a'_2, the parallactic angle increases and the
object is perceived to be nearer the eyes at A'. If the marks are moved farther apart to a''_1
and a''_2, the parallactic angle decreases and the brain receives an impression that the object
is farther away, at A''

This phenomenon of creating the three-dimensional or stereoscopic impression of
objects by viewing identical images of the objects can be achieved photographically.
Suppose that a pair of aerial photographs is taken from exposure stations L_1 and L_2 so
that the building appears on both photos as shown in Fig. 7-5. Flying height above
ground is H' and the distance between the two exposures is B, the *air base*. Object points
A and B at the top and bottom of the building are imaged at a_1 and b_1 on the left photo
and at a_2 and b_2 on the right photo. Now, if the two photos are laid on a table and
viewed so that the left eye sees only the left photo and the right eye sees only the right
photo as shown in Fig. 7-6, a three-dimensional impression of the building is obtained.
The three-dimensional impression appears to lie below the table top at a distance h from
the eyes. The brain judges the height of the building by associating depths to points A

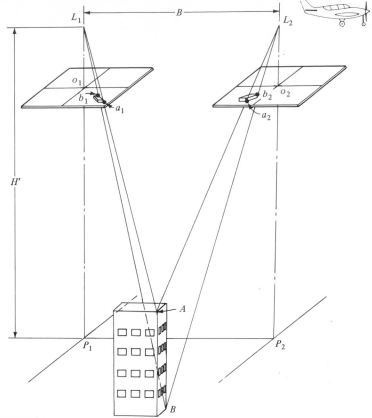

FIGURE 7-5
Photographs from two exposure stations with building in common overlap area.

and B with the parallactic angles ϕ_a and ϕ_b respectively. When the eyes gaze over the entire overlap area, the brain receives a continuous three-dimensional impression of the terrain. This is achieved by the continuous perception of changing parallactic angles of the infinite number of image points which make up the terrain. The three-dimensional model thus formed is called a *stereoscopic model* or simply a *stereomodel*, and the overlapping pair of photographs is called a *stereopair*.

7-5 STEREOSCOPES

It is quite difficult to view photographs stereoscopically without the aid of optical devices for the following two reasons: first, viewing the photos from the close range that is necessary causes eyestrain and focusing difficulty and, secondly, the eyes are focused at

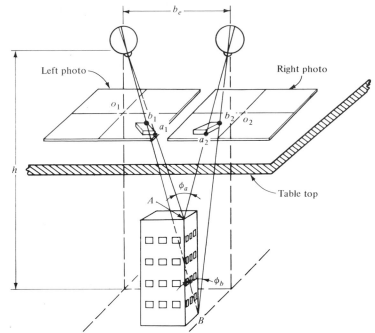

FIGURE 7-6
Viewing the building stereoscopically.

short range (approximately 6 inches) on the photos lying on the table while at the same time the brain perceives parallactic angles which tend to form the stereomodel at some depth below the table—a confusing situation to say the least. These difficulties in stereoscopic viewing may be overcome through the use of instruments called *stereoscopes*.

There is a wide selection of stereoscopes serving a variety of special purposes. All operate in essentially the same manner. The *lens* or *pocket* stereoscope shown in Fig. 7-7 is the least expensive and most commonly used stereoscope. It consists of two simple convex lenses mounted on a frame. The spacing between the lenses can be varied to accommodate various eye bases. The legs fold or can be removed so that the instrument is easily stored or carried—a feature which renders the pocket stereoscope ideal for fieldwork. The legs of the pocket stereoscope are slightly shorter than the focal length of the lenses, so that when the stereoscope is placed over the photos, light rays emanating from points on the photos converge slightly as they pass through each lens. (Recall from Chap. 2 that a bundle of light rays from a point exactly a distance f from a lens will converge and emerge through the lens parallel.) Longer object distances compatible with the distance at which the brain perceives the stereomodel are associated with the slightly converged light rays. The lenses also serve to magnify the images, thereby enabling detail to be seen more clearly.

FIGURE 7-7
Lens or pocket stereoscope. (*Courtesy Carl Zeiss, Oberkochen*)

In using a pocket stereoscope, the photos are placed so that corresponding images are slightly less than the eye base apart; usually about 2 inches. For normal 9-inch-square format photos taken with 60 percent end lap, the common overlap area of a pair of photos is a rectangular area 5.4 inches wide, as shown in Fig. 7-8a. If the photos are separated by 2 inches for stereoviewing with a pocket stereoscope as shown in Fig. 7-8b, there is a rectangular area shown double crosshatched in which the top photo obscures the bottom photo, thereby preventing stereoviewing. To overcome this problem, the top photo can be gently rolled up out of the way to enable viewing the corresponding imagery of the obscured area.

The *mirror* stereoscope shown in Fig. 7-9 permits the two photos to be completely separated when viewing stereoscopically. This eliminates the problem of one photo obscuring part of the overlap of the other, and it also enables the entire stereomodel to be viewed simultaneously. The operating principle of the mirror stereoscope is illustrated in

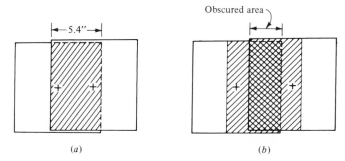

(a)   (b)

FIGURE 7-8
(a) The common overlap area of a pair of 9-inch format photos taken with 60 percent end lap (corresponding images coincident). (b) Obscured area when photos are oriented for viewing with pocket stereoscope.

FIGURE 7-9
ST-4 mirror stereoscope. (*Courtesy Wild Heerbrugg Instruments, Inc.*)

Fig. 7-10. The stereoscope has two large wing mirrors and two smaller eyepiece mirrors, all of which are mounted at 45° to the horizontal. Light rays emanating from image points on the photos such as a_1 and a_2 are reflected from the mirror surfaces, according to the principles of reflection discussed in Sec. 2-4, and are received at the eyes forming parallactic angle ϕ_a. The brain automatically associates the depth to point A with that

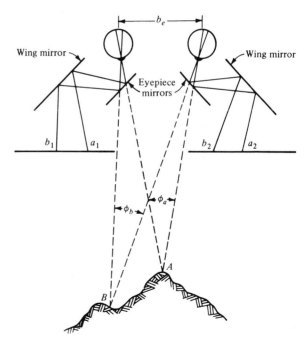

FIGURE 7-10
Operating principle of the mirror stereoscope.

parallactic angle. The stereomodel is thereby created beneath the eyepiece mirrors as illustrated in Fig. 7-10.

Simple lenses are usually placed directly above the eyepiece mirrors as shown in Fig. 7-9. Their separation may be changed to accommodate various eye bases. The focal length of these lenses is also slightly greater than the length of the reflected ray path from photo to eyes, and therefore they serve basically the same function as the lenses of the pocket stereoscope. Mirror stereoscopes may be equipped with binoculars which fasten over the eyepiece mirrors. The binoculars, which may be focused individually to accommodate each eye, permit viewing images at high magnification—a factor which is especially important and useful in photo interpretation or in identifying image points. High magnification, of course, limits the field of view so that the entire stereomodel cannot be viewed simultaneously. The stereoscope must therefore be moved about if all parts of the stereomodel are to be seen.

It is extremely important to avoid touching the first-surfaced mirrors of a mirror stereoscope. This is true because the hands contain oils and acids which can eat away the coatings on the mirrors, rendering them useless. If the mirrors are accidentally fingerprinted, they should be cleaned immediately, using a soft cloth and lens cleaning fluid.

A variation of the mirror stereoscope called the *Old Delft Scanning Stereoscope* has many conveniences. The photos are viewed through oculars via an optical path of prisms

FIGURE 7-11
Zoom 95 stereoscope. (*Courtesy Bausch and Lomb Co.*)

and lenses. The oculars can be individually focused and magnification of either 1.5 or 4.5X can be selected. At either of these magnifications the field of view includes only a limited portion of the stereomodel, but the entire stereomodel may be viewed without moving the stereoscope or photos. This is accomplished by turning knobs which rotate prisms in both optical paths, making it possible to scan the stereomodel in both the X and Y directions. By rotating one prism small residual y *parallaxes* (see Sec. 7-7) can be eliminated.

A different type of stereoscope called the *Zoom stereoscope* is shown in Fig. 7-11. A variety of these instruments are manufactured affording a choice of special features such as continuous zoom magnification up to 120X, capability of rotating images optically (which permits convenient correction for crab or alignment of photos), accommodation of various format sizes from 70 millimeters up to 9 inches, and individual focus and enlargement so that two photos of different scales can be viewed stereoscopically. For direct stereoscopic viewing of film negatives, these stereoscopes may be obtained mounted on a light table and equipped with a special scanning mechanism. A reel of film and a takeup reel are mounted on either end of the table. By turning a crank, the frames are brought into position for viewing.

7-6 THE USE OF STEREOSCOPES

Before attempting to use a stereoscope, it is important to study the operator's manual if one is available. This is especially true for stereoscopes having more elaborate optical viewing systems. Also, the lenses and mirrors should be inspected and cleaned if necessary.

In stereoscopic viewing, it is important to orient the photos so that the left and right eyes see the left and right photos respectively. If the photos are viewed in reverse, a *pseudoscopic view* results in which ups and downs are reversed; e.g., valleys appear as ridges and hills appear as depressions. This can be advantageous for certain work such as tracing drainage patterns, but normally the correct steroscopic view is desired. The photos should be oriented so that the shadows appear to fall to the right or toward the observer, and failure to do this can also cause a pseudoscopic view.

Accurate and comfortable stereoscopic viewing requires that the eye base, the line joining the centers of the stereoscope lenses, and the flight line all be parallel. Therefore, after the photos have been inspected and laid out so as to prevent a pseudoscopic view, the flight line is marked on both photos. For vertical photographs, the flight line is the line from the center of the left photo to the center of the right photo. In marking the flight line, the photo centers (principal points) are first located by joining opposite fiducial marks with straight lines. Principal points are shown at o_1 and o_2 on Fig. 7-12. *Conjugate principal points* (locations of principal points of adjacent overlapping photos) are marked next. This may be done satisfactorily by carefully observing images immediately surrounding the principal points, finding those corresponding images in the overlap area of the adjacent photos, and then marking the conjugate principal points by estimating their positions with respect to these surrounding images. The conjugate principal points are shown at o'_1 and o'_2 on Fig. 7-12.

The next step in orienting a pair of photos for stereoscopic viewing is to tape the left photo down onto the table. Then the right photo is oriented so that the four points defining the flight line (o_1, o'_2, o'_1, and o_2) all lie along a straight line as shown in Fig. 7-12. The right photo is retained in this orientation, and while viewing through the stereoscope, it is moved sideways until the spacing between corresponding images produces a comfortable stereoscopic view. Normally the required spacing between corresponding images is about 2 inches for a pocket stereoscope and about 10 inches for a mirror stereoscope.

It is not absolutely necessary to locate the flight lines and orient photos for stereoscopic viewing in the manner outlined above; in fact, for casual stereoviewing, it is normally done by a trial method in which the photos are simply shifted in position until a clear stereoscopic view is obtained. If accuracy and eye comfort is a consideration, however, orientation by the "flight line" procedure is recommended.

As previously stated, comfortable stereoscopic viewing requires that the line joining the stereoscope lens centers be parallel with the flight line. Once the photos are properly oriented, the operator can easily align the stereoscope by simply rotating it slightly until the most comfortable viewing position is obtained. The operator should look directly into the centers of the lenses, thereby holding the eye base parallel with the flight line.

7-7 CAUSES OF Y PARALLAX

An essential condition that must exist for clear and comfortable stereoscopic viewing is that the line joining corresponding images be parallel with the direction of flight. This condition is fulfilled with the corresponding images a_1 and a_2 shown in Fig. 7-12. When corresponding images fail to lie along a line parallel to the flight line, *y parallax* (p_y) is said to exist. Any slight amount of y parallax causes eyestrain, and excessive amounts prevent stereoscopic viewing altogether.

If a pair of truly vertical overlapping photos taken from equal flying heights is oriented perfectly, then no *y* parallax should exist anywhere in the overlap area. Failure of any of these conditions to be satisfied will cause *y* parallax. In Fig. 7-13, for example, the photos are improperly oriented and the principal points and conjugate principal points do not lie on a straight line. As a result, *y* parallax exists at both points *a* and *b*. This condition can be prevented by careful orientation.

In Fig. 7-14 the left photo was exposed from a lower flying height than the right

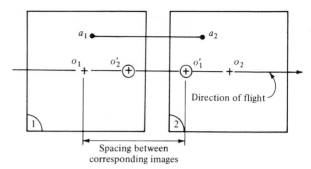

FIGURE 7-12
Pair of photos properly oriented for stereoscopic viewing.

photo, and consequently its scale is larger than the scale of the right photo. Even though the photos are truly vertical and properly oriented, y parallax exists at both points a and b due to variation in flying heights. To obtain a comfortable stereoscopic view, the y parallax can be eliminated by sliding the right photo upward transverse to the flight line when viewing point a and sliding it downward when viewing point b.

The effect of tilted photos is illustrated in Fig. 7-15. The left photo is truly vertical and shows positions of images a through d of a square parcel of property on flat terrain. The right photo was tilted such that the same parcel appears as a trapezoid. Y parallax exists throughout the stereoscopic model as a result of the tilt, as indicated for points a and c. In practice the direction of tilt is random, and therefore small y parallaxes from this source are likely to exist in variable amounts throughout most stereomodels. If it is the intent to obtain vertical photography from a constant flying height, however, these conditions are generally so well controlled that y parallaxes from these sources are hardly ever noticeable. Most serious y parallaxes usually occur from improper orientation of the photos, a condition which can easily be corrected.

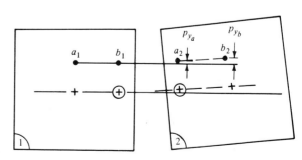

FIGURE 7-13
Y parallax caused by improper orientation of the photos.

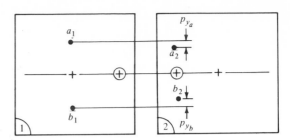

FIGURE 7-14
Y parallax caused by variation in flying
height.

7-8 VERTICAL EXAGGERATION IN STEREOVIEWING

Under normal conditions the vertical scale of a stereomodel will be greater than the
horizontal scale. This scale disparity is called *vertical exaggeration.* It is usually of greatest
concern to photo interpreters who must take this condition into account when estimating
heights of objects, calculating slopes, etc.

Although other factors are involved, vertical exaggeration is caused primarily by the
lack of equivalence of the B/H' ratio in obtaining the photography and the corresponding
b_e/h ratio in stereoviewing. B/H' is the *base-height* ratio, or the ratio of the *air base*
(distance between the two exposure stations) to flying height above average ground; b_e/h
is the ratio of the eye base to the distance from the eyes at which the stereomodel is
perceived. For 60 percent end lap photography taken with a 6-inch focal length, 9-inch
square format camera, the B/H' ratio is 0.60. The average adult eye base is about 2.6
inches, and although h is a difficult variable to measure, repeated tests with numerous
people indicate an average value of about 17 inches. Using these two average values, the
b_e/h ratio is approximately 0.15. The product of the B/H' ratio and the *inverse* of the
b_e/h ratio gives an approximation of vertical exaggeration, or

$$V = \left(\frac{B}{H'}\right)\left(\frac{h}{b_e}\right) \text{(approx.)} \qquad (7\text{-}1)$$

EXAMPLE 7-1 Calculate the approximate vertical exaggeration for vertical aerial photos

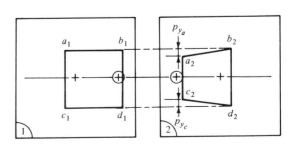

FIGURE 7-15
Y parallax caused by tilt of the photos.

taken with a 12-in (305-mm) focal length camera having a 9-in (23-cm)-square format if the photos were taken with 60 percent end lap from a flying height 3,000 ft above terrain.

SOLUTION   By Eq. (6-1),

$$\text{Scale} = \frac{f}{H'} = \frac{12 \text{ in}}{3,000 \text{ ft}} = \frac{1 \text{ in}}{250 \text{ ft}}$$

The total ground coverage of one photo is

$$9 \text{ in} \times 250 \text{ ft}/_{\text{in}} = 2,250 \text{ ft}$$

With 60 percent end lap there is a 40 percent advance between exposures, or the air base is

$$B = 0.40(2,250 \text{ ft}) = 900 \text{ ft}$$

By Eq. (7-1), assuming b_e/h to be 0.15,

$$V = \frac{900}{3,000} \times \frac{1}{0.15} = 2.0(\text{approx.})$$

REFERENCES

Ambrose, W. R.: Stereoscopes with High Performance, *Photogrammetric Engineering*, vol. 31, no. 5, p. 822, 1965.

American Society of Photogrammetry: "Manual of Photogrammetry," 3d ed., George Banta Co., Inc., Menasha, Wis., 1966, chap. 11.

Anson, A.: Significant Findings of a Stereoscopic Acuity Study, *Photogrammetric Engineering*, vol. 25, no. 4, p. 607, 1959.

Goodale, E. R.: An Equation for Approximating the Vertical Exaggeration Ratio of a Steroscopic View, *Photogrammetric Engineering*, vol. 19, no. 4, p. 607, 1953.

Gumbel, E. J.: The Effect of the Pocket Stereoscope on Refractive Anomalies of the Eyes, *Photogrammetric Engineering*, vol. 30, no. 5, p. 795, 1964.

Howard, A. D.: The Fichter Equation for Correcting Stereoscopic Slopes, *Photogrammetric Engineering*, vol. 34, no. 4, p. 386, 1968.

La Prade, G. L.: Stereoscopy—A More General Theory, *Photogrammetric Engineering*, vol. 38, no. 12, p. 1177, 1972.

Miller, C. I.: Vertical Exaggeration in the Stereo Space Image and its Use, *Photogrammetric Engineering*, vol. 26, no. 5, p. 815, 1960.

Nicholas, G., and J. T. McCrickerd: Holography and Stereoscopy: The Holographic Stereogram, *Photographic Science and Engineering*, vol. 13, no. 6, p. 342, 1969.

Palmer, D. A.: Stereoscopy and Photogrammetry, *Photogrammetric Record*, vol. 4, p. 391, 1964.

Raasveldt, H. C.: The Stereomodel, How It Is Formed and Deformed, *Photogrammetric Engineering*, vol. 22, no. 4, p. 708, 1956.

Scheaffer, C. E.: Stereoscope for Strips, *Photogrammetric Engineering*, vol. 34, no. 10, p. 1044, 1968.

Thayer, T. P.: The Magnifying Single Prism Stereoscope: A New Field Instrument, *Journal of Forestry*, vol. 61, p. 381, 1963.

Treece, W. A.: Estimation of Vertical Exaggeration in Stereoscopic Viewing of Aerial Photographs, *Photogrammetric Engineering*, vol. 21, no. 4, p. 518, 1955.

Yacoumelos, N.: The Geometry of the Stereomodel, *Photogrammetric Engineering,* vol. 38, no. 8, p. 791, 1972.

PROBLEMS

7-1 What are some of the monocular methods of perceiving depth?

7-2 What is a parallactic angle?

7-3 Compare the advantages and disadvantages of the pocket and mirror stereoscopes.

7-4 Give a step-by-step procedure for orienting photos for stereoscopic viewing.

7-5 What is y parallax? What are the causes of y parallax in a stereomodel?

7-6 Calculate the approximate vertical exaggeration in a stereomodel from photos taken with a 6-inch focal length camera having a 9-inch square format if the photos are taken at 55 percent end lap at a flying height of 8,000 feet above ground.

7-7 The problem is the same as Prob 7-6 except that 65 percent end lap and 10,000 feet flying height above ground are used in the calculation.

STEREOSCOPIC PARALLAX

8-1 INTRODUCTION

Parallax is the apparent displacement in the position of an object, with respect to a frame of reference, caused by a shift in the position of observation. A simple experiment will serve to illustrate parallax. If a finger is held in front of one's eyes and while gazing at the finger the head is quickly shifted from side to side without moving the finger, the finger will appear to move from side to side with respect to objects beyond the finger such as pictures on the wall. The closer the finger is held to the eyes, the greater will be its apparent shift. This apparent motion of the finger is parallax, and it is due to the shift in the position of observation.

If a person looked through the viewfinder of an aerial camera as the aircraft moved forward, he would see images of objects move across his field of view. This image motion is another example of parallax caused by shifting the location of the observation point. Again, the closer an object is to the camera, the more its image will appear to move.

An aerial camera exposing overlapping photographs at regular intervals of time obtains a record of positions of images at the instants of exposure. The change in position of an image from one photograph to the next caused by the aircraft's motion is termed *stereoscopic parallax, x parallax,* or simply *parallax.* Parallax exists for all images

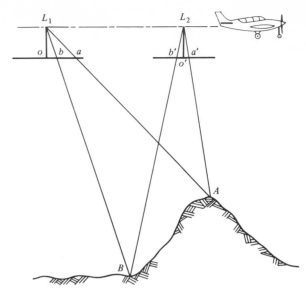

FIGURE 8-1
Stereoscopic parallax of vertical aerial photographs.

appearing on successive overlapping photographs. In Fig. 8-1, for example, images of object points A and B appear on a pair of overlapping vertical aerial photographs which were taken from exposure stations L_1 and L_2. Points A and B are imaged at a and b on the left-hand photograph. Forward motion of the aircraft between exposures, however, caused the images to move laterally across the camera focal plane parallel to the flight line, so that on the right-hand photo they appear at a' and b'. Because point A is higher (closer to the camera) than point B, the movement of image a across the focal plane was greater than the movement of image b; in other words, the parallax of point A is greater than the parallax of point B. This calls to attention two important aspects of stereoscopic parallax: (1) the parallax of any point is directly related to the elevation of the point and (2) parallax is greater for high points than for low points. Variation of parallax with elevation provides the fundamental basis for determining elevations of points from photographic measurements.

Figure 8-2 shows the two photographs of Fig. 8-1 in superposition. Parallaxes of object points A and B are p_a and p_b respectively. Stereoscopic parallax for any point such as A whose images appear on two photos of a stereopair, expressed in terms of "flight line" photographic coordinates, is

$$p_a = x_a - x'_a \qquad (8\text{-}1)$$

In Eq. (8-1), p_a is the stereoscopic parallax of object point A, x_a is the measured photocoordinate of image a on the left photograph of the stereopair, and x'_a is the

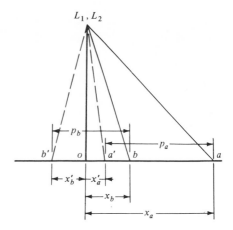

FIGURE 8-2
The two photographs of Fig. 8-1 shown
in superposition.

photocoordinate of image a' on the right photo. These photocoordinates *are not* measured with respect to the fiducial axis system. Rather, they are measured with respect to the "flight line" axis system described in Sec. 8-2. In Eq. (8-1) it is imperative that proper algebraic signs be given to measured photocoordinates in order to obtain correct values for stereoscopic parallax.

Figure 8-3 is a portion of a stereopair of vertical photographs taken over Washington, D.C., with a 6-inch focal length camera at a flying height of 6,000 feet above ground. On these photos, note how all images moved laterally with respect to the y axis from their positions on the left photo to their positions on the right photo. Note also how vividly the Washington Monument illustrates the increase in parallax with higher points; i.e., the top of the monument has moved farther across the focal plane than the bottom of the monument.

On Figure 8-3 the Washington Monument affords an excellent example for demonstrating the use of Eq. (8-1) for finding parallaxes. The top of the monument has an x coordinate ($x_t = 4.32$ inches) and an x' coordinate ($x'_t = 0.72$ inches). By Eq. (8-1), the parallax $p_t = 4.32 - 0.72 = 3.60$ inches. Also, the bottom of the monument has an x coordinate ($x_b = 3.96$ inches) and an x' coordinate ($x'_b = 0.67$ inches). Again by Eq. (8-1), $p_b = 3.96 - 0.67 = 3.29$ inches. In Sec. 8-8 it will be demonstrated how these parallaxes can be used to compute the height of the Washington Monument.

8-2 PHOTOGRAPHIC "FLIGHT LINE" AXES FOR PARALLAX MEASUREMENT

Since parallax occurs parallel to the direction of flight, the photographic x and x' axes for parallax measurement must be parallel with the flight line for each of the photographs of a stereopair. (Primed values denote the right-hand photo of a stereopair.) For a vertical

FIGURE 8-3
Overlapping vertical photographs taken over Washington, D.C., illustrating stereoscopic parallax. (*Photos Courtesy Alster and Associates, Inc.*)

photograph of a stereopair, the flight line is the line connecting principal point and conjugate principal point. Principal points are located in the usual manner by intersecting the x and y fiducial lines. A monoscopic method of establishing conjugate principal points was described in Sec. 7-6. Stereoscopic methods are discussed in Sec. 8-4. The y and y' axes for parallax measurement pass through their respective principal points and are perpendicular to the flight line.

All photographs except those on the ends of a flight strip may have two sets of flight axes for parallax measurements—one to be used when the photo is the left photo of the stereopair and one when it is the right photo. An example is shown in Fig. 8-4, where photographs 1 through 3 were exposed as shown. Parallax measurements in the overlap area of photos 1 and 2 are made with respect to the solid xy axis system of photo 1 and the solid $x'y'$ system of photo 2. However, due to the aircraft's curved path of travel, the flight line of photos 2 and 3 is not in the same direction as the flight line of photos 1 and 2. Therefore, parallax measurements in the overlap area of photos 2 and 3 must be made with respect to the dashed xy axis system on photo 2 and the dashed $x'y'$ system of photo 3. It is possible for the two axis systems to be coincident; however, this does not generally occur in practice. Henceforth in this chapter it shall be understood that photographic coordinates for parallax determination are measured with respect to the flight line axis system.

8-3 MONOSCOPIC METHODS OF PARALLAX MEASUREMENT

Parallaxes of points in a stereopair may be measured either monoscopically or stereoscopically. There are certain advantages and disadvantages associated with each method. In either method the photographic flight line axes must first be carefully located by marking principal points and conjugate principal points.

The simplest method of parallax measurement is the monoscopic approach in which Eq. (8-1) is solved after direct measurement of x and x' on the left and right photos respectively. A disadvantage of this method is that two measurements are required for each point.

Another monoscopic approach to parallax measurement is to fasten the photographs down on a table or base material as shown in Fig. 8-5. In this method the photographic flight lines $o_1 o_2$ and $o'_1 o'_2$ are marked as usual. A long straight line, AA', is drawn on the base material and the two photos are *carefully* mounted as shown so that the photographic flight lines are coincident with this line. Having fastened the photos down, the distance D between principal points is a constant which can be measured. The parallax of point B is $p_b = x_b - (-x'_b)$. However, by examining the figure, it is seen that parallax is also

$$p_b = D - d_b \qquad (8\text{-}2)$$

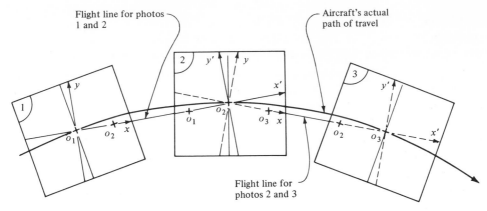

FIGURE 8-4
Flight line axes for measurement of stereoscopic parallax.

With D known in Eq. (8-2), to obtain the parallax of a point it is only necessary to measure the distance d between its images on the left and right photos. The advantage is that for each additional point whose parallax is desired, only a single measurement is required. With either of these monoscopic methods of parallax measurement, any of the simple scales described in Sec. 5-3 may be used, and the choice will depend upon the desired accuracy.

8-4 PRINCIPLE OF THE FLOATING MARK

Parallaxes of points can be measured while viewing stereoscopically with the advantages of speed and accuracy. Stereoscopic measurement of parallax makes use of the principle of the *floating mark*. While viewing a stereomodel through a stereoscope, two small identical marks etched on clear glass called *half marks* may be placed over the photographs—one on the left photo and one on the right photo as is illustrated in Fig. 8-6. The left mark is seen with the left eye and the right mark with the right eye. The half marks may be shifted in position until they fuse together into a single mark which appears to exist in the stereomodel and to lie at a particular elevation. If the half marks are moved closer together, the parallax of the half marks is increased and the fused mark will therefore appear to rise. Conversely, if the half marks are moved apart, parallax is decreased and the fused mark appears to fall. This apparent variation in the elevation of the mark as the spacing of half marks is varied is the basis for the term "floating mark."

The spacing of the half marks (parallax of the half marks) may be varied so that the floating mark appears to rest exactly on the terrain. This produces the same effect as though an object of the shape of the half marks had existed on the terrain when the

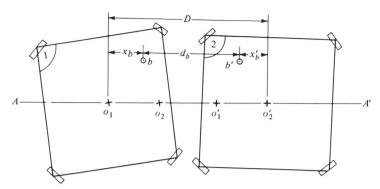

FIGURE 8-5
Parallax measurement using a simple scale.

photos were originally taken. The floating mark may be moved about the stereomodel from point to point, and as the terrain varies in elevation, the spacing of the half marks may be varied to make the floating mark rest exactly on the terrain. Figure 8-6 demonstrates the principle of the floating mark and illustrates how the mark may be set exactly on particular points such as *A, B,* and *C* by placing the half marks at *a* and *a', b* and *b',* and *c* and *c'* respectively.

The principle of the floating mark can be used to transfer principal points to their conjugate locations, thereby marking the flight line axes. In this procedure the principal points are first located as usual at the intersection of fiducial lines. Then by means of a point transfer device such as that shown in Fig. 8-7, these principal points are transferred to their conjugate locations. The point transfer device consists of two separate pieces containing identical half marks etched on glass. The left half mark of Fig. 8-7 is placed over one of the principal points, say the left point o_1, for example. While viewing with a mirror stereoscope, the right half mark is placed on the right photo and moved about until a clear stereoscopic view of the floating mark is obtained and the fused mark appears to rest exactly on the ground. The right half mark, which is hinged, is then raised to make way for lowering a hinged arm containing a pin. The pin comes down exactly on the position occupied by the right half mark. It is pressed into the photograph, thereby marking the conjugate principal point. This stereoscopic procedure is very accurate if carefully performed and it has the advantage that discrete images near the principal points are not necessary, as they are with the monoscopic method. Imagine, for example, the difficulty of monoscopically transferring a principal point which falls in the middle of a wheat field. This transfer could be done easily by the stereoscopic method, however.

A homemade version of the stereoscopic point transfer device described above consists of two small pieces of transparent plastic upon which identical crosses are inked.

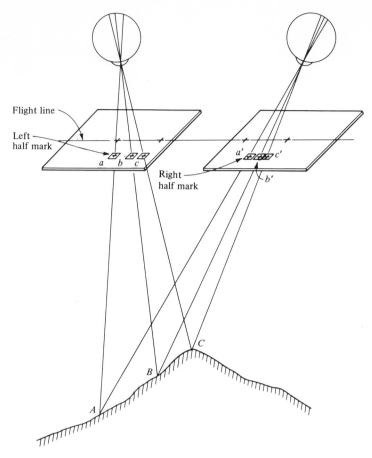

FIGURE 8-6
The principle of the floating mark.

When a half mark is stereoscopically located over a conjugate principal point, its photographic position is marked by pinpricking through the center of the cross.

8-5 STEREOSCOPIC METHODS OF PARALLAX MEASUREMENT

Through the principle of the floating mark, parallaxes of points may be measured stereoscopically. This method employs a stereoscope in conjunction with an instrument called a *parallax bar* and also frequently called a *stereometer*. A parallax bar consists of a metal bar to which are fastened two half marks. The right half mark may be moved with respect to the left mark by turning a micrometer screw. Readings from the micrometer

FIGURE 8-7
Simpson point transfer device. (*Courtesy Alan Gordon Enterprises, Inc.*)

are taken with the floating mark set exactly on points whose parallaxes are desired. From the micrometer readings, parallaxes or differences in parallax are obtained. A parallax bar is shown lying beneath a mirror stereoscope in Fig. 8-8.

When using a parallax bar, the two photos of a stereopair are first *carefully* oriented for comfortable stereoscopic viewing, in such a way that the flight line of each photo lies along a common straight line as shown in Fig. 8-5. The photos are then fastened securely and the parallax bar is placed on the photos. The left half mark, called the *fixed mark*, is unclamped and moved so that, when the floating mark is fused on a terrain point of average elevation, the parallax bar reading is approximately in the middle of the run of the graduations. The fixed mark is then clamped, where it will remain for all subsequent parallax measurements on that particular stereopair. Having positioned the fixed mark in this manner, the right half mark or *movable mark* may be moved left or right with respect to the fixed mark (increasing or decreasing the parallax) as required to accommodate high points or low points without exceeding the run of the parallax bar graduations.

Figure 8-9 is a schematic diagram of the operating principle of the parallax bar. Having oriented the photos and positioned the fixed half mark as just described, the *parallax bar constant, C,* for the setup is determined. For the setup, the spacing between principal points is a constant, D. Once the fixed mark is clamped, the distance from the fixed mark to the index mark of the parallax bar is also a constant, K. From Fig. 8-9, the parallax of point A is

$$p_a = x_a - x'_a = D - (K - r_a) = (D - K) + r_a$$

The term $D - K$ is C, the parallax bar constant for the setup. Also, r_a is the micrometer reading. Substituting C into the above equation, the expression becomes:

$$p_a = C + r_a \qquad (8\text{-}3)$$

Equation (8-3) assumes the parallax bar micrometer to be "forward-reading," i.e., readings increase with increasing parallaxes. Should the readings decrease with increasing parallax, the parallax bar is called "backward-reading" and the algebraic sign of r must be reversed.

FIGURE 8-8
Wild ST-4 mirror stereoscope with binocular attachment and parallax bar.
(*Courtesy Wild Heerbrugg Instruments, Inc.*)

In order to calculate the parallax bar constant, a micrometer reading is taken with the floating mark set on a point. The parallax of that particular point is also directly measured monoscopically and calculated using Eq. (8-1). Then with p and r for that point known, the value of C is calculated, using Eq. (8-3), as

$$C = p - r \qquad (8\text{-}4)$$

The parallax bar constant should be determined on the basis of micrometer readings and parallax measurements for two points. Then the mean of the two values of C may be adopted. Any two points may be selected for this purpose; however, the two principal points are convenient and often used. Figure 8-10 is a section through a pair of overlapping vertical photos. By Eq. (8-1), the parallax of the left photo ground principal point O_1 is $p_{o_1} = x_{o_1} - (-x'_{o_1}) = 0 - (-b') = b'$. (The x coordinate of o_1 on the left photo is zero.) Also, the parallax of the right photo ground principal point O_2 is

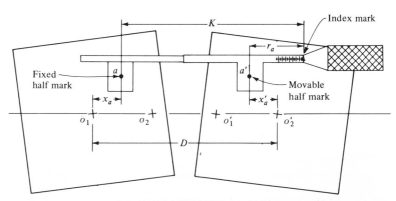

FIGURE 8-9
Schematic diagram of the parallax bar.

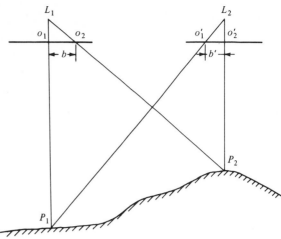

FIGURE 8-10
Parallax of the principal points.

$p_{o_2} = x_{o_2} - x'_{o_2} = b - 0 = b$. From the foregoing, it is seen that the parallax of the left ground principal point is photo base b' measured on the right photo and the parallax of the right ground principal point is photo base b measured on the left photo.

To determine the parallax bar constant using principal points, distances b and b' are first measured. Then the floating mark is stereoscopically fused on the left principal point o_1 and micrometer value r_{o_1} is read, from which we obtain $C_1 = b' - r_{o_1}$. The floating mark is then stereoscopically placed on the right principal point o_2 and micrometer value r_{o_2} is read, from which we obtain $C_2 = b - r_{o_2}$. Errors due to tilt in the photography, unequal flying heights, paper shrinkage, and measurement will generally give two slightly different values of C. The mean value is normally adopted.

In practice, the principal points sometimes become defaced so that stereoscopic measurements r_{o_1} and r_{o_2} are difficult to obtain. In that case, any two discrete images may be used. However, they should be chosen so that they lie on opposite sides of the flight line and equidistant from the flight line. This minimizes error in parallaxes due to faulty orientation of the photos. Also, since the parallax of a point depends only upon the elevation of the point and not on its location on the photograph, the parallaxes of two ground points lying at the same elevation will be equal. Therefore, if the principal points are slightly defaced, the floating mark may be stereoscopically set just slightly to the side of them when their micrometer readings are taken. This will not affect the micrometer readings if the elevation is the same, and it avoids the inaccuracy of setting the floating mark on defaced imagery.

One of the advantages of measuring parallax stereoscopically is increased speed, for once the parallax bar constant is determined, the parallaxes of all other points are quickly

FIGURE 8-11
N2 mirror stereoscope with binoculars and attached parallax bar. (*Courtesy Carl Zeiss, Oberkochen*)

obtained with a single micrometer reading for each point. Another advantage is increased accuracy, not only because binocular vision is used but also because the least reading of most parallax bar micrometer scales is 0.01 millimeter. A person's ability to set the floating mark, like learning to swim, improves with practice. An experienced person using quality equipment and clear photographs is generally able to obtain parallaxes to within approximately ± 0.03 millimeters of their correct values.

Instruments are available which incorporate a stereoscope and parallax bar into a single unit. Figures 8-11 and 8-12 illustrate, respectively, a mirror stereoscope and pocket stereoscope with attached parallax bars. Note the binocular attachment, for greater accuracy, on the unit of Fig. 8-11. The pocket stereoscope unit is especially handy for quick determinations of tree heights, building heights, etc. Although it has the advantage

FIGURE 8-12
TM pocket measuring stereoscope. (*Courtesy Carl Zeiss, Oberkochen*)

of simplicity and compactness, it does of course retain the inconvenience common to pocket stereoscopes that the top photo obscures part of the overlap area of the stereopair.

8-6 PARALLAX EQUATIONS

Figure 8-13 illustrates an overlapping pair of vertical photographs which have been exposed at equal flying heights above datum. Images of an object point A appear on the left and right photos at a and a' respectively. The planimetric position of point A on the ground is given in terms of ground coordinates X_A and Y_A. The XY ground axis system has its origin at the datum principal point O of the left-hand photograph; the X axis is in the same vertical plane as the photographic x and x' flight axes; and the Y axis passes through the datum principal point of the left photo and is perpendicular to the X axis. According to this definition, each stereopair of photographs has its own unique ground coordinate system.

By equating similar triangles of Fig. 8-13, formulas for calculating h_A, X_A, and Y_A may be derived. First of all, from similar triangles $L_1 o a_y$ and $L_1 A_o A_y$,

$$\frac{Y_A}{H - h_A} = \frac{y_a}{f}$$

from which we obtain

$$Y_A = \frac{y_a}{f}(H - h_A) \qquad (a)$$

And equating similar triangles $L_1 o a_x$ and $L_1 A_o A_x$,

$$\frac{X_A}{H - h_A} = \frac{x_a}{f}$$

from which we obtain

$$X_A = \frac{x_a}{f}(H - h_A) \qquad (b)$$

Also from similar triangles $L_2 o' a'_x$ and $L_2 A'_o A_x$,

$$\frac{B - X_A}{H - h_A} = \frac{-x'_a}{f}$$

from which we obtain

$$X_A = B + \frac{x'_a}{f}(H - h_A) \qquad (c)$$

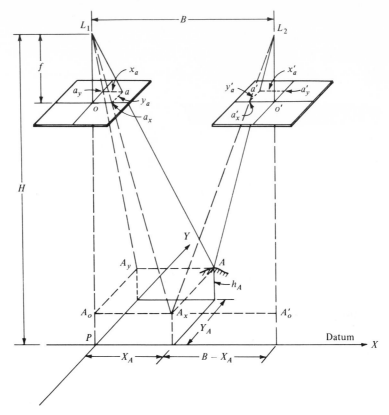

FIGURE 8-13
Geometry of an overlapping pair of vertical photographs.

Equating (*b*) and (*c*) and reducing:

$$h_A = H - \frac{Bf}{x_a - x'_a}$$

Substituting p_a for $x_a - x'_a$ into the above,

height of object $\qquad h_A = H - \frac{Bf}{p_a}$ $\qquad$ (8-5)

Now substituting Eq. (8-5) into each of Eqs. (*b*) and (*a*) and reducing,

X + Y coordinates $\qquad X_A = B\left(\frac{x_a}{p_a}\right)$ $\qquad$ (8-6)

$$Y_A = B\left(\frac{y_a}{p_a}\right) \qquad (8\text{-}7)$$

In Eqs. (8-5), (8-6), and (8-7), h_A is the elevation of point A above datum, H is the flying height above datum, B is the air base, f is the focal length of the camera, p_a is the parallax of point A, X_A and Y_A are ground coordinates of point A in the previously defined unique arbitrary coordinate system, and x_a and y_a are the photocoordinates of point a measured with respect to the flight line axes on the left photo.

Equations (8-5), (8-6), and (8-7) are commonly called the *parallax equations*. They are among the most useful equations to the photogrammetrist. These equations enable a complete survey of the overlap area of a stereopair to be made provided the focal length is known and sufficient ground control is available so the airbase B and flying height H can be calculated.

Equations (8-6) and (8-7) yield X and Y ground coordinates in the unique arbitrary coordinate system of the stereopair, which is not related to the true ground coordinate system. However, if arbitrary coordinates are determined using Eqs. (8-6) and (8-7) for two points whose true ground coordinates are known, then the arbitrary coordinates of all other points can be transformed into the true ground system through a two-dimensional coordinate transformation as described in Appendix B.

EXAMPLE 8-1   A pair of overlapping vertical photographs were taken from a flying height of 4,045 ft above sea level with a 152.4-mm focal length camera. The air base was 1,280 ft. With the photos properly oriented, parallax bar readings of 12.57 and 13.04 mm were obtained with the floating mark set on principal points o_1 and o_2 respectively. On the left photo b was measured as 93.73 mm and on the right photo b' was measured as 93.30 mm. Parallax bar readings of 10.96 and 15.27 mm were taken on points A and B. Also, the x and y photocoordinates of points A and B measured with respect to the flight axes on the left photo were $x_a = 53.41$ mm, $y_a = 50.84$ mm, $x_b = 88.92$ mm, and $y_b = -46.69$ mm. Calculate the elevations of points A and B and the horizontal length of line AB.

SOLUTION   By Eq. (8-4),

$$C_1 = b' - r_{o_1} = 93.30 - 12.57 = 80.73 \text{ mm}$$

$$C_2 = b - r_{o_2} = 93.73 - 13.04 = 80.69 \text{ mm}$$

$$C = \frac{80.73 + 80.69}{2} = 80.71 \text{ mm} \quad \text{constant.}$$

By Eq. (8-3),

$$p_a = C + r_a = 80.71 + 10.96 = 91.67 \text{ mm}$$

$$p_b = C + r_b = 80.71 + 15.27 = 95.98 \text{ mm} \quad \text{parallax.}$$

By Eq. (8-5),

$$h_A = H - \frac{Bf}{p_a} = 4,045 - \frac{1,280(152.4)}{91.67} = 1,917 \text{ ft above sea level} \quad \text{elevation}$$

$$h_B = H - \frac{Bf}{p_b} = 4,045 - \frac{1,280(152.4)}{95.98} = 2,012 \text{ ft above sea level}$$ *elevation*

By Eqs. (8-6) and (8-7),

$$X_A = B\left(\frac{x_a}{p_a}\right) = \frac{53.41(1,280)}{91.67} = 746 \text{ ft}$$

$$X_B = B\left(\frac{x_b}{p_b}\right) = \frac{88.92(1,280)}{95.98} = 1,186 \text{ ft}$$ *X coordinates*

$$Y_A = B\left(\frac{y_a}{p_a}\right) = \frac{50.84(1,280)}{91.67} = 710 \text{ ft}$$

$$Y_B = B\left(\frac{y_b}{p_b}\right) = \frac{-46.69(1,280)}{95.98} = -623 \text{ ft}$$ *Y.*

The horizontal length of line AB is,

$$AB = \sqrt{(X_B - X_A)^2 + (Y_B - Y_A)^2}$$
$$AB = \sqrt{(1,186 - 746)^2 + (-623 - 710)^2} = 1,404 \text{ ft}$$ ////

8-7   ELEVATIONS BY PARALLAX DIFFERENCES

Parallax differences between one point and another are caused by different elevations of the two points. While parallax Eq. (8-5) serves to define stereoscopic parallax and its relationship to flying height, elevation, air base, and camera focal length, parallax differences are more convenient for determining elevations. In Fig. 8-14, object point C is a control point whose elevation h_C above datum is known, The elevation of object point A is desired. Rearranging Eq. (8-5), parallaxes of both points can be expressed as

$$p_c = \frac{fB}{H - h_C} \qquad (d)$$

$$p_a = \frac{fB}{H - h_A} \qquad (e)$$

The difference in parallax, $p_a - p_c$, obtained by subtracting Eq. (d) from Eq. (e) and rearranging is

$$p_a - p_c = \frac{fB(h_A - h_C)}{(H - h_A)(H - h_C)} \qquad (f)$$

Let $p_a - p_c$ equal Δp, the difference in parallax. Substituting $(H - h_A)$ from Eq. (e) and Δp into Eq. (f) and reducing, the following expression for elevation h_A is obtained:

$$h_A = h_C + \frac{\Delta p(H - h_C)}{p_a} \qquad (8-8)$$

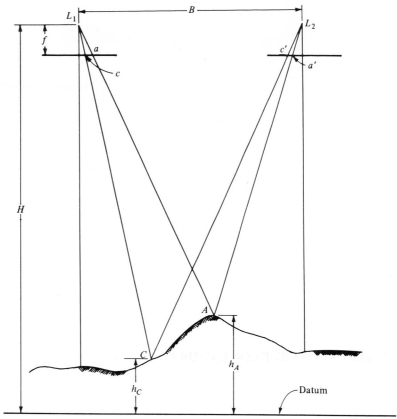

FIGURE 8-14
Elevations by parallax differences.

EXAMPLE 8-2 In Example 8-1, an additional parallax bar reading of 11.89 was taken on control point C, whose elevation is 1,938 ft above sea level. Calculate the elevations of points A and B of that example using parallax difference Eq. (8-8).

SOLUTION   By Eq. (8-3),

$$p_c = C + r_c = 80.71 + 11.89 = 92.60 \text{ mm}$$

For point A,

$$\Delta p = p_a - p_c = 91.67 - 92.60 = -0.93 \text{ mm}$$

By Eq. (8-8),

$$h_A = 1,938 + \frac{(-0.93)(4,045 - 1,938)}{91.67} = 1,917 \text{ ft above sea level}$$

For point B,

$$\Delta p = p_b - p_c = 95.98 - 92.60 = 3.38 \text{ mm}$$

By Eq. (8-8),

$$h_B = 1,938 + \frac{3.38(4,045 - 1,938)}{95.98} = 2,012 \text{ ft above sea level} \qquad ////$$

Note that these answers check the values computed in Example 8-1. Note also that in using Eq. (8-8), elevations to the nearest foot are readily calculated using only a slide rule.

In using Eq. (8-8), if a number of control points are located throughout the overlap area, elevations of unknown points are most accurately determined from the parallax difference of the nearest control point. This minimizes the effects of many errors including photographic tilt, imperfect alignment of the photos for parallax measurement, shrinkage and expansion of the photo papers, and camera-lens distortions.

8-8 APPROXIMATE EQUATION FOR ELEVATIONS FROM PARALLAX DIFFERENCES

The following approximate equation for elevation differences is obtained from Eq. (8-8) by (1) substituting the photo base b of the stereopair for p_a; (2) substituting average flying height above ground, H', for $(H - h_C)$; and (3) letting $\Delta h = h_A - h_C$:

$$\Delta h = \frac{\Delta p H'}{b} \qquad (8-9)$$

In Eq. (8-9), Δh is the difference in elevation between two points whose parallax difference is Δp. For photography in a 9-inch-square format taken with 60 percent end lap, the photo base b is approximately 90 millimeters. For moderate relief, parallaxes for all points are approximately equal to b, so that the substitution of b for p_a is valid. Furthermore, if flying height is not extremely low and if relief is moderate, the substitution of average flying height above ground, H', for $(H - h_C)$ is valid. For very low flying heights or in areas of significant relief, or both, the assumptions of Eq. (8-9) are not met; in these cases Eq. (8-8) should be used. Equation (8-9) is especially convenient in photo interpretation where rough elevations, building heights, tree heights, etc., are often needed.

EXAMPLE 8-3 The parallax difference between the top and bottom of a tree is measured as 1.32 mm on a stereopair of photos taken at 3,000 ft above ground. Average photo base is 88 mm. How tall is the tree?

SOLUTION   By Eq. (8-9),

$$\Delta h = \frac{1.32 \times 3,000}{88} = 45 \text{ ft}$$

EXAMPLE 8-4 Using parallax difference Eq. (8-9), determine the height of the Washington Monument from parallax measurements on Fig. 8-3. Flying height was 6,000 ft above ground and the photo base b was measured as 3.25 in.

SOLUTION   On Fig. 8-3 the parallax of the top of the monument was measured as 3.60 in and the parallax of the bottom was 3.29 in. Parallax difference is

$$\Delta p = 3.60 - 3.29 = 0.31 \text{ in}$$

By Eq. (8-9) the monument height is

$$\Delta h = \frac{6,000 \times 0.31}{3.25} = 572 \text{ ft}$$

(This agrees quite closely with its true height of 555 ft.)   ////

8-9 MEASUREMENT OF PARALLAX DIFFERENCES

Parallax differences may be determined in any of the following ways:

1) By monoscopic measurement of parallaxes followed by subtraction.

2) By taking differences in parallax bar readings. The validity of this approach is seen if parallaxes determined from parallax bar readings are subtracted, as

$$\Delta p = p - p_c = (C + r) - (C + r_c) = r - r_c$$

3) By *parallax wedge.*

A parallax wedge, as illustrated in Fig. 8-15, consists of a piece of transparent film upon which are drawn two converging lines. The left line is a reference line while the line on the right contains graduations from which readings can be made. The spacing of the two lines depends on whether the parallax wedge will be used with a mirror stereoscope or a pocket stereoscope. For a pocket stereoscope the spacing should vary from about $2\frac{1}{2}$ inches at the bottom to about $1\frac{3}{4}$ inches at the top. This spacing accommodates the usual spacing between corresponding images when a stereopair is oriented for viewing with a pocket stereoscope, and it gives a possible range of about $\frac{3}{4}$ inch in parallax differences that can be measured.

Suppose line spacings of a parallax wedge were exactly 2.50 inches at the bottom and 1.70 inches at the top, as shown in Fig. 8-15. If the total height, y, of the graduations was exactly 8 inches, then for graduations spaced at $\frac{1}{10}$-inch intervals along the line, each of the eighty graduations proceeding upward on the scale is 0.01 inches closer to the reference line than the next lower graduation. Graduations numbered from 0 to 80 on the parallax wedge therefore represent parallax differences in $\frac{1}{100}$-inch units, and with this particular parallax wedge a range of 0.80-inch of parallax difference can be accommodated.

In using a parallax wedge, the photos are first carefully oriented as usual and secured. The parallax wedge is placed in the overlap area, and while viewing stereoscopically, the two lines of the parallax wedge will fuse and appear as a single *floating line* in areas where the spacing of the lines is slightly less than the spacing of corresponding photo images. The floating line will appear to split where the parallax of the lines is equal to that of photo images. The position of the parallax wedge can be adjusted so that the floating line splits forming a wedge exactly at a point whose parallax is desired, and at that point a reading is taken from the scale. The parallax wedge reading at point *a* of Fig. 8-15, for example, is 1.93 inches. Parallax differences are obtained by simply taking differences in parallax wedge readings for different points.

An expedient means of producing a parallax wedge is to prepare an ink drawing on white paper, photograph it, and then prepare a film positive from the negative. The size of the positive must be carefully produced to obtain proper dimensions.

8-10 PARALLAX CORRECTION GRAPH

Errors in measured parallaxes due to photographic tilt, imperfect alignment of the photos for parallax measurement, shrinkage or expansion of the photo papers, and camera lens distortions can be effectively compensated for by constructing a *parallax correction graph*. To construct such a graph it is necessary to have a number of vertical control points evenly distributed throughout the stereo overlap area. Assume, for example, that six well-distributed control points *A* through *F* exist in the overlap area of a stereopair exposed from a flying height of 6,900 feet above datum. The elevations of the six points are given in column 2 of Table 8-1.

Based upon one selected *reference* control point, parallax differences Δp that theoretically must exist for the other control points are calculated using the following rearranged form of Eq. (8-8):

$$\Delta p = \left(\frac{h - h_C}{H - h_C}\right) p_c \qquad (8\text{-}10)$$

In Eq. (8-10), h_C and p_c are the elevation and parallax respectively of the reference control point, and h is the elevation of the other control points. Flying height above datum is H. The reference control point may be arbitrarily selected, but it is convenient to choose the point of lowest elevation, as parallax differences calculated from Eq. (8-10) are then all positive. Parallax differences $\Delta'p$ between the reference control point and the

FIGURE 8-15
Parallax wedge.

other control points are measured using a parallax bar. A correction, c_p, to be applied to the measured parallax of each of the other control points to obtain their theoretically correct parallax is simply

$$c_p = \Delta'p - \Delta p$$

Parallax bar readings and the data for calculating parallax corrections for the six points of this example are given in columns 3 through 6 of Table 8-1.

Table 8-1 PARALLAX CORRECTIONS   *problem 8-17.*

1	2	3	4	5	6
Control point	Elevation, ft	Parallax bar reading, mm	Measured parallax difference, $\Delta'p = (r - r_c)$, mm	Calculated parallax difference,* $\Delta p = \left(\dfrac{h - h_C}{H - h_C}\right)p_c,$ mm	Parallax correction, $c_p = \Delta'p - \Delta p,$ mm
A	1,071	19.85	0.63	0.54	0.09
B	1,135	20.78	1.56	1.43	0.13
C	1,032	19.22	. . .	. . .	. . .
D	1,100	20.26	1.04	0.95	0.09
E	1,184	21.60	2.38	2.12	0.26
F	1,116	20.55	1.33	1.17	0.16

*Parallax p_C of reference control point C is 81.62 mm

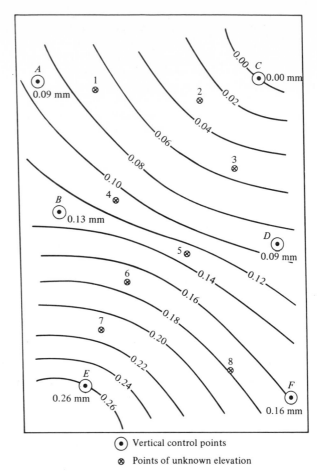

FIGURE 8-16
Parallax correction graph.

A transparent overlay is placed over one of the photos of the stereopair and the positions of all vertical control points are marked. The overlay for this example is shown in Fig. 8-16. Parallax corrections of all vertical control points are noted beside each point, and by interpolating between points, isolines connecting points of equal parallax correction are drawn in the same manner that contours of equal elevation are drawn.

Locations of points whose elevations are to be determined are also plotted on the transparent overlay, as are points 1 through 8 of Fig. 8-16. Corrections to be applied to measured parallaxes of each point are read from the parallax correction graph based upon the locations of the points in the overlap area. Elevations of the points are then calculated from the corrected parallaxes. Parallax bar readings, parallax corrections, and computed elevations for points 1 through 8 are given in Table 8-2.

Table 8-2   ELEVATIONS FROM CORRECTED PARALLAXES

1	2	3	4	5	6
Point	Parallax bar reading, mm	Measured parallax difference, $\Delta'p = (r - r_C)$, mm	Parallax correction (from graph), mm	Corrected parallax difference, $\Delta p = \Delta'p - c_p$, mm	Elevation,* $h = h_C + \dfrac{\Delta p (H - h_C)}{p_C}$, ft
1	19.82	0.60	0.07	0.53	1,070
2	19.32	0.10	0.03	0.07	1,037
3	18.63	− 0.59	0.05	− 0.64	986
4	19.01	− 0.21	0.11	− 0.32	1,009
5	21.67	2.45	0.13	2.32	1,199
6	20.60	1.38	0.17	1.21	1,119
7	21.01	1.79	0.21	1.58	1,146
8	21.75	2.53	0.18	2.35	1,201

*Parallax of reference control point C is 81.62 mm

8-11   COMPUTING FLYING HEIGHT AND AIR BASE

To use parallax equations, it is generally necessary to compute flying height and air base. Flying height may be calculated using any of the methods described in Sec. 6-9. For best results, the average of flying heights for the two photos of a stereopair should be used.

If the air base is known and if one vertical control point is available in the overlap area, flying height for the stereopair may be calculated using Eq. (8-5).

EXAMPLE 8-5   An overlapping pair of vertical photographs taken with a 152.4-mm focal length camera has an air base of 2,125 ft. The elevation of control point A is 927 ft above sea level and the parallax of point A is 89.40 mm. What is the flying height above sea level for this stereopair?

SOLUTION   By Eq. (8-5):

$$H = h + \frac{Bf}{p} = 927 + \frac{2,125(152.4)}{89.40} = 4,550 \text{ ft above sea level} \qquad ////$$

If the flying height above datum is known and if one vertical control point is available in the overlap area, the air base for the stereopair may be calculated using Eq. (8-5).

EXAMPLE 8-6   An overlapping pair of vertical photos was exposed with a 152.4-mm focal length camera from a flying height of 5,320 ft above datum. Control point C has an elevation of 865 ft above datum and the parallax of its images on the stereopair is 86.27 mm. Calculate the air base.

SOLUTION By rearranged Eq. (8-5),

$$B = (H - h)\frac{p}{f} = (5,320 - 865)(86.27)/152.4 = 2,522 \text{ ft} \qquad ////$$

If two control points are available in the overlap area or if a line of known horizontal length appears in the overlap area (the elevations of its end points being known), then the air base can be readily calculated. The horizontal length of a line may be expressed in terms of rectangular coordinates, according to the pythagorean theorem, as

$$AB = \sqrt{(X_B - X_A)^2 + (Y_B - Y_A)^2}$$

Substituting Eqs. (8-6) and (8-7) into the above for the rectangular coordinates,

$$AB = \left[\left(\frac{Bx_b}{p_b} - \frac{Bx_a}{p_a} \right)^2 + \left(\frac{By_b}{p_b} - \frac{By_a}{p_a} \right)^2 \right]^{1/2}$$

Solving the above equation for B,

for 1 photo

$$B = \left[\frac{(AB)^2}{\left(\dfrac{x_b}{p_b} - \dfrac{x_a}{p_a} \right)^2 + \left(\dfrac{y_b}{p_b} - \dfrac{y_a}{p_a} \right)^2} \right]^{1/2} \qquad (8\text{-}11)$$

If at least two control points are available in the overlap area, the air base may also be determined by radial line plotting. These principles are discussed in Chap. 9.

EXAMPLE 8-7 Images of the end points of ground line, AB, whose horizontal length is 2,134.1 ft, appear on a pair of overlapping vertical photographs. Photocoordinates measured with respect to the flight axis on the left photo were $x_a = 33.29$ mm, $y_a = 13.46$ mm, $x_b = 41.76$ mm, and $y_b = -95.76$ mm. Photocoordinates measured on the right photo were $x'_a = -52.32$ mm and $x'_b = -44.96$ mm. Calculate the air base for this stereopair.

SOLUTION By Eq. (8-1):

$$p_a = x_a - x'_a = 33.29 - (-52.32) = 85.61 \text{ mm}$$
$$p_b = x_b - x'_b = 41.76 - (-44.96) = 86.72 \text{ mm}$$

By Eq. (8-11):

$$B = \left[\frac{(2{,}134.1)^2}{\left(\dfrac{33.29}{85.61} - \dfrac{41.76}{86.72}\right)^2 + \left(\dfrac{13.46}{85.61} + \dfrac{95.76}{86.72}\right)^2}\right]^{1/2} = 1{,}687.2 \text{ ft}$$

////

8-12 MAPPING WITH STEREOSCOPE AND PARALLAX BAR

When accuracy requirements are low, suitable topographic maps may be compiled using a stereoscope and parallax bar. One method of accomplishing this is to use Eqs. (8-6) and (8-7) to compute planimetric positions of all map detail and "contour points" necessary for drawing elevation contours. Elevations of the contour points are preferably determined using parallax difference Eq. (8-8). These points can all be plotted in a planimetrically correct manner according to their coordinates. Elevation contours can then be interpolated between contour points.

The mapping procedure described above requires an excessive amount of time and work. A much faster method is simply to plot planimetric positions of points directly from the left photograph of the stereopair on a transparent overlay. Elevations of all necessary points may then be determined by measuring parallax differences. The contours can be interpolated and drawn directly on the overlay while viewing the stereomodel through the stereoscope. This affords the operator advantage of being able to actually see the terrain in three dimensions while drawing the contours. Since planimetric positions of points are directly traced from a photograph, however, this method has the disadvantage that the resulting map is a perspective projection. It varies in scale with terrain elevation and contains all the image positional errors of the left photo.

Another method of map compilation with stereoscope and parallax bar is to use one of the instruments designed specifically for *direct tracing* of topographic features and elevation contours. One such instrument is the *stereocomparagraph* shown in Fig. 8-17. It consists of a mirror stereoscope and parallax bar mounted together as a unit. The photos are oriented for clear stereoviewing, using the "flight line" method described in Sec. 7-6, and then they are taped securely. The stereocomparagraph may be attached to a parallel drafting arm and oriented so that the line through the half marks of the parallax bar is parallel to the flight line. The stereocomparagraph may then be moved about the stereomodel—tracing topographic features such as roads, fences, rivers, etc.—by keeping the floating mark constantly in contact with features being traced. A metal arm (not shown in Fig. 8-17) attached to the stereocomparagraph holds a pencil which enables direct tracing of the features onto a map sheet. With the proper parallax bar micrometer readings set, contours may be traced directly by keeping the floating mark in contact with the

FIGURE 8-17
Fairchild stereocomparagraph. (*Courtesy Alan Gordon Enterprises, Inc.*)

ground as it is moved about the stereomodel. Parallax bar settings required to trace each contour are readily computed.

EXAMPLE 8-8   A pair of overlapping vertical photographs were taken with a 152.00-mm focal length camera from a flying height of 6,885 ft above sea level. The air base was 3,240 ft. The stereopair was oriented for parallax measurements and the parallax bar constant was determined as $C = 67.45$ mm. Calculate the parallax bar micrometer settings necessary to trace the 750-, 800-, 850-, 900-, 950- and 1,000-ft contours.

SOLUTION   Eq. (8-5) is solved in tabular form as follows:

Contour, ft	$H - h$, ft	$p = \dfrac{Bf}{H-h}$, mm	$r = p - C$, mm
750	6,135	80.27	12.82
800	6,085	80.93	13.48
850	6,035	81.60	14.15
900	5,985	82.29	14.84
950	5,935	82.98	15.53
1,000	5,885	83.68	16.23

////

With parallax bar instruments such as the stereocomparagraph, the map substitute which results is a perspective projection containing the tilt and relief displacements of the left photo of the stereopair. In areas of little relief it may serve as a map, but in areas of accented terrain, considerable correction would be necessary to develop the map substitute into a map.

There are parallax-bar-type instruments available for mapping which correct for tilt and relief displacements, thereby providing an orthographic projection. Methods employed for making these corrections are ingenious and vary for different instruments. The K.E.K. plotter of Fig. 8-18 is an example of such an instrument. It is a portable instrument consisting basically of a mirror stereoscope, measuring half marks, and a pair of photo carriers. Each photo carrier may be rotated and tilted so that photographic tilt can be accounted for. Accommodations for scale variations are made by varying the spacing of the half marks. This raises the height of the vertical datum plane, the stereomodel being adjusted accordingly to that datum by raising or lowering the photo carriers. When the instrument is properly oriented to ground control, planimetry and contours can be traced by keeping the floating mark in contact with features being traced. A tracing pencil attached to the reference mark records the movement. A pantograph enables some enlargement or reduction from photo scale to map scale.

8-13 ERROR EVALUATION

Answers obtained using the various equations presented in this chapter will inevitably contain errors. It is important to be aware of the presence of these errors and to be able to assess their magnitudes. Some of the sources of error in computed answers using parallax equations are as follows:

1) Locating and marking the flight line on photos
2) Orienting the stereopair for parallax measurement
3) Parallax measurements
4) Measurement of photocoordinates
5) Shrinkage or expansion of photographs
6) Unequal flying heights for the two photos of the stereopair
7) Tilted photographs
8) Other errors of lesser consequence such as camera-lens distortion, atmospheric refraction distortion, errors in ground control, etc.

A general approach for determining the combined effect of several random errors in computed answers is presented in Sec. 6-10. The same simple and straightforward method is demonstrated in the following example.

EXAMPLE 8-9 In the computation of the elevation of point A in Example 8-1, suppose that the random errors were ± 5 ft in H, ± 5 ft in B and ± 0.03 mm in p_a. Compute the

FIGURE 8-18
K.E.K. plotter. (*Courtesy Philip B. Kail Assoc., Inc.*)

resulting error in h_A due to each of these error sources and compute the total combined effect of all three errors.

SOLUTION   The basic equation used was Eq. (8-5), and the derivatives of h_A in that equation taken with respect to each of the three error sources are

1) $\dfrac{dh_A}{dH} = 1$ from which $dh_A = dH$

Therefore dh_A, the error in h_A, caused by an error dH in the flying height, is dH, or ± 5 ft.

2) $\dfrac{dh_A}{dB} = \dfrac{f}{p_a}$ from which $dh_A = \dfrac{f}{p_a}\,(dB)$

Substituting numerical values into the above,

$$dh_A = \frac{152.4}{91.67}\,(\pm 5) = \pm 8.3 \text{ ft}$$

3) $\dfrac{dh_A}{dp_a} = \dfrac{Bf}{(p_a)^2}$ from which $dh_A = \dfrac{Bf}{(p_a)^2}\,(dp_a)$

Substituting numerical values into the above,

$$dh_A = \frac{1280(152.4)}{(91.67)^2}(\pm 0.03) = \pm 0.7 \text{ ft}$$

The combined effect in the computed elevation of point A of all three random errors is the square root of the sum of the squares of the individual contributions, or

$$dh_{A\,(total)} = \sqrt{5^2 + 8.3^2 + 0.7^2} = \pm 9.7 \text{ ft} \qquad ////$$

Errors in computed answers using any of the equations of this chapter can be analyzed in the fashion described above. It is, of course, necessary to estimate the magnitude of the random errors. It is more difficult to analyze errors caused by tilt in the photographs. The subject of tilted photographs is discussed in Chap. 13. For the present, however, suffice it to say that for normal photography intended to be vertical, errors in parallax equation answers from this source are compatible with errors from the other sources that have been considered.

REFERENCES

Aldred, A. H.: Wind-Sway Error in Parallax Measurements of Tree Height, *Photogrammetric Engineering,* vol. 30, no. 5, p. 732, 1964.

American Society of Photogrammetry: "Manual of Photogrammetry," 3d ed., George Banta Co., Inc., Menasha, Wis., 1966, chap. 2.

Avery, T. E.: Two Cameras for Parallax Height Measurements, *Photogrammetric Engineering,* vol. 32, no. 6, p. 576, 1971.

Bender, L. U.: Derivation of Parallax Equation, *Photogrammetric Engineering,* vol. 33, no. 10, p. 1175, 1967.

Hackman, R. J.: The Isopachometer—A New Type Parallax Bar, *Photogrammetric Engineering,* vol. 26, no. 3, p. 457, 1960.

Hadjitheodorou, C.: Elevation from Parallax Measurements, *Photogrammetric Engineering,* vol. 29, no. 5, p. 840, 1963.

Johnson, E. W.: The Limit of Parallax Perception, *Photogrammetric Engineering,* vol. 23, no. 5, p. 933, 1957.

Moessner, K. E.: Comparative Usefulness of Three Parallax Measuring Instruments in the Measurement and Interpretation of Forest Stands, *Photogrammetric Engineering,* vol. 27, no. 5, p. 705, 1961.

Nash, A. J.: Use a Mirror Stereoscope Correctly, *Photogrammetric Engineering,* vol. 38, no. 12, p. 1192, 1972.

Schut, G. H.: The Determination of Tree Heights From Parallax Measurements, *The Canadian Surveyor,* vol. 19, p. 415, 1965.

Visser, J.: The Construction of the Datum Correction Graph for Map Compilation with Stereometer-Type Instrument, *Photogrammetric Engineering,* vol. 20, no. 5, p. 849, 1954.

Welch, R.: Height Difference Measurement Errors, *Photogrammetric Engineering,* vol. 36, no. 6, p. 576, 1970.

PROBLEMS

(Note: All photocoordinates given for these problems are measured with respect to the flight line axes.)

8-1 Calculate the stereoscopic parallaxes of points *a* through *d* given the following measured photocoordinates:

Point	x (left photo)	x' (right photo)
a	2.15 in.	− 1.28 in.
b	70.25 mm	− 19.41 mm
c	3.80 in.	0.27 in.
d	102.87 mm	11.02 mm

Which point is highest in elevation? Which is lowest?

8-2 Calculate the elevations of points *a* through *d* of Prob. 8-1 if the camera focal length is 6 inches, flying height above datum is 12,050 feet, and the air base is 6,320 feet.

8-3 A pair of overlapping vertical photographs are mounted for parallax measurement as illustrated in Fig. 8-5. Distance *D* is measured as 10.24 inches. Calculate the stereoscopic parallaxes of the following points whose measured *d* values are as follows:

Point	d
a	6.71 in
b	6.95 in
c	6.28 in
d	6.49 in

Which point is highest in elevation? Which is lowest?

8-4 Assume that point *A* of Prob. 8-3 has an elevation of 1,230 feet above datum and that the photos were taken with a $3\frac{1}{2}$-inch focal length camera. If the air base is 3,705 feet, what are the elevations of points *b*, *c*, and *d*?

8-5 A pair of overlapping vertical photos are oriented for parallax measurement with stereoscope and forward-reading parallax bar. On the left photo, *b* measures 82.55 millimeters and on the right photo *b'* is 83.00 millimeters. The parallax bar readings on o_1 and o_2 were 20.77 millimeters and 20.88 millimeters respectively. (*a*) Calculate the parallax bar constant *C* based on the average for the two principal points. (*b*) Which principal point is higher in elevation? (*c*) Calculate the parallaxes of points *a* through *d*, given the following micrometer readings:

Point	Micrometer reading, mm
a	19.82
b	20.39
c	21.01
d	18.46

8-6 Assume that the photos of Prob. 8-5 were taken from a flying height of 9,610 feet above control point A, whose elevation is 648 feet above datum. Calculate the elevations of points b, c, and d using Eqs. (8-8) and (8-9) and compare the results of the two equations. (Assume average flying height above ground to be 9,610 feet.)

8-7 From the information given for Probs. 8-1 and 8-2, calculate the horizontal ground length of line AC. Measured y coordinates on the left photo are $y_a = -2.46$ inches and $y_c = 3.92$ inches.

8-8 From the data of Probs. 8-3 and 8-4, calculate the area on the ground contained within triangle ABC. Measured x and y photocoordinates of a, b, and c on the left photo were $x_a = -0.282$ inches, $y_a = 3.470$ inches, $x_b = 0.875$ inches, $y_b = -4.041$ inches, $x_c = 4.328$ inches, and $y_c = 1.178$ inches.

8-9 The air base of a pair of overlapping vertical photos was determined to be 1,838 feet. The focal length of the camera was 152.10 mm. The image coordinates of point A, whose elevation is 865 feet above datum, were determined on the left photo as $x_a = 1.68$ millimeters and on the right photo as $x_a' = -86.37$ millimeters. What is the flying height above datum for the stereopair?

8-10 The images of two control points A and B appear in the overlap area of a pair of vertical photographs which were taken with a camera having a focal length of 152.45 mm. The following photocoordinates and ground coordinates apply to points A and B. Calculate the air base of the stereopair using Eq. (8-11).

Point	Left photocoordinates		Right photocoordinates		Ground coordinates	
	x, mm	y, mm	x', mm	y', mm	X, ft	Y, ft
A	26.25	−96.00	−65.07	−95.99	256,335.4	91,741.6
B	−2.00	34.20	−92.62	34.18	256,616.4	89,626.1

8-11 Distances b on the left photo and b' on the right photo of a pair of overlapping vertical photos are 90.85 and 89.43 millimeters respectively. If the air base is 1,600 feet and the camera focal length is 88.22 mm, which ground principal point is higher and by how much?

8-12 A pair of overlapping vertical photos is taken from a flying height of 2,000 feet above ground with a 6-inch focal length camera. The x coordinates on the left photo of the base and top of a certain pine tree are 2.46 and 2.56 inches respectively. On the right photo these x' coordinates are -1.08 and -1.13 inches respectively. Determine the height of the tree.

8-13 A pair of overlapping vertical photos were taken with a 6-in focal length camera from a flying height of 7,630 feet above sea level. The air base was 3,683 feet. This pair was oriented for parallax measurements with a stereocomparagraph having a forward-reading parallax bar, and the parallax bar constant, C, was determined as

80.28 millimeters. Calculate the required micrometer settings for tracing the 1,500-, 1,600-, 1,700-, and 1,800-foot contours.

8-14 A pair of overlapping vertical photos were exposed with a camera having a 210 mm focal length. Calculate B and H from the following information on the ground points D and E:

Point	Elevation, ft	Left photocoordinates		Right photocoordinates	
D	1,875	x_d	− 0.685 in	x'_d	− 4.371 in
E	2,343	x_e	3.904 in	x'_e	0.064 in

8-15 A pair of overlapping vertical photos was exposed from a flying height of 12,050 feet above datum using an 88.84-mm focal length camera. The air base was determined as 9,830 feet. The following micrometer readings were taken (forward-reading parallax bar). Calculate the elevations of points 1 through 4 if the elevation of point A is 1,868 feet above datum.

Point	Micrometer reading, mm
A	12.76
1	18.29
2	19.06
3	10.20
4	20.73

8-16 A parallax wedge for use with a pocket stereoscope similar to that shown in Fig. 8-15 has a height of graduations, y, equal to 6.00 inches. The lateral spacing between reference line and the graduated line is 1.90 inches at the top and 2.30 inches at the bottom. What is the vertical spacing of adjacent graduations on the graduated line if the difference in parallax between adjacent graduations is 0.01 inch?

8-17 A vertical stereopair of aerial photos was exposed from 4,450 feet above datum. Five vertical control points whose elevations are given below appear in the stereo overlap area. Construct a parallax correction graph based on the parallax bar readings given below. The parallax bar was forward-reading and the constant was 73.35 mm. (Plot the positions of the control points in the overlap area using the given x and y photocoordinates taken from the left photo of the stereopair.)

half scale.

Point	Elevation, ft	Parallax bar reading, mm	Photocoordinates, left photo	
			x, mm	y, mm
A	1,438	27.81	11.7	96.5
B	1,507	29.75	95.5	88.9
C	1,218	21.61	78.7	9.1
D	1,390	26.24	− 9.1	− 90.9
E	1,116	18.77	93.0	− 89.8

8-18 Using the parallax correction graph constructed for Prob. 8-17, calculate elevations for points 1 through 5 whose parallax bar readings are given below. (Plot the positions of points 1 through 5 from the given photocoordinates measured on the left photo of the stereopair.)

Point	Parallax bar reading, mm	Photocoordinates, left photo	
		x, mm	y, mm
1	24.21	15.2	72.1
2	17.95	72.1	46.2
3	26.09	17.8	5.6
4	20.64	35.6	− 22.9
5	30.28	61.0	− 86.4

8-19 In Prob. 8-9, suppose that random errors were ± 2 feet in h_A, ± 5 feet in B, and ± 0.05 millimeters in each of x_a and x'_a. What is the expected resultant error in the calculated value of H due to these random errors?

8-20 In Prob. 8-12, assume that random errors existed in the amounts of ± 5 feet in H and ± 0.005 inch for each of the measured photocoordinates. What is the expected error in the calculated height of the tree due to these random errors?

9

RADIAL-LINE TRIANGULATION AND PLANIMETRIC MAP REVISION

9-1 INTRODUCTION

Radial-line triangulation is a method for extending or supplementing horizontal control. The techniques may also be applied to planimetric map compilation. Radial-line triangulation was one of the earliest photogrammetric mapping procedures, done initially by graphical methods called *radial-line plotting*. Slotted templates and mechanical devices were developed later which duplicated the graphical procedures. More recently radial-line triangulation has been performed numerically using electronic computers.

Radial-line triangulation is not used extensively today, having given way to other more accurate and convenient methods which are described in Chaps. 14, 15, and 18. The procedure is occasionally used, however, for providing supplemental control for small-scale charting, for controlling mosaic construction, and for limited planimetric map revision.

9-2   FUNDAMENTAL PRINCIPLE OF RADIAL-LINE TRIANGULATION

The fundamental principle upon which radial-line triangulation is based is that angles with vertexes at the principal point of a vertical photograph are true horizontal angles. The procedure therefore assumes truly vertical photos. In Fig. 9-1 the plane of the vertical photo is horizontal and parallel to the datum plane. Points A' and B' in the datum plane are vertically beneath object points A and B. Planes $LAA'P'$ and $LBB'P'$ are vertical, and therefore angle aob on the photo is equal to the true horizontal angle $A'P'B'$.

On a vertical photograph, relief displacement, radial-lens distortion, and atmospheric refraction all displace images along radial lines from the principal point and therefore do not affect sizes of photographic angles with vertexes at the principal point. Also variations in flying heights of vertical photos affect photo scale but not angle sizes.

Radial-line triangulation consists basically of two distinct operations: (1) *resection* to determine the planimetric positions of photo exposure stations and (2) *intersection* from two or more photos whose exposure stations have been established to determine the positions of new points. These operations may be performed separately, but more often they are done simultaneously.

9-3   GRAPHICAL METHODS

Radial-line triangulation by graphical techniques is an easily visualized procedure and will be used to introduce the subject. In Fig. 9-2, five photos of a flight strip are laid out in their overlapping positions. Principal points and conjugate principal points have been marked on the photos. Points a and b are images of two horizontal ground control points A and B. A transparent overlay is placed over photo no. 1 and a template is prepared as shown in Fig. 9-3a by ruling lines on the overlay from the principal point o_1 through points a, b, c, d, and conjugate principal point o_2. Angles with vertexes at o_1 are true horizontal angles on the template. A second, similar template is prepared for photo no. 2, as shown in Fig. 9-3b. In drawing the rays it is necessary to hold the overlays firmly and use a sharp, hard drawing pencil so that true angles are obtained between rays.

A base map upon which the radial-line triangulation will be performed is prepared next and ground control points A and B are plotted as shown on Fig. 9-4. The scale of the base map is chosen quite arbitrarily, but it should not normally differ greatly from photo scale. If map scale is chosen larger than photo scale, then the templates must be prepared larger in size than the photos to make possible an increase in scale from photo to map. Template no. 1 is oriented on the base map so that rays o_1a and o_1b simultaneously pass through their respective plotted control points A and B. At the same time template no. 2 is oriented on the map to make rays o_2a and o_2b pass through their respective plotted control points and, in addition, rays o_1o_2 on template no. 1 and o_2o_1 on template no. 2 are made to coincide. With these conditions established, the locations of o_1 and o_2 define

FIGURE 9-1
Horizontal angles on a vertical photograph.

the true planimetric map positions of ground principal points (exposure stations) P_1 and P_2. Their positions are marked on the map by pricking through the templates with a pin. The direction of P_1P_2 on the map represents the flight direction for that stereopair, and the distance from P_1 to P_2 represents the air base. This procedure for locating exposure station positions is called *resection*—more specifically *two-point resection,* since it requires two control points.

FIGURE 9-2
Five photos of a flight strip.

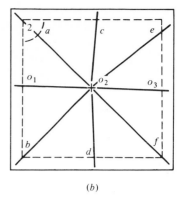

(a) (b)

FIGURE 9-3
(a) Template for photo no. 1. (b) Template for photo no. 2.

With the exposure stations of a pair of overlapping photographs fixed on the map, any number of other points whose images appear in the overlap area of the stereopair can be established by *intersection*. When the two templates were originally prepared, rays through new points c and d were also drawn. With the two templates oriented on the map as previously described, the intersection of rays $o_1 c$ and $o_2 c$ fixes the true planimetric position of point C. Likewise, the intersection of rays $o_1 d$ and $o_2 d$ locates point D. Map locations of any points in the overlap area can be established by this procedure.

Once points C and D are established on the map, they become new horizontal control points. These points were carefully selected so that their images appeared not only on photos no. 1 and 2 but also on no. 3. (This condition requires greater than 50 percent end lap in the photos.) By treating C and D as control points, a template can be prepared for photo no. 3 and resection performed, as previously described to locate exposure station P_3. With P_3 located, new points E and F can be fixed on the map by intersection from photos no. 2 and 3. Carefully selecting images e and f so that their images appear on photo no. 4 enables exposure station P_4 to be located. This procedure of successive resection and intersection may be continued through the entire strip of photos. The completed radial-line triangulation for the five-photo strip is shown in Fig. 9-4.

9-4 PASS POINTS *more than 1 flight lines*

Points C through J of the triangulated strip of Fig. 9-4 are points of extended horizontal control. They may be used for controlling subsequent photogrammetric procedures such as mosaic construction or planimetric mapping. These points were necessary, however, to continue the radial triangulation through the strip, and therefore they are

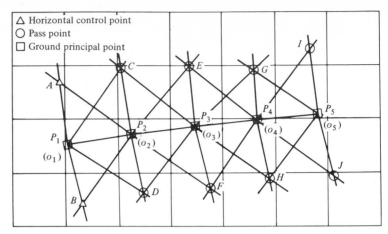

FIGURE 9-4
Radial-line triangulation assembly of five-photo strip.

called *pass points* because they enabled the triangulation to pass from one photo to the next.

To satisfactorily serve as pass points, images must be sharp and well defined on all photos in which they appear. They must be located in desirable positions on three successive overlapping photographs. The most ideal positions are opposite the principal points and conjugate principal points as illustrated in Fig. 9-2. This placement creates the strongest geometrical strength and yields highest accuracy. For radial-line triangulation of a block of two or more strips, pass points common to two strips should be chosen in the center of the side lap area.

Careful overall planning should precede a radial-line triangulation project. The photographs should be carefully studied and all pass points selected and labeled prior to constructing templates. When the templates are prepared, all rays should be labeled on the templates to prevent confusion when assembling them on the map.

9-5 THREE-POINT RESECTION

The two-point resection procedure described in Sec. 9-3 requires that a *stereopair* be resected simultaneously and that two horizontal control points appear in the overlap area of the stereopair. If three or more horizontal control points appear anywhere in a *single vertical photo*, its exposure station can be located by *three-point resection*. In Fig. 9-5a,

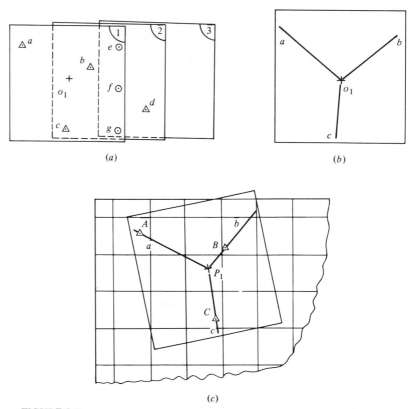

FIGURE 9-5

(*a*) Photos with ample control for three-point resection. (*b*) Template prepared for three-point resection. (*c*) Locating an exposure station by three-point resection.

for example, images *a, b,* and *c* of horizontal control points *A, B,* and *C* appear in vertical photo no. 1. A template is prepared for that photo by drawing rays from the principal point through the three image points, as shown in Fig. 9-5*b*. The template is placed on a base map upon which the three control points have been plotted, and it is oriented so that the three rays simultaneously pass through their respective plotted control points, as shown in Fig. 9-5*c*. This locates exposure station P_1, which is marked on the map by pinpricking. Greater accuracy is achieved if more than three points are used, and in that case all rays must simultaneously pass as nearly as possible through their respective plotted control.

If images of three or more horizontal control points also appear somewhere on adjacent photo no. 2, then its exposure station can also be located by three-point resection. Points *b, c,* and *d* of Fig. 9-5*a*, for example, could be used for photo no. 2. With the positions of the two photos of the stereopair settled, new pass points can be located by intersection. If pass points are selected whose images appear on photo no. 3—for example, at positions e, f, and g of Fig. 9-5a—then, with their positions known, they may be used in three-point resection to locate exposure station P_3. In this manner radial-line triangulation by three-point resection may be extended.

Radial-line triangulation by three-point resection has the advantage that conjugate principal points need not be used. A disadvantage of the method is the greater amount of ground control needed. Two-point resection is more convenient for graphical radial-line triangulation or when using slotted or mechanical templates. Three-point resection is useful in locating single photo exposure stations and in map revision as described in Sec. 9-12.

9-6 RADIAL-LINE TRIANGULATION OF A BLOCK

A block of photos may be assembled in a simultaneous radial-line triangulation by means of pass points located in the side lap of adjacent strips. If another strip below the strip of Fig. 9-4 were to be triangulated simultaneously with the upper strip, for example, then pass points d, f, h, and j would be chosen in the side lap area common to both strips. These pass points would also be chosen very carefully because their images may appear on as many as six photos.

Pass points which tie strips together are called *tie points*. In assembling templates of two or more strips, not only must the previously described ray intersections be adhered to, but rays from both strips common to tie points must also intersect simultaneously. Because of drafting errors in preparing templates and because certain assumptions such as vertical photos are not actually met, angles on templates may not be true horizontal angles. Therefore, some difficulties may be encountered in assembling templates of a block. In these cases, a best fit is forced which tends to adjust for discrepancies.

9-7 CONTROL POINT LOCATIONS

From foregoing discussions it should be apparent that a minimum of two horizontal control points are necessary for radial-line triangulation. More than two are desirable, however, for providing checks and improving accuracy. In the example of Fig. 9-4, control points A and B existed in the overlap area of a stereopair. Better overall stability in controlling that triangulation would have been obtained had more than two control points existed or had the two points been as widely spaced in the strip as possible, say at A and J. In general, best network stability is obtained with a uniformly distributed control network, an important consideration in performing field surveys for establishing control for radial-line triangulation.

In graphical radial-line triangulation, it is convenient but not necessary for two control points to occur within the overlap of one stereopair of the block. If there are no stereopairs in which two control points appear in the overlap area, graphical methods may still be performed, but either of two slightly different approaches must be taken. In the first approach, the assembly is begun at one control point. Scale and orientation are estimated, and the entire assembly is constructed so that, it is hoped, other control point ray intersections of the finished assembly occur near their respective plotted map positions. Based on discrepancies of plotted control points and their corresponding ray intersections, adjustments are made by trial and error to change scale and orientation until the assembly is fitted as closely as possible to all control.

In the second technique, the first two templates are oriented in an arbitrary location on the map by simply making lines o_1o_2 and o_2o_1 coincide. Scale is arbitrarily set by making map distance P_1P_2 some convenient value. Successive templates are oriented to this arbitrarily located stereopair until the entire network is assembled. Then the arbitrary positions of all points—including exposure stations, pass points, and control points—are pinpricked and their coordinates are scaled from the map. With coordinates of the control points known in both the ground system and arbitrary system, a two-dimensional conformal coordinate transformation may be performed as described in Appendix B to obtain ground coordinates of all exposure stations and pass points.

9-8 SLOTTED TEMPLATES

The slotted template method of radial-line triangulation is similar to the graphical method except that templates are prepared differently. In this method, long narrow slots are cut in a template material to represent rays radiating from the center of the photo. The template material is usually thin stiff cardboard, plastic, or metal. Figure 9-6 shows a cardboard template being prepared in a slotted template cutter.

In cutting a cardboard template with the instrument of Fig. 9-6, the photo is first placed over the cardboard and, while firmly holding both photo and cardboard together, pinpricks into the underlying cardboard are made through the photo to mark principal point, conjugate principal points, and all pass points. A hole centered on the pinprick of the principal point is made in the cardboard using a special punch. This hole serves as the center of rays. The cardboard is placed on the table of the template cutter with the center punch hole over the upright stud as shown in Fig. 9-6. By means of a sighting device, the cardboard is rotated and aligned so that each slot is cut in its correct position. Imaginary lines from the center of the principal point punch hole through the centers of the elongated slots represent rays which define horizontal angles. All slots should be labeled to avoid confusion in assembling the network.

When templates have been prepared for each photo, the network is assembled on a

FIGURE 9-6
Slotted template cutter. (*Courtesy Carl Zeiss, Oberkochen*)

base map which has been prepared to desired scale. All available horizontal control is first plotted on the map. The map is placed over a softwood board and headless pins called *control pins* are driven firmly into the wood through each plotted control point. The shafts of the pins should be perpendicular to the map surface. The templates are assembled by making all slots (rays) to common points intersect. The network is held together by means of hollow shafted studs which are placed at the intersections of slots to common points. To prevent play in the assembly, the shafts of the studs are the same diameter as the slot widths. An assembly of a small block of seven photos is shown in Fig. 9-7.

The scale of an entire assembly may be made larger or smaller by gently pulling apart or compressing the edges of the assembly. In this manner the scale of the assembly is adjusted until it is equal to map scale—a condition which exists when the hollow shafts of the control point studs fit over their respective control pins. In the assembly of Fig.

FIGURE 9-7
An assembly of slotted templates.

9-7, the centers of hollow studs capped with square washers mark the seven exposure stations, centers of circular washers are pass points, and the two triangles are control points. Once the network has been fitted to the control, map positions of all exposure stations and pass points are marked by pinpricking through the centers of the hollow-shafted studs.

In the example of Fig. 9-7, two control points were used to control the seven-photo assembly. The two points do not exist in the overlap of a stereopair, but this causes no difficulty. Any number of control points can be conveniently accommodated in the slotted template method by simply fitting all control point studs to their respective control pins simultaneously. Because of errors in template construction, nonvertical photos, etc., some difficulties may be encountered in assembling the network. Normally these errors are adjusted for by gently vibrating the network and forcing all intersection and control conditions.

9-9 MECHANICAL TEMPLATES

Radial-line triangulation may also be performed using mechanical templates constructed from kits called *lazy daisys*. Except for the manner of constructing templates, the procedure is the same as slotted template radial-line triangulation.

Some of the components of a lazy-daisy kit, labeled *A* through *K*, are shown in Fig. 9-8. Mechanical templates called *spiders* are constructed from these components. Each photo is placed individually on a softwood board and a headless pin (item *J* of Fig. 9-8) is carefully driven through the principal point firmly into the underlying wood using the hammer (item *A*). The shaft of the pin should be perpendicular to the photo surface. A small stud (item *H*) is placed over the headless pin and a threaded bolt (item *E*) is placed over the stud. The center bolt serves as the hub of rays of the template. Headless pins are also carefully driven into the board through the two conjugate principal points and all pass points. Studs are then placed over them. A line connecting the pin at the principal point and the pin at any pass point or conjugate principal point represents the ray through that point.

Slotted metal arms (items *D*) are selected for constructing rays. The round hole on one end of the arm is placed over the central bolt and long slots within the arms are placed over the studs at the pass points and conjugate principal points. The arm for each ray is chosen from a variety of lengths with two considerations in mind: first, excessive length should be avoided, as this may cause difficulties in assembling the network, and, second, enough slot length must exist on either side of all studs to allow for relief displacements and to allow for making a scale change from photo to map. The necessity of meeting these conditions will become clear upon actually constructing a triangulation network from spiders.

FIGURE 9-8
Components of Lazy Daisy kit.

Once all arms have been placed over their studs, a washer (item *G*) and a nut (item *F*) are placed over the bolt and tightened by means of special wrenches (items *B* and *C*). This should be done carefully to prevent buckling of the arms, which would result in erroneous angles between rays. All rays should be labeled directly on the arms to assist in assembly.

When spiders have been prepared for all photos, they are assembled into a network in exactly the same manner as that described for slotted templates. An assembly of eight spiders representing a small block of photos is shown in Fig. 9-9. The control is again indicated with triangles. Exposure stations and pass points occur at the positions of their respective studs, and they are marked on the map by pinpricking through the hollow shafted studs.

9-10   ERRORS IN RADIAL-LINE TRIANGULATION

Some of the principal sources of error in radial-line triangulation are (1) differential paper shrinkage, (2) graphical or mechanical construction errors, (3) faulty location of principal points, (4) faulty transfer of conjugate principal points, and (5) tilt in the photos. Differential paper shrinkage causes small errors, but these can be eliminated by using polyester-base materials for both photos and base map. Graphical errors can be minimized by using a sharp, hard drawing pencil and good straightedge. They cannot be entirely eliminated, however, for even a pencil line as thin as 1/100 inch represents 10 feet on a map plotted at a scale of 1,000 feet to the inch. Construction errors in preparing slotted templates and lazy-daisy spiders can be minimized only by exercising caution in preparing them.

If the terrain is flat, errors caused by faulty location of principal points is insignificant. If the terrain is rugged or rolling, however, principal points should be

FIGURE 9-9
An assembly of spiders.

carefully located by intersecting very fine fiducial lines, and conjugate principal points should be carefully located. On a tilted photo, as discussed in Chap. 13, relief displacement is radial from the nadir point and tilt displacement is radial from the isocenter. If a vertical photo is assumed when in fact the photo is tilted, angles between rays will not be true horizontal angles. For tilts up to $3°$ in photos taken over terrain with moderate relief, errors from this source are quite small. The errors become more severe as relief variations and tilts increase. Errors caused by tilted photography can be removed by rectifying the photos; however, for intended vertical photography, errors caused by tilt are usually no more serious than graphical or construction errors.

Accuracy in extending control by radial-line triangulation is very dependent upon the density and distribution of existing ground control. In order to evaluate accuracy of block radial-line triangulation versus number of ground control points, empirical tests were performed. On the basis of these tests, the following equation was developed which relates expected average error in pass point location to the number of photos and number of ground control points:

$k = 0.16$

Allowable
error

$$e = k \left(\frac{t}{c} \right)^{1/2} \qquad (9\text{-}1)$$

In Eq. (9-1), e is the average error expected in pass point location in millimeters at compilation scale, k is a constant which has been evaluated at 0.16 for careful slotted template radial triangulation, t is the total number of photos in the assembly, and c is the total number of ground control points used in the assembly. The equation is applicable only for a uniform distribution of control points throughout a block of photos.

Although Eq. (9-1) was based on slotted template assemblies, it is plausible to also apply it to carefully constructed graphical and lazy-daisy assemblies. The form of Eq.

(9-1) may be changed as follows in order to calculate the number of well-distributed ground control points necessary in a block to achieve a certain accuracy in locating points with radial triangulation:

$$c = t\left(\frac{k}{e}\right)^2 \qquad (9\text{-}2)$$

EXAMPLE 9-1   Suppose it is required that pass points be located within an average accuracy of 10 ft from a block of 40 photos whose average scale is 500 ft per in. How many well-distributed ground control points must be established by field survey to achieve the desired accuracy?

SOLUTION   (Assume map compilation is at photo scale.) At compilation scale, the acceptable error, e in millimeters is

$$e = \frac{10\,\text{ft}(25.4\,\text{mm/in})}{500\,\text{ft/in}} = 0.508\,\text{mm}$$

By Eq. (9-2):

$$c = 40\left(\frac{0.16}{0.508}\right)^2 = 3.9 \qquad (4\text{ control points required}) \qquad ////$$

9-11   NUMERICAL METHODS

Several methods have been developed for performing radial-line triangulation numerically. All these methods involve measurement of photocoordinates followed by the formation and solution of a mathematical model which duplicates the graphical or mechanical procedures. Regardless of the numerical method performed, the lengthy nature of the computations make this procedure most feasible when performed on an electronic computer. Descriptions of various numerical methods are given in references cited at the end of this chapter.

The primary advantage in numerical radial-line triangulation is an increase in accuracy which results from the elimination of graphical and mechanical construction errors. The accuracy with which ground control can be extended by numerical procedures depends upon several variables such as tilt in the photos, flying height, and terrain relief. With vertical photography taken over moderate terrain having a uniform distribution of horizontal control points, an accuracy in computed X and Y ground coordinates of approximately 1/500 of the flying height is generally attainable.

9-12 PLANIMETRIC MAP REVISION BY RADIAL-LINE PLOTTING

As a result of new construction or other changing conditions, it is often necessary to update portions of the planimetry of existing maps. If vertical photos showing the new construction or changes are available, the map revision may be accomplished by radial-line methods. Assume, for example, that it is desired to plot the map position of the building appearing in the stereopair of Fig. 9-10a. To accomplish this by radial-line methods, templates are prepared for each photo by ruling lines from principal points through conjugate principal points and through the corners of the building, as shown in Fig. 9-10a. All rays through building corners are labeled to avoid confusion in plotting. The template overlays are then placed on the map and oriented so that o_1 and o_2 are coincident with the map locations of exposure stations P_1 and P_2 respectively and so that line $o_1 o_2$ of overlay no. 1 coincides with line $o_2 o_1$ of overlay no. 2. In this orientation, intersections of lines to common points locate the building corners. Their positions are pinpricked and the building is drawn on the map by connecting adjacent corners with straight lines, as shown in Fig. 9-10b. This procedure yields correct planimetric positions in spite of relief displacements and scale variations of the photos.

The above procedure presumes known map locations for the exposure stations of the stereopair. These may have been located through radial-line triangulation, as previously described. On the other hand, it is often possible to locate exposure stations by either two-point or three-point resection, using discrete points common to both the existing map and the photos. Buildings, road intersections, or intersections of streams or power lines with roads are some points that may suffice for control points.

9-13 PLANIMETRIC MAP REVISION WITH REFLECTION
OR PROJECTION INSTRUMENTS

If a large amount of planimetric map detail is to be revised, the process described in Sec. 9-12 is very tedious and time-consuming. A more practical approach is direct tracing of photographic images that may be superimposed on the map by means of reflection or projection instruments. Using reflection or projection instruments, photo images can be made to match corresponding map images even though their scales are unequal.

A reflection instrument for planimetric map revision called a *vertical sketchmaster* is shown in Fig. 9-11. Its operating principle is illustrated in Fig. 9-12. A light ray from photo image a is reflected by a large mirror at a_1, reflected again by an eyepiece mirror at a_2, and received by an observer at o. Because the eyepiece mirror is half-silvered, the observer can also simultaneously view the map. By adjusting the position of the map, photo image a and its corresponding map point A can be made to coincide. This principle of operation is known as *camera lucida*.

(*a*)

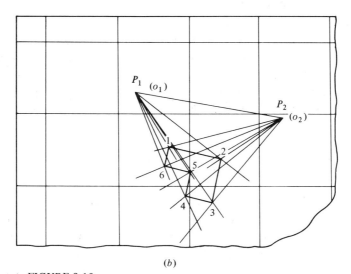

(*b*)

FIGURE 9-10
(*a*) Templates for locating a building by radial-line intersection. (*b*) Intersection on the base map.

The ratio of scales between photo and map is the ratio of ray path lengths aa_1a_2o and Aa_2o. This ratio can be changed using the adjustable legs of the instrument, although the range of scale change is quite limited. Each of the three legs may be adjusted to different lengths, thereby creating a tilted relationship between photo plane and map plane. By adjusting the legs, three photo images forming a triangle can be made

FIGURE 9-11
Vertical sketchmaster. (*Courtesy Keuffel & Esser Co.*)

coincident with their corresponding map images, and details in that triangular area can be traced on the map. The tilt of the photo plane does not represent the actual tilt of the photograph and does not completely eliminate errors from tilt displacement. It does, however, reduce the amount of tilt distortion in plotted planimetric detail. Of course, local relief displacements are still present.

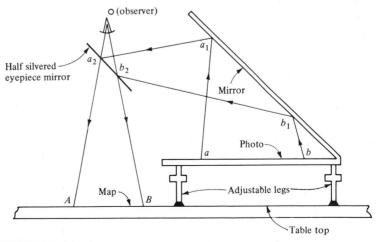

FIGURE 9-12
Operating principle of vertical sketchmaster.

FIGURE 9-13
Zoom transfer scope. (*Courtesy Bausch and Lomb*)

A horizontal sketchmaster similar to the vertical sketchmaster is also available. With this instrument the easel holding the photo may be tilted and rotated by means of a ball and socket to match photo images and map points. The horizontal sketchmaster enables making a rather large-scale change from photo to map.

The Zoom Transfer Scope (ZTS) of Fig. 9-13 is a versatile reflection instrument for planimetric map revision. With the ZTS an aerial photograph can be viewed in superposition with a map, and information from the photo may be readily transferred onto the map by direct tracing. The instrument can accommodate large differences in scale from photo to map. Its anamorphic optical system enables different magnification ratios to be applied in the x and y directions. It also has an image rotation system which operates by means of rotating prisms. These features facilitate adjusting photo images to coincide with map points or control points. The ZTS has zoom magnification providing continuous variations in magnification from 1 to 7X.

A *reflecting projector* may also be used for projecting photo images onto a map for direct tracing. The diagram of Fig. 9-14 illustrates the operating principle of this type of instrument. The photo is placed in a holder near the top of the instrument so that the imagery faces the mirror. Light rays carrying photo images are reflected from the mirror

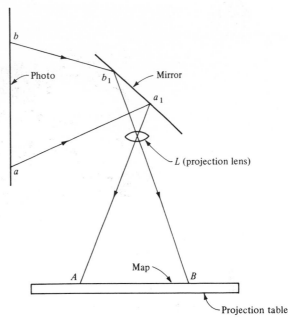

FIGURE 9-14
Operating principle of a reflecting projector.

through a lens and projected onto the map sheet on the projection table below. The magnification ratio from photo to map is the ratio of image distance aa_1L to object distance LA. When the magnification ratio is changed, a special mechanical arrangement automatically changes image and object distances in the required ratio to satisfy the lens formula—Eq. (2-5)—and maintain focus.

9-14   PLANIMETRIC MAP REVISION BY RADIAL PLOTTER

A radial plotter, as shown in Fig. 9-15, is an instrument for planimetric map revision which continuously solves the radial intersection problem mechanically. In using the radial plotter, a pair of overlapping vertical photos are placed on the stages of the instrument and pinned at their principal points. The stereopair is then oriented for stereoscopic viewing (the instrument incorporates a mirror stereoscope) by rotating the photos about their principal points until principal points and conjugate principal points lie along a common straight line. Two transparent arms, upon which a fine black line is etched, extend radially from the pinned principal points. The apparent intersection in the stereomodel of the black lines on the arms forms a cross which serves as a reference mark. The

FIGURE 9-15
Radial plotter. (*Courtesy Philip B. Kail Assoc., Inc.*)

radial arms are connected to a pencil chuck by means of a mechanical linkage; as the pencil is moved about, the reference mark appears to move about the stereomodel. When the radial plotter has been oriented to ground control, planimetric detail can be traced directly on a map beneath the instrument by moving the pencil so as to keep the reference mark in contact with objects being traced.

REFERENCES

American Society of Photogrammetry: "Manual of Photogrammetry," 3d ed., George Banta Co., Inc., Menasha, Wis., 1966, chap. 9.

Kail, P.: The Radial Planimetric Plotter, *Photogrammetric Engineering,* vol. 15, no. 3, p. 402, 1949.

Mikhail, E. M.: A Study in Numerical Radial Triangulation, *Photogrammetric Engineering,* vol. 34, no. 4, p. 358, 1968.

Trorey, L. G.: Slotted Template Error, *Photogrammetric Engineering,* vol. 13, no. 2, p. 227, 1947.

Turpin, R. D.: Numerical Radial Triangulation, *Photogrammetric Engineering,* vol. 32, no. 6, p. 1041, 1966.

Wolf, P. R.: Analytical Radial Triangulation, *Photogrammetric Engineering,* vol. 33, no. 1, p. 109, 1967.

PROBLEMS

9-1 Describe the different methods available for performing radial-line triangulation.

9-2 List the characteristics of good pass points for radial-line triangulation.

9-3 Prepare tracing-paper templates and perform a graphical two-point resection on the basis of the following ground coordinates and photocoordinates (with respect to the flight line axis) of control points *A* and *B*. Determine the ground length of the air base and the azimuth of the flight line. Use a base map scale of 1 inch = 1,000 feet.

base – 3,650

azimuth – 340°

Point	Photocoordinates				Ground coordinates	
	Left photo		Right photo			
	x, mm	y, mm	x', mm	y', mm	X, ft	Y, ft
A	38.15	71.12	– 41.15	70.85	2,168,518	91,159
B	46.97	– 76.98	– 38.10	– 77.47	2,174,662	93,701

9-4 For the stereopair of Prob. 9-3, perform a graphical intersection to determine the ground coordinates of pass points *C* and *D* given the following photocoordinates (with respect to the flight line axis).

Point	Photocoordinates			
	Left photo		Right photo	
	x, mm	y, mm	x', mm	y', mm
C	78.23	66.29	– 3.81	66.04
D	75.18	– 44.20	– 8.64	– 44.45

9-5 Prepare a tracing-paper template and perform a graphical three-point resection to determine the azimuth of the flight line and the ground coordinates of the exposure station of a vertical photograph. Three control points appear in the photo and their ground coordinates and photocoordinates (with respect to flight line axes) are as follows: (Use a base map scale of 1 inch = 500 feet.)

Point	Photocoordinates		Ground coordinates	
	x, mm	y, mm	X, ft	Y, ft
H_1	64.52	89.66	1,865,472	126,099
H_2	44.70	16.76	1,865,605	124,438
H_3	85.09	– 81.03	1,867,106	122,697

9-6 The problem is the same as Prob. 9-5 except for the following three horizontal control points:

Point	Photocoordinates		Ground coordinates	
	x, mm	y, mm	X, ft	Y, ft
A	– 69.85	93.47	2,203,296	88,813
B	– 55.63	19.56	2,202,638	87,622
C	– 39.88	– 82.04	2,201,721	86,072

9-7 Radial-line triangulation is to be performed to extend control through a block of photographs which consists of 8 flight strips with 15 photos per strip. Map compilation scale is 1 inch to 1,500 feet. If there are 12 well-distributed control points in the block, what error (in feet) can be expected in the map positions of pass points?

9-8 The problem is the same as Prob. 9-7 except that the block consists of 10 flight strips of 20 photos per strip, map compilation scale is 1:6,000, and there are 18 well-distributed horizontal ground control points in the block.

9-9 It is required to locate pass points on a map to an average accuracy of 10 feet from a block of 80 photographs. If map compilation scale is 1:6,000, how many well-distributed ground control points are needed to achieve the required accuracy?

9-10 Discuss the sources of error in radial-line triangulation.

9-11 Describe the various techniques available for planimetric map revision using vertical photographs.

PLANNING AERIAL PHOTOGRAPHY

10-1 INTRODUCTION

Successful execution of any aerial photogrammetric project depends upon good-quality photography. If the photography is to satisfactorily serve its intended purposes, the photographic mission must be carefully planned and faithfully executed according to the *flight plan*. A flight plan generally consists of two items: (1) a *flight map* which shows where the photos are to be taken and (2) *specificiations* which outline how to take them, including specific requirements such as camera and film requirements, scale, flying height, end lap, side lap, tilt and crab tolerances, etc. A flight plan which gives optimum specifications for a project can be prepared only after careful consideration of all the many variables which influence aerial photography.

An aerial photographic mission is an expensive operation involving two or more crewmen and expensive aircraft and equipment. In addition, in many areas periods of time that are acceptable for aerial photography are quite limited by weather and ground cover conditions which are related to season of the year. Failure to obtain satisfactory photography on a flight mission not only necessitates costly reflights but in all probability it will also cause long and expensive delays on the project for which the photos were ordered. For these reasons flight planning is one of the most important operations in the overall photogrammetric project.

100 acres or more – feasible   *gr ⁴⁵⁰/* } *acre*
                                    fl Big

10-2 END LAP AND SIDE LAP

Before discussing the many aspects which enter into consideration in planning an aerial photographic mission, it will be helpful to redefine the terms "end lap" and "side lap." As discussed in Sec. 1-4, vertical aerial photographic coverage of an area is normally taken as a series of overlapping flight strips. As illustrated in Fig. 10-1, *end lap* is the overlapping of successive photos along a flight strip. Figure 10-2 illustrates *side lap,* the overlap of adjacent flight strips.

In Fig. 10-1, *G* represents the dimension of the square of ground covered by a single photograph (assuming level ground and a square camera focal-plane format), and *B* is the air base or distance between exposure stations of a stereopair. The amount of end lap of a stereopair is commonly given in percent. Expressed in terms of *G* and *B*, it is

$$PE = \left(\frac{G - B}{G} \right) \times 100 \qquad (10\text{-}1)$$

In Eq. (10-1), *PE* is percent end lap. If stereoscopic coverage of an area is required, the absolute minimum end lap is 50 percent. However, in order to prevent gaps from occurring in the stereoscopic coverage due to crab, tilt, flying height variaitons, and terrain variations, end laps greater than 50 percent are used. Also, if the photos are to be used for photogrammetric control extension, images of some points must appear on three successive photographs—a condition requiring greater than 50 percent end lap. For these reasons aerial photography for mapping purposes is normally taken with about 60 percent end lap, plus or minus about 5 percent.

Crab, as explained in Sec. 4-10, exists when the edges of the photos in the *x* direction are not parallel with the direction of flight. It causes a reduction in stereoscopic coverage, as was indicated in Fig. 4-9*b.* Figures 10-3 through 10-5 illustrate reductions in

FIGURE 10-1
End lap, the overlapping of successive photos along a flight strip.

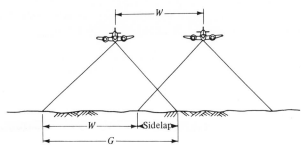

FIGURE 10-2
Side lap, the overlapping of adjacent flight strips.

end lap causing loss of stereoscopic coverage due to tilt, flying height variations, and relief variations respectively.

Side lap is required in aerial photography to prevent gaps from occurring between flight strips as a result of drift, crab, tilt, flying height variations, and terrain variations. *Drift* is the term applied to a failure of the pilot to fly along planned flight lines. It is often caused by strong winds. Excessive drifts are the most common cause for gaps in photo coverage; when this occurs, reflights are necessary.

In Fig. 10-2, G again represents the dimension of the square of ground coverage of a single photograph and W is the spacing between adjacent flight lines. An expression for PS, percent side lap in terms of G and W, is:

$$PS = \left(\frac{G - W}{G}\right) \times 100 \qquad (10\text{-}2)$$

Mapping photography is normally taken with a side lap of about 30 percent. An advantage realized from using this large a percentage is elimination of the need to use the extreme edges of the photography, where the imagery is of poorer quality. Photography for mosaic work is sometimes taken with greater than 30 percent side lap as this reduces the size of the central portion of the photograph that must be used, thereby

FIGURE 10-3
Failure to achieve stereoscopic coverage due to tilt.

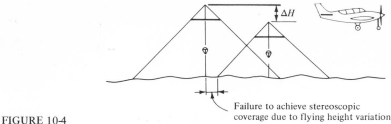

FIGURE 10-4
Failure to achieve stereoscopic coverage due to flying height variations.

lessening distortions of images due to tilt and relief. In some cases where aerial photography is to be used for very precise photogrammetric control extension, it may be taken with 60 percent side lap as well as 60 percent end lap.

EXAMPLE 10-1 The air base of a stereopair of vertical photos is 4,600 ft and flying height above average ground is 8,000 ft. The camera has a 6-in (152.4 mm) focal length and a 9-in (23 cm) format. What is the percent end lap?

> SOLUTION
>
> (a) Average photo scale $= \dfrac{f}{H'_{avg}} = $ 6 in/8,000 ft = 1 in/1,333 ft
>
> (b) Ground coverage dimension G = 9 in × 1,333 ft/in = 12,000 ft
>
> (c) Percent end lap—(by Eq. (10-1):
>
> $$PE = \left(\frac{12,000 - 4,600}{12,000}\right) \times 100 = 62\% \qquad ////$$

EXAMPLE 10-2 In Example 10-1, assume that the spacing between adjacent flight strips is 8,200 ft. What is the percent side lap?

> SOLUTION   By Eq. (10-2),
>
> $$PS = \left(\frac{12,000 - 8,200}{12,000}\right) \times 100 = 32\% \qquad ////$$

Failure to achieve stereoscopic coverage due to terrain variation

FIGURE 10-5
Failure to achieve stereoscopic coverage due to terrain variations.

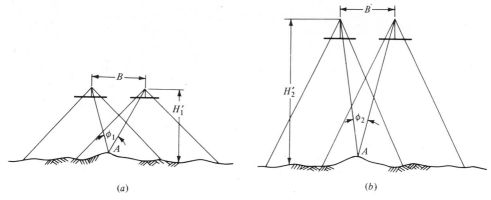

FIGURE 10-6
Parallactic angles increase with increasing B/H' ratios.

10-3 PURPOSE OF THE PHOTOGRAPHY

In planning aerial photographic missions, the first and foremost consideration is the purpose for which the photography is being taken. Only with the purpose defined can optimum equipment and procedures be selected. In general, aerial photographs are desired which have either good *metrical* qualities or high *pictorial* qualities. Photos having good metrical qualities are needed for topographic mapping or other purposes where precise quantitative photogrammetric measurements are required. High pictorial qualities are required for qualitative analysis such as photographic interpretation or for constructing aerial mosaics and photo maps.

Photographs of good metrical quality are obtained using calibrated cameras and films having fine-grained, high-resolution emulsions. For topographic mapping, photography is preferably taken with a wide or super-wide angle (short focal length) camera so that a large *base-height* (B/H') ratio is obtained. The B/H' ratio is the ratio of the air base of a pair of overlapping photographs to average flying height above ground. The larger the B/H' ratio, the greater the intersection angles or parallactic angles between intersecting light rays to common points. In Fig. 10-6a and b, for example, the air bases are equal but the focal length and flying height in Fig. 10-6a are half those of Fig. 10-6b. Photographic scales are therefore equal, but the B/H' ratio of Fig. 10-6a is double that of Fig. 10-6b, and parallactic angle ϕ_1 to point P in Fig. 10-6a is nearly double corresponding angle ϕ_2 in Fig. 10-6b.

It can be shown that errors in computed positions and elevations of points in a stereopair increase with increasing flying heights and decrease with increasing x parallax. Large B/H' ratios denote low flying heights and large x parallaxes, conditions favorable to higher accuracy. The photos of Fig. 10-6a are therefore superior to those of Fig. 10-6b from a mapping or quantitative point of view.

Photography of high pictorial quality does not require a calibrated camera, but the camera must have a good-quality lens. In many cases films having fast, large-grained emulsions produce desirable effects. For some photo interpretation work, normal color films are useful. For other special applications, black-and-white infrared or color infrared films are desirable. Special effects can also be obtained using filters in combination with various types of films. Timber types, for example, can be delineated quite effectively using a red filter in combination with black-and-white infrared film.

For mosaic work, relief displacements, tilt displacements, and scale variations produce objectionable degradations of pictorial quality. These may be minimized, however, by increasing flying height, thereby decreasing the B/H' ratio. Increased flying height, of course, reduces photo scale; but this can be compensated for by using a longer focal length camera. The photo of Fig. 10-7a was exposed at half the flying height of the photo of Fig. 10-7b. The scales of the two photos are equal, however, because the focal length f_2 of Fig. 10-7b is double f_1 of Fig. 10-7a. The photo of Fig. 10-7b is more desirable for mosaic construction because its scale variations and image distortions due to relief, tilt, and flying height variations are much less than those of the photo of Fig. 10-7a. On Fig. 10-7a, for example, relief displacement d_1 is double the corresponding relief displacement d_2 of Fig. 10-7b.

10-4 PHOTO SCALE

Average photographic scale is one of the most important variables that must be selected in planning aerial photography. It is normally fixed within certain limits by specific project requirements. For topographic mapping, photo scale is usually dictated by required map scale, required contour interval, and capabilities of the instruments that will be used in compiling the map. On the other hand, aerial photographic coverage for mosaic preparation or for photo interpretation must be planned at a scale which enables the smallest objects of importance to be resolved on the photos.

In topographic mapping with a stereoscopic plotting instrument, the enlargement ratio from photo scale to optimum map compilation scale must be considered. With some plotters the range of enlargement capability is quite wide; with others it is restricted within narrow limits (see Chap. 14). For many double-projection direct-viewing plotters, optimum enlargement ratio is five. If one of these instruments is to be used and if map scale is fixed, the optimum photo scale is automatically fixed at one-fifth map scale.

EXAMPLE 10-3 A map must be compiled at a scale of 1:6,000 using a Kelsh plotter whose optimum enlargement ratio from photo scale to map scale is five. What is optimum photo scale?

FIGURE 10-7
Reduction in relief displacement is achieved by increasing flying height.

SOLUTION Photo scale is one-fifth as large as map scale, therefore

$$S_{photo} = 1/6,000 \times 1/5 = 1/30,000; \text{ or } 1 \text{ in} = 2,500 \text{ ft}$$ ////

Selection of optimum map scale depends upon the purpose of the map. It should be carefully planned, because compilation at a larger scale than necessary is uneconomical, and compilation at too small a scale reduces the usefulness of the map or may even render it unsatisfactory. The accuracy to which planimetric positions of points can be measured from a map depends upon the scale of the map. Assume that map positions of planimetric features can be plotted correctly to within 1/30 inch, a condition necessary to meet National Map Accuracy Standards. Then if points must be accurate to within ± 1.0 foot on a cadastral map, required map scale is one inch to 30 feet. On the other hand, if points need only be accurate to within ± 10 feet on map, then a scale of 1 inch to 300 feet is all that is required.

Required contour interval for a map must be considered as well as planimetric accuracy in planning aerial photography. As with planimetric accuracy, contour interval also depends upon the intended use of the map. Assume that elevations can be interpolated correctly from a map to within one-half the contour interval, a condition required for meeting National Map Accuracy Standards. If elevations must be interpolated to within ± 0.5 foot on a highway design map, then a 1-foot contour interval is necessary. If elevations must be interpolated to ± 10 feet on a map prepared for studying the volume of water impounded in the reservoir of a large dam, then a 20-foot contour interval is all that is required.

Recommended contour interval depends not only on the use to be made of the map but also on the type of terrain. If the map is being prepared for planning a sewer system for a city such as Las Vegas, Nevada, which lies on very flat terrain, perhaps a 1-foot contour interval is required. On the other hand, if a topographic map of San Francisco is being prepared for the same purpose, because of the large range of relief in that city perhaps a 5- or 10-foot contour interval would be used. Photo scale and contour interval are closely related. As vertical mapping accuracy requirements increase (required contour interval decreases), flying height must decrease and hence photographic scale increases.

In large-scale mapping the following scale and contour interval (C.I.) relationships generally provide satisfactory compatibility: 1 inch = 50 feet with 1 foot C.I.; 1 inch = 100 feet with 2 foot C.I.; 1 inch = 200 feet with 5 foot C.I.; and 1 inch = 500 feet with 10 foot C.I. The minimum possible contour interval that can be reliably traced with a stereoscopic plotting instrument is generally given in terms of a *C factor* which is a ratio of flying height. This subject is discussed in more detail in Sec. 10-6.

10-5 FLYING HEIGHT

Once camera focal length and required average photo scale have been selected, required flying height above average ground is automatically fixed in accordance with scale Eq. (6-3).

EXAMPLE 10-4   Aerial photography having an average scale of 1:6,000 is required to be taken with a 6-in (152.4 mm) focal length camera over terrain whose average elevation is 1,400 ft above mean sea level. What is required flying height above mean sea level?

SOLUTION   By Eq. (6-3), (Note: 6 in = 0.5 ft.)

$$S = \frac{f}{H - h_{\text{avg}}} \qquad 1/6,000 = \frac{0.5}{H - 1,400}$$

$$H = 6,000(0.5) + 1,400 = 4,400 \text{ ft above sea level} \qquad ////$$

Flying heights above average ground may vary from a few hundred feet in the case of large-scale helicopter photography, to several hundred miles if satellites are used to carry the camera. Flying heights used in photographing for topographic mapping normally vary between about 1,500 and 30,000 feet. If a portion of the project area lies at a substantially higher or lower elevation than the other part, a different flying height above mean sea level for that portion may be necessary to maintain uniform flying height above ground.

Ground coverage per photo for high-altitude photography is greater than for low-altitude photography (see Table 10-1). Fewer high-altitude photos are therefore required to cover a given area. Very-high-altitude coverage is more expensive to obtain than low-altitude photography because of the special equipment that it requires. Some of the problems encountered at high flying heights are decreasing available oxygen, decreasing pressure, and extreme cold. When flying heights exceed about 10,000 feet, an oxygen supply system is necessary for the flight crew. At altitudes above 30,000 feet, pure oxygen under pressure is required. Also, the cabin must be pressurized and heaters are required to protect the crew against the cold. Most aerial photography is taken using single- or twin-engine aircraft. Supercharged single-engine aircraft can reach 20,000-feet altitudes, and supercharged twin-engine aircraft are capable of approaching 30,000 feet. Higher altitudes require turbocharged or jet aircraft.

During photography the pilot maintains proper flying height by means of an altimeter. Since altimeters give elevations above mean sea level, the proper reading is the sum of average ground elevation and required flying height above ground necessary to achieve proper photo scale. Altimeters are barometric instruments and consequently their readings are affected by varying atmospheric pressure. They must be checked daily and adjusted to base airport air pressure.

10-6 STEREOSCOPIC PLOTTER CONSIDERATIONS

If topographic mapping with a stereoscopic plotting instrument is to be performed, the photography must be planned in accordance with certain limiting factors of the particular plotter to be used. Important plotter considerations are (1) principal distance of the projectors, (2) optimum enlargement ratio from photo scale or diapositive scale to map compilation scale, (3) *C factor* of the plotter, and (4) vertical operating range of the plotter. These factors influence the choice of both camera and flying height.

In interior orientation, the principal distance of the plotter projectors must be set exactly equal to the principal distance of the diapositives. If the diapositives are prepared by contact printing or by one-to-one projection printing, then their principal distance is equal to the focal length of the taking camera (see Sec. 14-7). Some plotters are capable of accommodating a wide range of principal distances; others are limited either optically or mechanically to a very narrow range. Wide-angle Kelsh projectors, for example, accommodate a nominal principal distance of 152 millimeters (6-inch), and diapositive principal distances can vary only a few millimeters from this value. If a Kelsh or equivalent plotter is to be used, it is both logical and convenient to use a camera whose nominal focal length is equal to the nominal principal distance of the projectors. If the focal length of the taking camera is not within the range of the projector principal distance, the diapositives can be reduced or enlarged by projection printing to obtain the proper principal distance. Reduction causes a reduced model size, however, and enlargement may cause loss of imagery on the edges of the photos.

Optimum enlargement ratio of the stereoscopic plotter from photo scale to map compilation scale must be considered in planning aerial photography. If it is required that a topographic map be compiled to a certain scale, then, with the enlargement ratio of the plotter known, photo scale is fixed, and this in turn fixes flying height. Example 10-3 illustrates this condition.

Relative vertical accuracy capabilities of various stereoscopic plotters are commonly compared on the basis of their *C factors.* The *C* factor is the ratio of the flying height above ground of the photography to the contour interval that can be reliably plotted using that photography, or, in equation form,

$$C \text{ factor} = H'/C.I. \qquad (10\text{-}3)$$

The units of H' and C.I. (contour interval of Eq. (10-3) are the same. Based upon Eq. (10-3), if a plotter has a *C* factor of 1,000 and a map with a contour interval of 5 feet is required, then a flying height above ground of 5,000 feet *or less* is required. The more precise the plotter, the greater its *C* factor rating. Manufacturers commonly specify *C* factors for their instruments, and they may vary from 800 to about 1,800 depending upon the instrument. Contour accuracy depends not only on the plotting instrument but also upon the camera and its calibration, the quality of the photography, and the capability of the plotter operator. These conditions all combine to yield a total "system *C* factor."

In areas where terrain elevation varies considerably, mechanical or optical limitations of the stereoscopic plotter can place a limit on the lowest possible flying height. Kelsh and several other optical projection plotters, for example, can accommodate maximum relief variations in the stereoscopic model of about 20 percent of the projection distance. Projection distance is analogous to flying height above ground, and therefore flying height should be at least five times greater than the maximum terrain variations of any model. If, for example, an area has terrain variations of 600 feet, flying height must be at least 3,000 feet in order that the terrain variation does not exceed 20 percent of the flying height.

10-7 GROUND COVERAGE

Once average photographic scale and camera format dimensions have been selected, the ground surface area covered by a single photograph may be readily calculated. In addition, if end lap and side lap are known, the ground area covered by the stereoscopic

FIGURE 10-8
The area covered by a stereoscopic neat model.

neat model = B × W

neat model can also be determined. The neat model, as illustrated in Fig. 10-8, is the stereoscopic area between adjacent principal points and extending out sideways in both directions to the middle of the side lap. The neat model has a width of B and a breadth of W. Its coverage is important since it represents the approximate mapping area of each stereopair.

EXAMPLE 10-5 Aerial photography is to be taken from a flying height of 6,000 ft above average ground with a camera having a 6-in (152.4 mm) focal length and a 9-in (23 cm) format. End lap will be 60 percent and side lap will be 30 percent. What is the ground area covered by a single photograph and by the stereoscopic neat model?

SOLUTION By Eq. (6-1),

(a) S = 6 in/6,000 ft = 1 in/1,000 ft or 1:12,000

(b) The dimension, G of the square ground area covered by a single photo is

$$G = 1,000 \text{ ft/in} \times 9 \text{ in} = 9,000 \text{ ft}$$

(c) The area in acres covered on the ground by a single photo is

$$A = \frac{(9,000)^2}{43,560 \text{ sq ft per acre}} = 1,861 \text{ acres}$$

(d) At 60 percent, end lap B is 0.4 G and at 30 percent side lap W is 0.7 G. Therefore the dimensions of the rectangular stereoscopic neat model are

$$B = 0.4(9,000) = 3,600 \text{ ft}$$

$$W = 0.7(9,000) = 6,300 \text{ ft}$$

The area of the neat model is

$$A_N = \frac{3,600 \times 6,300}{43,560} = 521 \text{ acres}$$

Table 10-1

Photo scale	Photo scale in	Flying height, ft	G, ft	W (0.7 G) ft	B (0.4 G) ft	Acres per photo	Acres per neat model
1:1,800	1″ 150′	900	1,350	945	540	42	12
1:2,400	1″ 200′	1,200	1,800	1,260	720	74	21
1:3,000	1″ 250′	1,500	2,250	1,575	900	116	33
1:3,600	1″ 300′	1,800	2,700	1,890	1,080	168	47
1:4,200	1″ 350′	2,100	3,150	2,205	1,260	228	64
1:4,800	1″ 400′	2,400	3,600	2,520	1,440	298	83
1:5,400	1″ 450′	2,700	4,050	2,835	1,620	376	105
1:6,000	1″ 500′	3,000	4,500	3,150	1,800	465	130
1:6,600	1″ 550′	3,300	4,950	3,465	1,980	563	158
1:7,200	1″ 600′	3,600	5,400	3,780	2,160	669	187
1:7,800	1″ 650′	3,900	5,850	4,095	2,340	786	220
1:8,400	1″ 700′	4,200	6,300	4,410	2,520	911	255
1:9,000	1″ 750′	4,500	6,750	4,725	2,700	1,046	293
1:9,600	1″ 800′	4,800	7,200	5,040	2,880	1,189	333
1:10,800	1″ 900′	5,400	8,100	5,670	3,240	1,507	422
1:12,000	1″ 1,000′	6,000	9,000	6,300	3,600	1,861	521
1:15,000	1″ 1,250′	7,500	11,250	7,875	4,500	2,907	814
1:18,000	1″ 1,500′	9,000	13,500	9,450	5,400	6.5*	1.8*
1:24,000	1″ 2,000′	12,000	18,000	12,600	7,200	11.6*	3.3*
1:30,000	1″ 2,500′	15,000	22,500	15,750	9,000	18.2*	5.1*
1:40,000	1″ 3,333′	20,000	30,000	21,000	12,000	32.3*	9.0*
1:50,000	1″ 4,167′	25,000	37,500	26,250	15,000	50.4*	14.1*
1:60,000	1″ 5,000′	30,000	45,000	31,500	18,000	72.6*	20.3*

*Square miles

Table 10-1 gives ground dimensions and ground areas covered by a single photo and by the stereoscopic neat model for various commonly used photo scales. The table is based on a 6-inch (152.4 mm) focal length camera having a 9-inch (23-centimeter) square format. End lap and side lap of 60 percent and 30 percent respectively are assumed.

10-8   WEATHER CONDITIONS

The weather, which is always uncertain for any given day, is a very important consideration in aerial photography. An ideal day for aerial photography is one that is free from clouds; although if the sky is less than 10 percent cloud-covered, the day may be considered satisfactory. If clouds of greater than 10 percent coverage are present but are so high that they are above planned flying height, this is still objectionable since large shadows will be cast on the ground, obscuring features. The number of satisfactory cloudless days varies with time of year and locality.

A particular day can be cloudless and still be unsuitable for aerial photography due to atmospheric haze, smog, dust, smoke, high winds, or air turbulence. Atmospheric haze scatters almost entirely in the blue portion of the spectrum and it can therefore be effectively eliminated from the photographs by using a yellow filter in front of the camera lens. Smog, dust, and smoke scatter throughout the entire spectrum and cannot be filtered out satisfactorily. Best days for photographing over industrial areas which are susceptible to smog, dust, and smoke occur after heavy rains or during moving cold fronts which clear the air. Windy, turbulent days can cause excessive image motion and cause difficulties in keeping the camera oriented for vertical photography, in staying on planned flight lines, and in maintaining constant flying heights.

The decision to fly or not to fly is one that must be made daily. The flight crew should be capable of interpreting weather conditions and of making sound decisions as to when satisfactory photography can be obtained. If possible, the flight crew should be based near the project so that they can observe the weather firsthand and quickly take advantage of satisfactory conditions.

10-9   SEASON OF YEAR

The season of the year is a limiting factor in aerial photography because it affects ground cover conditions and the sun's altitude. If photography is being taken for topographic mapping, the photos should be taken when the deciduous trees are bare, so that the ground is not obscured by leaves. In many places this occurs twice a year for short periods in the late fall and in early spring. Oak trees tend to hold many of their leaves until spring, when the buds swell and cause them to fall. In areas with heavy oak cover, therefore, the most satisfactory period for aerial photography is that very short period in the spring between budding and leafing out. Sometimes aerial photography is taken for special forestry interpretation purposes, in which case it may be desirable for the trees to be in full leaf. Normally aerial photography is not taken when the ground is snow-covered. Snow not only obscures the ground but also causes difficulties in interpretation and in stereoviewing.

Another factor to be considered in planning aerial photography is the sun's altitude. Low sun angles produce long shadows which are objectionable because they obscure detail. Generally about a 30° sun angle is the minimum acceptable for aerial photography. During the winter months of November through February, the sun never reaches a 30° altitude in northern parts of the United States due to the sun's southerly declination. Aerial photography should therefore be avoided in those areas during these winter months if possible. For the other months, photography should be exposed during the middle portion of the day after the sun rises above 30° and before it falls below that altitude. For certain purposes, shadows may be desirable, as they aid in identifying objects. Shadows of trees, for example, help to identify the species. Shadows may also be helpful in locating photo-identifiable features such as fence posts, power poles, etc., to serve as photo control points.

10-10 FLIGHT MAP

A flight map, as shown in Fig. 10-9, gives the project boundaries and flight lines the pilot must fly to obtain the desired coverage. The flight map is prepared on some existing map which shows the project area. United States Geological Survey quadrangle maps are frequently used. The flight map may also be prepared on small-scale photographs of the area if they are available. In executing the planned photographic mission, the pilot finds two or more features on each flight line which he can identify both on the flight map and on the ground. He flies the aircraft so that his lines of flight pass over the ground points.

Rectangular project areas are most conveniently covered with flight lines oriented north and south or east and west. As illustrated in Fig. 10-9, this is desirable because the pilot can take advantage of section lines and roads running in the cardinal directions and fly parallel to them.

If the project area is irregular in shape or if it is long and narrow and skewed to cardinal directions, it may not be economical to fly north and south or east and west. In planning coverage for such irregular areas, it may be most economical to align flight lines parallel to project boundaries as nearly as possible. Flight planning templates are useful for determining best and most economical photographic coverage for mapping, especially for small areas. These templates, which show blocks of neat models, are prepared on transparent plastic sheets at scales which correspond to the scales of the base maps upon panel - painted X, cloth +, for corner monuments.

Job M-223
6 Flights, F/y at 4,050' Above
Sea Level. 60% Forward Lap.
6" Zeiss Camera.
1"=500' Negative Scale.
Hold Plan For Telephone
Go Ahead After Panels Are
Placed on Section Corner
Monuments.

FLIGHT CREW COPY

FIGURE 10-9
Example of a flight plan. (*Courtesy Alster & Associates, Inc.*)

211

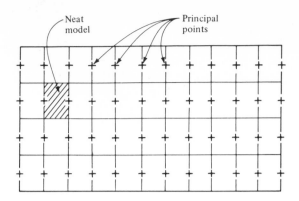

FIGURE 10-10
Transparent template of neat models used for planning aerial photography.

which the flight plan is prepared. The templates are then simply superimposed on the map over the project area and oriented in the position which yields best coverage with the fewest number of neat models. Such a template is shown in Fig. 10-10. The crosses represent exposure stations, and these may be individually marked on the flight map. This template method of flight planning is exceptionally useful in planning exposure station locations when artificial targets are used (see Sec. 11-10).

Once camera focal length, photo scale, end lap, and side lap have been selected, the flight map can be prepared. The following example illustrates flight map preparation for a rectangular project area.

EXAMPLE 10-6 A project area is 10 mi long in the east-west direction and $6\frac{1}{2}$ mi wide in the north-south direction (see Fig. 10-11). It is to be covered with vertical aerial photography having a scale of 1:12,000. End lap and side lap are to be 60 percent and 30 percent respectively. A 6-in (152.4 mm) focal length camera with a 9-in (23 centimeters) square format is to be used. Prepare the flight map on a base map whose scale is 1:24,000, and compute the total number of photographs necessary for the project.

SOLUTION

(a) Fly east-west to reduce the number of flight lines

(b) Dimension of square ground coverage per photograph

Photo scale = 1:12,000 (1 in = 1,000 ft)

$$G = 9 \text{ in} \times 1,000 \text{ ft per in} = 9,000 \text{ ft}$$

(c) Lateral advance per strip

$$W = 0.7 \, G \text{ at 30 percent side lap}$$
$$W = (0.7) \, 9,000 = 6,300 \text{ ft}$$

FIGURE 10-11
Project area for Example 10-6.

(d) Number of flight lines (Align the first and last line with $0.3G$ coverage outside the north and south project boundary lines as shown in Fig. 10-11. This ensures lateral coverage outside of the project area.)

Distance of first and last flight lines inside their respective north and south project boundaries (See Fig. 10-11).

$$\tfrac{1}{2}G - 0.3G = 4,500 - 2,700 = 1,800 \text{ ft}$$

$$\text{no. flight lines} = \frac{6\tfrac{1}{2} \text{ mi} \times 5,280 \text{ ft per mi} - 2 \times 1,800}{6,300 \text{ ft per strip}} + 1 = 5.9 (\text{use } 6)$$

Adjusted spacing between flight lines for integral number of flight lines

$$W_a = \frac{6\tfrac{1}{2} \times 5,280 - 2 \times 1,800}{5} = 6,144 \text{ ft}$$

(e) Linear advance per photo (air base)

$$B = 0.4\,G \text{ at } 60 \text{ percent end lap}$$

$$B = (0.4)\,9,000 = 3,600 \text{ ft}$$

(f) Number photos per strip (Take two extra photos beyond project boundary at each end of the strips to ensure coverage.)

$$\text{no. photos per strip} = \frac{10 \text{ mi} \times 5,280 \text{ ft per mi}}{3,600 \text{ ft per photo}} + 2 + 2 = 18.7 (\text{use } 19)$$

(g) Total no. of photos

$$19 \text{ photos per strip} \times 6 \text{ strips} = 114$$

(*h*) Spacing of flight lines on the map

$$\text{Map scale} = 1{:}24{,}000 \ (1 \text{ in} = 2{,}000 \text{ ft})$$

$$\frac{6{,}144 \text{ ft per strip}}{2{,}000 \text{ ft per in}} = 3.07 \text{ in}$$

(Draw the flight lines at 3.07 inches spacing on the map, with the first and last lines 0.9 inches—for 1,800 ft—inside the project boundaries.)

(*i*) Assuming the aircraft flies at a velocity of 120 mph, the intervalometer setting necessary to obtain the desired end lap is:

$$120 \text{ mph} \times \frac{5{,}280 \text{ feet per mile}}{3{,}600 \text{ seconds per hour}} = 176 \text{ feet per second}$$

$$\text{Intervalometer setting} = \frac{3{,}600 \text{ ft per photo}}{176 \text{ ft per sec}} = 20.45 \text{ sec (use 20 sec)} \qquad ////$$

10-11 SPECIFICATIONS

Most flight plans include a set of detailed specifications which outline the materials, equipment, and procedures to be used on the project. These specifications include requirements and tolerances pertaining to photographic scale (including camera focal length and flying height), end lap, side lap, tilt, crab, and photographic quality. The following is a sample set of specifications for aerial photography:

Detailed Specifications For Aerial Photography

A. General The Engineer shall perform the necessary flying and photography to provide photographic coverage of an area approximately 8 square miles in extent shown on the sketch map attached hereto as exhibit "A." The engineer may sublet this phase of the work to a qualified and experienced aerial photographic firm. The city, however, retains the right to approve or reject any or all such firms which the engineer may wish to engage.

B. Scale Flight height above average ground shall be such that the negatives will have an average scale of 1 inch equals 500 feet. Negatives having a departure from the specified scale by more than 5 percent because of tilt or abrupt changes in flying altitude must be corrected. The photographs shall be suitable for the compilation of the topographic maps specified herein, and the mapping flight height shall not vary from 3,000 feet above mean terrain, by more than 5 percent.

C. End lap and Side lap End lap shall be sufficient to provide full stereoscopic coverage of the area to be mapped. End lap shall average 63 percent, plus or minus 5 percent. End lap of less than 58 percent or more than 68 percent in one or more negatives shall be cause for rejection of the negatives in which such deficiency or excess occurs; unless within a stereoscopic pair, end lap exceeding 68 percent is necessary in areas of low elevation to attain the minimum 58 percent end lap in adjacent areas of high elevation. Wherever there is a change in direction of the flight lines, vertical photography on the beginning of a forward section shall end lap the photography of a back section by 100 percent. Any negatives having side lap of less than 20 percent or more than 55 percent may be rejected.

D. Tilt Negatives made with the optical axis of the aerial camera in a vertical position are desired. Tilt of any negative by more than three degrees, an average tilt of more than one degree for the entire project, or tilt between any two successive negatives exceeding four degrees may be cause of rejection.

E. Crab Crab in excess of three degrees may be cause of rejection of the flight line of negative or portions thereof in which such crab occurs.

F. Quality The photographs shall be clear and sharp in detail and of average uniform density. They shall be free from clouds, cloud shadows, light streaks, static marks, or other blemishes which would interfere with their intended use. All photography shall be taken when the area to be mapped is free of snow, before foliation, and at such time as to insure a minimum solar angle of 30 degrees, except upon written authorization to the contrary by the city.

G. Camera For topographic and contour mapping, photographs shall be exposed with a distortion free 6-inch focal length precision aerial mapping camera equipped with a between-the-lens element shutter to produce negatives 9 inches X 9 inches in size. The engineer shall furnish the city with a precision camera calibration report from the National Bureau of Standards for the camera to be used.

H. Contact Prints The contact prints from the vertical negatives shall be printed on double weight semimatte paper of suitable contrast.

I. Photo Index Photo indices shall be prepared by directly photographing on safety base film at a convenient scale, the assembly of contact prints from all indexed and evaluated prints used. One photo index map shall be delivered on cronapaque or equal. The photo index shall carry a suitable title, scale and north point.

J. Ownership of Negatives All negatives shall become the property of the city and shall be delivered to the city upon completion of this contract, or may be stored indefinitely in the film library of the engineer at no added charge.

(Courtesy Alster and Associates, Inc.)

REFERENCES

American Society of Photogrammetry: "Manual of Photogrammetry," 3d ed., George Banta Co., Inc., Menasha, Wis., 1966, chaps. 5 and 7.

Aguilar, A. M.: Cost Analysis of Aerial Surveying, *Photogrammetric Engineering,* vol. 33, no. 1, p. 81, 1967.

———: Management Planning for Aerial Surveying, *Photogrammetric Engineering,* vol. 35, no. 10, p. 1047, 1969.

Lund, H. G.: Factors in Computing Photo Coverage, *Photogrammetric Engineering,* vol. 35, no. 1, p. 61, 1969.

Pryor, W. T.: Specifications for Aerial Photography and Mapping by Photogrammetric Methods for Highway Engineering Purposes, *Photogrammetric Engineering,* vol. 16, no. 3, p. 439, 1950.

U.S. Dept. of Transportation, Federal Highway Administration: *Reference Guide Outline, Specifications for Aerial Surveys and Mapping by Photogrammetric Methods for Highways,* Washington, D.C., 1968.

Woodward, L. A.: Survey Project Planning, *Photogrammetric Engineering,* vol. 36, no. 6, p. 587, 1970.

Wright, M. S.: What Does Photogrammetric Mapping Really Cost?, *Photogrammetric Engineering,* vol. 26, no. 3, p. 452, 1960.

PROBLEMS

10-1 The air base of a stereopair of vertical photos is 3,250 feet and flying height above average ground is 5,200 feet. If the camera has a 6-inch focal length and a 9-inch square format, what is the percent end lap?

10-2 For Prob. 10-1, if adjacent flight lines are spaced at 6,000 feet, what is percent side lap?

10-3 An average photo scale of 1:14,000 is required of vertical photos. What air base is required in order to achieve 60 percent end lap if the camera has a 9-inch square format?

10-4 The problem is the same as Prob. 10-3 except that required photo scale is 1:6,000 and average end lap must be 55 percent.

10-5 Vertical photographs are exposed from 6,200 feet above average ground. If a B/H' ratio of 0.80 is required, what should be the length of the air base? What will percent end lap be for these photos if the camera focal length is $3\frac{1}{2}$ inches and the format is 90 inches square?

10-6 What is the B/H' ratio for vertical photography exposed with 65 percent end lap using a camera having a 6-inch focal length and a 9-inch square format?

10-7 The problem is the same as Prob. 10-6 except for 60 percent end lap and a $3\frac{1}{2}$ inch focal length camera.

10-8 A map to a scale of 1:8,000 is to be compiled from vertical aerial photographs using a Balplex (525) stereoplotting instrument. Optimum enlargement from photo to map is 3.5 for this instrument. If a 6-inch focal length camera is used, what should be flying height above average ground for the photography?

10-9 The problem is the same as Prob. 10-8 except that a Kelsh stereoplotting instrument with optimum enlargement of five is to be used to compile a map to a scale of 1 inch to 200 feet.

10-10 A stereoscopic plotting instrument having a C factor of 1,000 will be used to compile a map with a contour interval of 10 feet. What flying height is recommended, and what is corresponding photo scale if the camera has a 6-inch focal length?

10-11 A highway design map is to be compiled from aerial photography. The map is to have a scale of 1 inch to 100 feet and a 2-foot contour interval. The enlargement factor of the stereoscopic plotting instrument is five from photo to map, and the plotter's C factor is 1,200. If the camera focal length is 152.4 mm, what is the required flying height above average ground based upon required map scale? Based upon contour interval? Which conditions control flying height?

10-12   Vertical aerial photographs are taken from a flying height of 5,000 feet above average ground using a camera with a 210-mm focal length lens and a 9-inch square format. End lap is 60 percent at average terrain elevation. How many acres of ground are covered in a single photograph? In the neat model? (Assume 15 percent side lap.)

10-13   For Prob. 10-12, if low, average, and high terrain are 1,200, 1,600, and 2,000 feet above datum, what is percent end lap at low terrain? At high terrain? How many acres of ground are covered by a neat model at low terrain? At high terrain?

10-14   An aerial camera is equipped with an intervalometer that can be set to the nearest second only. Vertical aerial photos at a scale of 1:6,000 and with 60 percent end lap are required. If the camera format is 9 inches square and aircraft velocity is maintained at 130 miles per hour during photography, what is the required intervalometer setting?

10-15   A rectangular area 14 miles in the north-south direction by 8 miles in the east-west direction is to be covered with aerial photography having a scale of 1:8,000. End lap and side lap are to be 60 percent and 25 percent respectively. A camera having a 9-inch square format is to be used. Compute the total number of photographs in the project, assuming that the flight strips are parallel with the east and west project boundaries. Also add two photos at the ends of each strip to ensure complete coverage (see example Prob. 10-6).

10-16   If a flight map is to be prepared for Prob. 10-15 on a base map having a scale of 1:24,000, what should be the spacing in inches of flight lines on the map? What is the map distance between successive exposures along a flight line?

10-17   A transparent template of neat models, similar to that shown in Fig. 10-10, is to be prepared to overlay on a map having a scale of 1:20,000. What should be the dimensions of neat models on the template if the camera format is 9 inches square, photo scale is 1:12,000, end lap is 60 percent and side lap is 30 percent?

CONTROL FOR AERIAL PHOTOGRAPHY

11-1 INTRODUCTION

45-50% of cost

Photogrammetric control consists of any points whose positions are known in an object-space reference coordinate system and whose images can be positively identified in the photographs. In aerial photography the object space is the ground surface, and various reference ground coordinate systems are used to describe control point positions. Photogrammetric control, or "ground control" as it is commonly called in aerial photogrammetry, provides the means for orienting or relating aerial photographs to the ground. Almost every phase of photogrammetric work requires some ground control.

Photogrammetric control is generally classified as either *horizontal control* (the position of the point in object space is known with respect to a horizontal datum), or *vertical control* (the elevation of the point is known with respect to a vertical datum). Separate classifications of horizontal and vertical control have resulted primarily because of differences in horizontal and vertical reference datums, and because of differences in surveying techniques for establishing horizontal and vertical control. Also, horizontal and vertical control are often considered separately in photogrammetric processes. Some times both horizontal and vertical object space positions of points are known, so that these points serve a dual control purpose.

Field surveying for photogrammetric control is generally a two-step process. The first step consists of establishing a network of *basic control* in the project area. This basic control consists of horizontal control monuments and bench marks of vertical control which will serve as a reference framework for subsequent photo control surveys. The second step involves establishing object space positions of *photo control* by means of surveys originating from the basic control network. Photo control points are the actual image points appearing in the photos that are used to control photogrammetric operations. The accuracy of basic control surveys is generally higher than that of subsequent photo control surveys.

The establishment of good ground control is an extremely important aspect of the overall photogrammetric mapping operation. Depending upon conditions, the cost of establishing ground control for photogrammetric mapping can be expected to constitute between 20 and 50 percent of the total mapping cost. The accuracy of the finished map can be no better than the ground control upon which it was based. Many maps that have been carefully prepared in the office to exacting standards have failed to pass field inspection simply because the ground control was of poor quality. Because of its importance, the ground control phase of any photogrammetric project should be carefully planned and executed.

11-2 SELECTING PHOTO CONTROL IMAGES *can set before or after flight*

In general, images of acceptable photo control points must satisfy two requirements: (1) they must be sharp, well defined, and positively identified on all photos and (2) they must lie in favorable locations in the photographs. (Reasons for this latter requirement are described in Sec. 11-3.) Control surveys for photogrammetry are normally conducted after the photography has been obtained. This assures that the above two requirements can be met. Photo control images are selected after careful study of the photos. The study should include the use of a stereoscope to ensure a clear stereoscopic view of all points selected. This is important because many of the subsequent photogrammetric measurements will be made stereoscopically. A preliminary selection of photo control images may be made in the office, but it is often advantageous to make the final selection in the field with the photos in hand. This enables positive identification of objects to be made, and it also permits making a firsthand assessment of object point accessibility, terrain conditions, and surveying convenience.

Images for horizontal control have slightly different requirements than images for vertical control. Because their horizontal positions on the photographs must be precisely measured, images of horizontal control points must be very sharp and well defined horizontally. Some objects whose images are commonly satisfactory for horizontal control are intersections of sidewalks, intersections of roads, manhole covers, small lone bushes, isolated rocks, corners of buildings, fence corners, power poles, points on bridges, intersections of small trails or watercourses, etc. Care must be exercised to ensure that control points do not fall in shadowed areas on some photos.

Images for vertical control need not be so sharp and well defined horizontally. Points selected should, however, be well defined vertically. Best vertical control points are small flat or slightly crowned areas. The small areas should have some natural features nearby, such as trees or rocks, which help to strengthen stereoscopic depth perception. Large open areas such as the tops of grassy hills or open fields should be avoided, if possible, because of the difficulties they cause in stereoscopic depth perception. Intersections of roads and sidewalks, small patches of grass, small bare spots, etc., make excellent vertical control points.

The importance of exercising extreme caution in locating and marking objects in the field that correspond to selected photo images cannot be overemphasized. Mistakes in point identification are common and costly. A power pole for example, may be located in the field, but it may not be the same pole whose image was identified on the photos. Mistakes such as this can be avoided by identifying enough other details in the immediate vicinity of each point so that verification is certain. A pocket stereoscope taken into the field can be invaluable in point identification, not only because it magnifies images but also because hills and valleys which aid in object verification can be seen both on the photos and on the ground.

11-3 NUMBER AND LOCATION OF PHOTO CONTROL

The required number of control points and their optimum location in the photos depend upon the use that will be made of them. If the flying height of a photo which is assumed to be vertical is to be calculated, then the horizontal length of a line and the elevations of its end points are needed. A line of as great a length as possible should be chosen.

For controlling mosaics, only a sparse network of horizontal control may be needed. The network should be uniformly distributed throughout the block of photos. The balance of control needed may be filled in with radial-line triangulation (see Chap. 9) or by other photogrammetric control extension techniques (see Chap. 18).

In solving the *space resection* problem for determining the position and orientation of a tilted photo (see Chap. 13), a minimum of three vertical control points and two horizontal control points are required in each photo. Images of the vertical control points should ideally form a large equilateral triangle, and the horizontal control points should be widely spaced. Although these are required minimums for space resection, redundant control is recommended to increase the accuracy of the photogrammetric solution and to prevent mistakes from going undetected.

If photo control is being established for the purpose of orienting stereomodels in a

FIGURE 11-1

Ideal condition.

Control recommended for orienting stereomodels in a stereoscopic plotting instrument.

△ Horizontal control point
◯ Vertical control point
◬ Horizontal and vertical control point

plotting instrument for topographic map compilation, the absolute minimum amount of control needed in each stereomodel is the same as the minimum needed for space resection. Again, the prudent photogrammetrist will utilize some amount of redundant control. As a practical minimum, each stereomodel oriented in a plotter should have three horizontal and four vertical control points. The horizontal points should be fairly widely spaced and the vertical control points should be near the corners of the model. An ideal configuration is shown in Fig. 11-1. Some organizations require a fifth vertical control point in the center of each stereomodel.

If photogrammetric control extension is planned to supplement photo control, then lesser amounts of ground-surveyed photo control points are needed. Photogrammetric control extension, or *bridging* as it is often called, is a photogrammetric process for densifying or supplementing photo control from a sparse network of ground-surveyed photo control. The techniques of bridging are described in detail in Chap. 18. In many cases bridging affords the most economical solution to the photogrammetric control problem, and it has been gaining popularity in recent years.

The amount of ground-surveyed photo control needed in bridging will vary depending upon procedures, instruments, and personnel to be used. In general, the more dense the ground-surveyed network of photo control, the better the resulting accuracy in the supplemental control determined by bridging. There is an optimum amount of ground-surveyed photo control, however, which affords maximum economic benefit from bridging, and at the same time maintains a satisfactory standard of accuracy. On the average, if a strip of photos is to be bridged for the purpose of obtaining control for orienting stereomodels in a stereoplotter, a minimum of about two horizontal and four vertical ground-surveyed photo control points should appear in approximately every fifth

$\triangle$ Horizontal control point

$\bigcirc$ Vertical control point

$\textcircled{\triangle}$ Horizontal and vertical control point

FIGURE 11-2
Example control configuration for bridging a strip.

stereomodel along the strip. This configuration is shown in Fig. 11-2. For bridging blocks of photos, the ground-surveyed control should be systematically arranged throughout the block. Best control configurations consist of horizontal control along the periphery of the block with a uniform distribution of vertical control throughout the block. Experience generally dictates the best control configurations to use, and organizations involved in bridging normally develop their own standards which meet accuracy requirements for their particular combination of procedure, instruments, and personnel.

11-4 PLANNING THE CONTROL SURVEY

A great deal of planning should precede the photogrammatric control survey. A decision must be made early on required accuracy of the survey. The type of equipment needed and the field techniques to be used must also be settled. These aspects and many more are interrelated and must be considered simultaneously in reaching the best overall control survey plan. Previous experience in planning photogrammetric control surveys is a most valuable asset. A thorough understanding of surveying field techniques and a knowledge of instrument capabilities are also essential.

The accuracy required in any photogrammetric control survey will govern, to a large extent, the type of equipment and surveying techniques that can be used. Required accuracy of photo control depends primarily upon the accuracy required in the photogrammetric map or computation that it controls. This is not the only consideration, however, as accuracy may also depend upon whether the control will serve other purposes in addition to controlling the photogrammetric work. As an example, suppose a map is to be prepared by photogrammetric techniques for the purpose of planning and designing an urban transportation system. In that case the basic ground control should be accurate enough to also be used in describing property for right of way acquisition and to serve in precisely laying out the construction alignment, structures, etc. In this example the basic ground control should at least meet second-order standards and it should be referenced to the state plane coordinate system. Basic horizontal control points and bench marks should be permanently monumented and well described. If on the other hand, a map is being prepared photogrammetrically for purposes of forest inventory, not nearly so accurate a control survey is required; in fact, control taken directly from U.S. Geological Survey quadrangle maps is sometimes adequate.

The *national map standards of accuracy* govern accuracy requirements of maps, and therefore indirectly also govern control surveying accuracy. These standards require that 90 percent of the principal planimetric features be plotted to within $\frac{1}{30}$ inch of their true positions for map scales of 1:20,000 or larger, and to within $\frac{1}{50}$ inch for scales smaller than 1:20,000. On a map plotted at a scale of 1 inch to 50 feet, this represents an allowable horizontal map error of 1.6 feet on the ground. On a map at a scale of 1 inch to 2,000 feet, allowable horizontal map error is 40 feet. If national map accuracy standards are to be met, horizontal photo control must be located to better accuracy than the allowable horizontal map error. As a general rule of thumb, photo control should contain error no greater than one-half the horizontal map accuracy tolerance, e.g., no more than 0.01 inch at map scales of 1:20,000 or larger. Of course basic control must be more accurate than photo control.

National map standards of accuracy also require that 90 percent of all points tested for elevation be correct to within half the contour interval. A rule of thumb in topographic mapping states that elevations of vertical photo control points should be correct to within plus or minus one-fifth of the contour interval. According to this rule, a map being plotted with a contour interval of 10 feet requires vertical photo control accurate to within ± 2.0 feet. Of course the basic control must be more accurate than ± 2.0 feet.

A separate set of accuracy standards have been developed for highway mapping by photogrammetric methods. These are published by the Federal Highway Administration in the *Reference Guide Outline*, a reference cited at the end of this chapter. This publication also contains a great deal of other information relative to establishing ground control for aerial photography.

In planning the control survey, maximum advantage should be taken of existing control in the area. The National Geodetic Survey has established numerous first- and second-order triangulation monuments, traverse stations, and bench marks in their work of extending the national control network. The U.S. Geological Survey has also established a network of reliable horizontal and vertical control monuments in their topographic mapping operations. All this control can be trusted to be of high caliber.

Caution should be exercised in using other existing control of unknown accuracy, however.

In some locations, particularly in urban areas, rather dense networks of control exist. These may serve as basic control for originating field surveys to establish photo control. In some cases existing monuments can be targeted prior to flight so that their images appear on the photos; hence they may serve as photo control points themselves. Descriptions of their existing control in any area may be obtained from the National Geodetic Survey and the U.S. Geological Survey.

11-5 GROUND COORDINATE SYSTEMS FOR HORIZONTAL CONTROL

Horizontal control surveys consist of field measurements necessary for computing relative horizontal positions of points on the surface of the earth. These relative positions may be computed either in a *geodetic* coordinate system or a *plane* rectangular system. Positions of points in a geodetic coordinate system are expressed in terms of latitude and longitude. Geodetic coordinates have the advantage that relative positions of widely spaced points are not in error due to earth curvature; a situation which cannot be avoided in using plane rectangular coordinate systems. The mathematics of computing geodetic coordinates is quite complicated, however, and therefore special plane rectangular coordinate systems called *state plane coordinate* systems have been developed.

State plane coordinate systems retain the simplicity of plane rectangular coordinate computation yet permit coverage of large areas without introducing errors greater than one part in 10,000 between actual mean sea level distances and their equivalent distances as represented in the state plane coordinate systems. This has been accomplished by breaking the entire United States into numerous zones and limiting zone sizes. Contiguous zones overlap, and therefore calculations for surveys of large extent are readily carried from one zone to another.

State plane coordinates of any point can be computed from the latitude and longitude of the point, and conversely latitude and longitude of any point can be calculated given its state plane coordinates. The National Geodetic Survey has published tables containing the information necessary for computing positions of points in state plane coordinate systems. These tables are published in booklet form; a separate booklet being available for each of the 50 states.[1]

State plane coordinates have been computed for all triangulation and traverse stations of the National Control Network. State plane coordinates of new points may be established from surveys originating on these monuments. Because of their advantage of

[1] Available from the Superintendent of Documents, U.S. Government Printing Office, Washington, D.C., 20402.

simplicity of computation, together with the capability of wide coverage without significant loss in accuracy from earth curvature, state plane coordinates are the most commonly used reference ground coordinate systems for photogrammetric work in the United States.

For projects of a limited size, local plane rectangular coordinate systems which are related to an arbitrary or imaginary datum have sometimes been used. These arbitrary coordinate systems should be avoided, however, because they are unrelated to latitude and longitude or to any other absolute coordinate system.

Both geodetic and state plane coordinate systems are described in detail in the textbooks on surveying and geodesy cited at the end of this chapter, and students interested in further study in these areas should consult them.

11-6 VERTICAL DATUMS

Vertical positions or elevations of points in object space are given in terms of their vertical distances above or below some datum surface. The most commonly adopted vertical datum is *mean sea level,* although on some projects arbitrary datums have been used. Local vertical datums, for example, have been adopted by some United States cities. Their future use should be discouraged as much as possible, however, because they are not related to mean sea level and their use frequently causes confusion and leads to mistakes.

In the United States mean sea level has been determined on the basis of many years of observations at tidal gaging stations. These are located along the Pacific and Atlantic Oceans and the Gulf of Mexico. A general adjustment incorporating the observed data of these stations was made in 1929, and hence the vertical datum in current use in the United States is referred to as the *National Geodetic Vertical Datum of 1929.*

A network of bench marks has been established throughout the nation by the National Geodetic Survey. These bench marks were set by precise spirit leveling and their elevations are based upon the sea level datum of 1929. Because spirit leveling generally followed roads and railroads, these bench marks are readily accessible to local surveyors.

11-7 FIELD METHODS FOR ESTABLISHING HORIZONTAL CONTROL

Instruments and techniques for field surveying are numerous and varied. In this text only a very brief discussion of some basic methods is presented. The textbooks on surveying listed as references at the end of this chapter provide a much more thorough treatment of these subjects.

Horizontal control surveys, both for basic control and for photo control, may be conducted using any one of three conventional field methods: *traversing, triangulation, or trilateration.* Of these methods, traversing is most common. Regardless of the method used, however, the survey must originate from some existing reference control in the proximity of the project area. Existing control normally consists of a minimum of two intervisible points whose horizontal positions (e.g., state plane coordinates) are accurately known. The direction (e.g., azimuth from north) of the line connecting reference points is also normally known.

Traversing, as illustrated in Fig. 11-3a, consists of measuring horizontal angles and horizontal distances between consecutive stations of a closed network. The existing reference control stations are included in the network. Angles are measured with a theodolite or transit, while distances may be measured electronically or by taping. Based on the existing reference direction and measured angles, directions of all traverse lines may be determined. From the known directions, coordinates of all new stations may be calculated trigonometrically in the same rectangular coordinate system of the existing reference control.

Triangulation involves precise measurement of one or more "base lines" such as B_1 and B_2 of Fig. 11-3b. All possible horizontal angles between intervisible stations are also carefully measured. Then coordinates of new stations may be calculated trigonometrically. Trilateration is similar in concept to triangulation except that no angles are measured. Rather, all possible horizontal distances between intervisible stations in the network are measured, as illustrated in Fig. 11-3c. In trilateration, distances are generally measured electronically. Coordinates of all new stations may be calculated based upon the measured distances.

For any horizontal control survey, an important task which must precede taking field measurements is establishment of the network of stations in the project area whose positions are to be determined. In basic control surveys, the stations will normally be artificial monuments such as wooden stakes or iron rods driven into the ground. These are carefully referenced to permanent nearby features so that they can be recovered at a later date if lost. In photo control surveys, some of the stations will be artificial monuments and some of them will be the natural features selected for photo control points.

The particular combination of instruments and techniques that should be used for the horizontal control survey will depend upon the conditions of each project. Existing topography or the presence of certain man-made features such as roads and railroads may render one procedure more economical than others. If the project area is rugged or perhaps covers a river valley with bluffs on either side, triangulation or trilateration may prove to be the best approach. Triangulation and trilateration may also be best if the area is rather flat and densely wooded, although in this case towers may be required to raise the instruments above the trees to achieve intervisibility between stations. If a road or railroad runs along a strip of photographs in an area which provides satisfactory image point locations in the photos, or if the area is flat or gently rolling and is rather open for

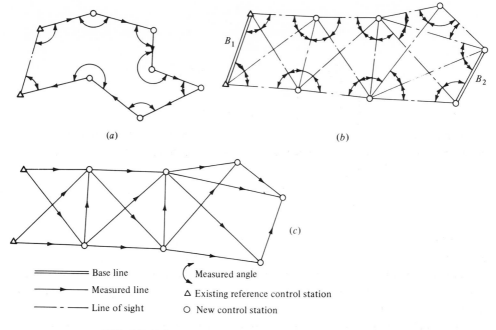

FIGURE 11-3
(a) Example of a traverse network. (b) Example of a triangulation network. (c) Example of a trilateration network.

also used stadia for low order accuracy

lines of sight, traversing may be most convenient. Accessibility of points, and surveying cost and convenience are aspects that must be kept in mind when originally selecting photo control images.

Accuracy required of photo control is another major consideration in deciding upon equipment and procedures to use. If a high accuracy standard for horizontal control is necessary, high standards of surveying will, of course, be required. Distance measurements by electronic means or by precise taping will be necessary, and angle measurements by precise theodolites will be required. Lower-order horizontal surveys may be adequately accomplished using rough taping or even stadia in some cases.

11-8   FIELD METHODS FOR ESTABLISHING VERTICAL CONTROL

For vertical control surveys, *spirit* or *differential* leveling is the most common field procedure, and where highest accuracy is required it is the method used. The basic equipment for spirit leveling is a leveling instrument and a graduated rod. A spirit level vial nearly filled with fluid is mounted on the leveling instrument. When the air bubble of

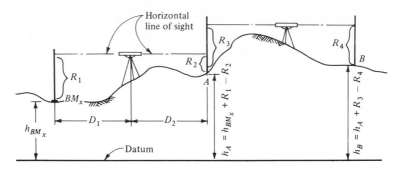

FIGURE 11-4
Spirit or "differential" leveling.

the vial is carefully centered, the telescopic line of sight is horizontal. The procedure of spirit leveling is illustrated in Fig. 11-4. The vertical control survey originates from a *bench mark* (monument of known elevation) such as BM_x. The elevation of BM_x above datum is h_{BM_x}. To establish the elevation of new point A, the leveling instrument is set up between BM_x and point A, the bubble is centered, and readings R_1 and R_2 are taken on the graduated rod held vertically at BM_x and A respectively. The elevation of point A is then equal to the elevation of BM_x, plus rod reading R_1, minus rod reading R_2.

To compensate for earth curvature and errors of atmospheric refraction of the line of sight, lengths D_1 and D_2 of sights to BM_x and A should be approximately equal. Then the magnitude of error from these sources will be equal in readings R_1 and R_2, and since the error is added in R_1 and subtracted in R_2, it is eliminated. With the elevation of point A known, the elevation of point B may be established by setting the instrument between A and B and taking rod readings R_3 and R_4. The elevation of B is then equal to the elevation of A plus rod reading R_3, minus rod reading R_4. This process is continued until elevations have been determined for all desired points. The leveling circuit should terminate on either the initial bench mark or on some other bench mark so that adjustments can be made for errors that accumulated in the rod readings.

Another technique for determining differences in elevation is *trigonometric leveling.* It may be used where moderate accuracy is required and is especially well suited for rugged terrain. In trigonometric leveling, as illustrated in Fig. 11-5, vertical angle α and horizontal distance D or inclined distance S between two points A and B are measured. Then difference in elevation is either $\Delta h = D \tan \alpha$ or $\Delta h = S \sin \alpha$. The distance may be measured electronically or by taping, but electronic methods are generally most convenient. The vertical angle is measured with a theodolite. On long sights, to compensate for earth curvature and atmospheric refraction, the vertical angle should be measured from each station and averaged.

For small-scale mapping which requires only rough elevations, *barometric* leveling,

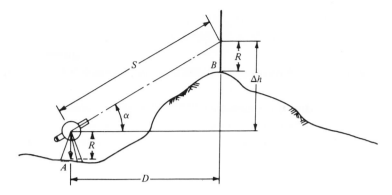

FIGURE 11-5
Trigonometric leveling.

airborne profile recording (APR) or *elevation metering* may provide satisfactory results. Barometric leveling is performed using two or more precise altimeters. The procedure can yield elevations having average errors less than 5 feet, and best accuracy is achieved during stable atmospheric conditions. An airborne profile recorder electronically determines a profile of the ground beneath the path of the aircraft in which it is carried. It is capable of achieving absolute elevations correct to within 10 feet, and it is particularly well adapted for use in inaccessible terrain. The elevation meter is a device attached to a wheeled vehicle which continually measures the inclination angle and length of travel as the vehicle moves. These parameters allow for an automatic recording to be made of differences in elevation from point to point. Accuracies to within plus or minus 2 feet have been obtained with this instrument.

11-9 AIRBORNE CONTROL SYSTEM

A unique system called the *Airborne Control System* ABC is in use by the U.S. Geological Survey for low-order horizontal and vertical control surveys. In this system, distances are measured electronically and horizontal and vertical angles are also measured by means of theodolites to a helicopter hovering over a station of unknown position and elevation. Measurements are taken from two or more established control points whose positions and elevations are known. The observations are taken while the pilot is aligned vertically above the unknown point by means of a special plumb line. The helicopter's distance above the point is read from graduations on the plumb line. This system is especially useful for small-scale mapping over rugged or inaccessible terrain.

11-10 ARTIFICIAL TARGETS

In some areas such as prairies, dense forests, deserts, etc., natural points suitable for photogrammetric control may not exist. In these cases artificial points called *panel points* may be placed on the ground prior to taking the aerial photography. Their positions are then determined by field survey or in some cases by photogrammetric control extension procedures. This procedure is called *premarking* or *paneling.*

Artificial targets provide the best possible photographic images, and therefore they are used for controlling the most precise photogrammetric work, whether or not natural points exist. Artificial targets are also used to mark section corners and boundary lines for photogrammetric cadastral work.

Besides their advantage of excellent image quality, their unique appearance makes misidentification of artificial targets unlikely. Disadvantages of artificial targets are that (1) extra work and expense are incurred in placing the targets, (2) the targets could be moved between the time of survey and the time of photography, and (3) the targets may not appear in favorable locations on the photographs. To guard against the second disadvantage, the photography should be obtained as near as possible to the time of the control survey. In order to obtain target images in favorable positions on the photographs, the coverage of each photo can be planned in relation to target locations, and the positions of ground principal points can be specified on the flight plan.

A number of different types of artificial targets have been successfully used for photogrammetric control. The main elements in target design are good color contrast, a symmetrical target that can be centered over the control point, and a target size that yields a satisfactory image on the resulting photographs. Contrast is best obtained using white targets against a black background. The target shown in Fig. 11-6 provides good symmetry for centering over the control point. The center panel of the target should be centered over the control point, since this is the image point to which measurements will be taken. The legs help in identifying targets on the photos, and they also help in determining the exact center of the target should the image of the center panel be unclear.

Target sizes must be designed on the basis of intended photo scale so that the target images are the desired size on the photos. An image size of about 0.03 millimeters to about 0.10 millimeters square for the central panel is generally ideal. As shown in Fig. 11-6, if the ground dimension of the central panel of the target is D, then the leg width should also be D, leg length should be $5D$, and the open space between the central panel and the leg should be D. Target sizes are readily calculated once photo scale and optimum target image size are selected. If, for example, a central panel size of 0.05 millimeters is desired and photography at a scale of 1:12,000 is planned, then D should be 2.0 feet.

Materials used for targeting are quite variable. In some cases satisfactory targets are obtained by simply painting white crosses on blacktop roads. In other cases targets are painted on plywood, masonite, or heavy cloth, in which case they may be salvaged and

FIGURE 11-6
Artificial photogrammetric target.

reused. Satisfactory targets have also been made by placing stones against an earth background in the shape of a cross. The stones may be painted white for added contrast. Lime placed in the shape of a cross against a dark background has also produced satisfactory targets. Old tires painted white are also good.

A procedure known as *post marking* can be performed if panel points are needed in an area after the photography has already been obtained. In this method, targets as described above are placed in the desired positions. Supplemental vertical photographs are taken of each target and its surrounding area with a small-format camera carried in a light aircraft flying at low altitude. Flying height can be calculated for the supplemental photography so that it has the same scale as the original photography. Locations of the targets can be transferred stereoscopically from the supplemental photography to the original photography using a point transfer device. Zoom magnification of the individual viewing systems of the point transfer device eliminates the need for having the scales of the supplemental and original photography equal.

11-11 INDEXING GROUND CONTROL *use alphabet or #'s*

For each project it is advisable to prepare a set of paper prints for indexing the ground control. This set of photos should be examined carefully and images of all control appearing on them should be identified from their field descriptions. When positive identification is made, the control point images should be lightly pricked with a pin to avoid the possibility of later misidentification mistakes; e.g., if a control point lies at a particular sidewalk intersection corner, pricking that corner will offset the possibility of mistakenly using a different corner at some later time simply because the written description was misinterpreted. The pinprick should just penetrate the emulsion and the pin should be held at right angles to the paper. Pricking should be done with the aid of a magnifying glass.

Control point images should be further marked by surrounding them with appropriate symbols, depending upon the type of control point. Triangles are commonly used to identify horizontal control points, while circles may be used for vertical control. A triangle inside a circle indicates both horizontal and vertical control on that point. Identifying numbers or names of control points should be written on the control photos beside the points. Some organizations have adopted numbering systems which correspond to the type of control point. As an example, vertical points may be given numbers from 1 to 999, horizontal points may be numbered from 1,000 to 1,999, and points of both vertical and horizontal control may be numbered from 2,000 to 2,999. Short written descriptions should be placed on the backs of the photos near the pinpricks. A set of control index photos carefully prepared can be a valuable asset in performing subsequent photogrammetric operations.

REFERENCES

American Society of Photogrammetry: "Manual of Photogrammetry," 3d ed., George Banta Co., Inc., Menasha, Wis., 1966, chap. 8.

Biege, R. R., Jr.: Photogrammetric Control Methods of the State Highway Commission of Kansas, *Surveying and Mapping,* vol. 29, no. 4, p. 679, 1969.

Bomford, G.: "Geodesy," 2d ed., Oxford University Press, Fair Lawn, N.J., 1962.

Brinker, R. C.: "Elementary Surveying," International Textbook Company, Scranton, Pa., 1969

Burger, T. D.: Use of the Elevation Meter in Topographic Mapping, *Surveying and Mapping,* vol. 21, no. 4, p. 481, 1961.

Danner, C. S.: Horizontal Control Problems in Private Practice, *Surveying and Mapping,* vol. 30, no. 2, p. 265, 1970.

Eckhardt, C. V.: Airborne Control for Topographic Mapping, *Surveying and Mapping,* vol. 26, no. 1, p. 49, 1966.

Federal Highway Administration: Reference Guide Outline, *Specifications for Aerial Surveys and Mapping by Photogrammetric Methods for Highways,* U.S. Dept. of Transportation, Washington, D.C., 1968.

Halliday, J.: The Vital Communications Link–Photoidentification of Horizontal Control, *Photogrammetric Engineering,* vol. 29, no. 5, p. 804, 1963.

Lee, D. R.: Vertical Control for Mapping the Okefenokee Swamp, *Surveying and Mapping,* vol. 27, no. 1, p. 73, 1967.

Loving, H. G.: Airborne Control System, *Surveying and Mapping,* vol. 23, no. 1, p. 91, 1963.

O'Leary, W. V.: A New Development Program for the Airborne Profile Recorder, *Photogrammetric Engineering,* vol. 29, no. 5, p. 872, 1963.

Theurer, C.: Control for Photogrammetric Mapping, *Photogrammetric Engineering,* vol. 23, no. 2, p. 318, 1957.

Thompson, M. M., and G. H. Rosenfeld: Map Accuracy Specifications, *Surveying and Mapping,* vol. 31, no. 1, p. 57, 1971.

Schwieder, W. H.: Laser Terrain Profiler, *Photogrammetric Engineering,* vol. 34, no. 7, p. 658, 1968.

VanWijk, M. C.: Test Areas and Targeting in the Hull Project, *Canadian Surveyor,* vol. 25, no. 5, p. 514, 1971.

Watts, R. G.: Simplicity of State Plane Coordinate System in Surveying, *Surveying and Mapping,* vol. 25, no. 4, p. 543, 1965.

PROBLEMS

11-1 Explain the difference between basic control and photo control.

11-2 Describe the characteristics of good horizontal photo control points.

11-3 Describe the characteristics of good vertical photo control points.

11-4 State the national map standards of accuracy for both horizontal positions and elevations.

11-5 What are the photographic dimensions in millimeters of a 30-inch-diameter manhole cover if photo scale is 1:6,000?

11-6 Describe the three conventional field methods used in horizontal control surveys.

11-7 Name the different field techniques used in establishing vertical control.

11-8 Discuss the advantages and disadvantages of using artificial targets as opposed to using natural images.

11-9 What must be the ground dimension D (see Fig. 11-6) of artificial targets if their corresponding photo dimension is to be 0.05 mm on photos exposed from 12,000 feet above ground with a 152-mm focal length camera?

11-10 The problem is similar to Prob. 11-9 except that photo dimension is 0.03 mm, flying height above ground is 8,000 feet and the camera focal length is 210 mm.

12

AERIAL MOSAICS

12-1 INTRODUCTION

An aerial mosaic is an assemblage of two or more individual overlapping photographs to form a single continuous picture of an area. The assembly is made by cutting and piecing together parts of photographs, being careful to make common images coincide as closely as possible at the match lines between adjacent photos. Mosaics are most commonly constructed from vertical aerial photos, although oblique photographs and terrestrial photographs have also been used. Well-constructed mosaics have the general appearance of a single enormous photograph. Figure 12-1 is an aerial mosaic of the entire San Francisco Bay area. More than 2,000 photos were assembled in producing this mosaic.

Mosaics are similar to maps in many respects and are frequently used as map substitutes. Mosaics have a number of advantages over maps. They show relative planimetric locations of an infinite number of objects. The objects are easily recognized by their pictorial qualities, whereas objects on maps—which are shown with symbols—must be limited in number. Mosaics of large areas can be prepared in much less time and at considerably lower cost than maps. Mosaics are easily understood and interpreted by people without photogrammetry or engineering backgrounds. For this reason mosaics are

FIGURE 12-1
Semicontrolled mosaic showing entire San Francisco Bay area. This mosaic consists of over 2,000 individual aerial photographs. (*Copyright photo, Courtesy Pacific Resources, Inc.*)

very useful in describing proposed construction or existing conditions to members of the general public, who would probably be confused by the same representations on a map.

Mosaics have the one serious disadvantage that they are not true planimetric representations. Rather, they are an assembly of numerous individual photographs, each of which is subject to image displacements and scale variations. The most serious image displacements and scale variations are caused by variations in the terrain elevation, tilting of the camera axis, and variations in the flying heights. Of course, some distortions result from shrinkage or expansion of the photo papers. Other small distortions, which are negligible for mosaics, are caused by film shrinkage or expansion and camera lens imperfections.

The effects of tilt and flying height variations can be eliminated by rectifying the photographs and ratioing them to a common scale. (This procedure is described in Sec. 13-14.) Rectification does not remove effects of topographic relief, however, and as a result the scale of a mosaic is never constant throughout unless the area shown is perfectly flat. Relief displacements can be minimized by using a high flying height, while at the same time the decrease in scale is compensated for by using a longer focal length camera. In measuring distances or directions from a mosaic, it must be remembered that, due to image displacements, the scaled values will not be true. Mosaics are often used for qualitative studies only, and in that case slight planimetric inaccuracies caused by image displacements are of little consequence.

12-2 USES OF MOSAICS

Because of their many advantages, mosaics are widely used. Their value is perhaps most appreciated in the field of planning, both in land-use planning and in planning for engineering projects. Mosaics which show an area completely and comprehensively can be rapidly and economically prepared. All critical features in the area which could affect the project can then be interpreted and taken into account. Alternate plans can be conveniently investigated, including considerations of soil types, drainage patterns, geologic features, land-use and associated right of way costs, etc. As a result of this type of detailed study, the best overall plan is finally adopted.

Mosaics are valuable in numerous other miscellaneous areas besides planning. They are used to study geologic features, to inventory natural resources, to record growth of cities and large institutions, to record construction activities at intervals of time, to record property boundaries, etc. Mosaics are used as planimetric map substitutes for many engineering projects. Highway departments, for example, that are engaged in preparing plans for extensive construction projects frequently use mosaics to replace topographic surveys. This not only eliminates most of the ground surveying but also does away with the painstaking procedure of plotting the planimetry in the office. Design drawings and construction specifications are superimposed directly over the mosaic. Mosaics used in this manner have resulted in a tremendous saving in time and cost with no significant loss of accuracy.

12-3 KINDS OF MOSAICS

Aerial mosaics generally fall into three classes: (1) *controlled,* (2) *semicontrolled,* and (3) *uncontrolled.* A controlled mosaic is the most accurate of the three classes. It is prepared from photographs which have been rectified and ratioed, i.e., all prints are made into equivalent vertical photographs which have the same scale. On the base board upon which the assembly will be laid, the horizontal positions of control points are plotted at the same scale as ratioed photo scale. The images of the control points must be recognizable on the photos. The coordinates of the ground control points may be obtained by field survey, by radial-line triangulation (see Chap. 9), or by other photogrammetric control extension procedures (see Chap. 18). The mosaic is laid by matching the control point images to their respective plotted positions on the base board. In spite of the precautions taken in preparing controlled mosaics, images of adjacent photographs will not match perfectly, nor will the scale of the mosaic be constant. Relief displacement is the chief reason for this condition. For certain small-scale controlled mosaic preparation, existing maps such as U.S. Geological Survey quadrangle maps may be used to provide the control. In this procedure the photos are ratioed to map scale. (If desired, map scale can first be altered to a convenient size by photographic enlargement or reduction.) The map is pasted to the mounting board and the mosaic is assembled by mounting the photos so that recognizable photo images coincide with their corrresponding map positions.

An uncontrolled mosaic is prepared by simply matching the image details of adjacent photos. There is no ground control, and vertical photographs which have not been rectified or ratioed are used. Uncontrolled mosaics are more easily and quickly prepared than controlled mosaics. They are not as accurate as controlled mosaics, but for many qualitative uses they are completely satisfactory.

Semicontrolled mosaics are assembled utilizing some combination of the specifications for controlled and uncontrolled mosaics. A semicontrolled mosaic may be prepared, for example, by using ground control but using photos that have not been rectified or ratioed. The other combination would be to use rectified and ratioed photos but no ground control. Semicontrolled mosaics are a compromise between economy and accuracy. The mosaic of Fig. 12-1 is a semicontrolled mosaic prepared from unrectified photos but assembled to fit U.S. Geological Survey quadrangle maps.

Mosaics are frequently categorized according to their use. In this type of classification are the *index* mosaic and *strip* mosaic. An index mosaic, or *photo index* as it is sometimes called, is illustrated in Fig. 12-2. It is an uncontrolled mosaic which has

FIGURE 12-2
Example of a "photo-index" or index mosaic.

been laid to very rough specifications. Its purpose is to serve as an index for correlating photo numbers and photo coverages. A quick check of the index mosaic makes it possible to determine which photos must be retrieved from the files to cover a particular area of interest. An index mosaic is assembled as soon as possible after the flight. In preparing them, no cutting or trimming of the photos is necessary. The assembly is made by matching images, being careful to keep the numbers of all photos clearly visible. A convenient method of assembling an index mosaic is to staple the photos to a fiber board such as Celotex. Upon completion, the assembly is photographed, and reduced prints are made for distribution. By assembling the index mosaic as soon as possible after the project, the photographic coverage of the project can be checked. Any gaps or missed areas will be visible, and arrangements can be made immediately for any necessary reflights.

A strip mosaic is the assembly of a series of photographs along a single flight strip. Strip mosaics are extremely useful in planning and designing linear engineering projects such as roads, railroads, pipelines, transmission lines, aqueducts, etc. Strip mosaics may be controlled, uncontrolled, or semicontrolled.

12-4 MATERIALS FOR PREPARING MOSAICS

The following materials are suggested for preparing mosaics:

Photographs For mosaic work, photographs should be taken with a minimum of about 60 percent end lap and 30 percent side lap. This makes it possible to use only the central portions of the photos, thereby reducing distortions due to relief and tilt. If the area is very flat, these percentages may be reduced; and if the area is rugged, they may be increased somewhat. The photographs should be printed on single-weight paper, and special care should be exercised in developing and printing to obtain uniform tones on all photos. This will result in an overall uniform tone on the mosaic.

Mounting boards These are the surfaces upon which the mosaic is to be laid. Mounting boards should have a smooth, hard, nonporous surface. Masonite makes an excellent mounting surface. Plywood may also be used, although it should be thoroughly moistened prior to laying the mosaic. Mounting boards should be large enough to accommodate the entire area of the assembly. After the mosaic has been completed and photographed for reproduction, the mounting board may be cleaned by soaking in water. In this manner it may be used repeatedly.

Adhesive Gum arabic is the most commonly used adhesive for mosaic construction. It is a slow-drying adhesive and therefore allows ample time for adjusting and shifting the prints to match images. Gum arabic adhesive may be purchased ready-mixed, or it may be mixed from ingredients according to the following recipe: Add $5\frac{1}{2}$ pounds of gum acacia to one gallon of warm water ($160°$ F). Stir until dissolved. Add 1 tablespoon of salicylic acid to serve as a preservative and $\frac{1}{2}$ pound of glycerine to prevent brittleness. The mixture should be thoroughly stirred, strained through a cloth or fine screen to remove lumps and foreign particles, and stored in large bottles until time of use. Another adhesive that is well suited for mosaic construction is made from a starch base. It is also slow-drying and can be purchased ready-mixed in bulk quantities.

Miscellaneous tools Among the tools useful in mosaic preparation are razor blades for cutting the photos, fine sandpaper for tapering match lines to a feather edge, a plastic squeegee for applying and removing the gum arabic, water and a water pail, sponges, drafting tape, and a touch-up kit for patching unavoidable image mismatches.

12-5 MOSAIC CONSTRUCTION

The definition of photogrammetry given in Sec. 1-1 implied that it was art as well as science. Mosaic construction is definitely one of those photogrammetric procedures where artistic capabilities may be utilized to advantage. Just as finger-painting is a messy procedure, mosaic preparation is also a messy task. Good-quality mosaic preparation requires a person who is not squeamish about getting his hands wet and covered with sticky adhesive. Because it is an art, a great deal of personal satisfaction can be derived from a successfully prepared mosaic.

The procedures of laying controlled and uncontrolled mosaics are essentially the same except for plotting control and matching corresponding photo images to that control. The following step-by-step procedure applies to the construction of an uncontrolled mosaic:

1) Lay out all the photographs on the mounting board so that common images overlap. Temporarily fasten them together with drafting tape to form a very crude mosaic. Shift the entire assembly so that it is centered on the mounting board and mark on the board the position of the center photo of the center strip. This photo will be laid first, and if it is laid in this marked position, the mosaic will be properly oriented on the board.

2) Remove the photos from the mounting board. Trim approximately $\frac{1}{2}$ inch from all four sides of the center photo of the center strip, tapering all four edges. This is done by lightly cutting through the emulsion with a razor blade as shown in Fig. 12-3. The sides to be discarded are torn off, using a downward twisting motion as shown in Fig. 12-4. If properly done, the edges of the central portion of the photo

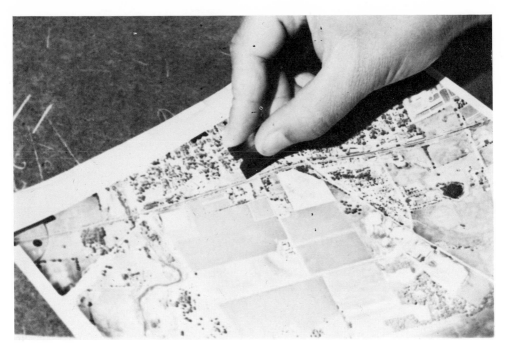

FIGURE 12-3
Making the razor cut.

should have approximately $\frac{1}{2}$-inch taper from full paper thickness to a feather edge. If a suitable taper is not obtained by tearing, light sanding with fine sandpaper may be necessary to obtain the desired feather edge. Tapering to a feather edge ensures the overall smooth appearance of the mosaic even though several layers of photos are mounted one on top of the other.

3) Moisten the mounting board, using a wet sponge. Apply adhesive in liberal amounts to both the back of the photo and to the mounting board. Place the first photo on the board in its premarked position and, with the fingers, rub it flat to the board. Remove all excess adhesive from on and under the photo with the squeegee, using firm strokes outward from the center of the photo as shown in Fig. 12-5. It is very important that all air bubbles be removed from under the photograph so that the mosaic lies flat. With a damp sponge, clean the working area in preparation for the next photo.

4) Place the second photo to be laid on the first photo with corresponding images overlapping. (The second photo can be the overlapping photo either left or right of the first photo laid.) Select the match line on the second photo along which the cut will be made. Match lines should be carefully chosen to obtain the best possible

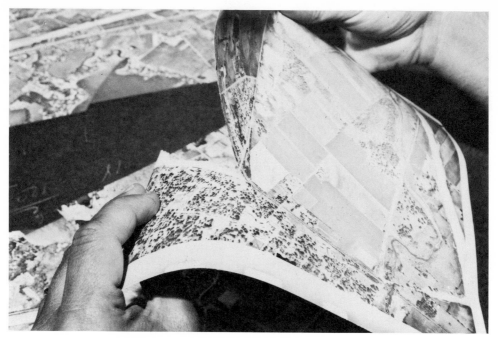

FIGURE 12-4
Carefully tearing a photo to obtain tapered edge.

matching of images and tones. If possible, they should be selected along roads, railroads, edges of fields, edges of roads, or other lines of definite tone demarcation. Avoid cutting at right angles to roads, railroads, etc., as this often creates noticeable mismatches in positions and tones. Match lines in the overlap of photos in the same strip should fall about midway between principal point and conjugate principal point, and match lines in the side lap between strips should fall approximately in the middle of the side lap. If match lines are selected in these general locations, only the central portions of photos actually show on the finished mosaic. Use of central areas minimizes image matching difficulties and produces a more uniform mosaic scale, since image displacements are minimal in these areas.

5) Using procedures of step 2, trim and taper the photo along the match line selected between the two photos. Also trim about $\frac{1}{2}$ inch from the other three sides of the photo and taper those edges.

6) Lay the second photo using procedures of step 3. In laying this and all remaining photos, particular care must be exercised to match images. In some cases all images cannot be matched, so that a best fit compromise is selected; but major features

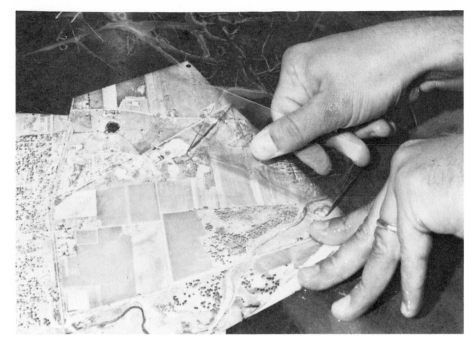

FIGURE 12-5
Using the squeegee.

whose mismatches would be most noticeable should be given preference in the compromise. If the photos are immersed in hot water, they may be stretched by small amounts to facilitate image matching. When gum arabic is used as the adhesive, the photos may be lifted and moved by small amounts for up to about 15 minutes after laying.

7) Continue laying photographs in a systematic procedure, progressing outward from the center photograph in all directions until the entire mosaic is laid. Figure 12-6a illustrates an overlapping five-photo strip prior to trimming, and Fig. 12-6b shows the general locations of the match lines and the order of laying the mosaic.

8) When the mosaic is completed, touchup any glaring image mismatches with a touch-up paint kit as shown in Fig. 12-7. A touch-up kit consists of a fine-pointed paintbrush and several colors of paint in shades of gray from black to white. With care in matching tones, it is possible to mask mismatches along roads, railroads, etc. Sometimes an area that should appear as one solid tone is so large that more than one photograph is required to cover it—e.g., large bodies of water. Unavoidable tonal variations from one photo to the next often cause such areas to appear

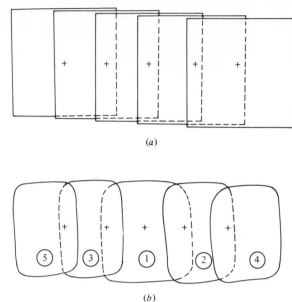

FIGURE 12-6

(a) Overlapping five-photo strip prior to trimming. (b) Strip mosaic illustrating match lines and order of laying photos.

patchy. In these cases the entire area may be painted a solid tone. The Pacific Ocean and San Francisco Bay in the mosaic of Fig. 12-1 were touched up in this manner.

12-6 AZIMUTH LINE METHOD

In constructing an uncontrolled mosaic by the procedures just described, tilt of the photos and topographic relief can cause cumulative mismatch errors which result in a twist or turn of the entire mosaic in one direction. By employing the *azimuth line* method, this objectionable twisting can be prevented. In this procedure, the photographs are first laid out and taped together in strips, matching corresponding images as carefully as possible by rapidly flipping the end lap areas up and down. A long straightedge is then placed over each strip so that it passes as nearly as possible through all photo centers, and a soft pencil line called an "azimuth line" is ruled across the photos. The strips are then disassembled and the lines are prolonged across the parts of the photos that were obscured by end lap.

A long straight line representing the azimuth line of the middle strip is drawn on

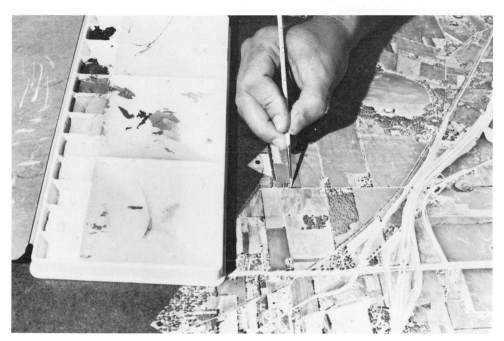

FIGURE 12-7
Final touch-up of a mosaic.

the mounting board. The middle strip is then laid by matching the azimuth line on the photos as closely as possible to the line on the board while at the same time matching image details as carefully as possible. If the mosaic consists of more than one strip, a straight line representing the azimuth line of the next side-lapping strip is drawn in its proper position on the mounting board. Proper position for the line is found by overlaying onto the center strip (which has been laid) the side lap area of approximately every fifth photo of the next strip. With the images of a least two widely spaced points of average elevation carefully matched in the side lap, the end of the azimuth line in each photo is transferred to the mounting board. A long straight line is then drawn on the mounting board so that it passes as nearly as possible through all points marking the azimuth line. This procedure is continued until all strips have been laid.

12-7 ORTHOPHOTOMOSAICS

An *orthophotomosaic* is an assembly of two or more *orthophotos* to form a continuous picture of the terrain. As implied by their name, orthophotos are orthographic representations of the terrain. They are derived from vertical aerial photographs using a

FIGURE 12-8
A portion of an orthophotomosaic with elevation contours superimposed.
(*Courtesy USDA Soil Conservation Service*)

differential rectification instrument. The method of producing orthophotos is discussed in detail in Chap. 15.

Orthophotos have had image displacements due to relief and tilt removed, so that they show features in their true planimetric positions. Distances, angles, and areas can therefore be measured directly from orthophotos just as from maps. Figure 12-8 shows a portion of an orthophotomosaic with elevation contours superimposed. In outward appearance it looks like an ordinary vertical aerial photograph with superimposed contours. Orthophotomosaics have the pictorial advantages of aerial mosaics and the geometric correctness of maps. In addition, they have the advantage that they can usually be prepared more rapidly and economically than line and symbol maps.

In general the procedures described in Sec. 12-3 for controlled mosaic assembly are used for assembling orthophotomosaics. In orthophotomosaic preparation, however, stable base materials (e.g., film) is generally used rather than paper base material as this maintains a higher degree of accuracy. Film orthopositives are carefully ratioed by scaling between control point images that appear in the orthonegatives. Because the ortho-positives have been ratioed and because they contain no distortions, very little difficulty should be encountered in matching corresponding images during mosaic assembly. In mosaic assembly with film base materials, featheredges must be sanded. Also, beeswax has been found to be the best adhesive.

12-8 REPRODUCTION

Prior to photographing for reproduction, a border and a title block are usually placed on the mosaic. The lettering of the title must be large enough to be visible at the intended reproduction size. The title is usually printed on white paper and then pasted onto the mosaic. It may also be desirable to add other information to the mosaic, such as grid lines or annotations of principal places or features. As shown in Fig. 12-8, contours may also be superimposed. If the average scale of the mosaic is given, it should be shown graphically so that it remains applicable for any reproduction size.

Reproduction of mosaics may be considered as a two-step process of (1) photographing the original mosaic with a copy camera to obtain a negative and (2) production of prints from the negative. Copy cameras used in step 1 are large, sometimes having focal planes with dimensions as great as 4 feet square. Copy cameras normally contain an easel plane upon which the object to be photographed is mounted. The easel plane may be tilted with respect to the optical axis of the camera lens—a procedure necessary in rectification. For photographing a mosaic prepared from vertical photos, however, the easel plane should be perpendicular to the optical axis. Copy cameras are normally mounted on a track so that object distances can be easily varied. The focal planes of these cameras can also be moved with respect to the lens so that the lens formula, Eq. (2-5), can be satisfied for varying object distances.

After the mosaic has been photographed and the negative developed, reproductions may be made in one of several ways. If a small number of copies are needed, noninking reproduction methods may be most economical. One such method is photographic reproduction (exposing sensitized photo paper through the negative and then developing the positives in a darkroom process). Another noninking process in common use is the *ozalid* process. In this procedure, prints are made from halftone positives which have been prepared from the original negatives (see Sec. 3-13). If a large number of copies of the mosaic are needed, an inking process such as lithography will be most economical.

REFERENCES

American Society of Photogrammetry: "Manual of Photogrammetry," 3d ed., George Banta Co., Inc., Menasha, Wis., 1966, chap. 17.

McNeil, G. T.: The Wet Process of Laying Mosaics, *Photogrammetric Engineering,* vol. 15, no. 2, p. 315, 1949.

Meyer, D.: Mosaics You Can Make, *Photogrammetric Engineering,* vol. 28, no. 1, p. 167, 1962.

Moranda, P. B.: A Study of the Propagation of Errors in a Simplified Photographic Mosaic, *Photogrammetric Engineering,* vol. 26, no. 4, p. 582, 1960.

Rosenfield, G. H.: The Accuracy of Mosaics, *Photogrammetric Engineering,* vol. 21, no. 5, p. 670, 1955.

PROBLEMS

12-1 Discuss the advantages and disadvantages of aerial mosaics as compared to conventional line and symbol maps.

12-2 Outline some of the uses of aerial mosaics.

12-3 Name and describe the various kinds of mosaics.

12-4 What is an index mosaic and what is it used for?

12-5 Describe the "azimuth line" method of laying mosaics.

TILTED PHOTOGRAPHS

13-1 INTRODUCTION

In spite of level vials and other stabilizing equipment, in practice it is impossible to maintain the optical axis of the camera truly vertical. Unavoidable aircraft tilts cause photographs to be exposed with the camera axis tilted slightly from vertical, and the resulting pictures are called *tilted photographs*. If vertical photography is intended, the amount by which the optical axis deviates from vertical is usually less then $1°$ and it rarely exceeds $3°$.

Six independent parameters called the *elements of exterior orientation* express the *space position* and *angular orientation* of a tilted photograph. The space position is normally given by X_L, Y_L, and Z_L, the three-dimensional coordinates of the exposure station in a ground coordinate system. Z_L is commonly called H, flying height above datum. Angular orientation is the amount and direction of tilt in the photo. Three angles are sufficient to define angular orientation, and in this book two different systems are described: (1) the *tilt-swing-azimuth* system (*t-s-α*) and (2) the *omega-phi-kappa* system (*ω-φ-κ*). The omega-phi-kappa system possesses certain computational advantages over the tilt-swing-azimuth system, and it is therefore more popular. The tilt-swing-azimuth system, however, is more easily understood and shall therefore be considered first.

13-2 ANGULAR ORIENTATION IN TILT, SWING, AND AZIMUTH

In Fig. 13-1, a tilted photograph is depicted showing the tilt-swing-azimuth angular orientation parameters. In the figure, L is the exposure station and o is the principal point of the photo positive. Ln is a vertical line, n being the *photographic nadir point* which occurs where the vertical line intersects the plane of the photograph. The extension of Ln intersects the ground surface at N_g, the *ground nadir point,* and it intersects the datum surface at N_d, the *datum nadir point.* Line Lo is the camera optical axis; its extension intersects the ground at P_g, the ground principal point, and it intersects the datum plane at P_d, the *datum principal point.* One of the orientation angles, *tilt*, is the angle t or nLo between the camera optical axis and the vertical line Ln. The tilt angle gives the magnitude of tilt of a photo.

Vertical plane Lno is called the *principal plane.* Its line of intersection with the plane of the photograph occurs along line *no,* which is called the *principal line.* The position of the principal line on the photo with respect to the reference fiducial axis system is given by s, the *swing* angle. "Swing" is defined as the clockwise angle measured in the plane of the photograph from the positive y axis to the downward or nadir end of the principal line, as shown in Fig. 13-1. The swing angle gives the direction of tilt on the photo.

The third angular orientation parameter, α or *azimuth*, gives the orientation of the principal plane with respect to the ground reference axis system. Azimuth is the clockwise angle measured from the ground Y axis (usually north) to the *datum principal line, N_dP_d.* Azimuth is measured in the datum plane or in a plane parallel to the datum plane. The three angles of tilt, swing, and azimuth completely define the angular orientation of a tilted photograph in space. If the tilt angle is zero, the photo is vertical. Thus a vertical photograph is simply a special case of the general tilted photograph.

13-3 AUXILIARY TILTED PHOTOCOORDINATE SYSTEM

In the tilt-swing-azimuth system, certain computations require the use of an auxiliary $x'y'$ rectangular photographic coordinate system. This system, as shown in Fig. 13-2a, has its origin at the photographic nadir point n and its y' axis coincides with the principal line (positive in the direction from n to o). Positive x' is $90°$ clockwise from positive y'. In solving tilted photo problems in the tilt-swing-azimuth system, photocoordinates are usually first measured in the fiducial coordinate system described in Sec. 5-2 and then converted to the auxiliary system numerically.

For any point in a tilted photo, the conversion from the xy fiducial system to the $x'y'$ tilted system requires (1) a rotation about the principal point through the angle θ

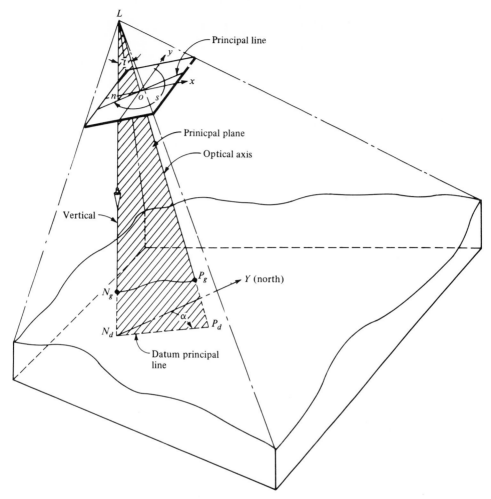

FIGURE 13-1
Geometry of a tilted photograph showing tilt-swing-azimuth angular orientation.

and (2) a translation of origin from o to n. The rotation angle θ is defined as:

$$\theta = s - 180° \qquad (13\text{-}1)$$

The coordinates of image point a after rotation are x'_a and y''_a, as shown on Fig. 13-2a. These are calculated using the following rotation equations:

$$x'_a = x_a \cos \theta - y_a \sin \theta$$
$$y''_a = x_a \sin \theta + y_a \cos \theta$$

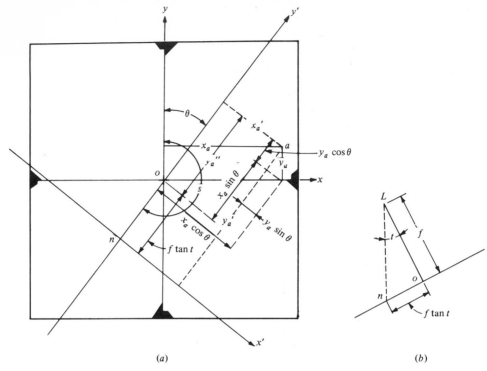

FIGURE 13-2
(a) Auxilliary $x'y'$ image coordinate system for a tilted photo. (b) Principal plane of a tilted photo.

The components of the above two rotation equations are illustrated in Fig. 13-2a. Auxiliary coordinate y'_a is obtained by adding the translation distance on to y''_a. From Fig. 13-2b, which is a view of the principal plane, on is $f \tan t$. Therefore the coordinates of a point in the required auxiliary coordinate system are

$$x'_a = x_a \cos \theta - y_a \sin \theta$$
$$y'_a = x_a \sin \theta + y_a \cos \theta + f \tan t \tag{13-2}$$

13-4 SCALE OF A TILTED PHOTOGRAPH

In Chap. 6 it was shown that scale variations in a vertical photograph are the result of variations in object distance (distance from camera to ground). The shorter the object distance, the larger the scale, and vice versa. For vertical photos, variations in object distances were caused only by topographic relief. In a tilted photograph, relief variations

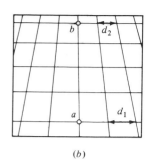

(a) (b)

FIGURE 13-3
(a) Principal plane of a tilted photo taken over flat ground. (b) Image on the tilted photo of a square ground grid.

also cause changes in scale, but scale in various parts of the photo is further affected by the magnitude and angular orientation of the tilt. Figure 13-3a illustrates the principal plane of a tilted photograph taken over a square grid on flat ground. Figure 13-3b illustrates the appearance of the grid on the resulting tilted photograph. Due to tilt, object distance LA in Fig. 13-3a is less than object distance LB and hence a grid line near A would appear larger (at a bigger scale) than a grid line near B. This is illustrated on Fig. 13-3b where photo distance d_1 appears longer than photo distance d_2, yet both are the same length on the ground.

The scale at any point on a tilted photograph is readily calculated if tilt and swing for the photograph and the elevation of the point are known. Figure 13-4 illustrates a tilted photo taken from a flying height H above datum. Lo is the camera focal length. The image of object point A appears at a on the tilted photo, and its photocoordinates in the auxiliary tilted photocoordinate system are x'_a and y'_a. The elevation of object point A above datum is h_A. Object plane $AA'KA''$ is a horizontal plane constructed a distance h_A above datum. Image plane $aa'kk'$ is also constructed horizontally. The scale relationship between the two parallel planes is the scale of the tilted photograph at point a because the image plane contains image point a and the object plane contains object point A. The scale relationship may be derived from similar triangles Lka' and LKA' as follows:

$$S_a = \frac{Lk}{LK} = \frac{ka'}{KA'} \qquad (a)$$

but

$$Lk = Ln - kn = f/\cos t - y'_a \sin t$$

also

$$LK = H - h_A$$

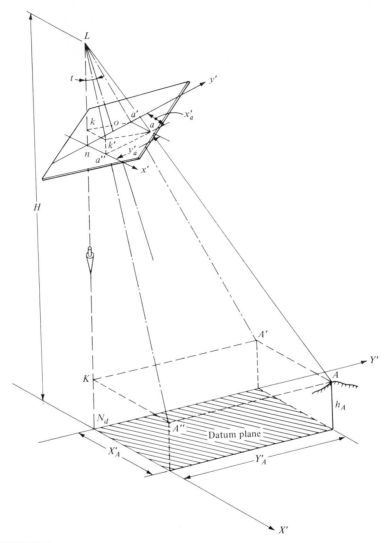

FIGURE 13-4
Scale of a tilted photo, and ground coordinate system.

Substituting Lk and LK into (a) and dropping subscripts:

$$S = \frac{f/\cos t - y' \sin t}{H - h} \qquad (13\text{-}3)$$

In Eq. (13-3), S is the scale on a tilted photograph for any point whose elevation is

h above datum. Flying height above datum for the photo is H, f is the camera focal length, and y' is the coordinate of the point in the auxiliary system calculated by Eq. (13-2). If the units of f and y' are inches and if H and h are feet, then the scale ratio is obtained in inches per foot. In examining Eq. (13-3), it is seen that scale increases with increasing terrain elevation. If the photo is taken over flat ground, then h is constant but scale still varies throughout the photograph with variations in y'.

EXAMPLE 13-1 A tilted photo is taken with a 6-in (152.4-mm) focal length camera from a flying height of 8,200 ft above datum. Tilt and swing are $2°\ 30'$ and $218°$ respectively. Point A has an elevation of 1,435 ft above datum, and its image coordinates with respect to the fiducial axis system are $x_a = -2.85$ in and $y_a = 3.43$ in. What is the scale at point a?

SOLUTION By Eq. (13-1);

$$\theta = s - 180° = 218° - 180° = 38°$$

By Eq. (13-2),

$$y'_a = -2.85(0.61566) + 3.43(0.78801) + 6.00(0.04366) = 1.21 \text{ in}$$

By Eq. (13-3),

$$S_a = \frac{6.00/0.99905 - 1.21(0.04362)}{8,200 - 1,435} = \frac{5.953 \text{ in}}{6,765 \text{ ft}} = \frac{1 \text{ in}}{1,140 \text{ ft}} \qquad\qquad ////$$

13-5 GROUND COORDINATES FROM A TILTED PHOTOGRAPH

If tilt and swing are known for a particular photograph, ground coordinates of any points appearing in the photograph may be calculated provided that their elevations are known. Ground coordinates are calculated in the unique $X'Y'$ rectangular coordinate system shown in Fig. 13-4. In this system the origin is at the datum nadir point, and the X' and Y' axes are in the same vertical planes and positive in the same directions as the x' and y' auxiliary photo axes respectively. In horizontal plane $aa'kk'$, distance $a'k$ is equal to y'_a $\cos t$. By proportionality of similar triangles LKA'' and Lkk',

$$\frac{KA''}{kk'} = \frac{LK}{Lk} \qquad\qquad (b)$$

Recognizing that $KA'' = X'_A$, $LK = H - h_A$, $kk' = x'_a$, and $Lk = f/\cos t - y'_a \sin t$, substituting into (b), and dropping subscripts, the following equation is obtained for the

X' ground coordinate of any point in a tilted photograph:

$$X' = \left(\frac{(H-h)}{f/\cos t - y' \sin t} \right) x' \qquad (13\text{-}4)$$

Also, by similar triangles LKA' and Lka',

$$\frac{KA'}{ka'} = \frac{LK}{Lk} \qquad (c)$$

Substituting $KA' = Y'_A$, $ka' = y'_a \cos t$, $LK = H - h_A$, and $Lk = f/\cos t - y'_a \sin t$ into (c) and dropping subscripts, the following equation is obtained for the Y' ground coordinate of any point in a tilted photograph:

$$Y' = \left[\frac{(H-h)}{f/\cos t - y' \sin t} \right] y' \cos t \qquad (13\text{-}5)$$

In Eqs. (13-4) and (13-5), X' and Y' are ground coordinates of any points appearing in a tilted photograph and all other terms are as previously defined. From X' and Y' ground coordinates, lengths of lines, angles, and areas can be calculated. Ground coordinates calculated by Eq. (13-4) and (13-5) are in the previously defined arbitrary coordinate system. However, if coordinates of two or more control points are also known in an absolute ground coordinate system (e.g., the state plane coordinate system) then coordinates of all points can be transformed from the arbitrary system into the absolute system using coordinate transformation equations described in Sec. B-2 of Appendix B.

EXAMPLE 13-2 Assume that image b of another object point B appears in the tilted photograph of Example 13-1, and that its measured photocoordinates with respect to the fiducial system are $x_b = 3.09$ in and $y_b = -1.78$ in. The elevation of B is 1,587 ft above datum. Calculate ground coordinates of A and B and the horizontal length of AB.

SOLUTION: By Eq. (13-2),

$$x'_a = -2.85(0.78801) - 3.43(0.61566) = -4.358 \text{ in}$$
$$x'_b = 3.09(0.78801) + 1.78(0.61566) = 3.531 \text{ in}$$
$$y'_b = 3.09(0.61566) - 1.78(0.78801) + 6.00(0.04366) = 0.762 \text{ in}$$
$$y'_a = 1.210 \text{ in (from Example 13-1)}$$

By Eq. (13-4) and (13-5),

$$X'_A = \frac{(8,200 - 1,435)(-4.358)}{6.00/0.99905 - 1.210(0.04362)} = \frac{6,765}{5.953}(-4.358) = -4,952 \text{ ft}$$

$$X'_B = \frac{(8,200 - 1,587)3.531}{6.00/0.99905 - 0.762(0.04362)} = \frac{23,350.5}{5.972} = 3,910 \text{ ft}$$

$$Y'_A = \frac{(8,200 - 1,435)1.210(0.99905)}{6.00/0.99905 - 1.210(0.04362)} = \frac{8,177.8}{5.953} = 1,374 \text{ ft}$$

$$X'_B = \frac{(8,200 - 1,587)0.762(0.99905)}{6.00/0.99905 - 0.762(0.04362)} = \frac{5,034.3}{5.972} = 843 \text{ ft}$$

From these coordinates length AB is found, using the pythagorean theorem, as follows:

$$AB = \sqrt{(3,910 + 4,952)^2 + (843 - 1,374)^2} = 8,878 \text{ ft} \qquad ////$$

13-6 RELIEF DISPLACEMENT ON A TILTED PHOTOGRAPH

Image displacements on tilted photographs caused by topographic relief occur much the same as they do on vertical photos. In Fig. 13-5, a is the image of an object point A. Point A' is in the datum plane vertically beneath A, and a' is its theoretical photographic position. Distance aa' is the image displacement due to the relief of point A. From geometry, it is known that two planes intersect along a straight line. Plane $LA''N_dA'A$ and the plane of the photograph intersect along line na. Planes $LA''N_dA'A$ and LN_dA' are coincident vertical planes because both contain the vertical line $LA''N_d$. Therefore plane LN_dA' intersects the plane of the photograph along line na'. Lines na and na' are coincident, and therefore aa' is along a radial line from n. The significance of the foregoing is that *relief displacements on tilted photographs occur along radial lines from the nadir point.* Relief displacements on a truly vertical photograph are also radial from the nadir point, but in that special case the nadir point coincides with the principal point.

On a tilted photograph, image displacements due to relief vary in magnitude depending upon flying height, height of object, amount of tilt, and location of the image in the photograph. Relief displacement is zero for images at the nadir point and increases with increased radial distances from the nadir.

In practice, tilted photos are nearly vertical and their nadir points are generally very near their principal points. Even for a photograph containing three degrees of tilt taken with a 6-inch focal length camera, distance *on* is only about 0.3 inches (8 millimeters). Relief displacements on tilted photos may therefore be calculated with satisfactory accuracy using Eq. (6-11) which applies to a vertical photograph. In using this equation, radial distances r are measured from the principal point, even though theoretically, they should be measured from the nadir point.

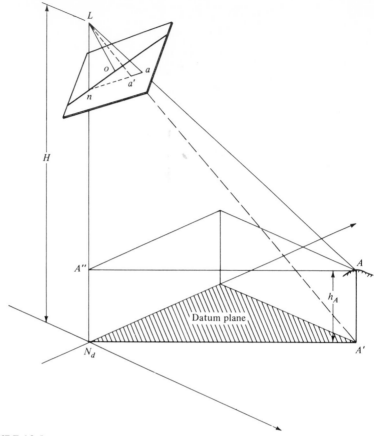

FIGURE 13-5
Relief displacement on a tilted photograph.

13-7 TILT DISPLACEMENT

Figure 13-6 illustrates the principal plane of a tilted photograph taken from exposure station L. Superimposed over the tilted photograph is an *equivalent vertical photograph*. An equivalent vertical photograph is an imaginary truly vertical photo taken from the same exposure station as the tilted photo with the same camera. The bisector of the tilt angle intersects the plane of the tilted photograph at point i, which is known as the *isocenter*. The line in the plane of the tilted photo, perpendicular to the principal line, and passing through the isocenter is called the *axis of tilt*. The axis of tilt is the line of intersection of the plane of the tilted photo and the plane of the equivalent vertical photo. Images along this line therefore have the same photographic positions in both photos. At all other locations in the tilted photo, image positions differ from their corresponding positions on the equivalent vertical photo.

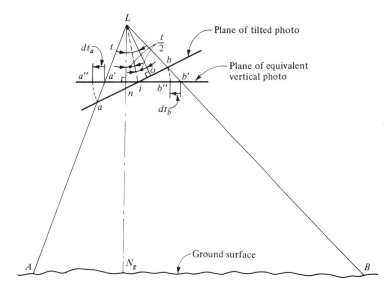

FIGURE 13-6
Tilt displacement in the principal plane of a tilted photograph.

Tilt displacement is the radial distance from the isocenter to an image on an equivalent vertical photo, minus the radial distance from the isocenter to the image on the tilted photo. In Fig. 13-6, a is the image of ground point A on a tilted photo and its image is at a' on the equivalent vertical photo. Point a'' is located in the plane of the equivalent vertical photograph such that distance $ia = ia''$. In this case tilt displacement is of magnitude dt_a, and it is outward from the isocenter. Similarly, images of ground point B occur at b and b' on the tilted and equivalent vertical photos respectively, and tilt displacement is inward toward the isocenter an amount dt_b. From this discussion it follows that tilt displacements are inward for images above the axis of tilt and outward for points below the axis of tilt. Tilt displacements occur even if the photo is taken over flat ground.

The amount of tilt displacement for any image on a tilted photo is given by

$$dt = \frac{(r_i)^2 \sin t \cos \lambda}{f - (r_i) \sin t \cos \lambda} \qquad (13\text{-}7)$$

In Eq. (13-7), dt is the amount of tilt displacement, r_i is the radial distance from the isocenter to the imaged point, f is the camera focal length, t is the tilt angle, and λ is the angle in the plane of the photograph between the principal line and the radial line from the isocenter to the imaged point. The algebraic sign of r_i is positive if the image lies above the axis of tilt and negative if it lies below. The units of dt will be the same as those used for r_i and f. The maximum value of λ is $90°$, which occurs when the point lies along the axis of tilt. When λ is $90°$ (i.e., for points on the axis of tilt), the numerator of Eq. (13-7) becomes zero and dt is therefore zero. This follows logically inasmuch as images on a tilted photo and its equivalent vertical photo coincide along the axis of tilt.

EXAMPLE 13-3 A photograph having a tilt of $3° 00'$ was exposed with a 152-mm focal length camera. Radial distance from the isocenter to a certain image point in the area above the axis of tilt measured 105 mm. The angle between the principal line and the radial line from the isocenter to the point was $40° 00'$. What is the tilt displacement for that image?

SOLUTION: By Eq. (13-7),

$$dt = \frac{(105)^2 (0.0523)0.7660}{152 - 105(0.0523)0.7660} = 3.0 \text{ mm}$$ ////

13-8 ANGULAR ORIENTATION IN OMEGA, PHI, AND KAPPA

As previously stated, besides the tilt-swing-azimuth system, angular orientation of a tilted photograph can also be expressed in terms of three rotation angles, *omega, phi,* and *kappa*. These three angles uniquely define the angular relationships between the three axes of the tilted photo (image) coordinate system and the three axes of the ground (object) coordinate system.

Figure 13-7 illustrates a tilted photo in space. The ground coordinate system is XYZ. The tilted photo image coordinate system is xyz (shown dashed), and its origin is at exposure station L. Consider an image coordinate system $x'y'z'$ with origin also at L and with its respective axes mutually parallel to the axes of the ground coordinate system, as shown in Fig. 13-7. As a result of three sequential rotations through the angles of omega, phi, and kappa, the $x'y'z'$ axis system can be made to coincide with the photographic xyz system. Each of the rotation angles omega, phi, and kappa is considered positive if counterclockwise when viewed from the positive end of the rotation axis.

The sequence of the three rotations is illustrated in Fig. 13-8. The first rotation, as illustrated in Fig. 13-8*a*, is about the x' axis through an angle omega. This first rotation creates a new axis system $x_1 y_1 z_1$. The second rotation phi is about the y_1 axis, as illustrated in Fig. 13-8*b*. As a result of the phi rotation a new axis system $x_2 y_2 z_2$ is created. As illustrated in Fig. 13-8*c*, the third and final rotation is about the z_2 axis through the angle kappa. This third rotation creates the xyz coordinate system which is the photographic image system. Equations which express these three rotations are developed in Sec. B-8 of Appendix B.

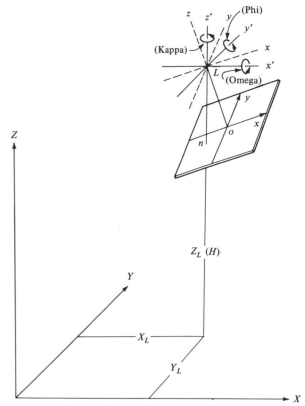

FIGURE 13-7
Orientation of a tilted photo in the omega-phi-kappa system.

For any tilted photo there exist a unique set of angles omega, phi, and kappa which explicitly define the angular orientation of the photograph with respect to the reference ground coordinate system. These three angles are related to the previously described tilt, swing and azimuth angles, and if either set of three orientation angles is known for any photo, the other three can be determined as described in Sec. C-8 of Appendix C. In the omega-phi-kappa system, as with the tilt-swing-azimuth system, the space position of any photo is given by the exposure station coordinates X_L, Y_L and Z_L (or H).

13-9 DETERMINING THE ELEMENTS OF EXTERIOR ORIENTATION

Many different methods, both graphical and numerical, are available for determining the six elements of exterior orientation of a tilted photograph. In general all methods require photographic images of at least three control points whose X, Y, and Z ground

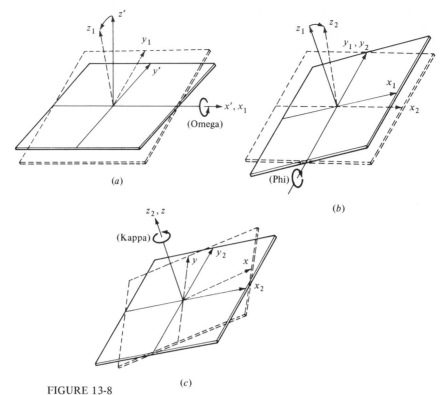

FIGURE 13-8
(*a*) Rotation about the x axis through angle omega. (*b*) Rotation about the y_1 axis through angle phi. (*c*) Rotation about the z_2 axis through angle kappa.

coordinates are known. Also the calibrated focal length of the camera must be known. Most procedures are iterative; i.e., a solution is obtained by successively making corrections to some initially assumed values for the unknown elements. All methods for determining the elements of exterior orientation are rather lengthy, but if one of the numerical procedures is programmed for an electronic computer, a solution is easily obtained.

In this text three methods for determining the elements of exterior orientation are considered: (1) the *Anderson scale-point* method, (2) the *Church* method, and (3) the method of *space resection by collinearity*. Students interested in studying other methods or in obtaining more details of the three methods presented herein are directed to references cited at the end of this chapter, principally Chap. 2 of the third edition of the *Manual of Photogrammetry*.

13-10 ANDERSON SCALE-POINT METHOD

The Anderson scale-point method is mainly a graphical procedure for determining tilt, swing, and flying height of a tilted photograph which requires only simple mathematics. When tilt, swing, and flying height have been determined, the remaining three elements of exterior orientation are readily calculated. The Anderson scale-point method cannot be applied to photos which are severely tilted. Also, because it is graphical, accuracy attainable with the method is limited. Since the emergence of the electronic computer, the Anderson scale-point method has had little practical value, and hence the method is only briefly discussed herein.

In the Anderson scale-point method three control lines must appear in the photograph whose tilt is being determined. An economical control configuration meeting that criterion is a large, nearly equilateral triangle. Relief displacements with respect to a selected "photo datum" (arbitrary datum chosen at the elevation of the lowest of the control points) are calculated for all control points. For these calculations, the photos are assumed to be vertical, relief displacement Eq. (6-11) is used, and radial distances r are measured from the principal point. *Photo datum positions* of the control images are then plotted by laying off the relief displacements along radial lines *toward* the principal point. The *photo datum scales* of the three lines are then calculated from the ratios of their measured *photo datum lengths* to their corresponding ground lengths. Since the image points have all been reduced to a common datum, the photo is truly vertical if the three scales are equal; otherwise tilt exists in the photo.

The amount and direction of tilt is a function of the magnitudes of the scale differences of the three lines and of the locations of the lines in the photograph. Based upon the scale differences, a graphical technique is applied to determine tilt, swing, and flying height. The procedure is described in references cited at the end of this chapter.

13-11 CHURCH METHOD

The late Professor Earl Church of Syracuse University developed various techniques for calculating the elements of exterior orientation of a tilted photograph. The method discussed herein is his two-part "space resection and space orientation" procedure. This method is applicable to oblique photographs as well as near verticals. Of available numerical techniques, it also requires perhaps the least amount of computation. The Church method is included within this text because it affords a precise numerical method of determining exterior orientation for students who do not have access to, or are not adept with electronic computers. If an electronic computer is available, however, the method of space resection by collinearity is recommended (see Sec. 13-12).

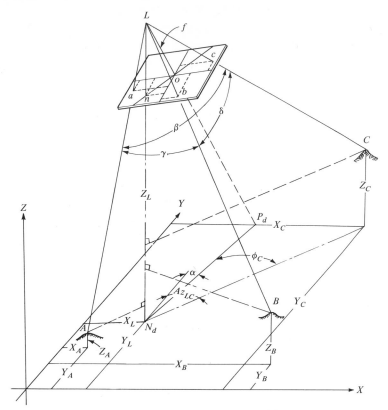

FIGURE 13-9
Control configuration for determining the elements of exterior orientation.

The two parts of the Church method consist of (1) determining the ground space coordinates of the exposure station and (2) determining the angular elements of orientation. In Fig. 13-9, images *a, b,* and *c* of ground control points *A, B,* and *C* appear in a tilted photo positive. Angles γ, δ, and β as shown in Fig. 13-9 have apexes at *L* and are the included angles between rays *LA, LB,* and *LC*. According to analytic geometry, the cosines of these angles are

$$\cos \gamma = \frac{(X_L - X_A)(X_L - X_B) + (Y_L - Y_A)(Y_L - Y_B) + (Z_L - Z_A)(Z_L - Z_B)}{(LA)(LB)}$$

$$\cos \delta = \frac{(X_L - X_B)(X_L - X_C) + (Y_L - Y_B)(Y_L - Y_C) + (Z_L - Z_B)(Z_L - Z_C)}{(LB)(LC)} \quad (13\text{-}8)$$

$$\cos \beta = \frac{(X_L - X_C)(X_L - X_A) + (Y_L - Y_C)(Y_L - Y_A) + (Z_L - Z_C)(Z_L - Z_A)}{(LC)(LA)}$$

In Eqs. (13-8), the X's, Y's and Z's are ground coordinates in feet (or meters) and LA, LB, and LC are the lengths of rays from the exposure station to the respective control points in feet (or meters). Ray lengths are calculated as $LA = \sqrt{(X_L - X_A)^2 + (Y_L - Y_A)^2 + (Z_L - Z_A)^2}$, etc.

Explicit values for $\cos \gamma$, $\cos \delta$, and $\cos \beta$, regardless of the tilt of the photograph, may be found with respect to focal length and photo image coordinates using the following similar analytic geometry equations:

$$\cos \gamma = \frac{x_a x_b + y_a y_b + f^2}{(La)(Lb)}$$

$$\cos \delta = \frac{x_b x_c + y_b y_c + f^2}{(Lb)(Lc)} \qquad (13\text{-}9)$$

$$\cos \beta = \frac{x_c x_a + y_c y_a + f^2}{(Lc)(La)}$$

In Eqs. (13-9), the x's and y's are image coordinates, f is focal length, and La, Lb, and Lc are lengths from the camera incident nodal point (exposure station) to the respective image points. The lengths are calculated as $La = \sqrt{x_a^2 + y_a^2 + f^2}$, etc., and are given in the same units as photocoordinates and focal length.

In the three Eqs. (13-8), having calculated $\cos \gamma$, $\cos \delta$ and $\cos \beta$ by Eqs. (13-9), there are only three remaining unknowns: X_L, Y_L, and Z_L. The equations may therefore be solved simultaneously to obtain the space position of the tilted photograph. Equations (13-8) are nonlinear, however, and therefore must be linearized. In this presentation Taylor's theorem is used for linearization. In using Taylor's theorem, initial estimates X_{L_o}, Y_{L_o}, and Z_{L_o} are made for the unknown exposure station coordinates, and corrections dX_L, dY_L, and dZ_L to be added to these initial estimates are calculated. (Taylor's theorem for linearizing nonlinear equations may be found in any standard textbook on differential calculus.) Applying Taylor's theorem to Eqs. (13-8) and rearranging, the following three linearized equations are obtained:

$$K_1 = a_{11} dX_L + a_{12} dY_L + a_{13} dZ_L$$
$$K_2 = a_{21} dX_L + a_{22} dY_L + a_{23} dZ_L \qquad (13\text{-}10)$$
$$K_3 = a_{31} dX_L + a_{32} dY_L + a_{33} dZ_L$$

In Eqs. (13-10), the a's (coefficients) and K's (constant terms) are defined as follows (zero subscripts signify that the estimated values for X_L, Y_L, and Z_L are used in the computation):

$$a_{11} = A_1 (X_L - X_B)_o + B_1 (X_L - X_A)_o$$
$$a_{12} = A_1 (Y_L - Y_B)_o + B_1 (Y_L - Y_A)_o$$
$$a_{13} = A_1 (Z_L - Z_B)_o + B_1 (Z_L - Z_A)_o$$

where

$$A_1 = \left[1 - \left(\frac{LA}{LB}\right)\cos\gamma\right]_o \quad \text{and} \quad B_1 = \left[1 - \left(\frac{LB}{LA}\right)\cos\gamma\right]_o$$

$$a_{21} = A_2(X_L - X_C)_o + B_2(X_L - X_B)_o$$

$$a_{22} = A_2(Y_L - Y_C)_o + B_2(Y_L - Y_B)_o$$

$$a_{23} = A_2(Z_L - Z_C)_o + B_2(Z_L - Z_B)_o$$

where

$$A_2 = \left[1 - \left(\frac{LB}{LC}\right)\cos\delta\right]_o \quad \text{and} \quad B_2 = \left[1 - \left(\frac{LC}{LB}\right)\cos\delta\right]_o$$

$$a_{31} = A_3(X_L - X_A)_o + B_3(X_L - X_C)_o$$

$$a_{32} = A_3(Y_L - Y_A)_o + B_3(Y_L - Y_C)_o$$

$$a_{33} = A_3(Z_L - Z_A)_o + B_3(Z_L - Z_C)_o$$

where

$$A_3 = \left[1 - \left(\frac{LC}{LA}\right)\cos\beta\right]_o \quad \text{and} \quad B_3 = \left[1 - \left(\frac{LA}{LC}\right)\cos\beta\right]_o$$

also

$$K_1 = [(LA)(LB)\cos\gamma - (X_L - X_A)(X_L - X_B) - (Y_L - Y_A)(Y_L - Y_B)$$
$$- (Z_L - Z_A)(Z_L - Z_B)]_o$$

$$K_2 = [(LB)(LC)\cos\delta - (X_L - X_B)(X_L - X_C) - (Y_L - Y_B)(Y_L - Y_C)$$
$$- (Z_L - Z_B)(Z_L - Z_C)]_o$$

$$K_3 = [(LC)(LA)\cos\beta - (X_L - X_C)(X_L - X_A) - (Y_L - Y_C)(Y_L - Y_A)$$
$$- (Z_L - Z_C)(Z_L - Z_A)]_o$$

Equations (13-10) are solved to obtain corrections dX_L, dY_L, and dZ_L. These corrections are added to X_{L_o}, Y_{L_o}, and Z_{L_o} to obtain improved estimates, and the procedure is repeated to determine new corrections to be added to the improved estimates. Iterations are continued until the corrections become negligible. The closer the initial estimates are to their true values, the faster a solution will be achieved. Usually if the estimates are carefully chosen, only two or three iterations will be necessary. If the photo is nearly vertical, initial estimates for X_L, Y_L, and Z_L are readily obtained as explained in Sec. 13-12.

Having completed the first part of the Church method, the remaining angular elements are readily determined. Expressions for the cosines of angles nLa, nLb, and nLc of Fig. 13-9, in terms of photographic nadir point coordinates x_n and y_n, photocoordinates of control points, and the camera focal length are:

$$(a) \quad \cos nLa = \frac{x_a x_n + y_a y_n + f^2}{(La)(Ln)}$$

$$(b) \quad \cos nLb = \frac{x_b x_n + y_b y_n + f^2}{(Lb)(Ln)} \qquad (13\text{-}11)$$

$$(c) \quad \cos nLc = \frac{x_c x_n + y_c y_n + f^2}{(Lc)(Ln)}$$

[Note that Eqs. (13-8), (13-9), and (13-11) are all similar and derived from the same analytic geometry equation for the cosine of an angle between two lines in space.] With X_L, Y_L, and Z_L known, explicit values for the cosines of angles nLa, nLb, and nLc may be calculated as follows (see Fig. 13-9):

$$\cos nLa = \frac{Z_L - Z_A}{LA}$$

$$\cos nLb = \frac{Z_L - Z_B}{LB} \qquad (13\text{-}12)$$

$$\cos nLc = \frac{Z_L - Z_C}{LC}$$

Rearranging Eqs. (13-11), eliminating Ln by equating (13-11a) to (13-11b), and equating (13-11b) to (13-11c), the following two equations result:

$$\left[\frac{x_a}{(La)\cos nLa} - \frac{x_b}{(Lb)\cos nLb} \right] x_n + \left[\frac{y_a}{(La)\cos nLa} - \frac{y_b}{(Lb)\cos nLb} \right] y_n$$

$$= \frac{f^2}{(Lb)\cos nLb} - \frac{f^2}{(La)\cos nLa}$$

$$\left[\frac{x_b}{(Lb)\cos nLb} - \frac{x_c}{(Lc)\cos nLc} \right] x_n + \left[\frac{y_b}{(Lb)\cos nLb} - \frac{y_c}{(Lc)\cos nLc} \right] y_n \qquad (13\text{-}13)$$

$$= \frac{f^2}{(Lc)\cos nLc} - \frac{f^2}{(Lb)\cos nLb}$$

In Eqs. (13-13) there are only two unknowns, x_n and y_n, and they may be determined by solving the equations simultaneously. Then, as can be seen from Fig. 13-10, the tilt angle is

$$t = \tan^{-1} \left(\frac{\sqrt{x_n^2 + y_n^2}}{f} \right) \qquad (13\text{-}14)$$

Also, with the nadir point located in the quadrant shown in Fig. 13-10, the swing

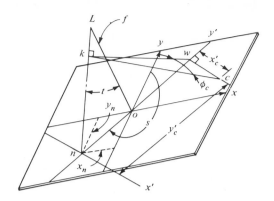

FIGURE 13-10
Tilt, swing, and azimuth by the Church
method.

angle may be calculated as

$$s = 180° + \tan^{-1}\left(\frac{x_n}{y_n}\right) \qquad (13\text{-}15)$$

It should be noted that Eq. (13-15) is not general, and the student must consider the quadrant in which the nadir point falls in order to determine swing properly. The final element of angular orientation is the azimuth of the principal line. In Fig. 13-10, plane kwc is constructed horizontal, therefore line cw is perpendicular to the principal line and is equal to x'_c. Also lines wk and ck are perpendicular to vertical line Ln. Horizontal angle ϕ_c is calculated as

$$\phi_c = \tan^{-1}\left(\frac{x'_c}{y'_c \cos t}\right) \qquad (13\text{-}16)$$

In Eq. (13-16), x'_c and y'_c are photocoordinates in the auxiliary tilted photocoordinate system as computed by Eqs. (13-2). From ground coordinates of the exposure station and of control point C, the azimuth of the ground line LC (see Fig. 13-9) is

$$Az_{LC} = \tan^{-1}\left(\frac{X_C - X_L}{Y_C - Y_L}\right) \qquad (13\text{-}17)$$

Finally the azimuth of the principal line, α, is calculated as:

$$\alpha = Az_{LC} - \phi_c \qquad (13\text{-}18)$$

(Note horizontal angle ϕ_c in the datum plane of Fig. 13-9.)

By using another control point, a check can be obtained for the azimuth of the principal line. As a final note on the Church method, correct algebraic signs must be applied to all photocoordinates and ground coordinates used in the equations.

13-12   SPACE RESECTION BY COLLINEARITY

The method of space resection by collinearity is a purely numerical method that simultaneously yields all six elements of exterior orientation. It is a versatile method enabling either the omega-phi-kappa or tilt-swing-azimuth angular elements to be determined. It also permits the use of redundant amounts of ground control; hence least squares computational techniques can be used to determine most probable values for the six elements.

Space resection by collinearity involves formulating the so-called *collinearity equations* for a number of control points whose X, Y, and Z ground coordinates are known and whose images appear in the tilted photo. The equations are then solved for the six unknown elements of exterior orientation which appear in them. The collinearity equations express the condition that for any given photograph the exposure station, any object point and its corresponding image all lie on a straight line. Figure 13-9 illustrates the collinearity condition that exists for each of three ground control points A, B, and C.

The mathematical development of the collinearity condition equations is given in detail in Appendix C. The basic equations are nonlinear and are linearized using Taylor's theorem. Collinearity equations of the linearized form [Eqs. (C-11) and (C-12) of Appendix C] can be written for each ground control point. Note, however, that since the object point coordinates of the control points are known, the unknowns dX_A, dY_A, and dZ_A drop out of Eqs. (C-11) and (C-12), hence the number of unknowns reduces to six, namely corrections $d\omega$, $d\phi$, $d\kappa$, dX_L, dY_L, and dZ_L. These are corrections to be applied to initial approximations for omega, phi, kappa, X_L, Y_L, and Z_L respectively. The linearized form of the space resection collinearity equations for a point A are

$$v_{x_a} = b_{11}\,d\omega + b_{12}d\phi + b_{13}d\kappa - b_{14}dX_L - b_{15}dY_L - b_{16}dZ_L + J \qquad (13\text{-}19)$$

$$v_{y_a} = b_{21}d\omega + b_{22}d\phi + b_{23}d\kappa - b_{24}dX_L - b_{25}dY_L - b_{26}dZ_L + K \qquad (13\text{-}20)$$

In Eqs. (13-19) and (13-20), the terms are as defined in Sec. C-4 of Appendix C. With two equations possible for each control point, a total of six equations are obtained from three control points. This system of equations is solved simultaneously for the six unknown corrections, and these corrections are then added to the initial values to obtain revised values. The solution is made again using the revised values as initial estimates, and new corrections are calculated. This procedure is iterated until the magnitudes of the corrections become negligible.

If more than three control points are available, then more than six equations can be formulated and their solution can be obtained by the method of least squares. If only three control points are available, the six equations that result afford a unique solution and therefore the residuals on the left-hand side of the equations, vx_a and vy_a, are zero.

After solving the collinearity equations iteratively and obtaining values for omega, phi, and kappa, values for tilt, swing, and azimuth (if they are desired) may be obtained.

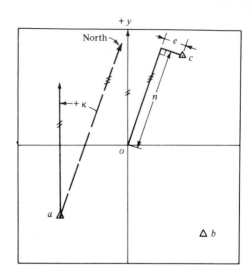

FIGURE 13-11
Graphical determination of initial approximations for determining the elements of exterior orientation.

The procedure for this conversion from omega, phi, and kappa to tilt, swing, and azimuth (or vice versa) is outlined in Sec. C-8 of Appendix C.

The use of Taylor's theorem in solving the collinearity equations requires initial approximations for all unknown elements of exterior orientation. These are easily obtained if the photos are nearly vertical. If a photo is assumed vertical, then the photo xy plane is parallel to the ground XY plane and values of zero may be taken for omega and phi. By plotting the direction of ground north on the photo, kappa may be estimated with sufficient accuracy by simply scaling the angle from ground north to the positive y photo axis. A counterclockwise angle is considered positive. In Fig. 13-11, for example, on the basis of ground coordinates of control points A and C, the direction of north is established and plotted from the image a of control point A. A line parallel to the y photo axis is also drawn from point a and angle kappa (counterclockwise and therefore positive) is measured. Usually a solution can be obtained if the initial approximations for omega, phi, and kappa are within about $10°$. It should be noted that corrections $d\omega$, $d\phi$ and $d\kappa$ in Eqs. (13-19) and (13-20) are in radian units and that initial values for omega, phi, and kappa must therefore also be in radians.

Initial values may be obtained for X_L and Y_L by scaling photo distances e (perpendicular to north) and n (parallel to north) from the principal point to a control point image such as c of Fig. 13-11. Then by multiplying e and n by average photo scale, incremental ground distances ΔX and ΔY are obtained as

$$\Delta X = e \, S_{avg}$$
$$\Delta Y = n \, S_{avg}$$

$$(13-21)$$

In Eqs. (13-21), if e and n are in inch units and S_{avg} is feet per inch, then ΔX and ΔY are in feet. By subtracting ΔX and ΔY from the X and Y ground coordinates of control point C, satisfactory values are obtained for X_L and Y_L, or:

$$
\begin{aligned}
X_L &= X_C - \Delta X \\
Y_L &= Y_C - \Delta Y
\end{aligned}
\qquad (13\text{-}22)
$$

An initial value for Z_L can be obtained by assuming a vertical photograph and solving the following modification of the scale equation:

$$
H = \left(\frac{AB}{ab}\right)f + h_{AB} \qquad (13\text{-}23)
$$

In Eq. (13-23), H (or Z_L) is flying height above datum, AB is the horizontal length of the ground control line, ab is its corresponding photo length, f is camera focal length, and h_{AB} is the average elevation of control points A and B.

13-13 POSITIONS OF NEW POINTS FROM MEASUREMENTS ON STEREOPAIRS OF TILTED PHOTOS

The collinearity equations may also be used to determine X, Y, and Z ground coordinates of new points whose images appear in the overlap area of a stereopair of tilted photos. The procedure is known as *space intersection*, so called because corresponding rays to the same object point from two overlapping photos must intersect at the point, as shown in Fig. 13-12. Space intersection requires that the six elements of exterior orientation for the two overlapping tilted photos be known. These elements may be calculated by methods described in Sec. 13-12. Collinearity equations of the linearized form [Eqs. (C-11) and (C-12) of Appendix C] can be written for each new point, such as point E of Fig. 13-12. Note, however, that since the six elements of exterior orientation are known, the only remaining unknowns in Eqs. (C-11) and (C-12) are dX_E, dY_E, and dZ_E. These are corrections to be applied to initial approximations for object space coordinates X_E, Y_E, and Z_E respectively for ground point E. The linearized form of the space intersection equations for point E are

$$
v_{x_e} = b_{14}dX_E + b_{15}dY_E + b_{16}dZ_E + J \qquad (13\text{-}24)
$$

$$
v_{y_e} = b_{24}dX_E + b_{25}dY_E + b_{26}dZ_E + K \qquad (13\text{-}25)
$$

In Eqs. (13-24) and (13-25), the terms are as defined in Sec. C-4 of Appendix C. Two equations [of the form of (13-24) and (13-25)] can be written for point e_1 of the left photo and two more for point e_2 of the right photo; hence four equations result. Any three will yield a unique solution for the three unknown corrections, but a better solution

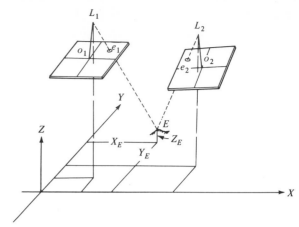

FIGURE 13-12
Space intersection with a stereopair of tilted photographs.

is obtained by using all four equations in a least squares solution. The corrections are applied to the initial approximations to obtain revised values for X_E, Y_E, and Z_E. The solution is then repeated until the magnitudes of the corrections become negligible.

Again because the equations are linearized using Taylor's theorem, initial approximations are required for each new point. Initial X and Y coordinates can be found satisfactorily using Eqs. (13-21) and (13-22) together with the procedures outlined in Sec. 13-12 for finding initial values for X_L and Y_L. An estimate for Z coordinates of new points can be made by assuming truly vertical photos and using the parallax equations described in Chap. 8.

13-14 RECTIFICATION OF TILTED PHOTOGRAPHS

Rectification is the process of making equivalent vertical photographs (*rectified photos*) from tilted photo negatives. Instruments used for rectification are called *rectifiers*. Rectified photos theoretically are truly vertical photos, and as such they are free from tilt displacements. They do contain image displacements due to topographic relief, however. Rectification requires the same amount of horizontal and vertical control as is required for computing tilt in photos.

Rectifiers operate on the principle of projection printing (see Sec. 3-12). Simultaneously with rectification, photos may also be *ratioed;* i.e., average scales of all photos in a strip or block are made uniform in spite of variations in flying heights. This is accomplished by varying projection distances to create a theoretically constant flying height above datum for all photos. Rectified and ratioed photos are used for the preparation of controlled mosaics. Rectified photos taken over flat terrain are also sometimes used as *photo maps*. Such photos have practically no relief displacements and, with their tilt displacements removed, their scale is nearly uniform throughout.

At the instant of exposure the negative plane of a tilted photo is inclined with respect to the datum plane. Figure 13-13 illustrates the principal plane of a tilted photo. Note that the magnitude of tilt between negative plane and datum plane is *t*, the tilt angle. If this same tilt relationship is created between *negative plane* and *rectifier easel plane* during projection printing, a rectified photo will be obtained. This is illustrated in Fig. 13-13, where the easel plane of a rectifier (shown dashed) is superimposed onto the sketch of the tilted photo. The easel plane (which holds the photographic emulsion upon which the rectified photo is exposed) is placed parallel to the datum plane, and therefore it makes an angle, *t*, with the negative plane. Inasmuch as the easel plane is in the same geometric position as the positive plane of a truly vertical photo exposed at *L*, the projection of negative images onto the easel plane produces a rectified (truly vertical) photo.

Unlike aerial photography where object distances are great compared to image distances, in rectification these distances are often comparable, and to achieve sharp focus for all images the Scheimpflug condition (see Sec. 2-8 and Fig. 2-14) must be satisfied. The Scheimpflug condition states that in projecting images through a lens, if the image and object planes are not parallel, the *image* plane, *object* plane, and *lens* plane must all intersect along a common line to satisfy the lens formula and achieve sharp focus for all images.

In practice different techniques are employed to arrive at rectifier settings necessary to achieve proper relationships between negative plane, easel plane, and lens plane. One method is to calculate numerically the elements of exterior orientation for each photo and from these values compute the required settings. Another possible method is to orient the photos in a stereoplotter, read the elements of exterior orientation, and from those values calculate the rectifier settings. This procedure requires a stereoplotter equipped with dials for reading the orientation elements, however.

Rectifier settings that are needed depend upon the particular rectifier. If an *automatic rectifier* is used, for example, the lens is canted by a special mechanical device which automatically provides sharp focus and satisfies the Scheimpflug condition regardless of the tilt angle or magnification ratio. With these instruments fewer computations and settings are needed. An automatic rectifier is shown in Fig. 13-14. Equations for calculating rectifier settings are beyond the scope of this text, but they are given in references listed at the end of this chapter.

For near vertical photography, a trial and error method of rectification which yields satisfactory results may be used. In this method three or more control points are plotted according to their ground control coordinates at the scale desired for the rectified photo.

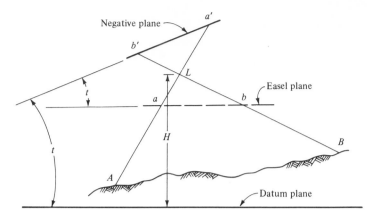

FIGURE 13-13
Principal plane of a tilted photograph with rectifier easel plane shown in super-position.

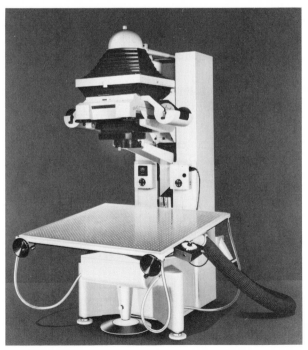

FIGURE 13-14
The SEG V enlarger rectifier. (*Courtesy Carl Zeiss, Oberkochen*)

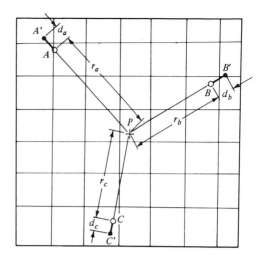

FIGURE 13-15
Plot of control points for rectification by
trial and error.

Such a plot is indicated in Fig. 13-15. The ground principal point of the photo must also
be located on the plot. Three-point resection may be used (see Sec. 9-5). (Theoretically
the ground nadir point should be plotted, but its position is unknown unless a
computation for tilt and swing is made.) Radial distances from ground principal point
(nadir point) to each plotted control point (like r_a, r_b, and r_c of Fig. 13-15, for example)
are measured in units of either inches or millimeters. Based on elevations h_A, h_B, and h_C
of the control points above datum, radial displacements d_a, d_b, and d_c are calculated
using the following relief displacement equation:

$$d = \frac{rh}{H - h} \qquad (13\text{-}26)$$

In the above equation, H is flying height above datum. Displacements calculated by
Eq. (13-26) are in inches or millimeters (the same units as the r values), and are laid off
outward along radial lines from the principal point (nadir point) to locate points A', B',
and C'. The plot is then placed on the easel and, by trial and error, the easel is adjusted in
orientation and elevation until projected images a, b, and c coincide with their respective
plotted points A', B', and C'. The trial-and-error adjustment also includes canting the
rectifier lens to achieve sharp focus. This automatically creates proper orientation of the
rectifier. The plot is then removed from the easel, a sheet of photographic paper is placed
there, and the rectified photo is exposed.

A less exact trial-and-error method of rectification that is frequently used follows
the procedure outlined above except that no corrections are made for relief displacement.

REFERENCES

American Society of Photogrammetry: "Manual of Photogrammetry," 3d ed., George Banta Co., Inc., Menasha, Wis., 1966, chaps. 2 and 16.

Anderson, R. O.: Scale-Point Method of Tilt Determination, *Photogrammetric Engineering,* vol. 15, no. 2, p. 311, 1949.

Berlin, L.: The Absolute Orientation of Near Verticals, *Photogrammetric Engineering,* vol. 30, no. 6, p. 1000, 1964.

Boge, W. E.: Resection Using Iterative Least Squares, *Photogrammetric Engineering,* vol. 31, no. 4, p. 701, 1965.

Clark, H. W.: The Geometry of Photorectification, *Photogrammetric Engineering,* vol. 15, no. 2, p. 288, 1949.

Church, E., and A. Quinn: *Elements of Photogrammetry,* Syracuse University Press, Syracuse, N.Y., 1944.

Gruner, H. E.: A Two Stage Rectification System, *Photogrammetric Engineering,* vol. 27, no. 4, p. 600, 1961.

Hallert, B.: Quality of Exterior Orientation, *Photogrammetric Engineering,* vol. 32, no. 3, p. 464, 1966.

Keller, M., and G. C. Tewinkel: *Space Resection in Photogrammetry,* ESSA Technical Report C&GS 32, U.S. Coast and Geodetic Survey, Washington, D.C., 1966.

Lehman, E. H., Jr.: Determining Exposure Point, Tilt, and Direction of Photograph From Three Known Ground Positions and Focal Length, *Photogrammetric Engineering,* vol. 29, no. 4, p. 702, 1963.

Moffitt, F. H.: "Photogrammetry," 2d ed., International Textbook Co., Scranton, Pa., 1967, chap. 9.

Rosenfeld, G. H.: The Problem of Exterior Orientation in Photogrammetry, *Photogrammetric Engineering,* vol. 25, no. 4, p. 536, 1959.

Wilson, K. R., and J. Vlcek: Analytical Rectification, *Photogrammetric Engineering,* vol. 36, no. 6, p. 570, 1970.

PROBLEMS

13-1 A particular tilted aerial photograph exposed with a 152-mm focal length camera has a tilt angle of $2°15'$ and its swing angle is $135°00'$. On this photograph, what are the auxiliary x' and y' photocoordinates for points a and b, whose photocoordinates measured with respect to the fiducial axes are $x_a = 72.08$ millimeters, $y_a = -32.59$ millimeters, $x_b = -39.27$ millimeters, and $y_b = 92.80$ millimeters?

13-2 The problem is the same as Prob. 13-1 except that camera focal length is 88 mm, tilt angle is $1°45'$, swing angle is $253°00'$, $x_a = -53.28$ millimeters, $y_a = 84.71$ millimeters, $x_b = -17.91$ millimeters, and $y_b = -77.48$ millimeters?

13-3 Calculate photographic scale for image points a and b of Prob. 13-1 if flying height above datum was 6,800 feet and if elevations of points A and B were 935 and 1,428 feet above datum respectively.

13-4 Calculate photographic scale for image points a and b of Prob. 13-2 if flying height above datum was 5,250 feet and if elevations of points A and B were 2,335 and 1,987 feet above datum respectively.

13-5 Calculate ground length of line AB for image points a and b of Probs. 13-1 and 13-3.

13-6 Calculate ground length of line AB for image points a and b of Probs. 13-2 and 13-4.

13-7 On a tilted photo, images a, b, and c of the three corners of a triangular tract of land have the following photocoordinates measured with respect to the fiducial axes: x_a = 47.66 millimeters, y_a = 71.25 millimeters, x_b = 21.89 millimeters, y_b = $- 84.92$ millimeters, x_c = -56.07 millimeters, and y_c = 10.63 millimeters. The tilt and swing angles of the photograph are $2°08'$ and $315° 00'$ respectively. Camera focal length is 152 mm and flying height above datum is 9,430 feet. Elevations above datum of points A, B, and C are 1,385, 1,017, and 1,490 feet respectively. What is the area of the tract of land in acres?

13-8 Compute the tilt displacements of the two points in Prob. 13-1.

13-9 Compute the tilt displacements of the two points in Prob. 13-2.

13-10 The images of three ground control points appear on a tilted aerial photograph taken with a camera having a focal length of 150.0 mm. Measured photocoordinates and corresponding ground control coordinates for the three points are:

Point	Photocoordinates		Ground coordinates		
	x, mm	y, mm	X, ft	Y, ft	Elevation, ft
A	2.23	−91.47	1,530,626.4	503,537.9	788.0
B	−100.78	71.11	1,531,256.2	500,302.1	600.6
C	106.19	76.02	1,528,113.9	501,719.1	923.3

Using the Church method, determine the six elements of exterior orientation for the photo.

13-11 The problem is the same as Prob. 13-10 except that the method of space resection by collinearity is to be used.

13-12 The problem is the same as Prob. 13-10 except that the camera focal length was 152.4 mm and measured photocoordinates and corresponding ground control coordinates for the three points are:

Photo	Photocoordinates		Ground coordinates		
	x, mm	y, mm	X, ft	Y, ft	Elevation, ft
D	1.36	−89.87	1,533,665.6	502,189.9	837.9
E	61.84	6.12	1,532,131.4	501,182.2	618.9
F	−6.06	76.69	1,532,747.3	499,757.7	920.9

13-13 Solve Prob. 13-12 using the method of space resection by collinearity.

STEREOSCOPIC PLOTTING INSTRUMENTS

14-1 INTRODUCTION

Stereoscopic plotting instruments (commonly called stereoplotters or simply plotters), are instruments designed to provide analogical solutions for object point positions from their corresponding image positions on overlapping pairs of photos. In general the optical and mechanical components of stereoplotters are manufactured to a high degree of precision and accurate results may be obtained from them. The primary use of stereoplotters is in compilation of topographic maps, and because this is currently the most widely practiced of photogrammetric applications, the subject of stereoplotters is one of the most important in the study of photogrammetry.

The basic concept underlying the design of a common type of stereoscopic plotting instruments is illustrated in Fig. 14-1. In Fig. 14-1*a,* an overlapping pair of aerial photos is exposed. Transparencies or *diapositives,* as they are called, carefully prepared to exacting standards from the negatives, are placed in two stereoplotter projectors as shown in Fig. 14-1*b.* This process is called *interior orientation.* Light rays are projected through the transparencies, and when rays from corresponding images on the left and right transparencies intersect below, they create a stereomodel (often simply called a *model*).

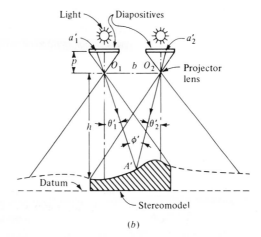

FIGURE 14-1
Basic concept of stereoscopic plotting instrument design. (*a*) Aerial photography; (*b*) stereoscopic plotting instrument.

By a process called *relative orientation,* the two projectors are oriented so that the diapositives bear the exact relative angular orientation to one another in the projectors that the negatives had in the camera at the instant they were exposed. Relative orientation creates, in miniature, a true three-dimensional stereomodel of the overlap area.

After relative orientation is completed, *absolute orientation* is performed. In this process the model is brought to the desired scale and leveled with respect to a reference datum. Figure 14-2 illustrates a stereomodel created by interior, relative, and absolute orientation of a stereopair in the projectors of a Balplex plotter. To retain simplicity of the figure, the framework of the instrument has been omitted.

When orientation is completed, measurements of the model may be made and recorded either graphically or digitally, depending upon the particular plotter and project. In either case, the position of any point is determined by bringing a reference mark into contact with the model point. For the plotter of Fig. 14-2, a reference mark in the center of the *platen* (white disk mounted on the tracing table) is brought into coincidence with model points. Planimetric positions of points are plotted by means of a pencil located vertically beneath the reference mark, and elevations are read directly from a dial which records up and down motion of the platen; the dial having been indexed to ground control during absolute orientation. Contours and other details may be traced directly, as shown on the manuscript map of Fig. 14-2, by moving the tracing table about while keeping the reference mark in contact with the model.

From an analysis of the preceding discussion, it should be apparent that stereoplotters combine three distinct systems: (1) a *projection* system, which creates the true three-dimensional stereomodel; (2) a *viewing* system, which makes it possible for an operator to see that model; and (3) a *measuring* (or tracing) system, which enables measurements of the stereomodel to be made and recorded.

14-2 CLASSIFICATION OF STEREOSCOPIC PLOTTERS

A variety of stereoscopic plotting instruments are currently available, each designed slightly differently. As an aid to understanding stereoplotters, it is helpful to classify them into groups having common characteristics. One common method of classification is by projection. This classification shall be divided into two broad categories: (1) *direct optical projection instruments* and (2) instruments with *mechanical* or *optical-mechanical projection.* Direct optical projection instruments create a true three-dimensional stereomodel by projecting transparency images through projector lenses. This is the type of projection illustrated in Figs. 14-1 and 14-2. The model is formed by intersections of light rays from corresponding images of the left and right diapositives. An operator is able to view the model directly and make measurements on it by intercepting projected rays on a viewing screen (platen).

Instruments of mechanical projection or optical-mechanical projection also create a true three-dimensional model from which measurements are taken. Their method of projection, however, is a simulation of direct projection of light rays by mechanical or optical-mechanical means. An operator views the diapositives stereoscopically directly through a binocular optical train.

Direct

FIGURE 14-2
Stereomodel created with a pair of Balplex projectors.

Other methods of classifying stereoplotters are (1) classification by accuracy capability (i.e., first-, second-, or third-order plotters) and (2) classification according to whether an "approximate" analogic solution or a "theoretically correct" analogic solution is obtained. The first of these classifications is unsatisfactory because of difficulties in assessing true accuracy capabilities of various instruments. Plotting accuracy is not solely a function of the instrument but also depends upon other variables such as quality of photography, operator ability, etc.

In the second of these classifications, instruments of the "approximate" category assume truly vertical photos and employ a parallax bar for measurement. These low-order instruments enable direct stereoscopic plotting, but the resulting map is a perspective projection, not an orthographic projection. For certain work, however, their accuracy is adequate. Some "approximate" plotters were discussed in Chap. 8. Plotters in the "theoretically correct" category are capable of creating a true stereomodel by means of interior, relative, and absolute orientation. This is the type of plotter discussed in this chapter.

Automated stereoplotters represent another class of instruments that has emerged in recent years. These instruments utilize automatic image correlators which replace human operators. Another type of instrument, called the *analytical plotter,* has also been recently perfected. It belongs in the automated stereoplotter class.

The first part of this chapter discusses direct optical projection stereoplotters. These instruments are simple in design and easily understood. They are also currently the most common type of stereoplotter in the United States. The second part describes instruments of mechanical and optical-mechanical projection. The final part of this chapter describes automated stereoplotting instruments.

It would be difficult if not impossible to describe each available instrument in detail in this chapter. For the most part, therefore, descriptions are general without reference to specific plotters and without comparisons of available instruments. In order to emphasize and clarify basic principles, however, examples are made of certain instruments and in some cases pictures are given. Omission of other comparable stereoplotters is not intended to imply any inferiority of these instruments. Operator's manuals which outline the details of each of the different instruments are provided by the manufacturers. Comprehension of the principles presented in this chapter should provide the background necessary for understanding these manuals.

PART I   DIRECT OPTICAL PROJECTION STEREOPLOTTERS

14-3   COMPONENTS

The principal components of a typical direct optical projection stereoplotter are illustrated in the schematic diagram of Fig. 14-3. The numbered parts are (1) the *main frame,* which supports the projectors rigidly in place, thereby maintaining orientation of a stereomodel over long periods of time; (2) the *reference table,* a large smooth surface which serves as the vertical datum to which model elevations are referenced and which also provides the surface upon which the manuscript map is compiled; (3) the *tracing table,* to which the platen and tracing pencil are attached; (4) the *platen,* the viewing screen which also contains the reference mark; (5) the *guide rods,* which drive the illumination lamps to illuminate desired areas of the diapositives; (6) *projectors;* (7)

FIGURE 14-3
Principal components of a typical direct optical projection stereoplotter.

illumination lamps; (8) *diapositives;* (9) *leveling screws,* which may be used to tilt the projectors in absolute orientation; and (10) the *projector bar,* to which the projectors are attached.

Although direct optical projection plotters of different manufacture vary somewhat in individual design and appearance, all are composed basically of these above parts. Reference to these parts will frequently be made in subsequent discussions in this chapter.

14-4 PROJECTION SYSTEMS

In the projection systems of direct optical projection stereoplotters, diapositives of a stereopair are placed in projectors and illuminated from above. Light rays are projected through the projector objective lenses and intercepted below on the reflecting surface of the platen. Stereoplotter projectors are similar to ordinary slide projectors, differing primarily in their optical precision, physical size, and capability of adjustment in attitude relative to one another. Since projection takes place through an objective lens, the lens formula, Eq. (2-5), must be satisfied in order to obtain a sharply focused stereomodel. In terms of the stereoplotter symbols of Fig. 14-1, the lens formula is expressed as:

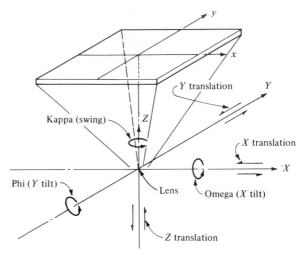

FIGURE 14-4
The six basic projector motions.

$$\frac{1}{f'} = \frac{1}{p} + \frac{1}{h} \qquad (14\text{-}1)$$

In Eq. (14-1), p is the *principal distance* of the projectors (distance from diapositive image plane to upper nodal point of the projector lens), h is the *projection distance* (distance from lower nodal point of the objective lens to the plane of optimum focus), and f' is the focal length of the projector objective lens. In order to obtain a clear stereomodel, intersections of projected corresponding rays must occur at a projection distance within the range of the *depth of field* of the projector lens (see Sec. 2-13).

In order to re-create the relative angular relationship of two photographs exactly as they were at the instant of their exposure (a process described in detail in Sec. 14-8), it is necessary that the projectors have rotational and translational movement capabilities. These motions, six in number for each projector, are illustrated in Fig. 14-4. Three of the movements are angular rotations about each of three mutually perpendicular axes: x rotation, called *omega* or *tilt*; y rotation called *phi* or *tip*; and z rotation called *kappa* or *swing*. The origin of the axis system about which the rotations take place is at the upper nodal point of the projector lens. The other three movements are linear translations along each of the three axes. In general, projectors of direct optical projection stereoplotters have all three angular rotations; however, they do not necessarily have all three linear translations. As a minimum they must have the x translation for changing the spacing between projectors, however.

Two different types of systems are used in illuminating diapositives: (1) those which illuminate the entire diapositive simultaneously and (2) those which illuminate

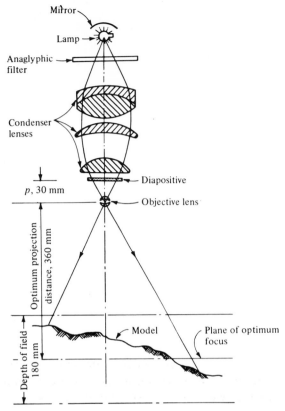

FIGURE 14-5
Projection system of the Multiplex instrument.

only a small area of the diapositive at one time. Multiplex and Balplex projectors illuminate the entire diapositive. This projection system does not require guide rods (item no. 5 of Fig. 14-3). To prevent excessive heat, both use reduced-sized diapositives and a system of forced air for cooling the projector housings.

The projection system of the Multiplex is illustrated in Fig. 14-5. The function of the condenser lenses is to distribute the light over the entire diapositive format and to condense all light rays through the small aperture of the objective lens. The principal distance of the commercial model of the Multiplex is 30.00 millimeters, and its optimum projection distance for satisfying Eq. (14-1) is 360 millimeters. Multiplex projectors have a depth of field of 90 millimeters up and down from optimum projection distance.

Figure 14-6 illustrates the projection system of the Balplex (ER-55) plotter. The light source is centered at one focal point of an ellipsoidal mirror, while the objective lens is placed at the other focal point. The ellipsoidal mirror acts as a condenser by virtue of

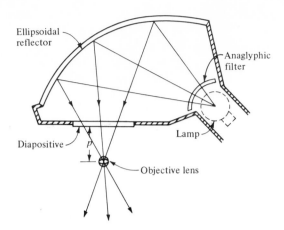

FIGURE 14-6
Cross section of the ellipsoidal reflector projection system of the Balplex instrument.

its property that any light ray emanating from a light source at one focal point is reflected through the other focal point. The principal distance of Balplex projectors is 55.00 millimeters. Three different models of Balplex projectors are available which provide choices in optimum projection distance of 760 millimeters, 525 millimeters, or 360 millimeters. Each of these different models uses a different objective lens to satisfy the lens formula. A 525-millimeter Balplex is shown in Fig. 14-7.

Projectors which illuminate only a small area of the diapositive at a time have the advantage that they can use full-sized diapositives, and they do not require a cooling system. This type of illumination system consists of a small, narrow-angle light source which illuminates an area on the diapositive about the size of a half dollar. When projected through the objective lens, an area slightly larger than the platen is illuminated in the model area. Driven by means of guide rods, the lamps swing above the diapositives, following the platen and illuminating it as it moves about the stereomodel. The Kelsh plotter shown in Fig. 14-8 utilizes this type of partial illumination. This instrument combines a nominal principal distance of 152 millimeters with an optimum projection distance of 760 millimeters; a combination which provides an enlargement ratio of five from diapositive scale to model scale.

14-5 VIEWING SYSTEMS

The function of the viewing system of a stereoplotter is to enable the operator to view the stereomodel three-dimensionally. Stereoviewing is made possible by forcing the left eye to view only the overlap area of the left photo while the right eye simultaneously sees

FIGURE 14-7
Balplex stereoplotting instrument with 525-millimeter optimum projection distance. (*Courtesy of Bausch and Lomb*)

only the overlap area of the right photo. The different stereoviewing systems commonly used in direct optical projection plotters are (1) the *anaglyphic* system, (2) the *stereo-image alternator* (SIA), and (3) the *polarized-platen viewing* (PPV) system.

An anaglyphic system uses filters of complementary colors, usually red and blue-green, to separate the left and right projections. Assume that a blue-green filter is placed over the light source of the left projector while a red filter is placed over the right. Then, if the operator views the projected images while wearing a pair of spectacles having blue-green glass over the left eye and red glass over the right eye, he will be able to see the stereomodel in three dimensions. The anaglyphic viewing system is simple and inexpensive; however, it precludes the use of color diapositives and causes considerable light loss, so that the model is not as bright as it could be if filters were not used.

The SIA system uses a system of synchronized shutters to achieve stereoviewing. A shutter is placed in front of each projector lens. Also, a pair of eyepiece shutters through

FIGURE 14-8
Kelsh stereoscopic plotting instrument. (*Courtesy of Kelsh Instrument Division, Danko Arlington, Inc.*)

which the operator must look, are situated in front of the platen. The shutters are synchronized so that the left projector and left eyepiece shutters are open simultaneously while the right projector and right eyepiece shutters are closed, and vice versa. An operator therefore sees only left projector images with the left eye and right projector images with the right eye. The shutters rotate at a rapid rate so tnat the operator is unaware of any discontinuity in the projection. An SIA system is shown attached to the Kelsh plotter pictured in Fig. 14-8.

The PPV system operates similarly to the anaglyphic system except that polarizing filters are used instead of colored filters. Filters of opposite polarity are placed in front of the left and right projectors, and the operator wears a pair of spectacles with corresponding filters on the left and right sides. In contrast to the anaglyphic system, the SIA and PPV systems both cause very little light loss, and both permit the use of color diapositives.

14-6 MEASURING AND TRACING SYSTEMS

A system for making precise measurements of the stereomodel is essential to every stereoplotter. Measurements may be recorded as direct tracings of planimetric features and contours of elevation, or they may be taken as X, Y, and Z model coordinates. One of the principal elements of the measuring system of a direct optical projection stereoplotter is a tracing table. The platen (white disk) contains a reference mark in its center; usually a tiny speck of light. The reference mark appears to float above the stereomodel if the platen is above the terrain, hence it is called the *floating mark*. The platen can be raised or lowered by turning a screw; the total vertical run of the threads being about 120 millimeters. Extension shafts of 50 millimeters can be added to increase this vertical range. Vertical movement of the platen is geared to a dial, and by varying gear combinations the dial can be made to record elevations directly in feet (or meters) for varying model scales.

A manuscript map, preferably of stable base material, is placed on top of the reference table, as illustrated in Fig. 14-2. The tracing table rests on the manuscript and is moved about manually in the X and Y directions. To plot the position of any point, the platen is adjusted in X, Y, and Z until the reference mark appears to rest exactly on the desired point in the model. A pencil point which is vertically beneath the reference mark is then lowered to record the planimetric position of the point on the map, and its elevation is read directly from the dial.

To trace a feature such as a creek, the pencil is lowered to the map and the tracing table is moved in the XY plane while the platen is moved up or down to keep the floating mark in contact with the stream. The pencil thereby records a continuous trace of the feature. Contours of elevation may also be traced by locking the dial at the elevation of the desired contour and then moving the tracing table about, keeping the floating mark in contact with the terrain.

For some projects it is desirable to obtain the record of measurements in digital form rather than graphic form. This is possible if the plotter is equipped with an XY *coordinatograph* such as that pictured in Fig. 14-9. The coordinatograph is mounted on the reference table, and the tracing table is connected to it. As the tracing table is moved about the model, X and Y coordinates can be read directly from the precisely graduated scales on the two rails of the coordinatograph. Elevations (Z coordinates) may be read directly from the tracing table dial as before. Special electronic equipment enables the

FIGURE 14-9
XY coordinatograph installed on a direct optical projection stereoplotter.
(*Courtesy Auto-trol Corp.*)

three coordinates at any point to be displayed visually and to be recorded automatically on magnetic tape or punched cards. In this era of electronic computers, significant computational advantages can be realized by systematically recording x, y, z coordinates of a dense network of points throughout the stereomodel, thereby obtaining a so-called *digital terrain model* (DTM).

Special "cross-sectioning" coordinatographs have been designed for taking terrain profiles at right angles to a center line; a procedure called *cross sectioning*. Cross sections are needed for computing earthwork volumes in the planning and design of highways, railroads, canals, etc. In taking photogrammetric cross sections, the adopted center line is plotted on the manuscript map. With the cross sectioning coordinatograph oriented with respect to the center line, the tracing table is constrained to move perpendicular to the center line at each desired station. Elevations and distances from center line are automatically recorded on tape or cards for each point on the terrain at which an operator sets the floating mark. These recorded cross sections may then be fed directly to a computer for processing earthwork volumes, etc. Prior to the emergence of photogrammetry, cross sectioning was done exclusively by field surveying. However photogrammetric cross sectioning is rapidly gaining popularity because it is many times faster, more economical, and produces results as accurate as those produced by field surveying.

14-7   INTERIOR ORIENTATION

As mentioned earlier, three steps are required to orient a stereoscopic plotter. The first of these, *interior orientation,* includes preparations necessary to re-create the geometry of the projected rays to duplicate exactly the geometry of the original photos, e.g., angles θ_1' and θ_2' of Fig. 14-1b must be exactly equal to angles θ_1 and θ_2 of Fig. 14-1a. This is necessary in order to obtain a true stereomodel. Procedures involved in interior orientation are: (1) preparation of diapositives, (2) compensation for image distortions, (3) centering diapositives in the projectors, and (4) setting off the proper principal distance in the projectors. These procedures are described individually as follows:

14-7.1   Preparation of Diapositives

Diapositives may be prepared either by *direct contact* printing or by *projection* printing. If contact-printed, their principal distances will be exactly equal to the focal length of the taking camera. For this reason contact-printed diapositives can be used only in plotters whose accommodation range in principal distance includes the focal length of the taking camera. Contact printing creates true geometry automatically as long as the principal distances of the projectors are set equal to the focal length of the taking camera.

In making diapositives by projection printing, principal distances of diapositives may be prepared to some value other than the focal length of the taking camera. Projection printing is necessary when diapositives for stereoplotting are being prepared from photography having a focal length outside of the plotter's range of principal distance accommodation. An example is preparation of Multiplex and Balplex diapositives (principal distances of 30 and 55 millimeters respectively) from 6-inch focal length photography. If diapositives are produced having principal distances other than the focal length of the taking camera, the dimensions of the diapositives will be reduced or enlarged in the ratio of p/f.

Geometric relationships that must exist in diapositive making by projection printing are illustrated in Fig. 14-10. By similar triangles of Fig. 14-10a,

$$\frac{f}{H'} = \frac{d}{D} \qquad (a)$$

Also by similar triangles of 14-10b,

$$\frac{d'}{d} = \frac{B}{A} \qquad (b)$$

And by similar triangles of Fig. 14-10c,

$$\frac{d'}{D'} = \frac{p}{h} \qquad (c)$$

Substituting (a) into (b), and in turn substituting into (c), the following relationship is obtained:

$$\frac{p}{f} = \frac{B}{A}\left(\frac{hD}{H'D'}\right) \qquad (d)$$

Now since true geometry must be retained from photography to stereoplotter projection, triangles ALB and $A'OB'$ of Figs. 14-10a and c are also similar, so that

$$\frac{H'}{D} = \frac{h}{D'} \qquad (e)$$

Substituting (e) into (d), the following equation is obtained expressing the condition that must be enforced in diapositive preparation by projection printing:

$$\frac{p}{f} = \frac{B}{A} \qquad (14\text{-}2)$$

In Eq. (14-2), p is the principal distance of the diapositive, f is the focal length of the taking camera, B is the distance in the projection printer from the emergent nodal point of the printer lens to the diapositive plane, and A is the distance from the negative plane to the incident nodal point of the printer lens. In order to get a diapositive that is in sharp focus, one further condition must be enforced, and this is that distances A and B in the projection printer must be set off so that the lens formula, Eq. (2-5), is satisfied for the printer lens, or

$$\frac{1}{f''} = \frac{1}{A} + \frac{1}{B} \qquad (14\text{-}3)$$

where f'' = focal length of projection printer lens.

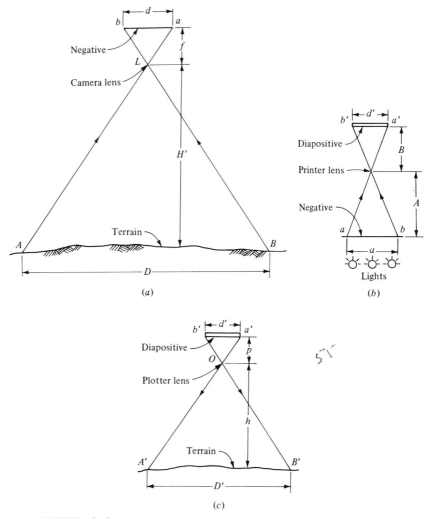

FIGURE 14-10
Geometric relationships required in making diapositives by projection printing.
(a) Photography; (b) projection printing; (c) stereoplotter projection.

EXAMPLE 14-1   It is desired to prepare diapositives having a principal distance of
153.00 mm from lunar photography taken with an 80.00-mm focal length Hasselblad
camera. If the projection printer lens has a focal length of 100.00 mm, what distances A
and B must be set off?

SOLUTION   By Eq. (14-2), $\dfrac{153.00}{80.00} = \dfrac{B}{A}$ $B = \left(\dfrac{153.00}{80.00}\right)A$

Substituting the above expression for B into Eq. (14-3),

$$\frac{1}{\dfrac{153.00}{80.00}\;A} + \frac{1}{A} = 1/100.00$$

Solving the above, $A = 152.29$ mm

Substituting and solving for B, $B = \left(\dfrac{153.00}{80.00}\right)152.29 = 291.25$ mm   ////

A projection printer manufactured especially for preparing enlarged or reduced diapositives having a wide range in versatility in distances A and B is pictured in Fig. 14-11.

If diapositives are contact-printed emulsion to emulsion, then the diapositives must be oriented emulsion up in the stereoplotter in order to re-create a geometrically correct model. This is a disadvantage with direct optical projection plotters because light rays carrying images are distorted in direction as they pass through the glass. This condition can be avoided by preparing diapositives by projection printing *through the film of the negative,* as shown in Fig. 14-12. Diapositives prepared in this manner are correctly oriented in the projectors *emulsion down,* thereby eliminating distortions due to rays passing through glass. (In Fig. 14-12 a dashed line for the letter F denotes that it is on the underside.)

Diapositives may be printed either on optically flat glass or on film. Some advantages can be realized by using film diapositives, e.g., lower cost, freedom from breakage, and less storage space required. A disadvantage in using film diapositives with many direct optical projection plotters is that for rigidity they must be placed in the projectors in a sandwich arrangement between two pieces of optically flat glass. This again creates distortions in ray paths which requires compensation.

14-7.2 Compensation for Image Distortions

Compensation for radial distortion of the lens of the taking camera may be accomplished in one of the following three ways: (1) elimination of the distortion with a "correction plate" in projection printing of the diapositives, followed by use of a distortion-free projector lens; (2) varying the projector principle distance by means of a cam, thereby reconstructing true geometry; and (3) use of a projector lens whose distortion characteristics negate the camera's distortion.

In the first method, a glass correction plate of varying thickness is placed in the projection printer in the ray path between negative and diapositive. Projected light rays passing through the correction plate are deflected along radial lines from the principal point by amounts necessary to remove radial distortion. Rather than placing the

correction plate in the projection printer, it can be placed in the stereoplotter projector
to accomplish the same effect. Different correction plates can be obtained which
accommodate lens distortions of different cameras. In addition to compensating for lens
distortions, correction plates are also available for removing distortions caused by
atmospheric refraction and earth curvature.

In the second method of lens distortion compensation, an aspheric cam
mechanically raises or lowers the projector lens (or the diapositive) so that, in spite of
distortions, projected rays make the same angle with the projector optical axis as they
made with the camera optical axis when they entered the camera. As a footnote to this
discussion it should be mentioned that most modern aerial camera lenses are so nearly
distortion-free that distortion compensation is often overlooked completely. The Zeiss
Pleogon lens is an example. Its near distortion-free characteristics are shown in the
radial-lens distortion curve of Fig. 4-13.

14-7.3   Centering the Diapositives in the Projectors

Diapositives must be centered in the projectors so that the principal point is on the
optical axis of the projector lens. Although this problem is solved slightly differently for
each instrument, it is basically done by aligning fiducial marks of the diapositives with
four calibrated collimation marks whose intersection locates the optical axis of the
projectors. Before diapositives are placed in the projectors, they are laid out so that their

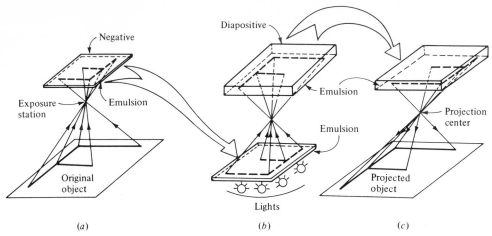

FIGURE 14-12
Printing diapositives by projection through the film base (note that correct model geometry is obtained with emulsion of diapositive facing down in the projector). (*a*) Original photography; (*b*) projection printing of diapositives; (*c*) stereoplotter projection.

common area overlaps. They are then separated, rotated 180° about the Z axis, placed on the plate holders of the projectors, and centered. In projection, the imagery is rotated 180°, which once again makes common areas of projected images overlap.

14-7.4 Setting Off the Proper Principal Distance in the Projectors

The final step in interior orientation is setting the diapositive principal distance on the projectors. This is unnecessary for plotters such as the Multiplex and Balplex, whose principal distances are permanently fixed and whose diapositives are prepared to conform with these principal distances. For other plotters the principal distance may be varied by either adjusting graduated screws or a graduated ring to raise or lower the diapositive image plane. These projectors are designed to accommodate a certain nominal principal distance and their range from that value is small; e.g., the Kelsh plotter pictured in Fig. 14-8 is designed for 6-inch (152-millimeter) photography, and its range in principal distance accommodation is only from 150 to 156 millimeters.

14-8 RELATIVE ORIENTATION

Imagine the camera frozen in space at the instants of exposure of two photographs of a stereopair. The two negatives in the camera would then bear a definite position and attitude relationship relative to each other. In relative orientation, this relative position

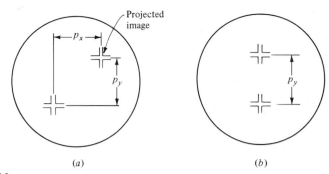

FIGURE 14-13
(*a*) Observing both *y* parallax and *x* parallax on the platen. (*b*) After removing *x* parallax, only *y* parallax remains.

and attitude relationship is re-created for the two diapositives by means of movements imparted to the projectors.

The condition that is fulfilled in relative orientation is that each model point and the two projection centers form a plane in miniature just like the plane that existed for the corresponding ground point and the two exposure stations. This condition is illustrated by corresponding planes $A'O_1O_2$ and AL_1L_2 of Fig. 14-1. Also, parallactic angle ϕ' for any point of the stereomodel of Fig. 14-1 must equal the point's original parallactic angle ϕ. The implication of the foregoing condition of relative orientation is that projected rays of all corresponding points on the left and right diapositives must intersect at a point, and this is the basis of the systematic relative orientation procedures described below.

Since relative orientation is unknown at the start, the two projectors are first positioned relative to one another by estimation. Usually, if vertical photography is being used, they are set so that the diapositives are nearly level and so their *x* axes lie along a common line. Also, the projectors are adjusted so that their *Y* and *Z* settings (distances from the projector bar in the *Y* and *Z* directions) are equal. When the projector lamps are first turned on, corresponding light rays will not intersect, and their projected images may appear on the platen as shown in Fig. 14-13*a*. Since the *X* component, p_x, of the mismatch of images is a function of the elevation of the point, it can be removed by raising or lowering the platen. The remaining *Y* component, p_y (see Fig. 14-13*b*), is called *y* parallax, and it must be removed or *cleared* for all points in the stereomodel in order to obtain a relatively oriented model.

Rather than attempting to clear *y* parallax at all points in the model, conventional procedure clears five standard points (plus a sixth for a check) located in the model, as shown in Fig. 14-14. If these five points are cleared of *y* parallax, then the entire model should be cleared. Points 1 and 2 are vertically beneath projector I (left projector) and projector II (right projector) respectively. Points 3 and 5 are on the *Y* axis through

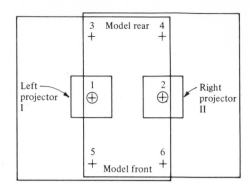

FIGURE 14-14
Stereomodel locations of six points conventionally used in relative orientation.

projector I and points 4 and 6 are on the Y axis through projector II. Points 1, 2, 3, and 4 roughly form a square, as do points 1, 2, 5, and 6.

Before describing relative orientation procedures, it will be helpful to consider the movement of projected images in the model area caused by each of the six projector motions. In Figs. 14-15a through f, these image movements are illustrated. Fig. 14-15a shows that an X translation imparts only X movement to all projected images, and therefore no y parallax could be cleared using this motion. In Fig. 14-15b, Y translation causes equal Y movement of all projected images; hence any point in the stereomodel could be cleared of y parallax using this motion. Figure 14-15c shows that all points move radially outward from the projection center if a projector is translated upward in Z. Image movement would be radially inward for a downward Z translation. Using Z translation, Y parallax could be cleared for any points except those along the X axis. In Fig. 14-15d omega rotation (tilt) causes Y movement of all projected images. This motion could therefore be used to clear y parallax anywhere in the model. As shown in Fig. 14-15e, a phi rotation (tip) causes an X movement for all projected images, but it also imparts a Y component for points not on the X and Y axes. And finally, in Fig. 14-15f, a kappa rotation (swing) imparts Y components to points everywhere in the model except along the Y axis. A clear grasp of these image movements will help to explain why y parallax can be removed and orientation achieved using the following procedures.

Two different systematic procedures for relative orientation will be discussed in this text: (1) the *two-projector* method, or what is commonly called the *swing-swing* method, and (2) the *one-projector* method. The steps involved in the two-projector method are as follows (refer to Figs. 14-14 and 14-15):

(a) Clear p_y at 1 with kappa (swing) of projector II.
(b) Clear p_y at 2 with kappa (swing) of projector I.
(c) Clear p_y at 3 with phi (tip) of projector II.
(d) Clear p_y at 4 with phi (tip) of projector I.

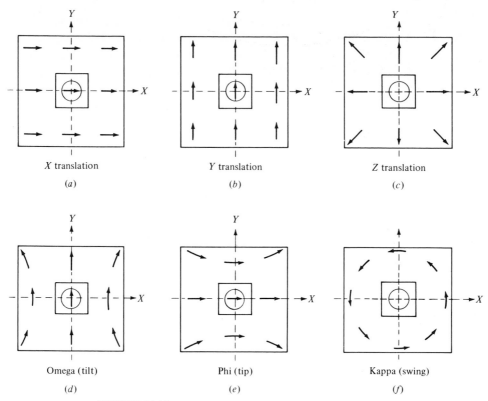

FIGURE 14-15
Movement of projected images in the model caused by the six projector motions.

(e) Observe p_y at 5 and overcorrect by introducing $\frac{1}{2} p_y$ in the opposite direction with omega (tilt) of either projector.

(f) Repeat steps a through e until no p_y exists at 5.

(g) Check 6 for p_y.

In analyzing the above steps, it should be noted that step b does not introduce y parallax at point 1 so that both points 1 and 2 are clear following this step. Also step c introduces no y parallax at either points 1 or 2, so that points 1, 2, and 3 are clear following this step. Furthermore, step d introduces no y parallax at points 1, 2, or 3, so that points 1 through 4 are clear following this step. Step e introduces y parallax at all points, but if steps a through d are repeated, the y parallax at point 5 will disappear. Several repetitions of steps a through e may be required to finally clear point 5, however. If points 1 through 5 are cleared, point 6 should also be clear, and if it is not, this is an indication that the other five points are not truly clear.

If the anaglyphic viewing system is used, y parallax for the first one or two repetitions of steps a through e may be cleared by matching corresponding red and blue-green images. Final repetitions are performed with the operator wearing the spectacles. When he is wearing the spectacles, the left and right eyes focus on the left and right projections respectively. Any y parallax in the projected images is unconsciously corrected for by a deviation of the optical axes of the two eyes. However, this causes an apparent y separation of the floating mark, which enables the operator to make a precise observation of the amount of y parallax present. Using the appropriate projector motions, y parallax is removed until the y separation of the two marks disappears and a single clear discrete floating mark is obtained.

The two-projector method described above requires rotations of both projectors. There are situations where it is necessary to retain the orientation of one projector, say the left, and to perform relative orientation with motions of the right projector only. An example of this is in orienting a strip of three or more photos on a projector bar holding three or more projectors. An eight-projector stereoplotter is shown in Fig. 18-1. After the first two photos are oriented, the third must be oriented to the second without upsetting the orientation of the second. The one-projector method outlined in the following steps may be used in this situation. All motions are imparted to the right-hand projector. (Refer to Fig. 14-14 for point locations.)

(*a*) Clear p_y at 2 with Y translation.
(*b*) Clear p_y at 1 with kappa (swing).
(*c*) Clear p_y at 4 with Z translation.
(*d*) Clear p_y at 3 with phi (tip).
(*e*) Observe p_y at 6 and overcorrect by introducing $\frac{1}{2} p_y$ in the opposite direction with omega (tilt).
(*f*) Repeat steps *a* through *e* until no p_y exists at 6.
(*g*) Check 5 for p_y.

14-9 ABSOLUTE ORIENTATION

After relative orientation is completed, a true three-dimensional model of the terrain exists. Although the horizontal and vertical scales of the model are equal, they are unknown and must be fixed at the desired value. Also the model is not yet level with respect to datum. Selecting model scale and fixing the model at that scale, and leveling the model are the purposes of absolute orientation.

14-9.1 Selecting Model Scale

Model scale is fixed within certain limits by the scale of the photography and by the characteristics of the particular stereoplotter. Comparing the geometry of Figs. 14-1*a* and *b*, model scale is seen to be the ratio of the sizes of triangles AL_1L_2 and $A'O_1O_2$. Equating these similar triangles, model scale may be expressed as

$$S_m = \frac{b}{B} = \frac{h}{H'} \qquad (14\text{-}4)$$

In Eq. (14-4), S_m is model scale, *b* is model air base, *B* is photographic air base, *h* is plotter projection distance, and H' is flying height above ground. From Chap. 6 it will be recalled that flying height above ground and camera focal length fix photo scale according to the following relationship:

$$S_p = \frac{f}{H'} \qquad (14\text{-}5)$$

In Eq. (14-5), S_p is photo scale and *f* is camera focal length. Substituting Eq. (14-5) into Eq. (14-4), the following convenient equation results for computing optimum model scale (given photo scale):

$$S_m = \frac{h}{f}\, S_p \qquad (14\text{-}6)$$

In Eq. (14-6), the term (h/f) is the ratio of projection distance to camera focal length, and it is also the enlargement ratio from photo scale to model scale. From the foregoing it is apparent, then, that for a given photo scale, *optimum model scale* is fixed for a particular stereoplotter by its *optimum projection distance.* A small aperature is used in objective lenses of projectors of direct optical projection stereoplotters so that a large depth of field results. A satisfactory model can therefore be obtained for a wide range in projection distance, and accordingly some flexibility is afforded in selecting model scale. The range in projection distance also makes it possible to accommodate topographic relief in the stereomodel. The actual model scale that is adopted should be chosen near optimum model scale, but it should be rounded to one of the commonly used even scales such as 1 inch to 100 feet, 1:1,000, etc. If the plotter is not equipped with a pantograph to change scale from model to map, then plotting scale is equal to model scale.

EXAMPLE 14-2 Mapping photography is taken with a 6-in (152-mm) focal length camera from a flying height of 3,000 ft above ground. What is optimum model scale, and what actual model scale would be adopted for (*a*) a Balplex (525) plotter and (*b*) a Kelsh (760) plotter?

SOLUTION By Eq. (14-5),

$$S_p = 6 \text{ in}/3{,}000 \text{ ft} = 1 \text{ in}/500 \text{ ft}$$

(*a*) Balplex (optimum h = 525 mm)
   By Eq. (14-6),

$$S_m = \left(\frac{525 \text{ mm}}{152 \text{ mm}}\right)\frac{1 \text{ in}}{500 \text{ ft}} = \frac{1 \text{ in}}{145 \text{ ft}}$$

Optimum model scale is 1 in/145 ft; Adopt 1 in/150 ft or 1:1,800

(*b*) Kelsh (optimum h = 760 mm)
   By Eq. (14-6),

$$S_m = \left(\frac{760 \text{ mm}}{152 \text{ mm}}\right)\frac{1}{500 \text{ ft}} = \frac{1 \text{ in}}{100 \text{ ft}}$$

Optimum model scale is 1 in/100 ft or 1:1,200; Adopt that value.   ////

When model scale has been adopted, an initial model air base (spacing between projectors) is set off. This is most conveniently done prior to relative orientation, so that model scale after relative orientation is close to required model scale. Model base is equal to photo base (distance between principal point and conjugate principal point) multiplied by the actual enlargement ratio S_m/S_p. The photo base can be measured directly from the photos, or it can be computed on the basis of percent end lap.

EXAMPLE 14-3 Assuming 9-in format and 60 percent end lap for the photography of Example 14-2, what should the initial model base be for (*a*) the Balplex (525) plotter and (*b*) the Kelsh (760) plotter?

SOLUTION At 60 percent end lap, the photo base is 40 percent of the 9-in format, or 0.4 × 9 = 3.6 in.

(*a*) Balplex

$$b = 3.6\left(\frac{S_m}{S_p}\right) = 3.6\left(\frac{1 \text{ in}/150 \text{ ft}}{1 \text{ in}/500 \text{ ft}}\right) = 12.0 \text{ in}$$

(*b*) Kelsh:

$$b = 3.6\left(\frac{1 \text{ in}/100 \text{ ft}}{1 \text{ in}/500 \text{ ft}}\right) = 18 \text{ in}$$ ////

14-9.2 Fixing Model Scale

If a preliminary model base is calculated as described above and the projectors are set accordingly, then after relative orientation the stereomodel will be near required scale. As shown in Fig. 14-16, model scale is changed by varying the model base. If the Y and Z

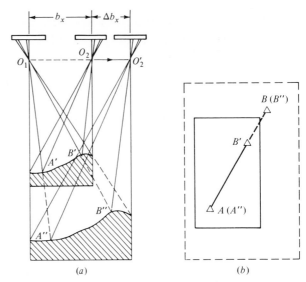

FIGURE 14-16
Changing model scale by adjusting model base. (*a*) Cross-sectional view; (*b*) plan view.

settings of the two projectors are equal, then model base is composed only of an X component called bx, and model scale is varied by simply changing model base by Δbx as shown in Fig. 14-16*a*.

A minimum of two horizontal control points is required to scale a stereomodel. These points are plotted at adopted model scale on the manuscript map as points A and B of Fig. 14-16*b*. The manuscript is then positioned under the model, and with the floating mark set on one model point, such as A', the manuscript is moved until map point A is directly under the plotting pencil. The floating mark is then set on model point B'. Holding the manuscript firmly with a fingertip at point A, it is rotated until map line AB is collinear with model line $A'B'$. If model line $A'B'$ is shorter than map line AB, model scale is too small and must be increased by increasing the model base until new model line $A''B''$ is equal in length to map line AB. The model base may be set to the required value by trial and error, or Δbx may be calculated directly using the following formula:

$$\Delta bx = bx \left(\frac{AB}{A'B'} - 1 \right) \qquad (14\text{-}7)$$

In Eq. (14-7), AB and $A'B'$ are scaled from the manuscript in any convenient units. If the algebraic sign of Δbx is negative, model scale is too large and bx must be reduced by Δbx. Once the model is scaled, it is recommended that a third horizontal control point be checked to guard against possible mistakes.

EXAMPLE 14-4 Assume that a map line AB scales 17.60 in and its corresponding model length is 16.94 in. The initial model base was set at 18.00 in with Y and Z base settings equal. What model base change is required to achieve desired model scale?

SOLUTION   By Eq. (14-7);

$$\Delta bx = 18.00\left(\frac{17.60}{16.94} - 1\right) = 0.70 \text{ in}$$

Model base must be increased by 0.70 in to bring the model to correct scale.   ////

14-9.3   Leveling the Model

The final step in absolute orientation is leveling the model. This procedure requires a minimum of three vertical control points distributed in the model so that they form a large triangle. Four points, one near each corner of the neat model, are preferred, however. A fifth point near the center of the model is also desirable. A model with a vertical control point near each corner that has not yet been leveled is shown in Fig. 14-17. Note that there are two components of tilt in the model, an X component and a Y component. The amount by which the model is out of level in each of these components is determined by reading model elevations of the vertical control points and comparing them with their known values.

Assuming four vertical control points in a model, as points A through D of Fig. 14-17, the following systematic procedure would be applied in leveling the model:

(a) Set the floating mark on model point A and index the tracing table dial to read the control elevation of that point.

(b) Read model elevation of control point D.

(c) From the difference between model elevation and control elevation, determine whether the model is X tilted up or down toward the rear. (If model elevation is higher than control elevation, the model is tilted up in the rear.)

(d) By one of the tilting methods to be discussed, introduce a corrective X tilt.

(e) Repeat steps a through d until the model is level in the direction from A to D.

(f) Re-index the tracing table dial to read the control elevation of point A with the floating mark set on model point A.

(g) Read model elevation of control point B.

(h) From the difference between model elevation and control elevation, determine whether the model is Y tilted up or down to the right.

(i) By one of the tilting methods to be discussed, introduce a corrective Y tilt.

(j) Repeat steps f through i until the model is level in that direction.

(k) Check point C to see if its model elevation conforms to its control elevation. (This helps to ensure that the model is truly level. If the model elevation of point C

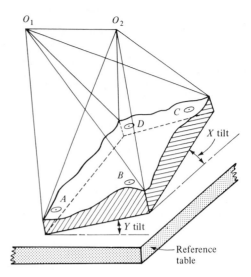

FIGURE 14-17
Stereomodel that is not level (note X and Y components of tilt).

does not agree with its control elevation, this could be an indication of model deformation caused by inaccuracies in relative orientation, or it could disclose blunders in the vertical control.)

There are different methods available for introducing the corrective X and Y tilts, and the choice will depend partly upon the particular stereoplotter and partly upon the amount of tilt necessary. A few plotters are designed so that their reference tables may be tilted in both the X and Y directions to make them parallel with the model datum. This method is easily visualized and is convenient because relative orientation is not altered since the projectors are not touched. The method may not be practical if a severe amount of tilt is necessary, however.

A second method for introducing corrective tilts in the model is tilting the projector bar by means of the leveling screws, as shown in Fig. 14-18. Both X and Y tilts can be introduced in this way. The method is convenient because it moves both projectors simultaneously and therefore does not upset relative orientation. Again, this method may not be practical if severe amounts of tilt exist.

A third method of introducing corrective tilts consists of X tilting each projector with equal amounts of omega rotation (tilt) and Y tilting each projector with equal amounts of phi rotation (tip), followed by a Z translation to remove the bz base component introduced by the phi rotations. This is illustrated in Fig. 14-19. In applying corrective X tilt, a trial amount of omega rotation is first introduced to the left projector. This, of course, introduces y parallax throughout the model, but if the Y and Z settings of the projectors are equal, this y parallax is entirely removed by introducing an equal

Side views

(a)   (b)

Front views

(c)   (d)

FIGURE 14-18
(a) and (b) Correcting X tilt of a model by X tilt of projector bar. (c) and (d) Correcting Y tilt of a model by Y tilt of projector bar.

amount of omega rotation to the right projector. If the operator clears y parallax for any point in the stereomodel when introducing omega to the right projector, the entire model will again be clear. In applying corrective Y-tilt, a trial amount of phi rotation is introduced equally into both projectors. This has the effect of creating a bz base component which is removed by raising or lowering either projector, the exact amount being just enough to clear y parallax for a point in one model corner. This third method has the advantage that large amounts of tilt are readily corrected, but its disadvantage is that small amounts of y parallax may remain in the model as a result of moving the projectors individually.

Regardless of the method of leveling, the previously established model scale will be upset, especially if large amounts of corrective tilts are required. Also, it is likely that absolute orientation will upset relative orientation. Therefore it is not practical to labor at great lengths with either relative or absolute orientation the first time through. Rather, quick orientations should be performed at first, followed by careful refinements the

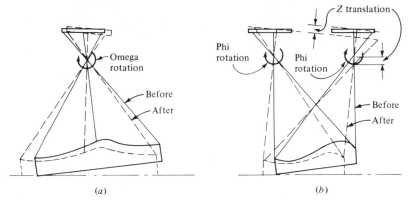

FIGURE 14-19
(*a*) Correcting X tilt of a model with equal omega rotations of both projectors.
(*b*) Correcting Y tilt of a model with equal phi rotations of both projectors followed by a Z translation.

second time through. When orientation is completed, the manuscript map should be firmly secured to the reference table in preparation for map compilation.

If the Y and Z settings of the projectors are not equal, in addition to base component bx, there will be Y and Z components to the model air base as shown in Fig. 14-20. This causes added difficulties in absolute orientation. If it were necessary to increase the model base in scaling, for example, projector II would have to be moved to II' along the base line joining I and II, otherwise y parallax would be introduced. This necessitates introducing Δbx, Δby, and Δbz components in scaling. Also, in leveling a model, equal amounts of omega and phi rotation of both projectors introduces y parallax that must be removed by translatory projector movements. These difficulties can be avoided by making the two Y projector settings equal and the two Z projector settings equal prior to starting orientation.

14-10 MAP COMPILATION

When the model has been completely oriented and the manuscript secured to the reference table, map compilation may be started. As a general rule in compilation, planimetric details and cultural features should be traced first, followed by contouring. This is because planimetry has a very significant effect on the location and appearance of contours (e.g., the v's of contours crossing streams must peak in the stream, contours crossing roads in cut cross the road at right angles and have their ditches on either side of the road, etc.). An example of carelessly compiled contours or planimetry is shown in Fig. 14-21*a*, while its corresponding correct rendition is shown in Fig. 14-21*b*.

FIGURE 14-20

Model base containing components b_x, b_y and b_z. (Note that an increase of b_x by Δb_x necessitates introducing Δb_y and Δb_z components as well.)

While planimetric features are traced, the floating mark should be kept in constant contact with the object. It is advisable to plot all features of a kind at once (e.g., all roads), before proceeding to another feature, as this reduces the likelihood of omissions. Generally, features are compiled in descending order of prominence. Any notes or labels that the compiler feels are necessary to avoid later misidentification should be made directly on the manuscript. A set of paper prints and a stereoscope are essential to the compiler as an aid in identifying features.

Contours are more difficult to compile than planimetry, especially for the beginner. But like learning to ride a bicycle, beginning frustrations are soon forgotten by those who persist. Generally, contouring can be approached in much the same way as the assembly of a jigsaw puzzle. Easier areas and prominent features are compiled first, and the more difficult detail is filled in later. It may be helpful to study the overall model for a time before beginning to compile contours. This gives a sense of familiarity much the same as one would get in making a field visit. Studying the model using paper prints and stereoscope can also be helpful. In more difficult areas or flat terrain, it is sometimes necessary to drop "spot elevations" and interpolate contours from them. This is helpful because spot elevations can be read to significantly greater accuracy than direct contour tracing. In areas covered with trees, it may be impossible to plot continuous contours. In these areas broken contours (contour lines plotted in open areas only) may be drawn, otherwise spot elevations can be plotted and contours interpolated. Densely vegetated areas occasionally must be field surveyed. When compiling contours, it is advisable to lock the tracing table dial at the desired contour elevation to prevent accidental movement of the platen.

Whether compiling planimetry or contours, the operator should occasionally check the orientation of the model, including scale and level. This is important especially when returning to the plotter after being away for a time.

When the manuscript is finished, it should be carefully checked for omissions and mistakes. It is then field-checked where any missing features are noted. Also, fea-

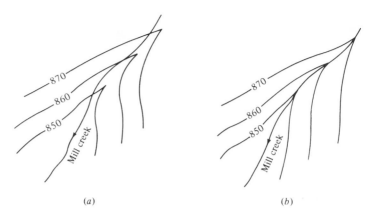

(a)   (b)

FIGURE 14-21
(a) Inconsistencies between planimetry and contour locations. (b) Consistent renditions of planimetry and contours.

tures are identified and local names are determined. An important part of any field check is an accuracy determination. In this procedure, photogrammetrically plotted distances and elevations are checked against field measurements.

With field inspection completed, the map is ready for drafting or scribing. If the map is drafted in ink, manuscript features are traced on stable base overlay material. Lettering is usually inked first, followed by planimetric features and finally contours. Features having straight lines or known geometric shapes are drawn with the aid of straightedges or templates. A certain amount of generalization is required, especially in smoothing contours. When inking is completed, the map may be reproduced on paper by a direct ozalid process, or it may be reproduced on stable base material by a contact photographic process known as *autopositive.*

Scribing is another convenient method of preparing negatives for map reproduction. This procedure requires sheets of transparent stable base material that have been coated with an opaque emulsion material. In a laboratory process, the manuscript map lines are transferred to the emulsion coating. Then, using special scribing tools, lines representing contours and features are made by cutting and scraping to remove the coating material. Special tools are also available for varying line weights and for scribing cartographic symbols used for features such as roads, schools, churches, mines, etc. Scribing is often faster and more convenient than ink drafting, and unlike inking it yields a negative directly; i.e., light passes through the clear areas where lines and symbols have been scribed. A person can generally become proficient at scribing much faster than he can at drafting with ink.

PART II STEREOPLOTTERS WITH MECHANICAL OR OPTICAL-MECHANICAL PROJECTION

14-11 INTRODUCTION

Mechanical projection stereoscopic plotting instruments simulate direct optical projection of light rays by means of two precisely manufactured metal *space rods*. These instruments are manufactured chiefly in Europe, but their use in the United States is rapidly increasing because of their versatility, convenience of operation, accuracy capabilities, and overall stability. As with direct optical projection instruments, the many slightly different designs of mechanical projection stereoplotters cannot be described in detail in this text. Rather, basic principles of mechanical projection are explained and a few instruments which typify these basic concepts are discussed briefly. Manuals provided by manufacturers outline the details of operation for their specific instruments.

The basic principles of mechanical projection are illustrated in the simplified diagram of Fig. 14-22. Diapositives are placed in *carriers* and illuminated from above. The carriers are analogous to projectors of direct optical projection instruments. Two space rods are free to rotate about *gimbal joints* O' and O'', and they can also slide up and down through these joints. The space rods represent corresponding projected light rays and the gimbal joints are mechanical projection centers, analogous to the objective lenses of projectors of direct optical projection stereoplotters. The model exposure stations are therefore represented by O' and O'', and the distance $O'O''$ is the model air base. Joints O' and O'' are fixed in position except that their spacing can be changed during orientation to obtain correct model scale.

The viewing system consists of two individual optical trains of lenses, mirrors, and prisms. The two optical paths are illustrated by dashed lines in Fig. 14-22. An operator looking through binocular eyepieces along the optical paths sees the diapositives directly and perceives the stereomodel. Objective lenses V' and V'' are situated in the optical trains directly beneath the diapositives. The lenses are oriented so that viewing is orthogonal to the diapositives; consequently the diapositive image planes (emulsion surfaces) can lie on the upper side of the diapositive glass with no refraction error being introduced because no rays pass obliquely through the glass. A reference half mark is superimposed on the optical axis of each of the lenses V' and V''. Movement is imparted to the lenses from the space rods by means of tie rods connected at another set of gimbal joints K' and K''. These joints are fixed in vertical position, and the vertical distance from lower gimbal joints O' and O'' to their corresponding upper gimbal joints K' and K'' is the principal distance p. During interior orientation, this distance is set equal to the principal distance of the diapositives.

The space rods intersect at the *tracing stand*. By manually moving the tracing stand, movement is imparted to the space rods, which in turn impels the viewing system and

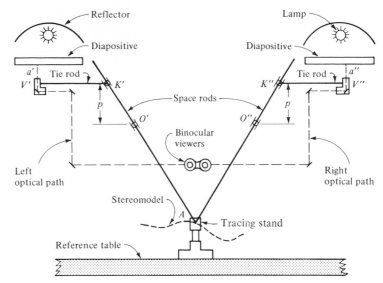

FIGURE 14-22
Basic principles of mechanical projection.

makes it possible to scan the diapositives. By manipulating the tracing stand in the X, Y, and Z directions, the optical axes of lenses V' and V'' can be placed on corresponding images such as a' and a''. This will occur when the reference half marks fuse into a single mark that appears to rest exactly on the model point. If orientation of the instrument has been carefully performed, with the floating mark fused on point a, the space rods have the same orientation that the incoming light rays from terrain point A had at the time of photography, and the intersection of space rods locates that model point. Each additional model point is located in this same manner.

By geometric comparison, the mechanical projection system illustrated in Fig. 14-22 is exactly the same as direct optical projection. Diapositives are placed in the carriers with their overlapping areas toward the outside. In scanning the diapositives, if the tracing stand is moved right, the viewing lenses move left, and vice versa. Also, if the tracing stand is pushed backward, the viewing lenses move forward, and vice versa. When the tracing stand screw is turned to raise the space rod intersection, the parallactic angle increases and the viewing lenses move apart, a manifestation of the increased x parallax which exists for higher model points.

The carriers of most mechanical projection stereoplotters are capable of rotations and translations, either directly or indirectly. These carrier motions are used to perform relative and absolute orientation. Many mechanical projection instruments are oriented using exactly the same procedures that were described for direct optical projection stereoplotters. Others which do not possess all three rotations and translations use slight variations from these basic orientation procedures.

The Wild *A-8 Autograph* shown in Fig. 14-23 is very similar in design to the hypothetical instrument of Fig. 14-22. There are some basic differences, however. Instead of the viewing lenses being connected to the space rods by tie rods, each is connected by a three-hinged parallellogram tong. The middle hinge of each tong is fixed in position. With this mechanism, a movement of the tracing stand to the right causes a corresponding movement of the viewing lenses to the right, and vice versa. Also an upward motion of the tracing stand causes an increase in parallactic angle at the intersection of space rods, but this causes the viewing lenses to move together. Unlike the previously described instrument, this necessitates placing the diapositives in the carriers with overlapping areas toward the inside.

A second basic difference is that the tracing stand is impelled in the X and Y directions by means of two handwheels in front of the instrument, while Z motion is introduced by pedaling a foot disk. Pictured with the A-8 Autograph is its standard coordinatograph, upon which map compilation is done. X and Y movements of the tracing stand are transmitted mechanically to the tracing pencil on the coordinatograph. By changing gear ratios, various enlargements or reductions from model scale to map scale may be achieved. Model coordinates can also be read directly from graduated X and Y scales on the coordinatograph. Z model coordinates are read directly from a scale graduated to record up and down motion of the tracing stand. The optional electronic equipment shown with the A-8 Autograph in Fig. 14-23 enables coordinates to be recorded automatically.

Interior orientation of the A-8 Autograph consists of preparing the diapositives either by contact printing or projection printing, centering the diapositives in the carriers by means of collimation marks, setting off the proper principal distance, and, if necessary, inserting distortion correction plates. With mechanical projection systems, a wide range of principal distances is readily achieved; the A-8 for example, will accommodate any distance between 98 and 215 millimeters.

Each projector of the A-8 is capable of the three rotations, but its only translation is an X translation needed for scaling models. Relative orientation of this instrument is by the two-projector method outlined in Sec. 14-8. The model is brought to scale by using the same procedure described in Sec. 14-9 except that the base is increased or decreased as required by increasing or decreasing the spacing of gimbal joints O' and O''. As described in Sec. 14-9, the model is checked for level by reading the elevations of at least three vertical control points. Corrective X tilts are introduced with equal amounts of omega rotation (tilt) to each carrier, and corrective Y tilts are applied using a common phi rotation (tip) which simultaneously rotates both carriers. Graduated dials which record omega, phi, and kappa rotations facilitate both relative orientation and absolute orientation.

FIGURE 14-23

Mechanical

Wild Autograph A-8. (*Courtesy Wild Heerbrugg Instruments, Inc.*)

Another stereoplotter utilizing mechanical projection is the Galileo-Santoni *Stereosimplex* IIC pictured in Fig. 14-24. The operation of this plotter is similar in principle to the hypothetical instrument illustrated in Fig. 14-22 except that the optical system is fixed and the space rods impel the diapositive carriers for scanning the model in the X and Y directions. X and Y scanning motions are introduced manually using a pantograph handle with one hand, while Z motions are introduced by turning the handwheel on the machine's left side. Movements in X and Y are transmitted to the plotting table at the desired enlargement or reduction ratio via the pantograph. The instrument is capable of omega rotations of up to 90°, so that it can handle horizontal (terrestrial) photographs in addition to aerial photos. Its range in principal distance accommodation is from 80 to 210 millimeters.

The Wild *B-8 Aviograph* shown in Fig. 14-25 is a mechanical projection instrument designed principally for mapping. A schematic diagram of its projection system is shown in Fig. 14-26. Gimbal joints O' and O'' are the projection centers, and they are fixed in position. The viewing system is driven by tie rods connected to the space rods at gimbal joints K' and K''. The unusual feature of this instrument is that joints K' and K'' are below projection centers O' and O''. The vertical distances between projection centers O' and O'' and their corresponding gimbal joints K' and K'' is the principal distance. The model is scanned in X and Y by manually pushing the tracing stand about while at the same time raising or lowering the floating mark with a finger screw on the tracing stand. If the tracing stand is pushed to the right, the viewing lenses V' and V'' also move to the right, and vice versa. Therefore the diapositives are centered in the carriers with their

FIGURE 14-24
Galileo-Santoni Stereosimplex IIC. (*Courtesy Galileo Corp. of America*)

overlap areas toward the inside, just as with the A-8 Autograph. A pantograph transmits X and Y motion to the tracing table. The B-8 has the same motions as the A-8 and is oriented in the same manner.

14-12 MECHANICAL PROJECTION INSTRUMENTS UTILIZING THE ZEISS PARALLELOGRAM

Imagine moving gimbal joint O'' of the hypothetical instrument of Fig. 14-22 to the right some arbitrary amount to O''_1, and in the process imagine that $O''_1 A_1$ is held parallel to $O''A$, as shown in Fig. 14-27. Also, instead of extending the length of the space rods to a point of intersection, suppose that their original length is retained but that the rods are joined near their ends by a *base bridge*. Then, by moving the base bridge as a whole in X, Y, and Z, the stereomodel could be scanned, and if a pencil were attached to the bridge, it would trace the scanning movement. The parallelogram $O''AA_1O''_1$ is the so-called *Zeiss parallelogram.* Its use in stereoplotters of mechanical projection is fairly common.

FIGURE 14-25
Wild B-8 Aviograph. (*Courtesy Wild Heerbrugg Instruments, Inc.*)

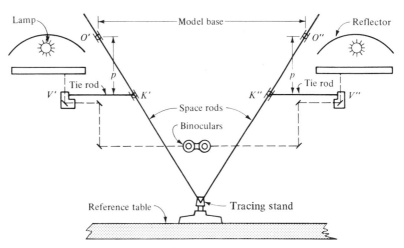

FIGURE 14-26
Schematic diagram of projection system of Wild B-8 Aviograph.

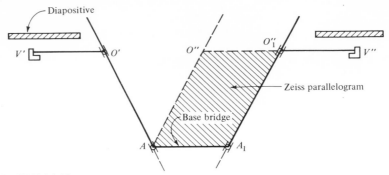

FIGURE 14-27
Zeiss parallelogram.

Theoretically, the model base of an instrument employing the Zeiss parallelogram is $O'O''$. The length of the model base can be changed, even though gimbal joints O' and O''_1 remain rigidly fixed, by varying the length of the base bridge. If the base bridge is lengthened from S to say S_L, as shown in Fig. 14-28, then theoretical position O'' moves to O''_L and the model base becomes shorter. This, of course, decreases model scale accordingly. If S is shortened, the effect is to lengthen the model base and increase model scale.

From the foregoing discussion it is seen that because of the Zeiss parallelogram, variations in the x component of the model base are introduced at the base bridge, and an increase in base bridge length causes a decrease in model base, and vice versa. Figures 14-29a and b illustrate that variations in y and z base components are also introduced at the base bridge. In Fig. 14-29a, imagine introducing a positive Δb_y at the right side of the base bridge. Since gimbal joint O''_1 is fixed in position, the space rod tilts. To complete the Zeiss parallelogram holding $O''A$ parallel to $O''_1 A_1$, negative Δb_y must exist at O''. Hence a positive Δb_y introduced at the right side of the base-bridge causes negative Δb_y

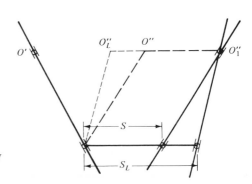

FIGURE 14-28
Decrease in model base is achieved by
increase of base-bridge length.

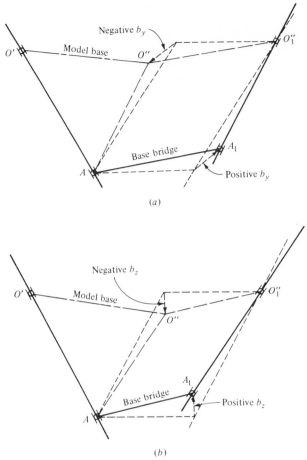

FIGURE 14-29
Introduction of b_y and b_z translations at base-bridge. Note that a positive b_y at base-bridge imparts a negative b_y to the right projector in (a) and positive b_z at base-bridge imparts negative b_z to the right projector in (b).

at the right carrier, and vice versa. Similar analysis of Fig. 14-29b illustrates that introducing positive Δb_z at the right end of the base bridge results in negative Δb_z at the right carrier, and vice versa. Translations in Y and Z to the left carrier are introduced at the left side of the base bridge.

Some advantages realized from using the Zeiss parallelogram design are stability because of the rigidly fixed positions of the perspective centers, a wide range in possible model bases (including zero base), and the capability of extending the base bridge to the so-called *base-out* position. As discussed in Chap. 18, this makes possible continuous orientation of all photos in a strip; a useful feature in extending control photogrammetrically.

FIGURE 14-30
Wild A-7 Universal Autograph. (*Courtesy Wild Heerbrugg Instruments, Inc.*)

The Wild *A-7 Universal Autograph* of Fig. 14-30 is a mechanical projection instrument which uses the Zeiss parallelogram and has the capability of extending its base bridge to the base-out position. Its viewing and measuring systems are similar to those of the A-8 Autograph. Its diapositive carriers each have the three rotations, and all three translations can be introduced at either end of the base bridge. The instrument may be relatively oriented using either the two-projector method or the one-projector method. The model base is adjusted for model scaling by translations at the base bridge. In leveling, if base components b_y and b_z are zero, corrective X tilts are applied by imparting equal omega rotations to both carriers, and corrective Y tilts are introduced with equal amounts of phi rotation to each carrier, followed by a b_z translation.

The Kern PG-2 stereoplotter shown in Fig. 14-31 also employs the Zeiss parallelogram. This instrument has the unique feature that the diapositive carriers remain horizontal throughout orientation. The instrument has the usual kappa rotations, but omega and phi are introduced by means of tilts applied to the space rods. The viewing system of the PG-2 is orthogonal to the diapositives. Relative orientation is accomplished using both projectors, but the procedure deviates slightly from the two-projector method described in Sec. 14-8 because the necessary rotations are not all available. The model is scaled by varying the length of the base bridge, and it is leveled by tilting the table. Scanning in X and Y is done by manually pushing the base carriage—these motions being transmitted to the plotting table by means of a pantograph. Z motion is imparted at the base bridge by means of a finger screw, and model elevations can be read directly from a dial geared to the base bridge.

FIGURE 14-31
Kern PG-2. (*Courtesy Kern and Co., Inc.*)

14-13 INSTRUMENTS WITH OPTICAL-MECHANICAL PROJECTION

Some stereoplotters have projection systems which are partly optical and partly mechanical, but these instruments are not as common as those of purely mechanical projection. The Zeiss *C-8 Stereoplanigraph* pictured in Fig. 14-32 is an instrument using a combination of optical and mechanical projection. With this instrument, diapositives are centered in the two projectors and illuminated from above. Corresponding images are optically projected through the projector objective lenses and come to focus on a pair of reference mirrors, as shown in the diagram of Fig. 14-33. The rays are reflected by the mirrors into two optical trains and are viewed by an observer through binoculars. A special mechanical linkage aligns the mirrors so that the reflected rays are received in the optical trains regardless of the area of the diapositives being viewed. Reference half marks superimposed at each reference mirror fuse into a floating mark that appears to rest exactly on a model point when the half marks are set on corresponding images.

An auxiliary *Bauersfeld* lens system attached beneath each projector objective lens, as illustrated in Fig. 14-34, assures perfect focus of projected rays on the reference

FIGURE 14-32
Zeiss C-8 Stereoplanigraph. (*Courtesy Carl Zeiss, Oberkochen*)

mirrors regardless of projection distance. Projector principal distances, p, are set equal to the focal length, f', of the projector lenses, and therefore projected rays emerge from the projector lenses parallel. These parallel rays enter the positive and negative Bauersfeld lens combination—the two lenses being separated by a spacing, e. Distance e is mechanically varied to maintain focus on the mirrors according to variations in the projection distance, h.

Each projector of the C-8 Stereoplanigraph has the customary three angular rotations, but translations are introduced as movements of the reference mirrors. This is the case because the instrument utilizes the Zeiss parallelogram, as illustrated in Fig. 14-33. Base components b_x, b_y, and b_z are varied in essentially the same manner as described for mechanical projection instruments that use the Zeiss parallelogram except that with the C-8 the reference half marks are translated instead of the ends of the base bridge.

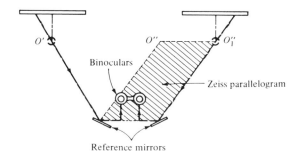

FIGURE 14-33
Schematic diagram of projection system
of C-8 Stereoplanigraph.

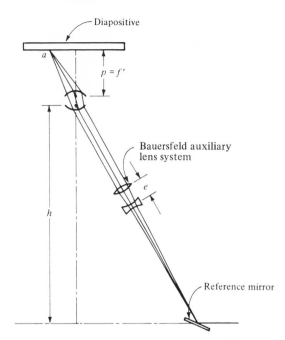

FIGURE 14-34
Auxiliary lens system which maintains sharp focus for all parts of the stereo-model.

Model scanning in the X and Y directions is introduced with the C-8 by means of handwheels, while Z motion is imparted by pedaling the foot disk. A unique feature of the Z motion of the C-8 is that the two projectors are raised or lowered to accommodate variations in terrain. The Y and Z motions of the C-8 can be interchanged for plotting from terrestrial photographs. This instrument is a universal stereoplotter capable of the base-in and base-out positions and is therefore suitable for continuous strip control extension as well as map compilation.

PART III   AUTOMATED STEREOPLOTTING INSTRUMENTS

14-14.   INTRODUCTION

"Automation" implies self-operation or the elimination of human operators in a process. All the stereoscopic plotting instruments discussed thus far, however, depend upon operators. In operating a stereoplotter, the operator's eye-brain combination continually performs *image correlation*, i.e., matching shapes, sizes, and densities of corresponding images from a stereopair of diapositives. In orienting a stereoplotter, image correlation is performed as the operator clears y parallax from projected rays of corresponding imagery.

Image correlation is also performed in map compilation as x parallax is cleared to keep the floating mark in contact with the model points.

In recent years ingenious instruments called electronic *image correlators* have been designed which can replace the human operator. These instruments can automatically correlate images and clear y parallax for plotter orientation or clear x parallax for map compilation. The chief potential advantages of such automated stereocompilation equipment over manually operated equipment are greatly increased speed, reduced mapping costs, and increased precision. Research in the field of automated mapping systems is active, and new developments loom on the horizon. At the present time initial cost of automatic stereocompilation equipment is high and the required capital outlay may not be justifiable to an organization unless their volume of mapping is correspondingly high. Military organizations must produce quantities of maps in short periods of time and consequently they have been intensely involved in the research and development of automatic stereocompilation equipment.

14-15 ELECTRONIC IMAGE CORRELATION AND AUTOMATIC STEREOPLOTTERS

The function of electronic image correlation systems is to automatically detect the presence of parallax between corresponding imagery. This function is performed in two steps: (1) conversion of imagery to electronic signals through an operation called *scanning* and (2) comparison of the electronic signals from the two diapositives of a stereopair, an operation called *correlation.*

The electronic image correlation system of the *B-8 Stereomat* is representative of image correlators used on many automatic stereoplotting instruments. The B-8 stereomat consists of a standard Wild B-8 mechancial projection stereoplotter (see Fig. 14-25), to which has been added an electronic image correlator and servomotors which perform the functions of a human operator. Figure 14-35 illustrates the principle of automatic operation of the electronic image correlator. The instrument contains two identical electronic scanning systems—one for each of the diapositives of a stereopair. A "flying spot" of light systematically scans back and forth across the face of each of the cathode ray tubes above the diapositives. The lens between the cathode ray tubes and the diapositives focus the flying spots of light onto the diapositives, and the lenses below the diapositives project the spots onto the photomultiplier tubes below. Electronic currents (I) generated by the photomultiplier tubes alternate according to the intensity of light received.

The flying spots above the two diapositives move synchronously with respect to the left and right diapositives. As the spots scan, if they cross corresponding light-dark borders of the two diapositives at different times, the resulting alternating currents

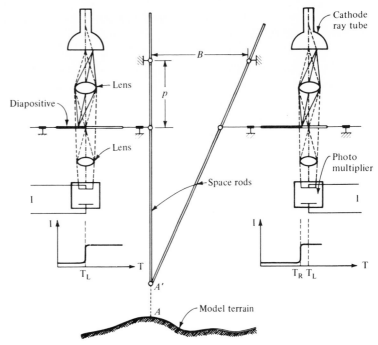

FIGURE 14-35
Automatic image correlator of the B-8 Stereomat.

generated by the photomultiplier tubes will have different phases. A difference in phase such as T_L and T_R of Fig. 14-35 indicates the presence of parallax, in which case the space rod intersection occurs at an incorrect model point such as A'. If any difference in phase is detected, a servomotor is automatically activated which moves the space rods to such position that the phase difference becomes zero. Then the flying spots will be simultaneously illuminating corresponding images and the space rod intersection will occur at correct model point A. This operation is exactly analogous to a human operator clearing parallax by manually moving the space rods until his two eyes simultaneously see corresponding images. The Stereomat does have an optical viewing system so that an operator can manipulate the instrument manually.

Since the flying spots have both x and y components, it is possible to automatically detect both x parallax and y parallax in a stereomodel. The instrument can relatively orient itself through automatic detection of y parallax. The presence of any y parallax activates servomotors that introduce projector motions to clear it. Automatic clearance of y parallax at the five standard points relatively orients a model. After a model has been oriented, automatic detection and elimination of x parallax enables profiles to be read, contours to be traced, and models to be digitized, i.e., recording X, Y, and Z model coordinates of a dense network of points throughout the model. Profiles can be scanned in either the X or Y direction.

Contours can be traced automatically by the B-8 Stereomat, but an operator must first bring the measuring mark in contact with the terrain at the desired starting contour elevation. The instrument will automatically compile the contour until it leaves the model, whereupon it will step to the next contour and begin tracing it. If a contour closes upon itself, the instrument would endlessly retrace that contour unless set to the next contour by an operator. In the automatic contouring mode, therefore, an operator is needed to monitor compilation.

It should be noted that an image correlator compares corresponding images and measures their respective positions on a stereopair of diapositives. It does not recognize or memorize forms or objects. Therefore if drastically differing corresponding imagery is encountered, as sometimes occurs in steep terrain, for example, the instrument may not be able to function. This, of course, would pose no problem for human operators who can associate common images even though they appear different. When contouring, the automatic image correlator may occasionally come to a point where it cannot find corresponding images. While attempting to find them, it may stray so far away that it cannot correct itself. An alarm alerts an operator to reset the instrument when this occurs.

14-16 ANALYTICAL PLOTTERS

The B-8 Stereomat incorporates an electronic image correlator and a mechanical projection stereoplotter. Automatic image correlators have also been successfully operated in conjunction with direct optical projection stereoplotters. Yet another class of automated stereoplotters called *analytical plotters* form neither an optical or mechanical stereomodel. Rather, a *mathematical model* is developed. Analytical plotters are accurate and highly flexible. They consist essentially of a precision *stereocomparator* (see Sec. 18-10) and coordinatograph interfaced with an electronic digital computer. Because they have no optical or mechanical limitations, analytical plotters are capable of handling a wide variety of photography including vertical, tilted, low oblique, convergent, high oblique, and panoramic photos. In addition, they can accommodate any focal length and correct for any combination of systematic errors caused by lens distortion, film shrinkage, atmospheric refraction, and earth curvature.

Early generations of analytical plotters required a certain amount of human intervention for their operation. More recent generations, however, incorporate electronic image correlators which enable them to operate almost completely automatically. Analytical plotters can be used for aerotriangulation, and they are also capable of automatic contouring and profiling. In addition, they can be equipped for automatic

FIGURE 14-36
Analytical plotter AP/C. (*Courtesy O.M.I. Corp. of America*)

printing of orthophotos. The Universal Automatic Map Compilation Equipment (UNAMACE) is an analytical plotter developed by the U.S. Army. A commercially available analytical plotter is the AP/C shown in Fig. 14-36.

In operating the AP/C analytical plotter, a stereopair of diapositives is placed on the viewing stages of the stereocomparator. Camera focal length and calibration characteristics are fed into the computer. Photocoordinates of diapositive fiducials are read, whereupon the computer automatically calculates principal point locations and corrections necessary for film deformation. For relative orientation, y parallax is measured at each of a minimum of five of the six standard relative orientation points (more than five is desirable). The computer then calculates the elements of relative orientation and stores them for future use. The computations are performed using least squares techniques if more than five points are used in the solution. For absolute orientation, model coordinates of a minimum of two horizontal and three vertical control points are measured, and their corresponding control coordinates are fed to the computer. The computer calculates the orientation elements necessary to scale and level the model and stores them. If more than the minimum number of control points are used, a least squares solution is performed.

When orientation is completed, measurements may be taken from the stereomodel, or a map may be compiled. The instrument operates by rapidly solving analytical equations for each model point based on the locations of the points and the stored orientation information. When operated in the automatic contouring or profiling mode, the electronic image correlation equipment automatically senses the stereomodel elevation and terrain slope. Output from the correlator activates servomotors to drive the coordinatograph which plots the contours or profiles.

REFERENCES

American Society of Photogrammetry: "Manual of Photogrammetry," 3d ed., George Banta Co., Inc., Menasha, Wis., 1966, chaps. 3, 12, 13, 14, and 15.

Bean, R. K.: Development of the ER-55 Projector, *Photogrammetric Engineering,* vol. 19, no. 1, p. 71, 1953.

Bertram, S.: The Universal Automatic Map Compilation Equipment, *Photogrammetric Engineering,* vol. 31, no. 2, p. 244, 1965.

Crabtree, J. S., and J. D. McLaurin: The BAI Image Correlator, *Photogrammetric Engineering,* vol. 36, no. 1, p. 70, 1970.

Danko, J. O., Jr.: Color, the Kelsh, and the PPV, *Photogrammetric Engineering,* vol. 38, no. 1, p. 83, 1972.

DeGraaf, R. M.: Automation Characteristics of the Stereomat B8, *Photogrammetric Engineering,* vol. 30, no. 5, p. 818, 1964.

Esten, R. S.: Automatic Photogrammetric Instruments, *Photogrammetric Engineering,* vol. 30, no. 4, p 544, 1964.

Forest, R. B.: AP-C Plotter Orientation, *Photogrammetric Engineering,* vol. 31, no. 6, p. 1024, 1966.

Ghosh, S. K.: *Theory of Sterophotogrammetry,* The Ohio State University Book Stores, Columbus, Ohio, 1968.

——:Photo/Model/Map Scales, *Photogrammetric Engineering,* vol. 32, no. 11, p. 1154, 1971.

Katibah, G. P.: Model Flatness-A Guide for Stereo-Operators, *Photogrammetric Engineering,* vol. 30, no. 2, p. 299, 1964.

Kasper, H.: The Wild B8 Aviograph-A Simple Photogrammetric Plotter, *Photogrammetric Engineering,* vol. 27, no. 4, p. 590, 1961.

Knauf, J. W.: The Stereoimage Alternator, *Photogrammetric Engineering,* vol. 33, no. 10, p. 1113, 1967.

Lawrence, C. H.: Stereomat 1V, Automatic Plotter, *Photogrammetric Engineering,* vol. 33, no. 4, p. 394, 1967.

Lyon, D.: Let's Optimize Stereoplotting, *Photogrammetric Engineering,* vol. 30, no. 6, p. 897, 1964.

Noonan, R. P.: A Systematic Procedure for Stereocompilers, *Photogrammetric Engineering,* vol. 36, no. 1, p. 56, 1970.

Sailor, S.: Demonstration Board for Stereoscopic Plotter Orientation, *Photogrammetric Engineering,* vol. 31, no. 1, p. 176, 1964.

Struck, L.: The Multiplex, Kelsh Plotter and Wild Autographs, *Photogrammetric Engineering,* vol. 18, no. 1, p. 84, 1952.

Tewinkel, G. C.: Stereoscopic Plotting Instruments, *Photogrammetric Engineering,* vol. 17, no. 4, p. 635, 1951.

Theis, J. B.: Automation and Photogrammetry, *Photogrammetric Engineering,* vol. 31, no. 2, p. 281, 1965.

Thompson, M. M., and J. G. Lewis: Practical Improvements in Steroplotting Instruments, *Photogrammetric Engineering,* vol. 30, no. 5, p. 802, 1964.

Trow, S. W., and M. Keller: Transfer of Absolute Orientation from One Type of Stereoscopic Plotting Instrument to Another, *Photogrammetric Engineering,* vol. 19, no. 5, p. 831, 1953.

Veres, S. A.: The Use and Adoption of Conventional Stereoplotting Instruments for Bridging and Plotting of Super Wide Angle Photography, *Canadian Surveyor,* vol. 23, no. 4, p. 359, 1969.

Whiteside, A. E., and C. W. Matherly: Recent Analytical Stereoplotter Developments, *Photogrammetric Engineering,* vol. 38, no. 4, p. 373, 1972.

PROBLEMS

14-1 Describe the basic differences between stereoplotters with direct optical projection and instruments with mechanical or optical-mechanical projection.

14-2 What is the focal length of the lens in a Balplex projector whose principal distance and optimum projection distance are 55 and 760 millimeters respectively?

14-3 The problem is the same as Prob. 14-2 except for a Kelsh plotter whose principal distance and optimum projection distance are 152 and 760 millimeters respectively.

14-4 Discuss the different viewing systems used in direct optical projection stereoplotters.

14-5 Outline the steps of interior orientation.

14-6 Photography is taken at 60 percent end lap with 152 mm focal length 9-inch square format camera from a flying height of 10,000 feet above average ground. If diapositives of this photography are to be prepared for use in a Balplex plotter, what values of A and B should be set off in the reduction printer if the reduction printer has a lens with a focal length of 100 mm?

14-7 For the photography of Prob. 14-6, what will be optimum model scale for a Balplex stereoplotter having an optimum projection distance of 525 mm?

14-8 If a plotting scale to the nearest 100 feet per inch is adopted for the stereomodel of Prob. 14-7, what will be the nominal dimensions of the neat model? (Assume 30 percent side lap.) What will projection distance be to average ground?

14-9 Photography is taken at 65 percent end lap with a 150-mm focal length 9-inch format camera from a flying height of 6,500 feet above average ground. What is optimum model scale for a Kelsh plotter having a 150-mm principal distance capability and a 760-mm optimum projection distance?

14-10   If a plotting scale to the nearest 100 feet per inch is adopted for the stereomodel of Prob. 14-9, what will be the nominal dimensions of the neat model? (Assume 25 percent side lap.) What will be the model dimensions of the entire overlap area? What will be the projection distance to average ground?

14-11   If the photography of Prob. 14-9 is to be used in a Multiplex plotter, what plotting scale will be adopted assuming a scale to the nearest 100 feet per inch is selected? What approximate base (bx) between projectors should be set off prior to relative orientation?

14-12   What are the advantages and disadvantages of using film diapositives in stereoplotters as opposed to glass diapositives?

14-13   Draw a sketch of the stereoscopic neat model and label the six points where y parallax is conventionally removed in relative orientation. For each of the left projector rotations and translations, list the point numbers at which y parallax may be introduced.

14-14   Outline the steps of the two-projector "swing-swing" method of relative orientation.

14-15   Outline the steps of the one-projector method of relative orientation.

14-16   Assume that a map line, AB, scales of 21.85 inches, and its corresponding model length, $A'B'$, prior to absolute orientation, measures 20.74 inches. If the initial model base was set at 16.5 inches, to what length should the model base be adjusted to scale the model? (Assume that Y and Z components of the model base are zero.)

14-17   Discuss the different methods of leveling a model in a stereoplotter.

14-18   Explain how a model can be leveled without using the leveling screws on the frame of the instrument. Under what conditions would this procedure be necessary?

14-19   Explain why it is convenient to set base components by and bz equal to zero prior to plotter orientation.

14-20   A Kelsh plotter having a usable depth of field of 12 inches (6 inches up and down from optimum projection distance) is oriented with average ground at optimum projection distance of 760 millimeters. What range in relief can be accommodated up and down from average ground if flying height was 3,000 ft above average ground? (Assume that the diapositive principle distance is equal to the 150 millimeter focal length of the taking camera.)

14-21   Same as Prob. 14-20 except that a Multiplex plotter is used. The plotter has a usable depth of field of 90 millimeters up and down from its optimum projection distance of 360 millimeters.

14-22   The Kern PG-2 stereoplotter has a range of principal distance from 85 to 172 millimeters, a nominal range in projection distance from 102 to 172 millimeters, and a pantograph enlargement ratio from model to map of from 1:1 to 1:3.33. If the diapositive principal distance is equal to camera focal length, what ranges in manuscript scales are possible for the photographs of Prob. 14-9?

14-23 The problem is similar to Prob. 14-22 except that a Wild A-8 instrument is used. It has a principal distance range of from 98 to 215 millimeters, a projection distance range of from 175 to 350 millimeters, and a coordinatograph enlargement ratio of from 4:1 up to 1:4.

14-24 Draw a sketch illustrating, the Zeiss parallelogram. How are b_x, b_y, and b_z base components varied for instruments incorporating the Zeiss parallelogram?

14-25 Describe the method of operation of electronic image correlators.

14-26 List the capabilities and advantages of analytical plotters.

ORTHOPHOTOGRAPHY

15-1 INTRODUCTION

An orthophoto is a photograph showing images of objects in their true orthographic positions. Orthophotos are therefore geometrically equivalent to conventional line and symbol planimetric maps which also show true orthographic positions of objects. The major difference between an orthophoto and a map is that an orthophoto is composed of images of features, whereas maps utilize lines and symbols plotted to scale to depict features. Because they are planimetrically correct, orthophotos can be used as maps for making direct measurements of distances, angles, positions and areas without making corrections for image displacements. This, of course, cannot be done with perspective photos.

Orthophotos are produced from perspective photos (usually aerial photos) through a process called *differential rectification*, which eliminates image displacements due to photographic tilt and relief. Tilt displacements, as described in Sec 13-7, exist in any photo if at the instant of exposure the photo plane is tilted with respect to the datum plane. Rectification eliminates the effects of tilt and yields an equivalent vertical photo. Unless the terrain is perfectly flat, however, a rectified equivalent vertical photo will still contain scale variations as a result of image displacements due to changes in relief. In the process of removing relief displacements from any photo, scale variations are also removed and scale becomes constant throughout the photo. Any photo which has a constant scale throughout is an orthophoto having the same planimetric correctness as a map. It should be mentioned that although relief displacements due to variable terrain are removed, a shortcoming of orthophotos is that relief displacements of vertical surfaces such as walls of buildings cannot be removed.

At first glance, an orthophoto looks the same as a perspective photo. But upon comparison of an orthophoto and a perspective photo of the same area, differences can usually be detected. Figure 15-1a is a portion of a perspective photo taken in Oklahoma. In Fig. 15-1b an orthophoto produced from that portion of the perspective photo is shown. Note in particular how relief displacement has made the power line on the perspective photo appear crooked, whereas it appears straight on the orthophoto because relief displacements have been removed.

The desirability of orthophotos over perspective photos has been recognized for many years. As early as 1903, Scheimpflug had conceived the idea of directly producing orthophotos from perspective photos. In the early 1930s, the Gallus-Ferber restitution machine was introduced in France. In addition to its use for stereoscopic plotting, this instrument could produce orthophotos directly from perspective photos. (Its operating principles were much the same as those incorporated into present-day orthophoto producing equipment.) Even though the instrument was operational, inefficiencies of the system together with a general lack of enthusiasm for the finished product caused orthophoto production to lie dormant until the 1950s.

In 1950 Russell Bean of the U.S. Geological Survey began experimenting with equipment for producing orthophotos, and his work led to the development of the instrument presently known as the *orthophotoscope*. The first orthophotoscope was introduced in 1953, and it was followed by several improved generations. Continued developments led to the model T-64 Orthophotoscope pictured in Fig. 15-2 which is currently used extensively by the Geological Survey in producing orthophotos.

15-2 ADVANTAGES AND USES OF ORTHOPHOTOS

Orthophotomaps prepared from orthophotos offer significant advantages over both line maps and aerial photos. This is because orthophotos possess the advantages of both air photos and line maps. On the one hand, orthophotos have the pictorial qualities of air photos because the images of an infinite number of ground objects can be recognized and identified. Furthermore, because of the planimetric correctness with which images are shown, measurements may be taken directly from orthophotos just as from maps.

The capability of being able to correlate images on the orthophotomap with what is observed on the ground is an asset in many fields of endeavor. Engineers, planners,

(a) (b)

FIGURE 15-1

(a) Portion of a perspective photo taken in Oklahoma. (Note the apparent crookedness of the power line caused by relief displacement.) (b) Orthophoto of same portion of perspective photo shown in (a). (Note straightness of the power line after relief displacement is eliminated.) (*Courtesy U.S. Geological Survey*)

Dark   Projector
curtain   bar

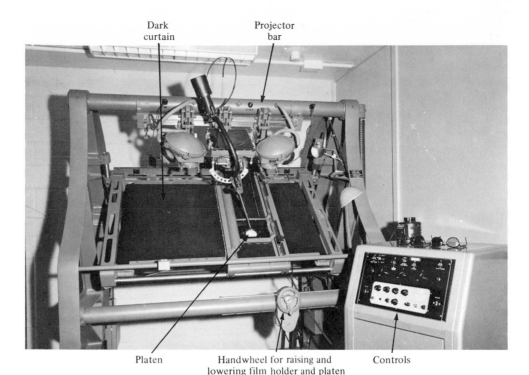

Platen   Handwheel for raising and   Controls
                lowering film holder and platen

FIGURE 15-2
Model T-64 Orthophotoscope. (*Courtesy U.S. Geological Survey*)

surveyors, foresters, geologists, agronomists, etc., can use orthophotos advantageously as base maps for plotting field observations. Foresters, for example, can classify and delineate different timber types in their true position directly on the orthophotomap by correlating images with what they observe in the field. Also, soil scientists can plot locations where soil samples were taken and delineate soil-type boundaries directly on orthophotomaps by correlating images with their corresponding objects on the ground. Property surveyors can utilize orthophotomaps to advantage because fence lines and other key items of evidence that can be field-identified are shown in true plan view on the orthophoto map.

Because images can be correlated with their corresponding objects on the ground, orthophotos make excellent base maps for preparing flight plan maps. Orthophotos are also very useful communication tools. Property owners and lay people can understand an orthophotomap, whereas they are frequently awestruck by a line and symbol map. Using orthophotos, engineers are better able to communicate with property owners to discuss right-of-way purchases, access to property, etc.

Orthophotomaps themselves offer no information as to elevations. They can serve as planimetric base maps upon which elevation contours are superimposed, however, and the resulting product is termed a *topographic orthophotomap*. Contours for topographic orthophotomaps are normally derived in a separate stereoplotting operation. The use of orthophotomaps as base maps for elevation contours eliminates the need for mapping planimetric data in stereoplotter compilation and can result in substantial time savings. An example of a topographic orthophotomap produced by the U.S. Geological Survey is shown in Fig. 15-3. This map of Prudhoe Bay on Alaska's north slope is one of an experimental series produced on the model T-64.

Orthophotos can be used as maps without cartographic treatment, or they can be enhanced and supplemented with lines, symbols, names, etc. It can be seen on Fig. 15-3 for example, that lines and names have been added. Colors may also be added to enhance the quality of the orthophotomap.

Compared to conventional line maps prepared through stereoplotter compilation, orthophotomaps can generally be prepared faster and at less cost. This is especially true for small-scale maps, maps of urban areas, or maps of areas with dense planimetric and cultural features. Added reproduction costs of orthophotomaps, however, offset savings in labor somewhat. Orthophotography has made it possible to map areas that would otherwise have gone unmapped, and it has made more frequent map revision plausible. It must be pointed out, however, that before an orthophotomap meeting national map accuracy standards can be produced, the same adequate ground control must be available for the orthophotoscope as for the conventional stereoplotter.

Orthophotos are still relatively new products but all indications now are that users are more than satisfied with them. It appears that orthophotos, with their many significant advantages, have an excellent chance of superseding, in large part, conventional line and symbol maps.

15-3 CLASSIFICATION OF INSTRUMENTS FOR PRODUCING ORTHOPHOTOS

Instruments used in the production of orthophotos can generally be classed into one of two broad categories: (1) those which produce images by direct optical projection, and (2) those which produce images electronically. Instruments that produce images by direct optical projection are basically modified versions of direct optical projection stereoplotters. They require an operator in order to function. Instruments that produce images electronically are generally automatic, but their cost is high and as a consequence a relatively limited number of them are currently in use.

Within the direct optical projection category, a distinction may be made between instruments which operate *on-line* and those which operate *off-line*. This on-line or off-line designation stems from the fact that two distinct operational phases are entailed in orthophoto production: (1) scanning profiles of the terrain of a stereomodel at

Orthophotomap prepared by the Geological Survey

Control by USC&GS and USCE

Orthophotomosaic by photogrammetric methods from aerial photographs taken Sept. 3, 1969. Topography from Army Map Service 1:50,000 series maps, surveyed 1955

Selected hydrographic data compiled from USC&GS Chart 9472 (1968) This information is not intended for navigational purposes.

Universal Transverse Mercator projection, 1927 North American datum 10,000-foot grid based on Alaska coordinate system, zone 4 1000-meter Universal Tranverse Mercator grid ticks zone 6, shown in blue

Township exteriors are surveyed. Township subdivisions are predetermined by the Bureau of Land Management. Folio U-3, Umiat Meridian

Lake elevations are unchecked

SCALE 1:24 000

CONTOUR INTERVAL 25 FEET.
DATUM IS MEAN SEA LEVEL
DEPTH CURVES AND SOUNDINGS IN FEET-DATUM IS MEAN LOWER LOW WATER
SHORELINE SHOWN REPRESENTS THE APPROXIMATE LINE OF MEAN HIGH WATER
THE MEAN RANGE OF TIDE IS APPROXIMATELY 0.5 OF A FOOT

UTM GRID AND 1969 MAGNETIC NORTH
DECLINATION AT CENTER OF SHEET

FIGURE 15-3
Topographic orthophotomap of Prudhoe Bay, Alaska. (*Courtesy U.S. Geological Survey*)

uniformly spaced increments and (2) exposing the orthonegative in a series of narrow strips, each having a width exactly equal to the spacing between adjacent profile scans. On-line instruments are those in which profile scanning and orthonegative exposure are combined into a single simultaneous operation. No record of profile elevations is retained, and the only product of on-line operation is the orthonegative. Off-line instruments, on the other hand, produce orthophotos in two separate operations. Profiles are first scanned and recorded in either graphical or digital form. Subsequently these profiles are read into an instrument which automatically exposes the orthonegative on the basis of the profiles. Some instruments are capable of operating either on-line or off-line. In discussing the details of operation of orthophoto producing instruments in the remaining sections of this chapter, it is assumed that the student has studied Chap. 14 or has an understanding of the principles of stereoscopic plotting instruments.

15-4 ON-LINE OPTICAL PROJECTION ORTHOPHOTO INSTRUMENTS

To introduce the subject of on-line optical projection orthophoto instruments, the U.S. Geological Survey's model T-64 Orthophotoscope will be discussed. This instrument is representative of instruments in the on-line optical projection category. Following the discussion of the model T-64, other similar instruments are described. Available space limits the discussion to only a few of the many ingenious instruments now available for orthophoto production. Inclusion or exclusion of any instrument in this text is no reflection of the author's opinion of the quality of that instrument. Orthophoto production is still in its infant stage and new innovative instruments are being introduced regularly. Although some of the instruments discussed herein may be superseded rather soon, the basic principles of differential rectification presented herein should prevail.

15-4.1 Model T-64 Orthophotoscope

The model T-64 Orthophotoscope of Fig. 15-2 contains three stereoplotter projectors supported on a projector bar. The center projector is a standard Kelsh projector which uses full-sized 9-inch diapositives. The other two are Balplex projectors which require diapositives reduced in size to achieve a 55 millimeter principal distance. Figure 15-4a illustrates a front view of the three projectors, and Fig. 15-4b shows a side view of the instrument. It, unlike an ordinary optical projection stereoplotter, has a flat *film holder* instead of a reference table. So that the operator can more conveniently see the rear of the model, the film holder (and projectors) are inclined upward at the rear of the model, making an angle of 40° with the horizontal.

Diapositives of three consecutive overlapping photographs of a flight strip, say photos 1, 2, and 3, are placed in the projectors and oriented using methods described in

FIGURE 15-4

(*a*) Front view of the projectors of the Model T-64 Orthophotoscope. (*b*) Side view of the Model T-64 Orthophotoscope.

Chap. 14. The three diapositives produce two stereomodels, models 1-2 and 2-3. The *two-projector* (swing-swing) method is first used to relatively orient one of the models, say model 1-2. That model is then leveled to ground control. The accuracy of the vertical ground control and the accuracy of the leveling operation need not be extremely precise, inasmuch as horizontal accuracy of the orthophoto is not appreciably affected by small leveling errors. When the first model is relatively oriented and leveled, model 2-3 is then relatively oriented to model 1-2 using the *one-projector* method. All motions are imparted to projector 3 so as not to upset previously oriented model 1-2. The second model is automatically leveled in the process of relatively orienting it to model 1-2. Finally, the scale of model 2-3 is made equal to the scale of model 1-2. This is achieved by adjusting model base 2-3 until the elevation of a *carry-over* point (point near the center of diapositive 2 and common to both models) is the same in model 2-3 as it is in model 1-2. It is unnecessary to scale the models absolutely to ground control because scaling is readily done later by photographic reduction or enlargement. For reasons which will be explained later, model scale is initially fixed by selecting a model base that produces an average projection distance of about 430 millimeters. When orientation is completed, a true three-dimensional stereomodel exists beneath the projectors, and, as shown in Fig. 14-4a, the stereomodel includes the entire area of the center diapositive.

The model T-64 Orthophotoscope uses the anaglyphic viewing system. Red filters are placed in front of the two outside projectors and a blue filter is placed over the center projector. An operator wearing spectacles with red and blue glasses over the left and right eye respectively can view model 1-2 stereoscopically. By reversing the spectacles, model 2-3 can be seen in three dimensions. When model 1-2 is viewed, the illumination lamp of projector 3 is turned off. Likewise, while viewing model 2-3 the lamp from projector 1 is off. At any one time an operator is able to see only the small portion of the stereomodel that is projected onto the reflecting surface of the circular platen (see Fig. 15-2).

The model T-64 Orthophotoscope must be operated under darkroom conditions. A large piece of unexposed film which will become the orthonegative is placed emulsion up on film holder. Because the film emulsion is sensitive only to blue light, a yellow or red "safe light" may be used to light the work area during operation. The unexposed film is covered by a dark curtain to protect it from undesired exposure (see Fig. 15-2). An operator systematically scans the stereomodel back and forth, and in the process the orthonegative is exposed in narrow strips through a thin slit in the center of the platen. This slit also serves as the operator's reference floating mark.

During the scanning process the film remains stationary. The platen is automatically motor-driven back and forth across the model in the y direction. A guide rod connecting the platen and illumination lamp of the center projector causes the lamp to continually follow and illuminate the platen as it scans. When a y scan is completed, the platen automatically "steps over" (moves sideways in the x direction) an amount equal to the width of the platen's scanning slit and begins scanning again in the opposite y direction. Each y scan exposes the negative to a narrow strip of terrain.

As illustrated in Fig. 15-5, the dark curtain protecting the unexposed film consists of two pieces which move with respect to one another during scanning. The platen is fixed to a narrow section (unshaded area) which is able to move back and forth in the y direction by means of rollers. This narrow y scanning section of curtain is attached to the large x scanning section (shaded), which covers the remainder of the film holder. This large curtain passes over two large rollers, thereby enabling the scanning platen to "step over" in the x direction at the completion of each y scan.

The scanning process is begun in a corner of one of the two stereomodels and is continued without interruption until that model is completed. The operator then switches the lighting to the other model and continues. The total time required to scan the entire area of the center diapositive is about two hours. Continuous scanning at constant speed is important to ensure uniform exposure throughout the orthonegative.

Since the emulsion of the film is sensitive only to blue light, the orthonegative is exposed only to images projected through the blue filter of the center projector. The center diapositive is full-sized and therefore no loss of detail occurs from reduction printing of diapositives, as would be the case if the center projector, like the side projectors, also used reduced-size diapositives. (An earlier generation of the model T-64 also used a Balplex projector in the center position.) Optimum projection distance for blue light through the lens of the center projector is 430 millimeters. This is the basis for

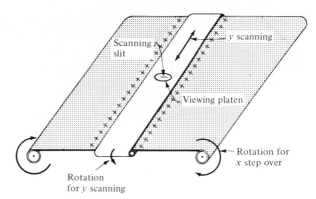

FIGURE 15-5
Scanning mechanism of the Model T-64 Orthophotoscope.

an earlier statement about scale being arbitrarily fixed during orientation so as to achieve an average projection distance of 430 millimeters.

By turning the handwheel on the front of the instrument (see Fig. 15-2) the film holder and platen can be raised and lowered. During the scanning process an operator views the steremodel on the platen and adjusts its height so as to keep the scanning slit continually in contact with the terrain. This is illustrated with points *A, B,* and *C* of Fig. 15-4*a*. The scale of the stereomodel is uniform throughout, and by keeping the platen continually in contact with the stereomodel, the entire orthonegative is exposed at model scale. The result is a negative of uniform scale throughout, which is, of course, an orthophoto.

In order to achieve a theoretically perfect orthophoto, each model point of varying elevation would have to be exposed at the proper height. Orthophotos obtained with the model T-64 are therefore approximations of theoretically perfect orthophotos because each individual point is not exposed separately. Rather, the width of a narrow strip is exposed simultaneously, a procedure which assumes equal model elevation for the width of the strip. The strips are sufficiently narrow so that, for practical purposes, the assumption is met and satisfactory results are achieved. Normally the width of the scanning slit is set at 5 millimeters. The slit width and also scan speed can be varied, however, depending upon the type of terrain in any model. Best results are achieved in rugged terrain by using a narrow strip. In flat terrain a wider strip may be scanned, thereby increasing the speed of the operation yet maintaining satisfactory accuracy.

The procedure described above is used for producing black-and-white ortho-negatives with the T-64 Orthophotoscope. If color orthophotos are desired, a somewhat different technique is necessary. Only a two-photo steromodel can be printed at one time. Three diapositives are used, two of them being of the same photo of the stereopair. The

Kelsh projector, which must contain a color diapositive, is moved to one side on the projector bar, say the left side. It is completely oriented to one of the Balplex projectors. This establishes the position and orientation of the Kelsh projector. The first Balplex projector is then moved along the projector bar to the far right. The other Balplex projector, which contains a diapositive of the same photo as that contained in the Kelsh projector, is placed on the projector bar between the other two projectors. The model is oriented again using the two Balplex projectors. The one-projector method is used and all motions are imparted to the center projector. This technique establishes the center Balplex projector in the same relative orientation as the Kelsh projector.

With orientation completed, scanning is performed by an operator who raises and lowers the platen and film holder following terrain profiles of the stereomodel beneath the Balplex projectors. Color film on the film holder beneath the Kelsh projector is exposed through an exposing slit which moves back and forth in unison with the viewing platen. In this way the orthonegative is simultaneously exposed to the same area viewed by the operator. The diapositives in the Balplex projectors can be black and white, and the operator can view the model using the anaglyphic system. However, white light must be projected through the color diapositive in the Kelsh projector to expose the color film.

15-4.2 SFOM 693

The Societe Francaise d'Optique et de Mechanique (SFOM) 693 orthophoto instrument is designed so that it can be attached to most optical projection stereoplotters. Its method of operation is similar to that of the model T-64 Orthophotoscope. Like the model T-64, the film holder is raised and lowered during scanning. However, scanning proceeds back and forth in the x direction with "step over" in the y direction. Scanning speed is varied electronically to provide uniform light intensity over the entire orthonegative in spite of light intensity variations within the stereomodel. The SFOM 693 is capable of producing color orthonegatives through the use of the stereo-image alternator (SIA) viewing system.

15-4.3 Kelsh K-320 Orthoscan

The Kelsh K-320 Orthoscan pictured in Fig. 15-6 is also similar to the model T-64 Orthophotoscope. This instrument contains three projectors and is capable of scanning the entire area of the center diapositive in a single setup. An operator varies the height of the platen to keep it in contact with the terrain as the instrument scans back and forth in the y direction. What is unique about the instrument is its use of coherent fiber optics. The relatively new science of fiber optics has enabled images to be conducted along a curved path through a coil of glass fibers. In the Kelsh K-320 Orthoscan, the film plane remains stationary, the exposure slit only is raised and lowered by the operator during

FIGURE 15-6
Kelsh K-320 Orthoscan. (*Courtesy Kelsh Instrument Div., Danko Arlington, Inc.*)

scanning, and images are transmitted through a fiber optic coil from the exposure slit to the orthonegative below. The K-320 provides an enlargement ratio of five from photo scale to orthonegative scale.

15-4.4   Zeiss Ortho-3 Projector

The Zeiss Ortho-3 Projector pictured in Fig. 15-7 combines a two-projector stereoplotter and a third orthoprojector into one instrument. This instrument introduces the concept of raising and lowering the projectors rather than the viewing platen during scanning to keep the floating mark in contact with the terrain. The stereomodel of the Ortho-3 instrument is formed in the two front projectors and the orthonegative is exposed through the rear projector. The rear projector contains a duplicate of one of the two diapositives contained in the front projectors, and it is placed in the same orientation as the front projector which contains the common diapositive. All three projectors are raised

FIGURE 15-7
Zeiss Ortho-3 projector. (*Courtesy Carl Zeiss, Oberkochen*)

and lowered during scanning by turning the handwheel in front of the instrument. An operator follows stereomodel profiles on the viewing platen as it moves back and forth in the y direction. An exposure slit beneath the rear projector moves back and forth in unison with the viewing platen and simultaneously exposes the orthonegative (which is protected from undesired light exposure by a dark curtain) to the same area viewed by the operator.

15-4.5 Wild PPO-8 and Zeiss Jena Orthophot

The Wild PPO-8 Orthophoto instrument is operated in conjunction with the Wild A-8 Autograph stereoscopic plotter, and the Zeiss Jena Orthophot is operated in conjunction with the Zeiss Jena Topocart stereoscopic plotter. The principles of operation of the PPO-8 instrument are as follows. By means of a handwheel an operator maintains the floating mark in contact with the terrain as the stereoplotting instrument automatically scans back and forth in the y direction. Imagery from the scans is projected via an optical train of lenses and prisms from the left diapositive of the stereopair to a drum in the rear of the instrument which contains the film. Exposure is made onto the film through a slit in the drum. The film rotates back and forth in the drum in synchronization with the y scanning motion in the stereomodel. Prisms within the optical train rotate the imagery to account for photographic tilt, and a variable magnification optical unit constantly corrects for scale variations in accordance with variations in model elevations along the scanned profiles. The Wild PPO-8 orthophoto instrument has the capabilities of varying scanning speed and slit width, and it can produce color orthophotos as well as black and white. The Orthophot instrument is similar in operation to the PPO-8.

15-5 OFF-LINE OPTICAL PROJECTION ORTHOPHOTO INSTRUMENTS

As previously stated, off-line instruments produce orthophotos in two separate operations. In the first operation, stereomodel profiles are scanned, recorded, and stored in either graphical or digital form. The second operation, which may take place at a later date, consists of reading these profiles into an instrument, which, in turn, automatically drives an orthoprojector and regulates projection distance according to these profiles, thereby continually achieving uniform scale of the orthonegative exposure.

Following are descriptions of some optical projection instruments capable of producing orthophotos off-line.

15-5.1 Kelsh K-320 Orthoscan

In addition to its capability of being operated on-line, the Kelsh K-320 Orthoscan can be operated off-line. With this instrument a stereomodel can be scanned without placing film in the holder. Each scan profile is recorded on punched tape. When the entire model has been scanned and all profiles recorded, film may be placed in the holder and the instrument switched to automatic scanning. In this mode only the center projector lamp is turned on. The exposure platen automatically follows the model terrain according to the information contained on the punched tape. Either color or black and white orthonegatives can be exposed.

15-5.2 U.S.G.S. Orthophotomat

In order to exploit the advantages of off-line production of orthophotos, the U.S. Geological Survey developed the orthophotomat pictured in Fig. 15-8. In using this instrument, profiles along each scan line are first generated in a separate stereoscopic plotting instrument. By means of a specially designed coordinatograph, these profiles are recorded in graphic form.

FIGURE 15-8
Orthophotomat. (*Courtesy U.S. Geological Survey*)

After the model is completely scanned and all profiles recorded, they are read through an instrument known as an *Autoline*. The Autoline follows the profile lines and automatically emits signals which control the projection distance of the orthophotomat as it scans and exposes the orthonegative. The Autoline follows profile lines by means of two photo cells which straddle the plotted profile line. The photo cells automatically and continually center themselves over the line by making the received light intensity in each photo cell equal. As the Autoline progresses along a profile line, any sensing of inequality of light intensity received by the photo cells activates a servomotor which recenters the two photo cells over the line.

The single projector of the orthophotomat is oriented by means of preselected image points projected onto a base sheet when the stereomodel was oriented in the stereoplotter for generating profiles. In orienting the orthophotomat, the projector is adjusted in elevation and orientation until the projected images match their corresponding plotted positions on the base sheet.

FIGURE 15-9
Gigas-Zeiss GZ-1 Orthoprojector. (*Courtesy Carl Zeiss, Oberkochen*)

15-5.3 Gigas-Zeiss GZ-1 Orthoprojector

The Gigas-Zeiss GZ-1 Orthoprojector shown in Fig. 15-9 contains only a single projector. It was designed expressly for orthophoto production. This projector is the same as those of the C-8 Stereoplanigraph and therefore incorporates the Bauersfeld auxiliary lens system for maintaining sharp focus regardless of variations in projection distance. The GZ-1 can either be operated on-line with a C-8 Stereoplanigraph or a Planimat stereoplotter, or it can be operated off-line from stored profiles. As with the Zeiss Ortho-3 Projector, the film holder remains stationary and the scale of imagery projected onto the orthonegative is kept constant by raising and lowering the projector to vary the projection distance.

An accessory called the Optical Interpolation System is available with the GZ-1 Orthoprojector. This accessory is used when the GZ-1 is operating in the off-line mode. The Optical Interpolation System reads two adjacent profiles simultaneously and interpolates across them to determine terrain slopes at right angles to the scan lines. With this instrument the scanning slit exposes the width between adjacent profiles instead of centering the scanning slit over a single profile. By means of coherent fiber optics, imagery is transmitted to the orthonegative.

Fig. 15-10 is a section taken at right angles to the scan lines which illustrates the concept of the Optical Interpolation System. Instead of imaging horizontal scans S_1, S_2, S_3, and S_4 which are centered on profiles P_1, P_2, P_3, and P_4, exposures are made onto

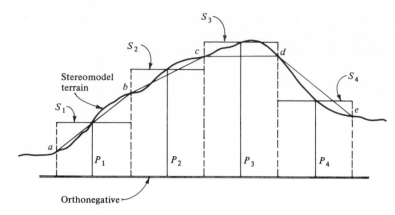

FIGURE 15-10
Concept of the Zeiss Optical Interpolation system.

the orthonegative of the sloping scans, *ab, bc, cd,* and *de.* An affine scale change is produced by the fiber optics in conducting images so that the sloping scans are imaged orthogonally onto the orthonegative film below. Advantages of this system are an orthophoto with greater planimetric accuracy, the possibility of increased scan width, and better matching of images on the orthophoto between adjacent scan lines. This latter advantage is particularly important in rugged terrain where great differences in terrain elevation from one side of the scan slit to the other cause noticeable mismatching of images. Note on Fig. 15-10 for example, that scan lines, *ab, bc, cd,* and *de* fit the terrain much better than do scans S_1, S_2, S_3, and S_4.

15-6 ADVANTAGES OF OFF-LINE ORTHOPHOTO PRODUCTION

Several significant advantages can be realized through the use of off-line orthophoto production techniques. First of all, greater accuracy results for the following reasons: (1) in scanning profiles the tiny speck of light on the platen may be used as a floating mark rather than the large exposure slit; (2) an operator can occasionally stop to rest so that the tedium of prolonged uninterrupted scanning is removed, thereby reducing errors arising from operator·fatigue; (3) scanning speed can be reduced to very slow speeds to accommodate profiling difficult areas; (4) errors made on any profile can be immediately corrected; and (5) spot checks can be made and profiles corrected before removing the model from the stereoplotter. (For on-line instruments of Sec. 15-4.5, advantages 1, 2 and 3 apply)

In addition to increased accuracy of the orthophoto, several other advantages result from off-line production techniques. Efficiency of orthophoto production can be increased because the rate at which an orthonegative can be exposed off-line is increased.

Profiles can be read from several stereoplotters and fed to one off-line orthoprojector. Double models (the entire area of the center diapositive of a triplet of photos) can be printed nonstop without the necessity of a three-projector stereoplotter. In this procedure, profiles from two adjacent models can be read independently and fed to the orthoprojector as a single set of data. Nonstop printing of the entire diapositive eliminates the visible match line that would result if the two independent models were printed separately and pieced together later as an orthophotomosaic.

Off-line orthophoto production enables profiles of an area to be stored for long periods of time and then reused for map revisions. Planimetric details, especially in heavily populated areas, may change a great deal over relatively short periods of time, but these changes rarely affect terrain profiles. Orthophotos for planimetric map revision can therefore generally be prepared from new photography, but using the old stored profiles of the same area. Off-line orthophoto production also gives rise to the possibility of digitizing contours from existing maps and then numerically deriving the profiles necessary for scanning stereomodels. Also contour locations can automatically be computed and plotted from the stored digitized profiles using a computer driven flat-bed XY plotter. One final advantage of off-line orthophoto production is the ease with which the procedure enables color orthophotos to be produced.

15-7 AUTOMATIC CONTOURING DURING ORTHOPHOTO PRODUCTION

During the process of exposing orthonegatives, locations of elevation contours can be marked by a technique called *linedropping*. Imagine that while scanning profiles, a pencil which moves with the scanning device is automatically lowered to a map sheet when the platen passes through the elevation of a desired contour. Suppose that the pencil stays in contact with the map, marking a line until another contour elevation is crossed by the platen, at which time the pencil is automatically raised. By alternately raising and lowering the pencil at contour elevation crossings, the spaces between adjacent contours are marked. Upon completion of scanning, the ends of the lines marking corresponding points of equal elevation can be joined to form continuous contours. Contour maps produced in this manner are satisfactory for some work, although they will not generally meet national map accuracy standards, nor will they be as accurate as maps compiled in the conventional manner in a stereoplotter.

It is sometimes difficult to decipher which lines correspond to equal elevations in drawing contours from the linedropped plots. This problem may be alleviated somewhat through a photographic linedropping technique. In this procedure, lines of varying width are recorded photographically on a separate film as contour elevations are crossed during profile scanning. The intensity of the light signal which exposes the line-drop film is varied each time a new contour elevation is crossed. This causes a variation in thickness of

(a)

(b)

(c)

FIGURE 15-11

(a) Portion of a line-dropped contour map produced in the GZ-1 Orthoprojector.
(b) Portion of an orthophoto (same area) produced by the GZ-1 Orthoprojector.
(c) Portion of a contour map (same area) produced by the Zeiss Automatic Contourliner in conjunction with the GZ-1.

dropped lines which greatly reduces the difficulty of drawing the contours. Figure 15-11a illustrates a portion of a line-dropped contour map produced in the GZ-1 Orthoprojector simultaneously with the production of the corresponding orthophoto pictured in Fig. 15-11b. Note that the contours on this map have already been manually drawn by connecting the ends of lines of common thickness.

The Automatic Contourliner is an accessory operated in conjunction with the GZ-1 Orthoprojector which affords another possibility in achieving automatic contours while exposing orthonegatives. The instrument simultaneously reads two adjacent profiles that have been read off-line, and it makes extremely high-speed interpolations between them. During interpolation, small dots marking positions where contour-line elevations exist are imaged photographically on a film by pulses of light. The density of imaged points is so great that the impression of continuous contour lines is achieved. Figure 15-11c shows a contour map of the area of Figs. 15-11a and b that was compiled by the Automatic Contourliner.

15-8   INSTRUMENTS FOR IMAGING ORTHOPHOTOS ELECTRONICALLY

Instruments which produce orthophotos by electronic imaging were developed more or less as by-products of efforts toward automating stereocompilation. These instruments utilize image correlation devices (see Sec. 14-15) which automatically scan model profiles and expose orthonegatives through cathode ray tubes. Electronic imaging instruments are capable of producing high-quality orthophotos very rapidly. In spite of these advantages, their high cost has prevented them from becoming as abundant as optical imaging instruments. Following is a brief description of some electronic imaging instruments:

15-8.1   B-8 Stereomat

The B-8 Stereomat, as described in Sec. 14-15, is an automated stereoplotting instrument. When operated in its automatic profiling mode, the instrument is capable of producing orthophotos. Orthonegatives are exposed in the printer unit located in the rear of the instrument. During profile scanning, imagery from the right-hand photo is electronically scaled, rectified, and transmitted to a cathode ray tube in the printer, where it is redisplayed and exposes the orthonegative.

During scanning for orthophoto production, contours can also be simultaneously produced by the B-8 Stereomat. For this procedure an emulsion is used that is both blue- and red-sensitive. Orthophoto imagery is exposed by a blue-printing cathode ray tube, and contours are imaged by a red-sensitive cathode ray tube. Each time a contour elevation is crossed during scanning, a short line segment is exposed on the orthonegative by the red phosphor tube. The line segments are oriented at right angles to maximum slope, and they are equal in length to the width of the scan strip. The contours are therefore not smooth lines but rather composed of a series of short, connected line segments. The orthophoto imagery and contours can be printed separately by filtering, and because they were exposed simultaneously onto the same film, they will be in perfect register.

15-8.2   Analytical Plotter AS11-C

The Analytical Plotter AS11-C is also equipped with an electronic imaging orthoprinter. Therefore, besides being able to perform its varied battery of photogrammetric tasks which include photogrammetric ground control extension, automatic contouring, automatic profiling, and automatic model digitizing, the AS11-C is also capable of automatically exposing orthonegatives. Initial setup procedures and orientation for printing orthophotos is the same as for operating in any of its modes (see Sec. 14-16).

The AS11-C orthoprinter has an xy carriage which enables the orthonegative to move back and forth in unison with the scanner. When operating in the automatic orthophoto mode, the image correlator scans in the y direction until it has advanced a preset distance. The computer then interrupts the scanner and transmits the scanned imagery to the printing cathode ray tube, which makes the exposure onto the ortho-negative. Prior to exposure, the imagery of each area is electronically rectified and scaled according to camera parameters, geometry of the stereopair, and terrain in that particular area. After exposure, the scanner resumes its scanning in the y direction until it has again advanced the preset distance, whereupon another exposure is made. Scanning is therefore performed in a series of parallel strips, but exposures are made onto the orthonegative film as a series of small, individual, contiguous rectangular areas or patches.

The AS11-C is also able to plot contours as a by-product of printing orthophotos. Each time a contour elevation is crossed by the scanner, a pulse is transmitted to the contour generator, which exposes a short line segment onto a separate sheet of film located on a separate stage in the orthoprinter. The scanner senses terrain slopes as well as heights, and consequently it is able to orient the line segments perpendicular to the direction of maximum slope. The resulting contours are therefore not smooth lines, but instead they are composed of a series of short connected line segments like those produced in the B-8 Stereomat orthoprinter.

15-8.3 Gestalt Photomapper GPM

The Gestalt Photomapper GPM produces orthophotos in a manner similar to that of the AS11-C described above. It exposes orthonegatives in small hexagonal-shaped contiguous patches. The size of the patch can be varied and controlled through the use of a mask. When each patch is scanned, it is electronically transformed into a scaled orthogonal pro-jection and transmitted to a cathode ray tube, which makes the exposure onto the orthonegative.

15-9 FLIGHT PLANNING FOR ORTHOPHOTOGRAPHY

Many of the principles discussed in Chap. 10 apply directly in planning aerial photography for orthophotos, and therefore it is recommended that the student review that chapter. There are some additional factors that must also be considered in planning aerial photography for orthophotos, however.

Aerial photography taken for orthophotography must be planned in accordance with the equipment to be used in exposing the orthonegatives. If an optical projection instrument will be used, diapositives must be prepared with the proper principal distance, the same as is necessary in preparing diapositives for stereocompilation. A 6-inch (150-mm) focal length camera should be used, for example, if the projectors are designed to accept nominal 6-inch focal length photography. Some orthophoto instruments such as the AS11-C Analytical Plotter do not restrict the choice of camera.

Photographic scale is of course of paramount consideration in planning any aerial photographic mission. Specific project requirements normally fix the scale of the orthophotomap, and unless photographic enlargement or reduction of the orthonegatives is planned, this fixes photo scale to within certain limits according to the enlargement ratio from photo scale to orthonegative scale that will occur with a given orthophoto instrument. Orthophotomaps may be produced at scales larger than orthonegative scale by projection printing, and this affords some latitude in planning aerial photo scale. This, of course, is an added expense, but in addition image quality is somewhat degraded with enlargement and therefore the limits of possible enlargement are restricted. Once camera focal length and photo scale are selected, flying height is also fixed.

In certain special situations, the ground coverage of each orthophoto may be a consideration that overrides other factors in planning the photography. With a 6-inch (150-mm) focal length camera and a flight height of approximately 40,000 feet, for example, an orthophoto printed from two adjacent neat models (using only approximately the center 7-inch square of the middle photo of a triplet) will cover an entire $7\frac{1}{2}$ minute quadrangle. In executing flights for *orthophotoquads,* as they are called by the U.S. Geological Survey, desired locations for ground principal points are marked on the flight map to ensure that the exposure station of the center photo of a triplet of photos occurs in the center of the quadrangle. By placing the center photo of the triplet in the center projector of the model T-64 Orthophotoscope, an orthonegative of the entire quadrangle is obtained by scanning the double model. This arrangement is not only most economical but also eliminates the possibility of a visible splice occuring if a mosaic of two or more orthonegatives was necessary to cover the quad. In cases where individual orthonegatives must be pieced together in mosaic form, it is most economical to plan the coverage of each orthonegative so as to minimize the total number of stereomodels that must be scanned.

End lap and side lap for orthophotography should generally be about the same as that for mapping photography. Sixty percent end lap and approximately 30 percent side lap allows for complete stereocoverage in spite of aircraft tilts, flying height variations, terrain variation, crab, and drift. Although the entire stereo overlap area can be scanned, deterioration of image quality along the edges of the picture format also add to the justification for using the end lap and side lap suggested above.

Although best results are usually obtained if aerial photography is planned specifically for orthophotography, the possibility of other uses should be considered. It is possible, for example, that aerial photos can serve both for orthophoto production and for stereoplotter compilation of contours.

After all factors have been considered, a flight plan including a flight map and specifications should be prepared to guide the aerial flight crew.

REFERENCES

Ahrend, M., W. Bruchlacher, and H. Meier: The Gigas-Zeiss Orthoprojector, *Photogrammetric Engineering*, vol. 31, no. 6, p. 1039, 1965.

American Society of Photogrammetry: "Manual of Photogrammetry," 3d ed., George Banta Co., Inc., Menasha, Wis., 1966, chap. 15.

Bean, R.: Development of the Orthophotoscope, *Photogrammetric Engineering,* vol. 21, no. 4, p. 529, 1955.

Blachut, T., and M. Van Wijk: 3-D Information From Orthophotos, *Photogrammetric Engineering*, vol. 36, no. 4, p. 365, 1970.

Chapelle, W., and J. Edmond: The AS-11C Automatic System, *Photogrammetric Engineering*, vol. 35, no. 10, p. 1059, 1969.

Collins, S. H.: The Accuracy of Optically Projected Orthophotos and Stereo Orthophotos, *Canadian Surveyor*, vol. 23, no. 5, p. 450, 1969.

Esten, R.: Automatic Photogrammetric Instruments, *Photogrammetric Engineering*, vol. 30, no. 4, p. 544, 1964.

Fleming, E. A.: Photo Maps as Part of a Map Series, *The Canadian Surveyor*, vol. 24, no. 2, p. 173, 1970.

Hughes, T., A. Shope, and F. Baxter: U.S.G.S. Automatic Orthophoto System, *Photogrammetric Engineering*, vol. 37, no. 10, p. 1055, 1971.

Landen, D.: Photomaps for Urban Planning, *Photogrammetric Engineering*, vol. 32, no. 1, p. 136, 1966.

Marsik, Z.: Use of Rectified Photographs and Differentially Rectified Photographs for Photo Maps, *Canadian Surveyor*, vol. 25, no. 5, p. 567, 1971.

O'Brien, T. J.: Orthophotomapping for Prudhoe Bay Development, *American Society of Civil Engineers, Journal of the Surveying and Mapping Division*, vol. 97, no. Su. 2, p. 199, 1971.

Parenti, G.: Orthophoto Printing with the Analytical Plotter, *Photogrammetric Engineering*, vol. 33, no. 4, p. 411, 1967.

Pumpelly, J. W.: Cartographic Treatments in the Production of Orthophotomaps, *Surveying and Mapping,* vol. 24, no. 4, 1964.

———: Color-Separation and Printing Techniques for Photomaps, *Surveying and Mapping*, vol. 27, no. 2, p. 277, 1967.

Radlinski, W.: Orthophotomaps Versus Conventional Maps, *Canadian Surveyor*, vol. 22, no. 1, p. 118, 1967.

Scher, M. B.: Research in Orthophotography, *Photogrammetric Engineering*, vol. 30, no. 5, p. 756, 1964.

———: Orthophotomaps for Urban Areas, *Surveying and Mapping,* vol. 29, no. 3, p. 413, 1969.

PROBLEMS

15-1 Explain the basic differences between an orthophoto and a perspective photo.

15-2 Discuss the advantages and uses of orthophotos.

15-3 What are the advantages of off-line orthophoto production as opposed to on-line production?

15-4 Describe the method of orienting black and white diapositives in the model T-64 Orthophotoscope.

15-5 Aerial photography taken with 60 percent end lap with a 6-inch focal length 9-inch square format camera is to be scanned in the model T-64 Orthophotoscope. How many scanning strips are necessary to cover the model of the entire center diapositive if a 5 millimeter scanning slit width is used and if the model is oriented with a projection distance of 430 millimeters for average ground?

15-6 Describe the "linedropping" technique of automatic contouring.

15-7 It is desired to cover a 6-mile-square township with a single orthophoto made from the center diapositive of the model T-64 Orthophotoscope. What must be flying height above ground for the overlapping aerial photography if a 6-inch focal length 9-inch square format camera is used? (Use only center 7-inch square area of diapositive.)

15-8 What will be the dimensions of the orthonegative of the center diapositive of Prob. 15-7 if it is scanned in a GZ-1 Orthoprojector using a projection distance of 550 millimeters?

OBLIQUE AND PANORAMIC PHOTOGRAPHS

PART I OBLIQUE PHOTOGRAPHS

16-1 INTRODUCTION

Oblique photographs are aerial photos taken with the camera axis intentionally inclined at an angle with the vertical. If the inclination angle is so great that the horizon shows in the pictures, the photos are termed *high obliques*. If the horizon does not show, the photos are called *low obliques*. Figure 16-1 shows a high oblique exposed over downtown Oakland, California. Note that the horizon appears in the distant background. Figure 16-2 is a low oblique showing the national capitol in Washington, D.C.

   Some of the advantages that oblique photos hold over vertical photos are demonstrated in Figs. 16-1 and 16-2. It is readily noticed, for example, that obliques provide far greater ground coverage than verticals exposed from the same altitude. Also, side views of objects afforded by obliques make them more valuable than vertical photos for some interpretation purposes. Tree species, for example, are often readily identified from obliques showing tree profiles, whereas identification may be difficult or even impossible on verticals. To the untrained person, imagery of vertical photos may be rather difficult

FIGURE 16-1
High oblique photograph exposed over Oakland, Calif. (*Courtesy Pacific Resources, Inc.*)

to interpret because the vertical view is unfamiliar. Oblique photos, on the other hand, show objects in more easily recognized forms.

Oblique photos have some disadvantages in comparison to vertical photos also. Obliques are more difficult to analyze numerically, and they are not as readily adapted to map compilation. Also, objects in the foreground of obliques frequently obscure other objects from view.

16-2 LOW OBLIQUE PHOTOS

Low oblique photos are most frequently taken for nonmapping purposes. They are especially valuable for use in reconnaissance and planning. They are also used for various special purposes in photo interpretation. The pictorial qualities of low obliques make

FIGURE 16-2
Low oblique photograph showing the National Capitol in Washington, D.C.
(*Courtesy Maps, Inc.*)

them excellent for showing city skylines, layouts of large industries, proposed
construction sites, construction progress and newly completed construction projects,
transportation routes, etc.

Since low oblique photos are simply aerial photos that contain large amounts of
tilt, the same equations developed in Chap. 13 for tilted photos may be used to analyze
them. If the magnitude and direction of tilt are known, together with the flying height
above datum, it is possible to determine scale, relief displacement, tilt displacement, and
ground point coordinates from measurements of image positions on low oblique photos.

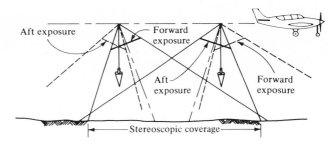

FIGURE 16-3
Convergent photography.

Convergent photography, as illustrated in Fig. 16-3, consists of stereopairs of low oblique photos taken with the camera axes converging toward one another. Cameras such as the one shown in Fig. 4-5 have been designed specifically for taking convergent photography. A single aerial camera can also be used for taking convergent photos, in which case the camera must be quickly tilted *fore* and *aft* to make the exposures.

Advantages of convergent photography in mapping are that up to 100 percent end lap can be obtained, and this results in larger coverage per stereomodel. Also, greater base-height ratios can be achieved, which increases parallactic angles of intersection of corresponding rays and makes possible greater accuracy in locating point positions photogrammetrically. Although not all stereoscopic plotting instruments are capable of handling convergent photography, many of them are. Orientation procedures for stereopairs of convergent photos are similar to those described in Chap. 14 for vertical photos. With optical projection plotters, however, in order to achieve optimum focus throughout the entire stereomodel, the *Scheimpflug condition,* described in Sec. 2-8, must be satisfied. Analytical computations with low oblique photos are performed in the same manner as with tilted photos. When the utmost in accuracy is desired in analytical computations, convergent photos are used because of their improved parallactic angles.

16-3 HIGH OBLIQUE PHOTOS

High oblique photos are now most frequently taken for nonmapping purposes. During the 1940s and 1950s, however, *trimetrogon* photography which utilized high oblique photos was used extensively for small-scale charting of vast areas of the world. Trimetrogon photography was so called because three cameras with *metrogon* lenses were used. Figure 16-4 illustrates the orientation of the three cameras of a trimetrogon system. The center camera exposed a vertical photo while the two side cameras exposed high oblique photos. The three cameras fired simultaneously and obtained ground coverage from horizon to

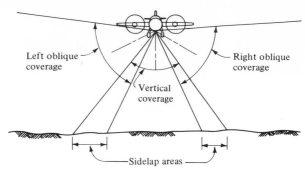

FIGURE 16-4
Orientation of three cameras used in trimetrogon photography.

horizon transverse to the direction of flight. As the aircraft progressed along a flight strip, successive exposures overlapped preceding ones. The coverage obtained with trimetrogon photography enabled rapid, small-scale planimetric map compilation of an extensive area.

In recent years, modern aircraft and space vehicles have made possible the acquisition of extremely high-altitude vertical photographs (see Fig. 20-17). These have almost completely supplanted high oblique photos for small-scale mapping. Obliques still retain their value, however, for interpretation, reconnaissance, and intelligence purposes.

High oblique photography has been used to supplement the ground control needed for small-scale mapping with vertical photography, especially in areas with difficult access for ground surveying. By exposing two high oblique photos (called *horizon* photos) simultaneously with each vertical exposure, magnitudes and directions of tilt of the vertical photos can be determined. This is possible because the two high oblique cameras are mounted with their optical axes tilted in planes perpendicular to one another; their orientations with respect to the vertical camera axis are known; and the tilt angles of the oblique camera axes are readily determined (see Eqs. 16-1 through 16-4).

Since high oblique photos are merely severely tilted photos, they can be analyzed using the tilted photo equations of Chap. 13. A slightly different approach is also convenient for analyzing them, however. Figure 16-5a illustrates the principal plane of a high oblique photograph, and Fig. 16-5b shows the resulting photo. The photograph was taken at exposure station L from a flying height H' above datum. The camera focal length was f. The datum nadir point, N, is the point on the datum plane vertically beneath the exposure station. The photographic nadir point, n, is the point where a vertical line from the exposure station pierces the photo plane. Because of the large tilts of high obliques, the photo nadir may not actually exist on the photo but rather fall on the extension of the photographic plane.

The following terms pertinent to a discussion of high obliques are described below and are illustrated on Figs. 16-5a and 16-5b:

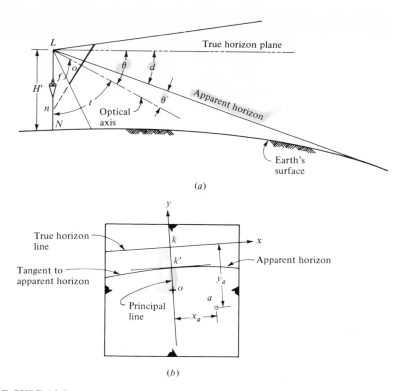

FIGURE 16-5
(*a*) Side view of the principal plane of a high oblique photograph. (*b*) Plan view of a high oblique photograph.

Apparent Horizon The actual line on the photograph indicating where the land and sky meet. As seen in Fig. 16-1, due to earth curvature the apparent horizon appears as a slightly curved line.

True Horizon The horizontal plane containing the exposure station. On the photograph, the line of intersection of the true horizon plane and the photo plane is the *true horizon line*.

Apparent Depression Angle The angle θ' measured in the principal plane between the camera axis and the apparent horizon. If the apparent horizon is visible on the photograph, the distance ok' from the principal point to the apparent horizon can be measured and θ' calculated as follows:

$$\theta' = \tan^{-1}\left(\frac{ok'}{f}\right) \qquad (16\text{-}1)$$

Dip Angle Angle d measured in the principal plane between the true and apparent horizons. The dip angle is due to the height of the camera above the earth. An equation for calculating its value in seconds may be developed with reference to Fig. 16-6.

In Fig. 16-6, O is the center of the earth and R is the mean radius of the earth. A high oblique photograph is exposed at L from a flying height H' above ground. N is the ground nadir point. Line LK is the true horizon, and LK' is the apparent horizon tangent to the earth at K'; therefore d is the dip angle. By geometry the angle at O subtended by arc NK' is also d. From the figure,

$$\tan d = \frac{LK'}{R} \qquad (a)$$

Also,
$$LK' = \sqrt{(R + H')^2 - R^2} \qquad (b)$$

Substituting (b) into (a) and reducing,

$$\tan d = \frac{\sqrt{2RH' + H'^2}}{R} \qquad (c)$$

Since H' is small compared to R, Eq. (c) reduces to

$$\tan d = \sqrt{\frac{2H'}{R}} \qquad (d)$$

Because the dip angle is always small, $\tan d$ is approximately d in radians. Also, due to atmospheric refraction, line LK' is bent such that d is reduced in size. Multiplying Eq. (d) by the constant 0.9216 to account for atmospheric refraction in a standard atmosphere, substituting into the equation the mean radius of the earth 20.9×10^6 feet, and converting radians to seconds, the following equation for dip angle in seconds results:

$$d'' = 58.8 \sqrt{H'} \qquad (16\text{-}2)$$

In Eq. (16-2), H' is the height of the camera above datum in feet.

True Depression Angle Angle θ measured in the principal plane between the camera optical axis and the true horizon. The true depression angle on Fig. 16-5a is seen to be the sum of the apparent depression angle and the dip angle, or

$$\theta = \theta' + d \qquad (16\text{-}3)$$

Tilt Angle Angle t measured in the principal plane between the camera axis and the vertical line through the exposure station. It is also the angle between the horizontal plane and the plane of the photo. The true depression angle and the tilt angle are related by the following expression:

$$t = 90° - \theta \qquad (16\text{-}4)$$

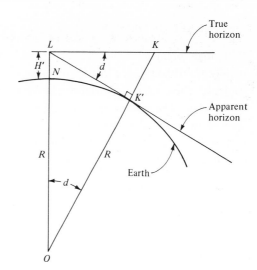

FIGURE 16-6
Dip angle of high oblique photograph.

16-4 PHOTOCOORDINATE SYSTEM FOR HIGH OBLIQUES

Locations of image points on oblique photos are commonly given with respect to the xy coordinate system shown in Fig. 16-5b. In this system, the x and y axes coincide with the true horizon line and principal line respectively, where the principal line is in the line of intersection of the principal plane and photo plane. The photographic position of any image point a may be given by its rectangular coordinates x_a and y_a, as shown in Fig. 16-5b. Points above the x axis have positive y coordinates and those below have negative y coordinates. Also, points to the right of the y axis have positive x coordinates and those to the left have negative x coordinates.

The x and y axes may be readily located on a high oblique photo if the apparent horizon shows as a nearly straight line such as that of Fig. 16-1. First, point k' of Fig. 16-5b is located by construction at the point where a tangent to the apparent horizon is perpendicular to a line passing through the principal point. The principal line (y axis) is drawn through principal point o and point k'. Length ok' (from principal point to apparent horizon) is measured, and from Eq. (16-1) the apparent depression angle θ' is calculated. From Eq. (16-2) the dip angle is computed, and the true depression angle θ is then determined from Eq. (16-3). Length ok from principal point to true horizon is then calculated using the following equation:

$$ok = f \tan \theta \qquad (16\text{-}5)$$

Distance ok is laid off to locate point k, and finally the true horizon line is drawn through k perpendicular to the principal line. If the apparent horizon is not visible on the photo, the *vanishing point* method described in Sec. 16-11 might possibly be used to locate the xy axes and to calculate angle θ.

16-5   SCALE OF HIGH OBLIQUE PHOTOS

With high oblique photos object distances vary from minimum distances of approximately the flying height in the foreground to extremely long distances near the apparent horizon. These extreme variations in object distances cause corresponding variations in photo scale. The scale at any point in a high oblique photo in the x direction differs from its scale in the y direction. On flat terrain scale is constant along any line in the x direction (along any line parallel to the true horizon), while it continually varies along any line in the y direction (along any line parallel with the principal line). The closer a point is to the true horizon—i.e., the smaller its y coordinate—the smaller will be its scale.

On Fig. 16-7 scale in the x direction at point a is the ratio of photo distance $a'a$ to corresponding ground distance $A'A$, or

$$S_{x_a} = \frac{a'a}{A'A} \qquad (e)$$

From similar triangles in Fig. 16-7,

$$\frac{a'a}{A'A} = \frac{La'}{LA'} = \frac{La''}{LA''} = S_{x_a} \qquad (f)$$

Substituting $y_a \cos \theta$ for La'' and $(H - h)$ for LA'' into (f) and dropping subscripts:

$$S_x = \frac{y \cos \theta}{(H - h)} \qquad (16\text{-}6)$$

In Eq. (16-6), S_x is the scale at any point on a high oblique photo in the x direction, y is the photocoordinate of the point measured from the true horizon of the photo, θ is the true depression angle, H is flying height above datum, and h is the elevation of the point above datum.

Again referring to Fig. 16-7, an expression for the scale in the y direction for any point on a high oblique photo may be developed. On the figure ground distance AB is considered infinitesimally small, and the scale in the y direction at point a may be expressed as the ratio of photo distance ab to corresponding ground distance AB. However, since $a'b' = ab$, and $A'B' = AB$;

$$S_{y_a} = \frac{a'b'}{A'B'} \qquad (g)$$

In Fig. 16-7 let ϕ be angle oLa', the vertical angle between the camera axis and ray LA'. Also, line $A'K$ is constructed perpendicular to the camera axis so that $A'K$ is parallel to $a'k$. In triangle $A'PK$ the angle at P is equal to θ, and the angle at A' is therefore $(90° - \theta)$. Since $A'B'$ is infinitesimally short, lines LA' and LB' are assumed parallel, and hence in triangle $A'B'B''$ the angle at B' is $(\theta + \phi)$. Therefore the angle at B'' is $(90° - \phi)$. By the law of sines in triangle $A'B'B''$,

$$A'B' = \frac{A'B'' \cos \phi}{\sin (\theta + \phi)} \qquad (h)$$

FIGURE 16-7
Scale of a high oblique photograph.

Substituting (h) into (g),

$$S_{y_a} = \frac{a'b' \sin(\theta + \phi)}{A'B'' \cos \phi} \qquad (i)$$

From similar triangles of Fig. 16-7,

$$\frac{a'b'}{A'B''} = \frac{La'}{LA'} \qquad (j)$$

Substitute (j) into (i),

$$S_y = \frac{La' \sin(\theta + \phi)}{LA' \cos \phi} \qquad (k)$$

But from (f), $La'/LA' = S_{x_a}$. Also from Fig. 16-7, $La' = f/\cos \phi$ and $LA' = (H - h/\text{Cos}\,(90° - \theta - \phi)$. Therefore,

$$S_{x_a} = \frac{f \sin(\theta + \phi)}{(H - h) \cos \phi} \qquad (m)$$

Rearranging (m),

$$\frac{S_{x_a}(H-h)}{f} = \frac{\sin(\theta + \phi)}{\cos \phi} \qquad (n)$$

Substituting $La'/LA' = S_{x_a}$, and Eq. (n) into (k),

$$S_{y_a} = \frac{(S_{x_a})S_{x_a}(H-h)}{f} \qquad (p)$$

Finally, substituting Eq. (16-6) into (p), dropping subscripts, and reducing,

$$S_y = \frac{y^2 \cos^2 \theta}{f(H-h)} \qquad (16\text{-}7)$$

In Eq. (16-7), S_y is the scale in the y direction at any point on a high oblique photo, and the remaining terms are as previously described.

EXAMPLE 16-1   A high oblique photo was exposed from a flying height of 10,000 ft above ground with a camera having a focal length of 6 in. The distance ok' was measured as 2.92 in. Find the scale in the x and y directions at the principal point.

SOLUTION   From Eqs. (16-1), (16-2), and (16-3),

$$\theta' = \tan^{-1}\left(\frac{2.92}{6.00}\right) = 25° \ 57'$$

$$d = 58.8 \sqrt{10,000} = 5,880'' = 1° \ 38'$$

$$\theta = 25° \ 57' + 1° \ 38' = 27° \ 35'$$

From Eq. (16-5),

$$ok = 6.00 \tan 27° \ 35' = 3.13 \text{ in.}$$

(ok is also the y coordinate of the principal point.)

From Eqs. (16-6) and (16-7),

$$S_x = \frac{(3.13)\cos 27° \ 35'}{10,000} = 1 \text{ in}/3,605 \text{ ft}$$

$$S_y = \frac{(3.13)^2 \cos^2 27° \ 35'}{(6.00)10,000} = 1 \text{ in}/7,800 \text{ ft} \qquad ////$$

16-6   LENGTHS OF LINES FROM SINGLE HIGH OBLIQUE PHOTOS

For a high oblique photo *taken over flat terrain*, the ground length of any line may be determined if the images of its end points appear on the photo. This is accomplished by determining its X and Y components and then applying the pythagorean theorem.

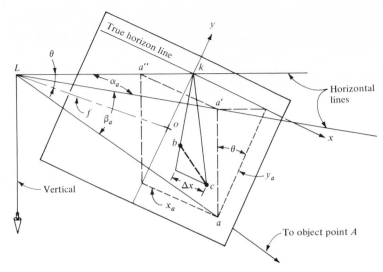

FIGURE 16-8
Lengths of lines, and horizontal and vertical angles from a high oblique photograph.

Consider, for example, determining ground length BC from images b and c which appear in the high oblique photo of Fig. 16-8. To determine the X and Y components, lines are first constructed on the photograph from point k through image points b and c. At point c, the x photo component Δx between the two lines is measured parallel to the x axis. Then the X ground component ΔX is calculated as (note that H' is flying height above average ground)

$$\Delta X = \Delta x \left(\frac{H'}{y_c \cos \theta} \right) \qquad (16\text{-}8)$$

Also ΔY, the Y ground component is calculated as

$$\Delta Y = \left(\frac{1}{y_c} - \frac{1}{y_b} \right) \left(\frac{fH'}{\cos^2 \theta} \right) \qquad (16\text{-}9)$$

Finally, the ground length of line BC is determined from its X and Y components by applying the pythagoren theorem as

$$BC = \sqrt{(\Delta X)^2 + (\Delta Y)^2} \qquad (16\text{-}10)$$

EXAMPLE 16-2 The focal length, flying height above average ground, and true depression angle for a high oblique photograph are 152 mm, 6,000 ft, and 30° 00′ respectively.

Find ground length AB of a line whose images a and b appear on the photo. The Δx photo component measured at b is 6.21 mm, and the y coordinates of a and b are -100.38 and -104.81 mm respectively.

SOLUTION From Eq. (16-8),

$$\Delta X = 6.21 \left(\frac{6,000}{104.81 \ \cos 30° \ 00'} \right) = 410 \ \text{ft}$$

From Eq. (16-9),

$$\Delta Y = \left(\frac{1}{-104.81} - \frac{1}{-100.38} \right) \left(\frac{152 \times 6,000}{\cos^2 30° \ 00'} \right) = 512 \ \text{ft}$$

From Eq. (16-10),

$$AB = \sqrt{(410)^2 + (512)^2} = 654 \ \text{ft} \qquad\qquad ////$$

16-7 HORIZONTAL AND VERTICAL ANGLES FROM HIGH OBLIQUE PHOTOS

Horizontal and vertical angles to points whose images appear in oblique photos may be readily determined provided the reference xy axes can be located. As depicted in Fig. 16-8, an oblique photo exposed from L has its camera axis inclined downward at a true depression angle θ. Image point a in the photo has coordinates x_a and y_a as illustrated. Line aa' is constructed vertical, a' being in the horizontal plane containing the exposure station. Plane Lko is the principal plane (a vertical plane), and plane Laa' is also vertical because it contains vertical line aa'. Line $a'a''$ is parallel to the x axis and is horizontal.

Angle α_a between vertical planes Lko and Laa' (horizontal angle between camera axis and ray to object point A) may be calculated as

$$\alpha_a = \tan^{-1} \left(\frac{a'a''}{La''} \right) = \tan^{-1} \left(\frac{x_a}{Lk - a''k} \right)$$

Substituting for $a'a''$ and La'',

$$\alpha_a = \tan^{-1} \left(\frac{x_a}{f \sec \theta + y_a \sin \theta} \right) \qquad (16\text{-}11)$$

After α_a has been calculated, vertical angle β_a between horizontal line La' and ray La may be calculated as follows:

$$\beta_a = \tan^{-1} \left(\frac{aa'}{La'} \right) = \tan^{-1} \left(\frac{y_a \cos \theta}{La'' \sec \alpha_a} \right)$$

Substituting for La'',

$$\beta_a = \tan^{-1}\left(\frac{y_a \cos\theta}{(f\sec\theta + y_a \sin\theta)\sec\alpha_a}\right) \qquad (16\text{-}12)$$

In both Eqs. (16-11) and (16-12), due regard must be given the algebraic signs of x_a and y_a. Horizontal angles therefore have negative signs if x_a is negative, and vertical angles have negative algebraic signs if y_a is negative. The algebraic sign of the true depression angle θ is considered positive in all equations of this chapter.

16-8   EXPOSURE STATION POSITION AND AZIMUTH OF CAMERA AXIS

If images of three control points appear on a high oblique photo, the horizontal and vertical position of the exposure station and azimuth of the camera axis can be determined. The horizontal position of the exposure station and camera axis azimuth are determined first. In this procedure horizontal angles between the camera axis and the three control points are calculated using Eq. (16-11). An example is illustrated in Fig. 16-9, where horizontal angles α_a, α_b and α_c to control points A, B, and C have been calculated. From the three α angles, the two horizontal angles δ_1 and δ_2 can be determined. Using angles δ_1 and δ_2, the horizontal position of exposure station L can be determined by three-point resection. Either graphical three-point resection (see Sec. 9-5) may be performed, or numerical methods may be used. Most surveying books describe numerical methods of three-point resection.

When ground coordinates X_L and Y_L have been determined, the azimuth of a ray from the exposure station to a control point, such as ray LA may be calculated from coordinate differences. By adding α_a to the azimuth of LA, the azimuth of the camera axis may be determined. A check can be obtained by repeating this procedure with another control point.

If the vertical angle is computed for one vertical control point whose horizontal position is also known, the height of the camera above the control point may be determined. This presumes exposure station coordinates X_L and Y_L are known. In calculating camera height, it may be necessary to account for atmospheric refraction and curvature of the earth. Figure 16-10 illustrates a high oblique photograph taken at a flying height H above datum. The image a of vertical control point A appears in the photo. The elevation of A above datum is h_A. Vertical angle β_a of the ray from the exposure station to the control point may be calculated using Eq. (16-12). With the horizontal positions of the exposure station and control point known, horizontal distance D from exposure station L to control point A can be calculated. Then vertical distance $(V = D \tan\beta_a)$ may be calculated.

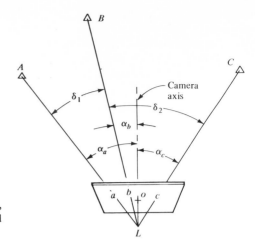

FIGURE 16-9
A high oblique photograph in space,
illustrating three-point resection method
of locating exposure station.

Due to atmospheric refraction, calculated vertical angle β_a is too small by an amount $\Delta\beta_a$, so that calculated V is not the true difference in elevation between L and A. Instead, due to atmospheric refraction, V is too small by an amount R. If R is added to V to obtain V', this is still not the true difference in elevation $(H - h_A)$, but is now too large by an amount C, which is due to earth curvature. The value of C is the amount of departure between a tangent to the earth's surface and the curved earth. It is proportional to the square of the distance D and is equal to $0.067\ M^2$, where M is the distance D in miles. The refraction correction R is approximately one-seventh the value of C but is in the opposite direction. The following expression yields the combined correction for the effects of refraction and curvature:

$$(R - C) = -0.574\,M^2 \qquad (16\text{-}13)$$

For small values of D, refraction and curvature is negligible, e.g., its value is only 0.57 feet for D equal to 1 mile. For large values of D, however, it becomes significant; e.g., it is 57 feet in 10 miles. The refraction and curvature correction, when added to computed V, yields the following equation for calculating flying height for a high oblique photo:

$$H = D \tan \beta_a + (R - C) + h_A \qquad (16\text{-}14)$$

EXAMPLE 16-3 Suppose that on the high oblique photo of Example 16-1, image a of vertical control point A has x and y coordinates of 3.83 and -2.94 in respectively. Calculate the flying height of the photo above datum if h_A is 1,460 ft and if the horizontal distance D from exposure station to point A is 6,550 ft.

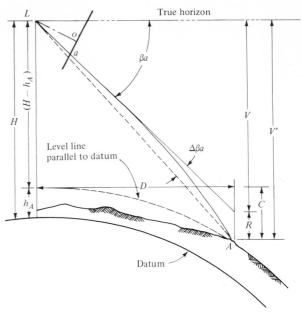

FIGURE 16-10
Earth curvature and atmospheric refraction corrections with high oblique photography.

SOLUTION   From Eq. (16-11), horizontal angle α_a is first calculated.

$$\alpha_a = \tan^{-1}\left(\frac{3.83}{6.00 \times \sec 27° 35' - 2.94 \times \sin 27° 35'}\right) = 35° 18'$$

·From Eq. (16-12), vertical angle β_a to control point A is

$$\beta_a = \tan^{-1}\left(\frac{-2.94 \times \cos 27° 35'}{(6.00 \times \sec 27° 35' - 2.94 \times \sin 27° 35') \sec 35° 18'}\right) = -21° 08'$$

From Eq. (16-13), the refraction and curvature correction is:

$$(R - C) = -0.574\left(\frac{6,550}{5,280}\right)^2 = -0.9 \text{ ft}$$

Finally, from Eq. (16-14), flying height for the photo is

$$H = 6,550 \tan 21° 08' - 0.9 + 1,460 = 3,990 \text{ ft above datum} \qquad ////$$

16-9   LOCATING POINTS FROM OVERLAPPING HIGH OBLIQUE PHOTOS

If images of an object point appear on two or more oblique photos whose positions and camera axis orientations are known, the horizontal and vertical position of the object point can be determined by the method of intersection. In Fig. 16-11, for example,

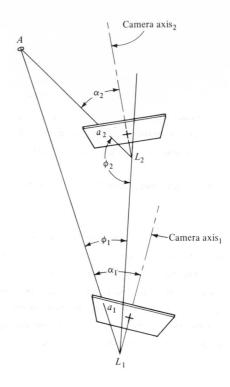

FIGURE 16-11
An overlapping pair of high oblique photographs in space, illustrating method of intersection for locating new points.

images a_1 and a_2 of object point A appear on oblique photos exposed at L_1 and L_2. If the positions and camera axis directions of both exposures are known, then the length and direction of the airbase L_1L_2 may be calculated from differences in ground coordinates. Horizontal angles α_1 and α_2 may be calculated from Eq. (16-11), from which horizontal angles ϕ_1 and ϕ_2 may be determined. The oblique triangle L_1AL_2, with its angles ϕ_1 and ϕ_2 and length L_1L_2 known, may be solved by the law of sines to obtain the horizontal ground position of A. Instead of using numerical techniques described above, graphical procedures can also be applied to obtain the position of point A.

If the flying height for the oblique photo is known, the elevation h_A of point A of Fig. 16-11 may be determined by first calculating vertical angle β_a using Eq. (16-12) and then solving for h_A in Eq. (16-14), or

$$h_A = H - D \tan \beta_a - (R - C) \qquad (16\text{-}15)$$

In order to solve Eq. (16-15), it is first necessary to determine the horizontal position of point A so that horizontal distance D from the exposure station to point A is available.

16-10 PERSPECTIVE GRIDS

To introduce the concept of a perspective grid, suppose a high oblique photo was exposed over flat terrain upon which existed a square grid pattern such as section lines of the U.S. Public Land System. If the camera were pointing in a northerly direction during exposure, all north-south section lines would appear to converge (vanish) at a point on the true horizon line of the photo. Such a point of convergence of parallel lines on an oblique photo is called the *vanishing point*. The square sections of land would appear on the photo as a pattern of quadrilateral grids. This grid pattern is properly called a *perspective grid*, because it represents a perspective view of a ground grid. In this case each perspective grid quadrilateral would represent a ground grid square of 1-mile dimensions.

Given flying height, focal length, and depression angle, it is possible to prepare a perspective grid for an oblique photo even though no ground grid actually exists. Ground dimensions of grid squares represented by quadrilaterals of the perspective grid can be selected at any convenient value. The grid is usually prepared on a transparent medium and, when superimposed on the photo, the perspective grid shows photo locations of imaginary ground squares. This provides a reference rectangular coordinate system for determining ground distances or for planimetric mapping by direct tracing.

In constructing a perspective grid for a high oblique photo, it is convenient to make one of the grid lines coincide with the principal line of the photo. The procedure involves first locating the true horizon line of the photo as described in Sec. 16-4. Then, as shown in Fig. 16-12, principal line *ko* is extended an arbitrary distance to establish point *e*. Because it corresponds to the principal line, ground line *EE* is the so-called *ground principal meridian*, and grid line *ke* is called the *grid principal meridian*.

A *base parallel* perpendicular to the grid principal meridian is established next by constructing a line parallel to the true horizon which passes through point *e*. Having selected *M*, the desired dimension of ground squares, it is necessary to find the required spacing, *m*, along the base parallel between adjacent grid meridians. (All grid lines of Fig. 16-12 that converge at *k*, such as *ck, dk, fk*, etc., are called *grid meridians*. They have corresponding ground lines *CC, DD, FF*, etc., called *ground meridians*, which are parallel to the ground principal meridian. Point *k* is the vanishing point for all ground meridians.) From similar triangles *kde* and *kDE* of Fig. 16-12,

$$\frac{m}{ke} = \frac{M}{kE}$$

Substituting $(H' \sec \theta)$ for kE into the above equation and solving for m,

$$m = \frac{Mke}{H' \sec \theta} \tag{16-16}$$

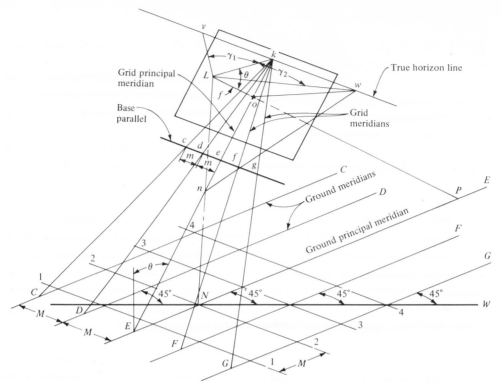

FIGURE 16-12
Constructing a perspective grid for a high oblique photograph.

In Eq. (16-16), m is the required spacing between adjacent grid meridians measured along the base parallel, M is the dimension of ground squares represented by grid quadrilaterals, ke is the length of the grid principal meridian from k to e, and H' is flying height above ground. The units of M and H' must be the same, and the units of m will be the same as the units of ke. Having calculated m, segments of length m are marked along the base parallel to locate points c, d, f, etc., and grid meridians ck, dk, fk, etc., are drawn. The spacing in the x direction on the oblique photo between adjacent meridians, no matter where measured, represents a ground distance of M.

It is next required to draw on the perspective grid a system of grid lines parallel to the base parallel. These lines are the so-called *grid parallels*. Consider a diagonal ground line NW of Fig. 16-12 which crosses ground principal meridian $ENPE$ at a $45°$ angle. Line NW also crosses all ground meridians at $45°$. Perpendiculars 1-1, 2-2, 3-3, etc., erected to ground meridians CC, DD, EE, etc., at the points where line NW intersects them forms a square ground grid of dimensions M.

The key to drawing parallels on the perspective grid is to find the perspective grid location of a diagonal ground line, such as *NW,* that makes a 45° angle with the principal plane. Perpendiculars (parallels) are then erected to the grid meridians where this diagonal crosses them. This produces the grid parallels. In Fig. 16-12, if distance *kw* is made equal to *Lk* where *Lk* is equal to $f \sec \theta$, then angle γ_2 is a horizontal angle of 45° and line *Lw* intersects the true horizon line at point *w.* The vertical plane containing line *Lw* also contains lines *nw* and *NW.* Line *nw* in the photo plane is therefore the perspective grid location of ground line *NW,* and point *w* is the vanishing point for line *NW.* According to perspective geometry, any system of lines that are parallel in the flat ground plane all vanish at the same vanishing point, provided they are not parallel to the horizon line. Point *w* is therefore the vanishing point for all lines in the ground plane that make an angle of 45° with the ground principal meridian. Hence grid line *wo* also represents a diagonal ground line that crosses ground meridians at 45°.

By similar analysis, the vanishing point for another set of parallel ground lines that make a 45° degree angle γ_1 with the ground principal meridian occurs at *v,* where distance *kv* is equal to $f \sec \theta$.

In applying the above principles to the construction of grid parallels, points *v* and *w* are first located on the true horizon line as illustrated in Fig. 16-13, where

$$vk = wk = f \sec \theta \qquad (16\text{-}17)$$

Diagonal lines *vv′* and *ww′* are then drawn, and where these diagonals intersect grid meridians, grid parallels are constructed as shown in Fig. 16-13. Meridians and parallels are drawn until the area of interest on the photo is covered. Once completed, the grid may be used to extrapolate distances, or it may be used for planimetric mapping. It should be noted that accuracy is highest in the picture foreground, and it diminishes rapidly toward the apparent horizon.

Diagonals *vv′* and *ww′* could be drawn at any random location as long as they converge at *v* or *w.* It is convenient, however, to draw them through the principal point, as this locates the ground principal point explicitly at a grid intersection on the map. The ground nadir point may then be located on the map by measuring back along the principal meridian on the map a distance *PN,* where

$$PN = \frac{H'}{\tan \theta} \qquad (16\text{-}18)$$

A technique of planimetric mapping called the *Canadian grid* method was used extensively in the past for small-scale planimetric mapping of much of Canada's flat wilderness area. The procedure involved preparing perspective grids for oblique photos such that each quadrilateral on the perspective grid represented a ground square of $\frac{1}{8}$ mile dimensions. Map compilation was done on a base sheet having a square grid of $\frac{1}{8}$ inch dimensions, so that the resulting map scale was 1 inch to the mile. Map compilation was

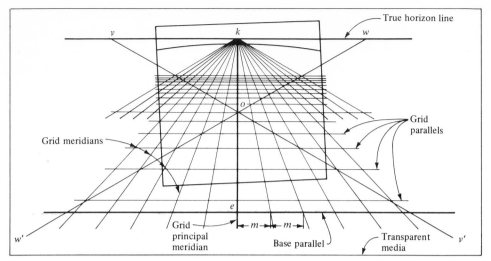

FIGURE 16-13
Constructing parallels of a perspective grid for a high oblique photograph.

done manually by transferring details appearing in each perspective grid quadrilateral to its corresponding map square.

16-11 TRUE HORIZON AND TRUE DEPRESSION ANGLE BY VANISHING POINT AND NADIR POINT METHODS

If a square or rectangular ground object such as a 1-mile square *section* of land appears on an oblique photo taken over flat terrain, the true horizon and true depression angle may be found even though the apparent horizon is not visible on the photo using the *vanishing point* method.

In Fig. 16-14, a square field, *abcd,* appears on an oblique photo as shown. Since parallel lines vanish at a point on the true horizon, lines *ab* and *cd* are extended until they intersect to locate vanishing point *v.* Likewise lines *ad* and *bc* are extended until they intersect to locate vanishing point *w.* The true horizon line *vw* may then be constructed. Principal point *o* is located from fiducial marks, and a perpendicular to the true horizon line is constructed which passes through the principal point. Point *k* where the perpendicular intersects the true horizon line is the origin of the oblique photocoordinate system. The *y* axis coincides with line *ok,* and the *x* axis coincides with line *vw.* Length *ok* is measured and the true depression angle calculated using Eq. (16-5).

If images of vertical objects such as tall buildings or telephone poles appear on an oblique photo, the true horizon and true depression angle may be determined by the

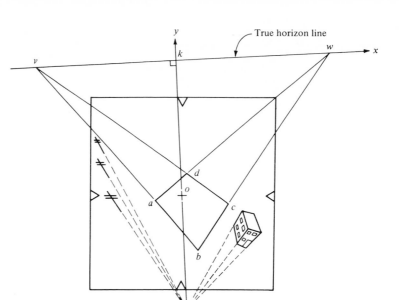

FIGURE 16-14
Locating the true horizon of an oblique photograph by vanishing points method
and by nadir point method.

nadir point method. In this technique, as illustrated in Fig. 16-14, image lines of vertical objects are extended to their intersection. This locates the photographic nadir point. Line *no* is then constructed (this is the *y* axis). Distance *no* is measured and the true depression angle is calculated as

$$\theta = 90° - \tan^{-1}\left(\frac{no}{f}\right) \quad (16\text{-}19)$$

With θ known, distance *ok* is calculated using Eq. (16-5), distance *ok* is laid off along the *y* axis to locate point *k*, and the true horizon is constructed by erecting a perpendicular to the *y* axis at point *k*.

PART II   PANORAMIC PHOTOGRAPHS

16-12   INTRODUCTION

A panoramic photograph is a picture of a strip of terrain taken transverse to the direction of flight. The exposure is made by a specially designed camera which scans laterally from one side of the flight path to the other. The lateral scan angle may be as great as 180°, in

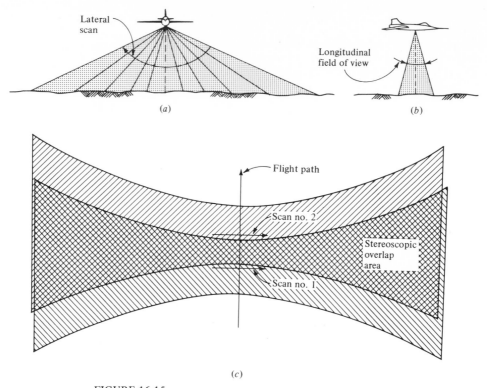

FIGURE 16-15
(a) Lateral scan of a panoramic photograph. (b) Longitudinal field of view of vertical panoramic photograph. (c) Ground coverage of overlapping vertical panoramic photos.

which case the photograph contains a panorama of the terrain from horizon to horizon. The longitudinal field of view of the scan (angular coverage in the direction of flight) is narrow, but the camera is capable of rapid cycling so that successive photos overlap the previous ones, thereby providing continuous stereoscopic coverage of the terrain.

Panoramic photos may be exposed either as *verticals* or *forward-looking obliques*. Figure 16-15a and b are front and side views illustrating lateral and longitudinal angular coverages of a vertical panoramic photograph, while Fig. 16-15c shows actual ground coverage of overlapping vertical paroramic photos. Figure 16-16 illustrates camera orientation for forward-looking oblique photos. Figure 16-17 is an example of a vertical panoramic photo. Note that scale decreases toward the horizons from its maximum scale directly beneath the flight path. This is, of course, expected, since scale decreases with an increase in object distance. This helps explain the "butterfly" appearance of ground coverage of a vertical panoramic photo shown in Fig. 16-15c. Figure 16-18 is a

FIGURE 16-16
Longitudinal field of view of forward-looking oblique panoramic photograph.

forward-looking oblique panoramic photo. The extreme curvature of the horizon in this photo is primarily due to the geometric nature of forward-looking oblique panoramic photos and only very slightly due to earth curvature.

In recent years increasing interest has been shown in panoramic photography. One reason for this interest is that compared to frame camera photos, panoramic photos cover a much greater area. Also because they utilize only the center portion of the camera lens, image resolution provided by panoramic photos may be as much as five times greater than that of frame camera photography. These advantages, together with more uniform illumination over the entire format, make panoramic photos exceptionally well suited for photo interpretation and for intelligence and reconnaissance purposes. Panoramic photos have the disadvantage that they lack the geometric fidelity of frame camera photos, a characteristic that is important for mapping.

16-13 PANORAMIC CAMERAS

Panoramic cameras are generally one of two types: those which scan by rotating the camera lens and those which scan by rotating a prism in front of the camera lens. These two basic scanning systems are illustrated in simplified diagrams of Figs. 16-19 and 16-20.

FIGURE 16-17
Vertical panoramic photograph taken over Marietta, Ohio, with a Perkin-Elmer KS-68A panoramic camera. (*Courtesy Perkin-Elmer*)

FIGURE 16-18
Forward-looking oblique panoramic photograph showing New York's World Fair grounds taken with a Fairchild F-415 panoramic camera. (*Courtesy Fairchild Space and Defense Systems*)

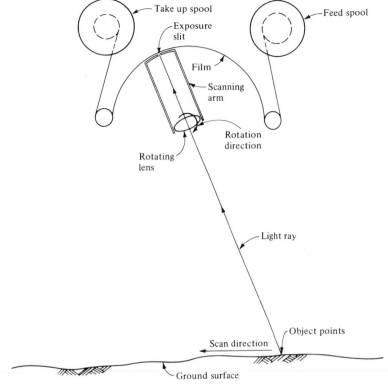

FIGURE 16-19
Schematic diagram of operation of rotating lens type of panoramic camera.

With the rotating-lens type shown in Fig. 16-19, the film is curved in the shape of a cylinder, and the camera lens is on the axis of this cylinder. The radius of the cylinder is equal to the focal length of the camera lens. The exposure is made on the film through a thin slit in a scanning arm which moves with the lens as it rotates in scanning from side to side. During exposure, the film is held fixed in position, except that it may be moved slowly backward opposite the flight direction to compensate for image motion caused by forward movement of the aircraft. After the scan is completed, the film is advanced into position for the next exposure.

With the rotating-prism type panoramic camera illustrated in Fig. 16-20, a double dove prism mounted in front of the camera lens rotates about its longitudinal axis, thereby scanning the terrain from side to side. The camera lens remains fixed during exposure. As the prism rotates, the film, which is stretched between two rollers, advances at a speed which is synchronized with the scanning rate of the rotating prism. The exposure is made through a narrow slit in front of the film. As with the rotating-lens

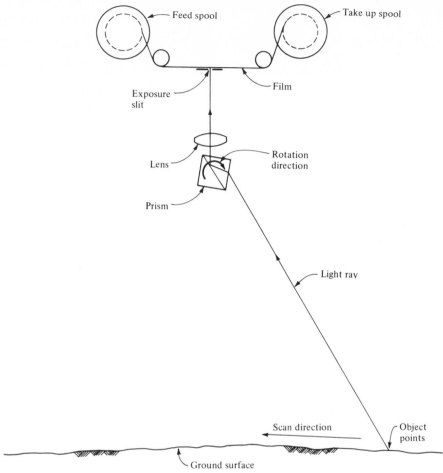

FIGURE 16-20
Schematic diagram of operation of rotating prism type of panoramic camera.

type, image motion due to aircraft advance may be compensated for by shifting the film slowly backward along the flight line as the exposure is made. Figure 16-21 shows a Fairchild KA-77 rotating-prism panoramic camera having a 6-inch focal length, a 180° lateral coverage, and a 40° longitudinal field of view. This camera uses roll film having a $4\frac{1}{2}$-inch width.

With both the rotating-lens and rotating-prism systems, the narrow scanning slit allows only light rays which pass through the center of the lens to expose the film. This accounts for the high resolutions and uniform light intensities which are characteristic of panoramic photos. Cameras of the rotating-prism type enable lateral scans to be made through 180°, an impossibility with rotating-lens types. Although the film in

FIGURE 16-21
Fairchild KA-77 rotating prism type panoramic camera. (*Courtesy Fairchild Space and Defense Systems*)

rotating-prism cameras is not actually curved in cylindrical form during exposure, this cylindrical geometrical equivalent is created by the scanning action of the prism.

16-14   GEOMETRY OF VERTICAL PANORAMIC PHOTOGRAPHS

Figure 16-22*a* is an isometric view illustrating the geometry of a vertical panoramic photo taken from exposure station *L*. The camera focal length is *f* and flying height above datum is *H*. The cylindrical surface of the photo positive is shown in Fig. 16-22*a*, while Fig. 16-22*b* shows the photo positive laid out flat. As shown in Fig. 16-22*a*, the scan angle ξ_a for any object point *A* may be defined as the angle between the vertical line *Lo* and line *La'* which is the projection of ray *La* onto the vertical plane containing the *y* axis.

For purposes of specifying image point positions on a vertical panoramic photo, an *xy* photocoordinate axis system is adopted. In this system the *x* axis is taken in the direction of flight passing through the position of zero scan angle. The *y* axis is taken along the trace of the intersection of the camera lens optical axis with the film during scanning. If the camera has no fiducial marks with which to locate the origin, *o*, of the *xy* axis system, it may be roughly located at the intersection of diagonals from the four corners of the format as shown by the dashed lines of Fig. 16-22*b*. The *y* axis is then constructed through *o* parallel to the long side of the format, and *x* is perpendicular to *y* passing through *o*. This reference *xy* axis system is shown in Fig. 16-22*b*.

The scan angle ξ_a corresponding to any image point *a* may be expressed in terms of the camera focal length and measured *y* photocoordinate of the point as

$$\xi_a = \left(\frac{y_a}{f}\right)\left(\frac{180°}{pi}\right) \qquad (16\text{-}20)$$

In Eq. (16-20), y_a and *f* must be in the same units and ξ_a is in degree units.

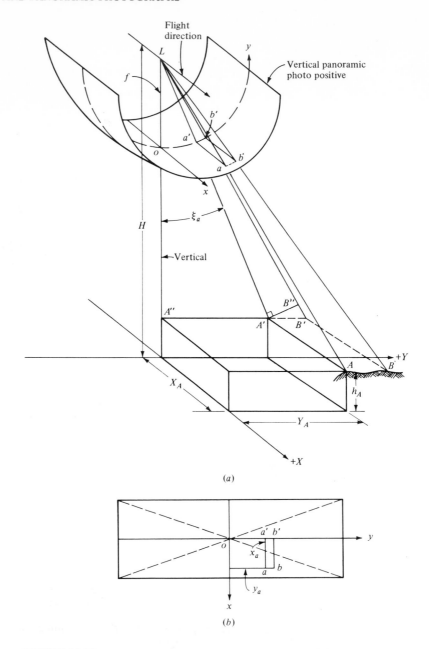

(a)

(b)

FIGURE 16-22

(a) Geometry of a vertical panoramic photograph. (b) Photocoordinate system of a vertical panoramic photograph.

16-15   SCALE OF A VERTICAL PANORAMIC PHOTOGRAPH

In Fig. 16-22a and b, a' is the orthogonal projection of image point a onto the y axis. In Fig. 16-22a, A' is in the vertical plane containing the y photo axis. From similar triangles $La'a$ and $LA'A$, the photo scale in the x direction at any point a on a vertical panoramic photo may be expressed as

$$S_{x_a} = \frac{aa'}{AA'} = \frac{f}{LA'}$$

But LA' is equal to $(H - h_A) \sec \xi_a$. Substituting this into the above equation and dropping subscripts, the following general equation is obtained for scale in the x direction at any point of a vertical panoramic photo:

$$S_x = \frac{f \cos \xi}{(H - h)} \qquad (16\text{-}21)$$

In Eq. (16-21), S_x is the scale in the x direction at any point on a vertical panoramic photo, f is the camera focal length, ξ is the scan angle computed from Eq. (16-20), H is flying height above datum, and h is the elevation of the object point above datum.

Also from Fig. 16-22, an expression for the scale in the y direction for any point on a panoramic photo may be obtained. Consider ground distance AB as being infinitesimally small. Then the scale in the y direction at image point a may be given as

$$S_{y_a} = \frac{ab}{AB} = \frac{a'b'}{A'B'}$$

Line $A'B''$ is constructed perpendicular to LA', and therefore, from similar triangles $La'b'$ and $LA'B''$,

$$\frac{La'}{LA'} = \frac{a'b'}{A'B''}$$

In the above expression, La'/LA' is S_{x_a}, which from Eq. (16-21) is equal to $f \cos \xi/(H - h)$. Also, $A'B''$ is equal to $(A'B') \cos \xi_a$. Substituting these values into the above expression, dropping subscripts, and reducing,

$$S_y = \frac{f \cos^2 \xi}{(H - h)} = S_x \cos \xi \qquad (16\text{-}22)$$

In Eq. (16-22), S_y is the scale at any point in the y direction on a panoramic photo. The other terms in the equation are as described for Eq. (16-21).

From an analysis of Eqs. (16-21) and (16-22), it is seen that as ξ increases, scale decreases. Near the horizons, where ξ approaches $90°$, cosine ξ approaches zero and photo scale becomes infinitely small. Most reliable quantitative information on a panoramic photo is therefore obtained near the center of the photo where scale is largest.

16-16 GROUND COORDINATES FROM MEASUREMENTS ON A VERTICAL PANORAMIC PHOTO

Positions of points whose images appear in a vertical panoramic photo may be calculated in a rectangular ground coordinate system from photocoordinate measurements. The ground coordinate system has its origin in the datum plane vertically beneath the exposure station. The X and Y ground axes are in the vertical planes containing the x and y photo axes respectively, and they are positive in the same directions as the photo axes. From similar triangles $La'a$ and $LA'A$ of Fig. 16-22a,

$$X_A = \frac{x_a(H - h_A)}{f \cos \xi_a} \qquad (16\text{-}23)$$

Also, from triangle $LA''A'$,

$$Y_A = (H - h_A) \tan \xi_a \qquad (16\text{-}24)$$

In Eqs. (16-23) and (16-24), X_A and Y_A are ground coordinates in the aforementioned arbitrary coordinate system and the other terms are as previously described. It should be noted that no provision is made in these equations for earth curvature or atmospheric refraction. Furthermore, unless corrections are made for the several types of distortions present in panoramic imagery, the accuracy with which points can be located from panoramic photos is limited. Near the horizons, scale becomes extremely small, so that accuracy is severely curtailed in those areas. Consequently the above scale and ground coordinate equations should not generally be considered as acceptable for mapping, but they can be used as guides to assist in interpretation from panoramic photography.

EXAMPLE 16-3   A vertical panoramic photo was exposed from a flying height of 10,000 ft above datum with a panoramic camera having a 6-in focal length lens. Two points, A and B, whose elevations are both 1,200 ft above datum, have the following photocoordinates measured on the positive with respect to a photo axis system pictured in Fig. 16-22b:

$$x_a = 27.08 \text{ mm} \qquad y_a = 98.43 \text{ mm}$$

$$x_b = -19.14 \text{ mm} \qquad y_b = -63.79 \text{ mm}$$

Calculate the scale of the photo at points a and b and calculate the ground distance AB.

SOLUTION   From Eq. (16-20) the scan angles are

$$\xi_a = \frac{(98.43)180°}{6(25.4)3.1416} = 37° \, 00'$$

$$\xi_b = \frac{(-63.79)180°}{6(25.4)3.1416} = -24° \, 00'$$

Photo scales from Eqs. 16-21 and (16-22) are

$$S_{x_a} = \frac{(6.00) \cos 37° \, 00'}{10,000 - 1,200} = 1 \text{ in}/1,840 \text{ ft}$$

$$S_{y_a} = \left(\frac{1 \text{ in}}{1,840 \text{ ft}}\right) \cos 37° \, 00' = 1 \text{ in}/2,305 \text{ ft}$$

$$S_{x_b} = \frac{(6.00) \cos 24° \, 00'}{10,000 - 1,200} = 1 \text{ in}/1,610 \text{ ft}$$

$$S_{y_b} = \left(\frac{1 \text{ in}}{1610 \text{ ft}}\right) \cos 24° \, 00' = 1 \text{ in}/1765 \text{ ft}$$

Ground coordinates from Eqs. (16-23) and (16-24) are

$$X_A = \frac{27.08(10,000 - 1,200)}{6(25.4) \cos 37° \, 00'} = 1,960 \text{ ft}$$

$$Y_A = (10,000 - 1,200) \tan 37° \, 00' = 6,630 \text{ ft}$$

$$X_B = \frac{-19.14(10,000 - 1,200)}{6(25.4) \cos 24° \, 00'} = -1,210 \text{ ft}$$

$$Y_B = (10,000 - 1,200) \tan - 24° \, 00' = -3,920 \text{ ft}$$

(Note that negative signs of X_B and Y_B correspond to negative x and y photocoordinates.)

By the pythagorean theorem,

$$AB = \sqrt{(-1,210 - 1,960)^2 + (-3,920 - 6,630)^2} = 11,020 \text{ ft} \qquad ////$$

16-17 IMAGE DISTORTIONS IN PANORAMIC PHOTOS

Panoramic photos contain several types of distortions not present in frame photography. First of all, there is a displacement of images called *panoramic distortion* which occurs because of the cylindrical shape of the film surface and because of the nature of scanning. If a square grid on flat ground is photographed with a panoramic camera in vertical orientation, panoramic distortions produce the characteristic trapezoidal grid pattern shown in Fig. 16-23.

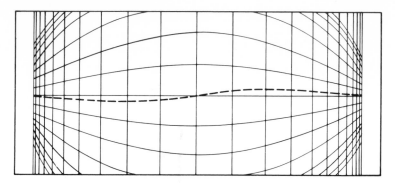

FIGURE 16-23
Panoramic distortion.

Scan positional distortion (also sometimes referred to as *sweep positional distortion*) is a displacement of images caused by the forward motion of the aircraft during the time of exposure. It causes a relative displacement in x coordinates for points which are separated in the y direction on the photo. Relative scan positional distortion for any two points is the product of photo scale and ground distance traveled in the elapsed time interval between exposure of the two points. The dashed line of Fig. 16-23 illustrates the nature of scan positional distortion for images along the y photo axis. Relative positions of images throughout the entire photo undergo similar distortions.

If the film or lens is translated during exposure to compensate for image motion due to aircraft advance, a relative displacement of images known as *image motion compensation distortion* results. Image motion compensation distortion tends to cancel the effects of scan positional distortion, although it does not compensate for it completely.

A distortion called *tipped panoramic distortion* results if the camera axis is tipped either forward or backward during exposure. Forward tipping is the case with the forward-looking oblique panoramic photos such as the one shown in Fig. 16-18. The extreme curvature of the apparent horizon in this photo is due primarily to tipped panoramic distortion.

The distortions described above can be removed and image positions rectified if enough information is known about camera and flight conditions. Necessary data include camera focal length, flying height, angular velocity of scanning, ground speed of the aircraft, and tip angle (angle camera axis makes with vertical). Rectification for selected image points may be accomplished analytically or, if performed by electronic rescanning or optical projection, all photo imagery may be rectified. If reliable quantitative photogrammetric data is to be taken from panoramic photos, image positions must be rectified. It is impossible to remove all distortions, however, due to the many unpredictable variables in panoramic photography. Film slippage, irregularities in angular scanning, film expansion or contraction, etc., create distortions which are difficult if not impossible to detect. New instrumentation is currently being developed which should, however, help to alleviate some of these uncertanties.

REFERENCES

Abraham, V.: Relative Geometric Strength of Frame, Strip, and Panoramic Cameras, *Photogrammetric Engineering,* vol. 27, no. 5, p. 755, 1961.

American Society of Photogrammetry: "Manual of Photogrammetry," 3d ed., George Banta Co., Inc., Menasha, Wis., 1966, chaps. 4 and 18.

Arena A., and M. Umlas: A New Panoramic Camera Development, *Photogrammetric Engineering,* vol. 34, no. 2, p. 169, 1968.

Donnelly, C. B. C.: Trimetrogon Photogrammetry, Some Usages in the Preparation of the Canadian Aeronautical Chart, *Photogrammetric Engineering,* vol. 15, no. 1, p. 22, 1949.

Gay, S. P., Jr.: Measurement of Vertical Heights From Single Oblique Aerial Photographs, *Photogrammetric Engineering,* vol. 23, no. 5, p. 900, 1957.

Griffin, E. P.: 20 Degree Convergent Versus Vertical Photography, *Photogrammetric Engineering,* vol. 26, no. 1, p. 59, 1960.

Hovey, S. T.: Panoramic Possibilities and Problems, *Photogrammetric Engineering,* vol. 31, no. 4, p. 727, 1965.

Itek Laboratories: Panoramic Progress, Part I, *Photogrammetric Engineering*, vol. 27, no. 5, p. 747, 1961.

Itek Laboratories: Panoramic Progress, Part II, *Photogrammetric Engineering,* vol. 28, no. 1, p. 99, 1962.

Kawachi, D. A.: Image Motion and its Compensation for the Oblique Frame Camera, *Photogrammetric Engineering,* vol. 31, no. 1, p. 154, 1965.

_____:Image Geometry of Vertical and Oblique Panoramic Photography, *Photogrammetric Engineering,* vol. 32, no. 2, p. 298, 1966.

Le Resche, J.: Analysis of the Panoramic Aerial Photograph, *Photogrammetric Engineering,* vol. 24, no. 5, p. 772, 1958.

McNeil, G. T.: Oblique Plotting Scale, *Photogrammetric Engineering,* vol. 15, p. 455, 1949.

_____: A Wide-Field Underwater Panoramic Camera, *Photogrammetric Engineering,* vol. 32, no. 1, p. 37, 1966.

Raisz, E.: Direct Use of Oblique Air Photos for Small Scale Maps, *Surveying and Mapping,* vol. 13, no. 4, p. 496, 1953.

Skiff, E. W.: "Analytical Treatment of Strip and Pan Photos," *Photogrammetric Engineering,* vol. 33, no. 11, p. 1290, 1967.

Stewart, R. A.: The Application of the Balplex Plotter to Trimetrogon Obliques, *Photogrammetric Engineering,* vol. 23, no. 4, p. 697, 1957.

PROBLEMS

16-1 A high oblique photograph was taken from a flying height of 5,900 feet above datum with a camera having a 210-mm focal length. Average ground elevation was 1,100 feet above datum. Distance ok' measured along the principal line from principal point to apparent horizon is 72.9 millimeters. What is the true depression angle for the photo?

16-2 The problem is similar to Prob. 16-1 except that flying height is 3,800 meters above datum, average ground is 800 meters above datum, camera focal length is 150 mm, and measured distance ok' is 3.16 inches.

16-3 For the photograph of Prob. 16-1, what is photo scale at the principal point in the x and y directions? (Assume average ground elevation at the principal point.)

16-4 For the photograph of Prob. 16-1, what are the scales in the x and y directions at the isocenter? (Assume average ground elevation at the isocenter.) What conclusion do you draw about scale at the isocenter?

16-5 A high oblique photograph taken from a flying height of 8,700 feet above datum with a 152-mm focal length camera has a true depression angle of $29°10'$. Images a and b have photocoordinates with respect to the xy high oblique photocoordinate system of $x_a = 77.5$ millimeters, $y_a = -43.4$ millimeters, $x_b = -54.9$ millimeters, and $y_b = -115.8$ millimeters. Calculate photo scale in the x and y directions for points a and b if ground points A and B have elevations of 930 feet and 760 feet above datum respectively.

16-6 Calculate the horizontal angle ALB at the exposure station between points A and B of Prob. 16-5.

16-7 Calculate the vertical angles from the exposure station to points A and B of Prob. 16-5.

16-8 A high oblique photograph is exposed with a 152.4-mm focal length camera. An altimeter reading at the exposure station provided an approximate flying height above datum of 4,900 feet. Average ground elevation was 1,050 feet. Images a, b, and c of horizontal control points A, B, and C appear on the photo. Their photocoordinates with respect to the xy high oblique photocoordinate axis system and their ground coordinates are given below. Photo distance ok' measured along the principal line from principal point to the apparent horizon is 73.9 millimeters. On a map, plot the control points A, B, and C. Compute horizontal angles ALB and BLC and determine the X and Y coordinates of the exposure station by graphical three-point resection (see Sec. 9-5).

Point	Photocoordinates		Ground coordinates	
	x, mm	y, mm	X, ft	Y, ft
A	101.4	− 88.2	1,829,562	77,718
B	17.2	− 64.8	1,824,579	78,184
C	− 71.7	− 69.2	1,819,618	77,488

16-9 Determine the camera axis direction for the photograph of Prob. 16-8.

16-10 Determine flying height above datum for the photograph of Prob. 16-8 if the elevation of control point A is 1,070 feet above datum.

16-11 Construct a perspective grid for the high oblique photograph of Prob. 16-1. Make the principal line coincide with one of the grid lines, and make perspective quadrilaterals represent ground squares of 500-foot dimensions. Make the photographic principal point occur at one of the perspective grid intersections and complete the grid from the picture foreground to about 1 inch above the principal point. Assume the photo has a 9-inch square format.

16-12 How do panoramic photographs differ from frame camera aerial photos?

16-13 List the advantages of panoramic photographs as compared to frame camera aerial photos. List the disadvantages.

16-14 Describe the different types of panoramic cameras.

16-15 A vertical panoramic photograph was taken with a 310-mm focal length camera from a flying height of 8,000 feet above ground. Calculate photographic scale in the x and y directions at points a and b, whose x and y photocoordinates are $x_a = 0.00$ millimeters, $y_a = 0.00$ millimeters, $x_b = 21.72$ millimeters, and $y_b = 134.80$ millimeters.

16-16 Calculate the ground length of line AB from image positions a and b of the panoramic photograph of Prob. 16-15. Assume level ground throughout the coverage of the panoramic photo.

16-17 Images c and d of ground points C and D appear on a vertical panoramic photograph taken with a 150-mm focal length camera from a flying height of 6,300 feet above datum. Points C and D have image coordinates of $x_c = -41.08$ millimeters, $y_c = 12.71$ millimeters, $x_d = 28.94$ millimeters, and $y_d = -127.13$ millimeters. Calculate the ground length of line CD if the elevations of C and D are 2,280 and 1,970 feet above datum respectively.

16-18 Discuss the various image distortions present in panoramic photographs.

17
TERRESTRIAL AND CLOSE-RANGE PHOTOGRAMMETRY

17-1 INTRODUCTION

Terrestrial photogrammetry is an important branch of the science of photogrammetry. It deals with photographs taken with a camera located on the surface of the earth. The term "close-range photogrammetry" has recently been adopted for terrestrial photographs having object distances of up to about 100 meters. Unlike aerial photography, with terrestrial photography the cameras are usually accessible, so that direct measurements can be made to obtain exposure station positions. Camera angular orientation can also usually be measured or set to fixed values, so that all elements of exterior orientation of a terrestrial photo are commonly known and need not be calculated. These known exterior orientation parameters are a source of control for terrestrial photos, replacing in whole or in part the necessity for locating control points in the object space.

Terrestrial photography may be *static* (photos of stationary objects) or *dynamic* (photos of moving objects). For static photography, slow, fine-grained, high-resolution films may be used and the exposures made by simply removing a lens cap for a short time. Stereopairs can be obtained by using a single camera and making exposures at both ends of a base line. In taking dynamic terrestrial photos, fast films and rapid shutter speeds are necessary. If stereopairs of dynamic occurrences are required, two cameras located at the ends of a base line must make simultaneous exposures.

17-2 APPLICATIONS OF TERRESTRIAL AND CLOSE-RANGE PHOTOGRAMMETRY

Historically the science of photogrammetry had its beginning with terrestrial photography, and topographic mapping was among its early applications. Terrestrial photos were found especially useful for mapping rugged terrain which was difficult to map by conventional field-surveying methods. Although it was known that topographic mapping could be done more conveniently using aerial photos, no practical method was available for taking aerial photographs until the airplane was invented. Following the invention of the airplane, emphasis in topographic mapping shifted from terrestrial to aerial methods. Terrestrial photogrammetry is still used in topographic mapping, but its application is usually limited to small areas and special situations such as deep gorges or rugged mountains that are difficult to map from aerial photography. Other applications of terrestrial photogrammetry are in mapping construction sites, areas of excavation, borrow pits, material stockpiles, etc.

Through the years terrestrial photogrammetry has continued to gain prominence in numerous diversified nontopographic applications. Examples of nontopographic applications occur in such areas as agriculture, conservation, ecology, forestry, archaeology, anthropology, architecture, geology, geography, engineering, criminology, oceanography, medicine, dentistry, and many more. In the field of medicine, x-ray photogrammetry has been utilized advantageously for measuring sizes and shapes of body parts, recording tumor growth, studying the development of fetuses, locating foreign objects within the body, etc.

Terrestrial photogrammetry holds a great deal of potential as a reliable means of investigating traffic accidents. Photos which provide all information necessary to reconstruct the accident may be rapidly obtained. Time-consuming sketches and ground measurements, which all too often are erroneous, are not needed, and normal traffic flow can more quickly be restored. Terrestrial photogrammetry has been widely practiced in accident investigation for many years in several European countries.

Time-lapse terrestrial photos have been used to record speeds of automobiles, directions and velocities of water currents, rate and manner of plant growth, etc. A unique and highly specialized application of terrestrial photogrammetry is in connection with the establishment of a worldwide satellite triangulation network. In this program positions of orbiting satellites are recorded as they pass through the fields of view of highly precise ballistic cameras such as the one shown in Fig. 1-3. Camera stations are distributed throughout the world and their positions are accurately determined on the basis of measurements taken from the photos. The camera stations will serve as a framework for a worldwide geodetic datum. In the space program terrestrial photos are also used to calibrate large parabolic antennas used in tracking spacecraft.

Terrestrial photogrammetry has become a very useful tool in many areas of scientific and engineering research for several reasons. One reason is that it makes possible measurements of objects which are inaccessible for direct measurement. Also, measurements can be obtained without actually touching delicate objects. In some experiments, such as measurements of water waves and currents, physical contact during measurement would upset the experiment and render it inaccurate. Cameras which freeze the action at a particular instant of time make possible measurements of dynamic occurrences such as deflections of beams under impact loads. Because of the many advantages and conveniences offered by terrestrial photogrammetry, its importance in the future seems assured.

17-3 TERRESTRIAL CAMERAS

A variety of cameras are used in terrestrial photography. All of them fall into one of two general classifications: *metric* or *nonmetric*. The term "metric camera," as used herein, includes those cameras manufactured expressly for photogrammetric applications. They have fiducial marks built into their focal planes, which enable accurate recovery of their principal points. Metric cameras are stably constructed and completely calibrated before use. Their calibration values for focal length, principal point coordinates, and lens distortions can be applied with confidence over long periods of time.

Nonmetric cameras are manufactured for amateur or professional photography where pictorial quality is important but geometric accuracy requirements are generally not considered paramount. These cameras do not contain fiducial marks, but they can be modified to include them. Nonmetric cameras can be calibrated and used with satisfactory results for many terrestrial photogrammetric applications. Where highest geometric accuracy is desired, however, metric cameras should be used.

Aerial cameras can be used for terrestrial applications, but this requires special tripod mounts. Aerial cameras used for terrestrial photography would, of course, be considered as metric cameras because of their stability and calibration characteristics. In general, all metric terrestrial cameras are fixed for focus at infinity and cannot produce sharp geometrically correct images at short ranges (under about 30 feet). These cameras can be modified, however, to permit sharp focus at short ranges. Exposures with metric cameras are usually made directly on glass plates; therefore film flattening devices are not necessary and the utmost in dimensional stability of the image is achieved.

Phototheodolites and *stereometric* cameras are two special types of terrestrial camera systems in the metric classification which are described in the following two sections. Of the many available terrestrial cameras, only a few are described and pictured herein as examples. Omission of other comparable cameras is not intended to imply any inferiority of these instruments.

FIGURE 17-1
Zeiss TMK phototheodolite. (*Courtesy
Carl Zeiss, Oberkochen*)

17-4 PHOTOTHEODOLITES

The term "phototheodolite" generally applies to a combination camera and theodolite. In a broader sense, however, a phototheodolite is any camera, usually metric, equipped for orienting its optical axis in a known direction with respect to a base line. Phototheodolites are generally mounted on tripods and centered over a desired camera station by means of a plumb bob.

The Zeiss TMK of Fig. 17-1 is a terrestrial camera of the phototheodolite classification. It has a telescope with cross hairs for sighting along a base line, and by means of a right angle prism, the camera axis may be oriented at 90° to a base line. If the camera optical axis is directed at 90° from both ends of a base line, as shown in Fig. 17-2, the photos of the resulting stereopair have their optical axes parallel. The TMK has a nominal focal length of 60 mm, and its pictures are exposed on glass plates of dimensions 90 by 120 millimeters.

The Wild P-30 which is shown in Fig. 1-1, fits the classical description of a phototheodolite. It combines a Wild T-2 theodolite and a metric camera. The theodolite

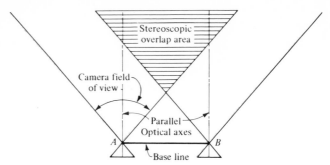

FIGURE 17-2
Stereo coverage obtained by exposing terrestrial photos at 90° to a base line from the ends of the base line.

has an upper and lower motion. With its upper motion locked and lower motion open, the camera and theodolite turn in azimuth as a unit. With the upper motion open and lower motion locked, the theodolite can be turned in azimuth while the camera retains its direction. The horizontal angle between the theodolite telescope axis and camera axis may be read from the horizontal circle. When the horizontal circle of the theodolite reads 0°00'00", the theodolite telescope axis and the camera axis point in the same direction. The camera axis can be set in any desired azimuth with respect to a base line. Stereopairs with parallel optical axes as shown in Fig. 17-2 can be obtained if desired by setting 90° on the horizontal circle with the upper motion and then sighting on the opposite end of the base line with the lower motion. The theodolite of the P-30 also has a vertical circle which facilitates determining camera station differences in elevation.

By leveling the theodolite, the camera of the P-30 is simultaneously leveled. The optical axis of the camera can be set horizontal, it can be tilted upward at an elevation angle of 7ᵍ (6° 18'), or it can be tilted downward at depression angles of 7ᵍ, 14ᵍ, 21ᵍ, or 28ᵍ. The camera's nominal focal length is 165 mm and exposures are made on glass plates of dimensions 100 by 150 millimeters. A terrestrial photo taken with the P-30 is shown in Fig. 1-2.

The Wild P-32 terrestrial camera shown in Fig. 17-3 has been designed to attach directly onto a standard surveying theodolite. The camera axis can be set at any desired vertical angle by making the appropriate setting on the theodolite's vertical circle, and it can be aimed at any horizontal angle with respect to the camera base line by means of the theodolite's horizontal circle. The P-32 camera has a 64-mm focal length and can make exposures either on glass plates of 65 millimeters by 90 millimeters size or on roll film, in which case a film flattening device is used.

The Zena Photheo 19/1318 of Fig. 17-4 is a phototheodolite of slightly different characteristics. With this camera the lens may be shifted vertically upward or downward to obtain the desired vertical coverage. An orientation attachment on top of the

FIGURE 17-3
Wild P-32 terrestrial camera mounted on
a T-2 theodolite. (*Courtesy Wild Heerbrugg Instruments, Ltd.*)

instrument makes it possible to align the camera axis in any desired azimuth and to measure vertical angles for determining camera station elevations. The Photheo 19/1318 camera has a nominal focal length of 190 mm and the dimensions of its photographic plates are 130 by 180 millimeters.

17-5 STEREOMETRIC CAMERAS

A stereometric camera consists of two identical metric cameras mounted rigidly at the ends of a fixed base so that their optical axes are parallel to one another. This means that relative orientation of the cameras is known after calibration, and it remains constant for all stereopairs taken. The shutters of both cameras are tripped simultaneously—a condition enabling dynamic occurrences to be photographed stereoscopically. A variety of stereometric systems are available, affording a wide choice in field of view, format dimensions, focusing distances, and fixed base lengths. Fixed bases are commonly available in 200-, 120-, and 40-centimeter lengths. Shorter base systems apply for photographing at closer range. The Zeiss SMK stereometric camera, consisting

FIGURE 17-4
Zena Photheo 19/1318 phototheodolite.
(*Courtesy Zena Co.*)

of two **TMK** cameras mounted at a fixed base of 120 centimeters, is shown in Fig. 17-5.

In terrestrial photogrammetry, *depth* is the distance from the camera base to photographed objects. *Base-depth ratios* (similar to base-height ratios of aerial stereopairs)

FIGURE 17-5
Zeiss SMK stereometric camera with 120-centimeter fixed base. (*Courtesy Carl Zeiss, Oberkochen*)

FIGURE 17-6
Horizontal stereopair of terrestrial photos taken for an auto accident investigation with a Wild C-120 stereometric camera. (*Courtesy Dr. T. M. Lillesand*)

provide a means of assessing relative geometric strengths of terrestrial stereopairs. Geometric strength is greater for large base-depth ratios because intersection angles between corresponding rays are greater. Because their bases are relatively short, stereometric cameras can attain strong base-depth ratios only when objects being photographed are at a rather close range. For longer ranges, stereopairs must be obtained by exposing single photos at the ends of a measured base line using cameras of the type described in Sec. 17-4.

Stereometric cameras are leveled for normal horizontal photography by means of level vials. Besides horizontal orientation of the cameras, however, special attachments available with most stereometric cameras permit the two cameras to be aimed vertically downward, vertically upward, or at various oblique angles in between. In each case the two camera axes remain parallel. Figure 17-6 shows a horizontal stereopair of terrestrial photos taken with a Wild C-120 stereometric camera. The stereopair was used to assist in reconstructing a traffic accident.

17-6 HORIZONTAL AND VERTICAL ANGLES FROM A HORIZONTAL PHOTO

A horizontal terrestrial photo is obtained if the camera axis is horizontal when the exposure is made. The plane of a horizontal photo is then vertical, and if the camera is properly leveled before exposure, the x and y photo axes (defined by the fiducial lines) are horizontal and vertical lines respectively. As with aerial photos, lines joining opposite fiducial marks should intersect at or very near the photographic principal point.

Figure 17-7 illustrates the positive of a horizontal terrestrial photo exposed at camera station L. The focal length of the camera is f, and o is the photographic principal point. Points A and B in the object space are imaged at a and b on the positive, and their photocoordinates are x_a, y_a, x_b, and y_b respectively. These photocoordinates may be

FIGURE 17-7
Horizontal and vertical angles from measurements on a horizontal terrestrial photo.

measured by any of the techniques described in Chap. 5. The horizontal angle α_a between the optical axis Lo and the ray to object point A is

$$\alpha_a = \tan^{-1}\left(\frac{x_a}{f}\right) \qquad (17\text{-}1)$$

Also, the vertical angle of inclination β_a between the horizontal plane and the ray to object point A is

$$\beta_a = \tan^{-1}\left[\frac{y_a}{(x_a^2 + f^2)^{1/2}}\right] \qquad (17\text{-}2)$$

In similar manner, the horizontal and vertical angles to point B are

$$\alpha_b = \tan^{-1}\left(\frac{x_b}{f}\right) \qquad (17\text{-}3)$$

and

$$\beta_b = \tan^{-1}\left[\frac{y_b}{(x_b^2 + f^2)^{1/2}}\right] \qquad (17\text{-}4)$$

Correct algebraic signs for these angles are automatically obtained by affixing proper algebraic signs to measured photocoordinates according to conventional procedure for rectangular coordinate systems. A horizontal angle to the left of the optical axis is therefore considered negative and one to the right is considered positive. Also, vertical angles above horizontal are positive and those below horizontal are negative. Horizontal angle A_hLB_h subtended at the exposure station by the two object points A and B is

$$A_hLB_h = \alpha_a - \alpha_b \qquad (17\text{-}5)$$

Horizontal and vertical angles determined by the above equations are the same angles that would be measured using a surveyor's transit at the camera station. An advantage of the photographic approach is that one click of the shutter produces an infinite number of points to which angles may later be determined. The photo measurements may be made in the comfort of an office, an important consideration if the alternative requires field surveying during times of adverse weather.

Horizontal and vertical angles may also be determined from horizontal terrestrial photos by graphical procedures. The results are likely to be less accurate than angles determined by analytical procedures, but in some cases they are satisfactory. Figure 17-8 illustrates the graphical construction of angles α_a, α_b, β_a, and β_b from the terrestrial photo in Fig. 17-7. To construct horizontal angle α_a, point a_h is located on the x axis by transferring point a parallel to the y axis. Distance oa_h therefore equals photocoordinate x_a. From point o distance Lo (equal to the camera focal length) is laid off perpendicular to the x axis. Line La_h is then drawn, and horizontal angle α_a is thus constructed.

Once α_a has been constructed, vertical angle β_a may be readily determined graphically. A perpendicular to line a_hL is constructed from point a_h and extended a distance equal to coordinate y_a to locate point a_v. Line La_v is then drawn, which yields angle a_vLa_h, the required vertical angle β_a. Angles α_b and β_b are constructed in similar manner, as shown in Fig. 17-8.

The photo may be used directly in graphical construction, as was done in Fig. 17-8. In this case it is affixed to a large piece of drafting paper. Another approach, which avoids defacing the photo, is to perform the construction on a separate piece of drafting paper after transferring x and y coordinates from the photo to the drafting paper, using dividers or an engineer's scale.

17-7   LOCATING POINTS BY INTERSECTION FROM TWO OR MORE HORIZONTAL PHOTOS

If images of an object point appear in two or more horizontal photos, the position and elevation of the point can readily be determined, provided the camera positions and directions of the optical axes are known. Figure 17-9a illustrates two horizontal photos taken from exposure stations L and L'. Figure 17-9b is a plan view of the situation. Images of object point A appear at a and a' on the two photos. Assume that angles δ and δ' of Fig. 17-9b have been measured with respect to the base line, so that relative directions of optical axes of the two exposure stations are known. Assume also that the

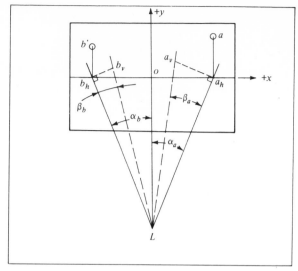

FIGURE 17-8
Horizontal and vertical angles from a horizontal terrestrial photo by graphical construction.

length of the base line has been measured and that the camera station elevations are known. An arbitrary XY object space coordinate system is adopted with origin at exposure station L and with the X axis coincident with the base line. It is required to determine the X and Y coordinates and elevation of point A.

This problem may be solved analytically or graphically. In the analytical solution, angles α_a, α'_a, β_a, and β'_a are calculated from Eqs. (17-1) and (17-2). Then angles ϕ, ϕ' and ϕ'' of Fig. 17-9b are calculated as follows:

$$\phi = \delta - \alpha_a$$
$$\phi' = \delta' - \alpha'_a \qquad (17\text{-}6)$$
$$\phi'' = 180° - \phi - \phi'$$

Applying the law of sines, distance LA in Fig. 17-9b may be calculated as

$$LA = \frac{B \sin \phi'}{\sin \phi''} \qquad (17\text{-}7)$$

Also, by the law of sines,

$$L'A = \frac{B \sin \phi}{\sin \phi''} \qquad (17\text{-}8)$$

Coordinates X_A and Y_A may then be calculated as

$$X_A = (LA) \cos \phi$$
$$Y_A = (LA) \sin \phi \qquad (17\text{-}9)$$

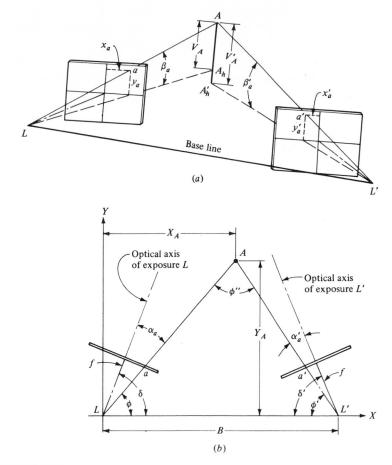

FIGURE 17-9
(*a*) Locating points by intersection from two horizontal terrestrial photos. (*b*) Plan view of intersection from two horizontal terrestrial photos.

A check on these coordinates may be obtained as follows:

$$X_A = B - (L'A) \cos \phi'$$
$$Y_A = (L'A) \sin \phi'$$

$$(17\text{-}10)$$

With reference to Fig. 17-9*a*, the elevation of point *A* is determined as

$$\text{elev } A = \text{elev } L + V_A \quad (17\text{-}11)$$

where $V_A = LA_h \tan \beta_a$, and LA_h is equal to horizontal length LA found in Eq. (17-7). A check may also be obtained on the elevation of *A* as follows:

$$\text{elev } A = \text{elev } L' + V'_A \quad (17\text{-}12)$$

where $V'_A = L'A'_h \tan \beta'_a$, and $L'A'_h$ is equal to horizontal length $L'A$ found in Eq. (17-8).

If images of an object point appear on more than two photos, additional check values on position and elevation may be obtained and the averages of several solutions can be adopted.

EXAMPLE 17-1 As illustrated in Figs. 17-9a and b, two horizontal terrestrial photos were taken with a phototheodolite having a focal length of 164.95 mm. The base line was measured as 250.0 ft and the exposure station elevations were 862.7 and 855.4 ft above mean sea level for the left and right exposures respectively. Angles δ and δ' were measured as $69° 30'$ and $66° 10'$ respectively. Images of object point A were measured on both photos with the following results: $x_a = 46.23$ millimeters, $y_a = 41.07$ millimeters, $x'_a = -17.83$ millimeters, and $y'_a = 48.20$ millimeters. Calculate the X and Y coordinates of point A in a rectangular coordinate system with origin at L and with the X axis coincident with the base line as shown in Fig. 17-9b.

SOLUTION Horizontal angles α_a and α'_a are calculated by Eq. (17-1),

$$\alpha_a = \tan^{-1}\left(\frac{46.23}{164.95}\right) = 15°39'$$

$$\alpha'_a = \tan^{-1}\left(\frac{-17.83}{164.95}\right) = -6° 10'$$

Vertical angles β_a and β'_a are calculated by Eq. (17-2),

$$\beta_a = \tan^{-1}\left\{\frac{41.07}{[(46.23)^2 + (164.95)^2]^{1/2}}\right\} = 13° 29'$$

$$\beta'_a = \tan^{-1}\left\{\frac{48.20}{[(-17.83)^2 + (164.95)^2]^{1/2}}\right\} = 16°12'$$

By Eqs. (17-6), angles ϕ, ϕ' and ϕ'' are

$$\phi = 69° 30' - 15° 39' = 53° 51'$$

$$\phi' = 66° 10' - 6° 10' = 60° 00'$$

$$\phi'' = 180° 00' - 53° 51' - 60° 00' = 66° 09'$$

Horizontal distances LA and $L'A$ by Eqs. 17-7 and 17-8 are

$$LA = \frac{(250.0) \sin 60° 00'}{\sin 66° 09'} = 236.7 \text{ ft}$$

$$L'A = \frac{(250.0) \sin 53° 51'}{\sin 66° 09'} = 220.7 \text{ ft}$$

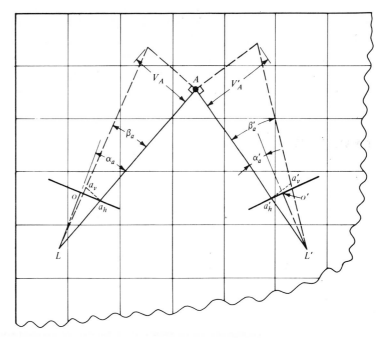

FIGURE 17-10
Map location of points by graphical intersection from two horizontal terrestrial photos.

The X_A and Y_A coordinates of point A by Eq. (17-9) are

$$X_A = (236.7) \cos 53° 51' = 139.6 \text{ ft}$$
$$Y_A = (236.7) \sin 53° 51' = 191.1 \text{ ft}$$

The elevation of point A by Eq. 17-11 is

elev $A = 862.7 + (236.7) \tan 13° 29' = 919.5$ ft above mean sea level

Applying Eqs. (17-10) and (17-12), checks may be obtained for the X_A and Y_A coordinates and for the elevation of A as follows:

$$X_A = 250.0 - (220.7) \cos 60° 00' = 139.6 \text{ ft (Check !)}$$
$$Y_A = (220.7) \sin 60° 00' = 191.1 \text{ ft (Check !)}$$

elev $A = 855.4 + (220.7) \tan 16° 12' = 919.5$ (Check !)   ////

The map position and elevation of point A may also be determined graphically. In this approach camera stations L and L' are plotted on a manuscript map with their optical axes also drawn in their correct directions, as illustrated in Fig. 17-10. With the apex of construction taken at the two exposure stations, horizontal angles α_a and α'_a are constructed as described in Sec. 17-6. Corresponding rays La_h and La'_h are extended to their intersection, which locates the map position of point A.

Vertical angles β_a and β'_a may also be constructed as shown in Fig. 17-9 and rays La_v and La'_v extended as illustrated. A perpendicular to line LA is established at A and extended until it intersects with extended line La_v. The distance from A to this intersection is V_A, the elevation of point A above camera station L. The elevation of point A is obtained by adding the scaled value of V_A to the elevation of station L. A check on the elevation of A is obtained by graphically determining V'_A and adding its scaled value to the elevation of camera station L'.

17-8 PARALLAX EQUATIONS

If a stereopair of *horizontal* terrestrial photos is exposed with the two camera axes perpendicular to the base line, parallax equations—similar to Eqs. (8-5) through (8-7) for vertical aerial photos—may be developed for calculating positions and elevations of points in the overlap area. Two cases must be considered in the terrestrial situation (1) where the exposing cameras have equal elevations and (2) where they have unequal elevations.

17-8.1 Equal Elevations of Camera Stations

Figure 17-11 illustrates a stereopair of horizontal photos exposed from camera stations L and L' *having the same elevations.* An arbitrary XYZ object space coordinate system is adopted with origin at exposure station L. The Y axis is horizontal and coincident with the optical axis of the left photo. X is horizontal and coincides with the base line, and Z points vertically upward.

Object point A appears in the overlap area of the stereopair. Its photocoordinates measured with respect to the fiducial axis systems are x_a and y_a on the left photo and x'_a and y'_a on the right photo. Note that for the adopted image and object axes, object X and image x are parallel, object Y and image z are parallel, and object Z and image y are parallel.

Parallax equations for calculating object space coordinates X_A, Y_A, and Z_A may be developed by equating similar triangles of Fig. 17-11. From similar triangles Lom and LOM,

$$\frac{X_A}{Y_A} = \frac{x_a}{f} \quad \text{from which} \quad X_A = \frac{x_a}{f} Y_A \qquad (a)$$

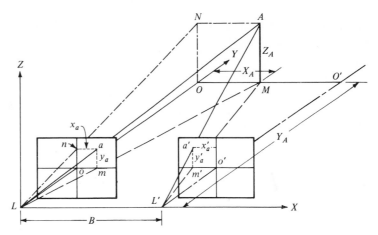

FIGURE 17-11
Stereopair of horizontal terrestrial photos exposed with camera axes parallel from exposure stations of equal elevation.

Also, from similar triangles $L'o'm'$ and $L'O'M$,

$$\frac{B - X_A}{Y_A} = \frac{-x'_a}{f} \quad \text{from which} \quad X_A = B + \frac{x'_a}{f} Y_A \qquad (b)$$

Equating (a) and (b), substituting $p_a = x_a - x'_a$, and reducing,

$$Y_A = \frac{Bf}{p_a} \qquad (17\text{-}13)$$

Now substituting Eq. (17-13) into (a),

$$X_A = \frac{Bx_a}{p_a} \qquad (17\text{-}14)$$

From similar triangles Lon and $LON,$

$$\frac{Z_A}{Y_A} = \frac{y_a}{f} \qquad (c)$$

Substituting Eq. (17-13) into (c),

$$Z_A = \frac{By_a}{p_a} \qquad (17\text{-}15)$$

Equations (17-13), (17-14), and (17-15) yield X, Y, and Z object space coordinates of any points whose parallaxes have been measured from a stereopair of terrestrial photos. If the assumed conditions of (1) horizontal photos, (2) equal camera station elevations, and (3) camera axes perpendicular to the base line are met, these equations are exact and very convenient. In practice, a properly leveled stereometric camera exposes stereopairs which automatically meet the assumed conditions. Also, if the terrain is nearly flat, these conditions can be established using a phototheodolite. The parallax equation approach has the advantages of simplified calculations and ease of measuring parallax, especially if a parallax bar is used. In using a parallax bar, the photos are oriented with their x axes along a common line, and parallax measurements are taken as described in Sec. 8-5.

EXAMPLE 17-2 A horizontal stereopair was exposed with a stereometric camera having a fixed base of 120 cm and a focal length of 64.00 mm. Images of object point A have photocoordinates x_a = 32.41 mm and y_a = 23.74 mm on the left photo and $x_{a'}$ = 28.06 mm and $y_{a'}$ = 23.73 mm on the right photo. Calculate the X, Y, and Z coordinates of point A. Find the elevation of point A if the cameras were at elevation 941.8 when the exposure was made.

SOLUTION   The parallax of point a is

$$p_a = x_a - x_{a'} = 32.41 - 28.06 = 4.35 \text{ mm}$$

From Eq. (17-13) through (17-15),

$$Y_A = \frac{(120.0)\,64.00}{4.35} = 1{,}766 \text{ cm} = 17.66 \text{ m}$$

$$X_A = \frac{(120.0)\,32.41}{4.35} = 894 \text{ cm} = 8.94 \text{ m}$$

$$Z_A = \frac{(120.0)\,23.74}{4.35} = 655 \text{ cm} = 6.55 \text{ m}$$

$$\text{elev } A = 941.8 + 6.55 \times 3.28 \text{ ft/m} = 963.3 \text{ ft above datum} \qquad ////$$

17-8.2 Unequal Elevations of Camera Stations

In some cases, usually because of terrain variations, equal camera heights are impossible. A stereopair taken with unequal camera heights is illustrated in Fig. 17-12. Even though the cameras are not at equal elevations, if the photos are horizontal and exposed with their optical axes parallel, parallax Eqs. (17-13) through (17-15) may still be used. As with the case of equal camera height, the object space coordinate system has its origin at the left exposure station. As shown in Fig. 17-12, the Y axis is coincident with the optical axis of the left exposure, X is horizontal and in the vertical plane containing the base line, and Z points vertically upward.

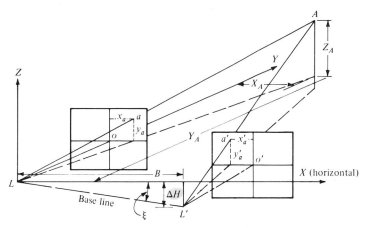

FIGURE 17-12
Stereopair of horizontal terrestrial photos exposed with camera axes parallel but
from exposure stations of unequal elevation.

Equations (17-13) through (17-15) may be used without modification for
horizontal stereopairs taken with unequal camera elevations. Parallaxes and photocoordinates, however, must be calculated with respect to the fiducial axis system. These
are not true parallaxes but rather projections of true parallaxes onto the X axis. If a
parallax bar is used for parallax measurement, the photos must be oriented as illustrated
in Fig. 17-13. The line joining principal points and conjugate principal points makes an
angle ξ with the x photo axes. Angle ξ is the inclination of the base line LL' with the
horizontal, and it may either be scaled from the photos or calculated as follows:

$$\xi = \tan^{-1}\left(\frac{\Delta H}{B}\right) \qquad (17\text{-}17)$$

In Eq. (17-17), ΔH is the difference in elevation of the two exposure stations and B
is the horizontal distance between them. Parallaxes measured with a parallax bar must be
multiplied by the cosine of ξ to obtain projections of true parallaxes onto the X axis.
Photocoordinates x_a and y_a for Eqs. (17-14) and (17-15) are measured with respect to
the fiducial x axis, and the value of B used in Eqs. (17-13) through (17-15) is the
horizontal distance between the two exposure stations.

If the camera axes for a stereopair are perpendicular to the base line but the camera
x axes are not horizontal, parallax equations can still be used. In this case, however,
principal points and conjugate principal points must be located to define the "photo base
line" axes in the same manner that "photo flight line" axes are located for the aerial
photographic case. Parallaxes and photocoordinates are then measured with respect to the
photo base line axes. If the camera elevations are unequal, these parallaxes and

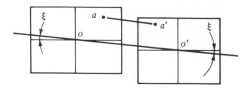

FIGURE 17-13
Orientation of photos of Fig. 17-12 for parallax measurement with a parallax bar.

photocoordinates must be projected onto the ground X axis by multiplying them by the cosine of ξ, which has been determined by Eq. (17-17).

17-9 OBLIQUE TERRESTRIAL PHOTOS

In order to center objects in the field of view, it is frequently necessary to incline the camera axis either up or down from the horizontal. The resulting photos are oblique terrestrial photos. With many terrestrial cameras the angle of inclination can be set or measured so that it is a known quantity. Figure 17-14 illustrates an oblique terrestrial photo with the camera axis inclined downward at a *depression* angle θ. To conform with usual sign convention, depression angles are considered negative in algebraic sign. If the camera axis is inclined upward, θ would be an *elevation* angle and considered positive.

In Fig. 17-14, L is the exposure station, and Lo is f, the camera focal length. Lk is a horizontal line intersecting the photo at k. If the camera is leveled before taking a photo, the x axis will be horizontal. A line in the plane of the photo through k and parallel to the x axis is also horizontal and termed the *horizon line*. The horizon line is the x^* axis, and the line to which y^* photocoordinates are referred. The y_a^* coordinate of image point a is given by

$$y_a^* = y_a + f \tan \theta \qquad (17\text{-}18)$$

In Eq. (17-18) the correct algebraic sign must be applied to θ. Also if an image point lies above the x^* axis, its y^* coordinate is considered positive; if it is below the x^* axis, its y^* coordinate is given a negative algebraic sign. In Fig. 17-14, aa' is a vertical line and a' lies in the horizontal plane of the exposure station and horizon line. Horizontal angle α_a between the vertical plane containing image point a and the vertical plane containing the camera axis is

$$\alpha_a = \tan^{-1} \frac{ha'}{Lk - hk} = \tan^{-1} \frac{x_a}{f \sec \theta - y_a^* \sin \theta} \qquad (17\text{-}19)$$

In Eq. (17-19) it should also be noted that correct algebraic signs must be applied to x_a, y_a^*, and θ. Algebraic signs of α angles are positive if they are clockwise from the optical axis and negative if they are counterclockwise. Also, sec is the secant.

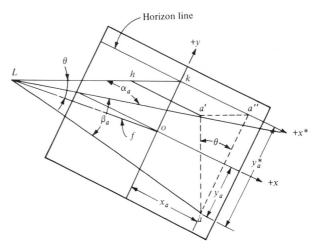

FIGURE 17-14
Horizontal and vertical angles from measurements on an oblique terrestrial photo.

Having determined horizontal angle α_a, vertical angle β_a to image point a can be calculated from the following equation:

$$\beta_a = \tan^{-1}\left(\frac{aa'}{La'}\right) = \tan^{-1}\left[\frac{aa'}{(Lk - hk)\sec\alpha_a}\right]$$

$$\beta_a = \tan^{-1}\left[\frac{y_a^* \cos\theta}{(f\sec\theta - y_a^* \sin\theta)\sec\alpha_a}\right] \qquad (17\text{-}20)$$

The algebraic signs of β angles are automatically obtained from the signs of the y^* coordinate used in Eq. (17-20). Using Eqs. (17-18) through (17-20) together with the intersection procedures described in Sec. 17-7, the positions and elevations of all points whose images appear in the overlap area of two or more oblique terrestrial photos may be determined.

EXAMPLE 17-3   An oblique terrestrial photo was exposed with the camera axis depressed at an angle of $30^{\text{g}}(-27°\ 00')$. The camera focal length was 60.00 mm. Compute the horizontal and vertical angles to an object point A whose image has photocoordinates $x_a = 27.41$ mm and $y_a = -34.90$ mm measured with respect to the fiducial axes.

SOLUTION   From Eq. (17-18) the y^* coordinate of point a is

$$y_a^* = -34.90 + 60.00\tan(-27°\ 00') = -65.47 \text{ mm}$$

From Eq. (17-19),

$$\alpha_a = \tan^{-1}\left[\frac{27.41}{60.00 \sec(-27°00') - (-65.47)\sin(-27°00')}\right] = 36°05'$$

From Eq. (17-20),

$$\beta_a = \tan^{-1}\left\{\frac{-65.47\cos(-27°00')}{[60.00\sec(-27°00') - (-65.47)\sin(-27°00')]\sec 36°05'}\right\} = -51°25' \quad ////$$

If images of an object point appear on two or more oblique terrestrial photos whose camera positions and orientations are known, horizontal and vertical positions of the object point may be determined. The procedure is the same as described in Sec. 16-9 for high oblique aerial photos. Also the perspective grid method of mapping, as described in Sec. 16-10 for high oblique aerial photos, may be applied to oblique terrestrial photos. The procedure assumes a flat object space plane and requires that the true horizon can be located. If the apparent horizon is not visible on the photo to enable locating the true horizon, it may be possible to locate the true horizon using the "vanishing point" or "nadir point" methods described in Sec. 16-11. The perspective grid method of mapping has proved very useful in certain areas such as mapping highway collisions. In this case a flat roadway may be taken as the object *XY* plane, and parallel road edges and cross joints may often be used for obtaining the true horizon by the vanishing point method.

17-10 EXPOSURE STATION LOCATION AND CAMERA AXIS DIRECTION

Sometimes the location of the exposure station and camera axis direction are unknown for a terrestrial photo and must be determined. A simple and convenient method for locating the horizontal position of the exposure station and the direction of the optical axis is *three-point resection*. It may be done either graphically or numerically, but in order to obtain the solution, the θ angle must be known and images of at least three horizontal control points must appear in the photo. Using Eq. (17-1), or (17-19) if the photo is oblique, horizontal angles between the camera axis and rays to the three control points are calculated. In the graphical three-point resection procedure described in Sec. 9-5, the three control points are plotted to scale on a base map. A transparent template containing the three rays and the camera axis is prepared based on the calculated horizontal angles. The template is placed in the base map and adjusted in position until the three rays simultaneously pass through their respective plotted control points. The exposure station position and direction of the optical axis are then marked on the map by

FIGURE 17-15
Determining elevation of camera station of terrestrial photo using one vertical
control point.

pinpricking through the template. Numerical techniques of three-point resection are
discussed in most textbooks on surveying and shall not be discussed herein.

The elevation of the exposure station is the height of the camera lens above datum.
If the elevation of the occupied station is known, the elevation of the camera lens is
usually determined by measuring the vertical distance from the ground point up to the
camera lens and adding it to the elevation of the ground point. If the exposure station
elevation is unknown, it may be determined from a vertical control point, provided that
the horizontal position of the camera and direction of its optical axis are known.

Assume that the position and elevation of point A in Fig. 17-15 are known. Vertical
angle β_a to control point A is calculated from Eq. (17-2), or Eq. (17-20) if the photo is
oblique. With the horizontal distance LA_h known, the camera station elevation may be
calculated from the following equation:

$$\text{elev } L = \text{elev } A - LA_h \tan \beta_a \qquad (17\text{-}21)$$

If more than one control point is available, the average of exposure station
elevations determined from all control points is adopted. If possible, it is best to measure
the position and orientation of the camera at the time of photography so that the
calculations described in this section are unnecessary.

17-11 STEREOSCOPIC PLOTTING INSTRUMENTS

In addition to analytical and graphical techniques, stereoscopic plotting instruments may
also be used to determine object point positions from stereopairs of terrestrial photos.
Although terrestrial photos can be used in all the plotters described in Chap. 14, there are

FIGURE 17-16
Wild A-40 Autograph for plotting from terrestrial stereopairs. (*Courtesy Wild Heerbrugg Instruments, Ltd.*)

certain critical limitations with many of them. One of the basic problems is that Y coordinates (depth) of horizontal and near-horizontal terrestrial stereomodels corresponds to Z coordinates (elevation) of aerial stereomodels. Normally the depth range required in terrestrial stereomodels far exceeds the elevation range encountered with aerial stereomodels. Many stereoplotters (including all direct optical projection instruments) designed specifically for aerial photography lack the depth range required for terrestrial photos because of both optical and mechanical limitations. If the depth range of a terrestrial stereopair is small, instruments designed for aerial photos may well prove satisfactory.

Another problem in accommodating terrestrial photos in direct optical projection plotters is that terrestrial camera focal lengths are not generally within the range of projector principal distance accommodation. Diapositives can be prepared with proper principal distances regardless of camera focal length (see Sec. 14-7.1). Printers are not commonly available, however, which handle the large variations in enlargement or reduction ratios that can result from the large disparities between terrestrial camera focal lengths and projector principal distances.

Most mechanical projection instruments are capable of accommodating a wide range in principal distances, so that diapositives are generally more easily prepared for them. In some cases contact-printed diapositives may be used. A number of stereoscopic plotters are designed to handle both aerial and terrestrial photos. With these instruments the Y and Z drives can be interchanged.

If the stereoplotter has dials for setting the projector rotations and translations and if the relative orientation and base line length are known for the stereopair, relative and absolute orientation can be accomplished by setting the dials to the known values. Difficulties will be encountered in relative and absolute orientation if the instrument lacks dials and if a large portion of the stereomodel lies above the horizon and is void of imagery. In these cases model points for relative orientation and control points for absolute orientation will not exist in the conventionally desirable locations of the stereomodel. With laboratory photography, this problem can often be overcome by placing artificial targets so that their images appear near the principal points and corners of the stereomodels.

Some stereoplotters have been designed specifically to handle terrestrial photography. The Wild A-40 of Fig. 17-16, for example, has been designed principally for use with stereopairs obtained from stereometric cameras. The instrument will also handle stereopairs obtained from single camera setups at the ends of a base line, provided the optical axes are aligned parallel. The Zeiss *Terragraph* is another instrument designed specifically for plotting from terrestrial photos.

17-12   CONTROL FOR TERRESTRIAL PHOTOGRAMMETRY

In terrestrial photogrammetry the object space is often relatively close to the camera; in fact, in many cases the photographs are taken in laboratories. Object distances vary from a few inches up to 1,000 feet or more and the objects photographed vary in size from articles as small as human teeth and smaller, to very large buildings or construction sites. If accurate photogrammetric maps are to be made of photographed objects, control will be required.

In terrestrial photogrammetry there are basically three different methods in establishing control: (1) imposing the control on the camera by measuring its position and orientation with respect to a coordinate system or with respect to the photographed object, (2) locating control points in the object space in a manner similar to locating control for aerial photography, and (3) combining camera control and object space control points.

In the first method, no control points need appear in the object space. Rather, the position and orientation of the camera or cameras are measured with respect to the object space coordinate system, or simply with respect to the object itself. If a plane object is being photographed from a single camera station, control requirements may be satisfied by measuring the distance from the camera to the plane surface and orienting the camera optical axis perpendicular to the surface. Perpendicular orientation can be accomplished by mounting a plane-surfaced mirror parallel to the object plane and then moving the camera about until the reflection of the camera lens occupies the center of the field of view. If the camera focal length is known, a complete planimetric survey of the object can then be made.

If stereopairs of photos are taken, the control survey can consist of measuring the horizontal distance and difference in elevation between the two camera stations and also determining the orientations of the camera optical axis for each photo. Phototheodolites enable a complete determination of camera orientation and direction of optical axis. Stereometric cameras automatically provide control by virtue of their known base-line length and relative orientation. In exposing stereopairs with less elaborate cameras, horizontal orientation can be enforced by using level vials and parallel orientation of the camera axes can be accomplished by reflection from parallel mirrors.

In the second method of controlling terrestrial photos, points should be selected in the object space which provide sharp and distinct images in favorable locations in the photographs. Their positions in the object space should then be carefully measured. If no satisfactory natural points can be found in the object space, artificial targets may be required. Targets should be designed so that their images appear sharp and distinct in the photos. White crosses on black cards may prove satisfactory. If the object space is small and the control points are close together, measurements for locating the targets may be made directly by means of graduated scales. If the object space is quite large or if the control points are inaccessible for direct measurement, triangulation with precise theodolites set up at the ends of a carefully measured base line may be necessary. In some cases a premeasured grid pattern may be placed in the object space and photographed along with the object, thereby affording the control.

If the object being photographed is stationary, control points may be located on the object. Corners of window frames, for example, may be used if a building is being photographed. If a dynamic occurrence is being photographed at increments of time, e.g., photographing beam deflections under various loads, then targets may have to be mounted on some stationary framework apart from the object. By means of engineer's levels, targets may be set at equal elevations, thereby providing a horizontal line in the object space. Vertical lines may be easily established by hanging plumb bobs in the object space.

The third method of controlling terrestrial photography is a combination of the first two methods. This third approach is generally regarded as prudent because it provides redundancy in the control which prevents mistakes from going undetected and also enables increased accuracy to be obtained.

17-13   A GENERAL SOLUTION

A general solution to any problem in terrestrial or close-range photogrammetry can be obtained by applying collinearity condition equations. Collinearity, as explained and developed in Appendix C, expresses the condition that an exposure station, any object point, and its corresponding image all lie on a straight line. The terrestrial collinearity condition is illustrated in Fig. 17-17. The equations for terrestrial photos are similar to Eqs. (C-5) and (C-6) of Appendix C for aerial photos; in fact, they can be written by inspection from these equations after comparing axis systems of the aerial and terrestrial cases.

If the terrestrial image and object space are defined as shown in Fig. 17-17, and if rotation angles omega, phi, and kappa are taken as counterclockwise rotations about image axes x, y, and z respectively, then there is only a slight difference between the terrestrial collinearity equations and the aerial collinearity equations. As shown in Fig. C-2, in developing collinearity for an aerial photograph, transformed image space axes x', y', and z' are parallel to the X, Y, and Z object space axes respectively. In the terrestrial case, however, image axis x' is parallel to object axis X, but image axes y' and z' are parallel to object axes Z and Y respectively, as shown in Fig. 17-17. Following a development similar to that given for the aerial photo in Sec. C-3 of Appendix C, the terrestrial collinearity equations are obtained as follows:

$$x_a = -f\left[\frac{m_{11}(X_A - X_L) + m_{12}(Z_A - Z_L) + m_{13}(Y_L - Y_A)}{m_{31}(X_A - X_L) + m_{32}(Z_A - Z_L) + m_{33}(Y_L - Y_A)}\right] \qquad (17\text{-}22)$$

$$y_a = -f\left[\frac{m_{21}(X_A - X_L) + m_{22}(Z_A - Z_L) + m_{23}(Y_L - Y_A)}{m_{31}(X_A - X_L) + m_{32}(Z_A - Z_L) + m_{33}(Y_L - Y_A)}\right] \qquad (17\text{-}23)$$

In Eqs. (17-22) and (17-23), the m's are elements of the rotation matrix and their values are given by Eqs. (B-21) of Appendix B.

Terrestrial collinearity Eqs. (17-22) and (17-23) are nonlinear and must be linearized using Taylor's theorem. Linearization follows the same steps as outlined in Sec. C-4 for linearizing the aerial collinearity equations and is left to the student.

The terrestrial collinearity equations are general and contain the six elements of exterior orientation (omega, phi, kappa, X_L, Y_L, and Z_L) as well as object space coordinates X_A, Y_A, and Z_A of points whose images appear in the photograph. These equations are applicable to almost any problem in terrestrial or close-range photogrammetry, including *space resection* to determine the position and orientation of a photograph or *relative orientation* and *absolute orientation* to determine coordinates of points whose images appear in the overlap area of a stereopair. The equations are applicable for overlapping photos regardless of camera orientation.

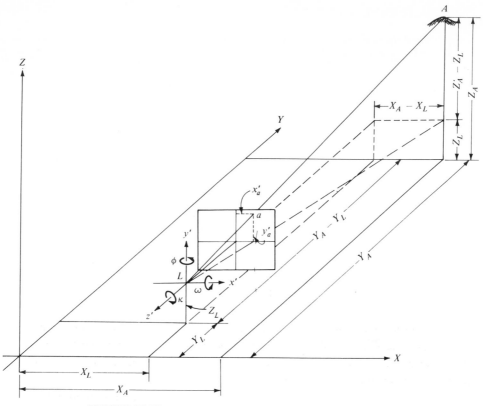

FIGURE 17-17
Geometry of the terrestrial collinearity condition.

17-14 X-RAY PHOTOGRAMMETRY

X-rays are invisible energy rays having a wavelength about 10,000 times shorter than visible energy. Because of their short wavelength, x-rays are capable of penetrating substances which normally absorb or reflect visible light. The shorter the x-rays, the greater their penetrating ability. X-rays are produced electronically in an x-ray tube. As illustrated in Fig. 17-18, when x-rays are directed toward an object such as the human body, if they pass through they create a latent image on the emulsion of a film held in a cassette below the object. Upon developing the exposed film, an x-ray negative called a *radiograph* is obtained. Bones or other solid objects which do not easily allow passage of x-rays cause less energy to reach the film, hence these areas show up light on the radiograph negative. Monoscopic measurements may be taken from individual radiographs, or objects may be viewed stereoscopically and measured three-dimensionally from stereopairs of radiographs. A stereoradiograph is shown in Fig. 17-19.

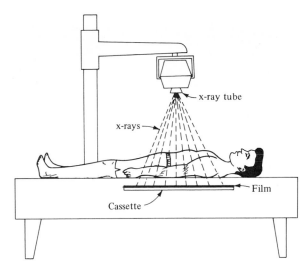

FIGURE 17-18
Exposing x-ray radiographs.

X-rays are used extensively in the medical profession to locate broken bones; to find foreign objects in the body such as bullets, pins, or tacks; to detect the presence of tumors, ulcers, and gallstones; and to examine the heart, lungs, liver, stomach, and digestive tract for disease or defects. Through stereoradiography, the position and depth in the body of defects can be accurately determined. X-rays are commonly used in dentistry for locating and determining sizes of cavities, for examining the roots of teeth, and to determine jawbone structure. X-rays are also used by orthodontists to plan and monitor corrective treatments. In industry, x-rays have a host of applications including examination of radioactive fuels, castings, and welds for defects; locating pipes and wires in buildings; and inspecting tires, radio tubes, etc.

Although radiographs may be analyzed using photogrammetric principles, there are several basic differences between radiographs and photographs. In radiography, for example, energy radiates through the object and onto the film, while in photography energy reflects from objects, is collected by a lens, and is focused onto the film. Also, images of radiographs are usually near the actual size of their corresponding objects, whereas in photography images are generally much smaller than the object they represent.

Figure 17-20a illustrates a side view of the geometry of the *normal case* of a stereopair of radiographs, and Figs. 17-20b and c show the left and right radiographs respectively. In the normal case, x-ray tubes at T and T' are equidistant from the film plane and the object reference plane and film plane are parallel. These conditions can be established in x-ray photography. *Object distance D* (perpendicular distance from object reference plane to the focal spots of the x-ray tubes) and *image distance d* (perpendicular

FIGURE 17-19
Stereopair of radiographs of human skull. (*Courtesy Dr. R. S. Singh*)

distance from the film plane to the focal spots of the x-ray tubes) are normally known. The focal spots of the x-ray tubes from which the x-rays emanate are separated by a base B, which is also assumed known. In Figs. 17-20b and c, points o and o' are the principal points of the radiographs (points where a perpendicular to the film plane from the focal spots intersect the film plane). Point A is a reference point situation on the object reference plane, and point P is any point in the object whose three-dimensional position is desired. From similar triangles TAT' and $a'Aa$ of Fig. 17-20a,

$$\frac{B}{D} = \frac{k - (m + n)}{d - D} \quad \text{from which} \quad k = \frac{B(d - D)}{D} + (m + n) \qquad (d)$$

Also, from similar triangles TPT' and $p'Pp$,

$$\frac{B}{D - h} = \frac{k}{h + d - D} \quad \text{from which} \quad k = \frac{B(h + d - D)}{D - h} \qquad (e)$$

Let Δp equal $(m + n)$, the difference in parallax between points P and A. Equating (d) and (e), substituting Δp for $(m + n)$, and reducing, the following equation is obtained for the height h of point P above the object reference plane:

$$h = \frac{D\Delta p}{Bd/D + \Delta p} \qquad (17\text{-}24)$$

In practice since d is approximately equal to D and Δp is generally small compared to B, the following approximate relationship is obtained:

$$h = \frac{D\Delta p}{B} \text{(approx)} \qquad (17\text{-}25)$$

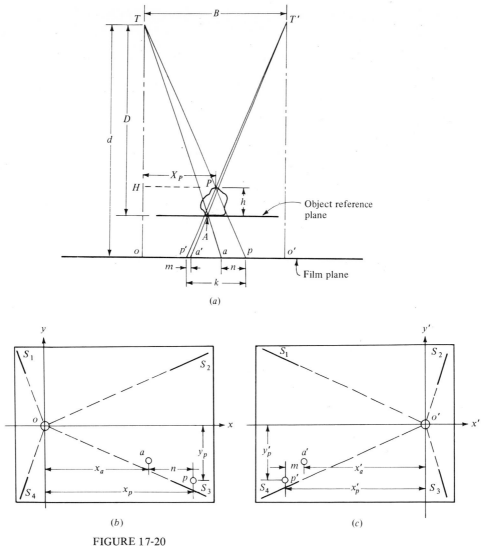

FIGURE 17-20
(a) Geometry of the normal case of stereoradiographs. (b) Left radiograph of stereopair; (c) right radiograph of stereopair.

The following expression for calculating the X object space coordinate of point P is obtained from similar triangles TPH and Tpo of Fig. 17-20a:

$$X_P = \frac{x_p(D - h)}{d} \qquad (17\text{-}26)$$

Similarly, an expression for the Y object space coordinate of point P is

$$Y_P = \frac{y_p(D-h)}{d} \qquad (17\text{-}27)$$

In Eqs. (17-26) and (17-27), the object space coordinate system is in the object reference plane, the origin occurs where line To of the left radiograph intersects the object reference plane, and the X axis is the intersection of plane $Too'T'$ with the object reference plane.

Radiographs contain no fiducial marks for locating principal points and coordinate axes, and therefore they must be located by some other means if Eqs. (17-26) and (17-27) are to be used. [Note that Eqs. (17-24) and (17-25) require only measurement of parallax differences from the radiographs and therefore it is not necessary to accurately locate principal points and coordinate axes if a parallax bar is used.] One simple method of locating principal points, although not extremely accurate, is by relief displacements. In this method, four thin wire studs are mounted perpendicular to the object reference plane so that they appear in the corners of the radiograms. As illustrated in Fig. 17-20b and c, these studs appear as lines on the radiographs at S_1, S_2, S_3, and S_4. Since the four lines are radial from the principal point, by extending the four lines to their common intersection the principal points are located. The x and x' axes are conveniently taken parallel to one side of the film. This presumes that the x-ray tube base B and the side of the film have been carefully arranged parallel to each other.

In practice, stereoradiographs have been taken in the following four different ways: (1) radiographing a stationary object using two stationary x-ray tubes; (2) exposing the left radiograph of a stationary object using one x-ray tube, then translating the tube to the right for the second exposure; (3) using one stationary x-ray tube and translating the object between exposures; and (4) using one stationary x-ray tube and rotating the object (which is on a tilting reference object platform) between exposures. Regardless of the method used, unless a simultaneous double exposure is made in method 1, there will be some elapsed time between exposures while the cassette is removed and replaced with a cassette containing unexposed film for the second radiograph, and while the x-ray tube or object is moved into position for the second radiograph. If the object moves with respect to its reference platform during the elapsed time between exposures, y parallax and other errors will be introduced into the system. Methods are available to compensate for these errors; however, they are rather complex and are beyond the scope of this text.

Radiograph image coordinates and parallaxes and parallax differences may be measured monoscopically to discrete points using any of the scales described in Chap. 5. Parallaxes and parallax differences may also be measured stereoscopically by parallax bar with the advantages that principal points and coordinate axes are not needed and nondiscrete points may be measured. Instruments have been designed specifically for making stereoscopic measurements of radiographs.

It is impossible to do the subject of x-ray photogrammetry justice in a short section such as this. Nevertheless this brief introduction explains some basic approaches in determining space positions of points and indicates some problem areas in x-ray photogrammetry. Students interested in further study in this area are referred to some of the references cited at the end of this chapter.

17-15 HOLOGRAMMETRY

Hologrammetry, a rather new development within the discipline of photogrammetry, uses *holograms* rather than photographs. Unlike the photographic approach which requires a stereopair of photos to achieve a three-dimensional effect, with hologrammetry a three-dimensional image can be obtained from a single hologram. These three-dimensional images, like the photogrammetric stereomodel, may be measured and mapped. Early applications of hologrammetry have been directed primarily to close-range (laboratory) applications, and for this reason the subject is presented in this chapter. Hologrammetry is also under study as a means for topographic mapping, and it is plausible that the technique will eventually have widespread applications in this area.

The science of hologrammetry is based upon the wave theory of light, which states that light is transmitted in regular sinusoidal oscillations. Because light transmits sinusoidally, it is possible to produce from two light sources brighter light by adding wave crest to wave crest, and it is also possible to produce darkness from the same two light sources by adding wave crest to wave trough. This principle, called *interference,* is illustrated in Fig. 17-21. In order for light to be capable of interference, it must be coherent and monochromatic, i.e., it must consist of energy of a uniform wavelength. Coherent light used in hologrammetry is commonly produced by *lasers.*

In producing holograms, two coherent light beams are produced from a single source by means of a beam splitter. In Fig. 17-22a, for example, coherent light is directed toward a beam splitter. Part of the light (reference beam) travels directly to the hologram, and part reflects from the object (object beam) and also impinges onto the hologram. The interference patterns created by interactions of reference and object beams are recorded on the hologram emulsion. The emulsion is developed in a darkroom to obtain a usable hologram.

Figure 17-22b illustrates reconstruction of the three-dimensional image of an object from the hologram. In reconstruction, a duplicate of the reference beam is directed toward the hologram at the same angle that it had in recording the hologram. An observer behind the hologram perceives a three-dimensional image of the object from the combination of the reference beam and interference patterns of the hologram. To the observer, the image appears exactly the same as if he were directly viewing the original object from behind a window. The image may be measured or mapped through the use of

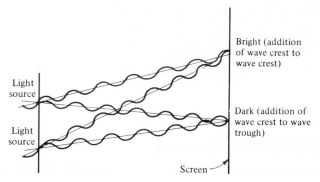

FIGURE 17-21
Principle of light interference.

a self-illuminated measuring mark and tracing system such as that of an optical projection stereoplotter.

The physical sizes of objects that can be directly recorded on holograms are limited by the size of the hologram plate. This is one of the reasons why holography has to date been used primarily in mapping small objects. If the same wavelength reference beam is used in recording and in reconstruction, the virtual image will be the same size as the original object. Magnification of the reconstructed image is possible if longer-wavelength coherent light is used in reconstruction than was used to record the hologram. Hologrammetry may be used for topographic mapping, but this procedure consists of first obtaining conventional stereophotography and then recording holograms of stereomodels created from these overlapping photos.

Hologrammetry possesses both advantages and disadvantages over conventional photography for mapping. Principal among its advantages is that since there are no lenses involved in either recording or in reconstruction, there are practically no optical limitations such as lens distortions, aberrations, focusing problems, or depth of field limitations. The latter two advantages make hologrammetry especially advantageous over conventional photogrammetry for very close-range work. Other advantages of holo-grammetry are that the three-dimensional model can be recorded on a single plate without relative orientation except for positioning the hologram relative to the reconstruction beam. If the hologram plate should be accidentally broken, the entire hologrammetric model can be recovered from any of the pieces with only a slight loss of resolution. Also, since the hologram contains only interference patterns and no imaged points, scratches or blemishes on the plate cause no particular difficulties.

Disadvantages of holographic recording systems are that they must use coherent monochromatic light, they require extreme stability, and their exposure times are relatively long. These requirements confine holographic systems to laboratories. Photo-

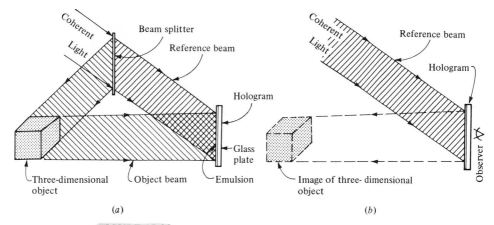

FIGURE 17-22
(*a*) Recording a hologram. (*b*) Reconstructing a three-dimensional virtual image from a hologram.

graphic systems, on the other hand, are very mobile and can operate in a variety of environments. Emulsions are available which can record energy from the ultraviolet to near infrared ranges of the spectrum, and any light source, including incoherent and monochromatic, can be used. Exposure times may be very short and cameras can be readily carried in aircraft for photographing terrain from high vantage points. Of course, one great advantage of photography is that the resulting images appear true and recognizable and can therefore be readily interpreted. Research is active in hologrammetry and new developments and applications are rapidly being introduced.

REFERENCES

American Society of Photogrammetry: "Manual of Photogrammetry," 3d ed., George Banta Co., Inc., Menasha, Wis., 1966, chap. 19.

Borchers, P. E.: The Photogrammetric Study of Structural Movements in Architecture, *Photogrammetric Engineering*, vol. 30, no. 5, p. 809, 1964.

Borrell, S. M.: Terrestrial Photography for Establishing Supplemental Control, *Photogrammetric Engineering*, vol. 23, no. 1, p. 58, 1957.

Brown, D. C.: Close-Range Camera Calibration, *Photogrammetric Engineering*, vol. 37, no. 8, p. 855, 1971.

Burgess, G. H., and J. Zulqar-Nain: Dental Research Using a Close-Range System, *Photogrammetric Engineering*, vol. 34, no. 7, p. 677, 1968.

Eastman Kodak Co.: "Fundamentals of Radiography," Rochester, N.Y., 1960.

Garbor, D.: Holography, 1948-1971, *Science*, vol. 177, no. 4046, p. 299, 1972.

Hallert, B.: Determination of Interior Orientation of Cameras for Non-Topographic Photogrammetry, Microscopes, X-ray Instruments and Television Images, *Photogrammetric Engineering,* vol. 26, no. 5, p. 748, 1960.

_____: "X-ray Photogrammetry, Basic Geometry and Quality," Elsevier Publishing Co., Amsterdam, 1970.

Halsman, J.: Stereoscopic Medical Photography, *Photogrammetric Engineering,* vol. 22, no. 2, p. 374, 1956.

Heyden, F. J.: Photogrammetry in Astronomy, *Photogrammetric Engineering,* vol. 16, no. 1, p. 66, 1950.

Karara, H. M.: Universal Stereometric Systems, *Photogrammetric Engineering,* vol. 33, no. 11, p. 1303, 1967.

_____: Simple Cameras for Close Range Applications, *Photogrammetric Engineering,* vol. 38, no. 5, p. 447, 1972.

Konecny, G.: Structural Engineering Application of the Stereometric Camera, *Photogrammetric Engineering,* vol. 31, no. 1, p. 96, 1965.

Leydolph, W. K.: Stereophotogrammetry in Animal Husbandry, *Photogrammetric Engineering,* vol. 20, no. 5, p. 804, 1954.

Malhotra, R. C.: Holography as Viewed by a Photogrammetrist, *Photogrammetric Engineering,* vol. 36, no. 2, p. 152, 1970.

McNeil, G. T.: X-ray Stereo Photogrammetry, *Photogrammetric Engineering,* vol. 32, no. 6, p. 993, 1966.

Merritt, E. L.: Selections of Camera Stations in Terrestrial Photogrammetry, *Photogrammetric Engineering,* vol. 14, no. 3, p. 421, 1948.

Moellman, D., and H. Karara: Close-Range Photogrammetric Data Reduction Scheme, *American Society of Civil Engineers, Journal of the Surveying and Mapping Division,* vol. 94, no. SU2, p. 211, 1968.

Mikhail, E. M., and Glaser: Mensuration Aspects of Holograms, *Photogrammetric Engineering,* vol. 37, no. 3, p. 267, 1971.

Salley, J. R.: Close Range Photogrammetry: A Useful Tool in Traffic Accident Investigation, *Photogrammetric Engineering,* vol. 30, no. 4, p. 568, 1964.

Schernhorst, J. N.: Close Range Instrumentation, *Photogrammetric Engineering,* vol. 33, no. 4, p. 377, 1967.

Singh, R. S.: Radiographic Measurements, *Photogrammetric Engineering,* vol. 36, no. 11, p. 1137, 1970.

Strasser, G. J.: Photogrammetric Engineering with a Wild Phototheodolite, *Photogrammetric Engineering,* vol. 19, no. 5, p. 834, 1953.

PROBLEMS

17-1 Discuss some of the uses of terrestrial or close-range photogrammetry.

17-2 Explain the differences between a phototheodolite and a stereometric camera.

17-3 A horizontal terrestrial photo was exposed with a phototheodolite having a focal length of 60.00 mm. Find the horizontal angle ALB at the exposure station subtended by points A and B if corresponding images a and b have photocoordinates of $x_a = 38.24$ millimeters, $y_a = -18.73$ millimeters, $x_b = -21.70$ millimeters, and $y_b = 30.86$ millimeters.

17-4 For the data of Prob. 17-3, calculate the vertical angles from the exposure station to points A and B.

17-5 Solve Prob. 17-3 graphically.

17-6 A stereopair of oblique terrestrial photos was exposed as illustrated in Fig. 17-9, The camera had a 164.96-mm focal length and the camera axis was inclined upward from horizontal at an angle of $6°\ 18'$ for both photos. Horizontal angles δ and δ' measured from the base line were $78°\ 18'$ and $79°\ 53'$ respectively. The horizontal length of the base line was 64.54 feet and the elevations of camera stations L and L' were 104.93 and 104.97 feet respectively. Calculate X and Y ground coordinates of point A if photocoordinates of image a on the left and right photo were $x_a = -1.61$ millimeters, $y_a = 26.17$ millimeters, $x_a' = -63.57$ millimeters, and $y_a' = 23.24$ millimeters. Assume the origin of ground coordinates to be at camera station L and that the X axis coincides with the base line as illustrated in Fig. 17-9.

17-7 Calculate the elevation of point A of Prob. 17-6.

17-8 On the overlapping pair of terrestrial photos of Prob. 17-6, a second point B has image coordinates on the left and right photos of $x_b = 63.42$ millimeters, $y_b = 22.51$ millimeters, $x_b' = 2.78$ millimeters, and $y_b' = 26.37$ millimeters. Calculate the horizontal length of line AB.

17-9 A horizontal stereopair of terrestrial photos was exposed using a stereometric camera having a base of 2.000 meters. The focal lengths of both cameras were 150.00 mm. Image coordinates of a church spire on the left and right photos were $x = 6.15$ millimeters, $y = 53.36$ millimeters, $x' = 0.79$ millimeters, and $y' = 53.35$ millimeters. Using the parallax equations, calculate X, Y, and Z coordinates of the church spire in a ground coordinate system with origin at the left camera station as indicated in Fig. 17-11.

17-10 The problem is similar to Prob. 17-9 except that the cameras had focal lengths of 64.00 mm, the camera base was 120 centimeters, and images of point A had measured photocoordinates on the left and right photos of $x_a = -8.12$ millimeters, $y_a = 4.83$ millimeters, $x_a' = -13.97$ millimeters, and $y_a' = 4.83$ millimeters.

17-11 A horizontal stereopair of terrestrial photos was exposed with unequal camera station elevations as illustrated in Fig. 17-12. The camera axes were oriented parallel, and the phototheodolite had a focal length of 164.96 mm. The horizontal length of the camera base line was 48.67 feet. Camera elevation was 105.88 feet at station L and 100.28 feet at L'. Using a parallax bar, parallaxes of 61.97 millimeters and 52.79 millimeters were obtained for image points a and b with the photos oriented as illustrated in Fig. 17-13. Photocoordinates of images a and b on the left photo measured with respect to the fiducial axes were $x_a =$

25.45 millimeters, $y_a = 19.26$ millimeters, $x_b = 32.46$ millimeters, and $y_b = 38.84$ millimeters. Calculate X, Y, and Z coordinates of points A and B in the ground coordinate system of Fig. 17-12 using the parallax equations. What is the length of line AB?

17-12 Discuss three basic approaches in establishing control for terrestrial or close-range photogrammetry.

17-13 What are some of the uses of x-ray photogrammetry?

17-14 Describe the different methods used in obtaining stereopairs of radiographs.

17-15 A stereopair of radiographs was exposed by shifting the x-ray tube 3.5 inches between exposures. Distances d and D from the x-ray tube to film plane and object reference plane are 36.0 and 35.5 inches respectively. Δp for image point p is measured as 0.25 inches. What is the height of object point P above the object reference plane? (Use both the exact and approximate formulas and compare the results.)

17-16 Discuss the advantages and disadvantages of hologrammetry as compared to conventional photographic photogrammetry for mapping.

PHOTOGRAMMETRIC CONTROL EXTENSION

18-1 INTRODUCTION

Many photogrammetric projects require an extensive amount of horizontal and vertical photo control. In compiling topographic maps with stereoplotters, for example, the absolute minimum number of control points necessary in each stereomodel is two horizontal and three vertical points, but practical minimums are three horizontal and four vertical. For large mapping projects, therefore, the number of control points needed is extensive, and the cost of establishing them can be extremely high if done exclusively by field survey methods. In recent years, with the advent of electronic computers and improved photogrammetric equipment and techniques, much of the needed control has been established by photogrammetric means from only a sparse network of field-surveyed ground control.

Photogrammetric control extension procedures (or *bridging*, as it is often called) can yield satisfactory accuracy for both horizontal and vertical photo control and at a substantial cost savings. Besides cost savings, however, bridging sometimes enables photogrammetric mapping to be achieved without actually setting foot on the property being mapped. This is an important point if property owners refuse to allow surveyors access to their land.

Photogrammetric methods of establishing control may be classified into one of two broad categories: *analogical* or *analytical*. Analogical procedures involve manual relative orientation and measurement of model coordinates using stereoscopic plotting instruments, while analytical methods consist of photocoordinate measurements followed by numerical relative orientation and computation of model coordinates using an electronic computer. Various specialized techniques have been developed within each of the two broad categories. This chapter briefly describes some of these techniques.

PART I   ANALOGICAL METHODS

18-2   STEREOTRIANGULATION WITH MULTIPROJECTOR INSTRUMENTS

Perhaps the most easily visualized (although not widely practiced) method of photogrammetric control extension is strip stereotriangulation using a multiprojector stereoplotter of the type shown in Fig. 18-1. In extending control by this method, adjacent stereomodels of a strip are successively oriented to each other to form a continuous "strip model." Coordinates of all pass points and control points are read from the strip model, and then all points are adjusted to a limited amount of field-surveyed ground control to arrive at their final coordinates.

The first step in stereotriangulation with a multiprojector instrument is preparation of a long manuscript map which will accommodate the strip model. All available field surveyed horizontal and vertical ground control is plotted thereon. The manuscript is placed on the plotting table, and assuming enough control exists in the first model, it is completely oriented. It is convenient, although not necessary, to have enough field-surveyed ground control in the beginning model of the strip to enable that model to be absolutely oriented.

After completing the orientation of the first model, the third diapositive of the strip is placed in projector III, as illustrated in Fig. 18-2. An initial model base $b'_{2\text{-}3}$ for model 2-3 is set approximately equal to the model base for model 1-2. The third photo is then relatively oriented to photo 2, using the one-projector method (see Sec. 14-8) to avoid upsetting previously oriented model 1-2. All motions during relative orientation of model 2-3 are imparted to projector III only.

Relative orientation of model 2-3 by the one-projector method automatically levels the model (it has the same datum as model 1-2), but model 2-3 is not yet at proper scale. In Fig. 18-2 point B', approximately vertically beneath projector II, has a lower elevation in model 2-3 than corresponding point B in model 1-2. This indicates that model base $b'_{2\text{-}3}$ is too large, causing the scale of model 2-3 to be too large. To give model 2-3 the same scale as model 1-2, the platen is raised until the tracing table dial reads the elevation of point B as determined in model 1-2. Model base $b'_{2\text{-}3}$ is then decreased by $\Delta b_{2\text{-}3}$ until

FIGURE 18-1
Multiprojector Balplex stereoplotting instrument. (*Courtesy Bausch and Lomb*)

the floating mark appears to rest exactly on point B. Points such as B are known as *carry-over* points because they make it possible to carry scale throughout the strip. If the model base contains b_y and b_z components, besides introducing a Δb_x correction, small Δb_y and Δb_z components will also be needed to clear y parallax in model 2-3. The procedure is repeated for each successive model of the strip until all photos have been oriented or until all projectors have been utilized.

Suppose that a control extension of the seven-model strip shown in Fig. 18-3*a* has been performed using the instrument pictured in Fig. 18-1. Positions of all horizontal and vertical control points have been plotted on the manuscript as they were measured from the model, as shown on the figure. Also, model locations of all pass points have been plotted, and model elevations of all control points and pass points have been read and recorded. Note that six pass points have been placed in each model, a standard procedure for stereotriangulation.

Except for the ground control in the first model, which was used to absolutely orient that model, discrepancies exist between plotted model positions of horizontal control points and their corresponding plotted field-surveyed positions. This is the result

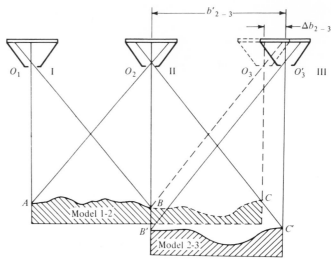

FIGURE 18-2
Scaling adjacent model 2-3 to model 1-2 by adjusting model base.

of various systematic and random errors that occur in the process of stereotriangulation. On the manuscript map of Fig. 18-3a, solid triangles represent model positions of horizontal control points and dashed triangles represent their corresponding "true" positions plotted from field-survey information. Note the discrepancies between model and true positions. If the X coordinate discrepancies (e_x) and Y coordinate discrepancies (e_y) for all horizontal control points are plotted versus their X strip coordinates, smooth curves such as those of Fig. 18-3b should result. Assuming that discrepancies along the entire strip correspond to these curves, corrections to pass points for X and Y discrepancies can be taken directly from the curves on the basis of their respective X strip coordinates. Pass point n, for example, would receive corrections of magnitude e_{x_n} and e_{y_n} as shown on Fig. 18-3b. Instead of obtaining the corrections graphically, they may be determined numerically by approximating the graphical curves with numerical polynomials. Strip adjustment by polynomials is readily performed using an electronic computer. The procedures are covered in some of the references cited for this chapter.

In similar fashion, by comparing measured model elevations of vertical control points with their field surveyed values, discrepancies will be noted as the strip progresses. These discrepancies (e_z) may also be plotted versus X strip coordinates and corrections made to pass point elevations on the basis of the curve. As shown on Fig. 18-3b, for example, pass point n would receive a correction of e_{z_n}. When the positions and elevations of the pass points have been corrected, they are ready for use as control points for map compilation or other photogrammetric operations.

△ Horizontal control point (true position)
o Vertical control point
+ Pass point
△ Horizontal control point (model position)

(a)

(b)

FIGURE 18-3
(a) Plan view of control extension of seven-model strip. (b) Smooth curves indicating accumulation of errors in X, Y, and Z coordinates during control extension of a strip.

If there is not enough ground control in the beginning model of the strip to enable absolute orientation, this first model may be set to some arbitrary scale and approximately leveled. Then the strip is formed as previously described and elevations are read and positions plotted on a manuscript as before for all ground control points and pass points. Pass point positions and elevations are finally adjusted by numerical methods according to differences between control coordinates and measured strip coordinates for all field-surveyed control points.

The amount of field-surveyed control needed in a strip depends upon the length of the strip. As a minimum, about two horizontal and three or four vertical points should exist in approximately every fifth model of the strip. The use of more control than this amount will generally improve accuracy of the control extension. A satisfactory control configuration for photogrammetric control extension of a strip was shown in Fig. 11-2.

18-3 PASS POINTS FOR ANALOGICAL CONTROL EXTENSION

Pass points for analogical control extension are normally selected in the general photographic locations shown in Fig. 18-4a. The points may be images of natural well-defined objects that appear in the required photo areas, or if no such points are available, pass points may be artificially marked using a special point marking device. Point marking devices make small holes in the emulsion which become the pass points.

Even though satisfactory natural points may exist in the required general locations on the photographs, many photogrammetrists prefer to mark pass points artificially for two reasons. First, a more discrete point is obtained so that more accurate measurements of its position can be obtained. Second, the likelihood of misidentifying pass points is greatly reduced. In analogical control extension only three pass points near the y axis of each photo are marked, as shown in Fig. 18-4a. When stereopairs of photos with pass points marked in this manner are oriented in a plotter, six points appear in each stereomodel, as shown in Fig. 18-4b.

18-4 STEREOTRIANGULATION WITH UNIVERSAL INSTRUMENTS

Continuous strip stereotriangulation by the previously described multiprojector technique is somewhat cumbersome and does not achieve the accuracy attainable from other photogrammetric control extension procedures. If a universal instrument is available, one which has only two projectors but which possesses *base-in* and *base-out* capabilities, continuous strip triangulation can be performed to a rather high degree of accuracy. The Wild A-7 Autograph and Zeiss C-8 Stereoplanigraph described in Chap. 14 are two universal instruments capable of continuous strip aerotriangulation.

The principles of strip formation using a universal instrument are illustrated in Fig. 18-5. Model 1-2 of the strip is relatively and absolutely oriented in the conventional manner with the instrument in the base-in mode. The geometry of this situation is illustrated in Fig. 18-5a. The base-in mode is said to exist when the space rods are pointing toward each other, and the two model base components b_L and b_R are to the inside of perspective centers O' and O''. With model 1-2 oriented, X, Y, and Z co-ordinates of all control points and pass points are read and recorded. With universal instruments these coordinates may be read directly from graduated scales so that errors due to a graphic plot are removed. A preferred data recording arrangement uses electronic equipment to automatically record model coordinates on punched cards, punched paper tape, or magnetic tape. This equipment avoids mistakes in reading and recording and saves a great deal of time.

After model 1-2 has been completed, photo 1 is replaced by photo 3 in the left projector and the base bridge is extended to the base-out mode shown in Fig. 18-5b. The

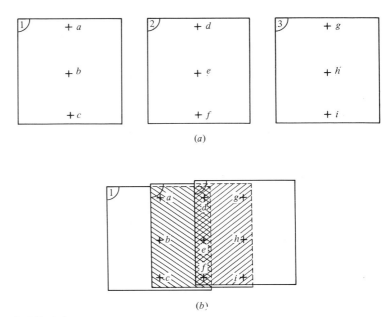

FIGURE 18-4

(*a*) Idealized pass point locations for analogical control extension. (*b*) Locations of pass points in two adjacent stereomodels.

base-out position is so called because the two base components b_L and b_R are to the outside of the perspective centers. In the base-out mode an optical switch enables switching the view of the left eye to the right diapositive and the right eye to the left diapositive. The net result of the base-out mode, in geometrical equivalence, is that the right projector is moved to the left, as shown dashed in Fig. 18-5*b*.

In the base-out mode, model 3-2 is relatively oriented using the one-projector method and imparting all motions to the left projector only. The model is then scaled as described in the previous article by changing the model base until the elevation of a carry-over point in model 3-2 reads the same as its elevation was in model 1-2. Coordinates of model points are then read and recorded. In model 3-2, Y and Z coordinates will be in the same coordinate system as model 1-2. Depending upon the instrument, there may be a discontinuity of X coordinates, however, and a numerical translation may be necessary.

When model 3-2 is completed, photo 2 is replaced by photo 4 in the right projector, the optical switch is flipped back, and the instrument is returned to the base-in mode as shown in Fig. 18-5*c*. Photo 4 is relatively oriented to photo 3 by the one-projector method and the model is scaled using a carry-over point as before. Model coordinates for model 3-4 are then read and recorded. This procedure of alternating base-in and base-out

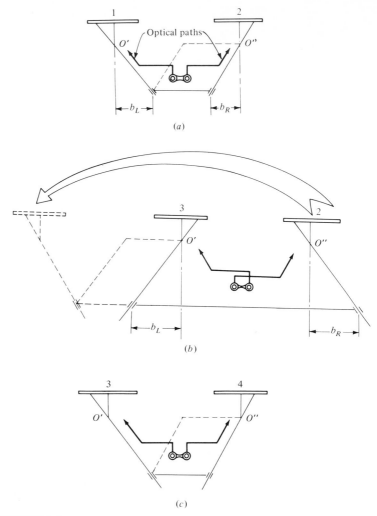

FIGURE 18-5
Principles of strip formation with a universal stereotriangulation instrument. (*a*) Model 1-2 oriented with base in; (*b*) model 2-3 oriented with base out; (*c*) model 3-4 oriented with base in. In (*b*) note that the equivalent of the base-in projector configuration (shown dashed) is achieved.

is continued until the strip has been completed. Strip coordinates are in the arbitrary coordinate system of model 1-2, which is an approximate and unadjusted coordinate system. When the strip is completed, an adjustment is made to all pass point coordinates according to discrepancies between field-surveyed coordinates of ground control points and their model coordinates. Because the recorded data is in digital form, this adjustment is most logically performed using numerical polynomials which approximate the graphical curves. After adjustment is made, the pass points are ready for use as control for other photogrammetric work.

Some advantages of the universal instrument method over the multiprojector approach are that there is no limit on the length of strip that can be handled, and accuracy is improved. In recent years both of these procedures have largely given way to the method of independent models, described in the next section.

18-5 INDEPENDENT MODEL STEREOTRIANGULATION

Independent model stereotriangulation, often referred to as *semianalytical* stereotriangulation, is an analogical procedure that emerged with the development of electronic computers. The most significant advantage of the method is that any stereoplotter can be used to perform the control extension provided that it is equipped with a coordinatograph for reading model coordinates. Another of its advantages is that absolute orientation is performed analytically and is therefore unnecessary in the plotter.

In the method of independent models, each stereopair of a strip is relatively oriented in the plotter. Model coordinates of all control points and pass points are then read and recorded for each stereomodel in turn. The coordinate system of each model is independent from the others. Figures 18-6a and b illustrate the first three relatively oriented stereomodels of a strip and show plan views of their respective independent coordinate systems. By means of pass points common to adjacent models, a three-dimensional coordinate transformation (see Sec. B-7 of Appendix B) is used to tie each successive model to the previous one. To gain needed geometrical strength in the transformations, the coordinates of the perspective centers (model exposure stations) are also determined in each independent model and included as common points in the transformation. The right exposure station of model 1-2, for example, is the same point as the left exposure station of model 2-3. To transform model 2-3 into model 1-2, therefore, coordinates of common points d, e, f and O_2 of model 2-3 are made to coincide with their corresponding model 1-2 coordinates.

By applying successive coordinate transformations, a continuous strip of stereomodels is formed, as illustrated in Fig. 18-6c. This strip may then be adjusted to ground control using polynomial methods to obtain corrected coordinates for all pass points.

Since model perspective centers are used in the strip formation coordinate transformations, their coordinates must be determined. Three different techniques are commonly applied for determining perspective center coordinates. The most convenient method is direct readout of their coordinates, but this requires a stereoplotter with equipment designed specifically for that purpose. This equipment, which at this writing is

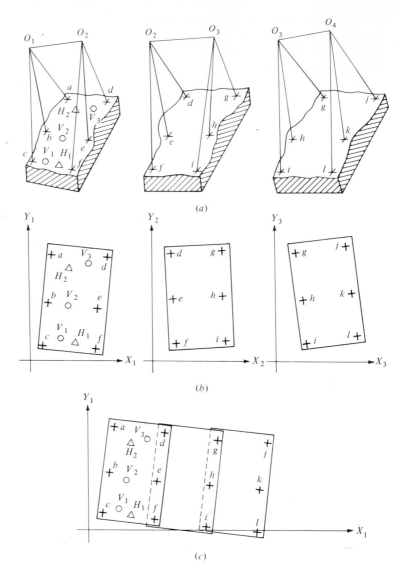

FIGURE 18-6
Independent model or semianalytical stereotriangulation. (*a*) Three adjacent relatively oriented stereomodels. (*b*) Individual arbitrary coordinate systems of three adjacent stereomodels. (*c*) Continuous strip of stereomodels formed by numerically joining the adjacent individual arbitrary coordinate systems into one system.

standard for only a few mechanical projection plotters, consists of a collimating telescope and mirror for aligning each space rod vertically by the autocollimation principle. With the space rods vertical, X and Y coordinates of the perspective center can be read. Also, by adjusting the Z motion of the base carriage, a reference mark on the space rod can be brought into coincidence with a reference mark on the plotter frame. By adding a calibrated constant to the measured Z value at this setting, the Z coordinate of the perspective center is obtained.

A second method, commonly called the *grid-plate* method, is illustrated in Fig. 18-7. A precisely manufactured grid plate is carefully centered in each projector, and X, Y, and Z model coordinates of a number of grid intersection points (preferably those in the corners of the projection) are read monoscopically. Treating the projector principal distance as analogous to the camera focal length, coordinates of the grid intersection points on the grid plate as analogous to photocoordinates, and model coordinates of grid intersections as ground coordinates, the space resection problem described in Sec. 13-12 is solved to obtain the X, Y, and Z coordinates of the perspective center. A minimum of three grid intersection points must be read for a solution but four corner points are recommended as a practical minimum. Tests show that no appreciable accuracy is gained by reading more than about ten points.

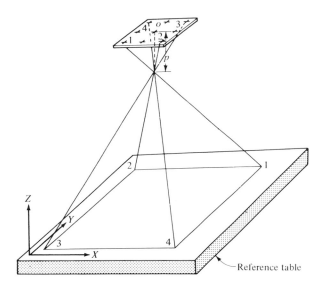

FIGURE 18-7
Grid plate method of determining model coordinates of perspective centers of stereoplotter projectors.

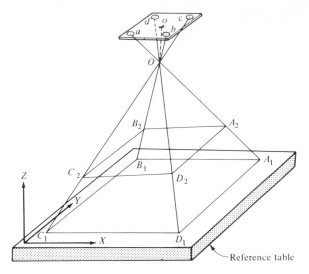

FIGURE 18-8
Two-point method of determining model coordinates of perspective centers of stereoplotter projectors.

A third method of perspective center coordinate determination, sometimes referred to as the *two-point* method, is depicted in Fig. 18-8. In this approach discrete points from any diapositive are read monoscopically at the extreme high and low levels of the stereoplotter's tracing table or base carriage Z range. The following two-point form of the equation for a straight line is then written for each point:

$$\frac{X_0 - X_{a1}}{X_{a2} - X_{a1}} = \frac{Y_0 - Y_{a1}}{Y_{a2} - Y_{a1}} = \frac{Z_0 - Z_{a1}}{Z_{a2} - Z_{a1}} \qquad (18\text{-}1)$$

In the above equation X_0, Y_0, and Z_0 are perspective center coordinates and X_{a_1}, Y_{a_1}, Z_{a_1}, X_{a_2}, Y_{a_2}, and Z_{a_2} are model coordinates for point a read at the two different Z levels as shown in Fig. 18-8. A minimum of two points must be read at two Z levels to obtain a solution, but again, as a practical minimum, four corner points should be read and the solution obtained using least squares. Any one of these three methods is capable of yielding perspective center coordinates to a high degree of accuracy.

PART II ANALYTICAL METHODS

18-6 INTRODUCTION

Analytical procedures in photogrammetric control extension, like analogical methods, involve the basic steps of (1) relative orientation of each stereomodel, (2) connection of adjacent models to form a continuous strip, and (3) adjustment of the strip to field-surveyed ground control. What is different about analytical methods is that the basic input consists of precisely measured photocoordinates of control points and pass points. Relative orientation is then performed analytically based upon the measured coordinates and known camera constants.

Analytically extended control tends to be more accurate than analogically extended control, largely because analytic techniques can more effectively eliminate systematic errors such as film shrinkage, atmospheric refraction distortions, camera-lens distortions, etc. Another advantage of analytical methods is freedom from the mechanical or optical limitations imposed by stereoplotters. Photography of any focal length, tilt, and flying height can be handled with the same efficiency. A disadvantage of analytical methods is that the computations are rather complicated and difficult to comprehend. Also a medium- or large-size computer is necessary to contain and compute the volume of data for extensive problems with economy and speed.

Several different variations in analytical control extension techniques have evolved. Basically, however, all methods consist of writing condition equations which relate the unknown elements of exterior orientation of each photo to camera constants and measured and refined photocoordinates. The equations are solved for the unknown orientation parameters, and either simultaneously or subsequently, coordinates of pass points are calculated. The most commonly used methods enforce one of two conditions: *collinearity* or *coplanarity*.

While some advanced analytical procedures simultaneously enforce collinearity or coplanarity conditions onto units such as triplets or small blocks of photos, the methods described in this text deal only with the stereopair as the basic unit. If photocoordinates are carefully measured and refined, these procedures yield a high degree of accuracy. It is not uncommon, for example, for pass point positions and elevations to be located analytically to an accuracy of within 0.0001 of the flying height.

18-7 COLLINEARITY CONDITION

Collinearity, as described in Appendix C, is the condition that the exposure station, any object point, and its photo image all lie along a straight line. The collinearity condition is illustrated in Fig. 18-9, where *L, a,* and *A* lie along a straight line. Two equations express the collinearity condition for any point; one equation for the x photocoordinate, and another for the y photocoordinate. The basic equations are Eqs. (C-5) and (C-6) of Appendix C, which are repeated here for convenience.

$$x = -f \left[\frac{m_{11}(X - X_L) + m_{12}(Y - Y_L) + m_{13}(Z - Z_L)}{m_{31}(X - X_L) + m_{32}(Y - Y_L) + m_{33}(Z - Z_L)} \right] \qquad (18\text{-}2)$$

$$y = -f \left[\frac{m_{21}(X - X_L) + m_{22}(Y - Y_L) + m_{23}(Z - Z_L)}{m_{31}(X - X_L) + m_{32}(Y - Y_L) + m_{33}(Z - Z_L)} \right] \qquad (18\text{-}3)$$

In Eqs. (18-2) and (18-3) x and y are photocoordinates of an image point; X, Y, and Z are ground coordinates of the object point; X_L, Y_L, and Z_L are ground coordinates of the exposure station; f is the camera focal length; and the m's (as described in Sec. B-7 of Appendix B) are functions of rotation angles omega, phi, and kappa.

The collinearity equations are nonlinear and are linearized using Taylor's theorem as described in Appendix C. The linearized forms are Eqs. (C-11) and (C-12) of Appendix C, and they are also repeated here for convenience:

$$v_x = b_{11}(d\omega) + b_{12}(d\phi) + b_{13}(d\kappa) - b_{14}(dX_L) - b_{15}(dY_L) - b_{16}(dZ_L)$$
$$+ b_{14}(dX) + b_{15}(dY) + b_{16}(dZ) + J \qquad (18\text{-}4)$$

$$v_y = b_{21}(d\omega) + b_{22}(d\phi) + b_{23}(d\kappa) - b_{24}(dX_L) - b_{25}(dY_L) - b_{26}(dZ_L)$$
$$+ b_{24}(dX) + b_{25}(dY) + b_{26}(dZ) + K \qquad (18\text{-}5)$$

In Eqs. (18-4) and (18-5), v_x and v_y are residual errors in measured x and y image coordinates, $d\omega$, $d\phi$, and $d\kappa$ are corrections to initial approximations for the orientation angles of the photo, dX_L dY_L, and dZ_L are corrections to initial approximations for the exposure station coordinates, and dX, dY, and dZ are corrections to initial values for the object space coordinates of the point. The b's are coefficients which are described in

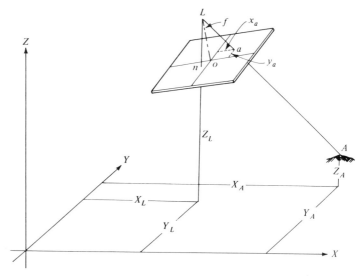

FIGURE 18-9
The *collinearity* condition.

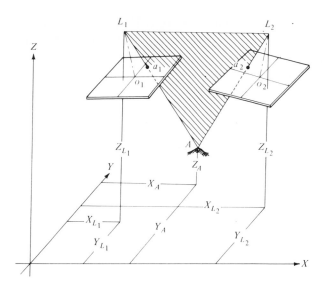

FIGURE 18-10
The *coplanarity* condition.

Appendix C. Because nonlinear terms are ignored in linearization by Taylor's theorem, the linearized forms of the equations are approximations. They are therefore solved iteratively, as described in Appendix C, until the magnitudes of corrections to initial approximations become negligible.

18-8 COPLANARITY CONDITION

Coplanarity, as illustrated in Fig. 18-10, is the condition that the two exposure stations of a stereopair, any object point, and its corresponding image points on the two photos all lie in a common plane. In the figure, for example, points L_1, L_2, a_1, a_2, and A all lie in a common plane. The coplanarity condition equation is

$$0 = B_X(D_1 F_2 - D_2 F_1) + B_Y(E_2 F_1 - E_1 F_2) + B_Z(E_1 D_2 - E_2 D_1) \qquad (18\text{-}6)$$

Where

$$B_X = X_{L_2} - X_{L_1}$$

$$B_Y = Y_{L_2} - Y_{L_1}$$

$$B_Z = Z_{L_2} - Z_{L_1}$$

$$D = (m_{12})x + (m_{22})y - (m_{32})f$$

$$E = (m_{11})x + (m_{21})y - (m_{31})f$$

$$F = (m_{13})x + (m_{23})y - (m_{33})f$$

In Eq. (18-6), subscripts 1 and 2 affixed to terms D, E, and F indicate that the terms apply to either photo 1 or photo 2. The m's again are functions of the three rotation angles omega, phi, and kappa. They are defined in Sec. B-7 of Appendix B. One coplanarity equation may be written for each object point whose images appear on both photos of the stereopair. The coplanarity equations do not contain object space coordinates as unknowns; rather, they contain only the elements of exterior orientation of the two photos of the stereopair. Therefore, after solving for the elements of exterior orientation, object point coordinates are calculated using collinearity equations but with all terms known except the object point coordinates.

Like collinearity equations, the coplanarity equation is nonlinear and must be linearized using Taylor's theorem. Linearization of coplanarity equations is somewhat more difficult than collinearity equations and is beyond the scope of this text. Coplanarity does have the advantage that the solution reduces to a smaller system of simultaneous equations and hence requires somewhat less computational time and computer storage.

18-9   PASS POINTS FOR ANALYTICAL CONTROL EXTENSION

In analytical photogrammetric control extension, pass points are located in the standard positions illustrated in Fig. 18-11. The pass points may be natural points, but artificially marked points are preferred for the same reasons cited in analogical control extension. If a stereocomparator is used for taking the photocoordinate measurements, only the three pass points along the y axis through the center of each photo need be marked, the same as for independent model stereotriangulation (see Fig. 18-4a). If a monocomparator is used, however, all nine points (six points on end photos of a strip) must be marked on each plate as shown in Fig. 18-11.

In marking pass points for monocomparator measurement, some points such as d, e, and f of Fig. 18-11, for example, appear on three successive photos. Each of these points may be located quite arbitrarily on one photograph, which is usually the center photo on which they appear; but once marked they must be *carefully* transferred to their corresponding locations on the two adjacent plates. The Wild PUG-4 point transfer instrument of Fig. 18-12 is a device designed specifically for marking corresponding pass points. With this instrument a stereopair of diapositives is placed on the illuminated carrier plate. The diapositives are viewed stereoscopically through a binocular viewing system which has a reference half mark superimposed on each of its optical paths. By means of slow-motion screws, the diapositives can be adjusted slightly in the x and y directions so that the floating mark appears to rest exactly on the point to be marked. Tiny drills which are collinear with the half marks are then lowered, and holes are drilled into the emulsion mark corresponding points. With any point marking and point transfer

FIGURE 18-11
Pass point locations for analytical control extension using a monocomparator.

instruments, it must be recognized that upon making the holes, the emulsion in those spots is destroyed. Thus no further refinement in the identification of the image position can be made, and any error in positioning is fixed. It must therefore be done with extreme caution.

18-10 PHOTOCOORDINATE MEASUREMENT

Once pass points have been marked on the diapositives, they are ready for comparator measurement. Image coordinates of all field-surveyed control points are also measured. Either *monocomparators* or *stereocomparators* may be used. Measurements with a mono-comparator are taken monoscopically using one plate at a time, as discussed in Sec. 5-7.

Stereocomparators simultaneously measure photocoordinates of corresponding points on a stereopair of diapositives. These instruments have two separate measuring

FIGURE 18-12
Wild PUG-4 stereoscopic point transfer instrument. (*Courtesy Wild Heerbrugg Instruments, Ltd.*)

FIGURE 18-13
Wild STK-1 Stereocomparator. (*Courtesy Wild Heerbrugg Instruments, Ltd.*)

systems, one for each photo. While viewing through binoculars along optical paths, the positions of the diapositives are adjusted until a reference floating mark appears to rest exactly on the desired point. In this position measurements are recorded for both photos. The basic measuring system of the Wild STK-1 stereocomparator shown in Fig. 18-13 consists of lead screws. Two measuring stages are utilized in the instrument: (1) a lower stage which carries both plates and records x_1 and y_1, the coordinates of a point on the left plate, and (2) an upper stage which records p_x and p_y, the small y translations and x translations necessary to place the floating mark in contact with the desired point. Coordinates x_2 and y_2 for the right photo are then given by

$$x_2 = x_1 + p_x$$
$$y_2 = y_1 + p_y \qquad \text{(18-7)}$$

The Zeiss PSK Stereocomparator of Fig. 18-14 uses a precisely graduated glass grid as its basic measuring device. Diapositives are mounted firmly against the grid and with the floating mark set, x and y increments from the point being measured to the nearest calibrated grid lines are measured by a micrometer. Both the STK-1 and PSK stereocomparators are capable of readings to the nearest micrometer (micron).

The O.M.I.-Nistri TA-3/P uses three plates simultaneously. An operator can view either the left stereopair or the right stereopair. Three separate measuring stages, each

FIGURE 18-14
Zeiss PSK Stereocomparator. (*Courstey Carl Zeiss, Oberkochen*)

operating on the lead screw principle, enable the simultaneous measurement and automatic recording of photocoordinates of any point on all three photos. This technique increases measurement efficiency, but perhaps its greatest advantage is the elimination of mistakes in misidentification of points from one stereopair to the next.

18-11 PHOTOCOORDINATE REFINEMENT

To obtain the highest possible degree of accuracy in analytical solutions, measured photocoordinates must be corrected for several systematic errors which cause distortions in image positions. This is true whether the measurements were taken by monocomparator or stereocomparator. The systematic image distortion corrections normally applied in analytical photogrammetry are (1) reduction of measured coordinates from the fiducial axis system to an axis system with origin at the principal point, (2) correction for film shrinkage or expansion, (3) compensation for radial-lens distortions, and (4) corrections for atmospheric refraction. If object point positions are to be determined in a plane coordinate system from high altitude super-wide angle photography, it may also be necessary to apply a correction for earth curvature. All these corrections are treated in detail in Secs. 5-8 through 5-14.

18-12 RELATIVE ORIENTATION BY COLLINEARITY

Analytical relative orientation of a stereopair is essentially a numerical duplication of the one-projector method of stereoplotter relative orientation. The left photo is held fixed in position, its orientation is also fixed, and model scale is initially set by selecting an arbitrary model base. The right photo is then adjusted by applying rotations and translations until all y parallax is cleared.

Analytical relative orientation is depicted in Fig. 18-15. As illustrated in the figure, the left photo is arbitrarily fixed in position and orientation by setting $\omega_1, \phi_1, \kappa_1, X_{L_1}$, and Y_{L_1} equal to zero. Z_{L_1} is also arbitrarily fixed at some rounded value, for example, approximately equal to the actual flying height of the photos. In addition, X_{L_2} is fixed at some arbitrary value, for example, approximately equal to the actual air base. This fixes the scale of the mathematical stereomodel approximately equal to true scale.

As with stereoplotter relative orientation, analytical relative orientation is achieved by enforcing the condition that corresponding rays intersect at a point. In Fig. 18-15, corresponding rays for six points A through F are shown satisfying this condition. The six points are located in basically the same areas as they were for stereoplotter relative orientation. The simultaneous enforcement of collinearity for intersecting corresponding rays is achieved by writing collinearity equations for both photos for at least five object points. Intersection of corresponding rays is automatically enforced because the equations from both photos for a given object point contain the same object space coordinates. The system of collinearity equations that is formulated contains five unknown elements of exterior orientation for photo 2 ($\omega_2, \phi_2, \kappa_2, Y_{L_2}$, and Z_{L_2}) plus three unknown object space coordinates, (X, Y, and Z) for each point used in the solution.

Each point used in relative orientation enables four collinearity equations to be written: an x and y equation of the form of Eqs. (18-4) and (18-5) for each photo of the stereopair. Using 5 object points, 20 equations can be written and a unique solution results because the number of unknowns is also 20, i.e., 5 unknown exterior orientation parameters for photo 2 plus 15 unknown object point coordinates. (Recall that 5 model points was also the minimum number required for relative orientation with a stereoplotter.) The solution of 20 simultaneous equations is obviously not a practical undertaking by hand methods, even for the most spirited photogrammetrist, and it should therefore be done on an electronic computer.

More than 5 points may be used in analytical relative orientation, and in that case each additional point adds 4 equations and only 3 new unknowns. Therefore each additional point adds 1 redundant equation. If redundancy exists in the system of equations, least squares techniques may be used to obtain most probable values. If 10 points were used for relative orientation, a system of 40 equations and 35 unknowns would result.

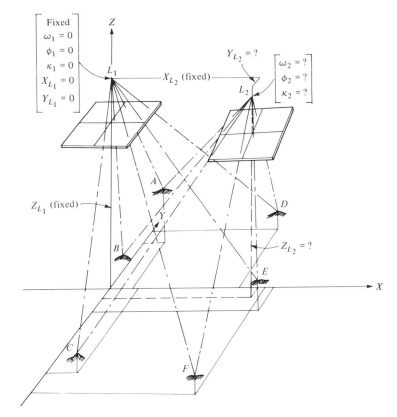

FIGURE 18-15
Analytical relative orientation.

Prior to solving the collinearity equations, initial approximations for all unknown values must be determined. Values of zero are commonly used for initial estimates of ω_2, ϕ_2, κ_2, and Y_{L_2}. An initial value for Z_{L_2} may be selected equal to the value used for Z_{L_1}. Approximations for object space coordinates may be scaled from the photographs, or more conveniently, they may be calculated using parallax Eqs. (8-5) through (8-7) assuming a vertical stereopair.

Suppose that the six points of Fig. 18-15 were used in analytical relative orientation. After relative orientation, the model coordinates of these points are known. They are the same values that would be read from a stereoplotter if a one-projector relative orientation were performed with the left projector and the model base fixed as described for the analytical procedure. The model coordinate system is arbitrary with its axes parallel to the left photo axis system and its origin a distance Z_{L_1} vertically beneath the left exposure station.

With the elements of exterior orientation known after relative orientation, model coordinates of any field-surveyed ground control or other points can be obtained by solving the collinearity equations. In this calculation all terms of Eqs. (18-4) and (18-5) are known except the object point coordinates. For each point, four equations are written involving its three ground coordinates, and the redundant system is solved using least squares.

18-13   STRIP FORMATION AND ADJUSTMENT

Each stereopair in a strip of photos may be relatively oriented in the manner described in Sec. 18-12. The result is a series of independent models, each having its own arbitrary coordinate system. Just as with the analogical method of independent models, adjacent models contain points that are common to both models. Using coordinates of common points and also using the common exposure station coordinates, three-dimensional coordinate transformations may be successively performed to join adjacent models and form a continuous model strip. This procedure is known as the *analytical method of independent models.*

As previously described for analogical control extension procedures, by comparing strip coordinates of horizontal and vertical control points to their corresponding field-surveyed values, corrections are applied to pass point coordinates and their final adjusted values become available for subsequent photogrammetric purposes.

Another approach to strip formation known as the *sequential method* is done simultaneously with relative orientation. It is more economical in terms of computational time because the need for strip formation by numerous three-dimensional coordinate transformations is eliminated. In the sequential method, the first model is relatively oriented as previously described. For stereopair 2-3, however, the elements of exterior orientation of the left photo are fixed equal to their values determined from relative orientation of model 1-2. This automatically retains the coordinate system of model 1-2 for the second model. The procedure is analogous to the multiprojector method of stereotriangulation. As with the multiprojector method of stereotriangulation, the scale of model 2-3 must initially be arbitrarily set by fixing a model base by estimation. Relative orientation is then performed and model coordinates for pass points calculated. The scale of model 2-3 is then checked against the scale of model 1-2 by computing lengths of lines common to both models. The scales are generally not equal because the initial estimate of model base is inexact. In Fig. 18-16, for example, points D and F are in model 1-2, and their corresponding locations computed in model 2-3 are at D' and F'. A scale factor relating the two models is calculated based on the two line lengths as follows:

$$S = \frac{DF}{D'F'} = \frac{\sqrt{(X_F - X_D)^2 + (Y_F - Y_D)^2 + (Z_F - Z_D)^2}}{\sqrt{(X'_F - X'_D)^2 + (Y'_F - Y'_D)^2 + (Z'_F - Z'_D)^2}} \qquad (18\text{-}8)$$

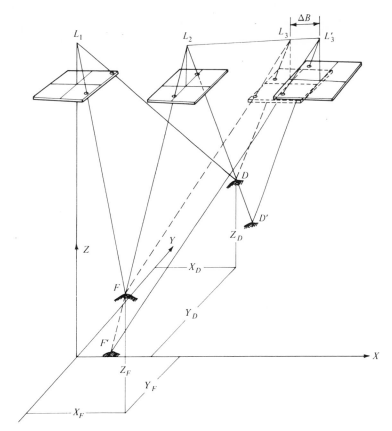

FIGURE 18-16
Analytical scaling of model 2-3 to model 1-2 by means of a scale line.

Generally the average of two or three scale factors determined from two or three different "scale lines" is used. All coordinates in model 2-3 are multiplied by the scale factor to obtain scaled coordinates. Model base components for model 2-3 are also multiplied by the scale factor and new exposure station coordinates for photo 3 obtained by adding the respective scaled base components to the X, Y, and Z coordinates for exposure station 2. In Fig. 18-16, L'_3 represents the original estimated exposure station and L_3 is the final exposure station obtained by scaling the model base.

Scaled coordinates of a carry-over point in model 2-3 are compared to the coordinates of the carry-over point in model 1-2, and any difference represents a translation that must be applied to all scaled model 2-3 coordinates to obtain final model coordinates for model 2-3.

Upon completion of model 2-3, model 3-4 is relatively oriented by holding the exterior orientation parameters of photo 3 fixed at their values determined in relative orientation of model 2-3. This procedure is continued until all models in the strip have been relatively oriented. The resulting strip will be continuous and in the coordinate system of the first stereopair. This strip is then adjusted to ground control as before.

18-14 BLOCKS OF PHOTOS

Thus far only control extension through a strip of photos has been considered. Control extensions can also be made through blocks of photos (two or more side lapping strips). In dealing with blocks, a number of pass points must be carefully selected so that they appear in the side lap area of adjacent strips as shown in Fig. 18-17. These points, called *tie-points,* make it possible to tie the individual strips together to form the continuous block.

Whether the control extension procedure is analogic or analytic, model coordinates are determined for all tie points as well as all pass points and control points. Using numerical methods, the strips are successively joined by matching common tie points and the block is adjusted to available horizontal and vertical field-surveyed ground control. As depicted in Fig. 18-17, control can be extended photogrammetrically through rather large areas using relatively few field-surveyed ground control points. As would be expected, experience has shown that the strongest solution is obtained when horizontal ground control points are located near the periphery of the block. Vertical control, however, must be uniformly distributed throughout the block.

A technique that has been successfully used in photogrammetric control extension is bridging from high-altitude photography to establish photo control for map compilation with lower-altitude photos. Supplemental control extended in this manner can be established to satisfactory accuracy, and the use of high-altitude photos enables greater coverage from fewer photos, thereby increasing the efficiency of photogrammetric control extension.

18-15 USE OF ELECTRONIC COMPUTERS

The magnitude of calculations involved in analytical photogrammetry makes the use of electronic computers imperative. The three basic computational steps in analytical photogrammetric control extension include (1) image coordinate refinement, (2) relative orientation and strip formation, and (3) strip and/or block adjustment. For greatest efficiency in data processing, computer programs for control extension should incorporate all of these steps into a single nonstop process. With such a combined program, camera parameters, measured image coordinates, and field-surveyed ground control coordinates are read into the computer at the beginning. The data are then processed without further

△   Horizontal control points

○   Vertical control points

+   Pass points

⊕   Tie points

FIGURE 18-17
Block of photos prepared for analytical control extension showing horizontal and
vertical ground control points, pass points, and tie points.

human intervention, and final adjusted ground coordinates of all pass points are printed
as output.

It is important to incorporate checking procedures into the computer program so
that mistakes in input data are screened out. Also, it is recommended that precisions of
computed pass point coordinates be calculated as a means of evaluating the solution.

18-16 BUNDLE METHOD

All of the preceeding discussions in this chapter have dealt with the so-called *polynomial*
methods of strip and block adjustment. As of now, in practice, these techniques have
most often been used. With the emergence of faster and larger capacity electronic
computers, however, another technique called the *simultaneous bundle block adjustment*
method, or simply the "bundle" method has become practical in analytical
photogrammetry. In this procedure all possible collinearity equations for an entire block
of photographs are formulated and solved simultaneously. Besides including the
conventional six pass points per model, equations are also formulated for all control
points. By solving both control and pass point collinearity equations simultaneously, a
numerical relative and absolute orientation of all stereomodels in the block is achieved.

The simultaneous solution of all collinearity equations produces a very large system of equations that is highly redundant and which is solved by the method of least squares. In theory this is mathematically more rigorous than polynomial methods, and in practice test results have shown that in fact the bundle method produces superior results. Use of the bundle method is expected to become more widespread in the future.

REFERENCES

Ackerman, F.: On the Theoretical Accuracy of Planimetric Block Adjustment, *Photogrammetria'*, vol. 21, no. 5, p. 145, 1966.

Anderson, J. M., and E. H. Ramey: Analytic Block Adjustment, *Photogrammetric Engineering*, vol. 39, no. 10, p. 1087, 1973.

Altenhofen, R. E.: Analytical Adjustment of Horizontal Aerotriangulation, *Photogrammetric Engineering,* vol. 32, no. 6, p. 1047, 1966.

American Society of Photogrammetry: "Manual of Photogrammetry," 3d ed., George Banta Co., Inc., Menasha, Wis., 1966, chaps. 2, 9, 10, 13, and 14.

Brandt, R. S.: Aerial Triangulation with the Stereoplanigraph, *Photogrammetric Engineering,* vol. 16, no. 4, p. 577, 1950.

Brucklacher, W.: Instruments for Marking Natural Points and Producing Artificial Points in the Preparation of Aerial Photography for Aerotriangulation, *Photogrammetric Engineering,* vol. 29, no. 5, p. 800, 1963.

Colcord, J. E.: Aerial Triangulation Strip Adjustment with Independent Geodetic Control, *Photogrammetric Engineering,* vol. 27, no. 1, p. 117, 1961.

Derenyi, E. E.: Triangulation with Super-Wide Angle Photographs, *Photogrammetric Engineering*, vol. 38, no. 1, p. 71, 1972.

Eden, J. A.: A New Fast-Working Approach to Analytical Photogrammetry, *Photogrammetric Record*, vol. 5, no. 3, p. 474, 1967.

Friedman, S. J.: Aerotriangulation with the Kelsh Plotter, *Photogrammetric Engineering*, vol. 19, no. 1, p. 51, 1953.

Ghosh, S. K.: Strip Triangulation with Independent Geodetic Control, *Photogrammetric Engineering*, vol. 28, no. 5, p. 801, 1962.

Harris, W. D., G. C. Tewinkel, and C. A. Whitten: Analytic Aerotriangulation, *Photogrammetric Engineering,* vol. 28, no. 1, p. 44, 1962.

Karara, H. M.: Maximum Bridging Distance in Spatial Aerotriangulation, *Photogrammetric Engineering,* vol. 27, no. 4, p. 542, 1961.

Keller, M.: Block Adjustment Operation at C and G S, *Photogrammetric Engineering,* vol. 33, no. 11, p. 1266, 1967.

Keller, M., and G. C. Tewinkel: "Aerotriangulation Strip Adjustment," Technical Bulletin no. 23, U.S. Coast and Geodetic Survey, Washington, D.C., 1964.

———: "Space Resection in Photogrammetry," Technical Report no. 32, U.S. Coast and Geodetic Survey, Washington, D.C., 1966.

Kratky, V.: Use of Aerotriangulation in Large Scale Mapping, *Canadian Surveyor,* vol. 25, no. 5, p. 542, 1971.

Matos, R. A.: Analytical Simultaneous Block Triangulation and Adjustment, *Photogrammetric Engineering,* vol. 30, no. 5, p. 786, 1964.

Merritt, E. L.: *Analytical Photogrammetry*, Pitman Publishing Co., New York, 1958.

Mikhail, E. M.: Use of Two-Directional Triplets in a Sub-Block Approach for Analytical Aerotriangulation, *Photogrammetric Engineering,* vol. 29, no. 6, p. 1014, 1963.

Morgan, P.: Rigorous Adjustment of Strips, *Photogrammetric Engineering,* vol. 37, no. 12, p. 1271, 1971.

Schmid, H. H.: Analytical Photogrammetric Instruments, *Photogrammetric Engineering,* vol. 30, no. 4, p. 559, 1964.

Schut, G. H.: Development of Programs for Strip and Block Adjustment at the National Research Council of Canada, *Photogrammetric Engineering,* vol. 30, no. 2, p. 283, 1964.

_____: Block Adjustment by Polynomial Transformations, *Photogrammetric Engineering,* vol. 33, no. 9, p. 1042, 1967.

_____: Formation of Strips from Independent Models, *Photogrammetric Engineering,* vol. 34, no. 7, p. 690, 1968.

Shmutter, B.: Triangulation with Independent Models, *Photogrammetric Engineering,* vol. 35, no. 6, p. 548, 1969.

Soliman, A. H.: Standard Error in Strip Adjustment, *Photogrammetric Engineering,* vol. 35, no. 1, p. 87, 1969.

Tewinkel, G. C.: Block Analytic Aerotriangulation, *Photogrammetric Engineering,* vol. 32, no. 6, p. 1056, 1966.

_____: Aerotriangulation for Control Surveys, *Surveying and Mapping,* vol. 32, no. 1, p. 39, 1972.

Thompson, E. H.: Aerial Triangulation by Independent Models, *Photogrammetria,* vol. 19, no. 7, p. 262, 1964.

Veres, S.: Aerial Triangulation Using Independent Photo Pairs, *American Society of Civil Engineers, Journal of the Surveying and Mapping Division*, vol. 91, no. SU2, p. 27, 1965.

Vlcek, J.: A Study of Analytical Models, *Photogrammetric Engineering,* vol. 33, no. 11, p. 1276, 1967.

Weissman, S.: Semi-Analytical Aerotriangulation, *Photogrammetric Engineering,* vol. 35, no. 8, p. 789, 1969.

Williams, H.: Analogue Aerial Triangulation, *American Society of Civil Engineers, Journal of the Surveying and Mapping Division,* vol. 90, no. SU2, p. 49, 1964.

Wolf, P. R.: Independent Model Triangulation, *Photogrammetric Engineering,* vol. 36, no. 12, p. 1262, 1970.

Wong, K.: Computer Programs for Strip Aerotriangulation, *American Society of Civil Engineers, Journal of the Surveying and Mapping Division,* vol. 95, no. SU1, p. 71, 1969.

PROBLEMS

18-1   In stereotriangulation with multiprojector instruments, explain how adjacent models are scaled after relative orientation by the one-projector method.

18-2   Briefly describe the "graphical error curves" method of adjusting strips of stereotriangulation to ground control.

18-3   Compare the multiprojector stereotriangulation method with stereotriangulation using universal instruments.

18-4   Discuss the advantages of independent model stereotriangulation over other methods of analogical stereotriangulation.

18-5   Describe the different methods available for determining model coordinates of perspective centers in independent model stereotriangulation.

18-6   Compute model coordinates of one of the perspective centers of a stereomodel using the two-point equation [Eq. (18-1)]. Model coordinates of two points A and B measured at two different elevations in the model are:

Point	X and Y at $Z = 70$ mm		X and Y at $Z = 310$ mm	
	X, mm	Y, mm	X, mm	Y, mm
A	606.03	510.62	604.12	508.69
B	245.84	504.65	410.32	505.51

18-7   Discuss the advantages of analytical methods of photogrammetric control extension as opposed to analogical methods.

18-8   Describe two different conditions that are commonly enforced in analytical photogrammetry.

18-9   Describe the different requirements in marking and transferring pass points for analytical photogrammetry when a monocomparator is used—as opposed to a stereocomparator—for measuring photocoordinates.

18-10   List the systematic errors in measured photocoordinates that are normally corrected for in analytical photogrammetry.

18-11   Perform analytical relative orientation using collinearity for the following stereomodel, given the refined photocoordinates for the left and right photos. In the solution set ω_1, ϕ_1, k_1, X_{L_1}, and Y_{L_1} all equal to zero, and set $Z_{L_1} = 11,000$ ft and $X_{L_2} = 6,000$ ft. The camera focal length is 152.00 mm. Compute ω_2, ϕ_2, k_2, Y_{L_2}, and Z_{L_2} and the X, Y, and Z model coordinates of points 1 through 6.

	Refined Photocoordinates			
	Left photo		Right photo	
Point	x, mm	y, mm	x, mm	y, mm
1	0.966	− 88.738	− 91.627	− 86.419
2	− 0.798	1.403	− 89.994	4.162
3	− 2.511	92.055	− 88.824	95.641
4	92.337	− 88.145	− 1.022	− 89.392
5	96.602	3.491	0.818	2.564
6	85.136	90.647	2.595	90.518

19

PHOTOGRAPHIC INTERPRETATION[1]

19-1 INTRODUCTION

Photographic interpretation is the act of examining photographic images for the purpose of identifying objects and judging their significance. It has been applied successfully in many areas including agriculture, archaeology, environmental engineering, ecology, forestry, geography, geology, meteorology, military intelligence, natural resource management, oceanography, soil science, and urban and regional planning.

Aerial photographs contain a detailed record of the ground at the time of exposure. A photo interpreter systematically examines the photos, but in addition he may also study other materials such as maps and reports of field trips. Based on this study an interpretation is made as to the objects appearing on the photos. Success in photo interpretation will vary with the training and experience of the interpreter, the nature of objects being interpreted, and the quality of the photographs being used. Generally the most capable photo interpreters have keen powers of observation plus imagination and a great deal of patience.

[1] By Dr. Ralph W. Kiefer, Professor of Civil and Environmental Engineering, The University of Wisconsin, Madison, Wis.

19-2 BASIC CHARACTERISTICS OF PHOTOGRAPHIC IMAGES

A systematic study of aerial photographs usually involves a consideration of the basic characteristics of photographic images. Seven of these characteristics are shape, size, pattern, shadow, tone, texture, and site.

Shape relates to the general form, configuration or outline of an individual object. Shape is probably the most important single factor in recognizing objects from their photographic images. A railroad is usually readily distinguished from a highway, for example, because its shape consists of long straight tangents and gentle curves as opposed to the curvy shape of a highway.

Size of objects on photographs will vary with photographic scale. Objects can be misinterpreted if their sizes are not evaluated properly. A dog house, for example, might be misinterpreted as a barn if size were not considered.

Pattern relates to the spatial arrangement of objects. The repetition of certain general forms or relationships is characteristic of many objects, both natural and man-made, and gives objects a pattern which aids the photo interpreter in recognizing them. An outdoor drive-in theater, for example, has a particular layout and pattern of parking spaces which aid in its identification.

Shadows are of importance to photo interpreters in two opposing respects: (1) the shape or outline of a shadow affords a profile view of objects, which aids interpretation; and (2) objects within shadows reflect little light and are difficult to discern on photographs, which hinders interpretation.

Tone refers to color or relative shades of gray of images on the photographs. It is related to reflectance of light from objects. Water, which absorbs nearly all incident light, photographs black, whereas a portland cement concrete highway reflects a high percentage of light and consequently photographs very light in tone. Without tonal differences, shapes, patterns, and texture of objects could not be discerned.

Texture is the frequency of tone change in the photographic image. Texture is produced by an aggregate of unit features which may be too small to be clearly discerned individually on the photograph. It is a product of their individual shape, size, pattern, shadow, and tone. As the scale of the photograph is reduced, the texture of a given object becomes progressively finer and eventually disappears. On large-scale photographs, for example, a stand of large-leaf tree species such as basswood or oak could likely be distinguished from small-leaf species such as poplar on the basis of their coarser texture.

Site or location of objects in relation to other features may be very helpful in identification. As an example, a ferris wheel might be difficult to identify if standing in a field near a barn, whereas it would be easy to identify if it were in an area recognized as an amusement park.

Figure 19-1 is a stereogram of aerial photos showing part of the Madison campus of the University of Wisconsin. The numbers on the figure refer to objects which can be

FIGURE 19-1
Stereogram of the University of Wisconsin, Madison Campus. Objects identified
are (1) lake, (2) deciduous trees, (3) parked cars, (4) multistory buildings, (5)
smokestack, (6) sidewalks, (7) building shadows, and (8) tree shadows. Photo
scale, 1:4,800 (*Courtesy Wisconsin Dept. of Transportation*)

identified by the amalgamation of their particular characteristics of shape, size, pattern,
shadow, tone, texture, and site. Some of the objects which can be identified are (1) lake,
(2) deciduous trees, (3) parked cars, (4) multistory buildings, (5) smokestack, (6)
sidewalks, (7) building shadows, and (8) tree shadows.

While a consideration of basic image characteristics is usually sufficient to identify rather obvious objects such as those specifically noted in Fig. 19-1, successful photo interpretation of complex situations requires specialized techniques. Determining tree species or estimating terrain conditions such as bedrock type, soil texture, and drainage characteristics are examples of complex tasks that cannot be solved by merely considering basic image characteristics.

19-3 PHOTOGRAPHIC INTERPRETATION FOR FORESTRY USES

Photographic interpretation can aid in mapping tree species; determining age, density, and sizes of trees; and it can be used in solving many other forestry related problems such as appraising fire, insect, and disease damage. The use of photographic interpretation for tree species identification will be illustrated here.[2]

Basic image characteristics of shape, size, pattern, shadow, tone, and texture described in Sec. 19-2 vary for different kinds of trees and can therefore be used by interpreters to aid in identification of tree species. Individual tree species have their own characteristic *size* and crown *shape.* Some species such as oak have rounded crowns, some such as balsam have cone-shaped crowns, and others such as white pine have star-shaped crowns. The arrangement of tree crowns produces a stand *pattern* that is quite distinct for many species. Tree *shadows* often provide a profile image of trees and can assist in species identification. *Tone* in aerial photographs depends on many factors, and it is not possible to correlate "absolute" tone values with individual tree species. "Relative" tones on a single photograph or strip of photographs, however, may be of great value in tree species identification. Variations in crown *texture* are important in species identification; e.g., some species have a tufted appearance, others appear smooth, and still others look billowy. *Site* can also play a key role in tree identification, as certain species occur only in highlands or on slopes while others are found only in lowlands or in swamps.

The success of photographic interpretation for tree species identification may depend on the various photographic parameters involved, such as time of year, time of day of photography, photographic scale, and film-filter combination used. The illustrations included here are vertical stereograms using panchromatic film.

A pure stand of black spruce (outlined area) surrounded by aspen is shown in Fig. 19-2. Black spruce are coniferous trees with very slender crowns and pointed tops. In pure stands, the canopy is regular in pattern and the tree height is even or changes gradually with the quality of the site. The crown texture of dense black spruce is

---

[2] Sec. 19-3 is based on material contained in the report by Victor G. Zsilinszky, "Photographic Interpretation of Tree Species in Ontario," 2d ed., revised, The Ontario Department of Lands & Forests, Canada, 1966. Mr. Zsilinszky supplied Figs. 19-2 and 19-3 and has given his kind permission to use materials from his report.

FIGURE 19-2
Black spruce (outlined area) and aspen, Ontario, Canada. Photo scale, 1:16,000.
(*Courtesy Ontario Dept. of Lands and Forests*)

carpetlike in appearance. In contrast to black spruce, aspen are deciduous trees with rounded crowns and there may be open space between trees. The striking difference in photo texture between black spruce and aspen is very clear in Fig. 19-2.

Stands of balsam fir and black spruce are shown in Fig. 19-3. Balsam fir are very symmetrical coniferous trees with sharply pointed tops. Since the crown widens rapidly toward the base with dense branching, balsam fir usually seems a thicker tree than the slender black spruce. Area 2 is a pure stand of black spruce. Area 1 is a mixed stand containing 60 percent balsam fir and 40 percent black spruce. Balsam fir stands often have erratic changes in size, forming an uneven stand profile and an irregular stand pattern. Note the contrast in Fig. 19-3 between the smooth, fine-textured (almost carpetlike) pattern of the black spruce as compared with the coarser-textured, more erratic pattern of the balsam fir.

The process of tree species identification using aerial photographic interpretation is not generally as simple as might be implied by the straightforward examples of Figs. 19-2 and 19-3. Results of photo interpretation work in Ontario have shown that it is difficult to identify tree species until the trees are over 20 years of age, although conifers can be distinguished from hardwoods at a younger age. In addition, individual stands are variable in appearance depending on age, site conditions, geographic location, geomorphic setting, and other factors. Other variables which complicate tree species identification are time of day of photography (direction and intensity of illumination), time of year (season), soil types, moisture content in the soil and topography. In spite of these variations and

FIGURE 19-3
Balsam fir (1) black spruce (2). Ontario, Canada. Photo scale, 1:16,000. (*Courtesy Ontario Dept. of Lands and Forests*)

complications, however, identification of tree species has generally been very successful when practiced by skilled and experienced interpreters.

19-4 BASIC ELEMENTS IN PHOTOGRAPHIC INTERPRETATION FOR TERRAIN ANALYSIS

Various terrain characteristics are important to soil scientists, geologists, geographers, civil engineers, urban and regional planners, landscape architects, and others seeking to understand the nature of soils and rocks. The principal terrain characteristics that can be estimated by means of air photo interpretation are geologic landform,[3] bedrock type, soil texture and plasticity, site drainage conditions, susceptibility to flooding, and depth of soil cover over bedrock.

In order to estimate the above terrain conditions, photo interpreters study individual characteristics of landscape elements separately and in relation to each other

---

[3]The term "landform" as used herein implies a specific topographic form, geologic origin, and soil or rock material. As an example, sand dunes have distinct topographic forms which can be recognized on aerial photographs; their geologic origin is *aeolian* (wind-deposited); and the soil particles in sand dunes are almost entirely sand-sized owing to the efficient wind sorting of particles during the formation of the sand dune. Other examples of geologic landforms are river terraces, drumlins, eskers, glacial moraines, etc.

and attempt to ferret out their meaning and interrelationship. A great deal of deductive and inductive reasoning is required to achieve success. In estimating terrain conditions, the following five basic elements are studied stereoscopically from aerial photos: (1) topographic form, (2) drainage, (3) erosion, (4) photo tone, and (5) vegetation and land use. These are briefly explained as follows:

1) Topographic Form The size and shape of a landform are probably its most important identifying characteristics. There is often a distinct topographic change at the boundary between two landforms, as can be seen in several of the illustrative example air photos that follow.

2) Drainage The drainage pattern and texture seen on aerial photographs are indicators of landform and bedrock type and also suggest soil characteristics and site drainage conditions. Figure 19-4 shows coarse- and fine-textured "dendritic" (treelike) drainage patterns. The dendritic drainage pattern is the most common drainage pattern found in nature. It develops under many terrain conditions including homogeneous unconsolidated materials and also in rocks with a uniform resistance to erosion, such as horizontally bedded sedimentary rocks and also granitic rocks. In a given climatic area, coarse-textured patterns would tend to develop where the soils and rocks have good internal drainage with little surface runoff, whereas a fine-textured pattern would tend to develop where the soils and rocks have poor internal drainage and surface runoff is high. Also, soft, easily eroded rocks, such as shale, would tend to develop fine-textured patterns, whereas hard, massive rocks, such as granite, would tend to develop coarse-textured patterns.

3) Erosion This term refers to the size and shape of the gullies (smallest drainage features that can be seen on aerial photographs). Gullies may be as small as a few feet deep and a few hundred feet long. Through an inspection of the *cross section, plan,* and *profile* characteristics of gullies, it is possible to estimate whether the soil is predominantly sand and gravel, silt, or clay. Figure 19-5 shows three typical gully cross-section shapes. Short gullies with V-shaped cross sections (Fig. 19-5*a*) develop in sand and gravel, gullies with U-shaped cross sections (Fig. 19-5*b*) develop in silty soils, and long gullies with gently rounded cross sections (Fig. 19-5*c*) develop in silty clay and clay soils.

4) Photo Tone The absolute value of the photo tone depends not only on certain terrain characteristics such as topography and soil moisture content but also on photographic factors such as film-filter combination, exposure, and photographic processing. Tone also depends on meteorological and climatological factors such as atmospheric haze, sun angle, and cloud shadows. Thus, as in the case of photo interpretation for forestry uses, photo interpretation for estimating terrain conditions relies on an evaluation of "relative" tone values. These relative tone

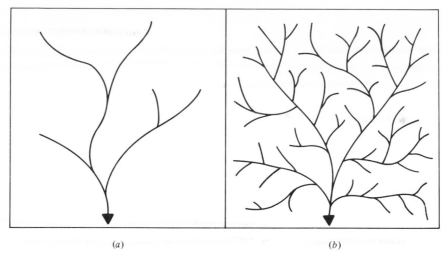

(a)   *(b)*

FIGURE 19-4
Illustrative drainage patterns. (*a*) Coarse-textured dendritic pattern; (*b*) fine-textured dendritic pattern.

values are very important because they form photographic patterns which may be of great significance. The striking mottled tonal patterns characteristic of fine-grained glacial till soils illustrated in Fig. 19-7 are good examples of the significance of photo tone patterns in the air photo interpretation process.

5) Vegetation and Land Use Differences in natural or cultivated vegetation often indicate differences in terrain conditions. As an example, orchards and vineyards are generally located on well-drained soils, whereas truck farming activities often take place on highly organic soils such as muck and peat deposits.

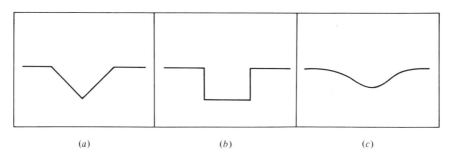

(a)   *(b)*   *(c)*

FIGURE 19-5
Illustrative gully cross sections. (*a*) Gully in sand and gravel; (*b*) gully in silt; (*c*) gully in silty-clay or clay.

19-5 INTERPRETATION OF LANDFORMS

As previously stated, one of the principal terrain characteristics that can be estimated by means of air photo interpretation is geologic landform. This section includes example air photos illustrating three different geologic landforms. Each of these is briefly described, and the basic elements described in Sec. 19-4 that are used in interpreting them are discussed.

19-5.1 Esker

Figure 19-6 shows an air photo of an *esker* (*A*) winding across an area of *glacial till* (*B*). An esker is a deposit of stratified sand and gravel formed by streams flowing on, within, or under glacial ice. After the glacial ice melted, sand and gravel remained in the form of a sinuous ridge. In many states, eskers are important sources of sand and gravel for construction materials. Glacial till is an unsorted mixture of varying amounts of gravel, sand, silt, and clay which were carried on and within glacial ice and deposited over the underlying materials as the glacial ice melted.

The *topographic form* of an esker is its single most important characteristic. It is a sinuous ridge about 300 feet wide which stands 20 to 40 feet above the surrounding glacial till. Because internal *drainage* is excellent through the sand and gravel, no drainage pattern has developed and *erosion* is virtually nonexistent. The *photo tone* on the esker is uniformly light as compared with the more mottled pattern on the glacial till. The *vegetation* and *land use* on the esker are different than those on the glacial till. The esker is not cultivated because of its steep slopes and excessively well-drained soils. However, the surrounding glacial till area is cultivated.

19-5.2 Glacial Till

Figure 19-7 shows poorly drained, fine-grained (silty clay) glacial till soils in Madison County, Indiana. The *topography* has very little relief. There is less than 20 feet difference in elevation between the lowest and highest points in the 1-square-mile area shown in Fig. 19-7. Because of the flat topography and the young age (geologically) of this landform, there is no well-developed surface *drainage* pattern and very little *erosion*. Artificial surface drainage (ditches) and subsurface drainage (buried tile drains) that appear in many places on this photograph are clues to the poor internal drainage of the soil. The *photo tone* differences create a mottled pattern which is characteristic of glacial till areas with fine-grained soils. The tonal differences, especially well developed in fields *C* and *D,* are caused by differences in sunlight reflection due to the varying moisture content of the soil. The soils on the small rises (2 to 3 feet high) are dryer and lighter in tone. The surrounding areas are wetter and darker in tone. Figure 19-7 was photographed

FIGURE 19-6
Esker in northern Wisconsin. Photo scale, 1:20,000. (*Courtesy U.S. Dept. of Agriculture, ASCS*)

when the crop cover was not heavy (mid-June). The *vegetation* and *land use* are characteristic of a rural area with nearly all of the area under cultivation. Fine-grained glacial till soils, especially those in the darker-toned depressions, have high moisture content and low strength. In these areas careful planning and design will be required to avoid highway pavement failures or unstable homesite foundation conditions.

19-5.3   Flood Plain

Figure 19-8 shows a river flood plain. Formation of flood plains is a normal part of the fluvial geomorphic cycle. Young streams have steep gradients and are actively engaged in the process of deepening and widening their valleys through erosion. Their courses are relatively straight, and they do not construct flood plains. Mature streams have flatter gradients and actively depositing flood plain materials during periods of flooding. Their

FIGURE 19-7
Fine-grained glacial till in northern Indiana. Photo scale 1:20,000. (*Courtesy U.S. Dept of Agriculture, ASCS*)

courses are meandering, with the width of the meander belt about equal to the valley width. Old streams have gentle gradients and the width of their flood plains is several times that of the meander belt width.

The construction of flood plains is a depositional process. Streams transport materials primarily through the traction (bed load) and suspension (suspended load) of materials. When a stream cannot transport the load imposed upon it (either because the total load exceeds the capacity of the stream or the particle sizes exceed the competence of the stream), deposition will occur. Flood plains are constructed through the normal processes of meander development and by over-the-bank flooding. Meander development results in the formation of a variety of features, including point bar deposits, channel scars, abandoned channels, and oxbow lakes. These features have a wide variety of associated soil types, from the sands and gravels of point bar deposits to the silts, clays, and organic soils of oxbows. Over-the-bank flooding deposits silts and clays in slack water

FIGURE 19-8
Flood plain in Indiana. The present channel of the stream can be seen at *PC*, an abandoned channel at *AC*, point bar deposits at *PB*, an oxbow lake at *OX*, and slack water at *SW*. Photo scale, 1:27,000. (*Courtesy U.S. Dept. of Agriculture, ASCS*)

(stillwater), and sands and coarse silts on and near the natural levees along the streams. Soils with a high organic content may develop in the slack water deposits.

Flood plain terrain has overall level relief with minor irregularities and a gentle downstream gradient. Soil deposits are complex and variable. Depth to bedrock is also variable, but wider flood plains generally have deeper soil deposits. Internal soil drainage is commonly poor due to the high water table.

The engineering significance of flood plains is that they are characterized by great variation in soils in both the horizontal and vertical direction and are subject to flooding at periodic intervals. Development and new construction on flood plains should proceed only when absolutely necessary, and then only after a careful study has been made of the soils present, the internal soil drainage and groundwater conditions, and the expected frequency and severity of flooding.

The flood plain shown on the airphoto of Fig. 19-8 is of the White River in Knox and Daviess Counties, Indiana. The topography is very flat on this flood plain (illustration is not a stereopair). Most of the flood plain features previously mentioned can be seen in this figure. The present channel of the stream can be seen at *PC*. An abandoned channel is seen at *AC*. Point bar deposits are shown at *PB*. The point bar deposits are small ridges of sand and gravel which photograph quite light in tone due to their sandy and well-drained nature. Shown at *OX* is an oxbow lake which contains shallow standing water that is gradually filling with organic growth. Fine-grained, poorly drained slack water deposits are shown at *SW*. There is a well-developed artificial drainage system, consisting of open ditches and "dead furrows," in the area of the slack water deposits. Without this drainage system, the soils would be too wet for cultivation.

In flood plain analysis, as with other areas of photo interpretation, many significant features that can be seen on the air photos may be completely overlooked by an observer on the ground. A limitation of air photos, however, is that they reveal primarily the surface soil conditions, and in the case of flood plain soils, there are often significant differences in soil characteristics at different depths. Buried granular deposits (e.g., point bar deposits) or buried organic soils (e.g., abandoned channels or oxbows) may occur on flood plains. It is usually necessary, and always desirable, to supplement the air photo interpretation process with selective fieldwork, especially when it is important to learn the characteristics of soils at depths.

19-6 INTERPRETATION OF BEDROCK TYPES

Through careful study of aerial photographs, skilled interpreters are able to identify different types of rocks. Figures 19-9 and 19-10 illustrate the striking differences in appearance of two different rock types. These differences in appearance are the result of

FIGURE 19-9
Sandstone in southern Utah. Photo scale, 1:20,000. (*Courtesy U.S. Geological Survey*)

variations in bedding, jointing, internal drainage, and resistance to erosion of these rocks. An interpreter must consider topography, drainage, and erosion characteristics in order to distinguish between different kinds of rocks.

Figure 19-9 shows sandstone, a sedimentary rock composed of cemented sand-sized particles arranged in horizontal layers. It is relatively pervious and resistant to erosion, and it is heavily "jointed" (cracked vertically) in two approximately perpendicular directions. Because of these characteristics, few surface streams have developed and the drainage is coarse-textured (see Fig. 19-4a). Those streams which have formed have cut deeply into the sandstone rock in directions which tend to align with the two principal directions of jointing.

FIGURE 19-10
Shale in southern Utah. Photo scale, 1:20,000. (*Courtesy U.S. Geological Survey*)

Figure 19-10 shows shale, a sedimentary rock composed of cemented silt and clay-sized particles arranged in horizontal layers which are thinner than the sandstone layers. Shale is impervious and easily eroded as compared with sandstone. Because of these characteristics, the streams have formed a fine-textured dendritic drainage pattern (see Fig. 19-4*b*) and a minutely dissected landscape has developed. Many other bedrock types such as limestone, granite, and basalt can also be identified using air photo interpretation approaches similar to those discussed above. However the student should not be misled into concluding that all rock identifications are as easy as those in the above examples. Indeed, many of them are extremely complex and require a great deal of study and background experience.

REFERENCES

American Society of Photogrammetry: "Manual of Photographic Interpretation," 1960.

Anson, A.: Color Photo Comparison, *Photogrammetric Engineering,* vol. 32, no. 2, p. 286, 1966.

Avery, T. E.: Evaluating the Potential of Photo Interpreters, *Photogrammetric Engineering,* vol. 31, no. 6, p. 1051, 1965.

_____: "Forester's Guide to Aerial Photo Interpretation," Agriculture Handbook No. 308, U.S. Department of Agriculture, Forest Service, December 1969.

_____: *Interpretation of Aerial Photographs,* 2d ed., Burgess Publishing Company, Minneapolis, 1968.

_____, **and H. Burkhart**: Screening Tests for Photo Interpreters, *Photogrammetric Engineering,* vol. 34, no. 5, p. 476, 1960.

_____, **and D. M. Richter**: An Airphoto Index to Physical and Cultural Features in Eastern U.S., *Photogrammetric Engineering,* vol. 31, no. 5, p. 896, 1965.

Colwell, R. N.: Aids for the Selection and Training of Photo Interpreters, *Photogrammetric Engineering,* vol. 31, no. 12, p. 327, 1965.

Fezer, F.: Photo Interpretation Applied to Geomorphology—A Review, *Photogrammetria,* vol. 27, no. 1, p. 7, 1971.

Howard, John A.: *Aerial Photo-Ecology,* American Elsevier Publishing Co., New York, 1970.

Kiefer, R. W.: Landform Features in the United States, *Photogrammetric Engineering,* vol. 33, no. 2, p. 174, 1967.

Lueder, D. R.: *Aerial Photographic Interpretation,* McGraw-Hill Book Company, New York, 1959.

Merifield, P. M.: Interpretation of Extraterrestrial Imagery, *Photogrammetric Engineering,* vol. 35, no. 5, p. 477, 1969.

Miller, V. C.: *Photogeology,* McGraw-Hill Book Company, New York, 1961.

Olson, C. E., Jr.: Photographic Interpretation in the Earth Sciences, *Photogrammetric Engineering,* vol. 29, no. 6, p. 968, 1963.

Rib, H. T., and R. D. Miles: Automatic Interpretation of Terrain Features, *Photogrammetric Engineering,* vol. 35, no. 2, p. 153, 1969.

Richter, D. M.: An Airphoto Index to Physical and Cultural Features in Western U.S., *Photogrammetric Engineering,* vol. 33, no. 12, p. 1402, 1967.

Sadacca, R.: Human Factors in Image Interpretation, *Photogrammetric Engineering,* vol. 29, no. 6, p. 978, 1963.

Scovell, O'Brien, McCormack, and Chapman: *Atlas of Landforms,* John Wiley & Sons, New York, 1966.

Strandberg, C. H.: *Aerial Discovery Manual,* John Wiley & Sons, New York, 1967.

Van Lopik, J., T. M. Merifield et al.: Photo Interpretation in the Space Sciences, *Photogrammetric Engineering,* vol. 31, no. 6, p. 1060, 1965.

von Bandat, H. F.: *Aerogeology,* Gulf Publishing Company, Houston, 1962.

Way, D.: *Terrain Analysis, A Guide to Site Selection Using Aerial Photographic Interpretation,* Dowden, Hutchinson & Ross, Inc., Stroudsburg, Pa., 1973.

Whitcher, G. H.: Canada's Air Photo Library, *Photogrammetric Engineering*, vol. 31, no. 5, p. 807, 1965.

Zsilinszky, V. G.: "Photographic Interpretation of Tree Species in Ontario," 2d ed., The Ontario Department of Lands and Forests, Ottawa, Ontario, Canada, 1966.

——— : The Practice of Photo Interpretation for a Forest Inventory, *Photogrammetria*, vol. 19, no. 5, 1964.

PROBLEMS

19-1 List the seven basic characteristics of photographic images that are considered in photographic interpretation and give an example of how each may be used to identify a particular object.

19-2 Briefly describe the techniques involved in tree species identification using aerial photographs.

19-3 List and briefly discuss the five principal elements studied stereoscopically in terrain analysis.

REMOTE SENSING[1]

20-1 INTRODUCTION

Broadly defined, remote sensing is any methodology employed to study from a distance the physical and or chemical characteristics of objects. Human sight, smell, and hearing are examples of rudimentary forms of remote sensing. A bat's guidance system is another type of remote sensor. Photographic interpretation is considered a form of remote sensing since it is used for identifying objects and judging their significance without physically touching them. Photo interpretation, however, is generally limited to a study of images recorded on photographic emulsions sensitive to energy in or near the visible portion of the electromagnetic spectrum. This chapter treats sensor systems which record energy in more quantifiable formats over a much broader range of the electromagnetic spectrum than those generally associated with photographic interpretation.

[1] By Dr. Thomas M. Lillesand, State University of New York, Syracuse, New York, and Dr. Alan R. Stevens, Tennessee Valley Authority, Chattanooga, Tenn.

Of particular value and interest to the engineer, planner, and resource manager are remote sensing systems that supply information about the terrestrial environment from an aerial or space vantage point. Historically this has been done by systematic extraction of data about objects from photographic emulsions sensitive only to visible light. As described in Chap. 3, emulsions are now available that extend photographic capabilities to include the near infrared portion of the electromagnetic spectrum. An additional wealth of information can be obtained, however, with systems that "see" or sense energy outside the visible or near visible range of electromagnetic radiation.

The technology of remote sensing has developed most rapidly during a time when man has become increasingly conscious of the need to preserve his environment. Remote sensing affords a practical means for frequent and accurate monitoring of the earth's natural and cultural resources and of determining the impact of man's activities on the air, water, and land. Data obtained from remote sensors have provided information necessary for making sound decisions and policy regarding resource development and land use. Remote sensing techniques have also been used in numerous special applications. Locating forest fires long before smoke appears, detecting diseased plants and trees before they can be noticed with the naked eye, detecting the presence of water pollutants and positioning icebergs are but a few of the many varied applications of remote sensors that have benefited mankind.

20-2   ELECTROMAGNETIC RADIATION

As discussed in Sec. 3-7, the sun and various artificial sources radiate electromagnetic energy of varying wavelengths. Light is a particular type of electromagnetic radiation that can be seen or sensed by the human eye. All electromagnetic radiation, whether visible or invisible, propagates in the form of sinusoidal waves traveling at the speed of light.

Electromagnetic energy does not interact with itself; rather, it can be perceived or sensed only through its interaction with matter. As an example, when one sees rays of light in a dark room, the perceived phenomenon is actually a manifestation of the interaction of light radiation with dust and other particulate matter in the air. When radiated energy strikes any object, it can interact with the object in any or all of five different ways. The incident energy can be *reflected, transmitted, absorbed, emitted,* or *scattered.* The extent and manner of interaction of electromagnetic energy with a given object is dependent upon the physical-chemical nature of the object. A green shirt can be distinguished from a red shirt, for example, because incident light is reflected highest in the green portion of the spectrum from the green shirt and highest from the red portion of the spectrum from the red shirt. If all electromagnetic energy were to interact with all matter in the same manner and to the same extent, electromagnetic discrimination, including human sight, would not exist. Different energy interactions that result from different types of matter can be discerned by using various types of remote sensors, and this enables different objects to be identified and in some cases quantified.

Interaction of electromagnetic energy with any object is selective by wavelength; i.e., different interactions occur for different wavelengths of energy. Because of the dependency of energy interaction on wavelength, remote sensors have been designed which respond to different wavelengths, a technique which aids in discriminating between different objects.

20-3   IDEALIZED REMOTE SENSING SYSTEMS

Practical remote sensing systems can perhaps be best understood by first considering an idealized remote sensing system or sequence. Such a sequence is illustrated in Fig. 20-1, wherein

1) Electromagnetic energy of all wavelengths and of known uniform intensity is produced by an ideal source.

2) The energy propagates from the source, without loss, to a homogeneous target.

3) The energy of various wavelengths selectively interacts with the target, resulting in a return signal of reflected and emitted energy.

4) The returned signal propagates without loss to a sensor that responds linearly to energy of all wavelengths of any intensity.

5) In real time, an intensity versus wavelength response is recorded, processed into an interpretable format, and recognized as being unique to the particular target in its particular physical-chemical state.

6) The information obtained about the particular target is made readily available, in a useful form, to users.

Unfortunately an ideal remote sensing system as described above does not exist. The constraints of nature and limitations of technology complicate each element of the ideal sequence. The nature of these complications becomes apparent upon considering the characteristics of energy sources, possible forms of target interactions, loss effects due to the atmosphere, the responsiveness of various sensor hardware, and the varied formats of sensor responses.

20-4   ENERGY SOURCES

All materials at temperatures above absolute zero ($-273°C$) continually emit electromagnetic radiation. The intensity and spectral character of this radiation is a function of the surface temperature of the emitting material. An object which would absorb all

FIGURE 20-1
Idealized remote sensing system.

energy incident upon it is called a *blackbody*. Since by definition a blackbody absorbs all incident energy, no energy is reflected and the body does indeed appear perfectly black. A blackbody is also a perfect radiator; i.e., it reemits all its absorbed energy. Inasmuch as a blackbody absorbs all incident energy and in turn emits all absorbed energy, it is in a state of equilibrium, growing neither hotter or colder. A blackbody radiates energy according to the following *Stefan-Boltzmann law*:

$$W_B = \sigma T^4 \qquad (20\text{-}1)$$

In Eq. (20-1), W_B is spectral radiant emittance per unit area for a blackbody source, T is temperature in degrees Kelvin, and σ is a proportionality constant. A radiating blackbody emits electromagnetic energy over a wide range of wavelength. The dominant wavelength, or wavelength at which maximum energy is radiated, is related to temperature by *Wein's Displacement law*, which is as follows:

$$\lambda_m = \frac{A}{T} \qquad (20\text{-}2)$$

In Eq. (20-2), λ_m is the wavelength of the emitted energy having maximum intensity, T is temperature in degrees Kelvin, and A is a constant. The relationship between temperature of a blackbody source and intensity and spectral character of its radiant emittance is depicted in Fig. 20-2. In the figure, radiant emittance curves are shown for blackbody sources at various temperatures. Note that with increasing temperature there is a marked increase in radiant emittance. Also, there is a progressive shift of the dominant radiated wavelength toward the lower end of the spectrum as the temperature of the source increases. Note for example that the peak of the 6000° curve occurs much to the left of the peak of the 200° curve. This phenomenon can be observed when a metal body such as a piece of iron is heated. As the iron becomes progressively hotter, it begins to glow and its color changes successively from dull red to orange to yellow and finally to white. As stated in Wein's displacement law, these changing colors are the result of dominance of shorted wavelength emission as the iron is heated.

Sunlight has the character of blackbody radiation at about 6000° K. Bodies at temperatures higher than 6000° K, such as certain stars, appear blue (their dominant wavelengths are in the blue region of the electromagnetic spectrum). Most incandescent lamps emit radiation typified by the 3000° K curve. (Note that the curve of Fig. 20-2 displays a relatively low level of blue energy, a characteristic readily detected by observing the lamps' orange color. Because light bulbs have a low level of blue energy as compared to the sun, blue filters or blue flashbulbs must be used for indoor photography with daylight or outdoor film.)

The earth's ambient temperature is about 300° K. It radiates energy that peaks in the 8- to 14-micrometer range, which is far beyond the visible or photographic part of the electromagnetic spectrum. To sense this energy, *thermal radiometers* and *scanners* (described in Secs. 20-10 and 20-11) are employed.

It is important to bear in mind that no perfect blackbody radiators exist in nature. Rather, most radiators are so-called "gray" bodies that emit varying proportions of the energy emitted by a theoretical blackbody. Radiant energy emittance for a gray body source is given by the following equation:

$$W_G = \xi \sigma T^4 \qquad (20\text{-}3)$$

In Eq. (20-3), W_G is the body radiant energy emittance, T is temperature in degrees Kelvin, and ξ is the *emissivity factor* of the source material. [Note that Eq. (20-3) for gray-body emittance differs from Eq. (20-1) for blackbody emittance only by the addition of the emissivity factor.] Emissivity factors are simply ratios of the emittance of a particular material to the emittance of a blackbody. If, for example, the radiant emittance for a blackbody at temperature T is W_B and radiant emittance for a gray body at the same temperature is W_G, then the emissivity factor ξ for that gray body is equal to W_G/W_B. Emissivity factors depend upon the composition of the material. Typical emissivity factors for common materials are water, 0.99; foliated trees, 0.96;

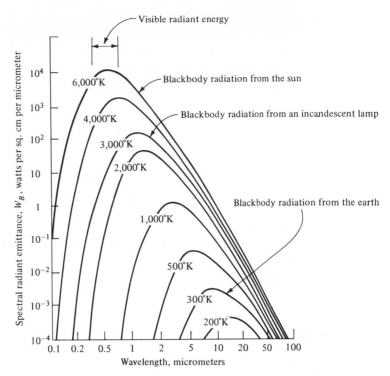

FIGURE 20-2
Spectral radiant emittance of blackbodies at various temperatures.

sand, 0.95; concrete, 0.92; dry soil, 0.90; snow, 0.85; and polished silver, 0.02. Polished silver is a good reflector but absorbs very little energy and consequently it is a poor radiator.

20-5 TARGET INTERACTIONS

As previously stated, electromagnetic energy can interact with an object in five ways. The nature of these possible interactions was schematically indicated in Fig. 20-1, with the exception of scatter which does not occur in an idealized remote sensing system. The five interactions include

1) *Reflection,* wherein the incident energy is returned to the medium of propagation fundamentally unchanged.

2) *Transmission,* where the energy propagates through the object.

3) *Absorption,* where incident radiation is converted to some other form of energy such as heat.

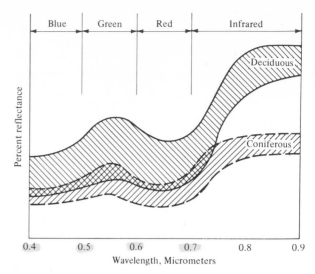

FIGURE 20-3
Spectral signature envelopes for deciduous and coniferous trees.

4) Emission, which is the reemission of some of the absorbed energy at the same or different wavelengths.

5) Scatter, which is the deflection of the radiation within the object resulting in further scattering and/or absorption.

The particular quantitative mix of these interactions displayed by any given object is dependent upon the wavelength of the incident energy and upon the atomic, molecular, and crystalline structure of the object. The amount of energy at various wavelengths that is returned to the sensor from a given object defines a theoretically unique *spectral signature* (analogous to the unique fingerprints of humans). Figure 20-3 shows typical spectral signature envelopes for deciduous trees and coniferous trees based upon their reflective interaction with sunlight over visible and near visible wavelengths. In the figure it can be seen that through all visible wavelengths, and particularly through the green region, the spectral signature envelopes overlap and therefore both types of trees can display identical reflectances; i.e., they have essentially the same color. In the infrared region, however, reflective interactions are much greater for deciduous trees than for conifers. This property makes infrared photography extremely useful for discriminating between these tree types. The aerial photos of Fig. 20-4*a* and *b* were exposed on panchromatic film (sensitive to only the visible portion of the electromagnetic spectrum) and infrared film respectively. On the infrared photo, note how easy it is to discern coniferous trees (dark areas) from deciduous trees (light areas). Except for a highly trained interpreter, these differences between tree types are not easily detected on the panchromatic photo.

FIGURE 20-4

(a) Aerial photo exposed with black-and-white panchromatic film. (b) Aerial photo exposed with black-and-white infrared film. On this photo note how easily coniferous trees (dark areas) can be discerned from deciduous trees (light areas). (*Courtesy Carl Zeiss, Oberkochen*)

20-6 ATMOSPHERIC EFFECTS

Discussion thus far has treated only interactions of electromagnetic energy with objects. However, the medium through which the energy propagates (usually the atmosphere) also has an effect upon the energy, and this effect must be considered before practical remote sensor systems can be fully understood.

Since the atmosphere contains a wide variety of suspended particles, it offers energy interaction capabilities just as "ground" objects do. In fact, in many meteorological applications of remote sensing, the atmosphere is the object of primary interest. For most engineering, planning, and resource management work, however, it is desirable to look *through* and not *at* the atmosphere. The extent to which the atmosphere transmits electromagnetic energy is dependent upon the wavelength of the source energy, as can be seen in the central portion of Fig. 20-5. This is a plot of percent atmospheric transmission of electromagnetic energy versus wavelength. Wavelengths in crosshatched areas are essentially not transmitted by the atmosphere. *Atmospheric windows* are said to exist in wavelength areas of high percentage transmission (noncrosshatched areas). Such a window exists in the 0.4 to 0.7 micrometer region of the electromagnetic spectrum—a situation enabling passage of the energy to which our eyes are sensitive. Note the low

FIGURE 20-5
Composite chart showing source energy, atmospheric transmission, and range of operation of various senors.

percentage of transmission in the range of 0.3 micrometers (ultraviolet) and shorter. This shows that the atmosphere effectively blocks passage of this short-wavelength energy.

The blocking effect of the atmosphere is the result of many complex interactions. These interactions consist of scatter and absorption of electromagnetic energy by particles that range in size and type from gas molecules, to aerosols and vapor, and up to water droplets. The effect of these interactions depends on the application, the type of sensor, and the amount of atmosphere through which the energy must pass. In photographic remote sensing, for example, scatter from gas molecules predominates at low wavelengths in accordance with the *Rayleigh effect,* which states that scatter is inversely proportional to the fourth power of wavelength. According to the Rayleigh effect, therefore, scatter increases rapidly as wavelength decreases. A blue sky is a manifestation of the Rayleigh effect, as we actually see the scattered blue wavelengths of sunlight. A red sun in the early morning or late evening results from the increased atmospheric path length of solar radiation. At these times the blue and green components of sunlight are nearly completely scattered, so that red is the only remaining portion of the visible spectrum penetrating the atmosphere.

All energy that finally reaches a sensing system must travel through the atmosphere. The effect of the atmosphere upon this energy is an important element that must be taken into account in the design of a practical remote sensing system.

20-7   PRACTICAL REMOTE SENSING SYSTEMS

Considering the varied nature of electromagnetic radiation, the character of its sources, its interaction with objects, and its interaction with the atmosphere, it can be appreciated that the design and utility of practical remote sensing systems also vary. Subsequent discussion in this chapter presents the salient characteristics of currently available basic sensor hardware. Multispectral photographic systems, radiometers, scanners, side-looking airborne radar systems, and passive microwave units are included. Figure 20-5 can be treated as a graphic frame of reference for discussion of these various systems. It shows spectral regions in which these various sensors operate, gives relative transparency of the atmosphere within these regions, and illustrates the relationship that these regions bear to energy from the sun and the earth at 300° K.

Before discussing individual sensor systems, a few characteristics illustrated by Fig. 20-5 are worthy of particular note. Photographic systems efficiently "look" through the atmosphere at energy supplied by the sun and *reflected* from targets. "Thermal" instrumentation senses energy *emitted* from the earth most efficiently through the 8- to 14-micrometer atmospheric window. Multispectral scanners can respond to both *reflected* and to *emitted* radiation. Both of these systems are said to be *passive* systems in that they do not generate their own energy source but rather respond to an externally supplied source of energy (the sun or, indirectly, the earth).

Radar systems, which operate in the 1-millimeter to 1-meter range of the electromagnetic spectrum are *active* systems because they respond to reflected self-generated source energy. Passive microwave units operate essentially in the radar range but respond to extremely low levels of naturally emitted energy.

20-8   GROUND TRUTH

As is the case with all of the sensor systems which follow, the validity of any quantitative information extracted from sensor images is a function of amount, geometric configuration, and accuracy of "ground truth" data. Ground truth encompasses any ground parameters that contribute to the calibration of the particular sensor and to the interpretation and evaluation of the remotely sensed data. Ground truth can vary from ground positions of objects whose images appear in the photo (see Chap. 11) to temperatures of water bodies that are undergoing study. It could also consist of laboratory reports from soil or water samples taken in the area, or the identification of tree species from an actual field study. In years to come, as hardware and the state of the art improve, the dependency of quantitative remotely sensed data upon ground truth will likely diminish. As with aerial photogrammetry, the significance of reliable ground truth must not be overlooked with any of the various nonphotographic sensors.

20-9   MULTISPECTRAL PHOTOGRAPHIC SYSTEMS

At the expense of decreased geometric accuracy relative to a mapping camera, 35- or 70-millimeter format cameras are often used in "banks" to acquire simultaneous *multispectral* photography. The advantage of making several simultaneous exposures of the same target using different emulsions is that discernible differences in the resulting imagery are not due to changes in atmospheric or target conditions. Rather, they are different responses generated by different wavelengths of energy selected by varied film and/or filters used on the various cameras in the bank. Multispectral cameras are of immense value in studies to determine the optimum filter-film combination for detecting or enhancing certain conditions. Figure 20-6 illustrates a multispectral photographic system consisting of a bank of four 70-millimeter format cameras.

The spectral limits of photographic remote sensing are fixed on the low end by atmospheric scatter and optical glass transmission at a wavelength of about 0.36 micrometers, and at the high end by the spectral sensitivity of currently available emulsions (approximately 1.0 micrometer). The spectral sensitivity of various emul-

FIGURE 20-6
Multispectral photographic system consisting of a bank of four 70-millimeter Hasselblad cameras. (*Courtesy Paillard, Inc.*)

sion types was presented in Secs. 3-7 through 3-9 and will therefore not be repeated here.

Response differences obtained from simultaneous photography using varying film and filter combinations in a multispectral camera have been used by agricultrualists for crop surveillance work, foresters for species identification and damage studies, geographers for urban growth studies, water resource managers for waste water plume identification and water quality studies, geologists for landform identification, and many more.

Quantitative analysis of multispectral photography in the form of densitometry (see Sec. 3-5) yields a "fourth dimension" from the photography. Emulsion density variations captured in each of the photographic bands has been used as an index for various identification problems such as vegetation types and vigor, soil types and moisture content, and effluent types and concentrations. In the assimilation of this quantitative spectral information from photographic emulsions, it must be realized that photographic density variations are normally a manifestation of a number of possible energy interactions and system parameters. Figure 20-7 illustrates this fact by depicting the energy-flow profile typical of photographic water quality monitoring systems. It can be seen from the figure that if it is desired to monitor effluent concentration variations at depth, one must take into account or remove density variations produced by atmospheric effects, water surface effects, and bottom effects, since these will tend to mask the response caused by the effluent concentration.

Multispectral photography is a relatively simple, efficient, and economical remote sensing device. Although photographic systems are currently the backbone of remote sensing, they have some serious limitations. Data acquisition is limited to a very small

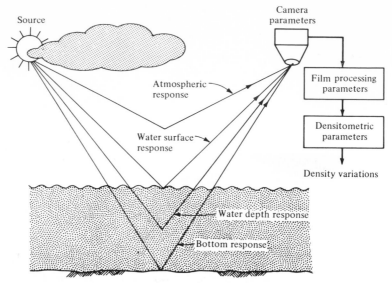

FIGURE 20-7
Energy-flow profile typical of photographic water quality monitoring systems.

portion of the electromagnetic spectrum, and it must be acquired in daylight during favorable weather conditions. The recording format consists of images which are not easily amenable to electronic processing in real time. The sensor systems described in the following sections have the capability of circumventing these shortcomings, but in order to do so they introduce some other undesirable characteristics—principally decreased resolution and geometric fidelity.

20-10 RADIOMETERS

A radiometer is a nonimaging sensor that responds electronically to radiant energy. The spectral sensitivity of radiometers ranges from 0.3 to 14 micrometers. Their physical characteristics vary with application. In general the following three components are common to all radiometers:

1) Energy collection optics
2) Wavelength selecting unit
3) Signal converting unit

The function of the energy collection optics is to establish the field of view and effective aperture of the radiometer and to transmit incoming energy to the wavelength selecting unit. Collecting optics of radiometers range from fiber optic devices for laboratory work or close-range field targets, to telescopic collectors for sensing at great distances.

The wavelength selecting unit isolates the incoming electromagnetic energy into discrete spectral bands. Incident energy in the 0.3- to 1.2-micrometer range is typically separated by refractive techniques using prisms (see Fig. 3-6) or diffraction gratings. Discrete energy bands in the 1.2- to 14 micrometer range are isolated using interference techniques because refractive optics are practically inoperable at these wavelengths. Both techniques "fan out" incoming energy, and, by placing the detector in the proper geometric position in the fan, it will sense only the energy band of interest.

Energy from the wavelength selecting unit is radiated to a detector in the signal conversion unit. The detector may be a photomultiplier tube for energy in the 0.3- to 1.2-micrometer wavelength range, or a heat sensitive transducer for energy in the middle or far infrared ranges. In any case, the energy is converted to an electrical signal, amplified, and recorded. For *static* radiometry, the signal is displayed as a meter reading whose variation with wavelength (when referred to a standard) describes the spectral signature for the target. In *dynamic airborne* radiometry, the detector signal is generally recorded as a continuous intensity profile on a strip chart recorder.

Of particular importance in airborne applications are "thermal radiometers," which provide a profile of thermal infrared emittance in the 8- to 14-micrometer region of the electromagnetic spectrum. Figure 20-8 illustrates the basic operation of such a system. In Fig. 20-8a, an aircraft carrying a radiometer flies over an area, the plan view of the path beneath the aircraft being shown in Fig. 20-8b. Figure 20-8c illustrates the typical expected output of the infrared emittance sensed by the thermal radiometer. This output can be converted to temperatures in accordance with Eq. (2-3) if the emissivities of the gray-body targets are known and atmospheric effects and sensor characteristics are taken into account. It is important to note that radiometric output does not indicate true temperatures directly. Rather, levels of emitted radiation are recorded, and these, when properly reduced and related to ground truth temperatures, yield temperatures accurate to within 1°C. For this reason thermal radiometers are often termed *airborne profiling thermometers*. The continuous record provided from thermal radiometers is an ideal calibration reference for other radiometric systems such as *thermal scanners*.

20-11 SCANNERS

A scanner is conceptually an airborne radiometer that senses a continuous strip of terrain beneath the path of the aircraft in which it is carried. The strip is composed of contiguous *scan lines* repeatedly taken transverse to the direction of flight, as illustrated in Fig. 20-9. The line-scanning process is analogous in many respects to the acquisition of

FIGURE 20-8
Basic operation of thermal radiometers.

panoramic photography (see Chap. 16). As the instrument scans the object space, responses are amplified and recorded at a rate proportional to the speed of the aircraft. The result is a series of electrical response profiles for contiguous scan lines.

Because detector signals are in electrical formats, they are conveniently utilized in a number of ways. In-flight monitoring is accomplished by displaying a time versus amplitude trace of detector responses on a cathode ray tube (CRT). The CRT display can be photographed using a strip camera, thereby producing "imagery" with tonal variations representing differential levels of reflected or emitted energy within the scanned scene. Simultaneous recording of the detector signal on magnetic tape permits further ground

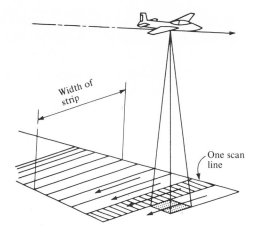

FIGURE 20-9
Scanner coverage.

manipulation of the sensor data. Such manipulation may include, for example, partial geometric rectification of the scanner display and image enhancement using electronic computers.

The collection and recording sequence employed in most "single channel" scanners is schematically represented by Fig. 20-10. The wavelength band sensed by a single-channel scanner is a function of its single detector. A "multispectral" scanner, on the other hand, employs multiple detectors and senses energy in various wavelength bands. Imagery prepared from the response of each channel shows the same scene viewed at the same time under the same conditions. Different responses at various wavelengths

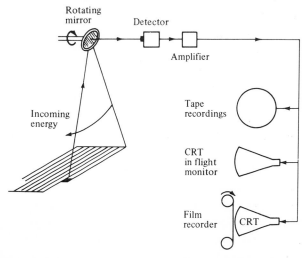

FIGURE 20-10
Schematic diagram of collection and recording sequence of single-channel scanners.

are therefore attributable to the physical-chemical nature of the target and not to changes in atmosphere or target.

The imagery shown in Fig. 20-11 is typical of output from airborne multispectral scanners. Comparison of the responses of corresponding multispectral images by trained interpreters or by the application of computer algorithms, has enabled rapid discrimination between various target types. Crop identification employing automated reduction of multispectral information has been shown to yield accuracies comparable to those obtained from human interpretation.

A particular type of scanner commonly applied in remote sensing work is a single-channel thermal scanner that operates in the 8- to 14-micrometer range of the electromagnetic spectrum. Thermal scanners depict variations of thermal energy *emitted* from the scene below the aircraft. They have been particularly valuable in studying thermal effluents from industrial processes. Figure 20-12*a* is a portion of a strip of thermal imagery showing the thermal plume of a power plant cooling effluent being discharged into a lake. In the figure, the lighter the tones, the hotter the water. This thermal imagery was analyzed in conjunction with thermal radiometer data to study the thermal structure of the plume and its related effect on the receiving body of water. Since thermal infrared energy is absorbed in the top few micrometers of any target, the indicated response is that of surface water temperatures only. Note the dark lines in the plume caused by power boats circulating cooler subsurface water to the surface. Note also on the figure that rough geometric outlines of buildings, cars, streets, etc., can be identified from their temperature differences detected by the thermal scanner.

Figure 20-12*b* is a black-and-white panchromatic aerial photo of the same area shown in Fig. 20-12*a*. Since panchromatic film is sensitive only to the visible portion of the electromagnetic spectrum, it was unable to record the presence of the thermal plume.

All thermal infrared systems can operate day or night; in fact, semidiurnal coverage of an area often yields differences in images that facilitate interpretation and identification. Objects subject to relatively rapid cooling during the night, for example, will generally appear drastically different on day imagery than on night imagery, and identifications can often be made based on knowledge of their cooling and heating rates as compared to other objects. An example of thermal scanner imagery obtained at night is shown in Fig. 20-13. Note that details are as readily interpreted from this image as they are from the daytime image of Fig. 20-12*a*.

As with aerial photography, imagery obtained from scanners is subject to scale variations and geometric distortions, but at a much larger rate. A complete discussion of these scale variations and image distortions is beyond the scope of this text. Figure 20-14*a* illustrates in a qualitative manner the nature of scale variations typical of scanner images. The figure shows the decrease in scale that occurs with an increase in distance from the *nadir line* (line of imagery representing terrain vertically beneath the aircraft's path). Figure 20-14*b* indicates the nature of relief displacement of scanner imagery. Note

FIGURE 20-11

Six simultaneously derived images of the same scene in different spectral ranges.
(*Courtesy Bendix Aerospace Systems Division, Ann Arbor, Michigan*)

489

(a)

(b)

FIGURE 20-12

(a) Thermal scanner image of the discharge plume of a power plant cooling effluent into a lake. Lighter tones indicate hotter water. (b) Black-and-white panchromatic aerial photo taken over the area of the plume. Note that the plume is not
visible because panchromatic film does not respond to thermal energy. (*Courtesy
Remote Sensing Program, University of Wisconsin, Madison*)

FIGURE 20-13

Thermal scanner image obtained at night. A great deal of intelligence data can be extracted from this image. Cars can be identified at *A*, commercial buildings at *B*, a highway interchange at *C*, sandy soil at *D*, bare soil at *E*, trees at *F*, grass at *G*, and residential area at *H*. (*Courtesy Remote Sensing Program, University of Wisconsin, Madison*)

that in all cases vertical lines in the object space are recorded as lines which diverge *perpendicular* to the nadir line.

From the examples presented herein, it should be apparent that scanner images depart radically from their photographic counterparts in terms of geometry, resolution, and fidelity. As remote sensing technology evolves, and as military systems become

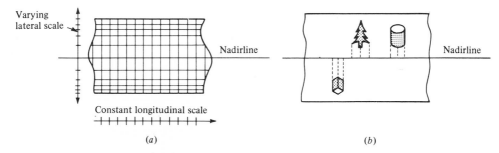

FIGURE 20-14

(*a*) Qualitative nature of scale variation of scanner imagery. (*b*) Relief displacement of scanner imagery.

declassified, resolution and geometric fidelity of scanners will improve. Their basic characteristics will remain essentially different from those of photographic systems, however.

ACTIVE- Radar

passive - sunlight

20-12 SIDE-LOOKING AIRBORNE RADAR

Radar is an acronym for *RA*dio *D*etecting *A*nd *R*anging systems. Some familiar forms of radar are *P*lan *P*osition *I*ndicator (PPI) typical of aircraft and ship installations, and doppler radar used in vehicle speed and control applications.

In many respects radar is similar to photography with a flashbulb. The flashbulb illuminates the object and the camera captures the rays of light that are reflected from the object. With radar, instead of using light, a narrow beam of radio energy is sent out by a directional antenna and a radio receiver captures the reflected radio waves. Because it generates and transmits its own energy, radar is an *active* system—as opposed to *passive* systems which generate no energy of their own but instead sense only natural radiation.

Of particular interest and utility in aerial remote sensing are *S*ide-*L*ooking *A*irborne *R*adar (SLAR) systems. As with all radar systems, SLAR units transmit radio signals in the 1-millimeter to 1-meter wavelength range and monitor the travel time for them to return as reflections from objects within the field of transmission. Since the propagation rate of the source energy is a known constant, travel times can be used directly to determine distances to reflecting targets. As shown in Fig. 20-15, the transmitting and receiving antenna, A, for SLAR systems directs and receives signals in thin slices approximately normal to the direction of flight. As the antenna advances in the direction of flight, transmitted pulses initiate the sweep of a CRT trace. Return signals corresponding to various terrain features appear on the trace and have their geometric positions on the CRT discretely defined on the basis of their respective travel times. Luminance of points recorded on the CRT are determined by the physical character and configuration of the targets. Individual CRT traces may be recorded on film by means of a strip camera directed at the display.

In Fig. 20-15 the antenna, A, is being repositioned longitudinally at aircraft velocity V_a. Each transmitted pulse, B, returns "echoes" from targets within the antenna beam. The time versus amplitude video signal, C, is imaged on a trace line, D, of the CRT. Ground objects such as the river at E are imaged on the film as it advances past the tube at a velocity V_f, which is proportional to the velocity of the aircraft. The resulting images have photographic clarity and reasonably good spatial orientation, as illustrated by the example in Fig. 20-16. Lateral ground coverages of SLAR strips are extensive, on the order of from 10 to 12 miles and greater.

Because they are active systems, SLAR units can operate day and night and in a variety of transmitting and receiving modes. Source wavelength and polarization can be

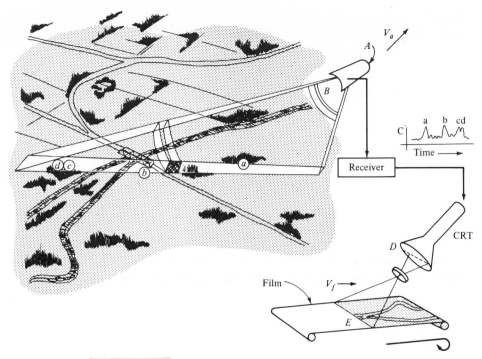

FIGURE 20-15
Recording sequence of side-looking airborne radar. (*Courtesy Westinghouse Electric Corporation*)

chosen to maximize target discrimination. Recorded returns are in an electrical format and therefore can be conveniently stored and manipulated. SLAR possesses the ability to penetrate clouds, precipitation, and light vegetation. For this reason it was used to map the perpetually overcast Panama Canal region of Central America. By flying the same region from opposite directions, stereoscopic SLAR coverage can be achieved. Stereoscopic SLAR imagery offers an uncommonly large "model" of terrain features, a condition of value to geologists. Geologic structural features such as faults, lineations, and large landforms may be detected from SLAR models that are often missed in ground observations or masked on other imagery.

20-13   PASSIVE MICROWAVE SYSTEMS

As previously mentioned, the earth is a source of emitted radiation that is closely approximated by a blackbody radiator at a temperature of 300° K. The radiation curve of a blackbody heated to 300° K peaks at a wavelength of about 10 micrometers, but energy

FIGURE 20-16
Side-looking airborne radar image showing the Ouchita Mountains, Oklahoma.
(*Courtesy Westinghouse Electric Corporation*)

of lesser intensity is emitted in wavelengths out to 1 meter and longer. As previously discussed, thermal radiometers and thermal scanners are used to sense energy in the areas of intense earth radiation near the peak of the curve. Passive microwave systems are employed to sense the extremely low-intensity energy of wavelengths from 1 millimeter to 1 meter. This is the same spectral region in which radar systems operate: however, passive microwave systems, as implied by their name, are passive systems, whereas radar systems are active.

As with radar, passive microwave units employ antennas to detect radiation. The output from these devices is essentially the same as that from thermal radiometers. The major difference is that the longer wavelength radiation sensed by passive microwave systems penetrates the surfaces of targets to a greater extent than does thermal infrared energy. For this reason, passive microwave systems have been used to obtain soil temperature data and related moisture conditions.

The fact that relatively little energy is radiated in the spectral region in which passive microwave operates would be of little consequence if the sensor could be held stationary so it could gather energy over a long period of time. Because of their forward motion, however, airborne passive microwave units cannot concentrate on a given area long enough to gather sufficient energy to achieve a satisfactory reading. To overcome this problem, the size of the *resolution cell* (area sensed at any instant of time) is increased to gather enough energy to get an adequate signal from each area sensed. As a consequence of the large resolution cells, the overall resolution of the passive microwave record is poor.

Passive microwave units may be of the *nonscanning* or *scanning* types. Nonscanning units sense only a strip of terrain directly below the aircraft, and the output is simply a profile indicating energy emitted by ground objects. This is essentially the same technique as that employed by nonscanning radiometers and thermal radiometers. Each system produces a temperature-related profile, the only difference being the wavelength of energy sensed.

Scanning passive microwave units differ from nonscanning units in that the antenna scans from side to side as the plane passes over the ground. The resulting series of profiles is usually recorded on magnetic tape and processed later in a computer. The computer can assign colors to different energy levels, thereby producing a false color picture in which particular colors correspond to given ranges of temperatures on the scanned terrain.

20-14 REMOTE SENSING FROM SPACE

The use of artificial satellites as sensor platforms has made possible the acquisition of high-resolution multispectral data of the earth's surface on a global basis. Satellite images not only cover very large areas, but they are also virtually free of image distortions due to relief because of the typically high flying heights. Figure 20-17 is an image obtained from the remote sensing system on board the first Earth Resources Technology Satellite (ERTS-1). It shows the San Francisco Bay area and a large portion of the Sacramento Valley recorded from a flying height of approximately 570 miles. Note the significant amount of detail that appears in the photo. The city of San Franciso in the lower left portion of the picture is partially obscured by a fog bank. It is of interest to compare the coverage of this single picture (with coverage of approximately 100 miles square), to the coverage of the 2,000-photo mosaic of the same area that is shown in Fig. 12-1.

Satellite sensor systems, to date, have included a combination of return beam vidicon (RBV) cameras and multispectral scanners (MSS). The ERTS-1 satellite system, for example, included three RBV cameras and a four-channel multispectral scanner. Film records of the video signals from each of the MSS bands can be used separately or in any combination. Figure 20-17 is actually a black-and-white reproduction of a "color composite" picture made from three bands of the multispectral scanner of ERTS-1. In accordance with the "color additive process," each of the three primary colors blue, green, and red were assigned to three of the satellite's recording bands and later

FIGURE 20-17
Imagery obtained from ERTS-1 satellite. This exposure, made from an approximately 570-mile flying height, shows the entire San Francisco Bay area and a major portion of the Sacramento Valley. (*Courtesy NASA*)

recombined in a single composite image. Blue on the composite image corresponds to channel 4, a green-sensitive channel; green corresponds to channel 5, a red-sensitive channel; and red corresponds to channel 6, a near-infrared-sensitive channel. The combination of these channels produces a color composite image very similar to an ordinary color-infrared photograph.

Figures 20-18 (*a*) and (*b*) are portions of black and white reproductions made from the responses of ERTS-1 MSS channels 5, (red channel) and 6 (near IR channel), respectively.

(a)

(b)

FIGURE 20-18

Imagery obtained from the multispectral scanner (MSS) of the ERTS-1 satellite. (*a*) is the response obtained in the red-sensitive channel 5, and (*b*) is the response from the near infrared-sensitive channel 6. Note that due to suspended material in the water, the lakes at 1 and 2 can hardly be discerned in (*a*), but these same lakes are readily discernible in (*b*). Note also that the city of Madison, Wisconsin, which is located at 3, is visible as a lighter toned area in (*a*), while there is practically no indication of urbanization in that area in (*b*). These examples illustrate how responses from different parts of the electromagnetic spectrum may be useful in accentuating different objects, thereby aiding in their interpretation and identification. (*Courtesy NASA*)

Some rather striking differences in the two responses can be seen. Note, for example, that the lakes at 1 and 2 (*a*) can hardly be discerned. This is primarily due to suspended material in the water which reflects red energy nearly the same as the surrounding area. These lakes absorb nearly all of the near IR energy, however, and therefore appear the same as the lakes at 3 in (*b*). There is also a marked difference in the responses obtained from urban areas. The city of Madison, Wisconsin, located at 3, for example, is visible as a lighter toned area on (*a*), while there is practically no indication of urbanization in that area on (*b*).

The reasonably good resolution, broad areal coverage, and synoptic character of satellite imagery is becoming increasingly useful in a number of applications. The continual updating of regional resource and land-use inventories is one of its most important applications.

20-15 CONCLUSION

Space has necessarily limited this discussion. Basic concepts that dictate design and utility of common civilian remote sensing systems have been presented. Most of the sensors discussed look at the terrestrial environment through "different eyes" and with ever increasing rates of data-generation capabilities. Processing of remotely sensed data into formats useful to those who monitor and manage the environment is a critical step in the remote sensing sequence and undoubtedly one that will receive much attention in future research. Continued evolution of automated storage and interpretation techniques, advances in sensor hardware, and an increasing awareness of remote sensing capabilities and applications, combined with a growing recognition of man's need to better understand the impact of his activities on his natural environment, should ensure a significant future for remote sensing.

REFERENCES

Aldrich, R. C.: Space Photos for Land Use and Forestry, *Photogrammetric Engineering*, vol. 32, no. 4, p. 389, 1971.

American Society of Photogrammetry: "Manual of Photographic Interpretation," George Banta Co., Inc., Menasha, Wis., 1960.

_____: "Manual of Photogrammetry," 3d ed., George Banta Co., Inc., Menasha, Wis., 1966, chaps. 2, 3, 4, 21, and 22.

_____: "Manual of Color Aerial Photography," George Banta Co., Inc., Menasha, Wis., 1968.

Anson, A.: Color Aerial Photos in the Reconnaissance of Soils and Rocks, *Photogrammetric Engineering*, vol. 36, no. 4, p. 343, 1970.

Barr, D. J., and R. D. Miles: SLAR Imagery and Site Selection, *Photogrammetric Engineering,* vol. 36, no. 11, p. 1155, 1970.

Bjornsem, R. L.: Infrared Mapping of Large Forest Fires, *Proceedings, Fifth Symposium on Remote Sensing of the Environment,* University of Michigan, Ann Arbor, Mich., 1968.

Bock, P., and J. G. Barmby: Survey Effectiveness of Spacecraft Remote Sensors, *Photogrammetric Engineering,* vol. 35, no. 8, p. 756, 1969.

Cochrane, G. R.: False Color Film Fails in Practice, *Photogrammetric Engineering,* vol. 34, no. 11, p. 1142, 1968.

Colvocoresses, A. P.: ERTS—A Satellite Imagery, *Photogrammetric Engineering,* vol. 36, no. 6, p. 555, 1970.

Colwell, R. N. et al.: Basic Matter and Energy Relationships Involved in Remote Reconnaissance, *Photogrammetric Engineering,* vol. 34, no. 5, p. 761, 1963.

——: Remote Sensing of Natural Resources, *Scientific American,* p. 54, 1968.

Eastman Kodak Company: "Kodak Wratten Filters for Scientific and Technical Use," 1st ed., Kodak Scientific and Technical Data Book No. B-3, Rochester, New York, 1970.

Fiore, C.: Side-Looking Radar Restitution, *Photogrammetric Engineering,* vol. 33, no. 2, p. 215, 1967.

Fritz, N. L.: Optimum Methods for Using Infrared-Sensitive Color Film, *Photogrammetric Engineering,* vol. 33, no. 10, p. 1128, 1967.

Gates, D. M.: Physical and Physiological Properties of Plants, in "Remote Sensing with Special Reference to Agriculture and Forestry," National Academy of Sciences, Washington, D.C., 1970, p. 224.

Gerbermann, A. H. et al.: Color and Color I.R. Films for Soil Identification, *Photogrammetric Engineering,* vol. 32, no. 4, p. 359, 1971.

Gregory, A. F.: Remote Sensing: A New Look at the Canadian Environment, *The Canadian Surveyor,* vol. 25, no. 2, p. 131, 1971.

Jensen, Niels: "Optical and Photographic Reconnaissance Systems," John Wiley & Sons, New York, 1968.

Kiefer, R. W., and J. P. Scherz: Applications of Airborne Remote Sensing Technology, *American Society of Civil Engineers, Journal of the Surveying and Mapping Division,* vol. 96, no. SU 1, p. 57, 1970.

Kruse, P., L. McGlauchlin, and R. McQuistan: *Elements of Infrared Technology,* John Wiley & Sons Inc., New York, 1963.

McLerran, J. H.: Infrared Thermal Sensing, *Photogrammetric Engineering,* vol. 33, no. 5, p. 507, 1967.

Molineux, C. E.: Multiband Spectral System for Reconnaissance, *Photogrammetric Engineering,* vol. 31, no. 1, p. 131, 1965.

Nunnally, N. R., and R. E. Witmer: Remote Sensing for Land Use Studies, *Photogrammetric Engineering,* vol. 36, no. 5, p. 449, 1970.

Pecora, W. T.: Surveying the Earth's Resources from Space, *Surveying and Mapping,* vol. 27, no. 4, p. 639, 1967.

Scherz, J. P. et al.: Photographic Characteristics of Water Pollution, *Photogrammetric Engineering* vol. 35, no. 1, p. 38, 1969.

Slater, P. N.: Multiband Cameras, *Photogrammetric Engineering,* vol. 38, no. 6, p. 543, 1972.

Smith, J. T., Jr.: Oil Slick Remote Sensing, *Photogrammetric Engineering,* vol. 37, no. 12, p. 1243, 1971.

Steiner, D.: Towards Earth Resources Satellites: The American ERTS and SKYLAB Programs, *Photogrammetria,* vol. 27, no. 6, p. 24, 1971.

Strandberg, C. H.: "Aerial Discovery Manual," John Wiley & Sons, New York, 1967.

Vikcsne, A. et al.: SLR Reconnaissance of Panama, *Photogrammetric Engineering,* vol. 36, no. 3, p. 253, 1970.

Weaver, K. F.: Remote Sensing: New Eyes to See the World, *National Geographic,* vol. 135, no. 1, p. 46, 1969.

Welch, R.: Remote Sensing for Water Pollution Control, *Photogrammetric Engineering,* vol. 37, no. 12, p. 1285, 1971.

_____: Quality and Applications of Aerospace Imagery, *Photogrammetric Engineering,* vol. 38, no. 4, p. 379, 1972.

Wilson, R. C.: Space Photography for Forestry, *Photogrammetric Engineering,* vol. 33, no. 5, p. 483, 1967.

Wolfe, E. W.: Thermal IR for Geology, *Photogrammetric Engineering,* vol. 37, no. 1, p. 43, 1971.

Yost, E., and S. Wenderoth: Multispectral Color for Agriculture and Forestry, *Photogrammetric Engineering,* vol. 32, no. 6, p. 590, 1971.

PROBLEMS

20-1   Define the term "remote sensing" and briefly discuss some of its applications.

20-2   In what ways can electromagnetic energy interact with matter?

20-3   Explain why blue flashbulbs are used for indoor photography with daylight film.

20-4   Describe the term "blackbody" as it relates to remote sensing.

20-5   Why is the aerial photographer concerned about scattered energy? What steps can he take to circumvent the problems caused by scattered energy?

20-6   What sensors would you use to monitor visible energy? Near-infrared energy? Near-thermal-infrared energy?

20-7   It is frequently desirable to use photographic imagery in conjunction with thermal scanners. Why?

20-8   Compare radiometers and scanners.

20-9   Explain the difference between active and passive remote sensing systems. Classify each of the sensors discussed in this chapter into either the active or passive category.

20-10   Discuss the advantages and disadvantages of Side-Looking Airborne Radar (SLAR).

20-11   What is ground truth? Discuss how its character might differ for a photographic mapping project as opposed to a thermal scanner pollution study.

APPENDIX A
RANDOM ERRORS AND LEAST SQUARES ADJUSTMENT

A-1 CLASSIFICATION OF ERRORS

In the processes of measuring any quantity, factors such as human limitations, instrumental imperfections, and instabilities in nature render the measured values inexact. Due to these factors, no matter how carefully a measurement is performed, it will always contain some error. Photogrammetry is a science that frequently requires measurements and therefore an understanding of errors—including how they occur and how they are treated in computation—is important. Before proceeding with an analysis of the treatment of errors, it will be helpful to classify errors as follows:

Systematic Error An error in a measurement which follows some mathematical or physical law. If the conditions causing the error are measured, a correction can be calculated and the systematic error eliminated. Systematic errors will remain constant in magnitude and algebraic sign if the conditions producing them remain the same. Because their algebraic sign tends to remain the same, systematic errors accumulate, and consequently they are often referred to as *cumulative* errors. Examples of systematic errors in photogrammetry are shrinkage or expansion of photographs, camera lens distortions and atmospheric refraction distortions.

Random Error   After systematic errors have been eliminated, the errors that remain are called random or *accidental* errors. Random errors are generally small, but they can never be avoided entirely in measurements. They do not follow physical laws like systematic errors, and therefore they must be dealt with according to the mathematical laws of probability. Random errors are as likely to be positive as negative; hence they tend to compensate each other and consequently are often called *compensating* errors. Examples where random errors occur in photogrammetry are in estimating between least graduations of a measuring scale or in indexing a scale.

Note that *mistakes* or blunders resulting from carelessness or confusion are not classified as errors. These must be eliminated by careful procedures and alertness. Henceforth in this discussion it will be assumed that all mistakes and systematic errors have been removed from measured values and only random errors remain. The treatment of these random errors is the subject of Appendix A.

A-2   DEFINITIONS

The following definitions of terms necessarily must precede a discussion of random errors:

True Value   The theoretically correct or exact value of a quantity. In measurements, however, the true value can never be determined because no matter how much care is exercised in measurement, small random errors will always be present.

Error   The difference between any measured quantity and the true value for that quantity. Since the true value of a measured quantity can never be determined, errors are likewise indeterminate, and hence they are strictly theoretical quantities.

Most Probable Value   That value for a measured quantity which, based upon the observations, has the highest probability. The most probable value may be obtained through *least squares adjustment,* which is based upon the mathematical laws of probability.

Residual   The difference between any measured quantity and the most probable value for that quantity. It is the value which is dealt with in adjustment computations, since errors are indeterminate. The term "error" is frequently used when "residual" is in fact meant, and although they are very similar, there is this theoretical distinction.

Degrees of Freedom   The number of redundant observations (those in excess of the number actually needed to calculate the unknowns). Redundant observations reveal discrepancies in observed values and make possible the practice of least squares adjustment for obtaining most probable values.

Weight   The relative worth of an observation compared to any other observation.

Measurements may be weighted in adjustment computations according to their precisions. A precisely measured value logically should be weighted heavily in an adjustment so that the correction it receives is smaller than that received by a less precise quantity.

Standard Deviation   A quantity used to express the precision of a group of measurements. Standard deviation is sometimes called the *root mean square error.* It may also be called the *68 percent error,* since according to the theory of probability, 68 percent of the observations in a group should have residuals smaller than the standard deviation. A general expression for standard deviation is

$$S_O = \sqrt{\frac{\Sigma p v^2}{r}} \qquad \text{(A-1)}$$

In Eq. (A-1), S_O is standard deviation, $\Sigma p v^2$ is the sum of the products of the individual weights of the measurements times their corresponding residuals squared, and r is the number of degrees of freedom. The units of standard deviation are the same as those of the original measurements. If the quality of all of the measurements is equal, they may be weighted equally by assigning each a weight of unity. In that case the p's drop out of Eq. (A-1).

If m independent direct measurements are taken of the same quantity, then the first measurement establishes a value for the unknown and all additional measurements, $(m - 1)$ in number, are redundant. For this special case (assuming equal weights), the standard deviation is

$$S_O = \sqrt{\frac{\Sigma v^2}{m - 1}} \qquad \text{(A-2)}$$

EXAMPLE A-1   The ten values listed in column (*a*) below were obtained in measuring a photographic distance with a glass scale. Each measured value is considered to be equally weighted. What is the most probable value and standard deviation of the group of measurements?

Measured values, mm (*a*)	*Residuals, mm (*b*)	Squared residuals, mm^2 (*c*)
105.27	− 0.005	25 × 10^{-6}
105.26	− 0.015	225
105.29	0.015	225
105.29	0.015	225
105.30	0.025	625
105.27	− 0.005	25
105.26	− 0.015	225
105.28	0.005	25
105.28	0.005	25
105.25	− 0.025	625
Σ = 1,052.75		Σv^2 = 2,250 × 10^{-6}

(*1*) The most probable value for a quantity which has been directly and independently measured several times is the mean, or

$$\text{mean} = MPV = \frac{1,052.75}{10} = 105.275 \text{ mm}$$

*(*2*) Residuals listed in column (*b*) above are obtained by subtracting the mean from each measurement. The squared residuals are listed in column (*c*).

(*3*) By Eq. (A-2), standard deviation is

$$S_O = \sqrt{\frac{0.002250}{10-1}} = \pm\,0.016 \text{ mm}$$

////

A-3 HISTOGRAMS

A *histogram* is a graphical representation of the distribution of a group of measurements or of the residuals for a group of measurements. It illustrates in an "easily digestible" form the nature of occurrence of random errors. A histogram is simply a bar graph of the size of measured values, or the size of residuals, as abscissas versus their frequency of occurrence as ordinates. An example histogram of residuals for 50 measurements of a photo distance is shown in Fig. A-1.

Histograms graphically display the following information about a particular group of measurements:

(*a*) Whether the measurements or residuals are symmetrically distributed about some central value.

(*b*) The total spread or dispersion in the measured values or in the residuals.

(*c*) The precision of the measured values. (A tall, narrow histogram represents good precision, while a short, wide one represents poor precision.)

Histograms of varying shape will be obtained for varying personnel and for variations in equipment used. The histogram of many comparator measurements of a photographic distance, for example, would likely produce a very narrow histogram body with a high ordinate at the center. A histogram of the same distance measured the same number of times with an engineers scale, and plotted at the same scale, would be wider, with a much lower ordinate value at the center.

In plotting a histogram of residuals, the residuals are calculated and classified into groups or *classes* according to their sizes. The range of residual size in each class is called the *class interval*. The width of bars on a histogram is equal to the class interval, and for the example of Fig. A-1 it is 3 micrometers. It is important to select a class interval that portrays the distribution of residuals adequately, and usually a class interval that produces about 15 bars (classes) on the graph is ideal. The number of residuals within

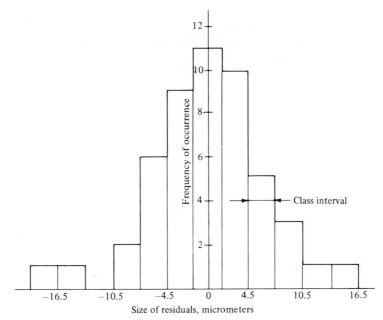

FIGURE A-1
Histogram for fifty measurements of a photographic distance.

each class (frequency of residuals) is then counted and plotted on the ordinate scale versus the residual size for the class on the abscissa scale.

A-4   NORMAL DISTRIBUTION OF RANDOM ERRORS

In the remaining discussion it shall be assumed that all error distributions are *normal*. This is a good assumption in photogrammetry as most distributions are in fact normal or very nearly normal.

A normal distribution, or *Gaussian distribution* as it is often called, is one which graphs as the typical bell-shaped curve shown in Fig. A-2. It is symmetrical about the ordinate for a residual of zero. For a very large group of measurements, this curve may be obtained in much the same way as a histogram except that the sizes of residuals are plotted on the abscissa versus their *relative frequencies* of occurrence on the ordinate. The relative frequency of residuals occurring within an interval Δv is simply the ratio of the number of residuals within that interval to the total number of residuals. If the number of measurements in the group is infinitely large and if the size of the interval is taken very small, the resulting curve becomes smooth and continuous as shown in Fig. A-2.

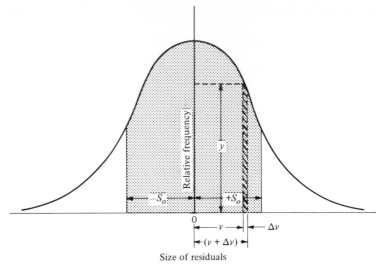

FIGURE A-2
Normal distribution curve.

The equation of the normal distribution curve is

$$y = \frac{he^{-h^2 v^2}}{\sqrt{\pi}} \qquad \text{(A-3)}$$

where y = the ordinate of the normal distribution curve and is equal to the relative
frequency of occurrence of residuals between the size of v and $(v + \Delta v)$
  e = the base of natural logarithms
  h = a constant which depends on the precision of the measurements and is equal to
$1/(\sqrt{2}\,S_o)$

The derivation of Eq. (A-3) is beyond the scope of this text, but it can be found in
references listed at the end of this appendix. In Fig. A-2 the probability of a residual
occurring between the limits of v and $(v + \Delta v)$ is equal to the crosshatched area under the
curve between those limits. It is the product of the ordinate y times the interval Δv. For
any single measurement of a group of measurements, the probability that its residual
occurs between any two abscissas on the curve (such as between $-S_o$ and $+S_o$ of Fig. A-2)
is equal to the area under the normal distribution curve between those abscissas. Since for
a group of measurements all residuals must fall somewhere on the abscissa scale of the
normal distribution curve, the total area under the curve represents total probability and
is therefore equal to 1.0. The area under the curve between any two abscissas may be
found by integrating Eq. (A-3) between those two abscissa limits. The integration is beyond the scope of this text, but it is pertinent to point out that the area between $-S_o$ and

$+S_o$ (shown shaded on Fig. A-2) is 68 percent of the total area under the curve. Hence S_o is called the 68 percent error, as previously mentioned.

A-5 INTRODUCTION TO LEAST SQUARES

Least squares is a procedure for adjusting observations containing random errors. It is by no means a new method. Karl Gauss, a German mathematician, used the method as early as the latter part of the eighteenth century. Until the invention of electronic computers, however, it was used rather sparingly because of the lengthy calculations involved.

For a group of equally weighted observations, the fundamental condition that is enforced in least squares adjustment is that *the sum of the squares of the residuals is minimized*. This condition, which has been developed from the equation for the normal distribution curve provides most probable values for the adjusted quantities. Suppose a group of m equally weighted measurements were taken having residuals v_1, v_2, v_3, ..., v_m. Then in equation form, the fundamental condition of least squares is expressed as

$$\sum_{i=1}^{m} (v_i)^2 = (v_1)^2 + (v_2)^2 + (v_3)^2 + \cdots + (v_m)^2 = \text{minimum} \qquad \text{(A-4)}$$

Some basic assumptions which underlie least squares theory are that the number of observations being adjusted is large and the frequency distribution of the errors is *normal*. Although these basic assumptions are not always met, least squares adjustment still provides the most rigorous error treatment available, and hence it has become very popular and important in many areas of modern photogrammetry. Besides yielding most probable values for the unknowns, least squares adjustment also enables precisions of adjusted quantities to be determined, and it reveals the presence of large errors and mistakes so that steps can be taken to eliminate them.

A-6 WEIGHTED OBSERVATIONS

Weights of individual observed values may be assigned according to a priori estimates, or they may be obtained from the standard deviations of the observations if they are available. An equation expressing the relation between standard deviation and weights is

$$p_i = \frac{1}{(S_i)^2} \qquad \text{(A-5)}$$

In Eq. (A-5), p_i is the weight of the ith observed quantity and $(S_i)^2$ is the square of the standard deviation or *variance* of that observation. Equation (A-5) states that *weights are inversely proportional to variances*. If measured values are to be weighted in least squares adjustment, then the fundamental condition to be enforced is that *the sum of the weights times their corresponding squared residuals is minimized*, or, in equation form,

$$\sum_{i=1}^{m} p_i(v_i)^2 = p_1 (v_1)^2 + p_2 (v_2)^2 + p_3 (v_3)^2 + \cdots + p_m (v_m)^2 = \text{minimum} \qquad \text{(A-6)}$$

A-7 APPLYING LEAST SQUARES

In the "observation equation" method of least squares adjustment, *observation equations* are written which relate measured values to their residual errors and the unknown parameters. One observation equation is written for each measurement. For a unique solution the number of equations must equal the number of unknowns. If redundant observations are made, then more observation equations can be written than are needed for a unique solution, and most probable values of the unknowns can be determined by the method of least squares. For a group of equally weighted observations, an equation for each residual error is obtained from each observation equation. The residuals are squared and added to obtain the function $\sum_{i=1}^{m} (v_i)^2$. To minimize the function, partial derivatives are taken with respect to each unknown variable and set equal to zero. This yields a set of equations called *normal equations* which are equal in number to the number of unknowns. The normal equations are solved to obtain the most probable values for the unknowns.

EXAMPLE A-2 As an elementary example illustrating the method of least squares adjustment by the observation equation method, consider the following three equally weighted measurements taken between points *A, B,* and *C* of Fig. A-3:

$$x + y = 3.0$$
$$x \quad\ = 1.5$$
$$y = 1.4$$

These three equations relate the two unknowns x and y to the observations. Values for x and y could be obtained from any two of these equations so that the remaining equation is redundant. Notice however, that the values obtained for x and y will differ

FIGURE A-3
Measurements for least squares adjustment example, Prob. A-2.

depending upon which two equations are solved. It is therefore apparent that the measurements contain errors. The equations may be rewritten as observation equations by including residual errors as follows:

$$x + y = 3.0 + v_1$$
$$x \quad = 1.5 + v_2$$
$$y = 1.4 + v_3$$

To arrive at the least squares solution, the observation equations are rearranged to obtain expressions for the residuals; these are squared and added to form the function $\sum_{i=1}^{m} (v_i)^2$ as follows:

$$\sum_{i=1}^{m} (v_i)^2 = (x + y - 3.0)^2 + (x - 1.5)^2 + (y - 1.4)^2$$

The above function is minimized, enforcing the condition of least squares, by taking partial derivatives with respect to each unknown and setting them equal to zero. This yields the following two equations:

$$\frac{\partial \Sigma v^2}{\partial x} = 0 = 2(x + y - 3.0) + 2(x - 1.5)$$

$$\frac{\partial \Sigma v^2}{\partial y} = 0 = 2(x + y - 3.0) + 2(y - 1.4)$$

The above equations are called *normal equations*. The reduced normal equations are

$$2x + \quad y = 4.5$$
$$x + 2y = 4.4$$

Solving the reduced normal equations simultaneously yields $x = 1.533$ and $y = 1.433$. According to the theory of probability, these values have the highest probability. This is indeed a simple example, but it serves to illustrate the method of least squares without complicating the mathematics. Least squares adjustment of large systems of observation equations is performed in the same manner.

A-8 SYSTEMATIC FORMULATION OF NORMAL EQUATIONS

In large systems of observation equations it is helpful to utilize systematic procedures to formulate normal equations. Consider the following system of m linear observation equations of equal weight containing n unknowns:

$$a_1 A + b_1 B + c_1 C + \cdots + n_1 N - L_1 = v_1$$
$$a_2 A + b_2 B + c_2 C + \cdots + n_2 N - L_2 = v_2$$
$$\cdots\cdots\cdots\cdots\cdots\cdots\cdots\cdots\cdots\cdots$$
$$a_m A + b_m B + c_m C + \cdots + n_m N - L_m = v_m$$

(A-7)

In Eqs. (A-7), the a's, b's, c's, etc., are coefficients of unknowns A, B, C, etc.; the L's are constants; and the v's are residuals. By squaring the residuals and summing them, the function Σv^2 is formed. Taking partial derivatives of Σv^2 with respect to each unknown A, B, C, etc., yields n normal equations. After reducing and factoring the normal equations, the following generalized system for expressing normal equations results:

$$[aa] A + [ab] B + [ac] C + \cdots + [an] N = [aL]$$
$$[ba] A + [bb] B + [bc] C + \cdots + [bn] N = [bL]$$
$$[ca] A + [cb] B + [cc] C + \cdots + [cn] N = [cL]$$
$$\cdots\cdots\cdots\cdots\cdots\cdots\cdots\cdots\cdots\cdots\cdots\cdots$$
$$[na] A + [nb] B + [nc] C + \cdots + [nn] N = [nL]$$

(A-8)

In Eqs. (A-8), the symbol [ ] signifies the sum of the products, e.g., $[aa] = a_1 a_1 + a_2 a_2 + a_3 a_3 + \ldots + a_m a_m$; $[ab] = a_1 b_1 + a_2 b_2 + a_3 b_3 + \ldots + a_m b_m$; etc.

It may be similarly shown that normal equations may be systematically formed from weighted observation equations in the following manner:

$$[paa] A + [pab] B + [pac] C + \cdots + [pan] N = [paL]$$
$$[pba] A + [pbb] B + [pbc] C + \cdots + [pbn] N = [pbL]$$
$$[pca] A + [pcb] B + [pcc] C + \cdots + [pcn] N = [pcL]$$
$$\cdots\cdots\cdots\cdots\cdots\cdots\cdots\cdots\cdots\cdots\cdots\cdots$$
$$[pna] A + [pnb] B + [pnc] C + \cdots + [pnn] N = [pnL]$$

(A-9)

In Eqs. (A-9) the terms are as described previously except that the p's are the relative weights of the individual observations. Examples of the bracket terms are $[paa] = p_1 a_1 a_1 + p_2 a_2 a_2 + \ldots + p_m a_m a_m$; $[pbL] = p_1 b_1 L_1 + p_2 b_2 L_2 + \ldots + p_m b_m L_m$; etc.

The formulation of normal equations from observation equations may be further systematized by handling the systems of Eqs. (A-8) or (A-9) in a tabular manner.

EXAMPLE A-3   Using the tabular method, form the normal equations for Example A-2.

SOLUTION

Equation no.	a	b	L	aa	ab	bb	aL	bL
1	1	1	3.0	1	1	1	3.0	3.0
2	1	0	1.5	1	0	0	1.5	0
3	0	1	1.4	0	0	1	0	1.4
				2	1	2	4.5	4.4
				$[aa]$	$[ab]$	$[bb]$	$[aL]$	$[bL]$

For this example, normal equations are formed by satisfying Eqs. (A-8) as follows:

$$[aa]x + [ab]y = [aL]$$
$$[ab]x + [bb]y = [bL]$$

Substituting the appropriate values from the above table yields the required normal equations as follows:

$$2x + y = 4.5$$
$$x + 2y = 4.4 \qquad ////$$

A-9 MATRIX METHODS IN LEAST SQUARES ADJUSTMENT

It has been previously mentioned that least squares computations are quite lengthy and are therefore most economically performed on an electronic computer. The algebraic approach—Eqs. (A-8) and (A-9)—for forming normal equations, and for obtaining their simultaneous solution, can be programmed for computer solution. The procedure is much more easily adapted to matrix methods, however.

In developing matrix equations for least squares computations, analogy will be made to the algebraic approach presented in Sec. A-8. First of all, observation Eqs. (A-7) may be represented in matrix form as:

$$_mA_n\, _nX_1 = {}_mL_1 + {}_mV_1 \qquad \text{(A-10)}$$

where:

$$
A = {}_m\begin{bmatrix} a_1\ b_1\ c_1\ \dots\ n_1 \\ a_2\ b_2\ c_2\ \dots\ n_2 \\ .\quad .\quad .\quad \dots \\ .\quad .\quad .\quad \dots \\ a_m b_m c_m \dots n_m \end{bmatrix}^n \;;\, X = {}_n\begin{bmatrix} A \\ B \\ C \\ . \\ . \\ N \end{bmatrix}^1
$$

$$
L = \begin{array}{c} \\ \\ \\ \\ \\ \\ \\ \\ m \end{array}\overset{1}{\begin{bmatrix} L_1 \\ L_2 \\ L_3 \\ . \\ . \\ . \\ L_m \end{bmatrix}} \quad \text{and} \quad V = \begin{array}{c} \\ \\ \\ \\ \\ \\ \\ \\ m \end{array}\overset{1}{\begin{bmatrix} v_1 \\ v_2 \\ v_3 \\ . \\ . \\ . \\ v_m \end{bmatrix}}
$$

Upon studying the following matrix representation, it will be noticed that normal Eqs. (A-8) are obtained as follows:

$$
A^T A X = A^T L \qquad \text{(A-11)}
$$

In the above equation, $A^T A$ is the matrix of normal equation coefficients of the unknowns. Premultiplying both sides of Eq. (A-11) by $(A^T A)^{-1}$ and reducing, there results:

$$
(A^T A)^{-1}(A^T A)X = (A^T A)^{-1} A^T L
$$
$$
IX = (A^T A)^{-1} A^T L
$$
$$
X = (A^T A)^{-1} A^T L \qquad \text{(A-12)}
$$

In the above reduction, I is the identity matrix. Equation (A-12) is the basic least squares matrix equation for *equally weighted* observations. The matrix X consists of most probable values for unknowns, A, B, C, . . . , N. For a system of *weighted* observations, the following matrix equation provides the X matrix of most probable values for the unknowns:

$$
X = (A^T PA)^{-1} A^T PL \qquad \text{(A-13)}
$$

In Eq. (A-13) the matrices are identical to those of the equally weighted equations except that the P matrix is a diagonal matrix of weights defined as follows:

$$
P = \begin{array}{c} \\ \\ \\ \\ \\ \\ \\ \\ \\ \\ m \end{array}\overset{m}{\begin{bmatrix} p_1 & & & & \text{zeros} \\ & p_2 & & & \\ & & p_3 & & \\ & & & . & \\ \text{zeros} & & & & . \\ & & & & \\ & & & & p_m \end{bmatrix}}
$$

EXAMPLE A-4   Solve example A-2 using matrix methods.

(*a*)   The observation equations of Example A-2 may be expressed in matrix form as follows:

$$_3A_2\,_2X_1 = {_3}L_1 + {_3}V_1$$

Where

$$A = \begin{bmatrix} 1 & 1 \\ 1 & 0 \\ 0 & 1 \end{bmatrix}_3^2 \quad ; \quad X = {_2}\begin{bmatrix} x \\ y \end{bmatrix}^1 \quad ; \quad L = \begin{bmatrix} 3.0 \\ 1.5 \\ 1.4 \end{bmatrix}_3^1 \quad ; \quad V = \begin{bmatrix} v_1 \\ v_2 \\ v_3 \end{bmatrix}_3^1$$

(*b*)   Solving matrix Eq. (A-12),

$$(A^TA) = \begin{bmatrix} 1 & 1 & 0 \\ 1 & 0 & 1 \end{bmatrix}\begin{bmatrix} 1 & 1 \\ 1 & 0 \\ 0 & 1 \end{bmatrix} = \begin{bmatrix} 2 & 1 \\ 1 & 2 \end{bmatrix}$$

$$(A^TA)^{-1} = \frac{1}{3}\begin{bmatrix} 2 & -1 \\ -1 & 2 \end{bmatrix} \quad ; \quad A^TL = \begin{bmatrix} 4.5 \\ 4.4 \end{bmatrix}$$

$$(A^TA)^{-1}A^TL = \frac{1}{3}\begin{bmatrix} 2 & -1 \\ -1 & 2 \end{bmatrix}\begin{bmatrix} 4.5 \\ 4.4 \end{bmatrix} = \begin{bmatrix} 1.533 \\ 1.433 \end{bmatrix} \qquad ////$$

Note that this solution yields exactly the same values for x and y as were obtained through the algebraic approach of Example A-2.

A-10   MATRIX EQUATIONS FOR PRECISIONS OF ADJUSTED QUANTITIES

The matrix equation for calculating residuals after adjustment, whether the adjustment is weighted or not, is

$$V = AX - L \qquad \text{(A-14)}$$

The standard deviation of unit weight for an unweighted adjustment is

$$S_o = \sqrt{\frac{(V^TV)}{r}} \qquad \text{(A-15)}$$

The standard deviation of unit weight for a weighted adjustment is

$$S_o = \sqrt{\frac{(V^T P V)}{r}} \qquad \text{(A-16)}$$

In Eqs. (A-15) and (A-16), r is the number of degrees of freedom and equals the number of observation equations minus the number of unknowns, or $r = (m - n)$.

Standard deviations of the adjusted quantities are

$$S_{X_i} = S_o \sqrt{(Q_{X_i X_i})} \qquad \text{(A-17)}$$

In Eq. (A-17), S_{X_i} is the standard deviation of the ith adjusted quantity, e.g., the quantity in the ith row of the X matrix; S_o is the standard deviation of unit weight as calculated by Eqs. (A-15) or (A-16); and $Q_{X_i X_i}$ is the element in the ith row and the ith column of the matrix $(A^T A)^{-1}$ in the unweighted case, or the matrix $(A^T P A)^{-1}$ in the weighted case. The $(A^T A)^{-1}$ and $(A^T P A)^{-1}$ matrices are the so-called *covariance* matrices.

EXAMPLE A-5   Calculate the standard deviation of unit weight and the standard deviations of the adjusted quantities x and y for the unweighted problem of Example A-4.

(a) By Eq. (A-14) the residuals are

$$V = \begin{bmatrix} 1 & 1 \\ 1 & 0 \\ 0 & 1 \end{bmatrix} \begin{bmatrix} 1.533 \\ 1.433 \end{bmatrix} - \begin{bmatrix} 3.0 \\ 1.5 \\ 1.4 \end{bmatrix} = \begin{bmatrix} -0.033 \\ 0.033 \\ -0.033 \end{bmatrix}$$

(b) By Eq. (A-15) the standard deviation of unit weight is

$$V^T V = \begin{bmatrix} -0.033 & 0.033 & 0.033 \end{bmatrix} \begin{bmatrix} -0.033 \\ 0.033 \\ 0.033 \end{bmatrix} = 0.0033$$

$$S_o = \sqrt{\frac{0.0033}{3 - 2}} = \pm 0.057$$

(c) Using Eq. (A-17), the standard deviations of the adjusted values for x and y are:

$$S_x = \pm 0.057 \sqrt{2/3} = \pm 0.046$$
$$S_y = \pm 0.057 \sqrt{2/3} = \pm 0.046 \qquad ////$$

In part (c) above, the numbers 2/3 under the radicals are the (1,1) and (2,2) elements of the $(A^T A)^{-1}$ matrix of Example A-2. The interpretation of the standard deviations computed under part (c) is that there is a 68 percent probability that the adjusted values for x and y are within ±0.046 of their true value. Note that for this simple example problem the three residuals calculated in part (*a*) were equal, and also the standard deviations of x and y were equal in part (*c*). This is due to the symmetric nature of this particular problem (illustrated in Fig. A-3), but it is not generally the case with more complex problems.

A-11   PRACTICAL EXAMPLE

The following example problem is presented to illustrate a practical application of least squares in photogrammetry. The example also shows the method of calculating coefficients of a polynomial which approximates the radial-lens distortion curve for an aerial camera (see Sec. 5-12).

EXAMPLE A-6   From the radial-lens distortion calibration data of an aerial camera given in the table below, calculate the coefficients of a polynomial which approximates the radial-lens distortion curve.

Radial distance, r, mm	Radial-lens distortion, Δr, mm
0.000	0.000
20.072	0.004
40.855	0.018
63.155	0.047
88.034	0.062
116.995	0.035
152.472	− 0.064

SOLUTION   As presented in Sec. 5-12, a polynomial of the following form satisfactorily defines radial-lens distortions:

$$\Delta r = k_1 r + k_2 r^3 + k_3 r^5 + k_4 r^7 \qquad \text{(A-18)}$$

////

In Eq. (A-18), Δr is the radial-lens distortion at a radial distance r from the principal point. The k's are coefficients which define the shape of the radial-lens distortion curve. One equation of the form of Eq. (A-18) can be written for each radial distance at which the distortion is known from calibration. Since there are four k's, four equations are required to obtain a unique solution for them. From calibration, radial-lens distortions are known for seven radial distances; hence seven equations can be written and the k's may be computed by least squares.

Based on the calibration data, the following seven observation equations may be written (note that residual errors are added for consistency):

$$0.000 + v_1 = (\quad 0.000)k_1 + (\quad 0.000)^3 k_2 + (\quad 0.000)^5 k_3 + (\quad 0.000)^7 k_4$$
$$0.004 + v_2 = (\quad 20.072)k_1 + (\quad 20.072)^3 k_2 + (\quad 20.072)^5 k_3 + (\quad 20.072)^7 k_4$$
$$0.018 + v_3 = (\quad 40.855)k_1 + (\quad 40.855)^3 k_2 + (\quad 40.855)^5 k_3 + (\quad 40.855)^7 k_4$$
$$0.047 + v_4 = (\quad 63.155)k_1 + (\quad 63.155)^3 k_2 + (\quad 63.155)^5 k_3 + (\quad 63.155)^7 k_4$$
$$0.062 + v_5 = (\quad 88.034)k_1 + (\quad 88.034)^3 k_2 + (\quad 88.034)^5 k_3 + (\quad 88.034)^7 k_4$$
$$0.035 + v_6 = (116.995)k_1 + (116.995)^3 k_2 + (116.995)^5 k_3 + (116.995)^7 k_4$$
$$-0.064 + v_7 = (152.472)k_1 + (152.472)^3 k_2 + (152.472)^5 k_3 + (152.472)^7 k_4$$

Using least squares Eq. (A-12) and an electronic computer, these seven equations were solved and the following values were obtained for the four coefficients:

$$k_1 = 1.99697 \times 10^{-4} \quad k_3 = -1.97388 \times 10^{-11}$$
$$k_2 = 1.94801 \times 10^{-7} \quad k_4 = \quad 0.43934 \times 10^{-15}$$

Using these k's in Eq. (A-18), radial-lens distortions for any value of r may be readily calculated.

REFERENCES

American Society of Photogrammetry: "Manual of Photogrammetry," 3d ed., George Banta Co., Inc., Menasha, Wis., 1966, chap. 2.

Benjamin, J. R., and C. A. Cornell: "Probability, Statistics and Decision for Civil Engineers," McGraw-Hill Book Company, New York, 1970.

Crandall, K. C., and R. W. Seabloom: "Engineering Fundamentals in Measurements, Probability and Dimensions," McGraw-Hill Book Company, New York, 1970.

Gale, L. A.: Theory of Adjustments by Least Squares, *Canadian Surveyor*, vol. 19, no. 1, p. 42, 1965.

Hallert, B.: "Photogrammetry," McGraw-Hill Book Company, New York, 1960.

Hirvonen, R. A.: "Adjustment by Least Squares in Photogrammetry and Geodesy," Frederick Ungar Publishing Co., New York, 1971.

Hamilton, W. C.: "Statistics in Physical Science," The Ronald Press Company, New York, 1964.

Konecny, G.: Classical Concepts of Least Squares Adjustment, *Canadian Surveyor*, vol. 19, no. 1, p. 16, 1965.

Kouba, J.: Principal Property and Least Squares Adjustment Design, *The Canadian Surveyor*, vol. 26, no. 2, p. 136, 1972.

Linnik, Y. V.: "Method of Least Squares and Principles of the Theory of Observation," Pergamon Press, New York, 1961.

Mikhail, E. M.: Parameter Constraints in Least Squares, *Photogrammetric Engineering*, vol. 36, no. 12, p. 1277, 1970.

Rainsford, H. F.: "Survey Adjustments and Least Squares," Frederick Ungar Publishing Company, New York, 1958.

Richardus, P.: "Project Surveying," North Holland Publishing Company, Amsterdam, 1966.

PROBLEMS

A-1 A photographic distance was measured ten times with the following results: 48.23, 48.26, 48.25, 48.24, 48.24, 48.27, 48.23, 48.25, 48.25, and 48.26 mm. Calculate the most probable value for the photo distance and the standard deviation of the group of measurements.

A-2 Solve the following observation equations using the tabular least squares method and calculate the standard deviations of the adjusted quantities.

$$2x_1 + 3x_2 + x_3 = 10$$
$$x_1 - 2x_2 + 3x_3 = 5$$
$$7x_1 + x_2 - 2x_3 = 3$$
$$-x_1 - x_2 - x_3 = -6$$

A-3 Suppose the constant terms 10, 5, 3, and -6 of the four equations of Prob. A-2 represent measurements having relative weights of 1, 2, 2, and 3, respectively. Using weighted least squares, calculate most probable values for x_1, x_2, and x_3 and determine standard deviations of these values.

APPENDIX B
COORDINATE TRANSFORMATIONS

B-1 INTRODUCTION

A problem frequently encountered in photogrammetric work is conversion from one rectangular coordinate system to another. This is because photogrammetrists commonly determine coordinates of unknown points in convenient *arbitrary* rectangular coordinate systems. These arbitrary coordinates may be the result of analytical computation, or they may be read from stereoscopic plotters. The arbitrary coodinates must then be converted into an *absolute* or ground coordinate system such as the state plane coordinate system. The procedure of converting from one coordinate system to another is known as *coordinate transformation*. The procedure requires that some points have their coordinates known in both the arbitrary and the absolute coordinate systems. Such points are called *control points*.

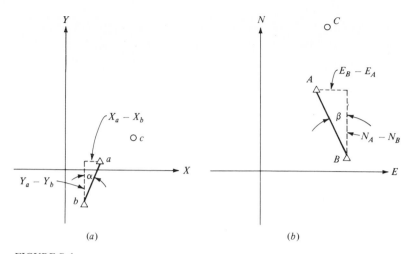

FIGURE B-1
(*a*) Arbitrary XY two-dimensional coordinate system. (*b*) Ground EN two-dimensional coordinate system.

B-2   TWO-DIMENSIONAL CONFORMAL TRANSFORMATION

The term "two-dimensional" means that the coordinate systems lie on plane surfaces. A *conformal* transformation is one in which true shape is preserved after transformation. To perform a two-dimensional conformal coordinate transformation, it is necessary that coordinates of at least two points be known in both coordinate systems. Accuracy in the transformation is improved by choosing the two points as far apart as possible. If more than two control points are available, an improved solution may be obtained by applying the method of least squares.

A two-dimensional conformal coordinate transformation consists of three basic steps: (1) scale change, (2) rotation, and (3) translation. The example illustrated in Fig. B-1 will be used to demonstrate the procedure. This example uses the minimum of two control points. Section B-4 describes the procedure when more than two control points are available. Figure B-1*a* shows the positions of points *a* through *c*, whose coordinates are known in an arbitrary XY system. Figure B-1*b* illustrates the positions of the same points, labeled *A* through *C* in a (ground) EN system. The coordinates of *A* and *B* are known in the ground system and it is required to determine the coordinates of *C* in the ground system.

Step 1, Scale Change

Comparing Fig. B-1*a* and *b*, it is evident that the lengths of lines *ab* and *AB* are unequal, hence the scales of the two coordinate systems are unequal. The scale of the XY system is made equal to the scale of the *EN* system by multiplying each *X* and *Y* coordinate by a scale factor, *s*. The scaled coordinates are labeled X' and Y'. Using the two control points, the scale factor is calculated in relation to the two lengths *AB* and *ab* as

$$s = \frac{AB}{ab} = \frac{[(E_B - E_A)^2 + (N_B - N_A)^2]^{1/2}}{[(X_b - X_a)^2 + (Y_b - Y_a)^2]^{1/2}} \tag{B-1}$$

Step 2, Rotation

If the scaled $X'Y'$ coordinate system is superimposed over the *EN* system of Fig. B-1*b* so that line *AB* in both systems coincides, the result is as shown in Fig. B-2. An auxiliary axis system $E'N'$ is constructed through the origin of the $X'Y'$ axis system parallel to the *EN* axes. It is necessary to rotate from the $X'Y'$ system to the $E'N'$ system, or in other words, to calculate $E'N'$ coordinates for the unknown points from their $X'Y'$ coordinates. The $E'N'$ coordinates of point *C* may be calculated in terms of the clockwise rotation θ by using the following equations:

$$\begin{aligned} E'_C &= X'_c \cos \theta - Y'_c \sin \theta \\ N'_C &= X'_c \sin \theta + Y'_c \cos \theta \end{aligned} \tag{B-2}$$

Rotation angle θ, shown in Fig. B-2, is the sum of angles α and β which are indicated on Fig. B-1*a* and *b*. From the coordinates of the two control points, these angles are calculated as

$$\begin{aligned} \alpha &= \tan^{-1}\left(\frac{X_a - X_b}{Y_a - Y_b}\right) \\ \beta &= \tan^{-1}\left(\frac{E_B - E_A}{N_A - N_B}\right) \end{aligned} \tag{B-3}$$

Step 3, Translation

The final step in the coordinate transformation is a translation of the origin of the $E'N'$ system to the origin of the *EN* system. The translation factors required are T_E and T_N, which are illustrated in Fig. B-2. Final *E* and *N* ground coordinates for point *C* then are

$$\begin{aligned} E_C &= E'_C + T_E \\ N_C &= N'_C + T_N \end{aligned} \tag{B-4}$$

Translation factors T_E and T_N are calculated as

$$\begin{aligned} T_E &= E_A - E'_A = E_B - E'_B \\ T_N &= N_A - N'_A = N_B - N'_B \end{aligned} \tag{B-5}$$

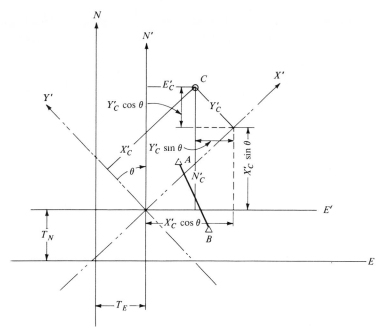

FIGURE B-2
Scaled $X'Y'$ coordinate system superimposed onto the EN ground coordinate system.

Note that these translation factors may be calculated in two different ways by using either control point A or B. It is advisable to calculate the translation factors using both points, however, in order to obtain a computation check.

Working sketches are recommended in computing coordinate transformations to aid in reducing the likelihood of mistakes. Caution should be exercised to ensure that correct algebraic signs are applied to the coordinates used in the transformation equations.

EXAMPLE B-1　Assume that in Fig. B-1a and b the arbitrary and ground coordinates of points A through C are as follows:

Point	Arbitrary coordinates		Ground coordinates	
	X	Y	E	N
A	632.17	121.45	1,100,64	1,431.09
B	355.20	-642.07	1,678.39	254.15
C	1,304.81	596.37		

It is required to compute the coordinates of point C in the ground EN system.

SOLUTION

(a) The scale factor is calculated from Eq. (B-1) as

$$s = \frac{[(1{,}678.39 - 1{,}100.64)^2 + (254.15 - 1{,}431.09)^2]^{1/2}}{[(355.20 - 632.17)^2 + (-642.07 - 121.45)^2]^{1/2}} = \frac{1{,}311.10}{812.20} = 1.61426$$

The arbitrary coordinates are then expanded to the $X'Y'$ system, which is equal in scale to the ground coordinate system, by multiplying each of the arbitrary coordinates by the scale factor. After multiplication, the $X'Y'$ coordinates are

	Scale coordinates	
Point	X'	Y'
A	1,020.49	196.05
B	573.39	−1,036.47
C	2,106.30	962.70

(b) The rotation angle, calculated by Eqs. (B-3), is

$$\alpha = \tan^{-1}\left[\frac{632.17 - 355.20}{121.45 + 642.07}\right] = 0.362753 \qquad \alpha = 19°\ 56'\ 18''$$

$$\beta = \tan^{-1}\left[\frac{1{,}678.39 - 1{,}110.64}{1{,}431.09 - 254.15}\right] = 0.490892 \qquad \beta = 26°\ 08'\ 46''$$

$$\theta = 19°\ 56'\ 18'' + 26°\ 08'\ 46'' = 46°\ 05'\ 04''$$

Rotation Eqs. (B-2) are then solved to obtain E' and N' coordinates. The solution in tabular form is as follows:

($\sin\theta = 0.720363$, $\cos\theta = 0.693597$)

Point	$X'\cos\theta$	$Y'\sin\theta$	$X'\sin\theta$	$Y'\cos\theta$	E'	N'
A	707.81	141.23	735.12	135.98	566.58	871.10
B	397.70	−746.63	413.05	−718.89	1,144.33	−305.84
C	1,460.92	693.49	1,517.30	667.73	767.43	2,185.03

(c) The translation factors T_E and T_N are calculated next, using Eqs. (B-5) as follows:

$$T_E = E_A - E'_A = 1{,}100.64 - 566.58 = 534.06$$

also
$$T_E = E_B - E'_B = 1{,}678.39 - 1{,}144.33 = 534.06 \text{ Check!}$$

$$T_N = N_A - N'_A = 1{,}431.09 - 871.10 = 559.99$$

also
$$T_N = N_B - N'_B = 254.15 + 305.84 = 559.99 \text{ Check!}$$

By adding the translation factors to E' and N', the following final transformed E

and N coordinates are obtained for point C:

$$E_C = 767.43 + 534.06 = 1301.49$$
$$N_C = 2185.03 + 559.99 = 2745.02$$

In the above example, although only one unknown point (point C) was transformed, any number of points could have been transformed using just the two control points.

B-3   ALTERNATE METHOD OF TWO-DIMENSIONAL CONFORMAL TRANSFORMATION

If an electronic computer is available, it is advantageous to compute coordinate transformations by an alternate method. In this method, equations involving four transformation coefficients are formulated in terms of the coordinates of the two or more points whose positions are known in both coordinate systems. The formation of the equations follows the same three steps discussed in Sec. B-2. The procedure consists first of multiplying each of the original coordinates of points a and b by a scale factor. The following four equations result:

$$
\begin{aligned}
X'_a &= sX_a \\
Y'_a &= sY_a \\
X'_b &= sX_b \\
Y'_b &= sY_b
\end{aligned}
\tag{B-6}
$$

Equations (B-6) are now substituted into Eqs. (B-2), except that subscripts of Eqs. (B-2) are changed to be applicable for points A and B. This substitution yields

$$
\begin{aligned}
E'_A &= sX_a \cos\theta - sY_a \sin\theta \\
N'_A &= sX_a \sin\theta + sY_a \cos\theta \\
E'_B &= sX_b \cos\theta - sY_b \sin\theta \\
N'_B &= sX_b \sin\theta + sY_b \cos\theta
\end{aligned}
\tag{B-7}
$$

Finally, translation factors T_E and T_N, as described previously, are added to Eqs. (B-7) to yield the following equations:

$$
\begin{aligned}
E_A &= sX_a \cos\theta - sY_a \sin\theta + T_E \\
N_A &= sX_a \sin\theta + sY_a \cos\theta + T_N \\
E_B &= sX_b \cos\theta - sY_b \sin\theta + T_E \\
N_B &= sX_b \sin\theta + sY_b \cos\theta + T_N
\end{aligned}
\tag{B-8}
$$

Let $\quad a = s \cos \theta$ and $b = s \sin \theta$

Making the substitution of a and b into Eqs. (B-8) and rearranging, there results

$$
\begin{aligned}
E_A &= aX_a - bY_a + T_E \\
N_A &= aY_a + bX_a + T_N \\
E_B &= aX_b - bY_b + T_E \\
N_B &= aY_b + bX_b + T_N
\end{aligned}
\qquad \text{(B-9)}
$$

Because both the XY and EN coordinates for points A and B are known, Eqs. (B-9) contain only four unknowns, the transformation factors a, b, T_E, and T_N. The four equations may be solved simultaneously to obtain the unknowns. When the four transformation factors have been computed, an E and an N equation of the form of Eqs. (B-9) may be solved to obtain the final coordinates of each point whose coordinates were known only in the XY coordinate system.

EXAMPLE B-2 Solve Example B-1 using the alternate method:

(*a*) Formulate Eqs. (B-9) for the points whose coordinates are known in both systems.

$$
\begin{aligned}
1{,}100.64 &= 632.17\,a - 121.45\,b + T_E \\
1{,}431.09 &= 121.45\,a + 632.17\,b + T_N \\
1{,}678.39 &= 355.20\,a + 642.07\,b + T_E \\
254.14 &= -642.07\,a + 355.20\,b + T_N
\end{aligned}
$$

(*b*) The simultaneous solution of the above four equations yields the following:

$$
\begin{aligned}
a &= 1.11965 \\
b &= 1.16285 \\
T_E &= 534.06 \\
T_N &= 559.99
\end{aligned}
$$

(*c*) Using the four transformation factors, the final EN ground coordinates of point C are calculated as follows:

$E_C = (1.11965)(1{,}304.81) - (1.16285)(596.37) + 534.06 = 1{,}301.49$

$N_C = (1.11965)(596.37) + (1.16285)(1{,}304.81) + 559.99 = 2{,}745.02$ \qquad ////

B-4 COORDINATE TRANSFORMATIONS WITH REDUNDANCY

In some instances more than two control points are available with coordinates known in both the arbitrary and ground systems. In that case redundancy exists and the transformation can be computed using a least squares solution. In this method, as discussed in

Appendix A, the sum of the squares of the residuals in the measurements are minimized, which, according to the theory of probability, produces the most probable solution. The least squares method has the additional advantages that any mistakes in the coordinates may be detected and the precisions of the transformed coordinates may be obtained. For these reasons it is advisable to use redundancy in coordinate transformations if possible.

In the least squares procedure, it is convenient to use the alternate method discussed in Sec. B-3. Two observation equations similar to those of Eqs. (B-9) are formed for each point whose coordinates are known in both systems. Residuals v are included in the equations to make them consistent, as follows:

$$aX - bY + T_E = E + v_E$$
$$bX + aY + T_N = N + v_N$$

(B-10)

If n points are available whose coordinates are known in both systems, $2n$ equations may be formed containing the four unknown transformation factors. The equations are solved by the method of least squares to obtain the most probable transformation factors. Transformed coordinates of all required points may then be found by using the transformation factors as illustrated in (c) of Example B-2.

It is theoretically correct in least squares to associate residuals with actual observations. In Eqs. (B-10), however, the X and Y coordinates are observed, yet the residuals have been associated with the E and N control coordinates. This is an easier approach and one that has been commonly used and found to yield entirely satisfactory results.

B-5   MATRIX METHODS IN COORDINATE TRANSFORMATIONS

Coordinate transformations involve rather lengthy calculations and are therefore best handled on an electronic computer. Matrix algebra is ideal for computer calculations and is therefore convenient for performing transformations.

To illustrate the application of matrix algebra in coordinate transformations, assume that coordinates of three control points, A through C, are known in both the XY system and the EN system. Let their coordinates be of equal reliability so that their weights are equal. Assume also that transformation into the EN system is required for points D through N, whose coordinates are known only in the XY system.

First of all, six observation equations of the form of Eqs. (B-10) are developed, two for each point A, B, and C, as follows:

$$X_A a - Y_A b + T_E = E_A + v_{E_A}$$
$$Y_A a + X_A b + T_N = N_A + v_{N_A}$$
$$X_B a - Y_B b + T_E = E_B + v_{E_B}$$

$$Y_B a + X_B b + T_N = N_B + v_{N_B}$$
$$X_C a - Y_C b + T_E = E_C + v_{E_C}$$
$$Y_C a + X_C b + T_N = N_C + v_{N_C} \qquad \text{(B-11)}$$

In matrix representation, the above six equations are

$$_6 A_4 \; _4 X_1 = \; _6 L_1 + \; _6 V_1 \qquad \text{(B-12)}$$

In matrix Eq. (B-12), A is the matrix of coefficients of the unknown transformation factors, X is the matrix of unknown transformation factors, L is the matrix of constant terms which is made up of control point coordinates, and V is the matrix of residual discrepancies in those coordinates brought about by measurement errors. More specifically these matrices are

$$A = \begin{bmatrix} X_A & -Y_A & 1 & 0 \\ Y_A & X_A & 0 & 1 \\ X_B & -Y_B & 1 & 0 \\ Y_B & X_B & 0 & 1 \\ X_C & -Y_C & 1 & 0 \\ Y_C & X_C & 0 & 1 \end{bmatrix}^4_{6} \qquad X = \begin{bmatrix} a \\ b \\ T_E \\ T_N \end{bmatrix}^1_{4} \qquad L = \begin{bmatrix} E_A \\ N_A \\ E_B \\ N_B \\ E_C \\ N_C \end{bmatrix}^1_{6} \qquad V = \begin{bmatrix} v_{E_A} \\ v_{N_A} \\ v_{E_B} \\ v_{N_B} \\ v_{E_C} \\ v_{N_C} \end{bmatrix}^1_{6}$$

As discussed in Appendix A, matrix Eq. (A-12) is used to solve this equally weighted system for the transformation factors. The final transformation of all points D through N into the EN system is performed as discussed in (c) of Example B-2. This phase of the computation is also readily adapted to matrix methods.

B-6   TWO-DIMENSIONAL AFFINE COORDINATE TRANSFORMATION

The two-dimensional *affine* coordinate transformation is only a slight modification of the two-dimensional conformal transformation to include different scale factors in the x and y directions. Although true shape is not retained, parallel lines remain parallel after affine transformation. A photogrammetry problem commonly solved using the two-dimensional affine transformation is conversion of measured photocoordinates from an arbitrary comparator axis system to the conventional xy fiducial axis system. Assume for example that comparator measurements have been taken with a diapositive oriented on the comparator as illustrated in Fig. B-3. Besides correcting for shrinkage by means of scale factors, the affine coordinate transformation also applies translations of X_o and Y_o to shift the origin from the XY comparator axis system to the xy photo system, and it applies a rotation through angle θ to orient the axes in the xy photo system. It is

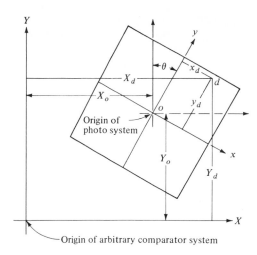

FIGURE B-3
Affine coordinate transformation from
arbitrary comparator XY axis system to
fiducial xy axis system.

entirely logical to use an affine transformation for this particular problem because it accounts for different magnitudes of film shrinkage or expansion that generally exist in the x and y directions. Following are the affine equations which transform from the XY comparator axes of Fig. B-3 to the xy photo system:

$$x = X + a_1 + a_2 X + a_3 Y$$
$$y = Y + b_1 + b_2 X + b_3 Y$$
(B-13)

As with the two-dimensional conformal transformation, the application of the affine transformation is a two-step procedure of (1) determining the a and b coefficients using points whose coordinates are known in both the XY and xy systems and (2) applying these coefficients to calculate transformed xy coordinates for all other points from their XY coordinates. In correcting photocoordinates, the four fiducial marks are used to perform step 1, since their calibrated xy coordinates are known from camera calibration, and their XY coordinates are available from comparator measurements. For a given photographic plate, a pair of equations of the form of Eq. (B-13) can be written for each fiducial mark. If there are four fiducials, four x and four y equations are obtained. Any three of the x equations will yield a solution for the unknown a coefficients, and any three of the y equations will yield a solution for the unknown b's. An improved solution may be obtained, however, if each set of four equations is solved simultaneously using least squares.

EXAMPLE B-3   Calibrated coordinates and comparator measured coordinates of the four fiducial marks for a certain photographic plate are given in the following table. The comparator-measured coordinates of other points 1, 2, and 3 are also given. It is required to compute the corrected coordinates of points 1, 2, and 3 using the affine transformation.

Point	Comparator coordinates		Calibrated coordinates	
	X, mm	Y, mm	x, mm	y, mm
Fiducial A	− 112.516	0.323	− 113.005	0.000
Fiducial B	0.016	− 112.904	0.000	113.000
Fiducial C	113.245	− 0.344	113.005	0.000
Fiducial D	0.702	112.869	0.000	− 113.000
1	10.711	− 70.715		
2	88.966	72.417		
3	109.564	− 70.953		

SOLUTION Equations of the form Eq. (B-13), with residuals added for consistency, are formulated first for the x coordinates of the four fiducial marks as

$$-113.005 + v_1 = -112.516 + a_1 - 112.516(a_2) + 0.323(a_3)$$

$$0.000 + v_2 = 0.016 + a_1 + 0.016(a_2) - 112.904(a_3)$$

$$113.005 + v_3 = 113.254 + a_1 + 113.245(a_2) - 0.344(a_3)$$

$$0.000 + v_4 = 0.702 + a_1 + 0.702(a_2) + 112.869(a_3)$$

Any three of the above four equations could be solved to obtain the three unknown a's. In this example, however, the v's were included and least squares Eq. (A-12) of Appendix A was used to obtain the three coefficients with the following results:

$$a_1 = -0.362 \qquad a_2 = 0.00110132 \qquad a_3 = -0.00304179$$

Now the corrected coordinates of unknown points 1 through 3 are calculated using these a's in Eq. (B-13) as follows:

$$x_1 = 10.711 - 0.362 + 0.00110132(10.711) - 0.00304179(-70.715) = 10.576$$

$$x_2 = 88.966 - 0.362 + 0.00110132(88.966) - 0.00304179(72.417) = 88.481$$

$$x_3 = 109.564 - 0.362 + 0.00110132(109.564) - 0.00304179(-70.953) = 109.538$$

In a similar manner, equations are written for the y coordinates of each of the four fiducial marks. These equations are solved to obtain the b's, whereupon the y-corrected coordinates of points 1 through 3 are calculated. These corrected y coordinates are

$$y_1 = -70.741 \qquad y_2 = 72.765 \qquad y_3 = -70.687 \qquad ////$$

If the fiducial marks are in the four corners, as is the case with Wild cameras, the very same procedures may be followed. Of course, it is required that calibrated coordinates and comparator coordinates be known for each of the four fiducial marks.

B-7   THREE-DIMENSIONAL CONFORMAL COORDINATE TRANSFORMATIONS

As implied by its name, a three-dimensional conformal coordinate transformation involves converting coordinates from one three-dimensional system to another. In the transformation, true shape is retained. This type of coordinate transformation is essential in analytical or computational photogrammetry for two basic problems: (1) to convert coordinates of points from a tilted photographic coordinate system to an equivalent vertical photographic system which is parallel to a ground or arbitrary object space system and (2) to form continuous three-dimensional "strip models" from independent stereomodels. Three-dimensional conformal coordinate transformation equations are developed here in general, while their application to specific photogrammetry problems is described elsewhere in the text where appropriate.

In Fig. B-4 it is required to transform coordinates of points from an xyz system to an XYZ system. The necessary transformation equations can be expressed in terms of seven independent transformation factors: three rotation angles, omega (ω), phi (ϕ), and kappa (κ); a scale factor (s); and three translation factors, T_x, T_y, and T_z. Before proceeding with the development of the transformation equations, it is important to define sign conventions. All coordinate systems shall be defined as right-handed, i.e., systems in which positive X, Y, and Z are defined as shown in Fig. B-4. Rotation angles ω, ϕ and κ are defined as positive if they are counterclockwise when viewed from the positive end of their respective axes. Positive ω rotation about the x' axis, for example, is shown in Fig. B-4.

The transformation equations shall be developed in the following two basic steps: (1) rotation and (2) scaling and translation.

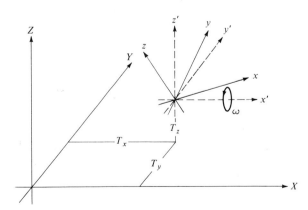

FIGURE B-4
XYZ and xyz right-handed three-dimensional coordinate systems.

Step 1   Rotation

In Fig. B-4 an $x'y'z'$ coordinate system parallel to the XYZ object system is constructed with its origin at the origin of the xyz system. In the development of rotation formulas, it is customary to consider the three rotations as taking place so as to convert from the $x'y'z'$ system to the xyz system. The rotation equations are developed in a sequence of three independent two-dimensional rotations. These rotations, illustrated in Fig. B-5, are first, ω rotation about the x' axis which converts coordinates from the $x'y'z'$ system into an $x_1y_1z_1$ system; second, ϕ rotation about the once rotated y_1 axis which converts coordinates from the $x_1y_1z_1$ system into an $x_2y_2z_2$ system; and third, κ rotation about the twice rotated z_2 axis which converts coordinates from the $x_2y_2z_2$ system into the xyz system of Fig. B-4. The exact amount and direction of the rotations for any three-dimensional coordinate transformation will depend upon the orientation relationship between the xyz and XYZ coordinate systems.

The development of the rotation formulas is as follows:

a)   First, rotation through the angle ω about the x' axis, as illustrated in Fig. B-6. The coordinates of any point A in the once rotated $x_1y_1z_1$ system, as shown graphically in Fig. B-6, are

$$x_1 = x'$$
$$y_1 = y' \cos \omega + z' \sin \omega \qquad \text{(B-14)}$$
$$z_1 = -y' \sin \omega + z' \cos \omega$$

Since this rotation was about x', the x' and x_1 axes are coincident and therefore the x coordinate of A is unchanged.

b)   Second, rotation through ϕ about the y_1 axis, as illustrated in Fig. B-7. The coordinates of A in the twice rotated $x_2y_2z_2$ coordinate system, as shown graphically in Fig. B-7 are

$$x_2 = -z_1 \sin \phi + x_1 \cos \phi$$
$$y_2 = y_1 \qquad \text{(B-15)}$$
$$z_2 = z_1 \cos \phi + x_1 \sin \phi$$

In this rotation about y_1, the y_1 and y_2 axes are coincident and therefore the y coordinate of A is unchanged. Substituting Eqs. (B-14) into (B-15):

$$x_2 = -(-y' \sin \omega + z' \cos \omega) \sin \phi + x' \cos \phi$$
$$y_2 = y' \cos \omega + z' \sin \omega \qquad \text{(B-16)}$$
$$z_2 = (-y' \sin \omega + z' \cos \omega) \cos \phi + x' \sin \phi$$

c)   Third, rotation through κ about the z_2 axis, as illustrated in Fig. B-8. The

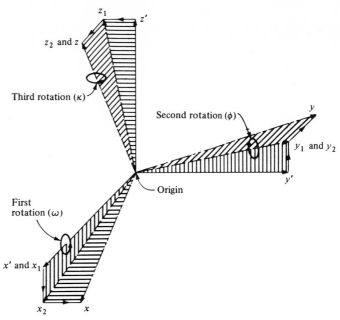

FIGURE B-5
The three sequential angular rotations.

coordinates of A in the three times rotated coordinate system, which has now become the *xyz* system as shown graphically in Fig. B-8, are

$$x = x_2 \cos \kappa + y_2 \sin \kappa$$
$$y = -x_2 \sin \kappa + y_2 \cos \kappa \qquad \text{(B-17)}$$
$$z = z_2$$

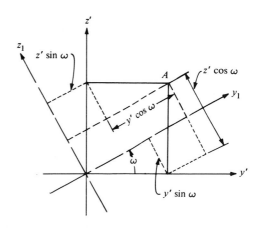

FIGURE B-6
Omega rotation about the x' axis.

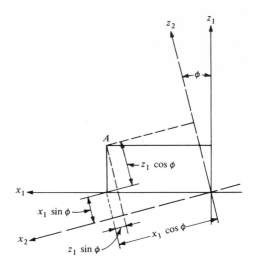

FIGURE B-7
Phi rotation about the y_1 axis.

In this rotation about z_2, the z_2 and z axes are coincident and therefore the z coordinate of A is unchanged. Substituting Eqs. (B-16) into (B-17):

$$
\left.\begin{aligned}
x &= [(y' \sin \omega - z' \cos \omega) \sin \phi + x' \cos \phi] \cos \kappa + (y' \cos \omega + z' \sin \omega) \sin \kappa \\
y &= [(-y' \sin \omega + z' \cos \omega) \sin \phi - x' \cos \phi] \sin \kappa + (y' \cos \omega + z' \sin \omega) \cos \kappa \\
z &= (-y' \sin \omega + z' \cos \omega) \cos \phi + x' \sin \phi
\end{aligned}\right\}
$$

(B-18)

Factoring Eqs. (B-18),

$$
\left.\begin{aligned}
x &= x'(\cos \phi \cos \kappa) + y'(\sin \omega \sin \phi \cos \kappa + \cos \omega \sin \kappa) + z'(- \cos \omega \sin \phi \cos \kappa \\
&\quad + \sin \omega \sin \kappa) \\
y &= x'(- \cos \phi \sin \kappa) + y'(- \sin \omega \sin \phi \sin \kappa + \cos \omega \cos \kappa) + z'(\cos \omega \sin \phi \sin \kappa \\
&\quad + \sin \omega \cos \kappa) \\
z &= x'(\sin \phi) + y'(- \sin \omega \cos \phi) + z'(\cos \omega \cos \phi)
\end{aligned}\right\}
$$

(B-19)

Substituting m's for the coefficients of $x', y',$ and z' in Eqs. (B-19), these equations are:

$$
\begin{aligned}
x &= m_{11}x' + m_{12}y' + m_{13}z' \\
y &= m_{21}x' + m_{22}y' + m_{23}z' \\
z &= m_{31}x' + m_{32}y' + m_{33}z'
\end{aligned}
$$

(B-20)

FIGURE B-8
Kappa rotation about the z_2 axis.

Where:

$$m_{11} = \cos \phi \cos \kappa$$

$$m_{12} = \sin \omega \sin \phi \cos \kappa + \cos \omega \sin \kappa$$

$$m_{13} = -\cos \omega \sin \phi \cos \kappa + \sin \omega \sin \kappa$$

$$m_{21} = -\cos \phi \sin \kappa$$

$$m_{22} = -\sin \omega \sin \phi \sin \kappa + \cos \omega \cos \kappa \qquad \text{(B-21)}$$

$$m_{23} = \cos \omega \sin \phi \sin \kappa + \sin \omega \cos \kappa$$

$$m_{31} = \sin \phi$$

$$m_{32} = -\sin \omega \cos \phi$$

$$m_{33} = \cos \omega \cos \phi$$

Equations (B-20) may be expressed in matrix form as

$$X = MX' \qquad \text{(B-22)}$$

Where
$$X = \begin{bmatrix} x \\ y \\ z \end{bmatrix} \quad M = \begin{bmatrix} m_{11} & m_{12} & m_{13} \\ m_{21} & m_{22} & m_{23} \\ m_{31} & m_{32} & m_{33} \end{bmatrix} \quad \text{and} \quad X' = \begin{bmatrix} x' \\ y' \\ z' \end{bmatrix}$$

The matrix M is commonly called the *rotation matrix*. The individual elements of the rotation matrix are *direction cosines* which relate the two axis systems. These matrix elements, expressed in terms of direction cosines are

$$M = \begin{bmatrix} \cos xx' & \cos xy' & \cos xz' \\ \cos yx' & \cos yy' & \cos yz' \\ \cos zx' & \cos zy' & \cos zz' \end{bmatrix} \qquad \text{(B-23)}$$

In the above matrix, cos xx' is the direction cosine relating the x and x' axes, cos xy' relates the x and y' axes, etc. Direction cosines are simply the cosines of the angles in space between the respective axes, the angles being taken between 0 and 180°. It is an important property that the sum of the squares of the three direction cosines of any straight line is unity. This property may be used to check the computed elements of the rotation matrix for correctness. The check is obtained if the sum of the squares of the elements of any row or of any column of the M matrix is equal to 1.

The rotation matrix is an *orthogonal* matrix, which has the property that its inverse is equal to its transpose, or

$$M^{-1} = M^T \qquad \text{(B-24)}$$

Using this property, Eq. (B-22) may be rewritten expressing $x'y'z'$ coordinates in terms of xyz coordinates as follows:

$$X' = M^T X \qquad \text{(B-25)}$$

In expanded form, this equation is:

$$
\begin{aligned}
x' &= m_{11}x + m_{21}y + m_{31}z \\
y' &= m_{12}x + m_{22}y + m_{32}z \qquad \text{(B-26)}\\
z' &= m_{13}x + m_{23}y + m_{33}z
\end{aligned}
$$

Step 2 Scaling and Translation

In order to arrive at the final three-dimensional coordinate transformation equations, i.e., equations which yield coordinates in the XYZ system of Fig. B-4, it is necessary to multiply each of Eqs. (B-26) by a scale factor s and add the translation factors T_x, T_y, and T_z. (Recall that the $x'y'z'$ coordinates given by Eqs. (B-26) are in a system that is parallel to the XYZ system.) This makes the lengths of any lines equal in both coordinate systems and translates from the origin of $x'y'z'$ to the origin of the XYZ system. Performing this step,

$$
\begin{aligned}
X &= sx' + T_x = s(m_{11}x + m_{21}y + m_{31}z) + T_x \\
Y &= sy' + T_y = s(m_{12}x + m_{22}y + m_{32}z) + T_y \qquad \text{(B-27)}\\
Z &= sz' + T_z = s(m_{13}x + m_{23}y + m_{33}z) + T_z
\end{aligned}
$$

In matrix form, Eqs. (B-27) are

$$\bar{X} = sM^T X + T \qquad \text{(B-28)}$$

In Eq. (B-28) matrixes M and X are as previously defined, s is the scale factor, and

$$\bar{X} = \begin{bmatrix} X \\ Y \\ Z \end{bmatrix} \quad \text{and } T = \begin{bmatrix} T_x \\ T_y \\ T_z \end{bmatrix}$$

In Eqs. (B-27), the nine m's are not independent of each other but rather, as seen in Eqs. (B-21), they are functions of the three rotation angles ω, ϕ, and κ. In addition to these three unknown angles, there are also three unknown translations and one scale factor in Eqs. (B-27), which makes a total of seven unknowns. A unique solution is obtained for the unknowns if the x and y coordinates of two horizontal points and the Z coordinates of three vertical points are known in both coordinate systems. If more than the minimum of seven coordinates are known in both systems, redundant equations may be written which make possible an improved solution through least squares techniques.

There are different approaches to the solution for the unknowns. Perhaps the easiest approach is to eliminate the three translation factors from the equations. Suppose there are three points, p, q, and r, whose coordinates are known in both systems. Then a total of nine equations of the type of Eqs. (B-27) may be written as follows:

$$
\begin{aligned}
&(1) \quad X_P = s(m_{11}x_p + m_{21}y_p + m_{31}z_p) + T_x \\
&(2) \quad Y_P = s(m_{12}x_p + m_{22}y_p + m_{32}z_p) + T_y \\
&(3) \quad Z_P = s(m_{13}x_p + m_{23}y_p + m_{33}z_p) + T_z \\
&(4) \quad X_Q = s(m_{11}x_q + m_{21}y_q + m_{31}z_q) + T_x \\
&(5) \quad Y_Q = s(m_{12}x_q + m_{22}y_q + m_{32}z_q) + T_y \\
&(6) \quad Z_Q = s(m_{13}x_q + m_{23}y_q + m_{33}z_q) + T_z \\
&(7) \quad X_R = s(m_{11}x_r + m_{21}y_r + m_{31}z_r) + T_x \\
&(8) \quad Y_R = s(m_{12}x_r + m_{22}y_r + m_{32}z_r) + T_y \\
&(9) \quad Z_R = s(m_{13}x_r + m_{23}y_r + m_{33}z_r) + T_z
\end{aligned}
\tag{B-29}
$$

If Eqs. (4), (5), and (6) above are subtracted from Eqs. (1), (2), and (3) respectively, and if Eqs. (7), (8), and (9) are subtracted from Eqs. (1), (2), and (3) respectively, the following six equations result:

$$
\begin{aligned}
X_P - X_Q &= s[m_{11}(x_p - x_q) + m_{21}(y_p - y_q) + m_{31}(z_p - z_q)] \\
Y_P - Y_Q &= s[m_{12}(x_p - x_q) + m_{22}(y_p - y_q) + m_{32}(z_p - z_q)] \\
Z_P - Z_Q &= s[m_{13}(x_p - x_q) + m_{23}(y_p - y_q) + m_{33}(z_p - z_q)] \\
X_P - X_R &= s[m_{11}(x_p - x_r) + m_{21}(y_p - y_r) + m_{31}(z_p - z_r)] \\
Y_P - Y_R &= s[m_{12}(x_p - x_r) + m_{22}(y_p - y_r) + m_{32}(z_p - z_r)] \\
Z_P - Z_R &= s[m_{13}(x_p - x_r) + m_{23}(y_p - y_r) + m_{33}(z_p - z_r)]
\end{aligned}
\tag{B-30}
$$

Equations (B-30) are nonlinear equations involving the four unknowns ω, ϕ, κ, and s. In order to solve these equations, they are linearized using Taylor's theorem. In accordance with Taylor's theorem, the linearized form of Eqs. (B-30) is

$$F_q = X_P - X_Q = (F_q)_0 + \left(\frac{\partial F_q}{\partial s}\right)_0 ds + \left(\frac{\partial F_q}{\partial \omega}\right)_0 d\omega + \left(\frac{\partial F_q}{\partial \phi}\right)_0 d\phi + \left(\frac{\partial F_q}{\partial \kappa}\right)_0 d\kappa$$

$$G_q = Y_P - Y_Q = (G_q)_0 + \left(\frac{\partial G_q}{\partial s}\right)_0 ds + \left(\frac{\partial G_q}{\partial \omega}\right)_0 d\omega + \left(\frac{\partial G_q}{\partial \phi}\right)_0 d\phi + \left(\frac{\partial G_q}{\partial \kappa}\right)_0 d\kappa$$

$$H_q = Z_P - Z_Q = (H_q)_0 + \left(\frac{\partial H_q}{\partial s}\right)_0 ds + \left(\frac{\partial H_q}{\partial \omega}\right)_0 d\omega + \left(\frac{\partial H_q}{\partial \phi}\right)_0 d\phi + \left(\frac{\partial H_q}{\partial \kappa}\right)_0 d\kappa$$

$$F_r = X_P - X_R = (F_r)_0 + \left(\frac{\partial F_r}{\partial s}\right)_0 ds + \left(\frac{\partial F_r}{\partial \omega}\right)_0 d\omega + \left(\frac{\partial F_r}{\partial \phi}\right)_0 d\phi + \left(\frac{\partial F_r}{\partial \kappa}\right)_0 d\kappa$$

$$G_r = Y_P - Y_R = (G_r)_0 + \left(\frac{\partial G_r}{\partial s}\right)_0 ds + \left(\frac{\partial G_r}{\partial \omega}\right)_0 d\omega + \left(\frac{\partial G_r}{\partial \phi}\right)_0 d\phi + \left(\frac{\partial G_r}{\partial \kappa}\right)_0 d\kappa$$

$$H_r = Z_P - Z_R = (H_r)_0 + \left(\frac{\partial H_r}{\partial s}\right)_0 ds + \left(\frac{\partial H_r}{\partial \omega}\right)_0 d\omega + \left(\frac{\partial H_r}{\partial \phi}\right)_0 d\phi + \left(\frac{\partial H_r}{\partial \kappa}\right)_0 d\kappa$$

$$(B-31)$$

In Eqs. (B-31), $(F_q)_0$, $(G_q)_0$, $(H_q)_0$, etc., are the right-hand sides of the respective Eqs. (B-30) evaluated at the initial approximations; $(\partial F_q/\partial s)_0$, $(\partial F_q/\partial \omega)_0$, $(\partial F_q/\partial \phi)_0$, etc., are partial derivatives with respect to the indicated unknowns evaluated at the initial approximations; and $ds, d\omega, d\phi$, and $d\kappa$ are corrections to the initial approximations. The units of $d\omega, d\phi$, and $d\kappa$ are radians while ds is a dimensionless scale factor.

In order to make all Eqs. (B-31) consistent, residual errors are added. Equations (B-31) are also simplified by substituting letters for the partial derivative coefficients as follows:

$$a_{11}ds + a_{12}d\omega + a_{13}d\phi + a_{14}d\kappa = [(X_P - X_Q) - (F_q)_0] + v_{X_q}$$

$$a_{21}ds + a_{22}d\omega + a_{23}d\phi + a_{24}d\kappa = [(Y_P - Y_Q) - (G_q)_0] + v_{Y_q}$$

$$a_{31}ds + a_{32}d\omega + a_{33}d\phi + a_{34}d\kappa = [(Z_P - Z_Q) - (H_q)_0] + v_{Z_q}$$

$$a_{41}ds + a_{42}d\omega + a_{43}d\phi + a_{44}d\kappa = [(X_P - X_R) - (F_r)_0] + v_{X_r}$$

$$a_{51}ds + a_{52}d\omega + a_{53}d\phi + a_{54}d\kappa = [(Y_P - Y_R) - (G_r)_0] + v_{Y_r}$$

$$a_{61}ds + a_{62}d\omega + a_{63}d\phi + a_{64}d\kappa = [(Z_P - Z_R) - (H_r)_0] + v_{Z_r}$$

$$(B-32)$$

Equations (B-32) may be expressed in matrix form as

$$_6A_4 \, _4X_1 = \, _6L_1 + \, _6V_1 \qquad (B-33)$$

Where

$$
A = \begin{bmatrix} a_{11} & a_{12} & a_{13} & a_{14} \\ a_{21} & a_{22} & a_{23} & a_{24} \\ a_{31} & a_{32} & a_{33} & a_{34} \\ a_{41} & a_{42} & a_{43} & a_{44} \\ a_{51} & a_{52} & a_{53} & a_{54} \\ a_{61} & a_{62} & a_{63} & a_{64} \end{bmatrix}_6^4 \quad X = \begin{bmatrix} ds \\ d\omega \\ d\phi \\ d\kappa \end{bmatrix}^1 \quad L = \begin{bmatrix} (X_P - X_Q) - (F_q)_0 \\ (Y_P - Y_Q) - (G_q)_0 \\ (Z_P - Z_Q) - (H_q)_0 \\ (X_P - X_R) - (F_r)_0 \\ (Y_P - Y_R) - (G_r)_0 \\ (Z_P - Z_R) - (H_r)_0 \end{bmatrix}_6^1 \quad V \begin{bmatrix} \nu_{X_q} \\ \nu_{Y_q} \\ \nu_{Z_q} \\ \nu_{X_r} \\ \nu_{Y_r} \\ \nu_{Z_r} \end{bmatrix}_6^1
$$

Equation (B-33) may be solved using least squares Eq. (A-12). The solution is iterated, due to the use of the Taylor series, until satisfactory values are obtained for s, ω, ϕ, and κ. Then the three translation factors are found by substitution into Eqs. (B-29). When all seven transformation factors have been found, the transformed coordinates of all points whose coordinates are known only in the original system may be found by applying equations of the type of Eqs. (B-29).

In order to clarify the coefficients of Eqs. (B-32), the partial derivatives for the first three equations are:

$$a_{11} = m_{11}(x_p - x_q) + m_{21}(y_p - y_q) + m_{31}(z_p - z_q)$$

$$a_{12} = 0$$

$$a_{13} = [(-\sin\phi\cos\kappa)(x_p - x_q) + \sin\phi\sin\kappa(y_p - y_q) + \cos\phi\,(z_p - z_q)]\,s$$

$$a_{14} = [m_{21}(x_p - x_q) - (m_{11})(y_p - y_q)]\,s$$

$$a_{21} = m_{12}(x_p - x_q) + m_{22}(y_p - y_q) + m_{32}(z_p - z_q)$$

$$a_{22} = [-m_{13}(x_p - x_q) - m_{23}(y_p - y_q) - m_{33}(z_p - z_q)]\,s$$

$$a_{23} = [(\sin\omega\cos\phi\cos\kappa)(x_p - x_q) + (-\sin\omega\cos\phi\sin\kappa)(y_p - y_q)$$
$$+ (\sin\omega\sin\phi)(z_p - z_q)]\,s$$

$$a_{24} = [m_{22}(x_p - x_q) - m_{12}(y_p - y_q)]\,s$$

$$a_{31} = m_{13}(x_p - x_q) + m_{23}(y_p - y_q) + m_{33}(z_p - z_q)$$

$$a_{32} = [m_{12}(x_p - x_q) + m_{22}(y_p - y_q) + m_{32}(z_p - z_q)]\,s$$

$$a_{33} = [(-\cos\omega\cos\phi\cos\kappa)(x_p - x_q) + (\cos\omega\cos\phi\sin\kappa)(y_p - y_q)$$
$$+ (-\cos\omega\sin\phi)(z_p - z_q)]\,s$$

$$a_{34} = [m_{23}(x_p - x_q) - m_{13}(y_p - y_q)]\,s$$

The coefficients for the last three equations from Eq. (B-32) are exactly the same as those for the first three with the exception that the subscripts q are replaced with subscripts r. In general, if there are n points whose X, Y, and Z coordinates are known in both systems, then $3(n - 1)$ equations of the type of Eqs. (B-32) may be formed. Three-dimensional conformal coordinate transformations involve lengthy calculations and therefore they are practical only when performed on an electronic computer.

REFERENCES

American Society of Photogrammetry: "Manual of Photogrammetry," 3d ed., George Banta Co., Inc., Menasha, Wisc., 1966, chap. 2.

Baetsle, P. L.: Conformal Transformations in Three Dimensions, *Photogrammetric Engineering*, vol. 32, no. 5, p. 816, 1966.

Blais, J. A. R.: Three-Dimensional Similarity, *Canadian Surveyor*, vol. 26, no. 1, p. 71, 1972.

Light, D. L.: The Orientation Matrix, *Photogrammetric Engineering*, vol. 32, no. 3, p. 434, 1966.

Mikhail, E. M.: Simultaneous Three Dimensional Transformation of Higher Degree, *Photogrammetric Engineering*, vol. 30, no. 4, p. 588, 1964.

———: Discussion Paper: Simultaneous Three Dimensional Transformation, *Photogrammetric Engineering*, vol. 32, no. 2, p. 180, 1966.

Schmidt, E.: "Transformation of Rectangular Space Coordinates," Technical Bulletin No. 15, U.S. Coast and Geodetic Survey, Washington, D.C., 1960.

Schut, G. H.: Conformal Transformations and Polynomials, *Photogrammetric Engineering*, vol. 32, no. 5, p. 826, 1962.

Tewinkel, G. C.: A Trigonometric Derivation of the Formulas for the Three-Dimensional Rotation Matrix, *Photogrammetric Engineering*, vol. 30, no. 4, p. 635, 1964.

Umbach, M. J.: "Aerotriangulation: Tranformation of Surveying and Mapping Coordinate Systems," Technical Report No. 34, U.S. Coast and Geodetic Survey, Washington, D.C., 1967.

Vlcek, J.: Discussion Paper: Simultaneous Three Dimensional Transformation, *Photogrammetric Engineering*, vol. 32, no. 2, p. 178, 1962.

PROBLEMS

B-1 The following table contains arbitrary X and Y coordinates of a group of points determined from radial-line triangulation. The table also includes state plane coordinates for three of the points. Using a *two-dimensional conformal* coordinate transformation, calculate state plane coordinates for the other points.

	Arbitrary coordinates from radial-line triangulation		State plane coordinates	
Point	X, ft	Y, ft	X, ft	Y, ft
A	60.811	− 64.033	2,098,844.8	102,178.4
B	70.614	93.859	2,098,827.9	99,318.6
C	87.901	67.864	2,098,489.9	99,769.9
1	87.074	− 60.131		
2	256.760	− 96.065		
3	377.222	− 33.853		
4	486.394	60.497		
5	534.059	80.812		

B-2 The following table contains X and Y comparator coordinates for four side fiducial marks and six additional photo images. The table also contains calibrated coordinates for the four fiducials. Using a *two-dimensional affine* coordinate transformation, determine corrected photocoordinates for the six image points.

	Comparator coordinates		Calibrated coordinates	
Point	X, mm	Y, mm	X, mm	Y, mm
A	55.169	159.893	− 113.000	0.000
B	167.716	273.482	0.000	113.000
C	281.000	160.706	113.000	0.000
D	168.580	46.939	0.000	− 113.000
1	228.498	105.029		
2	270.307	199.949		
3	259.080	231.064		
4	220.980	224.993		
5	123.952	234.036		
6	101.829	104.191		

B-3 Coordinates X_1, Y_1, and Z_1 for model I and X_2, Y_2, and Z_2 for model II of an independent model aerotriangulation are contained in the table below. Transform the model II coordinates into the model I coordinate system using a *three-dimensional conformal* coordinate transformation.

	Model I coordinates			Model II coordinates		
Point	X_1, mm	Y_1, mm	Z_1, mm	X_2, mm	Y_2, mm	Z_2, mm
R44	596.43	499.41	467.98	390.13	499.74	469.32
4401	578.87	630.14	81.70	371.46	630.95	81.14
367	632.54	419.06	82.39	425.43	419.18	82.38
4403	617.47	438.29	81.16	410.28	438.42	81.02
4402	655.16	295.94	97.18	448.00	295.94	97.68
4404	621.48	708.40	101.90	414.38	709.50	101.66
R45				611.15	499.09	470.34
3725				637.27	323.78	85.56
371				573.10	401.62	84.37
373				646.78	374.08	83.65
3705				533.29	285.12	87.02

APPENDIX C
DEVELOPMENT OF COLLINEARITY CONDITION EQUATIONS

C-1 INTRODUCTION

Collinearity as illustrated in Fig. C-1 is the condition that the exposure station of any photograph, an object point, and its photo image all lie on a straight line. The equations expressing this condition are called the *collinearity condition equations*. They are perhaps the most useful of all equations to the photogrammetrist.

In Fig. C-2 exposure station L of an aerial photo has coordinates X_L, Y_L, and Z_L with respect to the object (ground) coordinate system XYZ. Image a of object point A, shown in a *rotated* image plane, has image space coordinates x'_a, y'_a, and $-z'_a$, where the rotated image space coordinate system $x'y'z'$ is parallel to object space coordinate system XYZ.

FIGURE C-1
The collinearity condition.

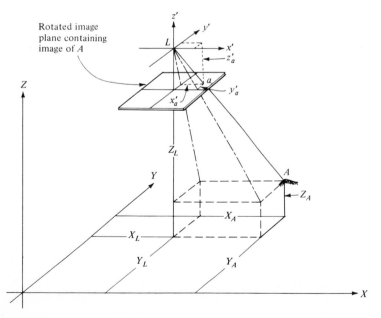

FIGURE C-2
Image coordinate system rotated such that it is parallel to the object space coordinate system.

C-2 ROTATION IN TERMS OF OMEGA, PHI, AND KAPPA

By means of the three-dimensional rotation formulas developed in Appendix B, an image point a having coordinates x_a, y_a, and $-z_a$ in a tilted photo such as that of Fig. C-1, may have its coordinates rotated into the $x'y'z'$ parallel coordinate system (parallel to XYZ) as shown in Fig. C-3. The rotated image coordinates x'_a, y'_a, and $-z'_a$ may be expressed in terms of measured photocoordinates x_a and y_a, the camera focal length f, and the three rotation angles omega, phi, and kappa. The rotation formulas are Eqs. (B-20), which were developed in Appendix B. For convenience they are repeated here.

$$x_a = m_{11}x'_a + m_{12}y'_a + m_{13}z'_a$$
$$y_a = m_{21}x'_a + m_{22}y'_a + m_{23}z'_a \qquad \text{(C-1)}$$
$$z_a = m_{31}x'_a + m_{32}y'_a + m_{33}z'_a$$

In Eqs. (C-1) the m's are functions of the rotation angles omega, phi, and kappa. These functions are given as Eqs. (B-21) in Appendix B. Also note on Fig. C-3 that the value for z_a is equal to $(-f)$.

C-3 DEVELOPMENT OF THE COLLINEARITY CONDITION EQUATIONS

The collinearity condition equations are developed from similar triangles of Fig. C-2 as follows:

$$\frac{x'_a}{X_A - X_L} = \frac{y'_a}{Y_A - Y_L} = \frac{-z'_a}{Z_L - Z_A}$$

Reducing,

$$x'_a = \left(\frac{X_A - X_L}{Z_A - Z_L}\right)z'_a \qquad (a)$$

$$y'_a = \left(\frac{Y_A - Y_L}{Z_A - Z_L}\right)z'_a \qquad (b)$$

Also, by identity,

$$z'_a = \left(\frac{Z_A - Z_L}{Z_A - Z_L}\right)z'_a \qquad (c)$$

Substituting (a), (b), and (c) into Eqs. (C-1),

$$x_a = m_{11}\left(\frac{X_A - X_L}{Z_A - Z_L}\right)z'_a + m_{12}\left(\frac{Y_A - Y_L}{Z_A - Z_L}\right)z'_a + m_{13}\left(\frac{Z_A - Z_L}{Z_A - Z_L}\right)z'_a \qquad \text{(C-2)}$$

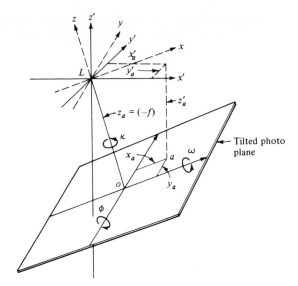

FIGURE C-3
Measurement x-y-z and rotated x'-y'-z' image coordinate systems.

$$y_a = m_{21}\left(\frac{X_A - X_L}{Z_A - Z_L}\right)z'_a + m_{22}\left(\frac{Y_A - Y_L}{Z_A - Z_L}\right)z'_a + m_{23}\left(\frac{Z_A - Z_L}{Z_A - Z_L}\right)z'_a \qquad \text{(C-3)}$$

$$z_a = m_{31}\left(\frac{X_A - X_L}{Z_A - Z_L}\right)z'_a + m_{32}\left(\frac{Y_A - Y_L}{Z_A - Z_L}\right)z'_a + m_{33}\left(\frac{Z_A - Z_L}{Z_A - Z_L}\right)z'_a \qquad \text{(C-4)}$$

Factoring the term $(z'_a/Z_A - Z_L)$ from Eqs. (C-2) through (C-4), dividing (C-2) and (C-3) by (C-4), and substituting $(-f)$ for z_a, the following collinearity equations result:

$$x_a = -f\left[\frac{m_{11}(X_A - X_L) + m_{12}(Y_A - Y_L) + m_{13}(Z_A - Z_L)}{m_{31}(X_A - X_L) + m_{32}(Y_A - Y_L) + m_{33}(Z_A - Z_L)}\right] \qquad \text{(C-5)}$$

$$y_a = -f\left[\frac{m_{21}(X_A - X_L) + m_{22}(Y_A - Y_L) + m_{23}(Z_A - Z_L)}{m_{31}(X_A - X_L) + m_{32}(Y_A - Y_L) + m_{33}(Z_A - Z_L)}\right] \qquad \text{(C-6)}$$

C-4 LINEARIZATION OF THE COLLINEARITY EQUATIONS

Equations (C-5) and (C-6) are nonlinear and involve nine unknowns: the three rotation angles omega, phi, and kappa which are inherent in the m's; the three exposure station coordinates X_L, Y_L, and Z_L; and the three object point coordinates X_A, Y_A, and Z_A.

The nonlinear equations are linearized using Taylor's theorem. In linearizing the collinearity equations, the Eqs. (C-5) and (C-6) are rewritten as follows:

$$F = 0 = qx_a + rf \qquad \text{(C-7)}$$

$$G = 0 = qy_a + sf \qquad \text{(C-8)}$$

Where

$$q = m_{31}(X_A - X_L) + m_{32}(Y_A - Y_L) + m_{33}(Z_A - Z_L)$$

$$r = m_{11}(X_A - X_L) + m_{12}(Y_A - Y_L) + m_{13}(Z_A - Z_L)$$

$$s = m_{21}(X_A - X_L) + m_{22}(Y_A - Y_L) + m_{23}(Z_A - Z_L)$$

According to Taylor's theorem, Eqs. (C-7) and (C-8) may be expressed in linearized form as:

$$0 = (F)_0 + \left(\frac{\partial F}{\partial x_a}\right)_0 dx_a + \left(\frac{\partial F}{\partial \omega}\right)_0 d\omega + \left(\frac{\partial F}{\partial \phi}\right)_0 d\phi + \left(\frac{\partial F}{\partial \kappa}\right)_0 d\kappa + \left(\frac{\partial F}{\partial X_L}\right)_0 dX_L$$

$$+ \left(\frac{\partial F}{\partial Y_L}\right)_0 dY_L$$

$$+ \left(\frac{\partial F}{\partial Z_L}\right)_0 dZ_L + \left(\frac{\partial F}{\partial X_A}\right)_0 dX_A + \left(\frac{\partial F}{\partial Y_A}\right)_0 dY_A + \left(\frac{\partial F}{\partial Z_A}\right)_0 dZ_A \qquad \text{(C-9)}$$

$$0 = (G)_0 + \left(\frac{\partial G}{\partial y_a}\right)_0 dy_a + \left(\frac{\partial G}{\partial \omega}\right)_0 d\omega + \left(\frac{\partial G}{\partial \phi}\right)_0 d\phi + \left(\frac{\partial G}{\partial \kappa}\right)_0 d\kappa + \left(\frac{\partial G}{\partial X_L}\right)_0 dX_L$$

$$+ \left(\frac{\partial G}{\partial Y_L}\right)_0 dY_L$$

$$+ \left(\frac{\partial G}{\partial Z_L}\right)_0 dZ_L + \left(\frac{\partial G}{\partial X_A}\right)_0 dX_A + \left(\frac{\partial G}{\partial Y_A}\right)_0 dY_A + \left(\frac{\partial G}{\partial Z_A}\right)_0 dZ_A \qquad \text{(C-10)}$$

In Eqs. (C-9) and (C-10), $(F)_0$ and $(G)_0$ are the functions F and G of Eqs. (C-7) and (C-8) evaluated at the initial approximations for the nine unknowns; the terms $(\partial F/\partial x)_0$, $(\partial F/\partial \omega)_0$, $(\partial F/\partial \phi)_0$, etc., are partial derivatives of the functions F and G with respect to the indicated unknowns evaluated at the initial approximations; and dx_a, $d\omega$, $d\phi$, etc., are unknown corrections to be applied to the initial approximations. The units of $d\omega$, $d\phi$, and $d\kappa$ are radians. Since dx_a and dy_a are corrections to measured photocoordinates x_a and y_a, they may be interpreted as residual errors in the measurements. These two terms may therefore be replaced by v_{x_a} and v_{y_a} which are the customary symbols adopted for residual errors. Note from Eqs. (C-7) and (C-8) that partial derivatives $\partial F/\partial x_a$ and $\partial G/\partial y_a$ are both equal to q. Substituting q for these terms in Eqs. (C-9) and (C-10), transposing qdx_a and qdy_a to the left-hand side of the equations, dividing each equation by q, and replacing dx_a and dy_a by v_{x_a} and v_{y_a} respectively, the following simplified forms of the linearized collinearity equations are obtained:

$$v_{x_a} = b_{11}d\omega + b_{12}d\phi + b_{13}d\kappa - b_{14}dX_L - b_{15}dY_L - b_{16}dZ_L + b_{14}dX_A$$

$$+ b_{15}dY_A + b_{16}dZ_A + J \tag{C-11}$$

$$v_{y_a} = b_{21}d\omega + b_{22}d\phi + b_{23}d\kappa - b_{24}dX_L - b_{25}dY_L - b_{26}dZ_L + b_{24}dX_A$$

$$+ b_{25}dY_A + b_{26}dZ_A + K \tag{C-12}$$

In Eqs. (C-11) and (C-12), J and K are equal to $(F)_o/q$ and $(G)_o/q$ respectively. The b's are coefficients equal to the partial derivatives. For convenience these coefficients are given below. In these coefficients ΔX, ΔY, and ΔZ are equal to $(X_A - X_L)$, $(Y_A - Y_L)$ and $(Z_A - Z_L)$ respectively. Numerical values for these coefficient terms are obtained by using initial approximations for the unknowns.

$$b_{11} = \frac{x}{q}(-m_{33}\Delta Y + m_{32}\Delta Z) + \frac{f}{q}(-m_{13}\Delta Y + m_{12}\Delta Z)$$

$$b_{12} = \frac{x}{q}[\Delta X \cos\phi + \Delta Y(\sin\omega \sin\phi) + \Delta Z(-\sin\phi \cos\omega)]$$

$$+ \frac{f}{q}[\Delta X(-\sin\phi \cos\kappa) + \Delta Y(\sin\omega \cos\phi \cos\kappa) + \Delta Z(-\cos\omega \cos\phi \cos\kappa)]$$

$$b_{13} = \frac{f}{q}(m_{21}\Delta X + m_{22}\Delta Y + m_{23}\Delta Z)$$

$$b_{14} = \frac{x}{q}(m_{31}) + \frac{f}{q}(m_{11})$$

$$b_{15} = \frac{x}{q}(m_{32}) + \frac{f}{q}(m_{12})$$

$$b_{16} = \frac{x}{q}(m_{33}) + \frac{f}{q}(m_{13})$$

$$J = \frac{(qx + rf)}{q}$$

$$b_{21} = \frac{y}{q}(-m_{33}\Delta Y + m_{32}\Delta Z) + \frac{f}{q}(-m_{23}\Delta Y + m_{22}\Delta Z)$$

$$b_{22} = \frac{y}{q}[\Delta X \cos\phi + \Delta Y(\sin\omega \sin\phi) + \Delta Z(-\cos\omega \sin\phi)]$$

$$+ \frac{f}{q}[\Delta X(\sin\phi \sin\kappa) + \Delta Y(-\sin\omega \cos\phi \sin\kappa) + \Delta Z(\cos\omega \cos\phi \sin\kappa)]$$

$$b_{23} = \frac{f}{q}(-m_{11}\Delta X - m_{12}\Delta Y - m_{13}\Delta Z)$$

$$b_{24} = \frac{y}{q}(m_{31}) + \frac{f}{q}(m_{21})$$

$$b_{25} = \frac{y}{q}\,(m_{32}) + \frac{f}{q}\,(m_{22})$$

$$b_{26} = \frac{y}{q}\,(m_{33}) + \frac{f}{q}\,(m_{23})$$

$$K = \frac{(qy + sf)}{q}$$

C-5 APPLICATIONS OF COLLINEARITY

The collinearity equations are applicable to the analytical solution of almost every aerial photogrammetry problem. Section 13-12 describes their use in *space resection*, in which the six elements of exterior orientation of a tilted photograph are computed. Section 18-12 explains how collinearity is applied in analytic *relative orientation*, which is necessary in analytically extending control photogrammetrically. Regardless of the particular problem, an *x* equation [Eq. (C-11)] and *y* equation [Eq. (C-12)] is written for each point whose image or images appear in the photo or photos involved in the problem. The equations will contain unknowns, the number of which will vary with the particular problem. If the number of equations is equal to or greater than the number of unknowns, a solution is possible.

Initial approximations are needed for all unknowns, and these are generally easily obtained by making certain assumptions, such as vertical photography. The initial approximations do not have to be extremely close, but the closer they are to the unknowns, the faster a satisfactory solution will be reached; and the result is a savings in computer time.

In solving a system of collinearity equations of the form of Eqs. (C-11) and (C-12) for any problem, the quantities which are determined are corrections to the initial approximations. After the first solution, the computed corrections are added to the initial approximations to obtain revised approximations. The solution is then repeated to find new corrections. This procedure is continued (iterated) until the magnitudes of the corrections become insignificant. With reasonable approximations to begin with, a satisfactory solution is usually obtained with about two or three iterations.

A system of collinearity equations of the form of Eqs. (C-11) and (C-12) may be expressed in matrix form as

$$_m V_1 = {_m A_n}\,{_n X_1} - {_m L_1} \qquad \text{(C-13)}$$

In Eqs. (C-13), m is the number of equations; n is the number of unknowns; V is the matrix of residual errors in the measured x and y photocoordinates; A is the matrix of b's, the coefficients of the unknowns; X is the matrix of unknown corrections to the initial approximations; and L is the matrix of constant terms J and K. If the number of equations exceeds the number of unknowns, a least squares solution may be obtained for the most probable values for the unknowns by using matrix Eq. (A-12) of Appendix A. Precisions of the unknowns may be computed by applying matrix Eqs. (A-14) through (A-17) of Appendix A.

C-6   ROTATION IN TERMS OF AZIMUTH, TILT, AND SWING

Instead of using omega, phi, and kappa as the rotation angles for transforming the tilted photocoordinates into an $x'y'z'$ coordinate system parallel to the ground system, rotation angles azimuth, tilt and swing may be used. A tilted photo illustrating the azimuth (α), tilt (t) and swing (s) angles is shown in Fig. C-4. In the figure the photo principal plane intersects the datum plane along line N_dP_d. The rotation formulas are developed by initially assuming an $x'y'z'$ coordinate system parallel to XYZ, and then, by means of rotations, converting it into the xyz photo measurement system. The origins of both image coordinate systems are taken at the exposure station L.

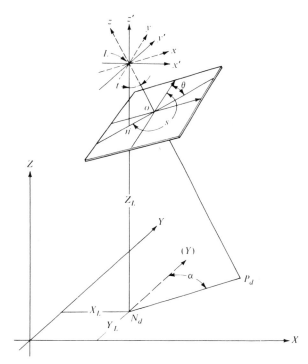

FIGURE C-4
Azimuth, tilt, and swing rotation angles.

The rotation equations are developed in a sequence of three separate two-dimensional rotations. The $x'y'z'$ coordinate system is first rotated about the z' axis through a clockwise angle α to create an $x^\alpha\text{-}y^\alpha\text{-}z^\alpha$ coordinate system. After rotation the y^α axis will be in the principal plane of the photo. With reference to Fig. C-5a the coordinates of any point in the $x^\alpha y^\alpha z^\alpha$ system are

$$x^\alpha = x' \cos \alpha - y' \sin \alpha$$
$$y^\alpha = x' \sin \alpha + y' \cos \alpha \qquad \text{(C-14)}$$
$$z^\alpha = z'$$

The second rotation is a counterclockwise rotation t about the x^α axis to create an $x^{\alpha t}\text{-}y^{\alpha t}\text{-}z^{\alpha t}$ coordinate system. After rotation, the $x^{\alpha t}$ and $y^{\alpha t}$ axes are in the plane of the tilted photograph. With reference to Fig. C-5b the coordinates of any point in the $x^{\alpha t}\text{-}y^{\alpha t}\text{-}z^{\alpha t}$ system are

$$x^{\alpha t} = x^\alpha$$
$$y^{\alpha t} = y^\alpha \cos t + z^\alpha \sin t \qquad \text{(C-15)}$$
$$z^{\alpha t} = -y^\alpha \sin t + z^\alpha \cos t$$

The third rotation is about the $z^{\alpha t}$ axis through the counterclockwise angle θ. Angle θ is defined as:

$$\theta = (s - 180°)$$

This third rotation creates an $x^{\alpha t\theta}\text{-}y^{\alpha t\theta}\text{-}z^{\alpha t\theta}$ coordinate system which coincides with the xyz tilted photo system. With reference to Fig. C-5c the coordinates of any point in the xyz system are

$$x = x^{\alpha t\theta} = x^{\alpha t} \cos \theta + y^{\alpha t} \sin \theta$$
$$y = y^{\alpha t\theta} = -x^{\alpha t} \sin \theta + y^{\alpha t} \cos \theta \qquad \text{(C-16)}$$
$$z = z^{\alpha t\theta} = z^{\alpha t}$$

Because $\sin \theta$ equals $- \sin s$, and $\cos \theta$ equals $- \cos s$, these substitutions may be made into Eqs. (C-16), from which

$$x = -x^{\alpha t} \cos s - y^{\alpha t} \sin s$$
$$y = x^{\alpha t} \sin s - y^{\alpha t} \cos s \qquad \text{(C-17)}$$
$$z = z^{\alpha t}$$

Substituting Eq. (C-14) into Eq. (C-15), in turn substituting into Eq. (C-17) and factoring, the following expressions result for the x, y, and z coordinates of any point:

$$x = m_{11}x' + m_{12}y' + m_{13}z'$$
$$y = m_{21}x' + m_{22}y' + m_{23}z' \qquad \text{(C-18)}$$
$$z = m_{31}x' + m_{32}y' + m_{33}z'$$

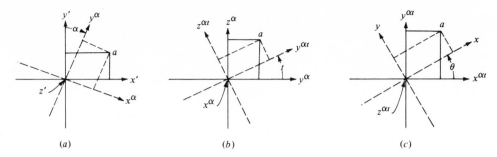

FIGURE C-5
Rotation in azimuth, tilt, and swing. (*a*) First rotation; (*b*) second rotation; (*c*) third rotation.

In Eqs. (C-18), the *m*'s are

$$m_{11} = -\cos \alpha \cos s - \sin \alpha \cos t \sin s$$
$$m_{12} = \sin \alpha \cos s - \cos \alpha \cos t \sin s$$
$$m_{13} = -\sin t \sin s$$
$$m_{21} = \cos \alpha \sin s - \sin \alpha \cos t \cos s$$
$$m_{22} = -\sin \alpha \sin s - \cos \alpha \cos t \cos s \qquad \text{(C-19)}$$
$$m_{23} = -\sin t \cos s$$
$$m_{31} = -\sin \alpha \sin t$$
$$m_{32} = -\cos \alpha \sin t$$
$$m_{33} = \cos t$$

C-7 COLLINEARITY EQUATIONS USING AZIMUTH-TILT-SWING ROTATION

By simply substituting azimuth-tilt-swing expressions [Eqs. (C-19)] for the *m*'s into Eqs. (C-5) and (C-6), collinearity equations are obtained which include azimuth, tilt, and swing as unknowns instead of omega, phi, and kappa. By applying Taylor's theorem, these azimuth, tilt, and swing equations can be linearized and used to solve photogrammetry problems analytically. More frequently, however, the omega-phi-kappa equations are used, and if the tilt, swing, and azimuth angles are desired, they are determined from omega, phi, and kappa as described in Sec. C-8.

C-8   CONVERTING FROM ONE ROTATION SYSTEM TO THE OTHER

Although the azimuth-tilt-swing expressions [Eqs. (C-19)] for the m's differ from their corresponding omega-phi-kappa expressions [Eqs. (B-21)], their numerical values are equal. This is true because the m's are actually direction cosines relating image and object coordinate systems as described in Sec. B-7 of Appendix B. Because of their equality, corresponding m's may be set equal to one another; e.g., $m_{11} = \cos \phi \cos \kappa = -\cos \alpha \cos s - \sin \alpha \cos t \sin s$. This equality of m's enables converting back and forth between the omega-phi-kappa and azimuth-tilt-swing systems.

If omega, phi, and kappa for a particular photograph are known, numerical values for the m's can be calculated and tilt, swing, and azimuth determined from the following:

$$\cos t = m_{33} \qquad \text{(C-20)}$$

$$\tan s = \frac{-\sin t \sin s}{-\sin t \cos s} = \frac{m_{13}}{m_{23}} \qquad \text{(C-21)}$$

$$\tan \alpha = \frac{-\sin \alpha \sin t}{-\cos \alpha \sin t} = \frac{m_{31}}{m_{32}} \qquad \text{(C-22)}$$

The quadrant of s is established on the basis of the algebraic signs of m_{13} and m_{23}. Since t is always between $0°$ and $90°$, $\sin t$ is always positive. Therefore algebraic signs of m_{13} and m_{23} are derived from the sine and cosine of s respectively. If both m_{13} and m_{23} are negative, then the sine and cosine of s are both positive and s is in quadrant I having a value between $0°$ and $90°$. Using similar analyses, the following table was developed to provide the proper quadrant for both s and α:

Algebraic sign of m_{13} or m_{31}	Algebraic sign of m_{23} or m_{32}	Quadrant of s or α
−	−	I
−	+	II
+	+	III
+	−	IV

If the tilt, swing, and azimuth are known for a particular photo, conversion to omega, phi, and kappa is also readily made as follows:

$$\sin \phi = m_{31} \qquad \text{(C-23)}$$

$$-\tan \omega = \frac{-\sin \omega \cos \phi}{\cos \omega \cos \phi} = \frac{m_{32}}{m_{33}} \qquad \text{(C-24)}$$

$$-\tan \kappa = \frac{-\cos \phi \sin \kappa}{\cos \phi \cos \kappa} = \frac{m_{21}}{m_{11}} \qquad \text{(C-25)}$$

In Sec. B-7 of Appendix B, a sign convention was adopted making omega, phi, and kappa positive if they were counterclockwise rotations when viewed from the positive end of their respective x, y, or z axes. Using this sign convention and recognizing that for aerial photography omega and phi cannot exceed $90°$, then phi is positive and counterclockwise if m_{31} is positive. Also, if m_{31} is negative, phi is negative and clockwise. Whether phi is positive or negative, since its value is less than $90°$, its cosine is always positive. Therefore if the quotient m_{32}/m_{33} is negative, omega is positive and counterclockwise, and if the quotient is positive, omega is negative and clockwise.

Kappa can take on any value between 0 and $360°$. If m_{11} is positive, then cos κ is positive because cos ϕ is always positive. Also if the quotient m_{21}/m_{11} is negative, tan κ is positive. Now if both the cosine and tangent of kappa are positive, then kappa is in quadrant I and between 0 and $90°$. Using similar analyses, the following table was derived for establishing the proper quadrant of kappa:

Algebraic sign of m_{11}	Algebraic sign of m_{21}/m_{11}	Quadrant of κ
+	−	I
−	+	II
−	−	III
+	+	IV

REFERENCES

American Society of Photogrammetry: "Manual of Photogrammetry," 3d ed., George Banta Co., Inc., Menasha, Wis., 1966, chap. 2.

Keller, M., and G. C. Tewinkel: "Space Resection in Photogrammetry," ESSA Technical Report C&GS 32, U.S. Coast and Geodetic Survey, Washington, D.C., 1966.

PROBLEMS

C-1 State the condition of collinearity in photogrammetry.

C-2 Explain why linearized collinearity equations must be iterated a number of times before a satisfactory solution is achieved.

For the following matrix M what are the values of omega, phi, and kappa? What are azimuth, tilt, and swing?

$$M = \begin{bmatrix} -0.9187 & 0.3921 & -0.0486 \\ -0.3923 & -0.9198 & -0.0060 \\ -0.0470 & 0.0136 & 0.9988 \end{bmatrix}$$

INDEX

Page numbers in *italic* indicate illustrations.